INTRODUCTION TO
corporate
finance

WILLIAM L MEGGINSON

SCOTT B SMART

BRIAN M LUCEY

INTRODUCTION TO
corporate
finance

SOUTH-WESTERN
CENGAGE Learning

Australia • Mexico • Singapore • Spain • United Kingdom • United States

Introduction to Corporate Finance
William Megginson, Scott Smart and Brian Lucey

Publishing Director: John Yates

Publisher: Patrick Bond

Development Editor: Rachael Sturgeon
                   Jenny Kedros

Production Editor: Leonora Dawson-Bowling

Manufacturing Manager: Helen Mason

Senior Production Controller: Maeve Healy

Marketing Manager: Anne-Marie Scoones

Typesetter: Newgen, India

Cover design: Keith Marsh, Fink Creative, St Ives, UK

Text design: Design Deluxe, Bath, UK

© 2008, Cengage Learning EMEA

For product information and technology assistance, contact **emea.info@cengage.com**

For permission to use material from this text or product, and for permission queries, email **clsuk.permissions@cengage.com**

British Library Cataloguing-in-Publication Data
A catalogue record for this book is available from the British Library.

ISBN: 978-1-84480-562-4

Cengage Learning EMEA
High Holborn House, 50-51 Bedford Row
London WC1R 4LR

Cengage Learning products are represented in Canada by Nelson Education Ltd.

For your lifelong learning solutions, visit
www.cengage.co.uk
Purchase e-books or e-chapters at:
http://estore.bized.co.uk

Printed by C&C Offset Printing Co. Ltd,
China
1 2 3 4 5 6 7 8 9 10 – 10 09 08

Brief contents

Contents

6 The trade-off between risk and return 190

7 Risk, return and the capital asset pricing model 220

PART 3 Capital budgeting 247

8 Capital budgeting process and techniques 250

9 Cash flow and capital budgeting 292

12 Capital structure 398

13 Dividend policy 432

PART 5 Additional topics in corporate finance 467

14 Entrepreneurial finance and venture capital 470

17 Mergers, acquisitions and corporate control 560

About the authors

WILLIAM L. MEGGINSON is Professor and Rainbolt Chair in Finance at the University of Oklahoma. Dr Megginson is co-author of the Thomson/South-Western MBA level text *Corporate Finance*, first published in 2004. He has published in the *Journal of Finance*, the *Journal of Financial Economics*, the *Journal of Economic Literature*, the *Journal of Financial and Quantitative Analysis*, the *Journal of Money, Credit, and Banking*, the *Journal of Applied Corporate Finance* and *Financial Management*. He received a Smith Breeden Distinguished Paper Awards for outstanding research published in the *Journal of Finance*. He is also a voting member of the Italian Ministry of Economics and Finance's Global Advisory Committee on Privatization. Dr Megginson has a Ph.D. in Finance from Florida State University. He has served as a consultant for the New York Stock Exchange, the OECD, the IMF, the World Federation of Exchanges and the World Bank.

SCOTT B. SMART has been a member of the finance faculty at Indiana University since 1990. He is co-author of *Corporate Finance*, an MBA level text published by Thomson/South-Western. Dr Smart has been recognized as a 'Master Teacher' by *Business Week* continuously over the last ten years, and has won more than a dozen teaching awards. He has published articles in scholarly journals such as the *Journal of Finance*, the *Journal of Financial Economics* and the *Review of Economics and Statistics*. He has appeared on CNBC and his research has been cited by the *Wall Street Journal*, *New York Post*, *Business Week*, *Fortune* and other major newspapers and periodicals. His consulting clients include Intel, Synopsys and Unext. Dr Smart has served on local boards of directors for Habitat for Humanity and other non-profit groups, and he currently serves as a trustee for the Skyhawk Small Cap Equity Fund. Dr Smart did his undergraduate work at Baylor University and received his Ph.D. from Stanford University.

BRIAN M. LUCEY is Professor at the School of Business, Trinity College Dublin, where he is Director of of the MSc in Finance. He has published many articles in journals such as the *Journal of International Money and Finance*, the *Journal of Multinational Financial Management*, the *Journal of International Financial Markets, Institutions and Money* and *Applied Financial Economics*. This research has been noted in the Financial Times and the Economist newspapers. A Fellow of Trinity College Dublin, Dr Lucey has previously been employed in the Central Bank of Ireland. He holds a Ph.D. in Finance from Stirling University.

Preface

M any finance textbooks, we have found, come in one of two versions. At one level there are texts that are very student friendly, but somewhat light on the theoretical and application aspects of finance. At the other end of the spectrum we have texts that are theory heavy, forbidding in aspect, and that require advanced mathematical and statistical skills to access. We have sought to make this the most student-friendly introductory finance textbook in the market today, but at no loss of rigour. We followed a set of core principles when writing the text and designing the overall support package that accompanies the book.

This edition is in part an adaptation of a textbook originally written for the US market. However, it is much more than just that. The book has been rewritten, restructured and reorganized to reflect a European-centric approach. Throughout we have striven to blend a balance of material – it is impossible and improper to ignore the interlinked nature of modern finance, and in adapting this book we have been conscious of this. Although the examples, terminology and currencies are mainly those of Europe and the UK, we have not shied away from including US and other third country examples where needed to illustrate a point. Students working through this text will, we trust, realize by the end that, while details may differ from country to country, the essential questions and concerns of corporate finance remain constant.

CORE PRINCIPLES

1. Create interest and relevance for students with real-world examples that make cutting-edge theories appealing, accessible and practical

We feel it is important to grab students' interest and attention from the beginning of the chapter with an interesting, relevant exposition of how the material in the chapter 'plays out' in reality. Every chapter of this book begins with a story pulled from recent headlines that illustrates a key chapter concept in an applied setting. An example is the introduction to Chapter 10, which discusses how BASF measures its weighted average cost of capital, or Chapter 14, which notes how a leisure company that operates a chain of dance venues benefited from venture capital.

We also strive to provide students with a smooth bridge between theory and practice by highlighting examples in a feature that we call 'Applying the Model'. These illustrations, many of which use real data from well-known companies, take concepts and make them easy to understand within an interesting and relevant context.

We have also recognized the importance of further cementing the linkage between real world and academic concepts with a feature we call simply 'Real World'. Each section of each chapter contains, as far as possible, an example that demonstrates the operation of the concept in reality. Thus, among many others, we have real world examples on the financing of the A1 racing circuit, the growth of currency spread betting, the expansion of Vodafone's operations in India, how interest rate swaps helped Bacardi to expand its rum operations and Ryanair dividends. All in all the dozens of real world examples provide a constant reinforcement of the ultimately applied nature of the issues being discussed.

2. Maximize the pedagogical and motivational value of technology

We have often experimented with technology packaged with textbooks, only to find that the included products tend to impede learning and classroom delivery more than they facilitate student interest and understanding. Some technology add-ons, created by subcontractors rather than the text's primary authors, seem to bear almost no relationship to the text they are meant to support. And of course, all too often a technology that we want to use inside or outside the classroom simply doesn't work.

With such experiences behind us, we wanted to develop an integrated technology package that engaged, motivated and at times entertained students, while helping them master financial concepts in their own time and at their own pace. We wanted to use technology to allow students to hear first-hand about exciting developments in financial research. We wanted students to hear from business professionals why the material contained in the text is relevant after the final exam is over. Most of all, as authors of the text, we wanted to take primary responsibility for creating the technology package to ensure that we seamlessly integrated technology with the text's most important concepts and techniques.

Tests with in-residence and online students have generated almost unanimous praise for these features. In fact, the most common complaint we have heard from students is, 'Why can't we see more of this?' Visit www.cengage.co.uk/megginson to see a sample of the Smart Finance resources that students can access. Access to the Smart Finance website is free with each new text.

Some examples of the fully integrated technology include (see page xxviii for more in-depth information):

- Animated Review Tutorials that explain key concepts.

- Problem Solving Animations that illustrate numerical solution methods as well as develop students' problem-solving intuition.

- Video Clips featuring European and American academics and practitioners, where each clip illustrates the conceptual bases of theory, theory in practice, and ethical issues that financial professionals routinely face.

- *Excel* Animations that walk students through problems or through particularly challenging aspects of problems that *Excel* helps to solve more easily.

In order to describe how to use these technologies in or out of class, and to provide syllabus integration suggestions, an informative *Resource Integration Guide* is available on the lecturer area of the companion website www.cengage.co.uk/megginson (see page xxix).

3. Provide a truly global perspective

The economic world is shrinking – particularly with regard to financial transactions. Europe has embarked on a brave experiment in international monetary coordination. Financial markets play an increasingly important role in the ongoing globalization of business and finance. Rather than grouping international issues into a chapter or two, we integrate a global consciousness throughout the text. Almost every chapter has a unique feature that we call 'Comparative Corporate Finance' designed to highlight similarities and differences among corporate finance practices around the world.

Within the global consciousness of the text we have, however, striven to provide a truly European textbook with an emphasis on the issues that are central to modern corporate finance. Examples, discussion of research, videos and real world concepts are in the main derived from European sources. Comparisons with finance and behaviour in the USA are used throughout to illustrate the similarity of underlying concepts and the crucial differences. We do not delve deeply into the minutiae of the different taxation, legal or regulatory systems, as the scope of the text is that of a survey at an introductory, accessible, but rigorous level. However, we do note the importance of these and other issues.

4. Connecting previous and present coursework to corporate finance

Experienced financial managers consistently tell us that they need people who can see the big picture and who can recognize connections across functional areas. To help students develop a larger sense of what finance is about, why it is relevant to their business studies and to ease the transition into their own chosen fields, we highlight concepts that most students learn in their introductory economics, statistics and accounting courses. We then connect these concepts to finance.

Our goal is to create a familiar starting point for students taking finance for the first time – for example, the marginal cost/marginal benefit framework they experienced in prerequisite economics courses. The marginal benefit versus marginal cost decision framework is classic microeconomics, recognizable to anyone who teaches finance. Most current finance textbooks fail to draw this vital connection for students: choose to fund only those projects for which the marginal benefits (MB) outweigh the marginal costs (MC). Finance is perhaps the discipline best suited to quantify and compare marginal costs (risk) against marginal benefits (returns on investment alternatives).

Several video clips early in the book also emphasize connections between finance and other disciplines. Beginning with what students know and building on that foundation allows us to use an approach that we have used successfully in our own teaching for many years. We wanted our book to reflect that teaching philosophy.

OTHER KEY FEATURES

Excel chapter appendices

Excel Appendices explicitly show students how to build *Excel* spreadsheets to solve finance problems more easily using modern tools rather than tables or even calculators. *Excel* is clearly the tool of choice for finance courses and for finance professionals today. These appendices are available on the student area of the companion website www.cengage.co.uk/megginson (see pages xxviii and xxix).

Thomson ONE – Business School Edition (BSE) problems

Thomson ONE – BSE is an online database that draws from industry-leading Thomson Financial's data sources, including Disclosure Datastream, and Securities Data Corporation databases. Analysts and other finance professionals use these tools every day to conduct research. To help motivate students to perform basic research and analysis without creating extra work for the instructor, the authors have written end-of-chapter problems that require students to use Thomson ONE – BSE. See page xxx for more in-depth information about using Thomson ONE – BSE.

Acknowledgements

Most people realize that creating a textbook is a collaborative venture. An adaptation of a successful text is even more so, and I first of all need to thank Bill Megginson and Scott Smart, without whose truly exceptional work this text would have been impossible to produce. I trust that the changes and adaptations made preserve the clarity and learning of the original while orientating the text towards a more European audience. It is humbling when one considers how many people are involved in planning, writing, editing, producing and launching a book. In the paragraphs that follow, I thank the many people who made significant contributions to this book. In particular, I wish to acknowledge the debt I owe to those who have worked so closely with me.

First, I wish to thank the team at Cengage Learning EMEA who pushed me to deliver a top-quality product. Great praise and thanks must go to Patrick Bond, Publisher, Cengage Learning EMEA and his team; to Jenny Kedros and Rachel Sturgeon, the Editors who had the unenviable job of keeping me on track; to Simon Perry for his copyediting skills and to the entire Cengage Learning EMEA marketing and production team.

Increasingly, the supplements are a key part of a textbook. In this regard huge thanks must go to Thomas Lagoarde-Segot of Trinity College Dublin and Euromed Marseille Ecole de Management. Thomas took responsibility for the re-writing of the Instructor's Manual, Study Guide, Test Bank and *Excel* appendices. As ever, it was a pleasure to work with Thomas.

Importantly, I thank the students of Applied Finance at Trinity College Dublin, who were the early recipients of many of the adapted concepts, real world examples and new thrusts of the text. Teaching and learning are intertwined and I hope that the students learned as much from my teaching them as I learned from my teaching of them.

The people and organizations who contributed their time to the video clips deserve a special thank you. It is my experience that these act as a significant learning aid, bringing home to students what the linkages are between the real world of business and the material covered.

This book could not have been written without the encouragement and understanding of my colleagues at the Institute for International Integration Studies at Trinity College Dublin. Particular thanks go to Colm Kearney, Elaine Hutson and Svitlana Voronkova for comments and encouragement. Most of all, however, thanks go to my wife, for listening over the last two years to more discussions on the pedagogic aspects of corporate finance than any woman should have to! Thanks Mary.

I would also like to thank the reviewers who assisted so diligently with the original research into the adaptation of this book and who throughout the process provided me with valuable, timely and pertinent feedback. Their perspectives and comments greatly improved the adaptation.

Ian Jackson, Staffordshire University, UK
Jenke R ter Horst, Tilburg University, Netherlands
Peter Moles, University of Edinburgh, UK
Jan Bartholdy, Aarhus School of Business, Denmark
Stefano Gatti, University of Bocconi, Milan, Italy
Christos Papahristodoulou, Malardalen University, Sweden
Michael Paserman, Hebrew University, Israel

Finally, thanks are due to those who were kind enough to reply to the questionnaire research conducted on corporate finance education that provided the springboard for the whole project: M B Adams, Swansea University, UK; Meziane Lasfer, Cass Business School, UK; Sheila Killian, University of Limerick, Ireland; Joel Branson, Vrije University Brussels, Belgium; Gerald Aranoff, College of Judea and Samaria, Israel; Simon Gao, Napier University, UK; Ben Heunes, Damelin School of Banking, South Africa; Chen-Yu Chang, University College London, UK; Kenneth Dyson, University of Ulster, UK; Suzette Viviers, University of Port Elizabeth, South Africa; Samuel Frankel, College of Management, Israel; Kossuth Mitchell, Pikeville College, USA; Libon Fung, Birkbeck College, UK; Jenny Robertson, University of Brighton, UK; Adri de Ridder, Royal Institute of Technology, Sweden; Ahron Rosenfeld, Ben-Gurion University of the Negev, Israel; Graham Diggle, Oxford Brookes University, UK; Sue Reed, Southampton Business School, UK; Robert Davidson, Glasgow Caledonian University, UK; A T Adams, University of Edinburgh, UK; John McLaren, Southampton Business School, UK; Jon Tucker, University of Exeter, UK; David Power, University of Dundee, UK; Brian Scroggie, Aberdeen Business School, UK; Clive Allen, University of Bournemouth, UK; Dimitrios Gounopoulos, University of Surrey, UK; M Tavakoli, University of St Andrews, UK; Heather Tarbert, Glasgow Caledonian University, UK; Olive Gardiner, Fife CFHE, UK; Kevin Campbell, University of Stirling, UK; Ruth Bender, Cranfield University, UK; Jackie Harvey, Newcastle Business School, UK; Niklas Strom, Uppsala University, Sweden.

Walk-through tour

Opening focus boxes appear at the beginning of each chapter describing a real world example introducing the topics to come.

Learning objectives appear at the beginning of each chapter to highlight the key ideas of that chapter.

Glossary terms are highlighted in the text and defined in the margin. All these terms are then provided in a full glossary at the back of the book.

Applying the Model boxes use real statistics to show how models explained in the text can be applied to corporate finance practices in the real world.

Smart Finance links appear in the margins, including Smart Concepts, Smart Solutions and Smart *Excel*, directing you to the Smart Finance section of the companion website for animated, step-by-step tutorials. See page xxviii for more information on the companion website and Smart Finance.

Smart Video logos in the margin direct you to the website at www.cengage.co.uk/megginson to see video clips of interviews with cutting-edge business and industry leaders. Choose from Smart Practices, Smart Ethics and Smart Ideas interviews. See page xxviii for more information on the companion website and Smart Finance.

Real World boxes describe topical examples from the world of corporate finance, applying the topics explained in the text and bringing them to life.

Comparative corporate finance boxes compare corporate finance practices and examples from around the world.

Concept review questions appear at the end of each section within chapters to test understanding of the material. These tie in directly with the learning objectives at the start of each chapter. Answers to the concept review questions are on the website at www.cengage.co.uk/megginson.

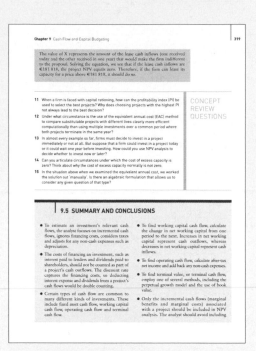

Summary and conclusions at the end of each chapter acts as a useful revision aid to what has been covered in each chapter.

Internet resources at the end of each chapter provides links to websites and companies related to topics in the chapter.

Key terms that have appeared in the text are included at the end of each chapter. These terms are all defined in the glossary at the end of the book.

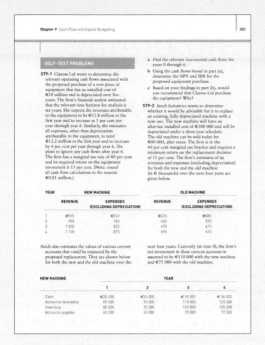

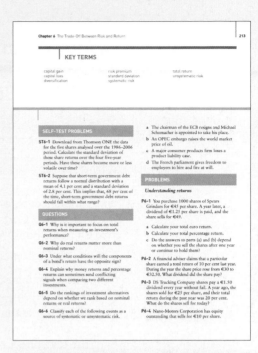

Self-test questions appear at the end of each chapter as a study aid to test your understanding of the key topics. Answers to the self-test questions are included in Appendix D at the end of the book and on the companion website at www.cengage.co.uk/megginson.

Questions and problems are included at the end of each chapter. These can be used for classroom discussion or assignments.

Minicases appear at the end of each chapter including an assignment to test understanding of the material in that chapter and to apply it to the real world.

Supplements and online resources

Visit www.cengage.co.uk/megginson for access to the Smart Finance animated resources and to further extensive teaching and learning material on the companion website.

Smart Finance is a fully integrated technology package created especially for *Introduction to Corporate Finance*, to aid learning and understanding of the topics covered in the book. Access to Smart Finance is free with each new purchase of the text.

- Smart Concepts

  These animated concept review tutorials, organized by chapter, explain key topics step-by-step, offering students the opportunity to review more difficult chapter material at their own pace. Students can also decide how much or what parts of the review they want to cover. Smart Concept icons in the margins of the text direct the student to www.cengage.co.uk/megginson to explore.

- Smart Solutions

  The Smart Solutions feature helps improve students' problem-solving skills by demonstrating animated solution steps and offering coaching about how to identify the right technique to apply to a particular problem. Smart Solutions icons in the margins of the text direct the student to www.cengage.co.uk/megginson to explore.

- Smart *Excel* Animations

  Excel animations walk students through problems or particularly challenging aspects of problems that *Excel* helps to solve more easily. Smart *Excel* icons in the margins of the text direct students to www.cengage.co.uk/megginson to view these resources.

- Smart Videos showing video clips of business and industry leaders.
  - Smart Practices video clips discuss how they maximize their companies' financial performance using cutting-edge practices.
  - Smart Ethics video clips show how both academics and business executives view ethics and the impact that ethical or unethical behaviour can have on the company's bottom line.
  - Smart Ideas clips show interviews with leading academic researchers discussing the theories and concepts discussed in the book. Smart Video icons in the margins of the text direct students to video clips relating to specific topics.
  - Smart Video icons in the margins of the text direct students to www.cengage.co.uk/megginson to view these videos.

Further teaching and learning resources are available on the companion website (www.cengage.co.uk/megginson) as follows:

For students
- Study plan for each chapter
- Multiple choice questions for each chapter

- Flashcards
- Answers to concept review questions
- Answers to self-test problems
- *Excel* appendices for ten chapters showing how to build *Excel* spreadsheets to solve finance problems
- Internet links to related websites for each chapter

For lecturers

- Instructor's manual
- *Resource Integration Guide* to using Smart Finance technologies
- PowerPoint lecture slides
- PowerPoint exhibit slides including the figures, tables and graphs from the text
- Testbank

Examview

This testbank and test generator provides a huge variety of different types of questions, allowing lecturers to create online, paper and local area network (LAN) tests. This CD-based product is available only from your Cengage sales representative.

Virtual learning environment

All of the web material is available in a format that is compatible with virtual learning environments such as Blackboard and WebCT. This version of the product is only available from your Cengage sales representative.

Thomson ONE – Business School Edition at http://tobsefin.swlearning.com

Want to bring concepts to life with real data? Do you assign research projects? Would you like your students to conduct research on the internet? Thomson ONE – Business School Edition meets all of these needs! This tool gives students the opportunity to use a business school version of an internet-based database that financial analysts and professionals around the world use every day. Relevant chapters include problems specifically for use with Thomson ONE – BSE so that your students find answers in real time. Thomson ONE – BSE includes access to ten-year financial statements down-loadable to *Excel*; one click Peer Set analysis; indices that students can manipulate or compare; and data for international, as well as domestic, companies. This resource is included *free* with each new text.

See **http://tobsefin.swlearning.com** for more information including an animated demonstration.

Guide to Thomson ONE – BSE

This helpful guide shows your students how to use the educational version of this valuable research and analysis tool. This guide allows students to learn for themselves how to use Thomson ONE – BSE at their own pace, saving professors precious class and office hour time. (ISBN: 0–324–31930–4).

PART 1

The Basic Tools of Finance

1 The scope of corporate finance

2 Financial statement and cash flow analysis

3 Present value

PART 1
Overview

Welcome to the study of corporate finance: a field that is rewarding financially and intellectually, with unmatched career opportunities that are as intellectually challenging as they are financially rewarding. In this book we try to explain how financial managers apply a few key principles as they weigh the marginal costs and marginal benefits of important business decisions. When managers take actions that have higher benefits than costs, they create value for shareholders. Our goals in introducing you to these principles are not only to impart useful knowledge, but also to convey our enthusiasm for our chosen field, as well as help you to explore whether a career in corporate finance is right for you.

Part 1 comprises three chapters, which lay the foundation for further work. Chapter 1 describes the roles that corporate finance experts play in a variety of businesses and industries. Most of what corporate finance professionals do on a day-to-day basis falls within one of the basic functions described in the chapter. We recommend that you revisit the list of five key functions as you work through this book. Most of the chapters place a heavy emphasis on just one or two of these functions and it is a useful exercise to map the key concepts from each chapter back to the five functions outlined in Chapter 1.

It has been said that accounting is the language of business, and certainly it is true that financial managers need to master basic accounting concepts and principles in order to do their jobs well. Chapter 2 offers a broad overview of the most important sources of accounting information – firms' financial statements. Our focus in this chapter is *not* on how accountants construct these statements. Instead, our goal is to illustrate why these statements are important to financial managers and why finance places so much emphasis on cash flow rather than on measures of earnings, such as net income or earnings per share. We also demonstrate how companies can use the information from financial statements to track their performance over time or to benchmark their results against those achieved by other firms. We also show how the emergence of harmonized accounting standards worldwide has made the task of comparing companies across national boundaries much easier.

Chapter 3 introduces one of the most fundamental concepts in finance called the time value of money. Simply put, the time value of money says that money today is worth more than money in the future. The reasoning behind this statement is straightforward. If you have money in hand today, you can invest it and earn interest, so receiving the money now is better than having to wait for it. Because business decisions typically involve costs and benefits that are spread out over many months and years, managers need a way to evaluate cash flows that the firm pays or receives at different times. For example, a firm spends €1 million today to purchase an asset that will generate a stream of cash receipts of €225 000 over the next several years. Do the costs of this investment outweigh its benefits, or are the benefits great enough to justify the costs? Chapter 3 explains how managers can make valid cost/benefit comparisons when cash flows occur at different times and using different rates of interest.

Chapter 1

The Scope of Corporate Finance

Apple succeeds with iTunes where others had failed

Ever since global sales of recorded music peaked in 1999, leading music companies have struggled to solve the difficult problem of how to set prices for their products that can compete with the same products for *free*! In 1999, the start-up company Napster pioneered file-sharing programs that allow music lovers to download song tracks over the internet for free. By 2004, some 900 million music files were available for sharing worldwide. Music companies' sales had been sliced by more than 20 per cent from their peak five years before. The challenge for music companies was this: to provide music on demand, at a price customers were willing to pay, while continuing to earn a profit. The recording industry may never discover how to make money selling music electronically – but Apple Computer did.

In April 2003, Apple launched a service called Apple iTunes Music Store from which customers could choose from among 500 000 music tracks provided by five major record labels. Steve Jobs, Apple's founder and chief executive officer (CEO), persuaded music companies to allow Apple to sell current and classic songs for 99 cents per track. The service was an immediate hit, selling 1 million songs during its first week alone and more than 70 million during its first 12 months. One customer reportedly spent more than €300 000! The service requires users to download songs using Apple's own software, directly promoting sales of Apple's stylish iPod MP3 player. This device retails for about $300, holds up to 7500 tracks, and has been widely applauded for its compact design and ease of use. Today, Apple sells more iPods than computers, and iPod sales reached $1800 million during 2006.

Perhaps surprisingly, the iTunes Music Store itself has thus far proven only marginally profitable for Apple. The company pays each record label between 60 and 65 cents per track. It spends an additional 25 cents in credit card fees and distribution costs, so the service yields a gross profit margin of only about 10 cents per song. On the other hand, iTunes clearly spurs iPod sales, which are very profitable and have allowed the company to rebrand itself from a computer company to one that is seen as a design house. And by keeping download prices so low, Apple both encourages the continued rapid growth of the music download market and discourages competitors from entering the market. In any case, the music companies don't seem to mind. They are at least receiving *some* revenue from songs downloaded over the internet.

Stories in the popular press tend to focus on the success of iTunes and iPod themselves. However, financial managers behind the scenes at Apple played a number of crucial roles in driving the success of the business. In this chapter, we explain how financial specialists interact with experts in fields as diverse as engineering, marketing, communications and law to help companies create wealth for their shareholders. We describe the types of activities that occupy financial managers day to day, and highlight some of the most promising career opportunities for finance students. The work that financial analysts do is intellectually challenging, as well as economically rewarding.

Sources: Multiple *Financial Times* articles from April 2003 to December 2006, downloaded from that company's paid internet service, FT.com (http://www.ft.com).

LEARNING OBJECTIVES

After studying this chapter you should be able to:

- Demonstrate an appreciation of how finance interacts with other functional areas of any business, see the diverse career opportunities available to finance students and outline the main professional financial qualifications available in business.

- Describe how modern companies obtain funding from financial intermediaries and markets, and discuss the five basic functions that modern financial managers must perform.

- Assess the costs and benefits of the three principal forms of business organization and explain why limited liability companies, with publicly traded shares, dominate economic life in most countries.

- Define agency costs and explain how shareholders monitor and encourage corporate managers to maximize shareholder wealth by choosing business opportunities for which the marginal benefits outweigh the marginal costs.

SMART FINANCE

Use the learning tools at www.cengage.co.uk/megginson

1.1 THE ROLE OF CORPORATE FINANCE IN MODERN BUSINESS

The example in the Opening Focus illustrates not only how managers conduct business in a modern, knowledge-based economy, but also shows the vital role that financial managers play in creating wealth. This story provides important insights into the theory and practice of corporate finance. Modern business involves people with many different skills and backgrounds working together towards common goals. Financial experts play a major role in achieving these goals. The importance (and status) of the finance function and the financial manager within business organizations has risen steadily over the past two decades. Business professionals in many different functional areas now recognize that competent financial professionals can do more than just keep the books and manage the firm's cash. Financial managers can create value in their own right.

This book focuses on the practising financial manager who is an integral part of the management team in a modern company. On the job, a financial manager must constantly apply financial tools to solve real business problems. Throughout this text, we highlight the one simple question that managers should ask when contemplating all business decisions: do the marginal benefits (MB) of taking a certain action outweigh the marginal costs (MC) of this action? For instance, at Apple Computer, the finance organization had to estimate the marginal benefits and costs of launching iTunes. By taking actions that generate benefits in excess of costs, firms generate wealth for their investors. Managers should take only those actions where the MB is at least equal to the MC.

As an introduction to what a financial manager's job entails, the next section discusses how various functional disciplines interact with financial managers. It describes the kinds of jobs that people with financial training generally take. Throughout this book, we assume that the managers we describe work for large, publicly traded corporations, but we maintain this assumption for convenience only. The skills and knowledge needed to contribute effectively towards achieving corporate business objectives are the same as those needed to be a successful entrepreneur, to manage family businesses, or to run a non-profit organization. Successful financial managers must be able to creatively manage both people and money.

SMART PRACTICES VIDEO

Tom Cole, Deutsche Bank, Leveraged Finance Group

'To be good at finance you have to understand how businesses work.'

See the entire interview at **www.cengage.co.uk/megginson**

How finance interacts with other functional business areas

Financial professionals interact with experts in a wide range of disciplines to drive successful businesses. Working with Apple's computer scientists, financial managers analysed the business potential of the iTunes service, as well as the sales potential of the iPod player. Financial managers:

- studied the economics of downloading music over the internet
- developed a strategy for providing a fee-based service that would attract customers
- negotiated licensing agreements with entertainment moguls from the recording industry
- worked with technical authorities to ensure that customers could seamlessly download songs.

Apple's financial managers also advised public relations professionals, who were asked to present the new service to a sceptical press and to answer journalists' questions about the service's financial aspects. Additionally, the company's financial managers worked with accounting and information systems staff. Together, they developed payment systems that allow the company to collect large numbers of small-denomination purchases by customers who use credit cards. As the iTunes service grows, financial managers must ensure that Apple will have the cash it needs to continue expanding the business, plus any follow-on services that might develop later.

In sum, although Apple's iPod was primarily a marketing and technology-driven project, the firm's financial organization played pivotal roles in every stage of the deal – from the initial assessment and funding of research, through the actual roll-out of iTunes, to managing the cash flows generated by the service, and then accumulating the capital needed to fund follow-on projects. In more ways than most people imagine, modern finance helps make high technology possible.

Career opportunities in finance

This section briefly surveys career opportunities in finance. Though different jobs require different specialized skills, the basic tools of corporate finance are vitally important for all business professionals, whether they work in industrial corporations, on Wall Street, or in the offices of a commercial bank or life insurance company. Three other skills that all finance jobs require are (a) good written, verbal and online communication and presentation skills; (b) teamwork; and (c) proficiency with computers and the internet. For an increasing number of finance jobs, an in-depth knowledge of international business has also become a prerequisite for career success.

We classify finance career opportunities as follows:

- corporate finance
- commercial banking
- investment banking
- money management
- consulting.[1]

Finance graduates in the European context can typically earn salaries that are at a premium over the average graduate. The exact salary you can attain will depend not only on the economic environment, but also on personal negotiating skills – and on how well you master the knowledge presented in this text!

Corporate finance Corporate (or what was traditionally called managerial) finance is concerned with the duties of the financial manager in a business. These managers handle the financial affairs of many types of businesses – financial and non-financial, private and public, large and small, profit seeking and not-for-profit. They perform such varied tasks as budgeting, financial forecasting, cash management, credit administration, investment analysis, and funds procurement. In recent years, changing economic and regulatory

---

[1] The basic job descriptions and duties are generally taken from the online resources *Careers in Business* (http://www.careers-in-business.com), *Careers in Finance* (http://www.careers-in-finance.com), and other career websites such as Monster.com (http://www.monster.com) that highlight the finance profession. Students seeking more detailed descriptions of the varying careers open to finance graduates, as well as in-depth analyses of the specific jobs and responsibilities of different positions, should join the Financial Management Association and obtain a copy of the paperback book entitled *Careers in Finance* (Financial Management Association International: Tampa, Florida, 2003). Salary levels for typical posts can be derived from *Financial Times* advertisements.

environments have increased the importance and complexity of the financial manager's duties. The globalization of business has also increased demand for people able to assess and manage the risks associated with volatile exchange rates and rapidly changing political environments. The major focus of this book is on the corporate finance function. In early 2007, advertisements in the *Financial Times* for trainee analysts suggested salaries of around €40 000 were routinely available.

Table 1.1 summarizes key facts relating to various entry-level and senior-level corporate finance positions.

Commercial banking Commercial banking is paradoxically an industry in decline in terms of the total number of entities, but one that has an increasing demand for graduates. Bank numbers, driven by consolidation worldwide, continue to decline. However, the value of banking products has increased very greatly, and so banks continue to hire large numbers of new business and finance graduates each year, and banking remains a fertile training ground for managers who later migrate to other

TABLE 1.1

Career opportunities in corporate finance

POSITION	DESCRIPTION
Financial analyst	Primarily responsible for preparing and analysing the firm's financial plans and budgets. Other duties include financial forecasting, performing financial ratio analysis, and working closely with accounting.
Capital budgeting manager	Responsible for evaluating and recommending proposed asset investments. May be involved in the financial aspects of implementing approved investments.
Cash manager	Responsible for maintaining and controlling the firm's daily cash balances. Frequently manages the firm's cash collection, short-term borrowing and banking relationships.
Project finance manager	In large firms, arranges financing for approved asset investments. Coordinates consultants, investment bankers and legal advisers.
Credit analyst/manager	Administers the firm's credit policy by analysing or managing the evaluation of credit applications, extending credit, and monitoring and collecting accounts receivable.
Assistant treasurer	Mid-level position in large firms, responsible for overseeing cash management (including banking relationships) and risk management/insurance needs.
Controller	Upper-mid-level position responsible for formulating and implementing integrated financial plans for companies or divisions. This includes supervising the firm's (or division's) accounting and treasury operations and providing foreign exchange exposure management.
Chief financial officer	Top management position charged with developing financial strategies for creating shareholder wealth. Responsible for developing policies covering all aspects of financial management, including dividends, capital structure, securities issuance, mergers and acquisitions, and international expansion. Often a member of the firm's board of directors.

fields. The key aptitudes required in most entry-level banking jobs are the same as in other areas. In addition to people, computer and international skills, apprentice bankers must master cash flow valuation along with financial and credit analysis.

Most commercial banks offer at least two basic career tracks – consumer and commercial banking. Consumer banking serves the financial needs of a bank's individual customers in its branch network, increasingly via electronic media such as the internet. Commercial banking, on the other hand, involves extending credit and other banking services to corporate clients, ranging from small, family-owned businesses to multinational behemoths. In addition, a great many technologically intensive support positions in banking require excellent finance skills and intimate knowledge of telecommunications and computer technology. Table 1.2 describes career opportunities in commercial banking.

TABLE 1.2

Career opportunities in commercial banking

POSITION	DESCRIPTION
Credit analyst	Entry-level position entails analysis of the creditworthiness of a corporate or individual loan applicant. Involves financial and ratio analysis of financial statements, making projections of future cash flows and often visiting applicants' businesses (corporate loan applicants). Generally a job for immediate graduates, but MBAs sometimes hired.
Corporate loan officer	Responsible for developing new loan business for the bank and for servicing existing accounts. Often called upon to help develop a long-term financing plan for customers and to work with borrowers encountering financial distress. Also expected to market other bank services (cash management, leasing, trust services) to clients.
Branch manager	For graduate trainees who select the retail side of commercial banking, this is an early position of real responsibility. Must manage personnel and customers of a bank branch and spearhead searches for new depositors and borrowers.
Trust officer	Responsible for providing financial advice and products to bank customers – often wealthy ones. Can involve estate planning and/or managing investment assets. Must have (or develop) knowledge of probate law, estate planning, investment planning and personal taxes.
Mortgage banker	Involves making and servicing mortgage loans to homebuyers and businesses. More senior positions involve arranging mortgages for larger real estate developments and commercial properties, as well as securitizing and selling mortgages to syndicators of mortgage-backed securities.
Leasing manager	One of many specialist positions responsible for managing banks' equipment leasing operations and developing new products and services. Other areas include buying accounts receivable and data processing services.
Operations officer	Generic classification for many specialist positions requiring knowledge of both banking and information-processing technology. For example, an electronic banking manager would develop the banks' internet presence and business strategy. Other positions are responsible for internal data processing; coordinating the bank's computer links to ATMs, other banks and the regulatory authorities; and ensuring security of the bank's electronic transactions.

Investment banking Along with consulting, investment banking is the career of choice for many highly qualified finance students because of its high income potential and the interesting nature of the work itself. When students consider finance as a career they typically are thinking of the work of an investment banker. Investment banking involves three main types of activities:

● Helping corporate customers obtain funding by selling securities such as shares and bonds to investors.

● Providing advice to corporate clients on strategic transactions such as mergers and acquisitions.

● Trading debt and equity securities for customers or for the firm's own account.

Investment banking was and remains extraordinarily profitable, and a small number of (mostly US-based) institutions have come to dominate the industry worldwide. But it remains a highly volatile industry. Investment banking is also notorious for being extremely competitive and for demanding long working hours from its professionals (especially the junior ones).

On the other hand, investment banking offers lucrative rewards for those who master the game. Most graduates hired by investment banks are assigned duties as financial analysts. In early 2007, starting salaries in the main European financial centres for entry-level analyst positions ranged from €40 000 upwards, plus bonuses that might average half of starting salaries. Employees who advance in the investment banking business find that their incomes often rise rapidly – sometimes exponentially.

In many ways, investment banking is a star system, like professional sports, where a handful of top producers receive seven-figure compensation packages, while regular employees earn merely comfortable incomes. Success in this industry demands good analytical and communication skills. Much of the growth in investment banking over the foreseeable future is likely to come from two sources – ongoing development of new financial products and services, and the continued internationalization of corporate finance.

Money management The past 25 years have been very good for stock market investors and finance professionals employed in the money management industry. This industry includes investment advisory firms, mutual fund companies, pension fund managers, trust departments of commercial banks and the investment arms of insurance companies. In fact, the money management industry encompasses any person or institution that acts as a **fiduciary** – someone who invests and manages money on someone else's behalf. Two powerful economic and demographic trends have created a rapidly growing demand for money management services. In the USA there has been a demographic bulge of those born in the 1940s and 1950s moving towards retirement, while in Europe we have seen significant new wealth creation in traditionally peripheral countries such as Ireland, Greece and the Iberian nations.

fiduciary
Someone who invests and manages money on someone else's behalf.

The second major force fuelling the growth of the money management industry has been the *institutionalization of investment*. Whereas in the past, individuals owned most financial assets (especially shares), today institutional investors dominate the markets. Of course, these money managers are not the final owners of the securities they invest in, but they do make almost all key investment decisions for their clients. This trend towards professional management of institutionally owned financial assets has created employment opportunities in the money management industry and this trend is likely to continue. Table 1.3 lists career opportunities in money management.

POSITION	DESCRIPTION
Securities analyst	Prepares company-specific and industry-wide analyses for various classes of publicly traded securities (especially shares and bonds). Also involves written and verbal presentations of research and recommendations.
Portfolio management, sales	Markets mutual fund shares to individual and/or institutional investors. Also supports pension fund's sales pitch to corporations, as needed. Stockbrokers develop their own client bases.
Portfolio manager	Selects and manages financial assets for inclusion in portfolios designed to meet specific investment preferences (such as growth, income, international and emerging markets). Relative performance of managers is continuously monitored and publicized.
Pension fund manager	Prudently manages assets held by employees' pension fund, controls appropriate administration expenses (trustee and consultant fees, brokerage commissions, etc.), allocates assets among investment managers and diversifies assets by type of security.
Financial planner	Provides budgeting, insurance, investment, retirement planning, estate planning and tax advice to individuals.
Investment adviser	Works for one of the many firms that specialize in providing investment advice, performance evaluation and quantitative analysis to the money management industry. Requires strong quantitative skills.

TABLE 1.3
Career opportunities in money management

Consulting As the name implies, consultants are hired by companies to analyse firms' business processes and strategies and then recommend how practices should change to make firms more competitive. Firms also hire consultants to implement recommendations. Consulting positions offer a unique opportunity early in your career to work with a broad range of businesses. In return, consultants can expect to spend the majority of their working life away from their base in clients' offices.

The above summaries certainly do not represent an exhaustive survey of financial career opportunities. Instead, they illustrate how you can establish a rewarding and satisfying career using the principles of corporate finance covered in this text. We now answer a perplexing question: What exactly should financial managers manage?

1 What is the 'marginal benefits greater than or equal to marginal costs' decision rule, and why should financial managers constantly seek to apply it to business decisions?

2 Think of another company or product besides Apple's iPod and note the connections between other functional areas and finance.

3 List and briefly describe five main career paths open to finance graduates.

4 Based on your own personal attributes and desires, which of these paths would you prefer?

CONCEPT REVIEW QUESTIONS

Real World

Financial theory and financial practice can sometimes be at odds, as you will see throughout this book. Each informs the other, however, and over time the theory and practice do evolve together. A great example of this is Dimensional Fund Advisers. DFA is a fund management company that was set up in the early 1980s to seek to exploit a phenomenon called the 'small cap' effect. This was the fact that, all other things being equal, the returns on smaller firms tend to be higher than those on larger firms. Over the years DFA has added strategies to its portfolio of funds. Each new strategy is informed by financial research, and DFA employs large numbers of analysts, fund managers and academics to both monitor and conduct research of their own.

1.2 CORPORATE FINANCE ESSENTIALS

Every business requires money to operate, and corporate finance seeks to acquire and manage this money. This section presents several basic concepts involved with the financial management of companies, beginning with a description of debt and equity capital, the two principal types of long-term funding for all businesses.

Debt and equity: The two flavours of capital

Even a casual reader of the financial section of a newspaper or watcher of the business news on television might conclude that businesses have access to many different types of long-term funding, or capital. In fact, only two broad types of capital exist – debt and equity. **Debt capital** includes all of a company's long-term borrowing from creditors. The borrower is obliged to pay interest, at a specified annual rate, on the full amount borrowed (called the loan's 'principal'), as well as to repay the principal amount at the debt's maturity. All of these payments must be made according to a fixed schedule, and creditors have a legally enforceable claim against the firm. If the company defaults on any of its debt payments, creditors can take legal action to force repayment. In some cases, this means that the creditors can force the borrowing firm into bankruptcy. Companies are forced out of business, and their assets are sold (liquidated) to raise cash, and the cash is then used to repay creditor claims. Recent developments in debt capital have greatly increased the complexity of the types available.

debt capital
Borrowed money.

equity capital
An ownership interest usually in the form of ordinary or preference shares.

The owners of the business contribute **equity capital**, which is expected to remain permanently invested in the company. The two basic sources of equity capital are (ordinary) shares and preference shares. When we hear that LMVH's shares have fallen, or that British Airways' have risen, we are hearing about how the market values ordinary shares. As discussed in greater depth in Section 1.3 and in Chapter 5, ordinary shareholders bear most of the firm's business and financial risk, because they receive returns on their investments only after creditors and preference shareholders are paid in full. Similar to creditors, preference shareholders are promised a fixed annual payment on their invested capital. Unlike debt, preference shareholders' claims are not legally enforceable, so these investors cannot force a company into bankruptcy if a preference share dividend is missed. If a company falls into bankruptcy and has to be liquidated, preference shareholders' claims are paid off before any money is paid back to common stockholders. Preference shares are not as common as ordinary shares, and their characteristics can usually be replicated by other financial instruments.

Financial intermediation and modern finance

In the modern economy companies can obtain debt capital by selling securities – effectively legally binding promises to pay – either directly to investors or through what are called financial intermediaries. A **financial intermediary** is an institution that raises capital by issuing liabilities against itself, and then using the funds raised in this way to make loans to companies and individuals. Commercial banks are the most well known of these institutions. Borrowers, in turn, repay intermediaries, meaning that debtors have no direct contact with the savers who actually funded the loans. Commercial banks issue liabilities such as demand deposits (checking or current accounts) to companies and individuals, and then loan funds to corporations, governments and households. While banks in the United States are prohibited from making equity investments, banks in other countries are allowed to purchase the shares of corporate customers. Other significant financial intermediaries include insurance companies, savings and loan institutions, and credit unions.

In addition to making loans, modern financial intermediaries provide a variety of financial services to businesses. By allowing companies and individuals to place their money in demand deposits, banks eliminate the need for everyone to hold large amounts of cash to purchase goods and services. Banks also act as the backbone of a nation's payments system by:

- Collecting payment on cheques sent to their corporate customers.
- Making payment on the cheques written by their customers to other parties.
- Providing information-processing services to small and medium-sized businesses.
- Handling large-volume transactions such as payroll disbursements.

The growing importance of financial markets Although modern financial intermediaries are generally very efficient, the role of these intermediaries as providers of debt capital to corporations has declined for decades. Instead, corporations have increasingly turned to capital markets for external financing, principally because the rapidly declining cost of information-processing makes it much easier for large numbers of investors to obtain and evaluate financial data for thousands of potential corporate borrowers and issuers of ordinary or preference shares. New types of financial intermediaries – especially pension funds and mutual funds – have come to prominence as corporate finance has shifted towards greater reliance on market-based external funding. These intermediaries are major purchasers of securities issued by non-financial companies.

When companies sell securities to investors in exchange for cash, they are said to raise capital in **primary market transactions**. In such transactions, firms actually receive directly the proceeds from issuing securities, so these are true capital-raising events. Once firms issue securities, investors can sell them to other investors. Trades between investors (called **secondary market transactions**) generate no new cash flow for the firm, so these are not true capital-raising events. Most stock market transactions are secondary market trades, whereas a much larger percentage of bond market transactions involve capital-raising primary offerings.

US markets are the most important capital markets in global finance. Over the last 15 years, US issuers have generally accounted for over 60 per cent of the total value of securities issued by corporations around the world each year. To put these 'market share' numbers in perspective, the United States represents only about 30 per cent of world gross domestic product (GDP) and only about one-eighth of the total value of world trade (exports plus imports). According to *Investment Dealers Digest* (January 2006), in 2005 global issues of securities, both debt and equity, totalled

financial intermediary
An institution that raises capital by issuing liabilities against itself, and then lends that capital to corporate and individual borrowers.

primary market transactions
Sales of securities to investors by a corporation to raise capital for the firm.

secondary market transactions
Trades between investors that generate no new cash flow for the firm.

corporate finance
The activities involved in managing money in a business environment.

external financing function
Raising capital to support companies' operations and investment programmes.

capital budgeting function
Selecting the best projects in which to invest the resources of the firm, based on each project's perceived risk and expected return.

financial management function
Managing firms' internal cash flows and their mix of debt and equity financing, both to maximize the value of the debt and equity claims on firms and to ensure that companies can pay off their obligations when they come due.

corporate governance function
Developing ownership and corporate governance structures for companies that ensure that managers behave ethically and make decisions that benefit shareholders.

risk management function
Managing firms' exposures to all types of risk, both insurable and uninsurable, in order to maintain optimum risk–return trade-offs and thereby maximize shareholder value.

venture capitalists
Professional investors who specialize in high-risk/high-return investments in rapidly growing entrepreneurial businesses.

initial public offering (IPO)
Corporations offer shares for sale to the public for the first time; the first public sale of company shares to outside investors.

$6.514 billion (up from $5.767 billion in 2004), of which $3.822 billion, or 58 per cent was from US issuers ($3.450 billion, or 59 per cent in 2004).

The five basic corporate finance functions

Although corporate finance is defined generally as the activities involved in managing cash flows (money) in a business environment, a more complete definition would emphasize that the practice of corporate finance involves five basic functions:

- Raising capital to support companies' operations and investment programmes (the external financing function).
- Selecting the best projects in which to invest firms' resources, based on each project's perceived risk and expected return (the capital budgeting function).
- Managing firms' internal cash flows, their working capital, and their mix of debt and equity financing, both to maximize the value of firms' debt and equity claims and to ensure that companies can pay off their obligations when due (the financial management function).
- Developing company-wide ownership and corporate governance structures that give incentives to managers to behave ethically and make decisions that benefit shareholders (the corporate governance function).
- Managing firms' exposures to all types of risk, both insurable and uninsurable, to maintain an optimal risk–return trade-off and therefore maximize shareholder value (the risk management function).

The following discussions provide a brief overview of the modern financial manager's five principal functions.

External financing Businesses raise money to support investment and other activities in one of two ways: either externally from shareholders or creditors, or internally by retaining and reinvesting operating profits. Although companies raise about two-thirds of their required funding internally each year, this section focuses on the external financing role – as does much of this book.

As we discuss in the next section, sole proprietorships and partnerships face very limited external funding opportunities, but companies enjoy richer and more varied opportunities to raise money externally. They can raise capital either by selling equity (ordinary or preference shares), or by borrowing money from creditors. When corporations are young and small, they usually must raise equity capital privately, either from friends and family, or from professional investors such as venture capitalists. These professionals specialize in making high-risk/high-return investments in rapidly growing entrepreneurial businesses. Once firms reach a certain size, they may decide to go public by conducting an initial public offering (IPO) – selling shares to outside investors and listing the shares for trading on a stock exchange. After IPOs, companies have the option of raising cash by selling additional stock in the future.

Capital budgeting The capital budgeting function represents firms' financial managers' single most important activity, for two reasons. First, managers typically evaluate very large investments in the capital budgeting process. Secondly, companies can prosper in a competitive economy only by seeking out the most promising new products, processes and services to deliver to customers. Companies such as Intel, British Airways, Shell, Samsung and Diageo regularly make huge outlays of money in capital investments. The pay-offs from these investments drive the value of their firms and the wealth of their shareholders. For these and other companies, the annual capital investment budget may run to several billion euros, so the consequences of flawed capital budgeting processes are serious indeed. Not only may the monies be wasted if incorrect decisions are made, but, more crucially, the company may find itself incorrectly positioned for future market or industry trends. A good analogy is the soccer industry – how much money should be paid to purchase a new player? Will he be a complete failure, or will the player be good, but unbalance the team and leave the whole less than the sum of its parts. Even for smaller companies, although the absolute value of the funds may not be as great, the importance is perhaps even higher.

The capital budgeting process breaks down into three steps:

1 *identifying* potential investments
2 *analysing* the set of investment opportunities and identifying those that create shareholder value, and
3 *implementing* and monitoring the investments selected in Step 2.

The long-term success of almost any firm depends on mastering all three steps. Not surprisingly, capital budgeting is also the area where managers most frequently and explicitly apply the marginal benefit versus marginal cost (MB $\geq$ MC) decision rule. Step 2 essentially describes precisely this kind of cost/benefit analysis. We cover capital budgeting in Part 3 of this book.

Financial management Financial management involves managing firms' operating cash flows as efficiently and profitably as possible. A key element of this process, known as the capital structure decision, is finding the right mix of debt and equity securities to issue that maximizes the firm's overall market value. A second part of the financial management function is ensuring that firms have enough working capital on hand for day-to-day operations. Managing working capital involves obtaining seasonal financing, building up enough inventories to meet customer needs, paying suppliers, collecting from customers and investing surplus cash, all while maintaining adequate cash balances. Managing working capital effectively requires not only technical and analytical skills, but also people skills. Almost every component of working capital management involves building and maintaining relationships with customers, suppliers, lenders and others.

Corporate governance Recent corporate scandals – such as financial collapses at Enron, Arthur Andersen, WorldCom and Parmalat – clearly show that establishing good corporate governance systems is paramount. Governance systems determine who benefits most from company activities; then they establish procedures to maximize firm value and to ensure that employees act ethically and responsibly. Good management does not develop in a vacuum. It results from corporate governance systems that hire and promote qualified, honest people, and that motivate employees to achieve company goals through salary and other incentives.

Developing corporate governance systems presents quite a challenge in practice because conflicts inevitably arise among shareholders, managers and other stakeholders. A firm's shareholders want managers to work hard and to protect shareholders' interests. But rarely is it in the interest of any *individual* shareholder to spend the time and money needed to ensure that managers act appropriately. If individual shareholders conducted this type of oversight, they would personally bear all the costs of monitoring management, but would share the benefits with all other shareholders. This is a classic example of the **collective action problem** that arises in most relationships between shareholders and managers. Likewise, though managers may wish to maximize shareholder wealth, they do not want to work harder than necessary, especially if others are going to reap most of the benefits. Finally, managers and shareholders may decide together to run a company to benefit themselves at the expense of creditors or other stakeholders who do not generally have a voice in corporate governance.

As you might expect, a variety of governance mechanisms designed to mitigate conflicts of interest have evolved over time. Strong boards of directors play a vital

collective action problem
When individual shareholders expend time and resources monitoring managers, bearing the costs of monitoring management while the benefit of their activities accrues to all shareholders.

role in any well-functioning governance system, because boards must hire, fire, pay and promote senior managers. Boards must also develop *fixed* (salary) and *contingent* (bonus and equity-based) remuneration packages that align managers' incentives with those of shareholders. In addition, a firm's auditors play a governance role by certifying the accuracy of financial statements. In the United States, accounting scandals and concerns about auditors' conflicts of interest prompted Congress to pass the **Sarbanes-Oxley Act of 2002 (SOX)**.

Just as all companies struggle to develop effective corporate governance systems, so do countries. Governments everywhere strive to establish legal frameworks for corporate finance that encourage both competitive businesses to develop and efficient financial markets to run properly. For example, a nation's legal system should allow mergers and acquisitions that increase economic efficiency, but block takeovers that significantly reduce competition. Commercial laws should provide protection for creditors and minority shareholders and limit opportunities for managers or majority shareholders to transfer corporate wealth from investors to themselves.

Risk management Historically, risk management has identified the unpredictable 'acts of nature' risks (fire, flood, collision and other property damage) to which firms are exposed and has used insurance products or self-insurance to manage those exposures. Today's risk management function identifies, measures and manages many more types of risk exposures, including predictable business risks. These exposures include losses that could result from adverse interest rate movements, commodity price changes and currency value fluctuations. The techniques for managing such risks are among the most sophisticated of all corporate finance practices. The risk management task attempts to quantify the sources and magnitudes of firms' risk exposure and to decide whether to simply accept those risks or to manage them.

Some risks are easily insurable, such as the risk of loss caused by fire or flood, employee theft or injury to customers by the company's products. Other corporate risks can be reduced through diversification. For example, rather than use a sole supplier for a key production input, a company may choose to contract with several suppliers, even if it means purchasing the input at slightly more than the lowest possible price. However, the focus of modern risk management is on the market-driven risks mentioned earlier, relating to interest rates, commodity prices and currency values. Many financial instruments – called derivatives because they derive their value from other, underlying assets – have been developed over the past two decades for use in **hedging** (i.e. offsetting) many of the more threatening market risks. These financial instruments are described in depth in Chapter 16.

We discuss each of the five major finance functions in this textbook, and we hope you come to share our excitement about the career opportunities that corporate finance provides. Never before has finance been as fast-paced, as technological, as international, as ethically challenging or as rigorous as it is today. These trends have helped make it one of the most popular majors for undergraduate students in US and international business schools.

Sarbanes-Oxley Act of 2002 (SOX)
Act of Congress that established new corporate governance standards for US public companies, and that established the Public Company Accounting Oversight Board (PCAOB).

SMART CONCEPTS
See the concept explained step-by-step at www.cengage.co.uk/megginson

hedging
Procedures used by firms to offset many of the more threatening market risks.

Source: Adapted from 'Brisk demand for graduates from across the board', *Financial Times*, 29 January 2007.

Real World

Finance specialism in MBA programmes has proved very popular over the years, with some universities offering deep specialization in aspects of finance. And this appears to have paid off. A report in early 2007 noted that over 40 per cent of MBA graduates from the London Business School were opting for careers in finance.

5 What is a financial intermediary? Why do you think these institutions have steadily been losing 'market share' to capital markets as the principal source of external financing for corporations?

6 List the five basic corporate finance functions. What is the general relationship among them?

7 Which of the five basic corporate finance functions might be considered 'non-traditional'? Why do you think these functions have become so important in recent years?

8 Do you consider that good corporate governance is something that can be legislated for or is it something that is emergent?

1.3 LEGAL FORMS OF BUSINESS ORGANIZATION

Companies exist so that people can organize to pursue profit-making ventures in a formal, legally secure manner. Although companies are organized in numerous ways, only a handful of forms have generally succeeded, and variations of these forms appear throughout the world. This section briefly examines how companies organize themselves legally, and discusses the costs and benefits that accrue to each major form.

Historically, three key legal forms of business organization in the developed world have been prominent: sole proprietorships, partnerships and companies/corporations. These have recently been joined by a fourth type in the United States, limited liability companies, or LLCs. Sole proprietorships are the most common form of organization. However, companies are by far the dominant form in terms of sales, assets and total profits. In addition to these classic forms, other 'hybrid' organizational forms exist.

Sole proprietorships

As the name implies, a sole proprietorship is a business with a single owner. In fact, in a proprietorship no legal distinction arises between the business and the owner. The business is the owner's personal property, it exists only as long as the owner lives and chooses to operate it, and all business assets belong to the owner personally. Furthermore, the owner/entrepreneur bears personal liability for all debts of the business and pays income taxes on the business's earnings.

Sole proprietorships are by far the most common type of business worldwide. Simplicity and ease of operation constitute the proprietorship's principal benefits. However, this organizational form suffers from severe weaknesses that usually limit the firm's long-term growth potential. These include the following:

- *Limited life.* By definition, a proprietorship ceases to exist when the founder dies or retires. Although entrepreneurs can pass the business assets on to their children (or sell them to someone else of their choice), the value of their business – such as business contracts and relationships – tie personally to the entrepreneurs.

- *Limited access to capital.* Proprietorships can obtain operating capital from only two sources – reinvested profits and owners' personal borrowing. In practice, both of these sources are easily exhausted.

- *Unlimited personal liability.* A sole proprietor is personally liable for all debts of the business, including any judgements awarded to plaintiffs in successful lawsuits. A single adverse verdict can impoverish even the most successful family business.

Partnerships

A (general) partnership is essentially a proprietorship with two or more owners who have joined their skills and personal wealth. As with sole proprietorships, no legal distinction exists between the business and its owners, each of whom can execute contracts binding on all the others, and each of whom is personally liable for all partnership debts. This is known as joint and several liability. Though owners are not required to formalize the terms of their partnerships in written partnership agreements, most do create such documents. In the absence of partnership agreements, businesses dissolve whenever one of the partners dies or retires. Furthermore, unless a partnership agreement specifies otherwise, each partner shares equally in business income and each has equal management authority. As with proprietorships, partnership income is taxed only once, at the personal level – a definite benefit in favour of these simple forms.

In addition to the tax benefits and ease of formation that partnerships share with proprietorships, partnerships allow a large number of people to pool their capital and expertise to form much larger enterprises. Partnerships enjoy more flexibility than proprietorships. Industries in which partnerships are a very important form of organization include accounting, consulting, engineering, law and medicine.

The drawbacks of partnerships resemble closely those of sole proprietorships and include the following:

- *Limited life.* Firms' lives can be limited, particularly if only a few partners are involved. Because partnerships are long-term, multi-person business associations, they are also plagued with instability problems as partners leave and others join the business.
- *Limited access to capital.* Firms remain limited to retained profits and personal borrowings if the partnership wants to expand or make capital investments.
- *Unlimited personal liability.* This disadvantage is even worse because the partners are subject to joint and several liability. If one partner makes an unwise or illegal decision, *all* the partners have to pay.

As firms grow larger, the competitive disadvantages of the proprietorship and partnership forms become increasingly severe. Almost all successful companies eventually become corporations. The recent history of the security brokerage industry in the United States shows this very clearly. All the major Wall Street brokerage firms were organized as partnerships before 1970, but during that year Merrill Lynch became a corporation and listed its own shares on the New York Stock Exchange. Over the next three decades, all of the large brokerage houses except Goldman Sachs either switched from partnership to corporate status or were acquired by other financial companies. The last major holdout, Goldman Sachs, finally adopted the corporate form and executed a very successful IPO in May 1999.

Limited partnerships In many ways, limited partnerships combine the best features of the (general) partnership and the corporate organizational forms. Most of the participants in the partnership (the limited partners) have the limited liability of corporate shareholders, but their share of the profits from the business is taxed as partnership income. In any limited partnership (LP), one or more general partners, each of whom has unlimited personal liability, must oversee the firm's activities. Because the general partners operate the business and they alone are legally exposed to the risk of ruin, they usually receive a greater share of partnership income than their capital contribution alone would merit. The limited partners must be totally passive. They contribute capital to the partnership, but they cannot have their names associated with the business, and they cannot take any active role in its operation, even as employees. In return for this passivity, limited partners do not face personal liability for the business's debts. This means limited partners can lose their equity

---

joint and several liability
A legal concept that makes each partner in a partnership legally liable for all the debts of the partnership.

limited partners
One or more totally passive participants in a limited partnership, who do not take any active role in the operation of the business and who do not face personal liability for the debts of the business.

investment in the business, but successful plaintiffs (or tax authorities) cannot look to the limited partners personally for payment of their claims above and beyond the limited partners' initial investments. Best of all, limited partners share in partnership income, which is taxed only once, as ordinary personal income for the partners.

Limited partnerships can provide tax benefits to the limited partners during the early years of the business. Disadvantages of LPs include lack of liquidity (that is, limited partnership interests may be difficult to sell) and problems with monitoring and disciplining the general partner(s). In the United States, in some cases registering an LP with the Securities and Exchange Commission allows (in very limited circumstances) secondary market trading of partnership interests, which reduces or eliminates the problem of low liquidity.

Corporations

By law, a corporation is a separate legal entity with many of the same economic rights and responsibilities as those enjoyed by individuals. Corporations can sue and be sued; they can own property and execute contracts in their own names; they can be tried and convicted for crimes committed by their employees. This organizational form has several key competitive advantages over other forms, including the following:

- *Unlimited life.* Once created, corporations have a perpetual life unless they are explicitly terminated.
- *Limited liability.* Firms' shareholders cannot be held personally liable for the firms' debts, although CEOs and chief financial officers (CFOs) can be held personally liable in the USA under the Sarbanes-Oxley Act if the debts result from improper accounting practices or fraudulent acts.
- *Individual contracting.* Corporations can contract individually with managers, suppliers, customers and ordinary employees, and each individual contract can be renegotiated, modified or terminated without affecting other stakeholders.
- *Unlimited access to capital.* The company itself, rather than its owners, can borrow money from creditors. It can also issue various classes of preference and other shares to equity investors. Furthermore, the ownership claims (ordinary and preference shares) of a public company can be freely traded among investors without obtaining permission from other investors. A **public company** has its shares listed for trading on a public securities market.

A **corporation** (or company) is a legal entity owned by the shareholders who hold its ordinary shares. Shares carry voting rights, and shareholders vote at annual meetings to elect **boards of directors**. These boards are then responsible for hiring and firing managers and setting overall corporate policies. The rules dictating voting procedures and other aspects of corporate governance appear in the firm's **corporate charter**, the legal document created at the company's inception to govern the firm's operations. (In the UK this is called the memorandum and articles of association; in Germany 'Gesellschaftsvertrag'; in France, 'statuts'.) The charter can be changed only by a shareholder vote. One important characteristic of the USA is that incorporation takes place at the state level. While most state incorporations are very similar, certain states such as Delaware and Florida are perceived to be more 'director friendly'. Elsewhere in the world there exist small legal jurisdictions such as Gibraltar, the Channel Islands and Aruba that have very flexible incorporation requirements, and some of these states derive a large percentage of their income from incorporation.

As explained in Chapter 5, those who hold shares own the firm's equity securities. These investors are called **shareholders** or stockholders (the terms are interchangeable). Often they are called **equity claimants** because they hold ownership claims.

public company
A corporation, the shares of which can be freely traded among investors without obtaining the permission of other investors and whose shares are listed for trading in a public securities market.

corporation
A separate legal entity with many of the same economic rights and responsibilities as those enjoyed by individuals.

boards of directors
Elected by shareholders to be responsible for hiring and firing managers and setting overall corporate policies.

corporate charter
The legal document created at the corporation's inception to govern its operations.

shareholders
Owners of ordinary and preference shares of a company.

equity claimants
Owners of a company's equity securities.

Generally, preference shareholders bear less risk than ordinary shareholders, because preference shares pay a fixed dividend yearly, and preference shareholders have a more senior claim on the firm's assets in the event of bankruptcy. Therefore, we refer to ordinary shareholders as the firm's ultimate owners. Ordinary shareholders vote periodically to elect members to the board of directors and to amend the firm's corporate charter when necessary. Directors typically include the company's top managers as well as outsiders, who are usually successful entrepreneurs or executives of other major corporations. The **chief executive officer (CEO)** is responsible for managing day-to-day operations and carrying out policies established by the board. In the United States the CEO is sometimes called the president of the company. Although not all companies split the roles of chairman and chief executive or president and CEO, increasingly it is seen as indicative of good corporate governance to do so. The board expects regular reports from the CEO about the firm's current status and future direction. Note the division between owners and managers in a large corporation, as shown by the red dashed horizontal line in Figure 1.1. This separation leads to **agency costs**, which arise because of conflicts of interest between shareholders (owners) and managers. Agency costs are discussed in greater depth later in this chapter.

Although corporations dominate economic life around the world, this form has some competitive disadvantages. Many governments tax corporate income at both company and personal levels. This treatment, commonly called the **double taxation problem**, has traditionally been the single greatest disadvantage of the corporate form.

Limited liability companies internationally Many countries distinguish two types of limited liability companies, the split being between limited liability companies that can be traded publicly on an organized exchange and those that are privately held. You should note that, even though a company may be private, this does not mean that its shares cannot be traded. The trading however is privately arranged and does not take place on an organized exchange. Thus, in Germany, Gesellschaft mit beschränkten Haftung (GmbH) are privately owned, unlisted, limited liability stock companies. In France, these types of private companies are called Société à Responsibilité Limitée (SARL). Private companies, particularly family-owned firms, play important roles in all market economies. For example, the German post-war 'economic miracle' was not propelled by giant companies, but rather by mid-sized, export-oriented companies that pursued niche marketing strategies at home and abroad. These Mittelstand (middle market) firms still account for some three quarters of all German economic activity. A similar set of relatively small, entrepreneurial companies has helped propel Taiwan, Singapore and other Asian nations to growth rates consistently higher than those achieved in the industrialized West.

Although public limited liability companies exist around the world, they too have different names in different countries. In the UK they are called public limited companies (plc); in Germany, Aktiengesellschaft (AG); in France, Société Générale (SG); and in Spain, Mexico and elsewhere in Latin America, Sociedad Anónima (SA). Given the complexity of national rules in European countries, the Societas Europaea, SE, or European Company form also exists, which allows incorporation in any European state with easy transfer of basis of incorporation to any other state. Key differences internationally revolve around tax treatment of business income and the amount of information that publicly traded companies must disclose. Tax rules are typically, though not always, harsher in the United States than elsewhere, and disclosure requirements are invariably greater for US than for non-US companies. The Comparative Corporate Finance panel shows how the firms' values of publicly quoted companies have surged in markets around the world over the past 20 years.

chief executive officer (CEO)
The top company manager with overall responsibility and authority for managing daily company affairs and carrying out policies established by the board.

agency costs
Costs that arise due to conflicts of interest between shareholders and managers.

double taxation problem
A situation where company profits (out of which dividends are paid) are subject to taxation, and the dividends themselves are also subject to taxation.

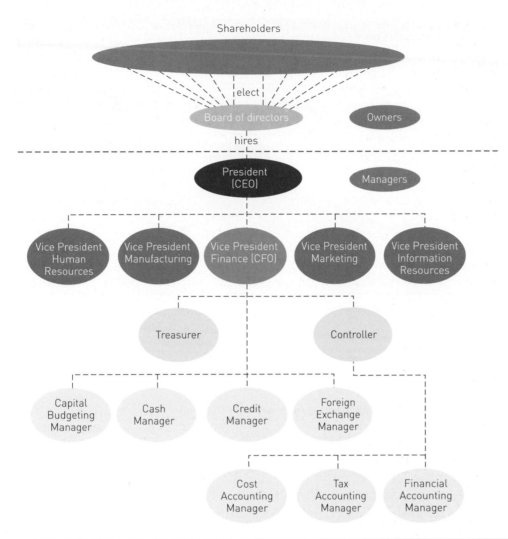

FIGURE 1.1

The finance function in the organizational structure of a typical large corporation

9 What are the advantages and disadvantages of the main types of organizational forms?

10 Comment on the following statement: 'Sooner or later, all successful private companies that are organized as proprietorships or partnerships must become corporations.'

CONCEPT REVIEW QUESTIONS

COMPARATIVE CORPORATE FINANCE
The growth of stock market capitalization

The world's stock markets have increased phenomenally in value and importance during the past 20 years. The figure traces the rise in the total value of the world's stock markets from 1990 to 2005. This period saw a total worldwide market capitalization increase of $8 trillion to about $44 trillion. As the figure shows, the market value of US stocks increased six-fold over this period, but non-US markets experienced even faster growth.

▶

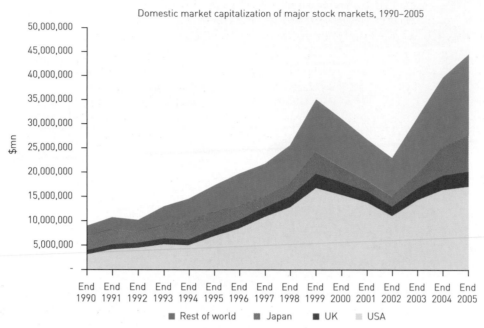

Domestic market capitalization of major stock markets, 1990–2005

Source: International Federation of Stock Exchanges (http://www.fibv.com).

1.4 THE CORPORATE FINANCIAL MANAGER'S GOALS

In large, publicly traded corporations, owners are typically distinct from managers. Traditionally, finance teaches that managers should act according to the interests of the firm's owners – its stockholders. In the sections that follow, we discuss varying ideas about what a corporate manager's goals should be. We first evaluate profit maximization and then describe shareholder wealth maximization. Next, we discuss the agency costs arising from potential conflicts between the stockholders' goals and the managers' actions. Finally, we consider the role of ethics in corporate finance and briefly discuss how the Sarbanes-Oxley Act is likely to affect financial management in the USA.

What should a financial manager try to maximize?

Maximize profit? Some people believe that the manager's objective always should be to try to maximize profits. To maximize profits, financial managers should take only those actions that are expected to increase the firm's revenues more than its costs. From a practical standpoint, this objective translates into maximizing earnings per share (EPS), defined as earnings available for ordinary shareholders divided by the number of shares outstanding.

Although it seems a reasonable objective for corporate managers, profit maximization as a goal suffers from several flaws:

- Figures for earnings per share are always historical, reflecting past performance rather than what is happening now or what will happen in the future.
- If managers seek only to maximize profits over a period of time, they may ignore the timing of those profits. Large profits that pay off many years in the future may be less valuable than smaller profits received next year.
- When firms compute profits, they follow certain accounting principles that focus on accrued revenues and costs. A firm that is profitable according to accounting principles may spend more cash than it receives, and an

unprofitable firm may have larger cash inflows than outflows. In finance, we place more emphasis on cash than on profits or earnings. Cash is king, but cash flow is perhaps an emperor. Profit cannot be used to pay bills, only cash.

● Finally, focusing only on earnings ignores variability, or risk. When comparing two investment opportunities, managers must consider both the risks and the expected return of the investments. Corporate finance presumes a trade-off between risk and expected return, and that risk and expected return are the key determinants of share prices. However, they affect share prices differently. Higher cash flow generally leads to higher share prices, while higher risk results in lower share prices.

Maximize shareholder wealth? Current theory asserts that the firm's proper goal is to maximize shareholders' wealth, as measured by the market price of the firm's shares. A firm's share price reflects the timing, magnitude and risk of the cash flows that investors expect the firm to generate over time. When considering alternative strategies, financial managers should undertake only those actions that they expect will increase the firm's share price – in other words, actions that will increase the value of the firm's future cash flows. This objective really brings us back to our basic premise for the book: financial managers should choose actions that generate benefits in excess of costs (MB ≥ MC).

Why does finance regard share value maximization as the primary corporate objective? Why not focus instead on satisfying the desires of customers, employees, suppliers, creditors or any other stakeholders? Theoretical and empirical arguments support the assertion that managers should focus on maximizing shareholder wealth. A firm's shareholders are sometimes called 'residual' claimants, meaning that they have claims only on any of the firm's cash flows that remain after employees, suppliers, creditors, governments and other stakeholders are paid in full. It may help to visualize all the firm's stakeholders standing in line to receive their allocation of the firm's cash flows. Shareholders stand at the very end of this line. If the firm cannot pay its employees, suppliers, creditors and tax authorities first, shareholders receive nothing. Furthermore, by accepting their position as residual claimants, shareholders agree to bear most of the risk of running the firm. If firms did not operate to maximize shareholder wealth, investors would have little incentive to accept the risks inherent in buying shares and providing the funds necessary for a business to thrive.

To understand this point, consider how a firm would operate if it were run in the interests of its creditors. Would such a firm ever make risky investments, no matter how profitable, given that its creditors receive only a fixed return if these investments pay off? Only shareholders have the proper incentives to make risky, value-increasing investments that maximize overall firm value. Thus, only shareholders can force the firm to take on risky, but potentially profitable, ventures.

Focus on stakeholders? Although the primary goal of managers should be maximizing shareholder wealth, many firms have broadened their focus in recent years to include the interests of other stakeholders – such as employees, customers, tax authorities and the communities where firms operate. A firm with a stakeholder focus consciously avoids actions that would prove detrimental to stakeholders by transferring other constituents' wealth to shareholders (e.g. driving down wages – the return to employee stakeholders – simply to increase shareholder value). The goal is not so much to maximize others' interests as it is to preserve those interests.

Considering other constituents' interests is part of the firm's 'social responsibility', and keeping other affected groups happy provides long-term benefit to shareholders. Such relationships minimize employee turnover, conflicts and litigation. In most cases, taking care of stakeholders translates into maximizing shareholder wealth. But conflict between these two objectives inevitably arises. In that case, the firm should ultimately be run to benefit equity holders. Companies are rarely required by law to act in a socially responsible manner, although the growth in corporate social responsibility (CSR) movements in recent years has begun to place a greater focus on this area. The EU Commission in 1995 set up a network on CSR, and the UK government has also led initiatives on CSR.

How can agency costs be controlled in corporate finance?

Control of modern corporations usually rests in the hands of professional, non-owner managers. We have seen that the goal of financial managers should be to maximize shareholder wealth; thus, managers act as agents of the owners, who have hired them to make decisions and to manage the firm for the owners' benefit. Technically, any manager who owns less than 100 per cent of the firm's stock is, to some degree, an *agent* of other owners.

In practice, managers also consider their own personal wealth, job security, lifestyle and prestige, and seek to receive perquisites, such as country club memberships, limousines, corporate jet usage and posh offices (provided at company expense, of course). Such concerns often motivate managers to pursue objectives other than shareholder wealth maximization. Voting shareholders, especially large institutional investors, recognize the potential for managers' self-interested behaviour, and use a variety of tools to limit such conflicts of interest. Financial economists recognize the agency costs that arise when the shareholders' interests and managers' interests conflict.

agency problems
The conflict between the goals of a firm's owners and its managers.

Types of agency costs Conflict between the goals of a firm's owners and managers gives rise to managerial **agency problems** – costs arising from the likelihood that managers may place personal goals ahead of corporate goals. Shareholders can attempt to overcome these agency problems by:

- relying on market forces to exert managerial discipline
- incurring the monitoring and bonding costs necessary to supervise managers
- structuring executive remuneration packages to align managers' interests with stockholders' interests.

Several market forces constrain a manager's opportunistic behaviour. In recent years large investors have become more active in management. This is particularly true for institutional investors such as mutual funds, life insurance companies and pension funds, which often hold large blocks of a firm's equity capital and thus have many votes to wield if issues arise. Institutional investor activists use their influence to pressure underperforming management teams, occasionally applying enough pressure to replace existing CEOs with new ones. The rise in investor activism, however, has not to date proven to dramatically affect value, but the evidence is more favourable as regards 'internal' corporate governance. Also, research from the London Business School/European Corporate Governance Institute in 2006 suggested that shareholder activism works for UK companies.

hostile takeover
The acquisition of one firm by another through an open-market bid for a majority of the target's shares where the target firm's senior managers do not support (or, more likely, actively resist) the acquisition.

An even more powerful form of market discipline is the **hostile takeover**. A hostile takeover involves the acquisition of one firm (the target) by another (the bidder) through an open-market bid, or tender offer, for a majority of the target's shares. By definition, a takeover attempt is hostile if the target firm's senior managers do not support (or, more likely, actively resist) the acquisition. The forces that drive hostile takeovers vary over time and from one acquisition to another, but poor financial performance is a common problem among targets of hostile bids. Bidders in hostile deals may believe they can improve the value of the target company, and thereby profit from their investment, by replacing incumbent management. Managers naturally see this as a threat and erect a variety of barriers to thwart potential acquirers. Nevertheless, the constant threat of a takeover provides additional motivation for managers to act in the firm owners' best interests. In 2005 and 2006 the threat of hostile takeovers caused significant tensions within the European Union, with a series of cross-border bids being stalled, blocked or criticized by national political figures, showing the importance of the implicit government stakeholder in many countries. Even in the USA, hostile takeovers are not always possible, as for example in the airline industry where a majority of ownership must vest with US citizens. In 2006 the state of Pennsylvania passed laws making it more difficult to remove directors. Such barriers to takeovers increase agency costs.

In addition to market forces, other devices can encourage managers to behave in shareholders' interests or limit the consequences when managers misbehave. 'Bonding expenditures' insure firms against the potential consequences of dishonest acts by managers. For example, managers could be required to accept a portion of their total pay in the form of delayed compensation that must be forfeited in the event of poor performance. 'Monitoring expenditures' pay for audits and control procedures that alert shareholders if managers pursue their own interests too aggressively. But, you may ask, 'Who monitors the monitors?' In the wake of Enron's bankruptcy, Enron's auditor, Arthur Andersen, experienced the consequences of failing to alert shareholders to the company's problems. Arthur Andersen's audit clients abandoned the firm in droves, and many of the firm's partners quit. The company was later convicted of criminal misconduct in a US court, which forced Arthur Andersen into bankruptcy.

Use of compensation contracts to control agency costs One of the most popular, powerful and expensive methods of overcoming agency costs and aligning managerial and shareholder interests is through the design of executive remuneration (or 'compensation') contracts. American companies have long used sophisticated (and potentially lucrative) executive compensation contracts, and the practice is spreading to other industrialized countries – though few European or Asian companies offer their managers pay levels that even approach what US managers receive. Remuneration contracts give managers incentives to act in the owners' best interests and allow firms to compete for, hire and retain the best managers available. For this reason, such pay packages are often called 'golden handcuffs', because they tie good managers to the firm.

Incentive remuneration plans attempt to tie managerial wealth directly to the firm's share price. This primarily involves making outright grants of shares to top managers or, more commonly, giving them share options, which we discuss later. Options give managers the right to purchase stock at fixed exercise prices, usually the market price of the shares at the time the manager receives the options. The idea is that managers who have incentives to take actions to maximize the share price above the exercise price will increase their own wealth along with that of other shareholders.

Although experts agree that linking pay to performance can effectively motivate management, the actual workings of many remuneration plans have been harshly criticized in recent years. Individual and institutional investors have publicly questioned the wisdom of awarding multi-million-dollar remuneration packages (which typically include salary, bonus and long-term remuneration) to executives of poorly performing corporations. For example, the highest paid US executives in 2006 were Richard Fairbank of Capital One Financial (with total pay of $249 million) and Terry Semel of Yahoo (total pay of $230 million). Average levels of CEO remuneration in other developed countries tend to be much lower – a fact that critics of CEO pay in the United States do not miss. For example, *The Guardian* newspaper in the UK publishes an annual pay survey and, for 2005, the highest paid UK-based CEO was Mick Davies of Xstrata, a mining company, on £15 million.

Are ethics important in corporate finance?

In recent years, actions by certain businesses have received major media attention. Examples include:

- A string of fines totalling more than $1.2 billion paid between 2002 and 2004 by major brokerage firms to investors (and the state of New York) for intentionally misleading investors with regard to buy-and-sell recommendations offered by brokerage firm analysts.
- The June 2002 insider trading arrest of Samuel Waksal, founder and CEO of the biotech firm ImClone Systems, who leaked information to family and friends on the failure of the Food and Drug Administration to approve ImClone's marketing application for the cancer drug Erbitux before that information was released to the public.

SMART ETHICS VIDEO

Andy Bryant, Executive Vice President of Finance and Enterprise Systems, Chief Financial Officer, Intel Corporation

'I never thought that ethics would be a value add to a company, but today I believe it counts as part of your market cap.'

See the entire interview at **www.cengage.co.uk/megginson**

- The January 2004 discovery that the Italian milk distribution company Parmalat had used forged documents to obtain loans and to issue bonds. These actions not only landed the company's top executives in jail but also triggered what may become the largest bankruptcy in financial history.
- The sensational 2004 trials of Dennis Koslowski (Tyco International Ltd) and Martha Stewart (Martha Stewart Living Omnimedia Inc.) on charges of misappropriation of company assets and conspiracy to obstruct justice, respectively.

Clearly, these and other similar actions, such as those involving Enron, Global Crossing, WorldCom and Adelphia, have focused attention on the question of ethics, or standards of conduct in business dealings. Today, society in general and the financial community in particular are developing and enforcing higher ethical standards. The US Congress passed the Sarbanes-Oxley Act in 2002 to enforce higher ethical standards and increase penalties for violators. The goal of these standards is to motivate businesspeople and investors alike to adhere to both the letter and the spirit of laws and regulations concerned with all aspects of business and professional practice.

More and more firms are directly addressing ethical issues by establishing corporate ethics policies and guidelines, and by requiring employee compliance with them. Frequently, employees must sign formal pledges to uphold firms' ethics policies. Such policies typically apply to employee actions in dealing with all corporate stakeholders, including the public at large.[2] Ethical behaviour is therefore viewed as necessary for the achievement of firms' goal of maximizing owner wealth.

CONCEPT REVIEW QUESTIONS

11 What are the relative advantages and disadvantages of using sophisticated management remuneration packages to align the interests of managers and shareholders?

12 Why are ethics important in corporate finance? What is the likely consequence of unethical behaviour by a corporation and its managers?

13 Why did the United States government pass the Sarbanes-Oxley Act of 2002, and what are its key provisions?

---

[2] Unfortunately, these steps are hardly enough. Enron had a detailed conflict-of-interest policy in place, but then waived it so that its executives could set up the special-purpose entities that subsequently caused Enron's failure. The result of a lack of effective ethics policies at Enron and numerous other firms has been an increased level of government oversight and regulation.

1.5 SUMMARY AND CONCLUSIONS

- When making financial decisions, managers should always ask whether the marginal benefits of the decision outweigh the marginal costs. Managers should take actions and accept projects only where the marginal benefits exceed or are equal to marginal costs.

- Finance graduates must interact with professionals trained in all other business disciplines. The five most important career paths for finance professionals are in corporate finance, commercial banking, investment banking, money management or consulting.

- Corporations can obtain external funding either from financial intermediaries, such as commercial banks, or by issuing securities directly to investors through capital markets. Intermediaries have been steadily losing financial market share to capital markets for several decades.

- The practice of corporate finance involves five basic, related sets of activities: external financing, capital budgeting, financial management, corporate governance and risk management.

- The three key legal forms of business organization are sole proprietorships, partnerships and limited liability companies. Sole proprietorships are most common, but limited liability companies dominate economically.

- Limited liability companies exist in virtually every country, and those in developed countries share many of the same basic traits.

- The goal of firm managers should be to maximize shareholder wealth rather than maximize profits, because the latter focuses on the past, ignores the timing of profits, relies on accounting values rather than future cash flows and ignores risk. Shareholder wealth maximization is socially optimal because shareholders are residual claimants who profit only after all other claims have been paid in full.

- Agency costs that result from the separation of ownership and control must be addressed satisfactorily for companies to prosper. These costs can be overcome, or at least reduced, by relying on market incentives or threats relating to corporate control, by incurring monitoring and bonding costs, and by using executive compensation contracts that align the interests of shareholders and managers.

- Ethics – the standards of conduct in business dealings – are important in corporate finance. Ethical behaviour is viewed as necessary for the achievement of firms' goal of maximizing owner wealth. The Sarbanes-Oxley Act of 2002 established rules and procedures in the United States aimed at eliminating the potential for unethical acts and conflicts of interest in public corporations.

INTERNET RESOURCES

Note: This textbook includes numerous internet links, both within the discussions and at the end of each chapter. Because some links are likely to change or be eliminated during the life of this edition, please go to the book's website (www.cengage.co.uk/megginson) to obtain updated links.

http://www.ft.com
Financial Times website. One of the best websites for international business and economic information.

http://www.careers.com http://www.monster.com http://www.usnews.com http://www.careers.wsj.com http://www.ft.com/jobs
Websites for career-related facts and figures.

http://www.sec.gov/edgar.shtml
US Securities and Exchange Commission's EDGAR website. Provides online access to all security registrations and financial documents filed by public companies with the SEC since 1994.

http://www.fsa.gov.uk/pubs/ukla/lr_comcode3.pdf
The combined code on good governance for UK listed companies.

http://www.treasurers.org
UK-based Association of Corporate Treasurers, including quizzes and a magazine.

http://www.jobs1.co.uk/directory/recruitment_finance.html
Repository of finance jobs.

http://www.gojobsite.ie/channels/graduate.html http://www.efinancialcareers.co.uk/
Contain profiles of financial service companies and links to recruitment.

KEY TERMS

agency costs	equity capital	limited partners
agency problems	equity claimants	president or chief executive
boards of directors	external financing function	officer (CEO)
capital budgeting function	fiduciary	primary market transactions
collective action problem	financial intermediary	public company
corporate charter	financial management function	risk management function
corporate finance	hedging	Sarbanes-Oxley Act 2002 (SOX)
corporate governance function	hostile takeover	secondary market transactions
corporation	initial public offering (IPO)	shareholders
double taxation problem	joint and several liability	venture capitalists

QUESTIONS

Q1-1 Why must a financial manager have an integrated understanding of the five basic finance functions? Why is the corporate governance function considered a finance function? Has the risk management function become more important in recent years?

Q1-2 Enter the home page of the Careers in Business website (http://www.careers-in-business.com), and page through the finance positions listed and their corresponding salaries. What skills sets or job characteristics lead to the variation in salaries? Which of these positions generally require prior work experience?

Q1-3 What are the advantages and disadvantages of the different legal forms of business organization? Could the limited liability advantage of a corporation also lead to an agency problem? Why? What legal form would a start-up entrepreneur likely prefer?

Q1-4 Can there be a difference between profit maximization and shareholder wealth maximization? If so, what could cause this difference? Which of the two should be the goal of the firm and its management?

Q1-5 Define a corporate stakeholder. Which groups are considered to be stakeholders? Would shareholders also be considered stakeholders? Compare the shareholder wealth maximization principle to the stakeholder wealth preservation principle in terms of economic systems.

Q1-6 What is meant by an 'agency cost' or 'agency problem'? Do these interfere with shareholder wealth maximization? Why? What mechanisms minimize these costs/problems? Are executive remuneration contracts effective in mitigating these costs/problems?

Q1-7 Are ethics critical to the financial manager's goal of shareholder wealth maximization? How are the two related? Is the establishment of corporate ethics policies and guidelines, and requiring employee compliance with them, enough to ensure ethical behaviour by employees?

PROBLEMS

Goals of the corporate financial manager

P1-1 Consider the following simple corporate example with one shareholder and one manager. There are two mutually exclusive projects in which the manager may invest and two possible manager remuneration contracts that the shareholder may choose to employ. The manager may be paid a flat €300 000 or receive 10 per cent of corporate profits. The shareholder receives all profits net of manager remuneration. Which project maximizes shareholder wealth? Which remuneration contract does the manager prefer if this project is chosen? Which project will the manager choose under a flat remuneration arrangement? Under a profit-sharing arrangement? Which remuneration contract aligns the interests of the shareholder and manager so that the manager will act in the best interest of the shareholder?

PROJECT #1		PROJECT #2	
PROBABILITY	GROSS PROFIT	PROBABILITY	GROSS PROFIT
33.33%	€0	50.0%	€600 000
33.33%	€3 000 000	50.0%	€900 000
33.33%	€9 000 000		

MINICASE *The scope of corporate finance*

The potential career paths for someone with expertise in finance are varied and exciting. Career possibilities include the areas of corporate finance, commercial banking, investment banking, asset management, mutual funds and brokerage, insurance, property and venture capital.

Assignment

Find descriptions for these and other finance-related careers on the following website: http://www.wetfeet.com/asp/careerlist.asp. Think of the ways that our core financial decision can be applied to each of these careers. Remember, our core financial decision takes the following approach: all financial decisions can be made by asking whether the marginal benefits (MBs) of taking a certain action are greater than or equal to the marginal costs (MCs) of this action.

Chapter 2

Financial Statement and Cash Flow Analysis

OPENING FOCUS

Accounting for the numbers

Accounting is the language of business, but, as we know, the elements of language can be changed and rearranged to make different stories. So too with accounting information. Studies by professors from Duke University in the USA have shown that executives are adept at making changes to accounting information, perfectly legally, which can have a dramatic impact on the 'bottom line'.

John Graham and Campbell Harvey, with their colleague Shivaram Rajgopal from Washington University, surveyed over 400 finance executives in large companies. What they discovered was that companies focus very heavily on 'bottom line' earnings, particularly earnings per share. The vast majority of companies would defer a good, profitable project if by taking it on in this accounting period they would impact on the earnings per share number in a manner that would surprise the stock market. Managers would trade off good value projects in favour of smoother earnings. None of these practices are in any way fraudulent or illegal. Rather they show how closely the managers watch the analysts who watch the earnings of the companies that the managers manage.

By contrast, other research, such as that by Rebecca Rosner, shows that companies that later go into bankruptcy engage pre bankruptcy in accounting manipulation of a more substantive nature.

This chapter provides you with the basic skills to analyse and interpret, from a finance perspective, the accounts of modern corporations.

Sources: Campbell Harvey, John Graham and Shivaram Rajgopal (2006) 'The Economic Implications of Corporate Financial Reporting', *Journal of Accounting and Economics*, 40; Rebecca Rosner (2003) 'Earnings Manipulation in Failing Firms', *Contemporary Accounting Research*, 20(2): 361–408.

LEARNING OBJECTIVES

After studying this chapter you should be able to:

- List and define the key financial statements that firms are required to provide to their shareholders.

- Evaluate a firm's cash flows using its financial statements, including the statement of cash flows.

- Calculate and interpret liquidity, activity and debt ratios.

- Review the popular profitability ratios and the role of the DuPont system in analysing the firm's returns.

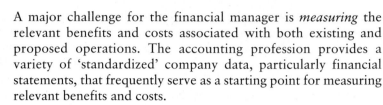

accrual-based approach
Revenues are recorded at the point of sale and costs when they are incurred, not necessarily when a firm receives or pays out cash.

cash flow approach
Used by financial professionals to focus attention on current and prospective inflows and outflows of cash.

A major challenge for the financial manager is *measuring* the relevant benefits and costs associated with both existing and proposed operations. The accounting profession provides a variety of 'standardized' company data, particularly financial statements, that frequently serve as a starting point for measuring relevant benefits and costs.

It is often said that accounting is the language of business. Corporate finance relies heavily on accounting concepts and language, but the primary focus of finance professionals and accountants differs significantly. Accountants apply generally accepted accounting principles (GAAP) to construct financial statements that attempt to portray fairly how a company has performed in the past. Accountants generally construct these statements using an **accrual-based approach**, which means that accountants record revenues at the point of sale and costs as they are incurred, not necessarily when a firm receives or pays out cash. These widely accepted accounting principles and practices allow corporate financial managers and others, barring fraud, to feel confident with the financial representation contained in audited financial statements.

In contrast to accountants, financial professionals use a **cash flow approach** that focuses more attention on current and prospective inflows (benefits) and outflows (costs) of cash. The financial manager must convert relevant accounting and tax information into cash outflows and cash inflows, which after adjustment for timing differences and risk factors, represent the relevant marginal costs and marginal benefits needed for decision making. This divergence is sometimes also characterized as an economic (cash flow and finance professional) perspective versus an accounting perspective.

This chapter describes how financial professionals use accounting information and terminology to analyse the firm's cash flows and financial performance. If accounting is the language of business, this chapter can be considered as a primer on how to use the language to say what is relevant to finance. We begin with a brief review of the major financial statements, then use them to demonstrate some of the key concepts involved in cash flow analysis. We give special emphasis to the firm's cash flows, free cash flows, the classification of inflows and outflows of cash, and the development and interpretation of statements of cash flows. Then, we discuss some popular financial ratios used to analyse the firm's financial performance.

2.1 FINANCIAL STATEMENTS

As noted in Chapter 1, financial managers focus primarily on cash flows rather than on accrual-based accounting data. In spite of this focus, it is important for financial managers to understand financial statements, which serve as a window through which outsiders – investors, lenders and others – view the firm's financial performance and position.

National governments require public companies to generate financial statements based on widely accepted accounting rules. In the United States, the Securities and Exchange Commission (SEC) is responsible for regulating publicly traded US companies, as well as the nation's stock and bond markets. Every other industrialized country has an agency similar to the SEC, and most developed countries mandate that companies generate financial statements that follow international accounting standards (IAS). An important force in the internationalization of accounting standards has been that the SEC has historically insisted that all non-US companies report results based on US rules if they wish to sell their securities directly to US investors. However, the corporate accounting scandals of 2001 and 2002 tarnished the reputation of these rules and enhanced that of IAS. More recently there has been an increased effort to harmonize internationally the rules underlying the presentation of accounting statements. Again, thinking of accounting as a language, the existence of different grammars – ways in which the language can be meaningfully put together – can cause confusion. Thus, in recent years the International Accounting Standards Board (IASB) has come to the forefront of the debate. In February 2006 the SEC reaffirmed its commitment to convergence and its wish to work with the IASB on the required convergence issues. Thus, the emergence of a world standard for accounting information, a world grammar, appears possible.

In this chapter we use data taken from the Thomson ONE database. Worldscope is a trade name of Thomson Financial, the providers of Banker One Business School Edition, a subscription to which is bundled with this text. In that package are accounts and statements from a large number of companies. However, the material in the package is a small sample of what is generally available from Worldscope, as the entire dataset covers 96 per cent by market value of world equity markets. Worldscope data are harmonized, based on analysis of original statements from companies. This harmonization is undertaken by the analysts at Thomson, and the resulting data are designed to be internationally comparable. Worldscope data are used worldwide by thousands of academics, analysts, bankers and investors. However, despite this de facto world standard, you should realize that the Worldscope data and accounts have no legal basis. A further issue is that the analysts at Worldscope on occasion use slightly different formulae for ratios from those that appear here. On the Thomson ONE site, right clicking on a number, ratio or element of a statement will show you how it is made up.

The key financial statements of any company are (1) the balance sheet, (2) the income statement and (3) the statement of cash flows. Companies may well, in their annual or quarterly reports, use different names. However, the information presented is the same. (In the USA an important further requirement is to provide a statement of retained earnings.) Our concern in this section is to review the information presented in these statements. Throughout, we present the financial statements from the 2006 annual report of LVMH, the French-based luxury goods producer, as an example of the use of standards and methods.

Balance sheet

A firm's balance sheet presents a 'snapshot' view of the company's financial position at a specific point in time – the financial year-end. By definition, a firm's assets must equal the combined value of its liabilities and shareholders' equity. Phrased differently, either creditors (lenders) or equity investors (owners) finance all of a firm's assets.

A balance sheet shows assets on the left-hand side and the claims of creditors and shareholders on the right-hand side. Both assets and liabilities by convention appear in descending order of liquidity, or the length of time it takes for accounts to be converted into cash in the normal course of business. The most liquid asset, cash, appears first, and the least liquid, fixed assets, comes last. Similarly, accounts payable represents the obligations the firm must pay with cash within the next year, whereas the last entry on the right-hand side of the balance sheet, shareholders' equity, quite literally never matures. This 'double entry' system is not new. Fra Luca Bartolomeo de Pacioli published the *Summa*, a coherent account of double entry bookkeeping and accounting, in 1494, but balance sheets in recognizably modern form are available from the early 14th century.

Table 2.1 presents LVMH's balance sheet as at 31 December 2006. As is standard practice in annual reports, the table also shows previous year accounts for comparison. Cash and cash equivalents are assets such as current account balances at commercial banks that can be used directly as a means of payment. 'Other current assets' represent very liquid, short-term investments, which financial analysts view as a form of 'near cash'. Such securities would include short, fixed-term deposit accounts. Accounts receivable represent the amount customers owe the firm from sales made on credit. Inventories include raw materials, work in progress (partially finished goods) and finished goods held by the firm. Note also that LVMH is obviously owed rebates on income tax paid, which it expects to receive within the year, which makes it a current asset.

The entry for property, plant and equipment is the book value of all real property, structures and long-lived equipment owned by the firm. Net property, plant and equipment represents the difference between this original value and accumulated depreciation – the cumulative expense recorded for the depreciation of fixed assets since their purchase. Tax authorities allow companies to depreciate, or charge against taxable earnings, a fraction of a fixed asset's cost each year to reflect a decline in the asset's economic value over time. The one fixed asset that is not depreciated is land, because it generally does not decline in value over time. To obtain the gross value of these assets for LVMH it is necessary to examine the account notes. Finally, brands and other intangibles include valuable items such as patents, trademarks, copyrights, exploration rights or other tradable assets. Although intangible assets are usually nothing more than legal rights, they are often extremely valuable, as the discussion of the market value of global brands in the Comparative Corporate Finance insert later in this chapter vividly demonstrates. In the case of LVMH, the value of the brands would reflect the world leading position it holds in areas of luxury goods, with brands such as Louis Vuitton, Pucci, Dior and Tag Heuer.

Turning our attention to the other side of the balance sheet, current liabilities include accounts payable, which are amounts owed for credit purchases by the firm; short-term borrowings comprise outstanding short-term loans, such as overdrafts and term loans typically from commercial bank, and also include the short-term component of long-term debt, in other words the part of long-term debt that will be repaid within one year;

TABLE 2.1

Balance sheet for LVMH, end-2004, 2005 and 2006 (€mn)

	2006	2005	2004		2006	2005	2004
Current assets	**9 165**	**8 516**	**7 412**	**Current liabilities**	**6 356**	**6 591**	**6 076**
Inventories and work in progress	4 383	4 134	3 598	Short-term borrowings	2 100	2 642	2 529
Accounts receivable	1 461	1 370	1 364	Accounts payable	1 899	1 732	1 581
Income tax	512	317	113	Income tax	692	373	201
Other current assets	1 587	1 225	1 302	Provisions	255	305	259
Cash and cash equivalents	1 222	1 470	1 035	Other current liabilities	1 410	1 539	1 506
Fixed assets	**19 620**	**19 537**	**18 105**	**Long-term liabilities**	**10 835**	**10 978**	**10 766**
Brands and other intangibles	8 227	8 530	7 838	Long-term borrowings	3 235	3 747	4 188
Goodwill	4 537	4 479	4 048	Provisions	983	949	883
Property, plant and equipment net	5 173	4 983	4 541	Deferred tax	2 862	2 925	2 458
Investments in associates	126	128	115	Other non-current liabilities	3 755	3 357	3 237
Non-current financial assets	504	451	718				
Other non-current assets	658	660	628	**Equity**	**11 594**	**10 484**	**8 675**
Deferred tax	395	306	217	Share capital	147	147	147
				Share premium account	1 736	1 736	1 736
				Treasury shares	−1 019	−972	−1 006
				Minority interests	991	1 025	893
				Translation adjustment	−119	292	−200
				Group share of net profit	1 879	1 440	1 194
				Reserves	7 979	6 816	5 911
Total assets	**28 785**	**28 053**	**25 517**	**Total liabilities and equity**	**28 785**	**28 053**	**25 517**

and 'other current liabilities', which are usually accrued expenses (costs incurred by the firm that have not yet been paid). Examples of accruals include taxes owed to the government and wages due to employees. Accounts payable and accruals are often called 'spontaneous liabilities' because they tend to change directly with changes in sales.

In many countries, laws permit firms to construct two sets of financial statements, one for tax purposes and one for reporting to the public. For example, when a firm purchases a long-lived asset, it can choose to depreciate this asset rapidly for tax purposes, resulting in large, immediate tax write-offs and smaller tax deductions later. When the firm constructs financial statements for release to the public, however, it may choose a different depreciation method, perhaps one that results in higher reported earnings in the early years of the asset's life and lower earnings later. The **deferred taxes** entry on the balance sheet is a long-term liability that reflects the discrepancy between the taxes that firms actually pay and the tax liabilities they report on their public financial statements. **Long-term debt** represents debt that matures more than one year in the future. Note also that LVMH has entries for provisions, which are monies due for liabilities such as pension fund reserve rebalancing and medical care of retirees. Some of these are due within the year, making them current, while others are longer term in nature.

The shareholders 'equity section provides information about the claims of investors who own preference and ordinary shares. LVMH has no **preference shares**, but if it had they would appear first in the shareholders' equity section, as they take precedence over ordinary shares Next, the amount paid in by the original purchasers of **ordinary shares**, the most basic form of corporate ownership, is shown by two entries – share capital and share premium account. The share capital entry equals the number of outstanding ordinary shares multiplied by the **par value** per share. The par value of a share is an arbitrary value with little or no economic significance. The **share premium account** equals the number of shares outstanding multiplied by the original selling price of the shares, net of the par value. Therefore, the combined value of ordinary shares and paid-in capital equals the proceeds the firm received when it originally sold shares to investors. **Reserves (retained earnings)** are the cumulative total of the earnings that the firm has reinvested since its inception. It is important to recognize that these retained earnings do not represent a reservoir of unspent cash. They represent shareholders' funds that they have decided to keep in the company rather than pay in dividends or spend on other investments.

In the case of LVMH there is another element of shareholders' equity, the **minority interest**, representing the value of shares that the company holds in subsidiaries of the company. The **treasury shares** entry records the value of ordinary shares that the firm currently holds in reserve. Usually, treasury shares appear on the balance sheet because the firm has reacquired previously issued shares through a share repurchase programme. We also see an item, 'Translation adjustment', which in the case of LVMH represents losses or gains on foreign exchange transactions, or incurred when translating foreign exchange. Equity consists of the total of all equity invested in the company.

Income statement

Table 2.2 presents LVMH's income statement for the year ended 31 December 2006. As with the balance sheet, LVMH's income statement also includes data from 2004 and 2005 for comparison.[1] In the vocabulary of accounting, income (also called profit,

deferred taxes Reflect the discrepancy between the taxes that firms actually pay and the tax liabilities they report on their public financial statements.

long-term debt Debt that matures more than one year in the future.

preference shares A form of ownership that has preference over ordinary shares with regard to income and assets.

ordinary shares The most basic form of corporate ownership.

par value (ordinary shares) An arbitrary value assigned to ordinary shares on a firm's balance sheet.

share premium account The number of ordinary shares outstanding times the original selling price of the shares, net of the par value.

reserves (retained earnings) The cumulative total of the earnings that a firm has reinvested since its inception.

minority interest The value of shares that a company holds in subsidiaries of the company.

treasury shares Shares that were issued and later reacquired by the firm through share repurchase programmes and are therefore being held in reserve by the firm.

---

[1] When reporting to shareholders, firms typically also include a common-size income statement that expresses all income statement entries as a percentage of sales.

TABLE 2.2
LVMH income statements for the years ended 31 December 2004–2006 (€mn)

	2006	2005	2004
Revenue	15 306	13 910	12 481
Cost of goods sold	5 481	5 001	4 373
Gross profit	**9 825**	**8 909**	**8 108**
Marketing and sales expenses	5 364	4 892	4 512
General and administrative expenses	1 289	1 274	1 224
Operating profit	**3 172**	**2 743**	**2 372**
Other income and expenditure	120	221	199
Earnings before interest and taxes (EBIT)	**3 052**	**2 522**	**2 173**
Net finance charges	53	143	220
Income tax	839	711	551
Net profit or income after taxes	2 160	1 668	1 402
Minority interest	281	228	208
Income to shareholders	**1 879**	**1 440**	**1 194**

earnings or margin) equals revenue minus expenses. LVMH's income statement, however, has several measures of 'income' appearing at different points. The first income measure is gross profit, which is the amount by which sales revenue exceeds the cost of goods sold (the direct cost of producing or purchasing the goods sold). Next, various operating expenses, including selling expense, general and administrative expense, are deducted from gross profits. The resulting operating profit of €3172 million represents the profits earned from the sale of products, although this amount does not include financial and tax costs. Other income, earned on transactions not directly related to producing and/or selling the firm's products, is added to operating income to yield earnings before interest and taxes (EBIT) of €3052 million. When a firm has no 'other income', its operating profit and EBIT are equal. Next, €53 million of interest expense – representing the cost of debt financing – is subtracted from EBIT to arrive at pre-tax income, in this case €2099 million. The final step is to subtract taxes from pre-tax income to arrive at net income, or net profit after taxes, of €2160 million. Net income is the proverbial 'bottom line' and the single most important accounting number for both corporate managers and external financial analysts. As we have seen earlier, LVMH has minority interests, and the share of income attributable to those outside interests is deducted in the last stage.

COMPARATIVE CORPORATE FINANCE
Assessing the market values of global brands

How much is a global brand name worth? Interbrand Corporation, a New York-based consulting firm, has been trying to answer this question for several years, and *Business Week* has been publishing the rankings annually since 2001. The accompanying table details what this firm considers the 25 most valuable brands of 2006. The total brand values are large and are dominated by brands of US-based companies. Additionally, the rankings are remarkably stable from year to year; the 2003 rankings listed the same top five, in order, and only one new brand entered the top 25 during 2004.

Although American companies are not required to disclose estimated brand values in their financial statements, large publicly traded British and Australian firms must do so. Brand values do, however, have a significant effect on US accounting rules in one important area – accounting for the 'goodwill' created when a firm is acquired by another company for more than the acquired firm's book value. This premium over book value represents the higher market (versus book) value of intangible assets such as patents, copyrights and trademarks, as well as brand names and business relationships that are not accounted for at all. Charges arising from goodwill impairment can have a dramatic effect on reported earnings.

RANK	BRAND	COUNTRY	SECTOR	VALUE ($mn)	CHANGE OVER YEAR
1	Coca-Cola	US	Beverages	67 000	−1%
2	Microsoft	US	Computer	56 926	−5%
3	IBM	US	Computer	56 201	5%
4	GE	US	Diversified	48 907	4%
5	Intel	US	Computer	32 319	−9%
6	Nokia	Finland	Telecom	30 131	14%
7	Toyota	Japan	Automotive	27 941	12%
8	Disney	US	Media/Entertainment	27 848	5%
9	McDonald's	US	Restaurants	27 501	6%
10	Mercedes	Germany	Automotive	21 795	9%
11	Citi	US	Financial	21 458	7%
12	Marlboro	US	Tobacco	21 350	1%
13	Hewlett-Packard	US	Computer	20 458	8%
14	American Express	US	Financial	19 641	6%
15	BMW	Germany	Automotive	19 617	15%
16	Gillette	US	Personal Care	19 579	12%
17	LVMH	France	Luxury	17 606	10%
18	Cisco	US	Computer	17 532	6%
19	Honda	Japan	Automotive	17 049	8%
20	Samsung	South Korea	Electronics	16 169	8%
21	Merrill Lynch	US	Financial	13 001	8%
22	Pepsi	US	Beverages	12 690	2%
23	Nescafé	Switzerland	Beverages	12 507	2%
24	Google	US	Internet	12 376	46%
25	Dell	US	Computer	12 256	−7%

Source: Interbrand Corporation.

Statement of cash flows

The statement of cash flows provides a summary of a firm's cash flows over the year. This is accomplished by isolating the firm's operating, investment and financing cash flows and reconciling them with changes in its cash and marketable securities during the year. LVMH's statement of cash flows for the year ended 31 December 2006, is presented in Table 2.4. We should also stress that other information presented in financial statements can be very useful to financial managers and analysts. This is especially true about the 'notes' to financial statements.

Notes to financial statements

A public company's financial statements include detailed explanatory notes keyed to the relevant accounts in the statements. These notes provide detailed information on the accounting policies, calculations and transactions underlying entries in the financial statements. Consider for example CRH, a cement, aggregates and building company with operations worldwide. In the firm's 2006 annual report the notes to the accounts consist of 42 pages in total. These contain a wealth of information on the geographical origin of sales, the operation of the company share option schemes, directors' remuneration, details on hedging and so forth.

Notes typically provide additional information about a firm's revenue recognition practices, income taxes, fixed assets, leases and employee remuneration plans. This information is particularly useful to professional security analysts who look for clues that shed more light on the firm's past and future performance.

CONCEPT REVIEW QUESTIONS

1 What role do the IASB and SEC play in determining the content and structure of financial statements?

2 Are balance sheets and income statements prepared with the same purpose in mind? How are these two statements different, and how are they related?

3 Which statements are of greatest interest to creditors, and which would be of greatest interest to shareholders?

4 Why does the balance sheet have to balance?

2.2 CASH FLOW ANALYSIS

Although financial managers are interested in the information contained in the firm's accrual-based financial statements, their primary focus is on cash flows. Remember, cash is king! Without adequate cash to pay obligations on time, to fund operations and growth, and to compensate owners, the firm will fail. The financial manager and other interested parties can gain insight into the firm's cash flows over a given period of time by using some popular measures of cash flow and by analysing the firm's statement of cash flows.

The firm's cash flows

Figure 2.1 illustrates the firm's cash flows. Note that the figure treats cash and marketable securities as perfect substitutes. Both cash and marketable securities represent a reservoir of liquidity that increases with cash inflows and decreases with cash outflows. Also note that the figure divides the firm's cash flows into (1) operating flows, (2) investment flows and (3) financing flows. The **operating flows** are cash inflows and outflows directly related to the production and sale of the firm's products or services. **Investment flows** are cash flows associated with the purchase or sale of both fixed assets and business equity. Clearly, purchases result in cash outflows, whereas sales generate cash inflows. The **financing flows** result from debt and equity financing transactions. Taking on new debt (short term or long term) results in a cash inflow, whereas repaying existing debt represents a cash outflow. Similarly, the sale of shares results in a cash inflow, whereas the repurchase of shares or payment of cash dividends generates a cash outflow. In combination, the firm's operating, investment and financing cash flows during a given period will affect the firm's cash and marketable securities balances.

Monitoring cash flow is important for financial managers employed by the firm and for outside analysts trying to estimate how much the firm is worth.

operating flows
Cash inflows and outflows directly related to the production and sale of a firm's products or services.

investment flows
Cash flows associated with the purchase or sale of both fixed assets and business equity.

financing flows
Result from debt and equity financing transactions.

Inflows and outflows of cash Table 2.3 classifies the basic inflows and outflows of cash for corporations (assuming other things are held constant). For example, if a firm's accounts payable increases by €1000 during the year, this change would be an inflow of cash. If the firm's inventory increases by €2500, the change would be an outflow of cash.

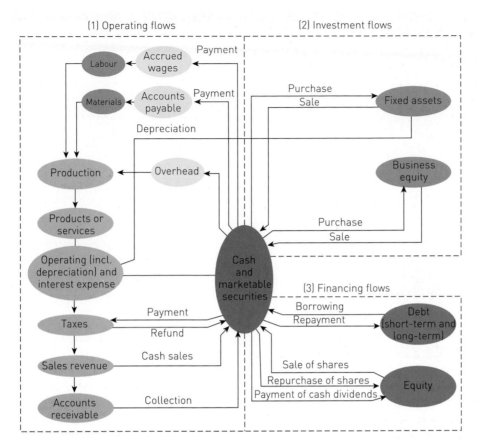

FIGURE 2.1

The pattern of cash flows through a firm

The firm's reservoir of liquidity, containing both cash and marketable securities, is impacted by changes in (1) operating flows, (2) investment flows and (3) financing flows.

INFLOWS	OUTFLOWS
Decrease in any asset	Increase in any asset
Increase in any liability	Decrease in any liability
Net income (profit after tax)	Net loss
Depreciation and other non-cash charges	Dividends paid
Sale of shares	Repurchase or retirement of shares

TABLE 2.3

The inflows and outflows of corporate cash

A few additional points can be made about the classification scheme in Table 2.3.

1 A *decrease* in an asset, such as the firm's inventory balance, is an *inflow of cash* because cash that has been tied up in the asset is released. Managers can use it for some other purpose, such as repaying a loan. In contrast, an *increase* in the firm's inventory balance (or any other asset) is an *outflow of cash* because additional inventory ties up more of the firm's cash. Similar logic explains why an increase in any liability is an inflow of cash, and a decrease in any liability is an outflow of cash.

2 Our earlier discussion noted why depreciation and other non-cash charges are considered cash inflows. Logic suggests that if net income is a cash inflow, then a net loss (negative net profits after taxes) is an outflow of cash. The firm must balance its losses with an inflow of cash, such as selling off some of its fixed assets (reducing an asset) or increasing external borrowing (increasing a liability). Note (from Equation 2.1, page 41) that a firm can have a net loss (EBIT – taxes) and still have positive cash flow when depreciation and other non-cash charges

during the period are greater than the net loss. Therefore, the statement of cash flows treats net income (or net losses) and non-cash charges as separate entries.

Applying the Model

Below we see the current assets and liabilities of Juventus Football Club for the financial years ending June 2004 and 2005 (in millions of euros).

ELEMENT	2005	2004
Cash	6.54	53.14
Short-term investments	2.04	2.04
Accounts receivable	71.08	61.04
Inventory	0	0
Accounts payable	17.01	12.57
Short-term debt	24.97	0

In terms of current assets, accounts receivable increased during the year, representing an outflow of cash for Juventus. Cash decreased, representing a cash inflow. It may seem strange to think of a decrease in cash balances as a source of cash, but that simply means that Juventus used some of its cash flow to 'disinvest in liquidity' rather than use the cash for another purpose. Not surprisingly, the club has no inventories (although some might consider the stock of players that are not gaining first team places as equivalent). On the liabilities side, accounts payable increased, representing a cash inflow for Juventus, while short-term debt increased, representing an inflow of cash for the club.

Developing and interpreting the statement of cash flows

The statement of cash flows summarizes the inflows and outflows of cash during a given period. Accountants construct the statement of cash flows by using the income statement for the year, along with the beginning- and end-of-year balance sheets. The procedure involves classifying balance sheet changes as inflows or outflows of cash; obtaining income statement data; classifying the relevant values into operating, investment and financing cash flows; and presenting them in the proper format.[2] The statement of cash flows for LVMH for the year ended 31 December 2006 appears in Table 2.4. Note that the statement assigns positive values to all cash inflows and negative values to all cash outflows. Notice under the investment activities section that the statement records the increase in gross fixed assets, rather than net fixed assets, as a cash outflow. Depreciation accounts for the difference between changes in gross and net fixed assets, but depreciation expense appears in the operating activities section of the statement. Thus, the focus on changes in gross fixed assets avoids double counting depreciation in the statement. For a similar reason, the statement does not show a specific entry for the change in retained earnings as an inflow (or outflow) of cash. Instead, the factors that determine the change in retained earnings – profits or losses and dividends – appear as separate individual entries in the statement.

---

[2] For a description and demonstration of the detailed procedures for developing the statement of cash flows, see any recently published financial accounting text.

By adding up the items in each category – operating, investment and financing activities – we obtain the net increase (decrease) in cash and marketable securities for the year. As a check, this value should reconcile with the actual yearly change in cash and marketable securities, obtained from the beginning- and end-of-year balance sheets. By applying this procedure to LVMH's income statement and balance sheets, we obtain the firm's statement of cash flows (see Table 2.4).

The statement of cash flows allows the financial manager and other interested parties to analyse the firm's cash flow over a period of time. Unusual changes in either the major categories of cash flow or in specific items offer clues to problems that a firm may be experiencing. For example, an unusually large increase in accounts receivable or inventories resulting in major cash outflows may signal credit or inventory problems, respectively. Financial managers and analysts can also prepare a statement of cash flows developed from projected, or pro forma, financial statements. They use this approach to determine whether the firm will require additional external financing or will generate excess cash that can be reinvested or distributed to shareholders. After you learn the concepts, principles and practices of corporate finance presented in the text, you will be able to glean a good amount of useful information from the statement of cash flows.

Free cash flow Free cash flow (FCF) is the amount of cash flow available to investors – the providers of debt and equity capital. It represents the net amount of cash flow remaining after the firm has met all operating needs and paid for investments – both long term (fixed) and short term (current). Free cash flow for a given period can be calculated in two steps.

First we find the firm's **operating cash flow (OCF)**, which is the amount of cash flow generated by the firm from its operations. It can be calculated using the following equation:

$$OCF = EBIT - Taxes + Depreciation$$

free cash flow (FCF)
The net amount of cash flow remaining after the firm has met all operating needs and paid for investments, both long term (fixed) and short term (current). Represents the cash amount that a firm could distribute to investors after meeting all its other obligations.

operating cash flow (OCF)
The amount of cash flow generated by a firm from its operations. Mathematically, earnings before interest and taxes (EBIT) minus taxes plus depreciation.

EQUATION 2.1

	2006	2005	2004
Operating activities			
Operating profit	3 052	2 522	2 173
Increase in depreciation and amortization	474	639	529
Other	−22	−72	6
Cash flow from operations before working capital changes	3 504	3 089	2 708
Interest and taxes paid	−174	−222	−215
Taxes	−784	−616	−389
Net cash from operations before working capital	2 546	2 251	2 104
Change in inventories	−351	−281	−252
Change in accounts receivable	−146	−67	29
Change in accounts payable	208	27	−88
Other	31	64	92
Net cash from operations	2 288	1 994	1 885
Investing activities			
Investing activities	−712	−818	−951
Operating investments	−749	−679	−588
Financial investments	37	−139	−363
Financing activities			
Financing activities	−1 153	−407	−76
Borrowings	785	1 192	1 599
Repayments	−1 757	−1 559	−1 686
Current investments	−181	−40	11

TABLE 2.4

Statement of cash flows for LVMH for the years ended 31 December 2004–2006 (€mn)

non-cash charges
Expenses, such as depreciation, amortization and depletion allowances, that appear on the income statement but do not involve an actual outlay of cash.

Note that because depreciation is a non-cash charge, it is added back to determine OCF. **Non-cash charges**, such as depreciation, amortization and depletion allowances, are expenses that appear on the income statement but do not involve an actual outlay of cash. Almost all firms list depreciation expense on their income statements, so we focus on depreciation rather than amortization or depletion allowances, but they are treated in a similar fashion. Substituting the values from the LVMH 2006 income statement (from Table 2.2) into Equation 2.1, we derive LVMH operating cash flow:

$$OCF = 3052 - 784 + 474 = 2742$$

LVMH OCF is €2742 million. Next, we convert this operating cash flow to free cash flow (FCF) by deducting the firm's net investments (denoted by the 'change' symbol Δ) in fixed and current assets from operating cash flow, as shown in the following equation:

EQUATION 2.2

$$FCF = OCF - \Delta FA - (\Delta CA - \Delta AP - \Delta accruals)$$

Note that because they occur automatically with changes in sales, only spontaneous current liability changes are deducted from current assets to find the net change in short-term investment. From the preceding calculation, we know that LVMH's OCF in 2006 was €2742 million. Using Table 2.1 we can calculate the changes in gross fixed assets, current assets, accounts payable and accruals between 2005 and 2006. Substituting these values into Equation 2.2, we derive the following:

$$FCF = 2742 - (-252) - (649 - 167 - (-138)) = 2374$$

LVMH thus has free cash flow in 2006 of €2374 million available to pay investors who provide the firm with debt and equity financing.

CONCEPT REVIEW QUESTIONS

5   How do depreciation and other non-cash charges act as sources of cash inflow to the firm? Why does a depreciation allowance exist in the tax laws? For a profitable firm, is it better to depreciate an asset quickly or slowly for tax purposes? Explain.

6   What is operating cash flow (OCF)? What is free cash flow (FCF), and how is it related to OCF?

7   Why is the financial manager likely to show great interest in the firm's statement of cash flows? What type of information can be obtained from this statement?

2.3 ANALYSING FINANCIAL PERFORMANCE USING RATIO ANALYSIS

Analysis of a firm's financial statements is of interest to shareholders, creditors and the firm's own management. In many cases, the constituents of a firm want to compare its financial condition to that of similar firms, but doing so can be very tricky. For example, suppose you are introduced to a new acquaintance named Bill who tells you that he runs a company that earned a profit of €10 million last year. Would you be impressed? What if you knew that Bill's last name was Gates? Most people would agree that a profit of €10 million would be a great disappointment for Microsoft, the firm run by Bill Gates.

The point here is that the sales, profits and other items that appear on a firm's financial statements are difficult to interpret unless we have some way to put the numbers in perspective. To analyse financial statements, we need relative measures that normalize size differences. Effective analysis of financial statements is thus based on the knowledge and use of ratios or relative values. Ratio analysis involves calculating and interpreting financial ratios to assess a firm's performance and status.

Using financial ratios

Different constituents will focus on different types of financial ratios. The firm's creditors are primarily interested in ratios that measure the short-term liquidity of the company and its ability to make interest and principal payments. A secondary concern of creditors is the firm's profitability; they want assurance that the business is healthy and will continue to be successful. Both current and prospective shareholders are interested in ratios that measure the firm's current and future levels of risk and return, because these two dimensions directly affect the firm's share price. The firm's managers must be concerned with all aspects of the firm's financial situation, so they use ratios to generate an overall picture of the company's financial health and to monitor the firm's performance from period to period. The managers carefully examine unexpected changes to isolate developing problems.

An additional complication of ratio analysis is that, for any given ratio, what is normal in one industry may be highly unusual in another. For example, by dividing a firm's earnings available for shareholders by its sales, we obtain the net profit margin ratio. Net profit margins vary dramatically across industries. An outstanding net profit margin in the retail grocery industry could look paltry in the software business. Therefore, when making subjective judgements about the health of a given company, analysts usually compare the firm's ratios to two benchmarks. First, analysts compare the financial ratios in the current year with previous years' ratios, hoping to identify trends that help them evaluate the firm's prospects. Secondly, analysts compare the ratios of one company with those of other 'benchmark' firms in the same industry (or to an industry average obtained from a trade association or third party provider).

We discuss the use of ratios by examining those for LVMH: note that the emphasis is on interpretation as opposed to detailed calculation. We focus on this company merely as an example, and you should note that the ratios presented in the remainder of this chapter can be applied to nearly any company. Of course, many companies in different industries use ratios that focus on aspects peculiar to their industry. For example, airlines pay close attention to the ratio of revenues to passenger miles flown. Retailers diligently track the growth in same-store sales from one year to the next. We cover the most common financial ratios and group them into five categories: liquidity, activity, debt, profitability and market ratios.

Liquidity ratios

Liquidity ratios measure a firm's ability to satisfy its short-term obligations as they come due. Because a common precursor to financial distress and bankruptcy is low or declining liquidity, liquidity ratios are good leading indicators of cash flow problems. The two basic measures of liquidity are the current ratio and the quick (acid-test) ratio.

The current ratio, one of the most commonly cited financial ratios, measures the firm's ability to meet its short-term obligations. It is defined as current assets divided by current liabilities, and thus presents in ratio form what net working capital measures by subtracting current liabilities from current assets. The end-2006 current ratio for LVMH is computed as follows:

$$CR = \frac{CA}{CL} = \frac{9165}{6356} = 1.44$$

How high should the current ratio be? The answer depends on the type of business under consideration and on the costs and benefits of having too much versus too

ratio analysis
Calculating and interpreting financial ratios to assess a firm's performance and status.

liquidity ratios
Measure a firm's ability to satisfy its short-term obligations as they come due.

current ratio
A measure of a firm's ability to meet its short-term obligations, defined as current assets divided by current liabilities.

net working capital
Profitability that represents the percentage of each sales euro remaining after all costs and expenses, including interest, taxes and preference share dividends, have been deducted.

little liquidity. For example, a current ratio of 1.0 is considered acceptable for a utility but may be unacceptable for a manufacturing firm. The more predictable a firm's cash flows, the lower the acceptable current ratio. Because LVMH is in the luxury goods business with highly cyclical annual cash flows, its current ratio of 1.44 indicates that the company takes a fairly aggressive approach to managing its liquidity.

The **quick (acid-test) ratio** is similar to the current ratio except that it excludes inventory, which is usually the least liquid current asset. The generally low liquidity of inventory results from two factors: (1) many types of inventory cannot be easily sold because they are partially completed items, special-purpose items and the like; and (2) inventory is typically sold on credit, which means that it becomes an account receivable before being converted into cash. The quick ratio is calculated as follows:

> **quick (acid-test) ratio**
> A measure of a firm's liquidity that is similar to the current ratio except that it excludes inventory, which is usually the least liquid current asset.

$$ATR(QR) = \frac{Cash + Receivables}{CL} = \frac{1222 + 1461}{6356} = 0.42$$

The quick ratio for LVMH in 2006 is 0.42. The quick ratio provides a better measure of overall liquidity only when a firm's inventory cannot be easily converted into cash. If inventory is liquid, the current ratio is a preferred measure of overall liquidity. Because LVMH inventory is mostly products that can be readily converted into cash, the firm's managers might consider it correct to focus on the current ratio rather than the quick ratio.

Activity ratios

> **activity ratios**
> A measure of the speed with which a firm converts various accounts into sales or cash.

Activity ratios measure the speed with which the firm converts various accounts into sales or cash. Managers and outsiders use activity ratios as guides to assess how efficiently the firm manages assets such as inventory, receivables and fixed assets, as well as the current liability, accounts payable.

> **inventory turnover**
> A measure of how quickly a firm sells its goods.

Inventory turnover provides a measure of how quickly a firm sells its goods. LVMH's 2006 inventory turnover ratio is as follows:

$$ITR = \frac{COGS}{Inventory} = \frac{5481}{4383} = 1.25$$

Notice that we use cost of goods sold rather than sales in the numerator because inventory is valued at its cost on the firm's balance sheet. Also note that in the denominator we use the ending inventory balance to calculate this ratio. If inventories grow over time or exhibit seasonal patterns, analysts sometimes use the average level of inventory throughout the year rather than the ending balance to calculate this ratio. This approach is used by default in Worldscope. The resulting turnover of 1.25 indicates that the firm basically sells outs its inventory just slightly more than one and a quarter times per annum. This value is only meaningful when it is compared with that of other firms in the same industry or with the firm's past inventory turnover. Inventory turnover is easily converted into an **average age of inventory** by dividing the turnover figure into 360. (Note 360 is used, purely by convention, rather than 365.)

> **average age of inventory**
> A measure of inventory turnover, calculated by dividing the turnover figure into 360.

Applying the Model

Inventory ratios, like most other financial ratios, vary a great deal from one industry to another. Looking at the Thomson ONE Banker data, we can see this if we compare company inventory ratios to peer groups. If we select three companies in three different industries, this becomes evident. In all cases we select as a peer group only those companies that are in the Europe/Africa region.

INDUSTRY	COMPANY	INVENTORY TURNOVER RATIO	PEER AVERAGE
Commercial printing	Wyndeham Press plc	19.22	19.03
Packaged foods and meats	Cadbury Schweppes	4.18	17.60
Gas distribution	Gaz de France	13.03	63.29

The **average collection period**, or average age of accounts receivable, is useful in evaluating credit and collection policies.[3] It measures the average amount of time that elapses from a sale on credit until the payment becomes usable funds for a firm. It is computed by dividing the firm's average sales per day into the accounts receivable balance. On average, in 2006 it took LVMH 34 days to receive payment from a credit sale.

$$ASPd = \frac{Sales\ Revenue}{360} = \frac{15306}{360} = 42.51$$

$$ACP = \frac{Accounts\ Receivable}{ASPd} = \frac{1461}{42.51} = 34.37$$

> **average collection period**
> The average amount of time that elapses from a sale on credit until the payment becomes usable funds for a firm. Calculated by dividing accounts receivable by average sales per day. Also called the average age of accounts receivable.

The average collection period is meaningful only in relation to the firm's credit terms. If LVMH extends 30-day credit terms to customers, an average collection period of 34.37 days may indicate a poorly managed credit or collection department, or both. The lengthened collection period could also be the result of an intentional relaxation of credit term enforcement in response to competitive pressures.

Firms use the **average payment period** to evaluate their performance in paying suppliers. It measures the average length of time it takes the firm to pay its suppliers. It equals the firm's average daily purchases divided into the accounts payable balance. To calculate average daily purchases, an analyst may have to estimate the firm's annual purchases, often by taking a specified percentage of cost of goods sold. This estimate is necessary because annual purchases are not reported on a firm's published financial statements. Instead they are embodied in its cost of goods sold. In a fashion similar to the average collection period, the average payment period is meaningful only when viewed in light of the actual credit terms extended to the firm by its suppliers.

> **average payment period**
> A measure of the average length of time it takes a firm to pay its suppliers.

The **fixed asset turnover** measures the efficiency with which a firm uses its fixed assets. The ratio tells analysts how many euros of sales the firm generates per euro of fixed asset investment. The ratio equals sales divided by net fixed assets (fixed assets less intangibles):

$$FAT = \frac{Sales}{NFA} = \frac{15306}{(19620 - 8227)} = 1.34$$

> **fixed asset turnover**
> A measure of the efficiency with which a firm uses its fixed assets, calculated by dividing sales by net fixed asset investment.

---

[3] The average collection period is sometimes called the days' sales outstanding (DSO). As with the inventory turnover ratio, the average collection period can be calculated using end-of-year accounts receivable or the average receivables balance for the year.

The fixed asset turnover for LVMH in 2006 is 1.34. This means that the company turns over its net fixed assets 1.34 times a year. Put another way, LVMH generates just over €1.34 in sales for every €1.00 of fixed assets. As with other ratios, the 'normal' level of fixed asset turnover varies widely from one industry to another.

An analyst must be aware that (when using this ratio and the total asset turnover ratio described next) the calculations use the *historical costs* of fixed assets. Because some firms have significantly newer or older assets than others, comparing fixed asset turnovers of those firms can be misleading. Firms with newer assets tend to have lower turnovers than those with older assets, which have lower book (accounting) values. A naïve comparison of fixed asset turnover ratios for different firms may lead an analyst to conclude that one firm operates more efficiently than another, when, in fact, the firm that appears to be more efficient simply has older (i.e. more fully depreciated) assets on its books. Also, for a company with large values of brands and other intangibles, it is not clear that excluding these from the analysis is in fact correct.

total asset turnover
A measure of the efficiency with which a firm uses all its assets to generate sales; calculated by dividing the value of sales a firm generates by the value of assets used.

The **total asset turnover** ratio indicates the efficiency with which a firm uses *all* its assets to generate sales. Like the fixed asset turnover ratio, total asset turnover indicates how many euros of sales a firm generates per euro of asset investment. All other factors being equal, analysts favour a high turnover ratio because it indicates that a firm generates more sales (and ideally more cash flow for investors) from a given investment in assets. LVMH's total asset turnover in 2006 equals 0.53, calculated as follows:

$$FAT = \frac{Sales}{TA} = \frac{15306}{28785} = 0.53$$

Debt ratios

Firms finance their assets from two broad sources – equity and debt. Equity comes from shareholders, whereas debt comes in many forms and from many different lenders. Firms borrow from suppliers, from banks and from widely scattered investors who buy publicly traded bonds. Debt ratios measure the extent to which a firm uses money from creditors rather than shareholders to finance its operations. Because creditors' claims must be satisfied before firms can distribute earnings to shareholders, current and prospective investors pay close attention to the debts on a firm's balance sheet. Lenders share these concerns because the more indebted the firm, the higher the probability that the firm will be unable to satisfy the claims of all its creditors.

In general, the more debt a firm uses in relation to its total assets, the greater its financial leverage. Fixed-cost sources of financing, such as debt and preference shares, create **financial leverage** that magnifies both the risk and the expected return on the firm's securities.[4] The more a firm borrows, the riskier its outstanding shares and bonds, and the higher the return that investors require on those securities. A detailed discussion of the effect of debt on the firm's risk, return and value is included in Chapter 12. Here we emphasize the use of debt ratios to assess a firm's indebtedness and its ability to meet the fixed payments associated with debt.

financial leverage
Using fixed-cost sources of financing, such as debt and preference shares, to magnify both the risk and expected return on a firm's investments.

Broadly speaking, there are two types of debt ratios. One type focuses on balance sheet measures of outstanding debt relative to other sources of financing. The other

---

[4] By fixed cost we mean that the cost of this financing source does not vary over time in response to changes in the firm's revenue and cash flow. For example, when a firm borrows money at a variable rate, the interest cost of that loan is not fixed through time, but the firm's obligation to make interest payments is 'fixed' regardless of the level of the firm's revenue and cash flow.

type, known as the **coverage ratio**, focuses more on income statement measures of the firm's ability to generate sufficient cash flow to make scheduled interest and principal payments. Investors and credit rating agencies use both types of ratios to assess a firm's creditworthiness.

The **debt ratio** measures the proportion of total assets financed by the firm's creditors. The higher this ratio, the greater the firm's reliance on borrowed money to finance its activities. The ratio equals total liabilities divided by total assets, and LVMH's debt ratio is 0.59. or 59 per cent. This figure indicates that the company has financed more than half of its assets with debt.

$$DR = \frac{TL}{TA} = \frac{17191}{28785} = 0.59$$

A close cousin of the debt ratio is the **assets-to-equity (A/E) ratio**, sometimes called the **equity multiplier**:

$$EM = \frac{TA}{Equity} = \frac{28785}{11594} = 2.49$$

The resulting value indicates that LVMH's assets in 2006 are two-and-a-half times greater than its equity.

An alternative measure of the firm's leverage that focuses solely on the firm's long-term debt is the **debt-to-equity ratio**, calculated by dividing long-term debt by shareholders' equity. The 2006 value of this ratio for LVMH is calculated as follows:

$$DER = \frac{LTD}{Equity} = \frac{3235}{11594} = 0.28$$

LVMH's long-term debts are therefore only around 30 per cent as large as its shareholders' equity. Note, however, that both the debt ratio and the debt-to-equity ratio use book values of debt, equity and assets. Analysts should be aware that the market values of these variables may differ substantially from book values. In addition, depending on which aspects of the company the analyst is focused on, certain elements of debt (such as convertible bonds) may be omitted from the debt figures.

The **times interest earned ratio**, which equals earnings before interest and taxes divided by interest expense, measures the firm's ability to make contractual interest payments. A higher ratio indicates a greater capacity to meet scheduled payments. The times interest earned ratio for LVMH in 2006 equals 57.58, indicating that the firm could experience a substantial decline in earnings and still meet its interest obligations:

$$TIE = \frac{EBIT}{Interest} = \frac{3052}{53} = 57.58$$

Profitability ratios

Several measures of profitability relate a firm's earnings to its sales, assets or equity. Profitability ratios are among the most closely watched and widely quoted financial ratios. Many firms link employee bonuses to profitability ratios, and share prices react sharply to unexpected changes in these measures.

The **gross profit margin** measures the percentage of each sales euro remaining after the firm has paid for its goods. The higher the gross profit margin, the better. Note

---

coverage ratio
A debt ratio that focuses more on income statement measures of a firm's ability to generate sufficient cash flow to make scheduled interest and principal payments.

debt ratio
A measure of the proportion of total assets financed by a firm's creditors.

assets-to-equity (A/E) ratio
A measure of the proportion of total assets financed by a firm's equity. Also called the equity multiplier.

equity multiplier
A measure of the proportion of total assets financed by a firm's equity. Also called the assets-to-equity (A/E) ratio.

debt-to-equity ratio
A measure of the firm's financial leverage, calculated by dividing long-term debt by shareholders' equity.

times interest earned ratio
A measure of the firm's ability to make contractual interest payments, calculated by dividing earnings before interest and taxes by interest expense.

gross profit margin
A measure of profitability that represents the percentage of each sales euro remaining after a firm has paid for its goods.

that Worldscope defines gross profit as Net sales less COGS less Depreciation, while the ratio below, as before, does not adjust for depreciation:

$$GPM = \frac{Gross\ profit}{Sales} = \frac{9825}{15306} = 0.64$$

operating profit margin
A measure of profitability that represents the percentage of each sales euro remaining after deducting all costs and expenses other than interest and taxes.

The **operating profit margin** measures the percentage of each sales euro remaining after deducting all costs and expenses other than interest and taxes. As with the gross profit margin, the higher the operating profit margin the better. This ratio is of interest because it tells analysts what a firm's bottom line looks like before deductions for payments to creditors and tax authorities.

The **net profit margin** measures the percentage of each sales euro remaining after all costs and expenses, including interest, taxes and payments to preference shareholders, have been deducted. Net profit margins vary widely across industries.

$$OPM = \frac{Operating\ profit}{Sales} = \frac{3052}{15306} = 0.19$$

$$NPM = \frac{Net\ income}{Sales} = \frac{1879}{15306} = 0.12$$

SMART ETHICS VIDEO

Frank Popoff, Chairman of the Board (retired), Dow Chemical
'Overstating or understating the performance of the enterprise is anathema . . . it's just not on.'

See the entire interview at **www.cengage.co.uk/megginson**

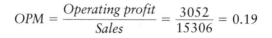

Probably the most closely watched financial ratio of them all is earnings per share (EPS). The earnings per share represent the monies earned on behalf of each outstanding ordinary share. The investing public closely watches EPS figures and considers them an important indicator of corporate success. Many firms tie management bonuses to meeting specific EPS targets. Earnings per share are calculated as follows:

SMART IDEAS VIDEO

John Graham, Duke University
'We asked companies, "Do you manage your earnings?"'

See the entire interview at **www.cengage.co.uk/megginson**

$$EPS = \frac{Net\ income}{\#\ Shares} = \frac{1879}{471.90} = 3.98$$

net profit margin
A measure of profitability that represents the percentage of each sales euro remaining after all costs and expenses, including interest, taxes and preference share dividends, have been deducted.

The value of LVMH's earnings per share outstanding in 2006 is €3.98. This figure represents the money amount earned on behalf of each share outstanding. The amount of earnings actually distributed to each shareholder is the dividend per share.

The **return on total assets (ROA)**, often called the return on investment (ROI), measures the overall effectiveness of management in using its assets to generate returns.[5] The return on total assets for LVMH in 2006 equals 6.53 per cent:

$$ROA = \frac{Net\ income}{TA} = \frac{1879}{28785} = 0.0653$$

return on total assets (ROA)
A measure of the overall effectiveness of management in generating returns to ordinary shareholders with its available assets.

A closely related measure of profitability is the **return on equity (ROE)**, which captures the return earned on the ordinary shareholders' (owners') investment in the firm. For a firm that uses only shares to finance its operations, the ROE and ROA figures are identical. With debt or preference shares on the balance sheet, these ratios usually differ. When the firm earns a profit, even after making interest payments to creditors and paying dividends to preference shareholders, the firm's use of leverage magnifies the return earned by ordinary shareholders, and ROE exceeds ROA.

return on equity (ROE)
A measure that captures the return earned on the ordinary shareholders' (owners') investment in a firm.

---

[5] Naturally, all other things being equal, firms prefer a high ROA. However, as we will see later, analysts must be cautious when interpreting financial ratios. We recall an old Dilbert comic strip in which Wally suggests boosting his firm's ROA by firing the security staff. The reduction in expenses would boost the numerator while the reduction in security would lower the denominator.

Conversely, if the firm's earnings fall short of the amount it must pay to lenders and preference shareholders, leverage causes ROE to be less than ROA. For LVMH, the return on equity for 2006 is 16.2 per cent, substantially above its return on total assets:

$$ROE = \frac{Net\ income}{SE} = \frac{1879}{11594} = 0.162$$

DuPont system of analysis Financial analysts sometimes conduct a deeper analysis of the ROA and ROE ratios using the **DuPont system**, which uses both income and balance sheet information to analyse the ROA and ROE ratios into component parts. This approach highlights the influence of the net profit margin, total asset turnover and financial leverage on a firm's profitability. In the DuPont system, the return on total assets equals the product of the net profit margin times total asset turnover. By definition, the net profit margin equals earnings available for ordinary shareholders divided by sales, and total asset turnover equals sales divided by total assets. When we multiply these two ratios together, the sales figure cancels, resulting in the ROA measure:

duPont system
An analysis that uses both income and balance sheet information to break down the ROA and ROE ratios into their component pieces.

$$\frac{Sales}{TA} \times \frac{Net\ income}{Sales} = \frac{Net\ income}{TA}$$

Naturally, the ROA value for LVMH using the DuPont system is the same value we calculated before, but now we can think of the ROA as a product of how much profit the firm earns on each euro of sales and of the efficiency with which the firm uses its assets to generate sales. Holding the net profit margin constant, an increase in total asset turnover increases the firm's ROA. Similarly, holding total asset turnover constant, an increase in the net profit margin increases ROA.

We can push the DuPont system one step further by multiplying the ROA by the ratio of assets-to-equity (A/E), or the equity multiplier. The product of these two ratios equals the return on equity. Notice that for a firm that uses no debt and has no preference shares, the ratio of assets-to-equity equals 1.0, so the ROA equals the ROE. For all other firms, the ratio of assets-to-equity exceeds 1. It is in this sense that the ratio of assets-to-equity represents a leverage multiplier.

$$ROE = ROA \times EM$$

We can apply this version of the DuPont system to LVMH in 2006 to recalculate its return on common equity:

$$ROE = 0.062 \times 2.48 = 0.162$$

Note that for LVMH the ratio of assets-to-equity is 2.49, which means that LVMH's return on equity is over twice as large as its return on total assets. Of course, using financial leverage has its risks. Notice what would happen if LVMH's return on total assets were a negative number rather than a positive one. The financial leverage multiplier would cause LVMH's return on equity to be even more negative than its ROA.

The advantage of the DuPont system is that it allows the firm to break down its return on equity into a profit-on-sales component (net profit margin) that ties directly to the income statement, an efficiency-of-asset-use component (total asset turnover) that ties directly to the balance sheet and a financial-leverage-use component (assets-to-equity ratio) that also ties directly to the balance sheet.

Market ratios

Market ratios relate the firm's market value, as measured by its current share price, to certain accounting values. These ratios provide analysts with insight into how investors think the firm is performing. Because the ratios include market values, they tend to reflect on a relative basis the shareholders' assessment of all aspects of the firm's past and expected future performance. Here we consider two popular market ratios, one that focuses on earnings and an other that considers book value.

price/earnings (P/E) ratio
A measure of a firm's long-term growth prospects that represents the amount investors are willing to pay for each euro of a firm's earnings.

The most widely quoted market ratio, the **price/earnings (P/E) ratio**, is often used as a barometer of a firm's long-term growth prospects. The P/E ratio measures the amount investors are willing to pay for each euro of the firm's earnings. The price/earnings ratio may indicate the degree of confidence that investors have in the firm's future performance. A high P/E ratio is believed to indicate that investors believe a firm will achieve rapid earnings growth in the future; hence, companies with high P/E ratios are referred to as 'growth stocks'. Simply stated, investors who believe that future earnings are going to be higher than current earnings are willing to pay a lot for today's earnings, and vice versa. The price of LVMH shares on the Euronext exchange at end-2006 was €79.95, which given the EPS of €3.98 reported earlier, gives a PE ratio of 20.1. This figure indicates that investors were paying €20.01 for each €1.00 of LVMH's earnings.

market/book (M/B) ratio
A measure used to assess a firm's future performance by relating its market value per share to its book value per share.

The **market/book (M/B) ratio** provides another assessment of how investors view the firm's past and, particularly, its expected future performance. It relates the market value of the firm's shares to their book value. The shares of firms that are expected to perform well – improving profits, growing market share, launching successful products and so forth – typically sell at higher M/B ratios than those firms with less attractive prospects. Simply stated, firms that investors expect to earn high returns relative to their risk typically sell at higher M/B multiples than those expected to earn low returns relative to risk.

CONCEPT REVIEW QUESTIONS

8 Which of the categories and individual ratios described in this chapter would be of greatest interest to each of the following parties?

   a Existing and prospective creditors (lenders)

   b Existing and prospective shareholders

   c The firm's management.

9 How could the availability of cash inflow and cash outflow data be used to improve on the accuracy of the liquidity and debt coverage ratios presented previously? What specific ratio measures would you calculate to assess the firm's liquidity and debt coverage, using cash flow rather than financial statement data?

10 Assume that a firm's total assets and sales remain constant. Would an increase in each of the ratios below be associated with a cash inflow or a cash outflow?

   a Current ratio   **d** Average payment period

   b Inventory turnover   **e** Debt ratio

   c Average collection period   **f** Net profit margin

11 Use the DuPont system to explain why a slower-than-average inventory turnover could cause a firm with an above-average net profit margin and an average degree of financial leverage to have a below-average return on equity.

12 How can you reconcile investor expectations for a firm with an above-average M/B ratio and a below-average P/E ratio? Could the age of the firm have any effect on this ratio comparison?

2.4 SUMMARY AND CONCLUSIONS

- The three key financial statements are (1) the balance sheet, (2) the income statement and (3) the statement of cash flows. Notes describing the technical aspects of the financial statements are normally included with them.

- Depreciation is the most common non-cash charge on income statements; others are amortization and depletion allowances. Depreciation is added back to EBIT after taxes to find a firm's operating cash flow. A measure of cash flow that is important to financial analysts is free cash flow, the cash flow available to investors. Free cash flow equals operating cash flow less the firm's net investment in fixed and current assets.

- The statement of cash flows, in effect, summarizes the firm's cash flows over a specified period of time, typically one year. It presents cash flows divided into operating, investment and financing flows. When interpreting the statement, an analyst typically looks for unusual changes in either the major categories of cash flow or in specific items to find clues to problems that the firm may be experiencing.

- Financial ratios are a convenient tool for analysing a firm's financial statements to assess its performance over a given period. A variety of financial ratios are available for assessing various aspects of a firm's liquidity, activity, debt, profitability and market value. The DuPont system is often used to assess various aspects of a firm's profitability, particularly the returns earned on both the total asset investment and the owners' equity in the firm.

- Financial decision makers must be conversant with basic corporate tax concepts, because taxes are a major measurement challenge that affect both benefits and costs. Taxes are a major outflow of cash to the profitable firm; they are levied on both ordinary income and capital gains. The marginal tax rate is more relevant than the average tax rate in financial decision making.

INTERNET RESOURCES

Note: This textbook includes numerous internet links, both within the discussions and at the end of each chapter. Because some links are likely to change or be eliminated during the life of this edition, please go to the book's website (www.cengage.co.uk/megginson) to obtain updated links.

http://www.carol.co.uk/
Free annual reports for many international companies.

http://www.iasb.org.uk/
The International Accounting Standards Board website.

http://www.quicken.com
A fairly extensive ratio analysis of a given company can be retrieved by typing in a ticker symbol.

http://www.rmahq.org/Ann_Studies/asstudies.html
Provides a sample of a Risk Management Association industry analysis and the material that explains the ratios, quartile, and other information that is available from RMA.

http://www.yahoo.com
Contains a link to Yahoo! Finance for retrieval of recent financial statements and a wide variety of other financial information for many firms.

KEY TERMS

accrual-based approach
activity ratios
assets-to-equity (A/E) ratio
average age of inventory
average collection period
average payment period
cash flow approach
coverage ratio
current ratio
debt ratio
debt-to-equity ratio
deferred taxes
DuPont system
equity multiplier
financial leverage

financing flows
fixed asset turnover
free cash flow (FCF)
gross profit margin
inventory turnover
investment flows
liquidity ratios
long-term debt
market/book (M/B) ratio
minority interest
net profit margin
net working capital
non-cash charges
operating cash flow (OCF)
operating flows

operating profit margin
ordinary shares
par value (of share)
preference shares
price/earnings (P/E) ratio
quick (acid-test) ratio
ratio analysis
reserves (retained earnings)
return on equity (ROE)
return on total assets (ROA)
share premium account
times interest earned ratio
total asset turnover
treasury shares

SELF-TEST PROBLEMS

ST2-1 Use the financial statements below to answer the questions about S&M Manufacturing's financial position at the end of the calendar year 2006.

S&M Manufacturing
Balance sheet at 31 December 2006 (€000)

Assets		Liabilities and equity	
Current assets		Current liabilities	
Cash	€ 140 000	Accounts payable	€ 480 000
Marketable securities	260 000	Notes payable	500 000
Accounts receivable	650 000	Accruals	80 000
Inventories	800 000	Total current	€1 060 000
Total current assets	€1 850 000	liabilities	
Fixed assets		Long-term debt	
Gross fixed assets	€3 780 000	Bonds outstanding	€1 300 000
Less: Accumulated	1 220 000	Bank debt (long-term)	260 000
depreciation		Total long-term debt	€1 560 000
Net fixed assets	€2 560,000	Shareholders' equity	
Total assets	**€4 410 000**	Preference shares	€180 000
		Par value of shares	200 000
		Paid-in capital	810 000
		in excess of par	
		Retained earnings	600 000
		Total shareholders'	€1 790 000
		equity	
		Total liabilities	**€4 410 000**
		and equity	

S&M Manufacturing
Income statement for year ended 31 December 2006 (€000)

Sales revenue		€6 900 000
Less: Cost of goods sold		4 200 000
Gross profits		€2 700 000
Less: Operating expenses		
Sales expense	€ 750 000	
General and administrative expense	1 150 000	
Leasing expense	210 000	
Depreciation expense	235 000	
Total operation expenses		2 345 000
Earnings before interest and taxes		€ 355 000
Less: Interest expense		85 000
Net profit before taxes		€ 270 000
Less: Taxes		81 000
Net profits after taxes		**€ 189 000**
Less: Preference shares dividends		10 800
Earnings available for		**€ 178 200**
ordinary shareholders		
Less: Dividends		75 000
To retained earnings		**€ 103 200**
Per share data		
Earnings per share (EPS)	€	1.43
Dividends per share (DPS)	€	0.60
Price per share	€	15.85

a How much cash and near cash does S&M have at year-end 2006?

b What was the original cost of all of the firm's real property that is currently owned?

c How much in total liabilities did the firms have at year-end 2006?

d How much did S&M owe for credit purchases at year-end 2006?

e How much did the firm sell during 2006?

f How much equity did the ordinary shareholders have in the firm at year-end 2006?

g What is the cumulative total of earnings reinvested in the firm from its inception through to the end of 2006?

h How much operating profit did the firm earn during 2006?

i What was the total amount of dividends paid out by the firm during the year 2006?

j How many shares did S&M have outstanding at year-end 2006?

ST2-2 The partially complete 2006 balance sheet and income statement for Challenge Industries are set out below, followed by selected ratio values for the firm based on its completed 2006 financial statements. Use the ratios along with the partial statements to complete the financial statements. *Hint*: Use the ratios in the order listed to calculate the missing statement values that need to be installed in the partial statements.

Challenge Industries
Balance sheet at 31 December 2006 (in €000)

Assets		Liabilities and equity	
Current assets		Current liabilities	
Cash	€ 52 000	Accounts payable	€150 000
Marketable securities	60 000	Notes payable	?
Accounts receivable	200 000	Accruals	80 000
Inventories	?	Total current liabilities	?
Total current assets	?	Long-term debt	€425 000
Fixed assets (gross)	?	Total liabilities	?
Less: Accumulated	240 000	Shareholders' equity	
depreciation		Preference shares	?
Net fixed assets	?	Par value of shares	150 000
Total assets	**?**	Paid-in capital in excess of par	?
		Retained earnings	390 000
		Total shareholders' equity	?
		Total liabilities and	**?**
		shareholders' equity	

Challenge Industries
Income statement for the year ended 31 December 2006 (in €000)

Sales revenue		€4 800 000
Less: Cost of goods sold		?
Gross profits		?
Less: Operating expenses		
Sales expense	€690 000	
General and administrative expense	750 000	
Depreciation expense	120 000	
Total operating expenses		1 560 000
Earnings before interest and taxes		?
Less: Interest expense		35 000
Earnings before taxes		?
Less: Taxes		?
Net income (Net profits after taxes)		**?**
Less: Preference dividends		15 000
Earnings available for ordinary shareholders		**?**
Less: Dividends		60 000
To retained earnings		**?**

Challenge Industries
Ratios for the year ended 31 December 2006

Ratio	Value
Total asset turnover	2.00
Gross profit margin	40%
Inventory turnover	10
Current ratio	1.60
Net profit margin	3.75%
Return on equity	12.5%

QUESTIONS

Q2-1 What information (explicit and implicit) can be derived from financial statement analysis? Does the standardization required by IFRS add greater validity to comparisons of financial data between companies and industries? Are there possible shortcomings to relying solely on financial statement analysis to value companies?

Q2-2 Distinguish between the types of financial information contained in the various financial statements. Which statements provide information on a company's performance over a reporting period, and which present data on a company's current position? What sorts of valuable information may be found in the notes to financial statements? Describe a situation in which the information in the notes would be essential to making an informed decision about the value of a company.

Q2-3 If you were a commercial credit analyst charged with the responsibility of making an accept/reject decision on a company's loan request, with which financial statement would you be most concerned? Which financial statement is most likely to provide pertinent information about a company's ability to repay its debt?

Q2-4 What is operating cash flow (OCF)? How is it calculated? What is free cash flow (FCF)? How is it calculated from OCF? Why do financial managers focus attention on the value of FCF?

Q2-5 Describe the common definitions of 'inflows of cash' and 'outflows of cash' used by analysts to classify certain balance sheet changes and income statement values. What three categories of cash flow are used in the statement of cash flows? To what value should the net value in the statement of cash flows reconcile?

Q2-6 What precautions must one take when using ratio analysis to make financial decisions? Which ratios would be most useful for a financial manager's internal financial analysis? Which for an analyst trying to decide which stocks are most attractive within an industry?

Q2-7 How do analysts use ratios to analyse a firm's financial leverage? Which ratios convey more important information to a credit analyst – those revolving around the levels of indebtedness or those measuring the ability to meet the contractual payments associated with debt? What is the relationship between a firm's levels of indebtedness and risk? What must happen for an increase in financial leverage to be successful?

Q2-8 How is the DuPont system useful in analysing a firm's ROA and ROE? What information can be inferred from the decomposition of ROE into contributing ratios? What is the mathematical relationship between each of the individual components (net profit margin, total asset turnover and assets-to-equity ratio) and ROE? Can ROE be raised without affecting ROA? How?

PROBLEMS

Financial statements

P2-1 Obtain financial statements for Microsoft for the last five years either from its website (http://www.microsoft.com) or from the SEC's online EDGAR site (http://www.sec.gov/edgar/searchedgar/webusers.htm). First, look at the statements without reading the notes. Then, read the notes carefully, concentrating on those about executive stock options. Do you have a different perspective after analysing these notes?

Cash flow analysis

P2-2 Given the balance sheets and selected data from the income statement of SMG Industries that follow, answer parts (a)–(c).

a Calculate the firm's operating cash flow (OCF) for the year ended 31 December 2004, using Equation 2.1.

b Calculate the firm's free cash flow (FCF) for the year ended 31 December 2004, using Equation 2.2.

c Interpret, compares and contrast your cash flow estimates in parts (a) and (b).

SMG Industries balance sheets (€mn)

Assets	31 December 2004	31 December 2003	Liabilities and shareholders' equity	31 December 2004	31 December 2003
Cash	€ 3 500	€ 3 000	Accounts payable	€ 3 600	€ 3 500
Marketable securities	3 800	3 200	Notes payable	4 800	4 200
			Accruals	1 200	1 300
Accounts receivable	4 000	3 800	Total current liabilities	€ 9 600	€ 9 000
			Long-term debt	€ 6 000	€ 6 000
Inventories	4 900	4 800	Ordinary shares	€11 000	€11 000
Total current assets	€16 200	€14 800	Retained earnings	6 400	5 800
			Total shareholders' equity	€17 400	€16 800
Gross fixed assets	€31 500	€30 100			
Less: Accumulated depreciation	14 700	13 100	Total liabilities and shareholders' equity	€33 000	€31 800
Net fixed assets	€16 800	€17 000			
Total assets	**€33 000**	**€31 800**			

Income statement data (2004, €mn)

Depreciation expense	€1 600
Earnings before interest and taxes (EBIT)	4 500
Taxes	1 300
Net profits after taxes	2 400

P2-3 Classify each of the following items as an inflow (I) or an outflow (O) of cash, or as neither (N).

Item	Change (€)	Item	Change (€)
Cash	+600	Accounts receivable	−900
Accounts payable	−1 200	Net profits	+700
Notes payable	+800	Depreciation	+200
Long-term debt	−2 500	Repurchase of shares	+500
Inventory	+400	Cash dividends	+300
Fixed assets	+600	Sale of shares	+1 300

Analysing financial performance using ratio analysis

P2-4 Manufacturers Bank is evaluating Aluminium Industries, which has requested a €3 million loan, to assess the firm's financial leverage and risk. On the basis of the debt ratios for Aluminium, along with the industry averages and Aluminium's recent financial statements (which follow), evaluate and recommend appropriate action on the loan request.

Aluminium Industries income statement for the year ended 31 December 2006

Sales revenue		€30 000 000
Less: Cost of goods sold		21 000 000
Gross profit		€ 9 000 000
Less: Operating expenses		
Selling expense	€3 000 000	
General and administrative expenses	1 800 000	
Lease expense	200 000	
Depreciation expense	1 000 000	
Total operating expense		6 000 000
Operating profit		€3 000 000
Less: Interest expense		1 000 000
Net profit before taxes		€2 000 000
Less: Taxes (rate = 40%)		800 000
Net profits after taxes		€1 200 000

Aluminium Industries balance sheet as at 31 December 2006

Assets		Liabilities and Stockholders' Equity	
Current assets		Current liabilities	
Cash	€ 1 000 000	Accounts payable	€ 8 000 000
Marketable securities	3 000 000	Notes payable	8 000 000
Accounts receivable	12 000 000	Accruals	500 000
Inventories	7 500 000	Total current liabilities	€16 500 000
Total current assets	€23 500 000	Long-term debt	€20 000 000
Gross fixed assets (at cost)		(including leases)	
Land and buildings	€11 000 000	Shareholders' equity	
Machinery and equipment	20 500 000	Preference shares (25,000 shares, €4 dividend)	€ 2 500 000
Furniture and fixtures	8 000 000		
Gross fixed assets	€39 500 000	Shares (1 million shares, €5 par)	5 000 000
Less: Accumulated depreciation	13 000 000		
Net fixed assets	€26 500 000	Paid-in capital in excess of par	4 000 000
Total assets	€50 000 000	Retained earnings	2 000 000
		Total shareholders' equity	€13 500 000
		Total liabilities and shareholders' equity	€50 000 000

Industry averages

Debt ratio	0.51
Debt-to-equity ratio	1.07
Times interest earned ratio	7.30

P2-5 Use the information below to answer the questions that follow.

Income statements for the year ended 31 December 2006

	Heavy Metal Manufacturing (HMM)	Metallic Stamping (MS)	High-Tech Software Co. (HTS)
Sales	€75 000 000	€50 000 000	€100 000 000
−Operating expenses	65 000 000	40 000 000	60 000 000
Operating profit	€10 000 000	€10 000 000	€ 40 000 000
−Interest expenses	3 000 000	3 000 000	0
Earnings before taxes	€ 7 000 000	€ 7 000 000	€ 40 000 000
−Taxes	2 800 000	2 800 000	16 000 000
Net income	€ 4 200 000	€ 4 200 000	€ 24 000 000

Balance sheets as of 31 December 2006

	Heavy Metal Manufacturing (HMM)	Metallic Stamping (MS)	High-Tech Software Co. (HTS)
Current assets	€ 10 000 000	€ 5 000 000	€ 20 000 000
Net fixed assets	90 000 000	75 000 000	80 000 000
Total assets	€100 000 000	€80 000 000	€100 000 000
Current liabilities	€ 20 000 000	€10 000 000	€ 10 000 000
Long-term debt	40 000 000	40 000 000	0
Total liabilities	€ 60 000 000	€50 000 000	€ 10 000 000
Shares	€ 15 000 000	€10 000 000	€ 25 000 000
Retained earnings	25 000 000	20 000 000	65 000 000
Total equity	€ 40 000 000	€30 000 000	€ 90 000 000
Total liabilities and equity	€100 000 000	€80 000 000	€100 000 000

a Use the DuPont system to compare the two heavy metal companies shown above (HMM and MS) during 2006. Which of the two has a higher return on equity? What is the cause of the difference between the two?

b Calculate the return on equity of the software company, HTS. Why is this value so different from those of the heavy metal companies calculated in part (a)?

c Compare the leverage levels between the industries. Which industry receives a greater contribution from return on total assets? Which industry receives a greater contribution from the financial leverage as measured by the assets-to-equity (A/E) ratio?

d Can you make a meaningful DuPont comparison across industries? Why or why not?

P2-6 Refer to Problem 2-5, and perform the same analysis with real data. Download last year's financial data from Air Liquide (http://www.airliquide.fr), ENI (www.eni.it) and BASF (www.basf.com) Which ratios demonstrate the greatest difference between Air Liquide and BASF? Which of the two is more profitable? Which ratios drive the greater profitability?

P2-7 A common-size income statement for Aluminium Industries' 2005 operations follows. Using the firm's 2006 income statement presented in Problem 2-4, develop the 2006 common-size income statement (see footnote 1) and compare it with the 2005 statement. Which areas require further analysis and investigation?

**Aluminum Industries common-size income statement for the year
ended 31 December 2005**

Sales revenue (€35 000 000)	100%
Less: Cost of goods sold	65.9
Gross profit	34.1%
Less: Operating expenses	
Selling expense	12.7%
General and administrative expenses	6.3
Lease expense	0.6
Depreciation expense	3.6
Total operating expense	23.2
Operating profit	10.9%
Less: Interest expense	1.5
Net profit before taxes	9.4%
Less: Taxes (rate = 40%)	3.8
Net profits after taxes	5.6%

P2-8 Use the following financial data for Greta's Gadgets to determine the effect of using additional debt financing to purchase additional assets. Assume that an additional €1 million of assets is purchased with 100 per cent debt financing with a 10 per cent annual interest rate.

**Greta's Gadgets
Income statement for the year ended 31 December 2006**

Sales	€4 000 000
−Costs and expenses @ 90%	3 600 000
Earnings before interest & taxes	€ 400 000
−Interest (0.10 × €1 000 000)	100 000
Earnings before taxes	€ 300 000
−Taxes @ 40%	120 000
Net income	€ 180 000

**Greta's Gadgets
Balance sheet as at 31 December 2006**

Assets		Liabilities and shareholders' equity	
Current assets	€ 0	Current liabilities	€ 0
Fixed assets	2 000 000	Long-term debt @ 10%	€1 000 000
Total assets	€2 000 000	Total liabilities	€1 000 000
		Shares equity	€1 000 000
		Total liabilities and shareholders' equity	€2 000 000

a Calculate the current (2006) net profit margin, total asset turnover, assets-to-equity ratio, return on total assets and return on equity for Greta's.

b Now, assuming no other changes, determine the effect of purchasing the €1 million in assets using 100 per cent debt financing with a 10 per cent annual interest rate. Further, assume that the newly purchased assets generate an additional €2 million in sales and that the costs and expenses remain at 90 per cent of sales. For the purposes of this problem, further assume a tax rate of 40 per cent. What is the effect on the ratios calculated in part (a)? Is the purchase of these assets justified on the basis of the return on equity?

c Assume that the newly purchased assets in part (b) generate only an extra €500 000 in sales. Is the purchase justified in this case?

d Which component ratio(s) of the DuPont system is (are) not affected by the change in sales? What does this imply about the use of financial leverage?

P2-9 Tracey White, owner of the Buzz Coffee Shop chain, has decided to expand her operations. Her 2006 financial statements follow. Tracey can buy two additional coffeehouses for €3 million, and she has the choice of completely financing these new coffeehouses with either a 10 per cent (annual interest) loan or the issuance of new shares. She also expects these new shops to generate an additional €1 million in sales. Assuming a 40 per cent tax rate and no other changes, should Tracey buy the two coffeehouses? Why or why not? Which financing option results in the better ROE?

Buzz Coffee Shops 2006 financial statements

Balance sheet		Income statement	
Current assets	€ 250 000	Sales	€500 000
Fixed assets	750 000	−Costs and expenses	200 000
Total assets	€1 000 000	@ 40%	
		Earnings before	€300 000
Current liabilities	€ 300 000	interest and taxes (EBIT)	
Long-term debt	0	−Interest expense	0
Total liabilities	€ 300 000	Net profit before taxes	€300 000
Equity	€ 700 000	−Taxes @ 40%	120 000
Total liabilities and shareholders' equity	€1 000 000	Net income	€180 000

P2-10 The financial statements of Access Corporation for the year ended 31 December 2006 follow.

Access Corporation income statement for the year ended 31 December 2006

Sales revenue		€160 000
Less: Cost of goods sold[a]		106 000
Gross profit		€ 54 000
Less: Operating expenses		
Sales expense	€16 000	
General and administrative expense	10 000	
Lease expense	1 000	
Depreciation expense	10 000	
Total operating expense		37 000
Operating profit		€ 17 000
Less: Interest expense		6 100
Net profit before taxes		€ 10 900
Less: Taxes @ 40%		4 360
Net profits after taxes		€ 6 540

[a] Access Corporation's annual purchases are estimated to equal 75 per cent of cost of goods sold.

Access Corporation balance sheet as at 31 December 2006

Assets			Liabilities and shareholders' equity		
Cash	€	500	Accounts payable	€	22 000
Marketable securities		1 000	Notes payable		47 000
			Total current liabilities	€	69 000
Accounts receivable		25 000	Long-term debt	€	22 950
			Total liabilities	€	91 950
Inventories		45 500	Shares[a]	€	31 500
Total current assets	€	72 000	Retained earnings		26 550
Land	€	26 000	Total liabilities and shareholders' equity		€150 000
Buildings and equipment		90 000			
Less: Accumulated depreciation		38 000			
Net fixed assets	€	78 000			
Total assets		**€150 000**			

[a] The firm's 3000 outstanding shares closed 2006 at a price of €25 per share.

a Use the preceding financial statements to complete the following table. Assume that the industry averages given in the table are applicable for both 2005 and 2006.

b Analyse Access Corporation's financial condition as it relates to (1) liquidity, (2) activity, (3) debt, (4) profitability and (5) market value. Summarize the company's overall financial condition.

Access Corporation's financial ratios

	Industry average	Actual ratio 2005	Actual ratio 2006
Current ratio	1.80	1.84	_____
Quick (acid-test) ratio	0.70	0.78	_____
Inventory turnover	2.50	2.59	_____
Average collection period[a]	37 days	36 days	_____
Average payment period[a]	72 days	78 days	_____
Debt-to-equity ratio	50%	51%	_____
Times interest earned ratio	3.8	4.0	_____
Gross profit margin	38%	40%	_____
Net profit margin	3.5%	3.6%	_____
Return on total assets (ROA)	4.0%	4.0%	_____
Return on equity (ROE)	9.5%	8.0%	_____
Market/book (M/B) ratio	1.1	1.2	_____

[a] Based on a 365-day year and on end-of-year figures.

P2-11 Given the following financial statements, historical ratios and industry averages, calculate UG Company's financial ratios for 2006. Analyse its overall financial situation both in comparison with industry averages and over the period 2004–2006. Break down your analysis into an evaluation of the firm's liquidity, activity, debt, profitability and market value.

UG Company income statement for the year ended 31 December 2006

Sales revenue		€10 000 000
Less: Cost of goods sold[a]		7 500 000
Gross profit		€ 2 500 000
Less: Operating expenses		
Selling expense	€300 000	
General and administrative expense	650 000	
Lease expense	50 000	
Depreciation expense	200 000	
Total operating expense		1 200 000
Operating profit (EBIT)		€ 1 300 000
Less: Interest expense		200 000
Net profits before taxes		€ 1 100 000
Less: Taxes (rate = 40%)		440 000
Net profits after taxes		€ 660 000
Less: Preference shares dividends		50 000
Earnings available for ordinary shareholders		€ 610 000
Earnings per share (EPS)		€ 3.05

[a] Annual credit purchases of €6.2 million were made during the year.

UG Company balance sheet as of 31 December 2006

Assets			Liabilities and shareholders' equity		
Current assets			Current liabilities		
Cash	€	200 000	Accounts payable	€	900 000
Marketable securities		50 000	Notes payable		200 000
Accounts receivable		800 000	Accruals		100 000
Inventories		950 000	Total current liabilities	€	1 200 000
Total current assets	€	2 000 000	Long-term debt	€	3 000 000
Gross fixed assets	€12	000 000	(including financial leases)		
Less: Accumulated depreciation		3 000 000	Shareholders' equity		
			Preference shares	€	1 000 000
Net fixed assets	€	9 000 000	(25,000 shares, €2 dividend)		
Other assets	€	1 000 000	Shares		600 000
Total assets	€12	000 000	(200,000 shares, €3 par)[a]		
			Paid-in capital in excess of par		5 200 000
			Retained earnings		1 000 000
			Total shareholders' equity	€	7 800 000
			Total liabilities and shareholders' equity	€12	000 000

[a] On 31 December 2006 the firm's shares closed at €27.50.

Ratio	Actual 2004	Actual 2005	Industry Average 2006
Current ratio	1.40	1.55	1.85
Quick (acid-test) ratio	1.00	0.92	1.05
Inventory turnover	9.52	9.21	8.60
Average collection period[a]	45.0 days	36.4 days	35.0 days
Average payment period[a]	58.5 days	60.8 days	45.8 days
Fixed asset turnover	1.08	1.05	1.07
Total asset turnover	0.74	0.80	0.74
Debt ratio	0.20	0.20	0.30
Debt-to-equity ratio	0.25	0.27	0.39
Times interest earned ratio	8.2	7.3	8.0
Gross profit margin	0.30	0.27	0.25
Operating profit margin	0.12	0.12	0.10
Net profit margin	0.067	0.067	0.058
Return on total assets (ROA)	0.049	0.054	0.043
Return on equity (ROE)	0.066	0.073	0.072
Earnings per share (EPS)	€ 1.75	€ 2.20	€ 1.50
Price/earnings (P/E) ratio	12.0	10.5	11.2
Market/book (M/B) ratio	1.20	1.05	1.10

Historical and industry average ratios for UG Company

[a] Based on a 365-day year and on end-of-year figures.

P2-12 Choose a company that you would like to analyse and obtain its financial statements. Next, select another firm from the same industry and obtain its financial data from the internet. Perform a complete ratio analysis on each firm. How well does your selected company compare with its industry peer? Which components of your firm's ROE are superior, and which are inferior?

SMART SOLUTIONS

See the problem and solution explained step-by-step at **www.cengage.co.uk/ megginson**

THOMSON ONE Business School Edition

Access financial information from the Thomson ONE – Business School Edition website for the following problem(s). Go to http://tabsefin.swlearning.com/. If you have already registered your access serial number and have a username and password, click **Enter**. Otherwise, click **Register** and follow the instructions to create a username and password. Register your access serial number and then click **Enter** on the aforementioned website. When you click Enter, you will be prompted for your username and password (please remember that the password is case sensitive). Enter them in the respective boxes and then click **OK** (or hit **Enter**). From the ensuing page, click **Click Here to Access Thomson ONE – Business School Edition Now!** This opens up a new window that gives you access to the Thomson ONE – Business School Edition database. You can retrieve a company's financial information by entering its ticker symbol (provided for each company in the problem(s)) in the box below 'Name/ Symbol/Key'. For further instructions on using the Thomson ONE – Business School Edition database, please refer to *A Guide for Using Thomson ONE – Business School Edition*.

P2-13 Compare the profitability of Ryanair and British Airways for the latest year. Using return on equity (ROE), determine which firm is more profitable. Use the DuPont system to determine what drives the difference in the profitability of the two.

P2-14 Analyse the financial condition of Puma over the last five years. Use financial ratios that relate to its liquidity, activity, debt, profitability and market value. In which areas has the company improved, and in which areas has the company's financial position worsened?

MINICASE *Financial statement and cash flow analysis*

You have been hired by EquiCredito Bank SA as a financial analyst. One of your first job assignments is to analyse the present financial condition of Bradley Stores. You are provided with the following 2006 balance sheet and income statement information for Bradley Stores. In addition, you are told that Bradley Stores has 10 000 000 shares outstanding, currently trading at €9 per share, and has made annual purchases of €210 000 000.

Your assignment calls for you to calculate certain financial ratios and to compare these calculated ratios with the industry average ratios that are provided. You are also told to base your analysis on five categories of ratios: (a) liquidity ratios, (b) activity ratios, (c) debt ratios, (d) profitability ratios and (e) market ratios.

Balance Sheet (in €000)

Cash	€ 5 000	Accounts payable	€ 15 000
Accounts receivable	20 000	Notes payable	20 000
Inventory	40 000	Total current liabilities	€ 35 000
Total current assets	€ 65 000	Long-term debt	€100 000
Net fixed assets	135 000	Shareholders' equity	€ 65 000
Total assets	€200 000	Total liabilities and equity	€200 000

Income statement (in €000)

Net sales (all credit)	€300 000
Less: Cost of goods sold	250 000
Earnings before interest and taxes	€ 50 000
Less: Interest	40 000
Earnings before taxes	€ 10 000
Less: Taxes (40%)	4 000
Net income	€ 6 000

Industry averages for key ratios

Net profit margin	6.4%
Average collection period (365 days)	30 days
Debt ratio	50%
P/E ratio	23
Inventory turnover ratio	12.0
ROE	18%
Average payment period (365 days)	20 days
Times interest earned ratio	8.5
Total asset turnover	1.4
Current ratio	1.5
Assets-to-equity ratio	2.0
ROA	9%
Quick ratio	1.25
Fixed asset turnover ratio	1.8

Assignment

Use the following guidelines to complete this job assignment. First, identify which ratios you need to use to evaluate Bradley Stores in terms of its (a) liquidity position, (b) business activity, (c) debt position, (d) profitability and (e) market comparability. Next, calculate these ratios. Finally, compare these ratios to the industry average ratios provided in the problem and answer the following questions.

1 Based on the provided industry average information, discuss Bradley Stores liquidity position. Discuss specific areas in which Bradley compares positively and negatively with the overall industry.

2 Based on the provided industry average information, what do Bradley Stores activity ratios tell you? Discuss specific areas in which Bradley compares positively and negatively with the overall industry.

3 Based on the provided industry average information, discuss Bradley Stores debt position. Discuss specific areas in which Bradley compares positively and negatively with the overall industry.

4 Based on the provided industry average information, discuss Bradley Stores profitability position. As part of this investigation of firm profitability, include a DuPont analysis. Discuss specific

areas in which Bradley compares positively and negatively with the overall industry.

5 Based on the provided industry average information, how is Bradley Stores viewed in the market-place? Discuss specific areas in which Bradley compares positively and negatively with the overall industry.

6 Overall, what are Bradley's strong and weak points? Knowing that your boss will approve new loans only to companies in a better-than-average financial position, what is your final recommendation (approval or denial of loan)?

Chapter 3
Present Value

OPENING FOCUS

What cost a child?

Over the latter part of 2005, the Republic of Ireland was gripped by the story of an adoption gone wrong. An Irish couple, the Dowses, had in 2001 adopted a child, later named Tristan, from Indonesia. Later, in 2003, claiming a failure to bond, the couple returned Tristan to the orphanage. At the time, Tristan was two years old.

The discovery of this case prompted questions in the Irish parliament, much public discussion and eventually a legal case. The Attorney General of Ireland took a case against the adoptive parents, acting on behalf of the child (as Tristan was and remains an Irish citizen), seeking redress. Eventually, in February 2006, the High Court made an order. In newspapers this was reported as the parents being required to pay €100 000 towards the upkeep of the child over the next 12 years, Tristan then being six years old.

However, this is not what the court ordered. The order was in fact a good example of a stream of cash flows, the valuation of which is the subject of this chapter. The court settlement had three parts. The first was an immediate €20 000 payment to the court, which would administer the monies until Tristan reached the age of 18. At age 18 (June 2019) he would also receive another lump sum of €25 000. Finally, a payment of €350 per month would be made, this to rise at the annual rate of inflation. The €100 000 reported in the newspapers comes from a straight addition of the sums of money. However, as we will see in this chapter, because the cash flows are spread out over time, such a straightforward addition is not generally correct.

That monies in the future differ from monies now is not something newly discovered. A long survey of the use of discounting is to be found in Parker's 1968 *Journal of Accounting* research article, called 'Discounted Cash Flow in Historical Perspective'.

LEARNING OBJECTIVES

After studying this chapter you should be able to:

- Understand how to find the future value of a lump sum invested today.

- Calculate the present value of a lump sum to be received in the future.

- Find the future value of cash flow streams – both mixed streams and annuities.

- Determine the present value of future cash flow streams, including mixed streams, annuities and perpetuities.

- Apply time-value techniques to compounding more frequently than annually, stated versus effective annual interest rates, and deposits needed to accumulate a future sum.

- Use time-value techniques to find implied interest or growth rates for lump sums, annuities and mixed streams, and an unknown number of periods for both lump sums and annuities.

SMART FINANCE

Use the learning tools at www.cengage.co.uk/megginson

Finance is primarily concerned with the voluntary transfer of wealth between individuals and across time. The transfer of wealth between individuals, which occurs in financial markets, can involve creditors lending money to borrowers in exchange for a promise of repayment with interest, or investors purchasing an ownership interest in a new business venture in exchange for a share in the venture's profits. Likewise, transferring wealth across time can take two forms. The first involves determining what the value of an investment made today will be worth at a specific future date, and the second determines the value today of a cash flow to be received at a specific date in the future. We refer to the first such computation as determining the future value and the second as determining the present value.

Because these wealth transfers are voluntary 'trades' of cash today for contractual promises of greater payments in the future, the ability to execute these trades makes all parties better off. The opportunity to borrow and lend using financial markets helps both savers and borrowers. By lending or investing money at a given interest rate, a saver can increase consumption in the future by foregoing some consumption today. The opportunity to receive cash today in exchange for a promise to repay that cash, plus interest, in the future also makes borrowers better off. These borrowers might be individuals, such as new university graduates, who want to obtain financing for new cars and are willing to commit a portion of their future incomes to paying off these loans. Alternatively, 'borrowers' might be entrepreneurs with great business plans and managerial talents, who need equity financing to turn their dreams into solid businesses. Perhaps the most relevant example of how borrowing can improve personal welfare is to consider the bargain students make with lenders. Students borrow sums of money (often sizeable) to finance their education, and the knowledge they gain increases their lifetime earnings potential by more than enough to repay the debt. In sum, financial markets improve the welfare of savers, entrepreneurs and ordinary citizens by allowing borrowing, lending and investing to occur efficiently.

Transfers of wealth occur between firms and investors just as they do between individuals. Because most decisions that financial managers face involve trading off costs and benefits that are spread out over time, managers need a framework for evaluating cash inflows and outflows that occur at different times. Adjusting for differences in the timing of benefits and costs is a major measurement challenge. This challenge is addressed using the **time value of money** techniques – which explicitly recognize that a euro received today is more valuable than a euro received in the future – presented in this chapter. Time value is one of the most important concepts in finance.

time value of money
The financial concept that recognizes the fact that a euro received today is more valuable than a euro received in the future.

Here we consider several objectives regarding the time value of money. The first is to show how to compute future values, beginning with the simple process of computing the future value of a lump sum, and then examining increasingly complex cash flow streams. Secondly, we demonstrate how to compute the present values of future cash flows, again beginning with a lump sum and then examining streams of future cash flows. Thirdly, we present some special applications of time-value techniques that financial managers commonly employ. The chapter concludes with several additional applications of time-value techniques.

3.1 FUTURE VALUE OF A LUMP SUM

The concept of future value

By consuming less than 100 per cent of their present incomes, investors can earn interest on their savings and thereby enjoy higher future consumption. A person who invests €100 today at 5 per cent interest expects to receive €105 in one year, representing €5 interest plus the return of the €100 originally invested. In this example, we say that €105 is the **future value** of €100 invested at 5 per cent for one year.

We can calculate the future value of an investment made today by applying compound interest over a specified period of time. **Compound interest** is interest earned both on the principal amount and on the interest earned in previous periods. **Principal** refers to the amount of money on which the interest is paid. To demonstrate these concepts, assume that you have the opportunity to deposit €100 into a risk-free account paying 5 per cent annual interest. For simplicity, we assume that interest compounds annually, though in later sections we show how to compute future values using semi-annual, quarterly and even continuous compounding periods.

At the end of one year, your account will have a balance of €105. This sum represents the initial principal of €100 plus 5 per cent (€5) in interest. This future value is calculated as follows:

$$\text{Future value at end of year 1} = €105 \times (1 + 0.05) = €105$$

If you leave this money in the account for another year, the investment will pay interest at the rate of 5 per cent on the new principal of €105. In other words, you will receive 5 per cent interest both on the original principal of €100 and on the first year's interest of €5. At the end of this second year, there will be €110.25 in your account, representing the principal at the beginning of year 2 (€105) plus 5 per cent of the €105, or €5.25, in interest. The future value at the end of the second year is computed as follows:

$$\text{Future value at end of year 2} = €105 \times (1 + 0.05) = €110.25$$

Substituting the first equation into the second one yields the following:

$$\text{Future value at end of year 2} = €100 \times (1 + 0.05) \times (1 + 0.05)$$
$$= €100 \times (1 + 0.05)^2 = €110.25$$

Therefore, €100 deposited at 5 per cent compound annual interest will be worth €110.25 at the end of two years. This represents two years' interest of 5 per cent paid on the original €100 principal, plus 5 per cent paid on the first year's €5 interest payment, or €0.25. It is important to recognize the difference in future values that results from compound versus simple interest. **Simple interest** is interest paid only on the initial principal of an investment, not on the interest that accrues in earlier periods. If the investment in our previous example pays 5 per cent simple interest, then the future value in any year equals €100 plus the product of the annual interest payment and the number of years. In this case, its value will be only €110 at the end of year 2 [€100 + (2 × €5)], €115 at the end of year 3 [€100 + (3 × €5)], €120 at the end of year 4 [€100 + (4 × €5)] and so on. Although the difference between a €110 account balance after two years at simple interest and €110.25 at compound interest seems rather trivial, the difference grows exponentially over time. For example, with simple interest this account would have a balance of €250 after 30 years [€100 + (30 × €5)], but with compound interest the account balance would be €432.19 in 30 years [€100 × (1 + 0.05)^{30}].

The equation for future value

Financial analysts routinely use compound interest. Throughout this book we generally use compound rather than simple interest. Equation 3.1 gives the general formula for calculating the future value, at the end of n years, of a lump sum invested today at an annual interest rate of r per cent:

$$FV = PV \times (1 + r)^n$$

EQUATION 3.1

future value
The value of an investment made today measured at a specific future date using compound interest.

compound interest
Interest earned both on the principal amount and on the interest earned in previous periods.

principal
The amount of money on which interest is paid.

simple interest
Interest paid only on the initial principal of an investment, not on the interest that accrues in earlier periods.

where FV = future value of an investment

PV = present value of an investment

r = annual rate of interest

n = number of years the PV is left on deposit.

The following Applying the Model illustrates an application of this equation by showing how you can use the concept of future value to evaluate an investment in a bank deposit account.

Applying the Model

In addition to having the opportunity to invest €100 in an open-ended savings account paying 5 per cent annual interest, you also have the chance to invest €100 in a deposit account at the bank paying 6 per cent annual interest. The difference is that you must leave your money in the account for five years to earn the full 6 per cent interest. If you withdraw the money early, you will face a substantial penalty. You would like to know how much your €100 deposit will be worth at the end of five years. Substituting $PV = €100$, $r = 0.06$, and $n = 5$ into Equation 3.1 gives the future value at the end of year 5, expressed as FV:

$$FV = €100 \times (1+0.06)^5 = €100 \times (1.3382) = €133.82$$

Your account will have an account balance of €133.82 at the end of the fifth year. This is shown on a **time line**, which is a graphical presentation of cash flows over a given period of time, at the top of Figure 3.1.

time line
A graphical presentation of cash flows over a given period of time.

FIGURE 3.1

Time line for €100 invested for five years at 6 per cent annual interest

This figure illustrates how €100 grows to €133.82 over five years if the annual interest rate is 6 per cent. The time line at the top shows the initial deposit as well as the accumulated value after five years. The lower right portion of the figure shows how to calculate the future value using Excel.

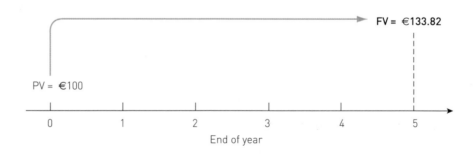

Column / Row	A	B
1	Present value	€100
2	Number of periods	5
3	Interest rate	6%
4	Future value	€133.82
5	*Formula B4*: FV(B3,B2,B1)	

PERIOD	INTEREST RATE (r)					
	1%	2%	3%	4%	5%	6%
1	1.010	1.020	1.030	1.040	1.050	1.060
2	1.020	1.040	1.061	1.082	1.102	1.124
3	1.030	1.061	1.093	1.125	1.158	1.191
4	1.041	1.082	1.126	1.170	1.216	1.262
5	1.051	1.104	1.159	1.217	1.276	1.338
6	1.062	1.126	1.194	1.265	1.340	1.419
7	1.072	1.149	1.230	1.316	1.407	1.504

TABLE 3.1

Format of a future-value factor (FVF) table

There are three popular methods for simplifying future-value calculations. One method is to use a future-value factor (FVF) table, such as Table A1 in Appendix A. Such a table provides future-value factors ($FVF_{r\%,n}$) for various interest rates (r) and holding periods (n). Table 3.1 reproduces a portion of Table A1 from the appendix. To find the future-value factor for 6 per cent interest and a five-year holding period ($FVF_{6\%,5}$), we simply move across the interest rates on the horizontal axis of the table until we reach the column labelled '6%', and then move vertically down this column until we find the row labelled 'Period 5'. We find that $FVF_{6\%,5}$ is equal to 1.338, and this is the number we would multiply by €100 to compute FV_5. Not surprisingly, this matches the previous FV_5 = €133.80, except for a small rounding difference.

A second method is to use a financial calculator. To compute FV in the example, you would simply input the number of years (5), the interest rate (6 per cent), and the amount of the initial deposit (€100), and then calculate the future value of €133.82. Consult the manual for the calculator you have purchased to see exactly how to input these figures.

The third method of simplifying time-value calculations involves using a financial spreadsheet such as *Excel*. The bottom of Figure 3.1 shows a simplified spreadsheet illustrating the key inputs, the cell formula for the output and the future value of €133.82.[1]

A graphic view of future value

Remember that we measure future value at the *end* of the given period. Figure 3.2 shows how quickly a €1.00 investment grows over time at various annual interest rates. The figure shows that (1) the higher the interest rate, the higher the future value and (2) the longer the period of time, the higher the future value. Note that for an interest rate of 0 per cent, the future value always equals the present value (€1), but for any interest rate greater than zero, the future value is greater than €1.

---

[1] The format of *Excel's* future-value formula is '=FV(rate,nper,pmt,pv,type)', where: rate = interest rate per period; nper = number of periods; pmt = the size of payments made each year in an annuity (in this case, set to 0 because we are calculating the future value of a lump sum rather than of an annuity); pv = the present-value or lump-sum amount; type = a 0/1 variable (omitted in our example) that indicates whether payments occur at the beginning or at the end of each period.

If you enter this formula in *Excel*, it will generate the answer, −133.82. You can force *Excel* to produce a positive future value simply by inserting a minus sign in front of the FV equation.

FIGURE 3.2

The power of compound interest: Future value of €1 invested at different annual interest rates

The figure shows that the future value of €1.00 increases over time as long as the interest rate is greater than 0 per cent. Notice that each line gets steeper the longer the money remains invested. This is the power of compound interest. For the same reason, the future value grows faster at higher interest rates. Observe how the lines get steeper as the interest rates increase.

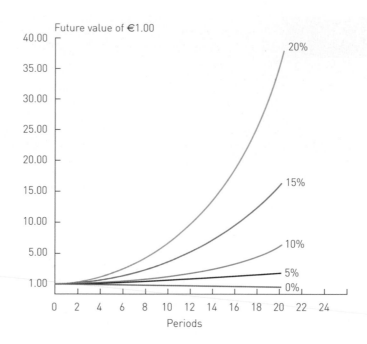

CONCEPT REVIEW QUESTIONS

1 Will a deposit made into an account paying compound interest (assuming compounding occurs once per year) yield a higher future value after one period than an equal-sized deposit in an account paying simple interest? What about future values for investments held longer than one period?

2 How would (a) a decrease in the interest rate or (b) an increase in the holding period of a deposit affect its future value? Why?

3 What would happen if someone had a negative rate of interest paid?

COMPARATIVE CORPORATE FINANCE

Me, save money?

This chapter shows how money grows over time as it earns interest. But before people can earn interest on their money, they have to save some money to invest. But just how different are the savings patterns of citizens in the major industrialized countries? As the accompanying chart makes clear, personal savings rates are strikingly different both between countries and within the same country at different points in time. Italy has the highest national savings rate (16 per cent) among rich countries in 2002, followed by Belgium, France and the Czech Republic. The ranking was somewhat different in 1992; while Italy was also the thriftiest rich country

then, with a savings rate exceeding 25 per cent, South Korean citizens had the second highest savings rate of 23 per cent. Although economists are divided about the determinants of varying national savings rates, systematic and enduring patterns can be observed and it seems clear that economic, demographic and cultural factors all play important roles in explaining the international differences.

The chart also shows that savings rates have declined between 1992 and 2002 for 15 of the 20 countries surveyed. For no country is this more true than the United States. The US savings rate was 8.7 per cent in 1992; by 2002 the savings rate of American households had declined to 3.7 per cent (and was actually negative during 2001). What is going on here? Why did people stop saving during a decade that encompassed the longest economic expansion in US history and that saw the stock market more than triple in value? An even more perplexing question is: how did American corporations finance the $8.5 trillion or so of capital investments they made between 1992 and 2002?

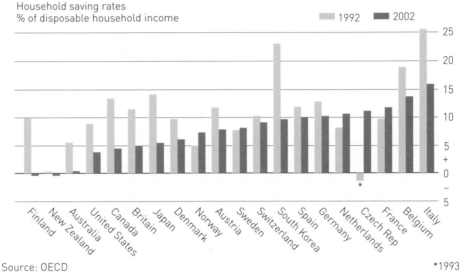

Household saving rates
% of disposable household income

1992   2002

Source: OECD   *1993

Source: 'Household Savings Rate', *The Economist* (July 2003), downloaded from http://www.economist.com.

3.2   PRESENT VALUE OF A LUMP SUM

We have examined how to project the amount of cash that builds over time as an initial investment earns interest. Now we want to reverse that focus and ask what an investor is willing to pay today to receive a given cash flow at some point in the future. In other words, we want to know the **present value** of the future cash flow. In this section, we focus on the problem of calculating the present value of a single future cash payment. In the previous section, we saw that the future value of a lump sum depended on the interest rate and on the amount of time that the money would earn that interest rate. Similarly, the present value depends largely on the investment opportunities of the recipient and the timing of the future cash flow.

present value
The value today of a cash flow to be received at a specific date in the future, assuming an opportunity to earn interest at a specified rate.

The concept of present value

In everyday language, we say that something is discounted to indicate that it is priced at less than full value. Discounting in finance is the same concept, but applied in a somewhat different manner. In finance, **discounting** describes the process we use to calculate the present value of future cash flows. To calculate the present value of future cash flows, we must discount the value of the cash flow because we lose the opportunity to earn interest on the money until we receive it. We also discount because from an economic perspective we forego the utility we would receive from having the money in hand now. That is, it is better to receive €100 today than to receive it in one year. If we have €100 now, we can earn interest. Therefore, the value right now of a €100 cash flow that will come at some future date is less than €100 – to determine how much less, we have to discount the future payment. This process is actually the inverse of compounding interest. Instead of finding the future value of present euros invested at a given rate, discounting determines the present

discounting
Describes the process of calculating present values.

value of a future amount, assuming an opportunity to earn a given return (r) on the money.[2]

To see how this works, suppose that an investment offers to pay you €300 one year from now. How much are you willing to spend today to acquire this investment if you earn 6 per cent on an alternative investment (of equal risk)? To answer this question, determine how much must be invested at 6 per cent today to have €300 one year from now. Let *PV* equal this unknown amount, and use the same notation as in the future-value discussion:

$$PV \times (1 + 0.06) = €300$$

Solving this equation for *PV* gives us the following:

$$PV = \left(\frac{€300}{(1 + 0.06)} \right) = €283.02$$

The present value of €300 one year from today is €283.02. That is, investing €283.02 today at a 6 per cent interest rate results in €300 at the end of one year. Therefore, you are willing to pay no more than €283.02 for the investment that pays €300 in one year.

The equation for present value

We can find the present value of a lump sum mathematically by solving Equation 3.1 for *PV*. In other words, the present value (*PV*) of some future amount (*FV*) to be received *n* periods from now, assuming an opportunity cost of *r*, is given by Equation 3.2:

EQUATION 3.2

$$PV = \left(\frac{FV}{(1 + r)^n} \right) = FV \times \left(\frac{1}{(1 + r)^n} \right)$$

The following Applying the Model illustrates the application of Equation 3.2, using a corporate investment opportunity as an example.

Applying the Model

Pam Verity, the financial manager of the Nordic Oil Drilling Company, was offered the chance to purchase the right to receive a €1700 royalty payment eight years from now. The offer came from Sam Long, the owner of the Petroleum Land Management Company. Pam believes that if she had the €1700 in hand now, she could invest it and earn 8 per cent. How much is she willing to pay for the right to receive this royalty payment? Substituting $FV = €1700$, $n = 8$, and $r = 0.08$ into Equation 3.2 yields the following:

$$PV = \left(\frac{€1700}{(1 + 0.08)^8} \right) = \left(\frac{€1700}{(1.85093)} \right) = €918.46$$

Pam finds that the present value of this €1700 royalty payment is €918.46. If Sam offers to sell Pam the royalty payment for €900 (or any amount less than

---

[2] This interest rate is variously referred to as the discount rate, required return, cost of capital, hurdle rate, or opportunity cost.

€918.46), Pam should accept the offer. In this case, the marginal cost of the investment (€900) is less than its marginal benefit (€918.46). At the top of Figure 3.3 is a time line graphically describing this process.

Real World

In the climate change discussions, a major report was the Stern Report, in late 2006, on the economics of climate change. Stern suggested that as the costs of doing nothing were so large we should take urgent action now. Central to this debate is the discount rate used. Stern suggested that a discount rate of 3–5 per cent would be inappropriate, as it would (as we have seen) result in very little weight being placed on the far-future costs and benefits. He argued for a discount rate of 0.1 per cent, saying, in defence: 'How can we say that our great-great-great grandchildren are worth less than we are worth ourselves?' So, while the climate debate may rage primarily on the science, there is also a close tie to the financial tools discussed in this chapter.

Source: Adapted from 'How To Value a Grandchild', *The Economist*, 4 December 2006.

There are three popular methods for simplifying present-value calculations. One method is to use a present-value factor (PVF) table, such as Table A2 in Appendix A. Part of Table A2 appears below as Table 3.2. Present-value factors for specific discount rates and compounding periods ($PVF_{r\%,n}$) are determined just as they were for future values. To find the relevant factor for the current example, $PVF_{8\%,8}$, move across the top of the table until you reach the 8 per cent column, then move down until you reach the row for eight years. The table indicates that the present value of €1 discounted for eight years at 8 per cent equals €0.540. Multiply that figure by €1700 to find the present value of the royalty payment, €918 (rounding to the nearest euro).

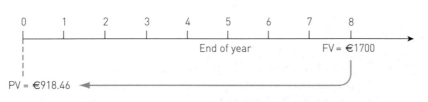

FIGURE 3.3

Present value of €1700 to be received in eight years at an 8 per cent discount rate

To calculate the present value of €1700, we must discount it to reflect the lost opportunity to earn 8 per cent interest on the money for eight years. In this example, the discounted value of €1700 equals just €918.46.

Calculator

Input	Function
1700	FV
8	N
8	I
	CPT
	PV
Solution	918.46

Spreadsheet

Column / Row	A	B
1	Future value	€1700
2	Number of periods	8
3	Interest rate	8%
4	**Present value**	**€918.46**
5	*Formula B4:* PV(B3,B2,0,B1)	

TABLE 3.2
The discount
factor for various
combinations
of interest rates
and time

PERIOD	DISCOUNT RATE (r)							
	1%	2%	3%	4%	5%	6%	7%	8%
1	0.990	0.980	0.971	0.962	0.952	0.943	0.935	0.926
2	0.980	0.961	0.943	0.925	0.907	0.890	0.873	0.857
3	0.971	0.942	0.915	0.889	0.864	0.840	0.816	0.794
4	0.961	0.924	0.888	0.855	0.823	0.792	0.763	0.735
5	0.951	0.906	0.863	0.822	0.784	0.747	0.713	0.681
6	0.942	0.888	0.837	0.790	0.746	0.705	0.666	0.630
7	0.933	0.871	0.813	0.760	0.711	0.665	0.623	0.583
8	0.923	0.853	0.789	0.731	0.677	0.627	0.582	0.540

Using financial calculators or spreadsheets, as shown in the lower portion of Figure 3.3, are two other popular methods for simplifying present-value calculations for a lump sum.[3]

A graphic view of present value

For investors who expect to receive cash in the future, Figure 3.4 contains two important messages. First, the present value of a future cash payment declines the longer investors must wait to receive it. Secondly, the present value declines as the discount rate rises. Note that for a discount rate of 0 per cent, the present value always equals the future value (€1). However, for any discount rate greater than zero, the present value falls below the future value.

CONCEPT
REVIEW
QUESTIONS

4 How are the present value and the future value of a lump sum related – in definition and in terms of mathematics? Notice that for a given interest rate (r) and a given investment time horizon (n), $PVF_{r,n}$ and $FVF_{r,n}$ are inverses of each other. Why?

5 How would (a) an increase in the discount rate or (b) a decrease in the time period until the cash flow is received affect the present value? Why?

3.3 FUTURE VALUE OF CASH FLOW STREAMS

Financial managers frequently need to evaluate streams of cash flows that occur in future periods. Although this is mechanically more complicated than computing the future or present value of a single cash flow, the same basic techniques apply. Two types of cash flow stream are possible – the mixed stream and the annuity. A **mixed stream** is a series of unequal cash flows reflecting no particular pattern, whereas an **annuity** is a stream of equal periodic cash flows. Either of these cash flow patterns can represent inflows earned on investments or outflows invested to earn future returns. Because certain shortcuts are possible when evaluating an annuity, we discuss mixed streams and annuities separately. While in general throughout this text we will deal

mixed stream
A series of unequal cash flows reflecting no particular pattern.

annuity
A stream of equal periodic cash flows.

---

[3] The format of the *Excel* function for present value is '=PV(rate,nper,pmt,fv,type)'. The terms in parentheses have similar interpretations to those in *Excel*'s future-value function. Note that in the present-value function, *Excel* produces an answer with the opposite sign to that of the value entered for the variable 'fv'. In other words, if a lump sum has a positive future value, *Excel* produces a negative estimate for the present value. You can change the sign of *Excel*'s answer simply by putting a minus sign in front of the PV equation.

FIGURE 3.4

The power of
discounting: Present
value of €1
discounted at
different interest
rates

*The present value of €1.00
falls as the interest rate
rises. Similarly, the longer
one must wait to receive a
€1.00 payment, the lower
the present value of that
payment.*

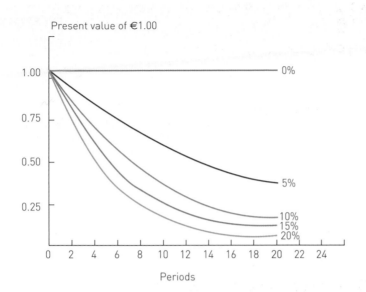

with cash flows as though they are annuities, this is only a convention, and in reality most financial flows are at best only approximate annuities.

Finding the future value of a mixed stream

The future value of any stream of cash flows measured at the end of a specified year is merely the sum of the future values of the individual cash flows at that year's end. This future value is sometimes called the terminal value. Because each cash flow earns interest, the future value of any stream of cash flows is greater than a simple sum of the cash flows.

Applying the Model

We wish to determine the balance at the end of five years in an investment account earning 9 per cent annual interest, given the following five end-of-year deposits: €400 in year 1, €800 in year 2, €500 in year 3, €400 in year 4 and €300 in year 5. These cash flows appear on the time line at the top of Figure 3.5, which also depicts the future-value calculation for this mixed stream of cash flows, followed by the spreadsheet solutions.

The future value of the mixed stream is €2930.70.[4] Note that the first cash flow, which occurs at the end of year 1, earns interest for four years (end of year 1 to end of year 5); the second cash flow, which occurs at the end of year 2, earns interest for three years (end of year 2 to end of year 5); and so on. As a result of the 9 per cent interest earnings, the five deposits, which total €2400 before interest, grow to more than €2900 at the end of five years.

---

[4] There is a €0.01 rounding difference between the future value given on the time line compared with the future-value calculation using a calculator or spreadsheet. As before, *Excel* reports the value €2930.71 as a negative number because the FV function always reverses the signs of the cash flows and the final answer. Notice that to calculate the stream's present value (a necessary input in the FV formula), we use the NPV function rather than the PV function because the latter does not accommodate mixed cash flow streams.

FIGURE 3.5

Future value at the end of five years of a mixed cash flow stream invested at 9 per cent

The future value of a mixed stream of cash flows is merely the sum of the future values of the individual cash flows. For the cash flows shown on the time line, the individual future values compounded at 9 per cent interest at the end of year 5 are shown at the end of the arrows. Their total of €2930.70 represents the future value of the mixed stream.

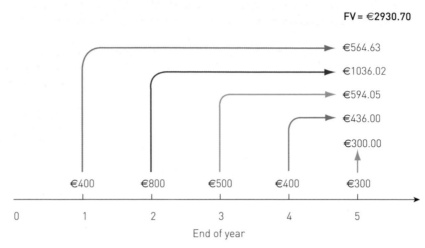

Letting CF_t represent the cash flow at the end of year t, the future value of an n-year mixed stream of cash flows (FV) is shown in Equation 3.3:

EQUATION 3.3

$$FV = CF_1 \times (1 + r)^{n-1} + CF_2 \times (1 + r)^{n-2} + \ldots + CF_n \times (1 + r)^{n-n}$$

Substitute the cash flows shown on the time line and the 9 per cent interest rate into Equation 3.3. The values shown to the right of the time line result. They total €2930.70.

Simplify the notation for Equation 3.3, as shown in Equation 3.3a, by using the Greek summation symbol, Σ, as a shorthand way of saying that the future value of this *n*-year mixed stream is equal to the sum of the future values of individual cash flows from periods 1, 2, 3, . . . , *n*:

$$FV = \sum_{t=1}^{n} CF_t \times (1 + r)^{n-t}$$

EQUATION 3.3A

Although summations economize on the notation needed to express most of the equations presented in this chapter, we present equations in their 'non-condensed' format for clarity wherever possible, and we use the summation notation sparingly. Mathematical purists can use their imaginations to construct the more succinct formulations.

Types of annuities

Before looking at future-value computations for annuities, we distinguish between the two basic types of annuities: these are known as an ordinary annuity and an annuity due. An **ordinary annuity** is an annuity for which the payments occur *at the end of each period*, whereas an **annuity due** is one for which the payments occur *at the beginning of each period*. To demonstrate these differences, assume that you choose the better of two annuities as a personal investment opportunity. Both are five-year, €1000 annuities. Annuity A is an ordinary annuity and annuity B is an annuity due. Although the amount of each annuity totals €5000, the timing of the cash flows differs; each cash flow arrives one year sooner with the annuity due than with the ordinary annuity. In fact, for any positive interest rate, the future value of an annuity due is always greater than the future value of an otherwise identical ordinary annuity.[5]

ordinary annuity
An annuity for which the payments occur at the end of each period.

annuity due
An annuity for which the payments occur at the beginning of each period.

Finding the future value of an ordinary annuity

The future value of an ordinary annuity can be calculated using the same method demonstrated earlier for a mixed stream.

Applying the Model

You wish to save money on a regular basis to finance an exotic holiday in five years. You are confident that, with sacrifice and discipline, you can force yourself to deposit €1000 annually, at the *end of each* of the next five years, into a savings account paying 7 per cent annual interest. This situation is depicted graphically at the top of Figure 3.6.

---

[5] Because ordinary annuities arise frequently in finance, we use the term 'annuity' throughout this book to refer to ordinary annuities, unless otherwise specified.

FIGURE 3.6

Future value at the end of five years of an ordinary annuity of €1000 per year invested at 7 per cent

The future value of the five-year €1000 ordinary annuity at 7 per cent interest at the end of year 5 is €5750.74, which is well above the €5000 sum of the annual deposits.

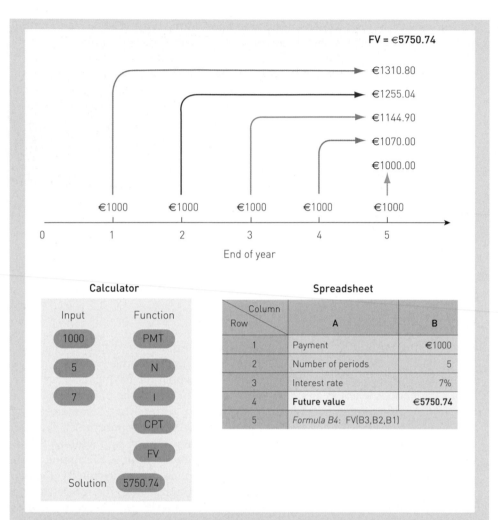

Compute the future value (FV) of this annuity, using Equation 3.3. Use the assumed interest rate (r) of 7 per cent and plug in the known values of each of the five yearly (n = 5) cash flows (CF_1 to CF_5), as follows:

$$
\begin{aligned}
FV &= CF_1 \times (1+r)^{n-1} + CF_2 \times (1+r)^{n-2} + \ldots + CF_n \times (1+r)^{n-n} \\
&= CF_1 \times (1+r)^{5-1} + CF_2 \times (1+r)^{5-2} + \ldots + CF_n \times (1+r)^{5-5} \\
&= €1000(1.07)^4 + €1000(1.07)^3 + €1000(1.07)^2 \\
&\quad + €1000(1.07)^1 + €1000 \\
&= €1310.80 + €1225.04 + €1144.90 + €1070 + €1000 \\
&= €5750.74
\end{aligned}
$$

The future value of the ordinary annuity is €5750.74. This is the amount of the money available to you to pay for your vacation. The year-1 cash flow of €1000 earns 7 per cent interest for four years, the year-2 cash flow earns 7 per cent interest for three years and so on.

Fortunately, a shortcut formula exists that simplifies the future-value calculation of an ordinary annuity. Using the symbol *PMT* to represent the annuity's annual payment, Equation 3.4 gives the future value of an annuity that lasts for *n* years (FV), assuming an interest rate of *r* per cent:

EQUATION 3.4

$$
FV = PMT \times \left(\frac{(1+r)^n - 1}{r} \right)
$$

Applying the Model

Demonstrate that Equation 3.4 yields the same answer obtained in the previous model by plugging in the values $PMT = €1000$, $n = 5$ and $r = 0.07$:

$$FV = €1000 \times \left(\frac{(1 + 0.07)^5 - 1}{0.07} \right)$$

$$= €1000 \times \left(\frac{1.4026 - 1}{0.07} \right)$$

$$= €1000 \times 5.7507$$

Once again, we find the future value of this ordinary annuity to be €5750.74.

In addition to using algebra, we can use a table such as Table A3 in Appendix A that details future-value factors for ordinary annuities at various interest rates for different holding periods. These are generically labelled $FVFA_{r\%,n}$; the factor corresponding to $r = 7\%$ and $n = 5$ equals $FVFA_{7\%,5}$, which equals 5.751. We can multiply this factor by €1000 to compute FV, which is €5751. Using financial calculators or spreadsheets, as shown below the time line in Figure 3.6, are two other popular methods for simplifying future-value calculations for annuities.

Finding the future value of an annuity due

The calculations required to find the future value of an annuity due involve only a slight change to those already demonstrated for an ordinary annuity. How much money will you have at the end of five years if you deposit €1000 annually at the *beginning of each* of the next five years into a savings account paying 7 per cent annual interest? This scenario is graphically depicted at the top of Figure 3.7. Note that the ends of years 0 through 4 are respectively equivalent to the beginnings of years 1 through 5. The €6153.29 future value of the annuity due is, as expected, greater than the €5750.74 future value of the comparable ordinary annuity discussed in the preceding section. Because the cash flows of the annuity due occur at the beginning of the year, the cash flow of €1000 at the beginning of year 1 earns 7 per cent interest for five years, the cash flow of €1000 at the beginning of year 2 earns 7 per cent interest for four years and so on. Comparing this to the ordinary annuity, it is clear that each €1000 cash flow of the annuity due earns interest for one more year than the comparable ordinary annuity cash flow. As a result, the future value of the annuity due is greater than the future value of the comparable ordinary annuity.

Because each cash flow of an annuity due earns one additional year of interest, the equation for the future value of an ordinary annuity, Equation 3.4, can be converted into an expression for the future value of an annuity due, FV (annuity due), simply by multiplying it by $(1 + r)$, as shown in Equation 3.5:

$$FV \text{ (annuity due)} = PMT \times \left(\frac{(1 + r)^n - 1}{r} \right) \times (1 + r)$$

EQUATION 3.5

Equation 3.5 demonstrates that the future value of an annuity due always exceeds the future value of a similar ordinary annuity for any positive interest rate. The future value of an annuity due exceeds that of an identical ordinary annuity by a factor of 1 plus the interest rate. We can check this by comparing the results from the two different five-year

FIGURE 3.7

Future value at the
end of five years of
an annuity due of
€1000 per year
invested at
7 per cent

*The future value at the end
of five years of a €1000
five-year annuity due that
earns 7 per cent annual
interest is €6153.29, which
exceeds the €5750.74
future value of the
otherwise identical
ordinary annuity (see
Figure 3.6). Each deposit in
the annuity due earns one
more year of interest than
the comparable deposit into
the ordinary annuity.*

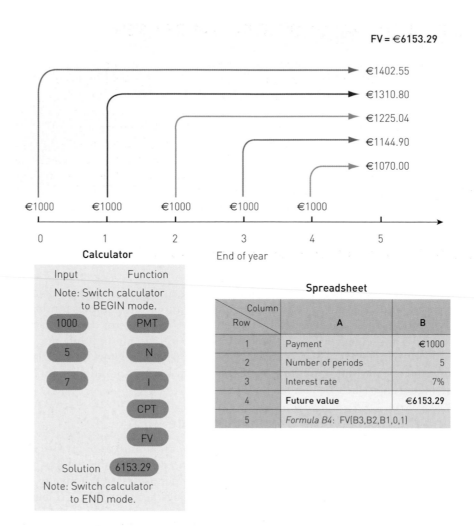

holiday savings plans presented previously. We determined that the future values of your
ordinary annuity and annuity due at the end of year 5, given a 7 per cent interest rate,
were €5750.74 and €6153.29, respectively. Multiplying the future value of the ordinary
annuity by 1 plus the interest rate yields the future value of the annuity due:

$$FV \text{ (annuity due)} = €5750.74 \times (1.07) = €6153.29$$

Because the cash flow of the annuity due occurs at the beginning of the
period rather than at the end, its future value is greater. In our illustration, you
earn about €400 more with the annuity due and can enjoy a somewhat more
luxurious holiday.

CONCEPT
REVIEW
QUESTIONS

6 How would the future value of a mixed stream of cash flows be calculated, given
the cash flows and applicable interest rate?

7 Differentiate between an ordinary annuity and an annuity due. How is the future
value of an ordinary annuity calculated, and how (for the same cash flows) can it
be converted into the future value of an annuity due?

8 What would happen to the relationship between the values of annuities due and
ordinary annuities if interest rates were to be negative?

3.4 PRESENT VALUE OF STREAMS OF CASH

Many decisions in corporate finance require financial managers to calculate the present values of cash flow streams that occur over several years. Decisions on how to finance an investment with the issuance of bonds, decisions on which project to spend investment on, decisions on how much credit to grant to customers, even decisions on mergers and acquisitions, all in effect rely on the concept of present value of streams of cash. In this section, we show how to calculate the present values of mixed cash flow streams and annuities. We also demonstrate the present-value calculation for a very important cash flow stream, known as a **perpetuity**. A perpetuity is a cash flow stream that continues forever. Perpetuities arise in many applications such as valuing a business as a going concern, or valuing a share with no definite maturity date. Perpetuities also arise, as we will see, when we consider certain types of bonds.

perpetuity
A level or growing cash flow stream that continues forever.

Finding the present value of a mixed stream

The present value of any cash flow stream is merely the sum of the present values of the individual cash flows. In other words, we apply the same techniques we used to calculate present values of lump sums to calculate the present values of all kinds of cash flow streams.

Applying the Model

Shortly after graduation you receive an inheritance that you use to purchase a small bed-and-breakfast inn as an investment. Your plan is to sell the inn after five years to finance an MBA. The inn is an old farmhouse, so you know that appliances, furniture and other equipment will wear out and need to be replaced or repaired on a regular basis. You estimate that these expenses will total €4000 during year 1, €8000 during year 2, €5000 during year 3, €4000 during year 4 and €3000 during year 5, the final year of your ownership. For simplicity, assume that the expense payments will be made at the end of each year. Because you have some of your inheritance left over after purchasing the inn (the deceased was indeed generous), you want to set aside a lump sum today from which you can make annual withdrawals to meet these expenses when they come due, as shown in Figure 3.8. Suppose you invest the lump sum in a bank account that pays 9 per cent interest. To determine the amount of money you need to put in the account, you must calculate the present value of the stream of future expenses, using 9 per cent as the discount rate.

The present value of the mixed stream is €19 047.58. The present-value factors corresponding to each annual cash flow are determined using present-value factor tables such as Table A2, using a financial calculator, or using an *Excel* spreadsheet. The more precise financial calculator and spreadsheet calculations are shown below the time line in Figure 3.8.

There is a general formula for computing the present value of a stream of future cash flows. Continuing to let CF_t represent the cash flow at the end of year t, the present value of an n-year mixed stream of cash flows (PV) is expressed as Equation 3.6:

$$PV = \left(CF_1 \times \frac{1}{(1+r)^1}\right) + \left(CF_2 \times \frac{1}{(1+r)^2}\right) + ... + \left(CF_n \times \frac{1}{(1+r)^n}\right)$$

$$= \sum_{t=1}^{n} CF_t \times \frac{1}{(1+r)^t}$$

EQUATION 3.6

FIGURE 3.8

Present value of a five-year mixed stream discounted at 9 per cent

The present value of the mixed stream is the sum of the present values of the individual cash flows discounted at the 9 per cent rate. The present values of the individual cash flows shown at the end of the arrows are summed to find the €19 047.58 present value of the stream of cash flows.

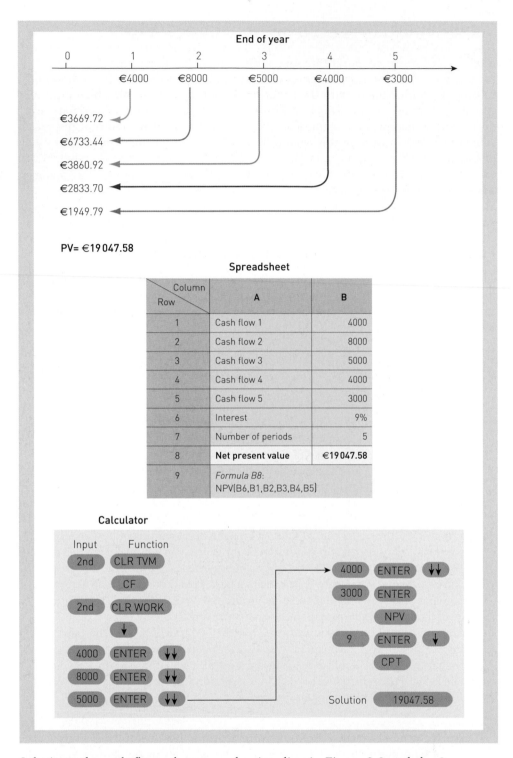

Substitute the cash flows shown on the time line in Figure 3.8 and the 9 per cent discount rate into Equation 3.6 to obtain the present-value figure, €19 047.58.

Finding the present value of an ordinary annuity

The present value of an ordinary annuity is found in a manner similar to that used for a mixed stream. Discount each payment and then add up each term to find the annuity's present value.

Applying the Model

Braden Company, a producer of plastic toys, was approached by its principal equipment supplier with an intriguing offer for a service contract. The supplier, the Extruding Machines Corporation (EMC), offered to take over all of Braden's equipment repair and servicing for five years in exchange for a onetime payment today. Braden's managers know their company spends €7000 at the end of every year, after the rush to create enough toys for the Christmas market, on maintenance. Taking EMC's service contract would reduce Braden's cash outflows by this €7000 annually for five years. Because these are equal annual cash benefits, Braden can determine what it is willing to pay for the service contract by valuing it as a five-year ordinary annuity with a €7000 annual cash flow. If Braden requires a minimum return of 8 per cent on all its investments, how much is it willing to pay for EMC's service contract? The calculation of the present value of this annuity is depicted on the time line presented at the top of Figure 3.9, followed by the spreadsheet solutions.

The present value of this ordinary annuity (EMC's service contract) is €27 948.97, calculated by applying the same method used previously to find the

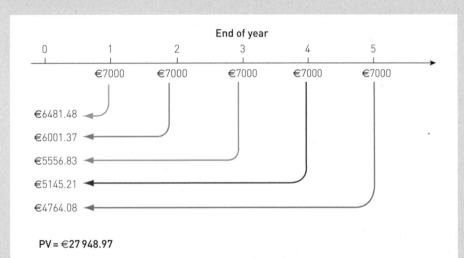

FIGURE 3.9

Present value of a five-year ordinary annuity discounted at 8 per cent

The present value of the five-year €7000 ordinary annuity discounted at 8 per cent is €27 948.97, which is merely the sum of the present values of the individual cash flows shown at the end of the arrows.

present value of a mixed stream. Each end-of-year €7000 cash flow is discounted back to time 0, and the present values of all five cash flows are summed to get the present value of the annuity. Therefore, if EMC offers the service contract to Braden for a lump-sum price of €27 948.97 or less, Braden should accept the offer. Otherwise, Braden should continue to perform its own maintenance.

As was the case with the future value of an annuity, a shortcut formula is available to simplify the present-value calculation for an annuity. Using the symbol *PMT* to denote the annual cash flow, the formula for the present value of an *n*-year ordinary annuity (*PV*) appears in Equation 3.7:

EQUATION 3.7

$$PV = \frac{PMT}{r} \times \left(1 - \frac{1}{(1+r)^n} \right)$$

Applying the Model

Use Equation 3.7 to calculate the present value of the service contract EMC has offered to the Braden Company. Substituting in $n = 5$ years, $r = 0.08$, and $PMT = €7000$, find the present value (*PV*) of this ordinary annuity to be €27 948.97, as shown below:

$$PV = \frac{€7000}{0.08} \times \left(1 - \frac{1}{(1.08)^5} \right) = \frac{€7000}{0.08} \times (1 - 0.6806) = €27948.97$$

By now, you know these computations can be simplified using a table such as Table A4 in Appendix A, which gives present-value factors for ordinary annuities at various discount rates for different holding periods. Many students find it easier to understand Equation 3.7 when the right-hand side of the equation is expressed simply as the annual cash flow (*PMT*) times the present-value factor for an annuity paying *r* per cent for *n* years, or $PVFA_{r\%,n}$. From Table A4, we get $PVFA_{8\%,5} = 3.993$. When multiplied by the €7000 annual cash flow, this results in a present value of €27 951, approximately equal to the present value obtained using more precise computations demonstrated beneath the time line in Figure 3.9.

Finding the present value of an annuity due

The present value of an annuity due is calculated in a fashion similar to that used for an ordinary annuity. Because each cash flow for an annuity due occurs one period earlier – at the beginning rather than at the end of the year – than for an ordinary annuity, an annuity due has a larger present value than an ordinary annuity with the same cash flows, discount rate and life. The expression for the present value of an annuity due, shown in Equation 3.8, is similar to the equation for the present value of an ordinary annuity (*PV*) given in Equation 3.7.

EQUATION 3.8

$$PV \text{ (annuuity due)} = \frac{PMT}{r} \times \left(1 - \frac{1}{(1+r)^n} \right) \times (1+r)$$

It is clear from a comparison of Equations 3.7 and 3.8 that the present value of an annuity due is merely the present value of a similar ordinary annuity multiplied by $(1 + r)$.

To demonstrate, assume that the Braden Company in the previous illustration wishes to determine the present value of the five-year, €7000 service contract at an 8 per cent discount rate, and that each of the cash flows occurs *at the beginning of the year.* To convert the service contract EMC offered the Braden Company into an annuity due, we assume that EMC would have to pay its annual maintenance cost of €7000 at the beginning of each of the next five years. This is not unreasonable, as the maintenance will have taken place at the end of the previous year. Braden is still evaluating what amounts to a five-year annuity; the company will just pay out each annual cash flow a year earlier. The present value of this annuity due is simply $(1 + r)$ times the value of the ordinary annuity: *PV* (annuity due) = €27 948.97 × (1.08) = €30 184.89. If Braden pays its maintenance costs at the start of each year, the most it is willing to pay EMC for the service contract increases by more than €2000 to €30 184.89.

Real World

One of the major uses in the finance world of annuities is the pensions market. Many people use their pension fund to purchase an annuity. In return for the lump sum the holder of the annuity pays the pensioner an annual sum. What makes this market complex is that the time over which the annuity is to be paid is uncertain in each individual case. Over a number of people, however, actuaries can predict the numbers that will live 5, 7, 10 etc. years, allowing the pension company to predict how much it can pay per annum. Many European countries (such as the UK, the Netherlands and Italy) require that all or part of a pension fund be annuitized. This means that the lump sum is used to purchase an annuity, a stream of income. Thus, saving for a pension involves annuities at both sides: we save a certain amount per annum to achieve a given lump sum, and at some stage that lump sum is used to purchase an annuity.

Source: Authors' own research.

Finding the present value of a perpetuity

As noted earlier, a perpetuity is a level or growing cash flow stream that continues forever. Here we focus on those with level streams, which can be viewed as annuities with infinite lives. In modern times the most famous perpetuity is perhaps the UK government consol bonds, the consol being short for consolidated. These bonds were first issued in 1752 when the existing debt of the UK government was consolidated into one issue, at 3.5 per cent. Over the years, other consolidations of UK government bonds took place. The last consol was issued in 1923, at 2.5 per cent. More information on this and other long-lived bonds can be found at www.dmo.gov.uk.

Currently, not many corporations or governments issue perpetual bonds.[6] Perhaps the simplest modern example of a perpetuity is preference shares issued by corporations. Preference shares promise investors a constant annual (or quarterly) dividend payment forever. It is also the case, however, that when dealing with the time value of money we find that with reasonable interest rates the value of an annuity approaches the value of a perpetuity as the lifespan of the perpetuity

---

[6] Some examples come close to being perpetuities. In July 1993, the Walt Disney Company sold €300 million of bonds that matured in the year 2093, 100 years after they were issued. The market dubbed these 'Sleeping Beauty bonds' because their maturity matched the amount of time that Sleeping Beauty slept before being kissed by Prince Charming in the classic story.

increases. Shown below is the value of a €100 annuity as a percentage of that of a €100 perpetuity, both valued at 8 per cent, as we increase the life of the annuity.

TABLE 3.3

The relationship between annuity and perpetuity values

YEARS	VALUE OF THE ANNUITY	VALUE AS A % OF PERPETUITY
1	€92.59	7%
5	399.27	32%
10	671.01	54%
20	981.81	79%
25	1 067.48	85%
50	€1 223.35	98%

In valuation of a perpetuity, although 'forever' is a difficult time period to measure, we simply express the lifetime (n) of this security as infinity (∞), and modify our basic valuation formulation for an annuity accordingly. For example, we wish to determine the present value of an annuity (PV) that pays a constant annual dividend amount (PMT) for a perpetual number of years ($n = \infty$) discounted at a rate r. Here, the Greek summation notation is helpful in expressing the formula in Equation 3.9:

EQUATION 3.9

$$PV = PMT \times \sum_{t=1}^{\infty} \frac{1}{(1+r)^t}$$

Fortunately, Equation 3.9 also comes in a simplified version, which says that the present value of a perpetuity equals the annual, end-of-year payment divided by the discount rate. Equation 3.10 gives this straightforward expression for the present value of a perpetuity (PV):

EQUATION 3.10

$$PV = PMT \times \frac{1}{r} = \frac{PMT}{r}$$

Applying the Model

Find the present value of the dividend stream associated with preference shares issued by the Alpha and Omega Service Company. A&O, as the company is commonly known, promises to pay €10 per year (at the end of each year) on its preference shares, and security analysts believe that the firm's business and financial risk merits a required return of 12.5 per cent. Substituting the values $PMT =$ €10 per year and $r = 0.125$ into Equation 3.10, we find the following:

$$PV = \frac{€10}{0.125} = €80$$

The present value of A&O's preference share dividends, valued as an annuity with a perpetual life, is €80 per share. In other words, the right to receive €10 at the end of every year for an indefinite period is worth only €80 today if a person can earn 12.5 per cent on investments of similar risk. If the person had €80 today and earned 12.5 per cent interest on it each year, €10 a year (0.125 × €80) could be withdrawn indefinitely without ever touching the initial €80.

Finding the present value of a growing perpetuity

As we have seen, perpetuities pay a constant periodic amount forever. However, few aspects of modern life are constant, and most of the cash flows we care about have a tendency to grow over time. This is true for items of income such as wages and salaries, dividend payments from companies and social security payments from governments.[7] Inflation is one, but only one, factor driving the increase in cash flows over time. We must therefore examine how to adjust the present value of a perpetuity formula to account for expected growth in future cash flows. Suppose we want to calculate the present value (PV) of a stream of cash flows growing forever ($n = \infty$) at the rate g. Given an opportunity cost of r, the present value of the **growing perpetuity** is given by Equation 3.11, which is sometimes called the **Gordon growth model**:

$$PV = \frac{CF_1}{r - g}, r > g$$

growing perpetuity
An annuity promising to pay a growing amount at the end of each year forever.

Gordon growth model
The valuation model, named after Myron Gordon, that views cash flows as a 'growing perpetuity'.

EQUATION 3.11

Note that the numerator in Equation 3.11 is CF_1, the first year's cash flow. This cash flow is expected to grow at a constant annual rate (g) from now to the end of time. The cash flow for any specific future year (t) can be determined by applying the growth rate (g) as follows:

$$CF_t = CF_1 \times (1+g)^{t-1}$$

Applying the Model

Gil Bates is a philanthropist who wants to endow a medical foundation with sufficient money to fund ongoing research. Gil is particularly impressed with the research proposal submitted by the Smith Cancer Institute (SCI). The institute requests an endowment sufficient to cover its expenses for medical equipment. Next year these expenses will total €10 million, and they will grow by 3 per cent per year in perpetuity afterwards. The institute can earn an 11 per cent return on Gil's contribution. How large must the contribution be to finance the institute's medical equipment expenditures in perpetuity? Equation 3.11 tells us that the present value of these expenses equals €125 million, computed as follows:

$$PV = \frac{10}{0.11 - 0.03} = \frac{10}{0.08} = 125$$

Note that Gil Bates would have to make an investment of only €90 909 090 (€10 000 000 ÷ 0.11, using Equation 3.10) to fund a non-growing perpetuity of €10 million per year. The additional investment of about €34 million is required to support the 3 per cent annual growth in the payout to SCI.

---

[7] Unfortunately, this is also true for expense items such as rent and utility expenses, car prices and tuition payments.

9   How would the present value of a mixed stream of cash flows be calculated, given the cash flows and an applicable required return?

10 Given the present value of an ordinary annuity and the applicable required return, how can this value be easily converted into the present value of an otherwise identical annuity due? What is the fundamental difference between the cash flow streams of these two annuities?

11 What is a perpetuity, and how is its present value conveniently calculated? How do you find the present value of a growing perpetuity?

12 What if we have a mixed stream of cash flows that also has a mixed set of interest rates? Can we handle this using the processes above?

SMART CONCEPTS

See the concept explained step-by-step at **www.cengage.co.uk/ megginson**

3.5 SPECIAL APPLICATIONS OF TIME VALUE

Financial managers frequently apply future-value and present-value techniques to determine the values of other variables. In these cases, the future or present values are known, and the equations presented earlier are solved for variables such as the cash flow (*CF* or *PMT*), interest or discount rate (*r*) or number of time periods (*n*). Here we consider four of the more common applications and refinements: (1) compounding more frequently than annually; (2) stated versus effective annual interest rates; (3) the calculation of deposits needed to accumulate a future sum; and (4) loan amortization. Then in the final section of this chapter we describe how time-value formulas and concepts can be used to determine interest or growth rates and an unknown number of time periods.

Compounding more frequently than annually

In many applications, interest compounds more frequently than once a year. Financial institutions compound interest semi-annually, quarterly, monthly, weekly, daily or even continuously. This section explores how the present-value and future-value techniques change if interest compounds more than once a year.

semi-annual compounding
Interest compounds twice a year.

Semi-annual compounding Semi-annual compounding means that interest compounds twice a year. Instead of the stated interest rate being paid once per year, half of the rate is paid twice a year. To demonstrate, consider an opportunity to deposit €100 in a savings account paying 8 per cent interest with semi-annual compounding. After the first six months, your account grows by 4 per cent to €104. Six months later, the account again grows by 4 per cent to €108.16. Notice that after one year, the total increase in the account value is €8.16, or 8.16 per cent (€8.16 ÷ €100.00). The return on this investment slightly exceeds the stated rate of 8 per cent because semi-annual compounding allows you to earn interest on interest during the year, increasing the overall rate of return. Table 3.4 shows how the account value grows

TABLE 3.4

The future value from investing €100 at 8 per cent interest compounded semi-annually over two years

PERIOD	BEGINNING PRINCIPAL (1)	FUTURE VALUE FACTOR (2)	FUTURE VALUE AT END OF PERIOD [(1) × (2)] (3)
6 months	€100.00	1.04	€104.00
12 months	104.00	1.04	108.16
18 months	108.16	1.04	112.49
24 months	112.49	1.04	116.99

every six months for the first two years. At the end of two years, the account value reaches €116.99.

Quarterly compounding As the name implies, **quarterly compounding** describes a situation in which interest compounds four times per year. An investment with quarterly compounding pays one-fourth of the stated interest rate every three months. Assume that after further investigation of your savings opportunities, you find an institution that pays 8 per cent interest compounded quarterly. After three months, your €100 deposit grows by 2 per cent to €102. Three months later, the balance again increases 2 per cent to €104.04. By the end of the year, the balance reaches €108.24. Compare that figure with the €108.16 you earn with semi-annual compounding. Table 3.5 tracks the growth in the account every three months for two years. At the end of two years, the account is worth €117.17.

Table 3.6 compares values for your €100 deposit at the end of years 1 and 2, given annual, semi-annual and quarterly compounding at the 8 per cent rate. As you should expect by now, the more frequently interest compounds, the greater the amount of money that accumulates.

quarterly compounding Interest compounds four times per year.

A general equation We can generalize the preceding examples in a simple equation. Suppose that a lump sum, denoted by *PV*, is invested at *r* per cent for *n* years. If *m* equals the number of times per year that interest compounds, the future value grows as shown in the following equation:

$$FV = PV \times \left(1 + \frac{r}{m}\right)^{m \times n}$$

EQUATION 3.12

Notice that if *m* = 1, Equation 3.12 reduces to Equation 3.1. The next several examples verify that this equation yields the same ending account values after two years, as shown in Tables 3.4 and 3.5.

PERIOD	BEGINNING PRINCIPAL (1)	FUTURE VALUE FACTOR (2)	FUTURE VALUE AT END OF PERIOD [(1) × (2)] (3)
3 months	€100.00	1.02	€102.00
6 months	102.00	1.02	104.04
9 months	104.04	1.02	106.12
12 months	106.12	1.02	108.24
15 months	108.24	1.02	110.41
18 months	110.41	1.02	112.62
21 months	112.62	1.02	114.87
24 months	114.87	1.02	117.17

TABLE 3.5
The future value from investing €100 at 8 per cent interest compounded quarterly over two years

| END OF YEAR | COMPOUNDING PERIOD | | |
	ANNUAL	SEMI-ANNUAL	QUARTERLY
1	€108.00	€108.16	€108.24
2	116.64	116.99	117.17

TABLE 3.6
The future value from investing €100 at 8 per cent for years 1 and 2 given various compounding periods

Applying the Model

In previous discussions, we calculated the amount that you would have at the end of two years if you deposited €100 at 8 per cent interest compounded semi-annually and quarterly. For semi-annual compounding, $m = 2$ in Equation 3.12; for quarterly compounding, $m = 4$. Substituting the appropriate values for semi-annual and quarterly compounding into Equation 3.12 yields the following results.

For semi-annual compounding:

$$FV = €100 \times \left(1 + \frac{0.08}{4}\right)^{2 \times 2} = €100 \times (1.04)^4 = €116.99$$

For quarterly compounding:

$$FV = €100 \times \left(1 + \frac{0.08}{4}\right)^{4 \times 2} = €100 \times (1.02)^8 = €117.17$$

These results agree with the values for FV_2 in Tables 3.4 and 3.5. If interest is compounded monthly, weekly or daily, m would equal 12, 52 or 365, respectively.

Continuous compounding As we switch from annual, to semi-annual, to quarterly compounding, the interval during which interest compounds gets shorter, while the number of compounding periods per year gets larger. In principle, there is almost no limit to this process – interest could be compounded daily, hourly or second by second. **Continuous compounding**, the most extreme case, occurs when interest compounds literally at every moment as time passes. In this case, m in Equation 3.12 would approach infinity, and Equation 3.12 converges to this expression:

continuous compounding
Interest compounds at literally every moment as time passes.

EQUATION 3.13

$$FV \text{ (continuous)} = PV \times e^{r \times n}$$

The number e is an irrational number, like π, which is useful in mathematical applications involving quantities that grow continuously over time. The value of e is approximately 2.7183. As before, increasing the frequency of compounding, in this case by compounding as frequently as possible, increases the future value of an investment.

Applying the Model

To find the value at the end of two years of your €100 deposit in an account paying 8 per cent annual interest compounded continuously, substitute $n = 2$, $PV = €100$ and $r = 0.08$ into Equation 3.13:

$$FV \text{ (continuous)} = €100 \times e^{0.08 \times 2} = €100 \times 1.1735 = €117.35$$

The future value with continuous compounding therefore equals €117.35, which, as expected, is larger than the future value of interest compounded semi-annually (€116.99) or quarterly (€117.17).[8]

---

[8] The *Excel* function for continuous compounding is '=exp(argument)'. For example, suppose you want to calculate the future value of €100 compounded continuously for five years at 8 per cent. To find this value in *Excel*, first calculate the value of $e(0.0835)$, using '=exp(0.08 × 5)', and then multiply the result by €100.

Stated versus effective annual interest rates

Both consumers and businesses need to make objective comparisons of loan costs or investment returns over different compounding periods. To put interest rates on a common basis for comparison, we must distinguish between *stated* and *effective* annual interest rates. The **stated annual rate** is the contractual annual rate charged by a lender or promised by a borrower. The **effective annual rate (EAR)**, also known as the 'true annual return', is the annual rate of interest actually paid or earned. The effective annual rate reflects the effect of compounding frequency, whereas the stated annual rate does not. We can best illustrate the differences between stated and effective rates with numerical examples.

Using the notation introduced earlier, we can calculate the effective annual rate by substituting values for the stated annual rate (r) and the compounding frequency (m) into Equation 3.14:

$$EAR = \left(1 + \frac{r}{m}\right)^m - 1$$

We can apply this equation using data from preceding examples.

stated annual rate
The contractual annual rate of interest charged by a lender or promised by a borrower.

effective annual rate (EAR)
The annual rate of interest actually paid or earned, reflecting the impact of compounding frequency. Also called the true annual return.

EQUATION 3.14

Applying the Model

Find the effective annual rate associated with an 8 per cent stated annual rate ($r = 0.08$) when interest is compounded annually ($m = 1$), semi-annually ($m = 2$) and quarterly ($m = 4$). Substituting these values into Equation 3.14 produces the following results.

For annual compounding:

$$EAR = \left(1 + \frac{0.08}{1}\right)^1 - 1 = (1 + 0.08) - 1 = 1.08 - 1 = 0.08 = 8\%$$

For semi-annual compounding:

$$EAR = \left(1 + \frac{0.08}{2}\right)^2 - 1 = (1 + 0.04)^2 - 1 = 1.0816 - 1 = 0.816 = 8.16\%$$

For quarterly compounding:

$$EAR = \left(1 + \frac{0.08}{4}\right)^4 - 1 = (1 + 0.02)^4 - 1 = 1.0824 - 1 = 0.0824 = 8.24\%$$

The results mean that 8 per cent compounded quarterly is equivalent to 8.24 per cent compounded annually. These values demonstrate two important points: (1) the stated and effective rates are equivalent for annual compounding; and (2) the effective annual rate increases with increasing compounding frequency.

Not surprisingly, the maximum effective annual rate for a given stated annual rate occurs when interest compounds continuously. The effective annual rate for this extreme case can be found by using the following equation:

$$EAR \text{ (continuous)} = e^r - 1$$

EQUATION 3.14A

For the 8 per cent stated annual rate ($r = 0.08$), substitution into Equation 3.14a results in an effective annual rate of 8.33 per cent, as follows:

$$EAR(\text{continuous}) = e^{0.08} - 1 = 1.0833 - 1 = 0.0833 = 8.33\%$$

annual percentage rate (APR)
The stated annual rate calculated by multiplying the periodic rate by the number of periods in one year.

annual percentage yield (APY)
The annual rate of interest actually earned reflecting the impact of compounding frequency. The same as the effective annual rate.

In most countries there are legal requirements, particularly for credit cards and consumer loans, to disclose the **annual percentage rate (APR)**. The APR is the stated annual rate found by multiplying the periodic rate by the number of periods in one year. For example, a bank credit card that charges 1.5 per cent per month has an APR of 18 per cent (1.5% per month × 12 months per year). However, the actual cost of this credit card account is determined by calculating the **annual percentage yield (APY)**, which is the same as the effective annual rate. For the credit card example, 1.5 per cent per month interest has an effective annual rate of $[(1.015)^{12} - 1] = 0.1956$, or 19.56 per cent. If the stated rate is 1.75 per cent per month, as is the case with many credit card accounts, the APY is a whopping 23.14 per cent. In other words, if you are carrying a positive credit card balance with an interest rate like this, pay it off as soon as possible!

Deposits needed to accumulate a future sum

Suppose that someone wishes to determine the annual deposit necessary to accumulate a certain amount of money at some point in the future. Assume that you want to buy a house five years from now and estimate that an initial down payment of €20 000 will be required. You want to make equal end-of-year deposits into an account paying annual interest of 6 per cent, so you must determine what size annuity results in a lump sum equal to €20 000 at the end of year 5. The solution can be derived from the equation for finding the future value of an ordinary annuity.

Earlier in this chapter, we found the future value of an n-year ordinary annuity (FV) by applying Equation 3.4. Solving that equation for PMT, in this case the annual deposit, we get Equation 3.15:

EQUATION 3.15

$$PMT = \left[\frac{FV}{\left[\dfrac{(1+r)^n - 1}{r} \right]} \right]$$

Once this is done, we substitute the known values of FV, r and n into the right-hand side of the equation to find the annual deposit required.

Applying the Model

Demonstrate the calculation using the situation in which you want to determine the equal annual end-of-year deposits required to accumulate €20 000 (FV) at the end of five years ($n = 5$), given an interest rate of 6 per cent ($r = 6\%$), as follows:

$$PMT = \left[\frac{€20000}{\left[\dfrac{(1.06)^5 - 1}{0.06} \right]} \right] = €3547.93$$

You can also use the future-value annuity factor to calculate the required deposit. Note that the denominator of Equation 3.15 is equivalent to the future-value factor for a 6 per cent, five-year annuity, which Table A3 shows as $FVFA_{6\%,5} = 5.637$. Dividing the future amount needed ($FV = €20\,000$) by this factor again gives (except for rounding) an annual cash flow of €3547.99. The amount of the annual deposit can alternatively be found using either a financial calculator or spreadsheet, as shown in Figure 3.10.

Loan amortization

Loan amortization refers to a situation in which a borrower makes equal periodic payments over time to fully repay a loan. For instance, with a 30-year home mortgage, the borrower makes the same payment each month for 30 years until the mortgage is completely repaid. To amortize a loan (i.e. to calculate the periodic payment that pays off the loan), you must know the total amount of the loan (the amount borrowed), the term of the loan, the frequency of periodic payments and the interest rate. To be more specific, the loan amortization process involves finding a level stream of payments (over the term of the loan) with a present value calculated at the loan interest rate equal to the amount borrowed. Lenders use a **loan amortization schedule** to determine these payments and the allocation of each payment to interest and principal.

loan amortization
A borrower makes equal periodic payments over time to fully repay a loan.

loan amortization schedule
Used to determine loan amortization payments and the allocation of each payment to interest and principal.

For example, suppose that you borrow €25 000 at 8 per cent annual interest for five years to purchase a new car. To demonstrate the basic approach, we first amortize this loan assuming that you make payments at the end of years 1 through 5. We then modify the annual formula to compute the more typical monthly car loan payments. To find the size of the annual payments, the lender determines the amount of a five-year annuity discounted at 8 per cent that has a present value of €25 000. This process is actually the inverse of finding the present value of an annuity.

Earlier, we found the present value (PV) of an n-year ordinary annuity using Equation 3.7. Solving that equation for PMT, the annual loan payment, we get Equation 3.16:

$$PMT = \left[\frac{PV}{\left[\frac{1}{r} \times \left[1 - \frac{1}{(1+r)^n} \right] \right]} \right]$$

EQUATION 3.16

Calculator

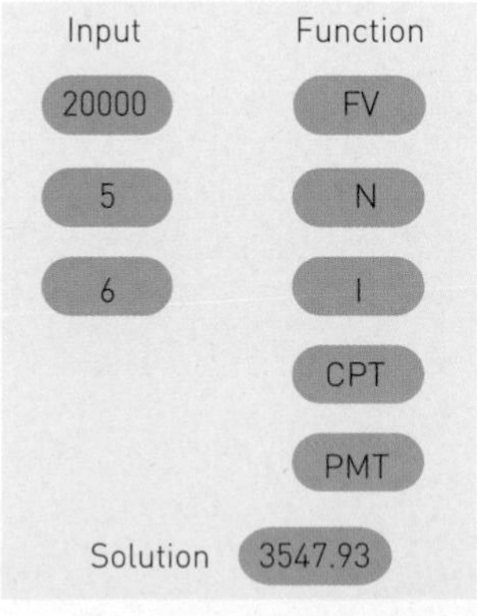

Input	Function
20000	FV
5	N
6	I
	CPT
	PMT
Solution	3547.93

Spreadsheet

	Column		
Row		A	B
1		Future value	€20 000
2		Number of periods	5
3		Interest rate	6%
4		Payment	€3547.93
5		*Formula B4*: Pmt(B3,B2,0,B1)	

FIGURE 3.10

Deposits (annuity) needed to accumulate a future sum

Applying the Model

To find the annual payment required on the five-year, €25 000 loan with an 8 per cent annual rate, we substitute the known values of PV = €25 000, r = 0.08 and n = 5 into the right-hand side of the equation:

$$PMT = \left[\frac{€25000}{\left[\left[\frac{1}{0.08}\right] \times \left[1 - \frac{1}{(1.08)^5}\right]\right]}\right] = €6261.41$$

Five annual payments of €6261.41 are needed to fully amortize this €25 000 loan.

As before, calculate the annual cash flow (*PMT*) by recognizing that the denominator of Equation 3.16 is equal to the present-value factor of an *r* per cent, *n*-year annuity ($PVFA_{r\%,n}$). Because Table A4 shows $PVFA_{8\%,5}$ = 3.993, again determine that the payment required to fully amortize this loan is €6260.96 (slight rounding difference) per year (*PMT* = €25 000 ÷ 3.993). The amount of the annual loan payment can alternatively be found, using either a financial calculator or spreadsheet, as shown in Figure 3.11.

The allocation of each loan payment of €6261.41 to interest and principal appears in columns 3 and 4 of the loan amortization schedule in Table 3.7. The portion of each payment representing interest (column 3) declines over the repayment period, and the portion going to principal repayment (column 4) increases. This pattern is typical of amortized loans; with level payments, the interest component declines as the principal falls, leaving a larger portion of each subsequent payment to repay principal.

Though computing amortized loan payments may seem a rather esoteric exercise, it is in fact the basis of the present-value formulation that people use most frequently in their personal lives. In addition to calculating car loan payments, it is used to compute mortgage payments on a home purchase. These consumer loans typically require monthly payments. We now demonstrate how to do the amortization calculations

FIGURE 3.11

Calculating loan amortization payments

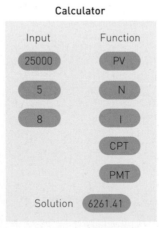

Calculator

Input	Function
25000	PV
5	N
8	I
	CPT
	PMT
Solution	6261.41

Spreadsheet

Row \ Column	A	B
1	Present value	€25 000
2	Number of periods	5
3	Interest rate	8%
4	**Payment**	**€6261.41**
5	*Formula B4*: Pmt(B3,B2,B1)	

END OF YEAR	LOAN PAYMENT (1)	BEGINNING OF YEAR PRINCIPAL (2)	PAYMENTS INTEREST [0.08 X (2)] (3)	PRINCIPAL [(1) – (3)] (4)	END-OF-YEAR PRINCIPAL [(2) – (4)] (5)	
1	€6 261.41	€25 000.00	€2 000.00	€4 261.41	€20 738.59	
2	6 261.41	20 738.59	1 659.09	4 602.32	16 136.27	
3	6 261.41	16 136.27	1 290.90	4 970.51	11 165.76	
4	6 261.41	11 165.76	893.26	5 368.15	5 797.61	
5	6 261.41	5 797.61	463.80	5 797.61	0	
6	1.062	1.126	1.194	1.265	1.340	1.419
7	1.072	1.149	1.230	1.316	1.407	1.504

TABLE 3.7

Loan amortization schedule €25 000 principal, for 8 per cent interest, five-year repayment period

using monthly rather than annual payments. First, Equation 3.16a is simply a modified version of Equation 3.16:

$$PMT = \left[\frac{r}{(1 + r)^n - 1} \right] \times (1 + r)^n \times PV$$

EQUATION 3.16A

Secondly, we generalize this formula to more frequent compounding periods by dividing the interest rate by m and multiplying the number of compounding periods by m. This changes the equation as follows:

$$PMT = \left[\frac{\frac{r}{m}}{(1 + \frac{r}{m})^{m \times n} - 1} \right] \times (1 + \frac{r}{m})^{m \times n} \times PV$$

EQUATION 3.16B

Applying the Model

Use Equation 3.16b to calculate what a monthly car payment will be if you borrow €25 000 for five years at 8 per cent annual interest. PV will again be the €25 000 amount borrowed, but the periodic interest rate ($r \div m$) will be 0.00667, or 0.667 per cent per month (0.08 per year ÷ 12 months per year). There will be $m \times n = 60$ compounding periods (12 months/year × 5 years = 60 months). Substituting these values into Equation 3.16b yields a monthly car loan payment of €506.91:

$$PMT = \left[\frac{\frac{0.08}{12}}{\left(1 + \frac{0.08}{12}\right)^{12 \times 5} - 1} \right] \times \left[1 + \frac{0.08}{12} \right]^{12 \times 5} \times €25\,000$$

$$= \left[\frac{0.00667}{(1.00667)^{60} - 1} \right] \times (1.00667)^{60} \times €25\,000$$

$$= €506.91$$

See if you can compute the monthly mortgage payment for a home purchased using a 30-year, €100 000 loan with a fixed 7.5 per cent annual interest rate. Note that there are 360 compounding periods (12 months/year × 30 years).[9]

CONCEPT
REVIEW
QUESTIONS

13 What effect does increasing compounding frequency have on (a) the future value of a given deposit and (b) its effective annual rate (EAR)?

14 Under what condition would the stated annual rate equal the effective annual rate (EAR) for a given deposit? How do these rates relate to the annual percentage rate (APR) and annual percentage yield (APY)?

15 How would you determine the size of the annual end-of-year deposits needed to accumulate a given future sum, at the end of a specified future period? What effect does the magnitude of the interest rate have on the size of the deposits needed?

16 What relationship exists between the calculation of the present value of an annuity and amortization of a loan? How can you find the amount of interest paid each year under an amortized loan?

3.6 ADDITIONAL APPLICATIONS OF TIME-VALUE TECHNIQUES

As you have probably already guessed, there are a vast number of applications of time-value techniques in modern finance. All are variations of the basic future-value and present-value formulas described earlier in this chapter. Here we expand our repertoire of computational methods to discuss two of the most important specialized uses of time-value techniques: determining (1) implied interest or growth rates and (2) the number of compounding periods.

Implied interest or growth rates

Analysts often need to calculate the compound annual interest or growth rate (annual rate of change in values) of a series of cash flows. Because the calculations required for finding interest rates and growth rates, given known cash flow streams, are the same, this section refers to the calculations as those required to find interest or growth rates. We examine each of three possible cash flow patterns – lump sums, annuities and mixed streams.

Lump sums The simplest situation is one in which a person wants to find the interest or growth rate of a single cash flow over time. As an example, assume that you invested €1000 in a stock market-based fund in December 2003 and that this investment December 2008, is worth €2150. You are interested to know what was your compound annual rate of return over this five-year period? This is easy to determine, as we are unconcerned about the investment's value during any of the intervening years. We simply want to determine what compound rate of return (r) converted a

---

[9] The amount of the mortgage payment is €699.21. To find this solution, just enter the formula '=pmt(0.00625,360 100 000)' in *Excel*. The first argument in this function is the monthly interest rate, 7.5 per cent divided by 12.

€1000 investment (*PV*) into a future amount (*FV*) worth €2150 in five years (n). Note that the number of years of growth (or interest) is the difference between the latest and earliest year number. In this case, $n = 5$ years. Although the period 2003 through 2008 includes six years, there are only five years of growth because the earliest year (2003) serves as the base year (i.e. time 0) and is then followed by five years of change: 2003 to 2004, 2004 to 2005, 2005 to 2006, 2006 to 2007 and 2007 to 2008. Finding r involves manipulating Equation 3.1 so that we have the value to be determined, in this case $(1 + r)^n$, on the left-hand side of the equation and the two known values, *PV* and *FV*, on the right-hand side of the equation, as shown in Equation 3.17:

$$(1 + r)^n = \frac{FV}{PV}$$

EQUATION 3.17

Substituting in the known values, we obtain the following:

$$(1 + r)^n = \frac{€2150}{€1000} = 2.15$$

This says that 1 plus the rate of return $(1 + r)$, compounded for five years ($n = 5$), equals 2.150. Our final step is to calculate the fifth root of 2.150, which is done simply by raising 2.150 to the one-fifth power using the y^x key on a financial calculator, and then subtracting 1:

$$r = \sqrt[5]{2.15} - 1 = 2.15^{0.2} - 1 = 1.1654 - 1 = 0.1654 = 16.54\%$$

We can use a financial calculator or spreadsheet to more directly solve for a growth of interest rate of a lump sum, as shown in Figure 3.12.

Annuities Sometimes you may need to find the interest rate associated with an annuity, which represents the equal annual end-of-year payments on a loan. To demonstrate, assume that your friend John Jacobs can borrow €2000 to be repaid in equal annual end-of-year amounts of €514.18 for the next five years. He wants to find the interest rate on the loan and asks you for assistance. You realize that he is really asking you an annuity valuation question, so you use a variant of the present value of an annuity formula shown in Equation 3.7:

$$PV = PMT \times \left[\frac{1}{r} \times \left[1 - \frac{1}{(1 + r)^n}\right]\right]$$

Calculator

Input	Function
1000	PV
-2150	FV
5	N
	CPT
	I
Solution	16.54

Spreadsheet

Row \ Column	A	B
1	Present value	€1000
2	Future value	-€2150
3	Number of years	5
4	**Interest rate**	**16.54%**
5	Formula B4: RATE (B3,0,B1,B2)	

FIGURE 3.12
Calculating an interest rate for a lump sum

You try to determine the interest rate (r) that will equate the present value of a five-year annuity ($PV = €2000$) to a stream of five equal annual payments ($PMT = €514.18$ per year). Because you know PV and PMT, you can rearrange Equation 3.7, putting the unknown value on the left-hand side and the known values on the right:

$$\left[\frac{1}{r} \times \left(1 - \frac{1}{(1+r)^n} \right) \right] = \frac{PV}{PMT} = \frac{€2000}{€514.18} = 3.8897$$

Unfortunately, the term on the left-hand side is very difficult to solve directly, but there is an easy shortcut to obtaining the solution. Equation 3.7 can also be expressed using present-value factors as the annual cash flow (PMT) times the present-value factor for an annuity paying r per cent for n years, or $PVFA_{r\%,n}$, which is the unknown value on the left-hand side of the preceding equation. Substituting, we get the following:

$$PVFA_{r\%,5} = \frac{PV}{PMT} = \frac{€2000}{€514.18} = 3.8897$$

We can then solve this equation by determining the appropriate five-year $PVFA$ having a value of 3.8897. Table A4 in Appendix A shows that $PVFA_{9\%,5} = 3.890$, so we can tell John Jacobs that he is being charged about 9 per cent on his loan.

We can use a financial calculator or spreadsheet to more directly solve for a growth of interest rate of an annuity, as demonstrated in Figure 3.13.

Mixed streams As shown in the previous discussion, finding the unknown interest or growth rate for a lump sum or an annuity is relatively simple, using the formulas presented here, the present-value tables, or a financial calculator or spreadsheet. But finding the unknown interest or growth rate for a mixed stream is very difficult to do using formulas or present-value tables. It can be accomplished by using an iterative trial-and-error approach to find the interest rate that could cause the present value of the stream's inflows to just equal the present value of its outflows. This calculation is often referred to as finding the yield-to-maturity or internal rate of return (IRR). A more efficient way to make this type of calculation is to use a financial calculator or spreadsheet that has the IRR function built into it. With this approach, you can input (with all outflows input as negative numbers) all the cash flows – both outflows

FIGURE 3.13

Calculating an interest rate for an annuity

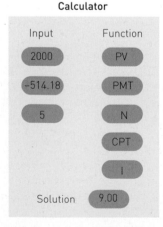

Calculator			Spreadsheet		
Input	Function		Column / Row	A	B
2000	PV		1	Present value	€2000
–514.18	PMT		2	Payment	–€514.18
5	N		3	Number of periods	5
	CPT		4	Interest rate	9.00%
	I		5	Formula B4: Rate (B3,B2,B1)	
Solution	9.00				

and inflows – and then use the IRR function to calculate the unknown interest rate. Because this approach is discussed and demonstrated in Chapter 4 with regard to bonds and in Chapter 8 with regard to its use in capital budgeting, a detailed description of its application is not included here. We will return to the issue of the internal rate of return when we discuss how firms make decisions about which projects to take on.

Number of compounding periods

Occasionally, for either a lump sum or an annuity, the financial analyst wants to calculate the unknown number of time periods necessary to achieve a given cash flow goal. We briefly consider this calculation here for both lump sums and annuities.

Lump sums If the present (PV) and future (FV) amounts are known, along with the interest rate (r), we can calculate the number of periods (n) necessary for the present amount to grow to equal the future amount. For example, assume that you plan to deposit €1000 in an investment that is expected to earn an 8 per cent annual rate of interest. Determine how long it will take to triple your money (to accumulate €3000). Stated differently, at an 8 per cent annual interest rate, how many years (n) will it take for €1000 (PV) to grow to €3000 (FV)? This can be expressed by simply rearranging the basic future-value formula, Equation 3.1, to express the unknown value, n, on the left-hand side and then plugging in the known values, FV, PV and r:

$$FV = PV \times (1 + r)^n$$

$$(1.08) = \frac{FV}{PV} = \frac{€3000}{€1000} = 3$$

Now what? How do you find the exponent value (n) that turns 1.08 into 3.000? Take natural logarithms of both sides of this formula and then express the unknown number of years (n) as a ratio of two log values, as follows:

$$n = \frac{\ln(€3000)}{\ln(1.08)} = \frac{1.0986}{0.0770} = 14.275$$

You thus find the number of years to be 14.275, which means that at an 8 per cent annual rate of interest, it will take about 14.3 years for your €1000 deposit to triple in value to €3000. Solving for an unknown number of periods for a lump sum using a financial calculator or a spreadsheet is demonstrated in Figure 3.14.

Annuities Occasionally, we want to determine the unknown life (n) of an annuity that is intended to achieve a specified objective, such as to repay a loan of a given amount (PV) with a stated interest rate (r) and equal annual end-of-year payments (PMT). To illustrate, assume that you can borrow €20 000 at a 12 per cent annual interest rate with annual end-of-year payments of €3000. You want to determine how long it will take to fully repay the loan's interest and principal. In other words, how many years (n) will it take to repay a €20 000 (PV), 12 per cent (r) loan if the payments of €3000 (PMT) are made at the end of each year? This is similar to the problem of determining the unknown interest rate in an annuity we addressed earlier, except we now know that $r = 12$ per cent, and that we are trying to determine the number of years (n). Once again, rearrange the equation that expresses

FIGURE 3.14

Calculating an unknown number of years for a lump sum

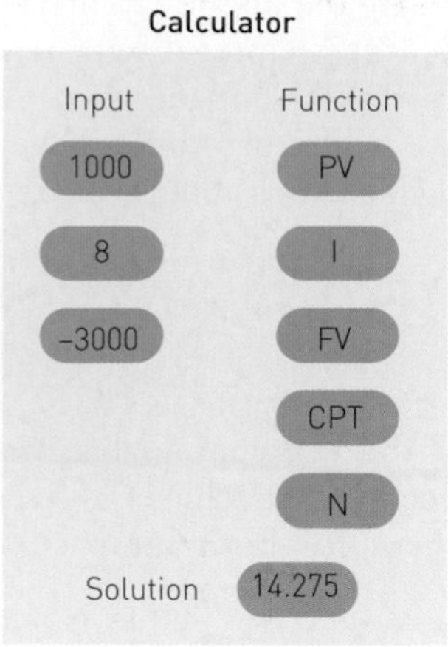

Calculator

Input	Function
1000	PV
8	I
-3000	FV
	CPT
	N

Solution 14.275

Spreadsheet

Row \ Column	A	B
1	Present value	€1000
2	Interest rate	8%
3	Future value	-€3000
4	**Number of years**	**14.275**
5	*Formula B4:* Nper (B2,0,B1,B3)	

FIGURE 3.15

Calculating an unknown number of years for an annuity

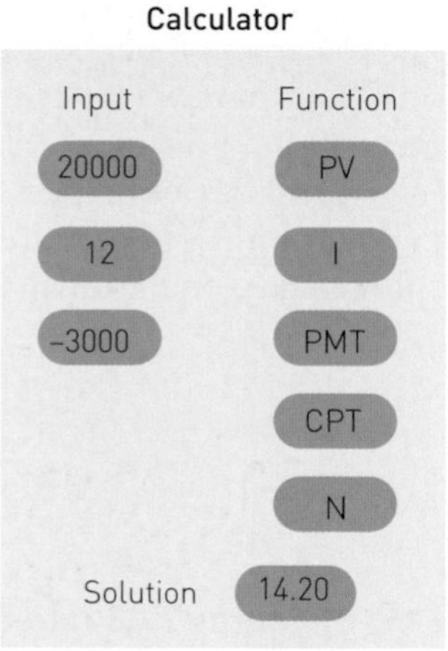

Calculator

Input	Function
20000	PV
12	I
-3000	PMT
	CPT
	N

Solution 14.20

Spreadsheet

Row \ Column	A	B
1	Present value	€20 000
2	Interest rate	12%
3	Future value	-€3000
4	**Number of years**	**14.20**
5	*Formula B4:* Nper (B2,B3,B1)	

the present value of an annuity (PV) as the product of its payment (PMT) and the present-value factor for an annuity paying r per cent for n years ($PVFA_{r\%,n}$):

$$PVFA_{12\%,n} = \frac{PV}{PMT} = \frac{€20000}{€3000} = 6.6667$$

We can solve this by finding the 12 per cent $PVFA$ value in Table A4 that most closely corresponds to 6.667, which is between 14 years ($PVFA_{12\%,14} = 6.628$) and 15 years ($PVFA_{12\%,15} = 6.811$). Using a financial calculator or spreadsheet, as shown in Figure 3.15, we find the number of years to be 14.20, which means that you have to repay €3000 at the end of each year for 14 years and about €600 ($0.20 \times €3000$) at the end of 14.20 years to fully repay the €20 000 loan at 12 per cent.

CONCEPT REVIEW QUESTIONS

17 How can you find the interest or growth rate for (a) a lump sum amount, (b) an annuity and (c) a mixed stream?

18 How can you find the number of time periods needed to repay (a) a single-payment loan and (b) an instalment loan requiring equal annual end-of-year payments?

3.7 SUMMARY AND CONCLUSIONS

- Financial managers can use future-value and present-value techniques to equate cash flows occurring at different times in order to compare decision alternatives. Managers rely primarily on present-value techniques and commonly use financial calculators or spreadsheet programs to streamline their computations.

- The future value of a lump sum is found by applying compound interest to the present value (the initial investment) over the period of concern. The higher the interest rate and the further in the future the cash flow's value is measured, the higher its future value.

- The present value of a lump sum is found by discounting the future value at the given interest rate. It is the amount of money today that is equivalent to the given future amount, considering the rate of return that can be earned on the present value. The higher the interest rate and the further in the future the cash flow occurs, the lower its present value.

- The future value of any cash flow stream – mixed stream, ordinary annuity or annuity due – is the sum of the future values of the individual cash flows. Future values of mixed streams are most difficult to find, whereas future values of annuities are easier to calculate because they have the same cash flow each period. The future value of an ordinary annuity (end-of-period cash flows) can be converted into the future value of an annuity due (beginning-of-period cash flows) merely by multiplying it by 1 plus the interest rate.

- The present value of a cash flow stream is the sum of the present values of the individual cash flows. The present value of a mixed stream is the most difficult to find, whereas present values of annuities are easier to calculate because they have the same cash flow each period. The present value of an ordinary annuity can be converted to the present value of an annuity due merely by multiplying it by 1 plus the interest rate. The present value of an ordinary perpetuity – a level stream that continues forever – is found by dividing the amount of the annuity by the interest rate.

- Some special applications of time value include compounding interest more frequently than annually, stated and effective annual rates of interest, deposits needed to accumulate a future sum and loan amortization. The more frequently interest is compounded at a stated annual rate, the larger the future amount that will be accumulated and the higher the effective annual rate.

- The annual deposit needed to accumulate a given future sum is found by manipulating the future value of an annuity equation. Loan amortization – determination of the equal periodic payments necessary to fully repay loan principal and interest over a given time at a given interest rate – is performed by manipulating the present value of an annuity equation. An amortization schedule can be prepared to allocate each payment to principal and interest.

- Implied interest or growth rates can be found using the basic future-value equations for lump sums and annuities and require an iterative trial-and-error approach for mixed streams. Using a financial calculator or spreadsheet can greatly simplify these calculations.

- Given present and future cash flows and the applicable interest rate, the unknown number of periods can be found using the basic equations for future values of lump sums and annuities. Using a financial calculator or spreadsheet greatly simplifies these calculations.

INTERNET RESOURCES

For updates to links in this section and elsewhere in the book, please go to the book's website at www.cengage.co.uk/megginson.

http://www.fastfindmortgages.ie/amortization.htm
A useful, java applet-type, graphical illustration of loan amortization that allows you to solve for payment present and future values.

http://www.tcalc.com
Contains numerous financial calculators that can be purchased and added to a website.

http://www.moneychimp.com
You can try the 'How Finance Works' link to learn about many applications of present and future value mathematics; the site has a number of useful, interactive graphs.

http://www.financialplayerscenter.com
Provides helpful tutorials on time value concepts.

KEY TERMS

annual percentage rate (APR)	future value	present value
annual percentage yield (APY)	Gordon growth model	principal
annuity	growing perpetuity	quarterly compounding
annuity due	loan amortization	semi-annual compounding
compound interest	loan amortization schedule	simple interest
continuous compounding	mixed stream	stated annual rate
discounting	ordinary annuity	time line
effective annual rate (EAR)	perpetuity	time value of money

SELF-TEST PROBLEMS

ST3-1 Starratt Alexander is considering investing specified amounts in each of four investment opportunities described below. For each opportunity, determine the amount of money Starratt will have at the end of the given investment horizon.

Investment A: Invest a lump sum of €2750 today in an account that pays 6 per cent annual interest and leave the funds on deposit for exactly 15 years.

Investment B: Invest the following amounts at the beginning of each of the next five years in a venture that will earn 9 per cent annually and measure the accumulated value at the end of exactly five years:

BEGINNING OF YEAR	AMOUNT
1	€ 900
2	1000
3	1200
4	1500
5	1800

Investment C: Invest €1200 at the end of each year for the next ten years in an account that pays 10 per cent annual interest and determine the account balance at the end of year 10.

Investment D: Make the same investment as in investment C but place the €1200 in the account at the beginning of each year.

ST3-2 Gregg Snead has been offered four investment opportunities, all equally priced at €45000. Because the opportunities differ in risk, Gregg's required returns (i.e. applicable discount rates) are not the same for each opportunity. The cash flows and required returns for each opportunity are summarized below.

OPPORTUNITY	CASH FLOWS	REQUIRED RETURN
A	€7500 at the end of 5 years	12%
B	Year Amount	15%
	1 €10 000	
	2 12 000	
	3 18 000	
	4 10 000	
	5 13 000	
	6 9 000	
C	€5000 at the end of each year for the next 30 years.	10%
D	€7000 at the beginning of each year for the next 20 years.	18%

a Find the present value of each of the four investment opportunities.

b Which, if any, opportunities are acceptable?

c Which opportunity should Gregg take?

ST3-3 Assume you wish to establish a university scholarship of €2000 paid at the end of each year for a deserving student at the school you attended. You would like to make a lump-sum gift to the school to fund the scholarship into perpetuity. The school's treasurer assures you that they will earn 7.5 per cent annually forever.

a How much must you give the school today to fund the proposed scholarship programme?

b If you wanted to allow the amount of the scholarship to increase annually after the first award (end of year 1) by 3 per cent per year, how much must you give the school today to fund the scholarship programme?

c Compare, contrast and discuss the difference in your response to parts (a) and (b).

ST3-4 Assume that you deposit €10 000 today into an account paying 6 per cent annual interest and leave it on deposit for exactly eight years.

a How much will be in the account at the end of eight years if interest is compounded

1 annually?

2 semi-annually?

3 monthly?

4 continuously?

b Calculate the effective annual rate (EAR) for (1) to (4) above.

c Based on your findings in parts (a) and (b), what is the general relationship between the frequency of compounding and EAR?

ST3-5 Imagine that you are a professional personal financial planner. One of your clients asks you the following two questions. Use time value of money techniques to develop appropriate responses to each question.

a I borrowed €75 000, am required to repay it in six equal (annual) end-of-year instalments of €3344 and want to know what interest rate I am paying.

b I need to save €37 000 over the next 15 years to fund my three-year-old daughter's university education. If I make equal annual end-of-year deposits into an account that earns 7 per cent annual interest, how large must this deposit be?

QUESTIONS

Q3-1 What is the importance for an individual of understanding time value of money concepts? For a corporate manager? Under what circumstance would the time value of money be irrelevant?

Q3-2 From a time value of money perspective, explain why the maximization of shareholder wealth and the maximization of profits may not offer the same result or course of action.

Q3-3 If a firm's required return were 0 per cent, would time value of money matter? As these returns rise above 0 per cent, what effect would the increasing return have on future value? Present value?

Q3-4 What would happen to the future value of an annuity if interest rates fell in the late periods? Could the future value of an annuity factor formula still be used to determine the future value?

Q3-5 What happens to the present value of a cash flow stream when the discount rate increases? Place this in the context of an investment. If the required return on an investment goes up, but the expected cash flows do not change, are you willing to pay the same price for the investment, or to pay more or less for this investment than before interest rates changed?

Q3-6 Look at the formula for the present value of an annuity. What happens to its value as the number of periods increases? What distinguishes an annuity from a perpetuity? Why is there no future value of a perpetuity?

Q3-7 What is the relationship between the variables in a loan amortization calculation and the total interest cost? Consider the variables of interest rates, amount borrowed, down payment, prepayment and term of loan in answering this question.

Q3-8 Why is it so difficult to find unknown interest or growth rates and numbers of periods when all other variables are known? When must you use trial-and-error techniques?

PROBLEMS

Future value of a lump sum

P3-1 You have €1500 to invest today at 7 per cent interest compounded annually.

a How much will you have accumulated in the account at the end of the following number of years?

  1 three years

  2 six years

  3 nine years.

b Use your findings in part (a) to calculate the amount of interest earned in

  1 the first three years (years 1 to 3)

  2 the second three years (years 3 to 6)

  3 the third three years (years 6 to 9).

c Compare and contrast your findings in part (b). Explain why the amount of interest

earned increases in each succeeding three-year period.

Present value of a lump sum

P3-2 A local government state savings bond can be converted to €100 at maturity six years from purchase. If the state bonds are to be competitive with central government savings bonds, which pay 8 per cent annual interest (compounded annually), at what price must the state sell its bonds? Assume no cash payments on savings bonds before redemption.

P3-3 You just won a lottery that promises to pay you €1 million exactly ten years from today. Because the €1 million payment is guaranteed by the state in which you live, opportunities exist to sell the claim today for an immediate lump-sum cash payment.

a What is the least you will sell your claim for if you could earn the following rates of return on similar risk investments during the ten-year period?

  1 6 per cent

  2 9 per cent

  3 12 per cent.

b Rework part (a) under the assumption that the €1 million payment will be received in 15 rather than ten years.

c Based on your findings in parts (a) and (b), discuss the effect of both the size of the rate of return and the time until receipt of payment on the present value of a future sum.

Future value of cash flow streams

P3-4 Dixon Shuttleworth is offered the choice of three retirement-planning investments. The first investment offers a 5 per cent return for the first five years, a 10 per cent return for the next five years and a 20 per cent return thereafter. The second investment offers 10 per cent for the first ten years and 15 per cent thereafter. The third investment offers a constant 12 per cent rate of return. Determine, for each of the given number of years, which of these investments is the best for

Dixon if he plans to make one payment today into one of these funds and to retire in the following number of years:

a 15 years

b 20 years

c 30 years.

P3-5 Robert Blanding's employer offers its workers a two-month paid sabbatical every seven years. Robert, who just started working for the firm, plans to spend his sabbatical touring Europe at an estimated cost of €25 000. To finance his trip, Robert plans to make six annual end-of-year deposits of €2 500 each, starting this year, into an investment account earning 8 per cent interest.

a Will Robert's account balance at the end of seven years be enough to pay for his trip?

b Suppose Robert increases his annual contribution to €3150. How large will his account balance be at the end of seven years?

P3-6 Robert Williams is considering an offer to sell his medical practice, allowing him to retire five years early. He has been offered €500 000 for his practice and can invest this amount in an account earning 10 per cent per year, compounded annually. If the practice is expected to generate the following cash flows, should Robert accept this offer and retire now?

END OF YEAR	CASH FLOW
1	€150 000
2	150 000
3	125 000
4	125 000
5	100 000

P3-7 Gina Coulson has just contracted to sell a small parcel of land that she inherited a few years ago. The buyer is willing to pay €24 000 at the closing of the transaction or will pay the amounts, shown in the following table, at the *beginning* of each of the next five years. Because Gina does not really need the money today, she plans to let it accumulate in an account that earns 7 per cent annual interest. Given her desire to buy a house at the end of five years after closing on the sale of the land, she decides to choose the payment

alternative – €24 000 lump sum or the mixed stream of payments in the following table – that provides the highest future value at the end of five years.

MIXED STREAM

BEGINNING OF YEAR (t)	CASH FLOW (CF_t)
1	€ 2 000
2	4 000
3	6 000
4	8 000
5	10 000

a What is the future value of the lump sum at the end of year 5?

b What is the future value of the mixed stream at the end of year 5?

c Based on your findings in parts (a) and (b), which alternative should Gina take?

d If Gina could earn 10 per cent rather than 7 per cent on the funds, would your recommendation in part (c) change? Explain.

P3-8 For the following questions, assume an ordinary annuity of €1000 and a required return of 12 per cent.

a What is the future value of a ten-year ordinary annuity?

b If you earned an additional year's worth of interest on this annuity, what would be the future value?

c What is the future value of a ten-year annuity due?

d What is the relationship between your answers in parts (b) and (c)? Explain.

P3-9 Kim Edwards and Chris Phillips are both newly graduated 30-year-old MBAs. Kim plans to invest €1000 per month into her retirement plan beginning next month. Chris intends to invest €2000 per month, but he does not plan to begin investing until ten years after Kim begins investing. Both Kim and Chris will retire at age 67, and the retirement fund they both choose has growth that averages a 12 per cent annual return, compounded monthly. Who will have more retirement plan money at retirement?

Present value of cash flow streams

P3-10 Given the mixed streams of cash flows shown in the following table, answer parts (a) and (b):

CASH FLOW STREAM

YEAR	A	B
1	€50 000	€10 000
2	40 000	20 000
3	30 000	30 000
4	20 000	40 000
5	10 000	50 000
Totals	€150 000	€150 000

a Find the present value of each stream, using a 15 per cent discount rate.

b Compare the calculated present values, and discuss them in the light of the fact that the undiscounted total cash flows amount to €150 000 in each case.

P3-11 As part of your personal budgeting process, you have determined that in each of the next five years you will have budget shortfalls. In other words, you need the amounts shown in the following table at the end of the given year to balance your budget – that is, to make inflows equal outflows. You expect to be able to earn 8 per cent on your investments during the next five years and want to fund the budget shortfalls over these years with a single initial deposit.

END OF YEAR	BUDGET SHORTFALL
1	€ 5 000
2	4 000
3	6 000
4	10 000
5	3 000

a How large must the lump-sum deposit into an account paying 8 per cent annual interest be today to provide for full coverage of the anticipated budget shortfalls?

b What effect does an increase in your earnings rate have on the amount calculated in part (a)? Explain.

P3-12 Ruth Nail receives two offers for her seaside home. The first offer is for €1 million today. The second offer is for an owner-financed sale with a payment schedule as follows:

END OF YEAR	PAYMENT
0 (Today)	€200 000
1	200 000
2	200 000
3	200 000
4	200 000
5	300 000

Assuming no differential tax treatment between the two options and that Ruth earns a rate of 8 per cent on her investments, which offer should she take?

P3-13 Melissa Gould wants to invest today to assure adequate funds for her son's university education. She estimates that her son will need €20 000 at the end of 18 years, €25 000 at the end of 19 years, €30 000 at the end of 20 years and €40 000 at the end of 21 years. How much does Melissa have to invest in a fund today if the fund earns the following interest rate?

a 6 per cent per year with annual compounding

b 6 per cent per year with quarterly compounding

c 6 per cent per year with monthly compounding.

P3-14 Assume that you just won the state lottery. Your prize can be taken either in the form of €40 000 at the end of each of the next 25 years (i.e. €1 million over 25 years) or as a lump sum of €500 000 paid immediately.

a If you expect to be able to earn 5 per cent annually on your investments over the next 25 years, ignoring taxes and other considerations, which alternative should you take? Why?

b Would your decision in part (a) be altered if you could earn 7 per cent rather than 5 per cent on your investments over the next 25 years? Why?

c On a strict economic basis, at approximately what earnings rate would you be indifferent when choosing between the two plans?

P3-15 For the following questions, assume an end-of-year cash flow of €250 and a 10 per cent discount rate.

a What is the present value of a single cash flow?

b What is the present value of a five-year annuity?

c What is the present value of a ten-year annuity?

d What is the present value of a 100-year annuity?

e What is the present value of a €250 perpetuity?

f Do you detect a relationship between the number of periods of an annuity and its resemblance to a perpetuity? If so, explain it.

P3-16 Use the following table of cash flows to answer parts (a)–(c). Assume an 8 per cent discount rate.

END OF YEAR	CASH FLOW
1	€10 000
2	10 000
3	10 000
4	12 000
5	12 000
6	12 000
7	12 000
8	15 000
9	15 000
10	15 000

a Solve for the present value of the cash flow stream by summing the present value of each individual cash flow.

b Solve for the present value by summing the present value of the three separate annuities (one current and two deferred).

c Which method is better for a long series of cash flows with embedded annuities?

P3-17 Joan Wallace, corporate finance specialist for Big Blazer Bumpers, is responsible for funding an account to cover anticipated future warranty costs. Warranty costs are expected to be €5 million per year for three years, with the first costs expected to occur four years from today. How much does Joan have to place into an account today earning 10 per cent per year to cover these expenses?

P3-18 Albert Mornoto, facilities and operations manager for the local soccer team, has come up with an idea for generating income. He wants to expand the stadium by building skyboxes sold with lifetime (perpetual) season tickets. Each skybox is guaranteed ten season tickets at a cost of €200 per ticket per year for life. If each skybox costs €100 000 to build, what is the minimum selling price that Albert will need to charge for the skyboxes to break even, if the required return is 10 per cent?

P3-19 Log on to Hugh Chou's financial calculator web page (http://www.interest.com/hugh/calc/simple.org) and look over the various calculator links available. Refer to some of the earlier time-value problems and rework them with these calculators. Run through several numerical scenarios to determine the effect of changing variables on your results.

Special applications of time value

P3-20 You plan to invest €2000 in a personal pension today at a stated interest rate of 8 per cent, which is expected to apply to all future years.

a How much will you have in the account at the end of ten years if interest is compounded as follows?

1 annually

2 semi-annually

3 daily (assume a 365-day year)

4 continuously.

b What is the effective annual rate (EAR) for each compounding period in part (a)?

c How much greater will your account balance be at the end of ten years if interest is compounded continuously rather than annually?

d How does the compounding frequency affect the future value and effective annual rate for a given deposit? Explain in terms of your findings in parts (a)–(c).

P3-21 Jason Spector has shopped around for the best interest rates for his investment of €10 000 over the next year. He has found the following:

STATED RATE	COMPOUNDING
6.10%	annual
5.90%	semi-annual
5.85%	monthly

a Which investment offers Jason the highest effective annual rate of return?

b Assume that Jason wants to invest his money for only six months, and the annual compounded rate of 6.10 per cent is not available. Which of the remaining investments should Jason choose?

P3-22 Answer parts (a)–(c) for each of the following cases.

CASE	AMOUNT OF INITIAL DEPOSIT (€)	STATED ANNUAL RATE, r (%)	COMPOUNDING FREQUENCY, m (TIMES/YEAR)	DEPOSIT PERIOD (YEARS)
A	2 500	6	2	5
B	50 000	12	6	3
C	1 000	5	1	10
D	20 000	16	4	6

a Calculate the future value at the end of the specified deposit period.

b Determine the effective annual rate (EAR).

c Compare the stated annual rate (r) to the effective annual rate (EAR). What relationship exists between compounding frequency and the stated and effective annual rates?

P3-23 Tara Cutler is newly married and preparing a surprise gift of a trip to Venice for her husband on their tenth anniversary. Tara plans to invest €5000 per year until that anniversary and to make her first €5000 investment on their first anniversary. If she earns an 8 per cent rate on her investments, how much will she have saved for their trip if the interest is compounded in each of the following ways?

a annually

b quarterly

c monthly.

P3-24 John Tye was hired as the new corporate finance analyst at I-Ell Enterprises and received his first assignment. John is to take the €25 million in cash received from a recent divestiture, use part of these proceeds to retire an outstanding €10 million bond issue, and use the remainder to repurchase shares. However, the bond issue cannot be retired for another two years. If John can place the funds necessary to retire this €10 million debt into an account earning a 6 per cent annual return compounded monthly, how much of the €25 million remains to repurchase shares?

P3-25 Find the present value of a three-year, €20 000 ordinary annuity deposited into an account that pays 12 per cent annual interest, compounded monthly. Solve for the present value of the annuity in the following ways:

a as three single cash flows discounted at the stated annual rate of interest

b as three single cash flows discounted at the appropriate effective annual rate of interest

c as a three-year annuity discounted at the effective annual rate of interest.

P3-26 To supplement your planned retirement in exactly 42 years, you estimate that you need to accumulate €220 000 by the end of 42 years from today. You plan to make equal annual end-of-year deposits into an account paying 8 per cent annual interest.

SMART SOLUTIONS

See the problem and solution explained step-by-step at **Smart Finance**

a How large must the annual deposits be to create the €220 000 fund by the end of 42 years?

b If you can afford to deposit only €600 per year into the account, how much will you have accumulated by the end of the year 42?

P3-27 Determine the annual deposit required to fund a future annual annuity of €12 000 per year. You will fund this future liability over the next five years, with the first deposit to occur one year from today. The future €12 000 liability will last for four years, with the first payment to occur seven years from today. If you can earn 8 per cent on this account, how much will you have to deposit each year over the next five years to fund the future liability?

P3-28 Mary Sullivan, capital outlay manager for Waxy Widgets, was instructed to establish a two-year contingency fund to cover the expenses associated with repairing defective widgets from a new production process. Waxy Widgets' controller wants to make equal monthly cash deposits into this fund. If Mary faces the following monthly repair costs and has €1 million to start the fund today, what will be her monthly payments into the fund to ensure that all repair costs are covered? Mary will make her first payment one month from today, and the fund will earn 6 per cent, compounded monthly.

MONTHS	REPAIR COSTS PER MONTH
1–4	€500 000
5–12	250 000
13–24	100 000

P3-29 Craig and LaDonna Allen are trying to establish a university fund for their son Spencer, who just turned three today. They plan for Spencer to withdraw €10 000 on his 18th birthday and €11 000, €12 000 and €15 000 on his subsequent birthdays. They plan to fund these withdrawals with a ten-year annuity, with the first payment to occur one year from today, and expect to earn an average annual return of 8 per cent.

a How much will the Allens have to contribute each year to achieve their goal?

b Create a schedule showing the cash inflows (including interest) and outflows of this fund. How much remains on Spencer's 21st birthday?

P3-30 Joan Messineo borrowed €15 000 at a 14 per cent annual interest rate to be repaid over three years. The loan is amortized into three equal annual end-of-year payments.

a Calculate the annual end-of-year loan payment.

b Prepare a loan amortization schedule showing the interest and principal breakdown of each of the three loan payments.

c Explain why the interest portion of each payment declines with the passage of time.

P3-31 You are planning to purchase a building for €40 000, and you have €10 000 to apply as a down payment. You may borrow the remainder under the following terms: a ten-year loan with semi-annual repayments and a stated interest rate of 6 per cent. You intend to make €6000 payments, applying the excess over your required payment to the reduction of the principal balance.

a Given these terms, how long (in years) will it take you to fully repay your loan?

b What will be your total interest cost?

c What would be your interest cost if you made no prepayments and repaid your loan by strictly adhering to the terms of the loan?

P3-32 Compute the monthly mortgage payment for a home purchased using a 30-year, €100 000 loan with a fixed 7.5 per cent annual interest rate.

P3-33 Use a spreadsheet to create amortization schedules for the following five scenarios. What happens to the total interest paid under each scenario?

a **Scenario 1:**
Loan amount: €1 million
Annual rate: 5 per cent
Term: 360 months
Prepayment: €0

b **Scenario 2:** Same as 1, except annual rate is 7 per cent

c **Scenario 3:** Same as 1, except term is 180 months

d **Scenario 4:** Same as 1, except prepayment is €250 per month

e **Scenario 5:** Same as 1, except loan amount is €125 000

P3-34 Go to the home page of your chosen bank and obtain current average mortgage rates. With this information, go to Hugh Chou's mortgage calculator (http://www.interest.com/hugh/calc/simple.org). Provide the requested variables to create an amortization schedule. Recreate the schedule with different prepayment amounts. What effect does the prepayment have on total interest and the term of the loan?

P3-35 To analyse various retirement-planning options, check out the financial calculator at Bloomberg (http://www.bloomberg.com). Determine the effect of waiting versus immediate planning for retirement. What is the effect of changing interest-rate assumptions on your retirement 'nest egg'?

P3-36 For excellent qualitative discussions of the value of compounded interest on saving for future (retirement) obligations, see the following websites:

http://www.prudential.com/retirement (Prudential Financial)
http://www.vanguard.com (The Vanguard Group)
http://www.fid-inv.com (Fidelity Investments)
http://www.bloomberg.com (Bloomberg)

What can you conclude about the timing of cash flows and future values available for retirement, considering the information provided on these websites?

Additional applications of time-value techniques

P3-37 Find the rates of return required to do the following:

a double an investment in four years
b double an investment in ten years
c triple an investment in four years
d triple an investment in ten years.

P3-38 You are given the series of cash flows shown in the following table:

CASH FLOWS

YEAR	A	B	C
1	€ 500	€ 1500	€ 2500
2	560	1550	2600
3	640	1610	2650
4	720	1680	2650
5	800	1760	2800
6		1850	2850
7		1950	2900
8			2060
9			2170
10			2280

a Calculate the compound annual growth rate associated with each cash flow stream.
b If year 1 values represent initial deposits in a savings account paying annual interest, what is the annual rate of interest earned on each account?

c Compare and discuss the growth rate and interest rate found in parts (a) and (b), respectively.

P3-39 Determine the length of time required to double the value of an investment, given the following rates of return.

a 4 per cent
b 10 per cent
c 30 per cent
d 100 per cent.

P3-40 You are the pension fund manager for Tanju's Toffees. Your CFO wants to know the minimum annual return required on the pension fund in order to make all required payments over the next five years and not diminish the current asset base. The fund currently has assets of €500 million.

a Determine the required return if outflows are expected to exceed inflows by €50 million per year.
b Determine the required return with the following fund cash flows.

END OF YEAR	INFLOWS	OUTFLOWS
1	€ 55 000 000	€ 100 000 000
2	60 000 000	110 000 000
3	60 000 000	120 000 000
4	60 000 000	135 000 000
5	64 000 000	145 000 000

c Consider the cash flows in part (b). What will happen to your asset base if you earn 10 per cent? 20 per cent?

P3-41 Jill Chew wants to choose the best of four immediate retirement annuities available to her. In each case, in exchange for paying a single premium today, she will receive equal annual end-of-year cash benefits for a specified number of years. She considers the annuities to be equally risky and is not concerned about their differing lives. Her decision will be based solely on the rate of return she will earn on each annuity. The key terms of each of the four annuities are shown in the following table:

ANNUITY	PREMIUM PAID TODAY	ANNUAL BENEFIT	LIFE (YEARS)
A	€ 30 000	€ 3 100	20
B	25 000	3 900	10
C	40 000	4 200	15
D	35 000	4 000	12

a Calculate to the nearest 1 per cent the rate of return on each of the four annuities Jill is considering.

b Given Jill's stated decision criterion, which annuity would you recommend?

P3-42 Determine which of the following three investments offers you the highest rate of return on your €1000 investment over the next five years.

Investment 1: €2000 lump sum to be received in five years
Investment 2: €300 at the end of each of the next five years
Investment 3: €250 at the beginning of each of the next five years.

a Which investment offers the highest return?

b Which offers the highest return if the payouts are doubled (i.e. €4000, €600 and €500)?

c What causes the big change in the returns on the annuities?

P3-43 Consider the following three investments of equal risk. Which offers the greatest rate of return?

	INVESTMENT		
END OF YEAR	A	B	C
0	−€ 10 000	−€ 20 000	−€ 25 000
1	0	9 500	20 000
2	0	9 500	30 000
3	24 600	9 500	−12 600

P3-44 You plan to start saving for your son's university education. He will begin university when he turns 18 and will need €4000 then and in each of the following three years. You will make a deposit at the end of this year in an account that pays 6 per cent compounded annually and an identical deposit at the end of each year, with the last deposit occurring when he turns 18. If an annual deposit of €1484 will allow you to reach your goal, how old is your son now?

P3-45 Log on to MSN Money (http://www.investor.msn.com) and select five stocks to analyse. Use their returns over the last five years to determine the value of €1000 invested in each stock five years ago. What is the compound annual rate of return for each of the five stocks over the five-year period?

P3-46 The viatical industry offers a rather grim example of present-value concepts. A firm in this business, called a viator, purchases the rights to the benefits from a life insurance contract from a terminally ill client. The viator may then sell claims on the insurance payout to other investors. The industry began in the early 1990s as a way to help AIDS patients capture some of the proceeds from their life insurance policies for living expenses.

SMART SOLUTIONS

See the problem and solution explained step-by-step at
www.cengage.co.uk/megginson

Suppose a patient has a life expectancy of 18 months and a life insurance policy with a death benefit of €100 000. A viator pays €80 000 for the right to the benefit and then sells that claim to another investor for €80 500.

a From the point of view of the patient, this contract is like taking out a loan. What is the compound annual interest rate on the loan if the patient lives exactly 18 months? What if the patient lives 36 months?

b From the point of view of the investor, this transaction is like lending money. What is the compound annual interest rate earned on the loan if the patient lives 18 months? What if the patient lives just 12 months?

THOMSON ONE **Business School Edition**

Access financial information from the Thomson ONE – Business School Edition website for the following problem(s). Go to http://tobsefin.swlearning.com/. If you have already registered your access serial number and have a username and password, click **Enter**. Otherwise, click **Register** and follow the instructions to create a username and password. Register your access serial number and then click **Enter** on the aforementioned website. When you click Enter, you will be prompted for your username and password (please remember that the password is case sensitive). Enter them in the respective boxes and then click **OK** (or hit **Enter**). From the ensuing page, click **Click Here to Access Thomson ONE – Business School Edition Now!** This opens up a new window that gives you access to the Thomson ONE – Business School Edition database. You can retrieve a company's financial information by entering its ticker symbol (provided for each company in the problem(s)) in the box below 'Name/Symbol/Key'. For further instructions on using the Thomson ONE – Business School Edition database, please refer to *A Guide for Using Thomson ONE – Business School Edition*.

P3-47 Compare the performance of SAP and Infosys. Calculate the five-year growth in sales and net income and determine the compound annual growth rate for each company. Does one company dominate the other in growth in both categories?

P3-48 Compare the market performance of Kimberly Clark and Procter & Gamble Company. Calculate the three-year growth in share price and the compound annual growth rate in share price for each company. If you had invested €10 000 in each share three years ago, what is the current value of each investment?

MINICASE *Present value*

FoamedAir SA is building a €25 million office building in Girona and is financing the construction at an 80 per cent loan-to-value ratio, where the loan is in the amount of €20 million. This loan has a ten-year maturity, calls for monthly payments and is contracted at an interest rate of 8 per cent.

Assignment

Using the above information, answer the following questions.

1 What is the monthly payment?

2 How much of the first payment is interest?

3 How much of the first payment is principal?

4 How much will FoamedAir SA owe on this loan after making monthly payments for three years (the amount owed immediately after the 36th payment)?

5 Should this loan be refinanced after three years with a new seven-year 7 per cent loan, if the cost to refinance is €250 000? To make this decision, calculate the new loan payments and then the present value of the difference in the loan payments.

6 Returning to the original ten-year 8 per cent loan, how much is the loan payment if these payments are scheduled quarterly rather than monthly?

7 For this loan with quarterly payments, how much will FoamedAir SA owe on this loan after making quarterly payments for three years (the amount owed immediately after the 12th payment).

8 What is the annual percentage rate on the original ten-year 8 per cent loan?

9 What is the effective annual rate (EAR) on the original ten-year 8 per cent loan?

PART 2

Valuation, Risk and Return

PART 2
Overview

Chaucer, the great early English poet, is alleged to have said, 'nothing ventured, nothing gained'. Financial markets give us ample evidence that Chaucer knew what he was talking about. Over time, high-risk investments typically tend to earn higher returns than low-risk investments do. When managers invest corporate funds, or when individuals decide how to allocate their money between different types of investments, they must weigh the potential benefit of higher returns against the cost of taking higher risk. The purpose of the following chapters is to explore in depth the relationship between risk and return. We begin in Chapters 4 and 5 by describing two of the most common types of investments available in the market – bonds and shares.

The bond market is vast, and it plays an extremely important role in the economy. Governments issue bonds to finance all kinds of public works projects and to cover budget deficits. Corporations sell bonds to meet daily operating needs and to pay for major investments. Chapter 4 describes the basic bond features and explains how investors value bonds.

Chapter 5 examines the stock market. Valuing shares is more complex than valuing bonds because shares typically do not promise fixed payment streams as bonds do – unless they are a particular type of share, called a preference share. Therefore, Chapter 5 discusses methods that investors and analysts use to estimate share values. The chapter also provides a brief explanation of how firms work alongside investment bankers to sell shares to the public and how investors can trade shares with each other.

With the essential features of bonds and shares in hand, Chapter 6 explores the historical returns earned by different classes of assets. The data illustrate that a fundamental trade-off between risk and return confronts investors. Chaucer was right. Investors who want to get rich have to accept risk as part of the deal.

Chapter 7 quantifies exactly what we mean by the term 'risk'. The chapter also introduces one of the most important theories in finance called the capital asset pricing model, or CAPM. The CAPM estimates the incremental return that investors or corporate managers can expect if they invest in an asset that is risky rather than one that is safe. That is, the CAPM is a tool that lets us evaluate the marginal benefits (higher returns) and marginal costs (higher risk) of alternative investments. It can be useful to individual investors who are trying to decide whether to save for retirement by investing in bonds, in shares or in a portfolio that contains both shares and bonds. But the CAPM also helps corporate managers decide whether it is better to invest a firm's money in a high-risk venture, like building a manufacturing plant in a foreign country, or in a low-risk undertaking, such as upgrading old equipment.

Chapter 4
Valuing Bonds

OPENING FOCUS

The bond that fell to earth?

One of the most interesting type of bonds is associated with a high net worth individual whom many consider as a musical genius. Not only has David Bowie been credited with reinventing popular music in the early 1970s, he also spawned intellectual property securitization. While that may sound like the name of one of his songs, it in reality is a simple transaction. In exchange for foregoing his royalties from 25 albums and over 200 songs recorded before 1990 he received a one-off payment of $55 million. The buyer of the bonds secured, or got the right to hold, the future revenue generated by Bowie's catalogue until the principal plus 8 per cent interest was repaid. The bonds were all purchased by Prudential Insurance.

While the industry expected a flood of similar transactions, the combination of the internet boom and the resulting boom in online piracy resulted in few such deals being made, and the quality of the bonds (the ratings, which we discuss below in more detail) suffered. Bowie, however, was thus insulated from the serious downturn. While the bond issue generated huge publicity for Bowie, and prompted the securitization of the catalogues of a number of other artists such as James Brown, the Isley Brothers and Marvin Gaye, the music industry has not flocked to this method of raising monies. The company that issued the bonds, Pullman, has however securitized other entertainment and literature revenue streams. Other entertainment companies that have raised bonds on the basis of revenues include a number of soccer clubs such as Lazio and Newcastle United, along with Madam Tussauds in London and Bernie Ecclestone on the future of Formula One racing.

In this chapter we will outline bond pricing and value. Be aware, however, that the area is extremely complex and what we show here is the basics and nothing but.

Source: http://www.pullmanco.com/.

LEARNING OBJECTIVES

After completing this chapter you should be able to:

- Recall the fundamental concepts that determine how we value assets.
- Understand the vocabulary that describes bonds and the markets in which they trade.
- Interpret the relationship been bond prices and interest rates.
- Explain the meaning of the 'term structure of interest rate'.

SMART FINANCE

Use the learning tools at www.cengage.co.uk/megginson

In the popular imagination, finance is closely associated with share, bond and other security markets. References to the closing level of the Dow Jones Industrial Average, the Nikkei 225, the Financial Times Stock Exchange 100 and other market indexes form part of the daily barrage of information that citizens of the world's largest economies absorb. Billions of people understand that these numbers can have a profound influence on their personal and professional lives as more and more countries adopt market-oriented economic policies. However, relatively few people understand the fundamental forces that determine security prices. Though we do not want to understate the complexities of security valuation, a relatively straightforward framework exists that investors can use to value many types of financial assets, including bonds and shares. This framework says that *the value of any asset equals the present value of future benefits accruing to the asset's owner.*

Notice the importance of the term 'present value' in the previous sentence. In Chapter 3, we learned the mechanics of converting a sequence of future cash flows into a single present value. In this chapter and in Chapter 5, we see that calculating present values is fundamental to the process of valuing financial assets. Chapters 8–10 illustrate the use of present-value calculations in valuing physical assets such as a new manufacturing plant or state-of-the-art computer equipment. Time and effort spent mastering present-value concepts earns its return over these chapters.

Our primary objective in this chapter is to describe models used to value debt securities, often called bonds. In the next chapter, we learn about pricing shares. Why do corporate managers need to understand how to price bonds and shares? First, firms must occasionally approach bond and stock markets to raise capital for new investments. Understanding how investors in these markets value the firm's securities helps managers determine how to finance new projects. Secondly, firms periodically make investments by acquiring privately held companies, just as they unload past investments by selling divisions. In either case, knowing how the market values an enterprise guides a manager's expectations regarding the appropriate price for an acquisition or divestiture. Thirdly, a company's share price provides an external, independent performance assessment of top management, one that a diligent board of directors watches closely. Surely managers who will be judged (and remunerated) based on the value of their firm's share price need to understand the determinants of that price. Fourthly, finance theory suggests that the objective of corporate management is to maximize the share price by correctly weighing the marginal benefits and costs of alternative actions. How can managers take actions to maximize share prices if they don't know what causes share prices to rise or fall?

This chapter presents an introduction to bonds and bond valuation. We begin by laying out the principles of valuation – principles that can be applied to a wide variety of valuation problems. After that, we describe the essential features of bonds and show how to apply the principles of valuation to calculate bond prices.

4.1 VALUATION BASICS

In a market economy, ownership of an asset confers the rights to the stream of benefits generated by the asset. These benefits may be tangible, such as the interest payments on Bowie's bonds mentioned in the 'Opening focus' section, or intangible, such as the pleasure one experiences when viewing a beautiful painting. Either way, the value of any asset equals the present value of all its future benefits. Finance theory focuses primarily on tangible benefits, typically the cash flows that an asset pays over time. For instance, a landlord who owns an apartment complex receives a stream of rental payments from tenants. The landlord is also responsible for maintaining the complex, paying taxes and covering other expenses. If the landlord wants to sell the apartment complex, what price should he expect to receive? According to our fundamental valuation principle above, the price should equal the present value of all future net cash flows. Investors value financial assets such as bonds and shares in much the same way. First, they estimate how much cash a particular investment distributes over time. Secondly, investors discount the expected cash payments using the time value of money mathematics covered in Chapter 3. The investment's value, or its current market price, equals the present value of its future cash flows.

This implies that pricing an asset requires knowledge of both its future benefits and the appropriate discount rate that converts future benefits into a present value. For some assets, investors know with a high degree of certainty what the future benefit stream will be. For other investments, the future benefit stream is much harder to predict. Generally, the greater the uncertainty about an asset's future benefits, the higher the discount rate investors will apply when discounting those benefits to the present.

Consequently, the valuation process links an asset's future benefits and the uncertainty surrounding those benefits to determine its price. Holding future benefits (cash flows) constant, an inverse relationship exists between risk and value. If two investments promise identical cash flows in the future, investors will pay a higher price for the one with the more credible promise. Or, to state that relationship another way, if a risky asset and a safe asset trade at the same price, the risky asset must offer investors higher future cash flows.

The fundamental valuation model

Chapters 6 and 7 present an in-depth analysis of the relationship between risk and return. For now, take as given the market's **required rate of return** on a specific investment. The term 'required rate of return' is the rate of return that investors expect or require an asset to earn given its risk. The riskier the asset, the higher will be the return required by investors in the market-place. We can also say that the required rate of return on an asset is the return available in the market on another equally risky investment. When someone purchases a specific investment, they lose the opportunity to invest their money in another asset. The return on the alternative investment represents an 'opportunity cost'.

required rate of return
The rate of return that investors require from an investment given the risk of the investment.

How do investors use this required rate of return to determine the prices of different types of securities? Equation 4.1 expresses the fundamental valuation model mathematically, as follows:

$$P_0 = \frac{CF_1}{(1+r)^1} + \frac{CF_2}{(1+r)^2} + \cdots + \frac{CF_n}{(1+r)^n}$$

EQUATION 4.1

This should be familiar to you, as it is the present value formula from Chapter 3. In this equation, P_0 represents the asset's price today (at time 0), CF_t represents the asset's expected cash flow at time t, and r is the required return – the discount rate that reflects the asset's risk. The marginal benefit of owning this asset is the right to receive the cash flows that it pays, and the marginal cost is the opportunity cost of committing funds to this asset rather than to an equally risky alternative. Therefore, Equation 4.1 establishes a price that balances the asset's marginal benefits and costs. The letter n stands for the asset's life, the period over which it distributes cash flows to investors, usually measured in years. As you will see, n may be a finite number, as in the case of a bond that matures in a certain number of years, or it may be infinite, as in the case of a share with an indefinite lifespan. In either case, this equation provides us with a vehicle for valuing almost any type of asset.

Applying the Model

Throughout the 1990s litigation in the USA between health officials and tobacco companies continued. Finally, in 1998 a general agreement was made. Following from the 1998 Master Settlement Agreement seven tobacco makers agreed to pay roughly $206 billion to the seven states party to the agreement over the next 25 years. States began to receive payments in 1999, but as the softening US economy resulted in reduced state tax collections, many states looked for ways to cash in early on the tobacco lawsuit. 'Tobacco bonds' were the solution. By selling the rights to the cash flows from their future tobacco settlement to investors who purchased tobacco bonds, states could capture the present value of future settlement proceeds immediately. Wisconsin closed its 2002–2003 budget shortfall by raising $1.6 billion in one such deal. How did the market determine the value of tobacco bonds in Wisconsin and other states? Suppose that the settlement decreed that a particular state would receive $250 million per year for 20 years, and suppose that the market's required return on investments with this level of risk was 6.5 per cent. The present value of this state's settlement proceeds was determined using the shortcut formula for an annuity's present value from Chapter 3 as follows:

$$P_0 = \frac{\$250m}{(1.065)^1} + \frac{\$250m}{(1.065)^2} + \cdots + \frac{\$250m}{(1.065)^{20}}$$

$$= \$250m \left[\frac{1 - \dfrac{1}{1.065^{20}}}{0.065} \right] = \$2.754 \text{ billion}$$

The state could sell bonds today worth €2.75 billion, using the settlement proceeds to repay bondholders over the next 20 years. To meet its needs for more immediate cash inflow, the state has effectively paid 6.5 per cent annual interest to exchange its 25-year, $250 million annuity for an immediate $2.75 billion.

With this simple framework in hand, we turn to the problem of pricing bonds. Though bond-pricing techniques can get very complex, we focus on 'plain-vanilla' bonds: those that promise a fixed stream of cash payments over a finite time period. Among the largest issuers of such 'fixed-income' securities are national, state and local governments, and multinational corporations.

CONCEPT
REVIEW
QUESTIONS

1 Why is it important for corporate managers to understand how bonds and shares are priced?

2 Holding constant an asset's future benefit stream, what happens to the asset's price if its risk increases?

3 Holding constant an asset's risk, what happens to the asset's price if its future benefit stream increases?

4 Keeping in mind Equation 4.1, discuss how you determine the price per acre of farmland in a particular region.

4.2 BOND PRICES AND INTEREST RATES

Bond vocabulary

Fundamentally, a bond is just a loan. Unlike car loans and home mortgages, which require borrowers to make regular payments, including both an interest component and some repayment of the original loan amount or **principal**, bonds make interest-only payments until they mature. On the **maturity date**, a bond's life formally ends, and both the final interest payment and the original principal amount are due. The principal amount of a bond, also known as the bond's **par value** or face value, is typically €1000 for corporate bonds.

Though bonds come in many varieties, most bonds share certain basic characteristics. First, many bonds promise to pay investors a fixed amount of interest, called the bond's **coupon**.[1] Most bonds make coupon payments every six months, or semi-annually. Because a bond's cash flows are contractually fixed, traders often refer to bonds as fixed-income securities. The legal contract between the borrower who issues bonds and the investors who buy them, called the bond **indenture**, specifies the euro amount of the coupon and when the borrower must make coupon payments. Secondly, a bond's **coupon rate** equals its annual coupon payment divided by its par value. Thirdly, a bond's **coupon yield** equals the coupon divided by the bond's current market price (which does not always equal its par value).

To illustrate, suppose that a government entity or a firm issues a bond with a €1000 par value and promises to pay investors €35 every six months until maturity. The bond's coupon is €70 per year, and its coupon rate is 7 per cent (€70 ÷ €1000). If the current market value of this bond is €980, then its coupon yield is 7.14 per cent (€70 ÷ €980).

Understanding how to price bonds is important in part because the bond market forms such a large sector of the modern financial system. An excellent source of international data on the bond (and other financial) markets is the Bank for International Settlements (BIS). As at the end of 2005, the BIS estimates (http://www.bis.org/statistics/secstats.htm) that there were some $58.6 trillion outstanding in debt securities across all nations. The vast majority of this amount is domestic, that is to say it is issued 'within' a particular country. Thus a Belgian company or municipality that floats a bond on the Belgian securities market would be issuing domestic debt, but were it to raise funds on the US markets that would be classed as international.

principal
The amount of money on which interest is paid.

maturity date
The date when a bond's life ends and the borrower must make the final interest payment and repay the principal.

par value (bonds)
The face value of a bond, which the borrower repays at maturity.

coupon
A fixed amount of interest that a bond promises to pay investors.

indenture
A legal document stating the conditions under which a bond has been issued.

coupon rate
The rate derived by dividing the bond's annual coupon payment by its par value.

coupon yield
The amount obtained by dividing the bond's coupon by its current market price (which does not always equal its par value).

A bond pricing equation (assuming annual interest)

We can value ordinary bonds by developing a simplified version of Equation 4.1. Remember that a bond makes a fixed coupon payment each year. Assume that the bond makes annual coupon payments of €C for n years, and at maturity the bond makes its final coupon payment and returns the face value, €F, to investors. Using these assumptions, we can replace Equation 4.1 with the following:

$$P_0 = \frac{C}{(1+r)^1} + \frac{C}{(1+r)^2} + \cdots + \frac{C}{(1+r)^n} + \frac{F}{(1+r)^n}$$

EQUATION 4.2

---

[1] Historically, bond certificates were printed with coupons attached that the bondholder would literally clip (like coupons in a newspaper) and mail in to receive an interest payment. That is the origin of the term 'coupon'. In modern times, bonds are registered, meaning that the issuer keeps a record of who owns a given bond. Interest payments are mailed directly to registered owners with no coupon clipping required. Many investors hold their bonds in a street name, meaning that a brokerage firm registers the bonds in its own name. Because brokerage firms have developed a comparative advantage in processing financial market transactions, holding securities in street name speeds the flow of money between bond issuers and buyers.

Equation 4.2 says that the bond's price equals the present value of an *n*-year ordinary annuity plus the present value of the lump-sum principal payment. Referring to our equation for the present value of an annuity in Chapter 3, we write the bond-pricing equation as follows:

$$P_0 = C\left[\frac{1 - \dfrac{1}{(1+r)^n}}{r}\right] + \frac{F}{(1+r)^n}$$

Applying the Model

On 1 January 2006, Worldwide United had outstanding a bond with a coupon rate of 9.125 per cent and a face value of €1000. At the end of each year this bond pays investors €91.25 in interest (0.09125 × €1000). The bond matures at the end of 2016, 11 years from now. Figure 4.1 illustrates the sequence of

FIGURE 4.1

Time line for bond valuation (assuming annual interest payments)

Worldwide United $9\frac{1}{8}$ per cent coupon, €1000 par value bond, maturing at the end of 2016; required return assumed to be 8 per cent.

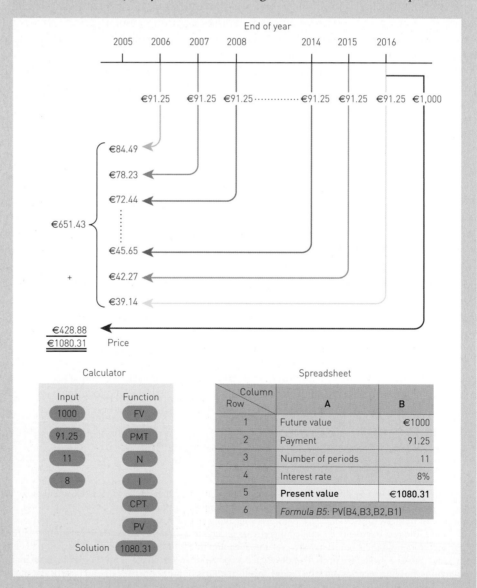

cash flows that the bond promises investors over time. Notice that we break up the bond's cash payments into two separate components. The first component is an 11-year annuity of €91.25 annual payments. The second component is a lump-sum payment of €1000 at maturity.

To calculate the price of this bond, we need to know what rate of return investors demand on bonds that are as risky as Worldwide's bonds. Assume that the market currently requires an 8 per cent return on these bonds. At that discount rate, the present value of 11 coupon payments of €91.25 plus the principal repayment equals:

$$PV\ coupon = 91.25 \times \left[\frac{1 - \frac{1}{(1.08)^{11}}}{0.08} \right] = €651.43$$

$$PV\ principal = \frac{1000}{(1.08)^{11}} = €428.88$$

$$Total = €1080.31$$

We calculate the price of this bond directly from our fundamental valuation Equation 4.1 as follows:

$$P_0 = \frac{91.25}{(1.08)^1} + \frac{91.25}{(1.08)^2} + \cdots + \frac{1091.25}{(1.08)^{11}}$$

Notice that this bond sells *above* par value. When a bond sells for more than its par value, we say that the bond trades at a **premium**. Why are Worldwide's bonds trading at a premium? By assumption, the market's required return on an investment like this is just 8 per cent, but Worldwide's bonds offer a coupon rate of 9.125 per cent. Therefore, if Worldwide's bonds sold at par value, they would offer investors a particularly attractive return, and investors would rush to buy them. As more and more investors purchase Worldwide bonds, the market price of those bonds rises.

premium
A bond that sells for more than its par value.

Think about the return that an investor earns if she purchases Worldwide bonds today for €1080.31 and holds them to maturity. Every year, the investor receives a €91.25 cash payment. At the current market price, this represents a coupon yield of about 8.4 per cent (€91.25 ÷ €1080.31), noticeably above the 8 per cent required return in the market. However, when the bonds mature, the investor receives a final interest payment plus the €1000 par value. In a sense, this bond has a built-in loss of €80.31 (€1000 par value less the €1080.31 purchase price) at maturity because the bond's principal is less than the current price of the bond. The net effect of receiving an above-market return on the coupon payment and realizing a loss at maturity is that the investor's overall return on this bond is exactly 8 per cent, equal to the market's required return.

In the example above, 8 per cent is the required rate of return on the bond in the market, also called the bond's **yield to maturity**. The yield to maturity (YTM) is simply the discount rate that equates the present value of a bond's future cash flows to equal its current market price. As a general rule, when a bond's coupon rate exceeds its YTM, the bond will trade at a premium as Worldwide's bonds do. Conversely, if the coupon rate falls short of the YTM, the bond will sell at a **discount** to par value. For example, suppose the market's required return on Worldwide bonds is 10 per cent

yield to maturity
The discount rate that equates the present value of the bond's cash flows to its market price.

discount
A bond sells at a discount when its market price is less than its par value.

rather than 8 per cent. This changes the price of Worldwide bonds as follows:

$$PV\ coupon = 91.25 \times \left[1 - \frac{\frac{1}{(1.1)^{11}}}{0.1} \right] = €592.68$$

$$PV\ principal = \frac{1000}{(1.1)^{11}} = €350.49$$

$$Total = €943.17$$

In this case the bonds trade at a *discount* because each month investors receive a coupon yield of about 9.7 per cent (€91.25 ÷ €943.17), a little less than the required rate of 10 per cent. Offsetting that, the bond has a built-in gain at maturity of €56.83 (€1000 par value less the €943.17 purchase price). The net effect of the below-market coupon payments and the gain at maturity is that investors who buy and hold this bond earn a yield to maturity of exactly 10 per cent.

Applying the Model

Verhoeven Enterprises has an outstanding bond issue that pays a 6 per cent annual coupon and matures in five years. The current market value of one Verhoeven bond is €1021.35. What yield to maturity do these bonds offer investors? Because the bond sells at a premium, we can infer that the yield to maturity is less than the bond's coupon rate.

We can use a financial calculator or spreadsheet program to calculate the answer very quickly, but let's try a trial-and-error approach first to strengthen our intuition about the relationship between a bond's price and its YTM. Suppose the bond offers a YTM of 5 per cent. At that rate, the price of the bond would be the following:

$$PV\ coupon = 60 \times \left[1 - \frac{\frac{1}{(1.055)^{5}}}{0.05} \right] = €256.22$$

$$PV\ principal = \frac{1000}{(1.05)^{5}} = €783.53$$

$$Total = €1043.30$$

Our guess produces a price that exceeds the market price of Verhoeven's bond. Because we calculated a price that is too high, we need to try again using a higher YTM. Discounting the bond's cash flows at a higher YTM results in a lower price. Suppose the YTM equals 5.5 per cent. Now we have:

$$PV\ coupon = 60 \times \left[1 - \frac{\frac{1}{(1.055)^{5}}}{0.05} \right] = €256.22$$

$$PV\ principal = \frac{1000}{(1.055)^{5}} = €765.13$$

$$Total = €1021.35$$

The YTM equals 5.5 per cent because that is the discount rate that equates the present value of the bond's cash flows with its current market price.

Semi-annual compounding

Most bonds issued in the United States make two interest payments per year rather than the European tradition of paying once per annum. Adjusting our bond-pricing framework to handle semi-annual or other frequencies of interest payments is easy. If the bond matures in n years and the annual coupon equals €C, then the bond now makes $2n$ payments equal to €$C \div 2$. Similarly, if the bond's annual yield to maturity equals r, we replace that with a semi-annual yield of $r \div 2$. This produces a modified version of Equation 4.2:[2]

$$P_0 = \frac{C/2}{(1 + r/2)^1} + \frac{C/2}{(1 + r/2)^2} + \cdots + \frac{C/2}{(1 + r/2)^{2n}} + \frac{F}{(1 + r/2)^{2n}}$$

EQUATION 4.3

Expressing this equation as a sum of the present value of an ordinary annuity and the present value of a lump sum, we have the following:

$$P_0 = C/2 \left[\frac{1 - \dfrac{1}{(1 + r/2)^{2n}}}{r/2} \right] + \frac{F}{(1 + r/2)^{2n}}$$

For example, the Peterson Fishing Company issues a three-year bond that offers a 6 per cent coupon rate paid semi-annually. This means that the annual coupon equals €60, and there are two €30 payments each year. Suppose that 6 per cent per year is also the market's required return on Peterson bonds. The market price of the bonds equals €1000.

$$PV\ coupon = 30 \times \left[1 - \frac{\dfrac{1}{(1.03)^6}}{0.03} \right] = €162.52$$

$$PV\ principal = \frac{1000}{(1.03)^6} = €837.48$$

$$Total = €1000$$

Because this bond offers investors a return exactly equal to the required rate in the market, the bond sells at par value. Notice, too, that the effective annual yield on this bond is slightly higher than 6 per cent. If the semi-annual yield is 3 per cent, the effective annual yield equals 6.09 per cent ($1.03^2 - 1$).

Again, we emphasize the fundamental lesson: *the price of a bond equals the present value of its future cash flows*. The complexity of bond pricing then arises from the choice of discount rate, assuming that we are reasonably certain about the cash flows. Therefore, we now turn to a more in-depth development of the concepts underlying bond valuation, starting with a discussion of interest rate risk.

---

[2] The yield to maturity on a bond is typically quoted like an APR. That is, the bond's annual YTM equals the semi-annual yield times 2. This implies that the effective annual YTM is slightly above the quoted YTM.

Bond prices and interest rates

A bond's market price changes frequently as time passes. Whether a bond sells at a discount or a premium, its price will converge to par value (plus the final interest payment) as the maturity date draws near. Imagine a bond that matures one day from now. The bond's final cash flow consists of its par value plus the last coupon payment. If this payment arrives just one day in the future, you determine the bond's price by discounting this payment for one day. Therefore, the price and the final payment are virtually identical.

Economic forces affecting bond prices A variety of economic forces can change bond prices, but the most important factor is the prevailing market interest rate. When the market's required return on a bond changes, the bond's price changes in the opposite direction. The higher the bond's required return, the lower its price, and vice versa. How much a bond's price responds to changes in required returns depends on several factors, especially the bond's maturity.

Figure 4.2 shows how the prices of two bonds change as their required returns change. Both bonds pay a 6 per cent coupon, but one matures in two years, whereas the other matures in ten years. As the figure shows, when the required return equals the coupon rate, 6 per cent, both bonds trade at par. However, as the required return increases, the bonds' prices fall. The decline in the ten-year bond's price exceeds that of the two-year bond. Likewise, as the required return decreases, the prices of both bonds increase. But the ten-year bond's price increases faster than does that of the two-year bond. The general lessons are: (1) bond prices and interest rates move in opposite directions; and (2) the prices of long-term bonds display greater sensitivity to changes in interest rates than do the prices of short-term bonds.

interest rate risk
The risk that changes in market interest rates will cause fluctuations in a bond's price. Also, the risk of suffering losses as a result of unanticipated changes in market interest rates.

Interest rate risk Figure 4.2 illustrates the importance of **interest rate risk** – that changes in market interest rates will move bond prices. Figure 4.3 shows just how volatile interest rates have been over the past four decades in Germany, the UK and

FIGURE 4.2

The relationship between bond prices and required returns for bonds with differing times to maturity but the same 6 per cent coupon rate

Bond prices move in the opposite direction to market interest rates. This figure shows that the prices of two-year and ten-year bonds fall as the required return rises (and vice versa), but the magnitude of this effect is much greater for the ten-year bond. Typically, long-term bond prices are much more sensitive to rate changes than short-term bond prices.

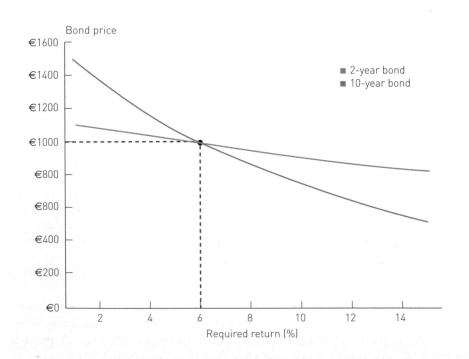

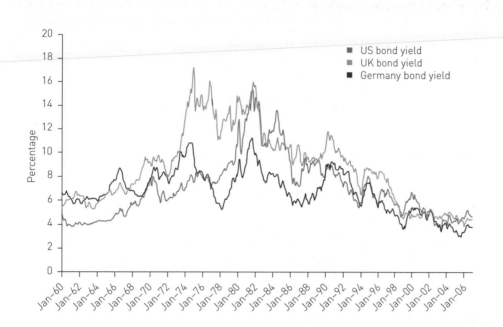

FIGURE 4.3

Government bond yelds, 1960–2006

This figure shows how volatile interest rates have been over this long period. Because changes in interest rates cause bond prices to fluctuate, bond investors must be aware of interest rate risk.

Source: *ecowin data.*

the USA. We can distinguish three 'regimes' in these rates. Up to the mid-1970s rates were low. During the 1970s, in response to oil shocks, macroeconomic instability and inflation, interest rates rose to their peak. Germany's peak rate was reached at 14 per cent in 1974 and 1982, while the peak in the USA was 16 per cent, again in 1982. For the UK the peak, also at 16 per cent, was reached in both 1974 and 1982. More recent decades have seen generally declining bond yields with rates now down to levels comparable to the early 1960s. The point of the graph is simple – because interest rates fluctuate widely, investors must be cognizant of the interest rate risk inherent in these instruments.

One of the main factors causing interest rate movements is inflation. When investors buy financial assets, they expect these investments to provide a return that exceeds the inflation rate. This is important to people because they want to achieve a better standard of living by saving and investing their money. If asset returns do no more than keep up with inflation, then investors are not really better off having invested their funds. For example, suppose you want to expand your (legally) downloaded music collection. You have €150 to spend, and each set costs €15, so you can purchase ten new downloaded sets. Alternatively, suppose you save your money and invest it in an asset earning a 10 per cent return. You reason that after one year, you will have €165 (€150 × 1.10), and with that you can buy 11 sets rather than ten. However, suppose that while your money is invested, the price of downloads increases by 10 per cent from €15 to €16.50. This means that at the end of the year, your €165 still just enables you to purchase just ten sets, exactly what you could have purchased a year earlier. In real terms, you are no better off at the end of the year than you were at the start.

The lesson here is that the bond yields must offer investors a positive **real return**. The real return on an investment *approximately* equals the difference between its stated or **nominal return** and the inflation rate. In the previous example, the nominal return on your investment is 10 per cent, but so is the inflation rate, so the

real return
Approximately, the difference between an investment's stated or nominal return and the inflation rate.

nominal return
The stated return offered by an investment unadjusted for the effects of inflation.

investment's real return is zero. Mathematically, if r equals the nominal return, i equals the inflation rate and r_{real} equals the real rate, then we can write the following:

$$(1 + r) = (1 + i)(1 + r_{real})$$

$$\frac{(1 + r)}{(1 + i)} - 1 = r_{real}$$

$$\frac{(1.10)}{(1.10)} - 1 = 0 = r_{real}$$

Changes in issuer risk When macroeconomic factors change, yields may change simultaneously on a wide range of bonds. But the market's required return *on a particular bond* can also change because the market reassesses the borrower's ability to repay investors. For example, if investors perceive that a certain firm is experiencing financial problems that could make it difficult for the company to repay its debts, the required return will increase and the price of the firm's bonds will fall. Conversely, when the market is more optimistic about a bond issuer's financial health, the required return will fall and the issuer's outstanding bonds will increase in value.

Real World

The experience of France Telecom illustrates what can happen to corporate bonds when business conditions deteriorate. To refinance its massive short-term debt, France Telecom conducted the largest corporate bond offering in history up to that time in March 2001 by selling the equivalent of $16.4 billion worth of bonds to investors around the world. France Telecom issued bonds in three different currencies – US dollars, euros and British pounds. Days after successfully floating its bonds, the firm announced that it could not retire as much short-term debt as it had originally anticipated, thereby signalling to the market that its cash flows were weaker than expected. Prices and yields of France Telecom bonds responded accordingly. The required return on France Telecom's five-year dollar bonds, issued with a 7.2 per cent coupon, rose to 8.5 per cent. The following equation shows that this increase in the required return was associated with a decline in price of $52.07, or 5.2 per cent, from the original $1000 par value:

$$P_0 = \frac{72}{2}\left[\frac{1 - \dfrac{1}{(1 + \frac{0.085}{2})^{10}}}{\frac{0.085}{2}}\right] + \frac{1000}{(1 + \frac{0.085}{2})^{10}} = \$947.93$$

Fortunately, the same effect can occur in reverse. Consider what might have happened if France Telecom's business had improved suddenly after the bond issue. Suppose that the bond market became convinced that France Telecom's brighter cash flow outlook lowered the risk of the five-year bonds. If investors lowered their required return on these bonds to 6.5 per cent, the price of the five-year bonds would have risen to $1029.48.

Source: Authors' own research

You might argue that this entire discussion is irrelevant if an investor holds a bond to maturity. If a bond is held to maturity, there is a good chance that the investor will receive all interest and principal payments as promised, so any price decrease (or increase) that occurs between the purchase date and the maturity date is just a 'paper loss'. Though the tax code may ignore investment gains and losses until investors realize them, financial economists argue that losses matter, whether investors realize them by selling assets or whether the losses exist only on paper. For example, when the France Telecom dollar bond's value falls from $1000 to $947.93, an investor holding the bond experiences an opportunity loss. Because the bond's price has fallen, the investor no longer has the opportunity to invest $1000 elsewhere.

CONCEPT REVIEW QUESTIONS

5 How is a bond's coupon rate different from its coupon yield?

6 In general, when will a bond sell at a discount?

7 Explain the meaning of the term 'interest rate risk'.

8 Why do bond prices and bond yields move in opposite directions?

9 What sort of company would be one where the issuer risk and interest rate risk changes offset each other in their bond pricing?

4.3 TYPES OF BONDS

The variety of bonds trading in modern financial markets is truly remarkable. In this section, we offer a brief description of the most common types of bonds available today. Many investors see bonds as a rather unexciting investment that provides a steady, predictable stream of income. That description fits some bonds reasonably well, but many bonds are designed with exotic features that make their returns as volatile and unpredictable as shares.

Bond trading occurs in either the primary or secondary market. Primary market trading refers to the initial sale of bonds by firms or government entities. Primary market trading varies depending on the type of bond being considered. For example, the US and UK governments both sell bonds through an auction process. Most go to a relatively small group of authorized government bond dealers, though individual investors can participate in the auctions, too. When corporations and state and local government bodies issue bonds in the primary market, they do so with the help of investment bankers, who assist bond issuers with the design, marketing and distribution of new bond issues.

Once bonds are issued in the primary market, investors trade them with each other in the secondary market. However, many bonds issued in the primary market are purchased by institutional investors who hold the bonds for a long time. For example, consider the needs of an insurance company that specializes in life policies, or a pension fund. In both cases the company is purchasing an asset with a long maturity, which makes sense as they have contingent liabilities that are also on a long timeframe. As a result, secondary market trading in bonds can be somewhat limited. For instance, if Zurich Insurance raises money by conducting a new bond offering, it is likely that their bonds will not trade as actively as Zurich Insurance shares. Although some specific bond issues do not trade a great deal once they are issued, the sheer size of the bond market means that investors interested in adding bonds to their portfolio have a wide range of choices. We now turn to an overview of the choices available to bond investors. There are several ways to structure an overview of the bond market, beginning with the types of bond issuers.

By issuer

Bonds come in many varieties and are classified in different ways. Perhaps the simplest classification scheme puts bonds into categories based upon the identity of the issuer.

corporate bonds
Bonds issued by corporations.

Large companies who need money to finance new investments and to fulfil other needs issue **corporate bonds**. Corporations issue bonds with maturities ranging from one to 100 years. When a company issues a debt instrument with a maturity of one to ten years, that instrument is usually called a note rather than a bond, but notes and bonds are essentially identical instruments. Most corporate bonds have a par value of €1000 and pay interest semi-annually.

municipal bonds
Issued by US state and local governments. Interest received on these bonds is exempt from federal income tax.

In the United States, federal law gives local and state governments a significant break by exempting interest received on **municipal bonds** from the bondholder's federal income tax. Obviously, this makes municipal bonds especially attractive to investors who face high marginal tax rates. In effect, the tax exemption on municipal bond interest allows state and local governments to raise money at lower interest rates than they would otherwise be able to do.

The largest single category of issuer of bonds in the world are governments, and within that the largest single issuer is the US government. The debt instruments issued by governments range in maturity from a few weeks to 50 years. Traditionally there was a split between **Treasury bills**, **Treasury notes** and **Treasury bonds**. In the USA this split is still used, and refers to various maturities of bonds. However, in Europe in general the split in nomenclature is not as common.

Treasury bills
Debt instruments issued by the US federal government that mature in less than one year.

Treasury notes
Debt instruments issued by the US federal government with maturities ranging from one to ten years.

Some government agencies and governmental organizations issue their own bonds, called **agency bonds**, to finance operations. In the USA these agencies include the Federal Home Loan Mortgage Corporation (Freddie Mac) and the Federal National Mortgage Association (Fannie Mae). In the European context this type of issue is much less common, but state-backed bonds are issued on behalf of other agencies.

Treasury bonds
Debt instruments issued by the US federal government with maturities longer than ten years.

Table 4.1 shows the amount outstanding in domestic and international markets of bonds issued by the three main sectors. As can be seen, government bonds dominate corporate bonds in terms of domestic issues, while the opposite is the case for international issues.

agency bonds
Bonds that are issued by an agency of government, such as a housing, investment or other quasi-commercial entity.

To date our focus has been on bond issues. Why do firms and government entities sell bonds? The simple answer is that bond issuers need money – money to finance a deficit, to build public infrastructure or to pay for expanded manufacturing facilities. An important characteristic that distinguishes corporations from government entities is that when the latter group needs to issue a security to raise funds, they are essentially limited to issuing a bond or other debt instrument. Corporations, on the other hand, can issue either debt (bonds) or equity (shares).

TABLE 4.1

Outstanding debt securities by sector of issuer ($ billion), September 2006

Source: Bank of International Settlements.

	USA	UK
Domestic		
Corporate	2 695.7	24.2
Government	19 839.4	1 022.4
Financial	11 356.2	317.8
International		
Corporate	401.3	203.0
Government	3.2	6.0
Financial	3 034.3	1 293.2

Debt securities offer a series of cash payments that are, for the most part, contractually fixed. The cash payout that bond investors expect from a firm generally does not fluctuate each quarter as the firm's earnings do, and if a firm fails to live up to its promise to make interest and principal payments, bondholders can take legal action against the company and force it into bankruptcy.

In contrast, shares, which we cover in the next chapter, represent an ownership or equity claim on the firm's cash flows. Unlike bondholders, shareholders generally have the right to vote on corporate matters ranging from electing a board of directors to approving mergers and acquisitions. However, shareholders have no specific legal entitlement to receive periodic cash payments. Whether shareholders receive any cash payments at all depends on the firm's profitability and on the board of directors' decision to distribute cash to investors. As we will see, some bonds have features that put them into a grey area between pure debt and equity. In the rest of this section, we discuss a wide range of bond features commonly observed in the corporate bond market.

By features

Fixed versus floating rates As we have already discussed, most bonds require the borrower to make periodic coupon payments and to repay the bond's face value at maturity. The coupon payments themselves may be fixed over the bond's life, or the coupons may adjust occasionally, if market interest rates change while the bond is outstanding. **Floating-rate bonds** provide some protection against interest rate risk for investors. If market interest rates increase, then eventually, so do the bond's coupon payments. Of course this makes borrowers' future cash obligations somewhat unpredictable, because the interest rate risk of floating-rate bonds is effectively transferred from the buyer to the issuer.

The interest rate on floating-rate bonds is typically tied to a widely quoted market interest rate. Benchmark interest rates that are used to determine how a floating-rate bond's interest rate changes over time include the one-year Treasury rate, the prime rate, and the London Interbank Offered Rate. The **prime rate** is the interest rate charged by large banks to 'prime' customers, usually businesses that have an excellent record of repaying their debts on time. The **London Interbank Offered Rate (LIBOR)** is a rate at which large banks can borrow from one another, and it is perhaps the most common benchmark interest rate for short-term debt. The equivalent of LIBOR in the United States is the **federal funds rate**, the rate for overnight lending between banks.

The interest rate on floating-rate bonds is typically specified by starting with one of the benchmark rates above and then adding a **spread**. The spread, also called the credit spread, is added to the benchmark interest rate, according to the risk of the borrower. Lenders charge higher spreads for less creditworthy borrowers.

Real World

In January 2007 the Dubai Holding Corporation, which groups together hotels and other entertainment businesses of the rulers of Dubai, raised $500 million in London, with repayments tied to LIBOR. Reflecting the high quality of the issuer, the coupon rate was 42 basis points (or 0.42 per cent) over three-month LIBOR. At that time three-month LIBOR stood at 5.36 per cent.

In addition to the fixed-rate notes and bonds that it issues, the US Treasury also offers a floating-rate debt instrument called Treasury Inflation-Protected Securities (TIPS). In the UK these are known as Interest Linked Bonds (ILBs). Rather than

floating-rate bonds
Bonds that make coupon payments that vary over time. The coupon payments are usually tied to a benchmark market interest rate. Also called variable-rate bonds.

prime rate
The rate of interest charged by banks on loans to business borrowers with excellent credit records.

London Interbank Offered Rate (LIBOR)
The interest rate that banks in London charge each other for overnight loans. Widely used as a benchmark interest rate for short-term floating-rate debt.

federal funds rate
The interest rate that US banks charge each other for overnight loans.

spread
The difference between the rate that a lender charges for a loan and the underlying benchmark interest rate. Lenders charge higher spreads to less creditworthy borrowers.

making coupon payments that are tied to a specific market interest rate such as LIBOR, these bonds pay a variable coupon that depends on the inflation rate. Some investors find these securities attractive because they offer a return that is protected against unexpected increases in inflation. For example, suppose an investor buys a ten-year inflation-indexed note with a par value of $1000 and a coupon rate of 2 per cent. If there is no inflation, the investor will receive a coupon payment of $10 (2% × $1000 × $\frac{1}{2}$) every six months. However, suppose that in the first six months after the investor bought this note, the United States experienced a 10 per cent increase in prices (i.e. a 10 per cent inflation rate). When the first coupon payment is due, the US Treasury increases the note's par value by the inflation rate, from $1000 to $1100. The 2 per cent coupon rate then applies to the new principal value. The first coupon payment will be $11 (2% × $1100 × $\frac{1}{2}$). Notice that the coupon payment increases at the rate of inflation (from $10 to $11, a 10 per cent increase). This means that TIPS and ILBs offer investors a constant *real* coupon rather than the constant *nominal* coupon guaranteed by ordinary government securities.

Secured versus unsecured
What assurances do lenders have that borrowers will fulfil their obligations to make interest and principal payments on time? In the case of unsecured debt, the only assurance is the borrower's promise to repay, combined with the recourse offered by the legal system if the borrower does not make all promised payments. An unsecured corporate bond is usually called a **debenture**. If a corporation has conducted more than one offering of debentures, some issues may have a lower priority claim than others. The term **subordinated debentures** refers to unsecured bonds that have legal claims inferior to, or subordinate to, other outstanding bonds. The terms *senior* and *junior* describe the relative standing of different bond issues, with senior bonds having a higher priority claim than junior bonds.

In some cases, however, firms pledge **collateral** when they issue bonds. Collateral refers to assets the bondholders can legally claim if a borrower defaults on a loan. When a bond is backed by collateral, we say that the bond is 'secured'. Examples of secured bonds are **mortgage bonds**, which are bonds secured by property or buildings. In Europe the most well known of these are Pfandbrief, bonds issued by German mortgage banks; **collateral trust bonds**, which are bonds secured by financial assets held by a trustee; and **equipment trust certificates**, which are bonds secured by various types of physical equipment and are typically related to transportation.

Zero-coupon bonds
Most bonds make periodic interest payments called coupons, but a few bonds, called zero-coupon bonds, pay no interest at all. Why would anyone purchase a bond that pays no interest? The incentive to purchase zero-coupon bonds is that they sell below face value. For that reason, zero-coupon bonds are also called discount bonds or **pure discount bonds**.[3] An investor who purchases a discount bond receives a capital gain when the bond matures and pays its face value.

The best-known example of a pure discount bond is a US Treasury bill, or T-bill. T-bills are issued by the US government, like Treasury notes and bonds discussed earlier, but they mature in one year or less, have a par value of $10 000 and distribute cash only at maturity. There are no intermediate coupon payments such as those paid by notes and bonds. For example, the Treasury sells a $10 000 face value bill that matures in six

debentures
Unsecured bonds backed only by the general faith and credit of the borrowing company.

subordinated debentures
An unsecured bond that has a legal claim inferior to other outstanding bonds.

collateral
The specific assets pledged to secure a loan.

mortgage bonds
A bond secured by real estate or buildings.

collateral trust bonds
A bond secured by financial assets held by a trustee.

equipment trust certificates
A secured bond often used to finance transportation equipment.

pure discount bonds
Bonds that pay no interest and sell below par value. Also called zero-coupon bonds.

---

[3] Be sure you understand the difference between a pure discount bond – a bond that makes no coupon payments at all – and an ordinary bond that sells at a discount. An ordinary bond sells at a discount when its coupon rate is below the rate of return that investors require to hold the bond.

months. The selling price of this T-bill was $9950.70. An investor who purchases the bill and holds it to maturity earns a return of 0.5 per cent over the next six months.

$$\frac{\$10\,000 - \$9950.7}{\$9950.7} = 0.005 = 0.5\%$$

We can convert that return to an annual rate by multiplying it by 2, so the annual (simple interest) return on the T-bill equals about 1 per cent.

Another example of a zero-coupon bond is a **Treasury STRIP**. The Treasury creates STRIP securities by issuing an ordinary coupon-paying note or bond, then stripping off the individual coupon and principal payments the security makes, and selling them as separate securities. For example, suppose a five-year, $1000 par Treasury note offers a coupon rate of 5 per cent. This means that the note will make ten coupon payments of $25 each at six-month intervals (5% $\times$ $1000 $\times$ $\frac{1}{2}$) and one $1000 payment at maturity. The Treasury can create 11 distinct STRIP securities by selling each of these payments separately. Suppose an investor pays $765.13 for the right to receive the $1000 principal payment in five years. Calculate the investor's return on this instrument by solving for its yield to maturity:

$$\$765.13 = \frac{\$1000}{(1 + r)^5}$$

$$r = 0.055 = 5.5\%$$

STRIPS are by no means limited to the USA. The general principle holds in any case where the underlying bond is a zero-coupon. By some measures, STRIP bonds are the most popular bonds traded in Canada, and they are also traded in the UK and New Zealand.

Convertible and exchangeable bonds Some bonds issued by corporations combine the features of debt and equity. Like ordinary bonds, **convertible bonds** pay investors a relatively safe stream of fixed coupon payments. But convertible bonds also give investors the right to convert their bonds into the shares of the firm that issued the bonds. This means that if the share prices increases, bondholders can share in that gain.

Treasury STRIP
A zero-coupon bond representing one coupon payment or the final principal payment made by an existing Treasury note or bond.

convertible bond
A bond that gives investors the option to redeem their bonds for the issuer's shares rather than cash.

Real World

On 10 February 2004, the parent company of American Airlines, AMR Corporation (ticker, AMR), announced a $300 million offering of convertible bonds maturing in 2024. The bonds offered investors a coupon rate of 4.5 per cent, paid semi-annually, and bondholders also received the right to exchange each $1000 par value bond for 45.3515 AMR common shares. At what share price does it make sense for bondholders to exercise the right to convert their bonds into shares? Consider that each bond is worth either $1000 or 45.3515 times AMR's share price. The breakeven point occurs when AMR's share price equals $22.05 ($1000 ÷ 45.3515). At any lower price, bondholders are better off taking $1000 in cash, but at any higher price, the shares are worth more than the bonds' face value. Moreover, there is no upper limit to the return that AMR convertible bondholders can earn. Once the price of AMR shares exceeds $22.05, each additional $1 increase in the price is worth an additional $45.3515 to bondholders.

Source: Adapted from American Airlines website, investor information section: www.aa.com.

exchangeable bonds
Bonds issued by corporations that may be converted into shares of a company other than the company that issued the bonds.

Exchangeable bonds work in much the same way as convertible bonds, except that exchangeable bonds are convertible into the shares of a company other than the company that issued the bonds. Exchangeable bonds are often used when one company owns a large block of shares in another firm that it wants to divest. Although the option to convert bonds into shares generally resides with the investor who holds a convertible bond, exchangeable bonds' conversion rights can vary. Sometimes the bond indenture requires that, at maturity, bondholders accept shares in the underlying firm. In that case, the securities are called mandatory exchangeable bonds.

callable
Bonds that the issuer can repurchase from investors at a predetermined price known as the call price.

call price
The price at which a bond issuer may call or repurchase an outstanding bond from investors.

Callable and putable bonds Most corporate bonds and some government bonds are callable. This means that the bond issuer retains the right to repurchase the bonds in the future at a predetermined price known as the call price. That right is valuable when market interest rates fall. Recall that bond prices generally rise as market interest rates fall. A firm that issued non-callable bonds when rates were high may want to retire those bonds and reissue new ones after a decline in interest rates. However, retiring the outstanding bonds requires paying a significant premium over par value. With callable bonds, the call price establishes an upper limit on how much the firm must pay to redeem previously issued bonds. Investors recognize that the call feature works to the advantage of the bond issuer, so callable bonds must generally offer higher coupon rates than otherwise similar non-callable bonds.

putable bonds
Bonds that investors can sell back to the issuer at a predetermined price under certain conditions.

Putable bonds work in the opposite way. Putable bonds allow investors to sell their bonds back to the issuing firm. This option is valuable to bondholders because it protects them against a decline in the value of their bonds. Therefore, putable bonds can offer lower coupon rates than otherwise similar non-putable bonds.

default risk
The risk that the corporation issuing a bond may not make all scheduled payments.

Protection from default risk Besides interest rate risk, bond investors also have to worry about default risk. Default risk refers to the possibility that a bond issuer may not be able to make all scheduled interest and principal payments on time and in full. The bond indenture, – the contract between a bond issuer and its creditors – usually contains a number of provisions designed to protect investors from default risk. We have already discussed some of these features, including a bond issue's seniority and whether it is secured or unsecured. Additional examples of these provisions include sinking funds and protective covenants. A sinking fund provision requires the borrower to make regular payments to a third-party trustee. The trustee then uses those funds to repurchase outstanding bonds. Usually sinking fund provisions require the trustee to retire bonds gradually, so that by the time a bond issue's maturity date arrives, only a fraction of the original issue remains outstanding. The trustee may purchase previously issued bonds on the open market, or the trustee may repurchase bonds by exercising a call provision, as described above.

sinking fund
A provision in a bond indenture that requires the borrower to make regular payments to a third-party trustee for use in retiring the bond.

Protective covenants
Provisions of the bond indenture that stipulate actions that the borrower must do (positive covenants) or actions that the borrower must not do (negative covenants).

Protective covenants, included in the bond indenture, specify requirements that the borrower must meet as long as bonds remain outstanding. Positive covenants specify things that the borrower must do. For example, positive covenants may require a borrower to file quarterly audited financial statements, to maintain a minimum amount of working capital or to maintain a certain level of debt coverage ratios. Negative covenants specify things that the borrower must not do, such as pay unusually high dividends, sell off assets or issue additional senior debt.

Clearly investors have a lot of choices when they consider buying bonds. The number and variety of fixed-income investments available in the market is truly astounding and far exceeds the number of shares available for trading. Let us turn now to the bond markets to see how bonds are traded, how bond prices are quoted and what external information is available to bond traders to help them make investment decisions.

10 What are the main types of issuers of bonds?

11 What is the difference between a pure discount bond and an ordinary bond that
sells at a discount?

12 Explain who benefits from the option to call a bond, and who benefits from the
option to convert a bond into shares.

4.4 BOND MARKETS

In terms of the monetary volume of securities traded each day, the bond market is
much larger than the stock market. Though some bonds are listed on stock exchanges,
most bonds trade in an electronic over-the-counter (OTC) market. The OTC market
is not a single physical location where bonds are traded. It is a collection of dealers
around the world who stand ready to buy and sell bonds. Dealers communicate with
one another and with investors via an electronic network. Because trades are
decentralized and negotiated privately, it is usually difficult to obtain accurate, up-to-date
price information on most bonds. Nevertheless, it is useful to see how bond prices
are quoted in different segments of the market.

Bond price quotations

By convention, in the USA Treasury note and bond prices are quoted as a percentage
of par value and in increments of 32nds of a dollar. For example, consider a note that
matures in August 2009. It has a bid price of 109:20, which means that an investor
who owned this note could sell it for 109 and 20/32nds per cent of par value. The
fraction 20/32 equals 0.625, so this bond's dollar bid price equals $1096.25 ($1000 ×
1.09625). In the UK and Europe bonds are generally quoted in decimal form, which
is rather easier to consider.

Applying the Model

In June 2006 a note offering a coupon rate of 5.5 per cent and maturing in May
2011 has an ask price of 107:14. This bond has a yield of 3.83 per cent. To derive
this yield, let us make a simplifying assumption and assume that the most recent
coupon payment was just made. This means that the next coupon payment will
arrive in six months.[4] Each semi-annual coupon payment equals $27.50. The
Treasury pays the next coupon in November 2006 and the final one in May 2011,
so ten payments remain. The ask price in dollar terms equals 107 and 14/32nds
per cent of par value. Because 14/32 equals 0.4375, the ask price is:

$$1000 \times 1.074375 = \$1074.375$$

[4] In fact, the May coupon payment was made a few weeks before 5 June, so the next coupon payment
would come in a little less than six months. By making an assumption about the timing of this note's cash
flows that is incorrect by a couple of weeks, we derive a yield that is slightly different from the quoted yield.
However, we stick with our assumption because it allows us to keep the discounting simple, with cash
flows arriving exactly every six months.

Now apply Equation 4.3 or use *Excel* or a financial calculator to find the note's ask yield to maturity:

$$1074.375 = \frac{27.50}{(1 + \frac{r}{2})^1} + \frac{27.50}{(1\frac{r}{2})^2} + \cdots + \frac{1027.50}{(1 + \frac{r}{2})^{10}}$$

$$r = 0.0385 = 3.85\%$$

Our solution is within 0.02 percentage points (or 2 basis points) of the actual yield of the bond. The slight difference occurs because of our simplifying assumption that the next coupon will arrive in exactly six months.

TABLE 4.2

Market data for actively traded corporate bonds, April 2006

Source: http://www.Ft.com/Marketdata accessed 6 April 2006.

COMPANY	CURRENCY	REDEMPTION DATE	COUPON (%)	MOODY'S RATING	PRICE	YIELD (%)	YIELD SPREAD
DaimlerChrysler	$	September 2009	7.20	A3	105.20	5.50	68bp
Deutsche Telekom	$	July 2013	5.25	A3	97.91	5.60	77bp
Volkswagen	€	May 2009	4.13	A3	101.17	3.72	31bp
Electricité de France	€	October 2010	5.75	Aa1	108.31	3.72	7bp
Boots	£	May 2009	5.50	Baa1	100.87	5.12	66bp
France Telecom	£	March 2011	7.50	Baa1	110.36	5.10	64bp

yield spread
The difference in yield to maturity between two bonds or two classes of bonds with similar maturities.

Table 4.2 shows market data for some heavily traded corporate bonds.

Traders often refer to the **yield spread** on a particular bond. The yield spread equals the difference in yield to maturities between a corporate bond and a government bond of roughly the same maturity. By convention, yield spreads are quoted in terms of basis points, where one basis point equals 1/100 of 1 per cent. Because corporate bonds are riskier than government bonds, they offer higher yields, so the yield spread is always a positive number. It is important to correctly match the maturity of the government and corporate bond. Corporate bonds that have a maturity far in the future should be matched with long-term government bonds, while those that are close to maturity should be matched with shorter-term government issues.

As you might expect, bond spreads reflect a direct relationship with default risk. The greater the risk that the borrower may default on its debts, the higher the spread that bonds issued by the borrower must offer investors to compensate them for the risk that they take. For investors, estimating the default risk of a particular bond issue is a crucial element in determining what the required return on the bond should be. Fortunately, bond investors have several resources at their disposal to help them make this evaluation.

Bond ratings

For information on the likelihood that a particular bond issue may default, investors turn to bond rating agencies such as Standard & Poor's, Moody's and Fitch. These

RATING DESCRIPTION	MOODY'S	S&P AND FITCH	
Highest quality	Aaa	AAA	Investment grade
High quality	Aa1, Aa2, Aa3	AA+, AA, AA−	
Upper medium	A1, A2, A3	A+, A, A−	
Medium	Baa1, Baa2, Baa3	BBB+, BBB, BBB−	
Non-investment grade	Ba1	BB+	
Speculative	Ba2, Ba3	BB, BB−	Junk bonds
Highly speculative	B1, B2, B3	B+, B, B−	
Very risky, default	Caa1 or lower	CCC+or lower	

TABLE 4.3
Bond ratings

Bond rating agencies such as Moody's, Standard and Poor's and Fitch assign bond ratings based on their assessment of the borrower's ability to repay. Bonds in the top four ratings categories are investment grade bonds, while those rated lower are junk bonds.

organizations provide an independent assessment of the risk of most publicly traded bond issues, and they assign a letter **bond rating** to each issue to indicate its degree of risk. Table 4.3 lists the major bond rating categories provided by each of the agencies and the interpretation associated with each rating class. Bonds rated BBB− or higher by S&P and Fitch, and Baa3 or higher by Moody's, fall into the investment grade category. Bonds rated lower than that are called non-investment grade or **junk bonds**. The term 'junk bonds' has a pejorative connotation but simply means that these bonds are riskier than investment grade bonds. For example, for bonds in the investment grade category, the probability of default is extremely low, perhaps as low as 1 per cent. A recent study put the probability of a B-rated bond defaulting in its first year at almost 8 per cent.[5]

Table 4.4 shows the relationship between bond ratings and yield spreads for corporate bonds at different maturities.[6] As before, the yield spreads are quoted in basis points. The first entry in the top left corner of the table shows a corporate bond with the highest possible Aaa/AAA rating and a maturity of one year. At end-March 2006 this form of bond offered a yield that was just five basis points above the one-year US Treasury rate. Moving across the row, we see that yield spreads increase with time to maturity. As expected, yield spreads increase as you move down the rows, as the default risk rises the lower the rating. The bottom row shows that the lowest-rated bonds, those that are at or near the point of default, offer yields that are more than 10 per cent higher than comparable maturity Treasury securities. To illustrate an extreme case, suppose that the yield to maturity on a ten-year Treasury equals 3 per cent. The next-to-last entry in Table 4.4 shows that a ten-year corporate bond rated Caa/CCC must offer a yield that is 14 per cent higher than the Treasury bond, or 17 per cent. If that seems like an attractive return, remember the risk dimension. An investor who buys a large number of bonds rated Caa/CCC will almost certainly not earn an average yield of 17 per cent, because some of these bonds will default. When default occurs, bondholders typically do not receive all the payments

bond ratings
Grades assigned to bonds by specialized agencies that evaluate the capacity of bond issuers to repay their debts. Lower grades signify higher default risk.

junk bonds
Bonds rated below investment grade (also known as high yield bonds).

---

[5] 'Default Curves and the Dynamics of Credit Spreads', by Wesley Phoa, in *Professional Perspectives on Fixed Income Portfolio Management*, Frank J. Fabozzi, ed., John Wiley & Sons, 2002.
[6] Here, we focus only on corporate bonds – that is, bonds issued by companies. We do not look at other forms of bonds, such as those issued by state agencies, municipalities and so on. These usually have features and tax treatments that make them difficult to compare.

TABLE 4.4

The relationship between bond ratings and spreads at different maturities

The table shows the difference in yields, as of March 2006, between bonds in different ratings categories and Treasury securities having the same maturity. For instance, five-year bonds with a AAA rating offered a yield that was 20 basis points higher than the five-year Treasury note in February 2006. Note that yield spreads rise with maturity just as they rise as the bond rating falls.

Source: http://www.ejv. com/publicspreads.cgi? *Industrial*, 31 March 2006.

RATING	1 YEAR	2 YEAR	3 YEAR	5 YEAR	7 YEAR	10 YEAR	30 YEAR
Aaa/AAA	5	10	15	20	27	31	55
Aa1/AA+	10	15	20	30	37	50	77
Aa2/AA	15	25	30	35	47	62	92
Aa3/AA−	20	30	35	45	55	75	101
A1/A+	25	35	40	50	59	82	112
A2/A	35	44	55	60	69	90	117
A3/A−	45	59	70	75	84	106	146
Baa1/BBB+	55	65	80	90	98	120	163
Baa2/BBB	60	75	100	105	116	137	182
Baa3/BBB−	75	90	110	115	128	165	225
Ba1/BB+	115	125	140	165	190	215	270
Ba2/BB	140	185	210	220	230	275	360
Ba3/BB−	165	205	230	245	260	295	385
B1/B+	195	220	250	275	300	360	400
B2/B	220	230	275	320	355	385	430
B3/B−	270	320	365	420	455	485	505
Caa/CCC	1 100	1 200	1 225	1 200	1 200	1 275	1 400

they were originally promised, so the yield they realize on their bonds falls short of the promised yield to maturity.[7]

Thus far, we have maintained a simplifying assumption in our valuation models. You can see that assumption embedded in Equations 4.1 and 4.2. Both equations assume that we can apply a single discount rate, r, to determine the present value of cash payments made at any and all future dates. In other words, the models assume that investors require the same rate of return on an investment that pays cash one year from now and on one that pays cash ten years from now. In reality, required rates of return depend on the exact timing of cash payments, as the next section illustrates.

CONCEPT REVIEW QUESTIONS

13 Calculate a bond's yield to maturity using the ask price, then repeat the calculation using the bond's bid price. Which yield to maturity is higher?

14 The price of a certain Treasury note is quoted as 98:10. What is the dollar price of this note if its par value is $1000?

15 Explain why the yield spread on corporate bonds versus Treasury bonds should always be positive.

---

7 According to The Salomon Center for the Study of Financial Institutions, the default rate among junk bonds reached a record 12.8 per cent in 2002. In a very rough sense, this means that one of eight junk bond issues in the market defaulted that year. The Center estimates that investors who held defaulted bonds recovered only 25 per cent of par value. With the improving economy in 2003, the default rate fell to 4.6 per cent and the recovery rate increased to 45 per cent.

4.5 THE TERM STRUCTURE OF INTEREST RATES

The yield curve

Table 4.4 reveals an important fact: bond yields vary with maturity. The difference in the yield spread between a one-year and a 30-year bond varies from 50 basis points for Aaa/AAA bonds to 300 basis points, or more, for junk bonds. Though Table 4.4 reports yield spreads rather than yields, the data suggest that a positive relationship exists between time to maturity and yield to maturity for bonds in any risk category.

Financial experts refer to the relationship between time to maturity and yield to maturity for bonds of equal risk as the **term structure of interest rates**. The term structure of interest rates indicates whether yields rise, fall or remain constant across bonds with different maturities. The simplest way to communicate information about the term structure is to draw a graph that plots yield to maturity on the *y*-axis and time to maturity on the *x*-axis. Each day, many financial publications show this graph, usually for a sample of government securities. A graph showing the term structure of interest rates is called the **yield curve**.

The yield curve changes over time. Figure 4.4 shows how the German yield curve looked at different dates; typically, long-term bonds offer higher yields do than short-term bonds, and the yield curve slopes up. As investors' expectations about future inflation change, so too does the yield curve. Higher inflation expectations lead to higher bond yields. The shape of the yield curve changes over time also.

Why the yield curve sometimes slopes up and at other times slopes down is a complex problem. However, there is an interesting link between the slope of the yield curve and overall macroeconomic growth. Historically, when the yield curve inverts (i.e. switches from an upward slope to a downward slope), a recession usually follows. In fact, several research studies show that economic forecasts based on the yield curve's slope more accurately predict recessions than many forecasts produced using complex statistical models. One reason for this pattern is as follows. Suppose a firm receives new information from its salesforce indicating that orders for the firm's

term structure of interest rates
The relationship between yield to maturity and time to maturity among bonds having similar risk.

yield curve
A graph that plots the relationship between yield to maturity and maturity for a group of similar bonds.

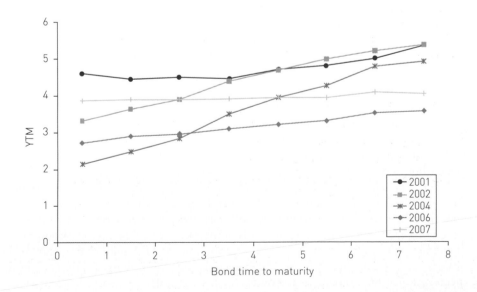

FIGURE 4.4

The term structure of interest rates

The figure shows how the German yield curve looked on different dates. Most of the time, the yield curve slopes up because long-term bond yields exceed short-term bond yields. However, bond yield curves can flatten or even invert at times.

products are likely to fall in the near term. This prompts the firm to cut back on planned investment. That means the firm's need for long-term borrowing to finance new investment is diminished. If this happens to just a few firms, it is not likely to have a noticeable effect on financial markets. But if it happens to many firms simultaneously (because demand is falling for many products at once, as happens during a recession), the aggregate demand for new financing to pay for investment will fall. Firms will not need to issue long-term bonds to borrow money for new factories or new equipment. A reduction in the demand for long-term borrowing can cause long-term interest rates to fall relative to short-term rates, and the yield curve may invert. The yield curve may also invert because short-term rates rise above long-term rates. This may occur when a central bank increases short-term rates to fight inflation. The yield curve works well as a predictor of economic activity in all the large industrialized economies.

Expectations theory

Economists have studied the yield curve intensely for several decades, trying to understand how it behaves and what it portends for the future. As a result of that research, we know that economic growth forecasts that include the slope of the yield curve perform well relative to forecasts that ignore the yield curve. Can the yield curve also tell us something about the direction in which interest rates are headed? The answer is a highly qualified yes. To understand the logic underlying the hypothesis that the slope of the yield curve may predict interest rate movements, consider the following example.

Russell wants to invest €1000 for two years. He does not want to take much risk, so he plans to invest the money in short-term government securities: one-year securities currently offer a 5 per cent YTM, and two-year a 5.5 per cent YTM. At first, Russell thinks his decision about which investment to purchase is easy. He wants to invest for two years, and the two-year bond pays a higher yield, so why not just buy that one? Thinking further, Russell realizes that he could invest his money in a one-year bond and reinvest the proceeds in another one-year bond when the first bond matures. Whether that strategy will ultimately earn a higher return than that of simply buying the two-year bond depends on what the yield on a one-year bond will be one year from now. For example, if the one-year bond rate rises to 7 per cent, Russell will earn 5 per cent in the first year and 7 per cent in the second year, for a grand total of 12 per cent (12.35 per cent after compounding). Over the same period, the two-year bond offers just 5.5 per cent per year or 11 per cent total (11.30 per cent after compounding). In this scenario, Russell earns more by investing in two one-year bonds than in one two-year bond. But what if the yield on a one-year bond is just 5 per cent next year? In that case, Russell earns 10 per cent over two years (or 10.25 per cent after compounding), and he is better off buying the two-year bond. If next year's yield on the one-year bond is about 6 per cent, then Russell will earn approximately the same return over the two years no matter which investment strategy he chooses.

expectations theory
In equilibrium, investors should expect to earn the same return whether they invest in long-term government bonds or a series of short-term government bonds.

This example illustrates the **expectations theory** of the term structure: in equilibrium, investors should expect to earn the same return whether they invest in long-term Treasury bonds or a series of short-term Treasury bonds. If the yield on two-year bonds is 5.5 per cent when the yield on one-year bonds is 5 per cent, then investors must expect next year's yield on a one-year bond to be 6 per cent. If they expected a yield higher than 6 per cent, investors are better off purchasing a series of one-year bonds than from buying the two-year bond. Conversely, if investors expect next year's bond rate to be less than 6 per cent, they will flock to the two-year bond. Equilibrium occurs when investors' expectations are such that the expected return on a two-year bond equals the expected return on two one-year bonds. In this example, equilibrium occurs when investors believe that next year's interest rate will be 6 per cent.

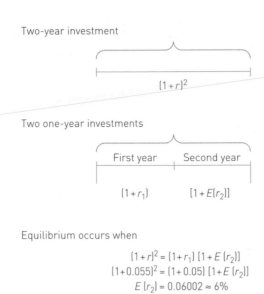

FIGURE 4.5

The expectations hypothesis

The expectations hypothesis says that investors should earn the same expected return by purchasing one two-year bond or two one-year bonds. In this example, equilibrium occurs when the expected return on a one-year bond next year, $E(r_2)$, is 6 per cent. Only then do the two investment strategies provide the same expected return.

Figure 4.5 illustrates this idea. The first part of the figure shows that the value of €1 invested in one two-year bond will grow to $(1 + r)^2$. In this expression, r represents the current interest rate on a two-year bond. Next, the figure shows that investors expect €1 invested in a sequence of two one-year bonds to grow to $(1 + r_1)$ $[1 + E(r_2)]$. Here, r_1 represents the current one-year bond rate, and $E(r_2)$ represents the expected one-year bond rate in the second year. Equilibrium occurs when the two strategies have identical expected returns, or when the expected one-year interest rate is about 6 per cent.

SMART CONCEPTS

See the concept explained step-by-step at **Smart Finance**

COMPARATIVE CORPORATE FINANCE
Is the yield curve a good economic predictor?

Economists have known for many years that the slope of the yield curve – that is, the difference between yields on short-term and long-term Treasury securities – helps predict future economic growth in the United States. The same is true in many other countries, although the reliability of growth forecasts based on the yield curve varies internationally. The accompanying chart measures the reliability of forecasts based on the yield curve in 11 different countries.

For each country, the chart shows the ability of the yield curve to predict, one year in advance, changes in three different measures of economic activity: the percentage change in real gross domestic product (GDP), the percentage change in industrial production and the change in the unemployment rate. The vertical height of the bars measures forecast reliability. A forecast that perfectly predicted future economic activity plots at 100 per cent, whereas an utterly useless forecast plots at 0 percent.

The chart indicates that the yield curve is most useful in predicting future economic activity in the United States and Canada. The yield curve's predictive power is weaker, but still significant, in most European countries. Curiously, the yield curve's performance is worst outside the Western economies, showing almost no ability to predict changes in economic variables in Japan and Australia.

▶

Explanatory power of the yield spread for different measures of economic activity

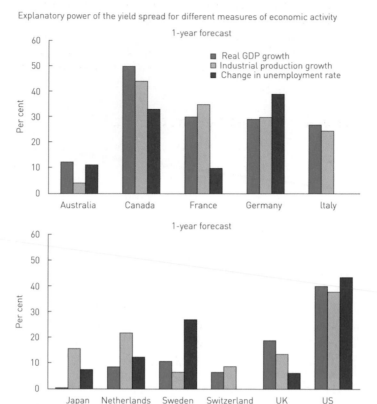

Source: Adapted from Catherine Bonser-Neal and Timothy R. Morley (1997) 'Does the Yield Spread Predict Real Economic Activity? A Multicountry Analysis: Federal Reserve Bank of St. Louis, *Economic Review*, 82(3):37–53.

Applying the Model

Suppose a one-year bond currently offers a yield of 5 per cent, and a two-year bond offers a 4.5 per cent yield. Under the expectations hypothesis, what interest rate do investors expect on a one-year bond next year? Remember that the expectations hypothesis says that investors should earn the same expected return by investing in either two one-year bonds or one two-year bond. Therefore, the breakeven calculation is:

$$(1 + 0.05)(1 + E(r_2)) = (1 + 0.045)^2$$
$$1 + E(r_2) = (1.045)^2/1.05$$
$$E(r_2) = 0.04 \text{ or } 4\%$$

The term $E(r_2)$ refers to the expected return on a one-year bond next year (year 2). On the left-hand side of the equation, we have the return that an investor expects to earn by purchasing a one-year bond this year and another one next year. That should equal the return earned by purchasing a two-year bond today and holding it to maturity. Only when the expected one-year bond rate is 4 per cent are investors indifferent between these two strategies.

Expectations theory implies that when the yield curve is sloping upward – that is, when long-term bond yields exceed short-term bond yields – investors must expect short-term yields to rise. According to the theory, only if investors expect short-term rates to rise will they be willing to forego the higher current yield on a long-term instrument by purchasing a short-term bond. Conversely, when the yield curve inverts, and short-term yields exceed long-term yields, investors must expect short-term rates to fall. Only then would investors willingly accept the lower yield on long-term bonds.

Liquidity preference and preferred habitat theories

Unfortunately, the slope of the yield curve does not always provide a reliable signal of future interest rate movements, perhaps because expectations theory ignores several factors that are important to investors and that influence the shape of the yield curve. The first factor is that investors may have a preference for investing in short-term securities. As we have seen, when market interest rates change, the prices of long-term bonds fluctuate more than the prices of short-term bonds. This added risk might deter some investors from investing in long-term bonds. To attract investors, perhaps long-term bonds must offer a return that exceeds the expected return on a series of short-term bonds. Therefore, when the yield curve slopes up, we cannot be sure whether this is the result of investors expecting interest rates to rise in the future, or simply a reflection of compensation for risk. The liquidity preference theory of the term structure recognizes this problem. It says that the slope of the yield curve is influenced not only by expected interest rate changes but also by the liquidity premium that investors require on long-term bonds.

A second factor clouds the interpretation of the slope of the yield curve as a signal of interest rate movements if certain investors always purchase bonds with a particular maturity. For instance, pension funds that promise retirement income to investors and life insurance companies that provide death benefits to policyholders have very long-term liabilities. These companies may have a strong desire to invest in long-term bonds (the longest available in the market) to match their liabilities, even if long-term bonds offer low expected returns relative to a series of short-term bonds. Economists use the preferred habitat theory (or the market segmentation theory) to describe the effect of this behaviour on the yield curve. If short-term bond rates exceed long-term rates, the cause may be that the demand for long-term bonds is very high relative to their supply. This demand drives up long-term bond prices and drives down their yields. If the investors purchasing long-term bonds have a strong preference for investing in those securities, despite their low yields, then a yield curve that slopes down does not necessarily imply that investors expect interest rates to fall.[8]

Conclusion

Valuing assets – both financial assets and real assets – is what finance is all about. In this chapter, we have learned some simple approaches for pricing bonds, which are among the most common and most important financial instruments in the market. A bond's price depends on how much cash flow it promises investors, how that cash flow is taxed, how likely it is that the issuer will fulfil its promises (i.e. default risk), whether investors expect high or low inflation and whether interest rates rise or fall over time. In the next chapter we apply many of these same ideas to the pricing of shares.

liquidity preference theory
States that the slope of the yield curve is influenced not only by expected interest rate changes, but also by the liquidity premium that investors require on long-term bonds.

preferred habitat theory
A theory that recognizes that the shape of the yield curve may be influenced by investors who prefer to purchase bonds having a particular maturity regardless of the returns those bonds offer compared to returns available at other maturities.

---

[8] Do you have a favourite place to go to enjoy a beer with your peers? Is the price of beer there the lowest price in town? If not, you are behaving according to the preferred habitat theory. You prefer to go to a particular establishment to socialize, even though you could buy the same beer at another location for less money. In the same way, some investors prefer to invest in long-term bonds even though a series of sort-term bonds might offer a higher expected return.

16 Explain why the height of the yield curve depends on inflation.

17 Suppose the government issues two five-year bonds. One is an ordinary bond that offers a fixed nominal coupon rate of 4 per cent. The other bond is an inflation-indexed bond. When the inflation-indexed bond is issued, will it have a coupon rate of 4 per cent, more than 4 per cent or less than 4 percent?

18 If the yield curve does act as a good predictor of future economic conditions, can the government use this as a tool to manage the economy?

4.6 SUMMARY AND CONCLUSIONS

- Valuation is a process that links an asset's return with its risk. To value most types of assets, one must first estimate the asset's future cash flows and then discount them at an appropriate discount rate.

- Pricing bonds is an application of the general valuation framework. A bond's price equals the present value of its future cash flows, which consist of coupon and principal payments.

- The yield to maturity is a measure of the return that investors require on a bond. The YTM is the discount rate that equates the present value of a bond's cash flows to its current market price.

- Bond prices and interest rates are inversely related. When interest rates rise (fall), bond prices fall (rise), and the prices of long-term bonds are more responsive in general to changes in interest rates than short-term bond prices are.

- Bonds are categorized based on who issues them or on any number of features such as convertibility, callability, maturity and so on.

- Bond rating agencies help investors evaluate the risk of bonds. Bonds with lower ratings must offer investors higher yields.

- The return that is most important to investors is the real, or inflation-adjusted, return. The real return is roughly equal to the nominal return minus the inflation rate.

- The 'term structure of interest rates' describes the relationship between time to maturity and yield to maturity on bonds of equivalent risk. A graph of the term structure is called the yield curve. The slope of the yield curve is highly correlated with future economic growth.

INTERNET RESOURCES

For updates to links in this section and elsewhere in the book, please go to the book's website at www.cengage.co.uk/megginson.

http://www.bondmarkets.com
An extremely comprehensive site with extensive coverage of current events, policy issues and research related to the bond markets. It has an extensive list of links to other bond sites on the web.

http://www.bondsonline.com
Provides an enormous amount of information on the bond markets.

http://www.financenter.com
A consumer-oriented site offering various online financial calculators that allow you to calculate a bond's after-tax yield to maturity, the effect of interest rate movements on a bond's price and many other figures.

http://www.isma.co.uk/
The international body that acts as a guardian of best practice in corporate bonds.

http://www.stockcharts.com/charts/YieldCurve.html
Offers a Java-animated yield curve juxtaposed to a plot of the S&P 500, a share index that includes 500 of the biggest and most important firms in the US market. It allows you to watch historical movements in share and bond markets simultaneously.

http://epp.eurostat.cec.eu.int/cache/ITY_PUBLIC/EYC/EN/page2.htm
Information on European yield curves, their creation and the different types of yield curves that exist.

KEY TERMS

agency bonds	federal funds rate	protective covenants
bond ratings	floating-rate bonds	pure discount bonds
call price	indenture	putable bonds
callable	interest rate risk	real return
collateral	junk bonds	required rate of return
collateral trust bond	liquidity preference theory	sinking fund
convertible bond	London Interbank Offered Rate	spread
corporate bonds	(LIBOR)	subordinated debentures
coupon	maturity date	term structure of interest
coupon rate	mortgage bonds	rates
coupon yield	municipal bonds	Treasury bills
debentures	nominal return	Treasury bonds
default risk	par value (bonds)	Treasury notes
discount	preferred habitat theory	Treasury STRIP
equipment trust certificates	premium	yield curve
exchangeable bonds	prime rate	yield spread
expectations theory	principal	yield to maturity

SELF-TEST PROBLEMS

ST4-1 A five-year bond pays interest annually. The par value is €1000 and the coupon rate equals 7 per cent. If the market's required return on the bond is 8 per cent, what is the bond's market price?

ST4-2 A bond that matures in two years makes semi-annual interest payments. The par value is €1000, the coupon rate equals 4 per cent and the bond's market price is €1019.27. What is the bond's yield to maturity?

ST4-3 Two bonds offer a 5 per cent coupon rate, paid annually, and sell at par (€1000). One bond matures in two years and the other matures in ten years.

   a What are the YTMs on each bond?

   b If the YTM changes to 4 per cent, what happens to the price of each bond?

   c What happens if the YTM changes to 6 per cent?

QUESTIONS

Q4-1 What is the relationship between the price of a financial asset and the return that investors require on that asset, holding other factors constant?

Q4-2 Define the following terms commonly used in bond valuation: (a) par value, (b) maturity date, (c) coupon, (d) coupon rate, (e) coupon yield, (f) yield to maturity (YTM) and (g) yield curve.

Q4-3 Under what circumstances will a bond's coupon rate exceed its coupon yield? Explain in economic terms why this occurs.

Q4-4 What is the difference between a pure discount bond and a bond that trades at a discount? If issuers successfully sell pure discount bonds in the market, investors must want them. Can you explain why any bond purchaser might prefer to purchase a pure discount bond rather than a bond that pays interest?

Q4-5 A firm issues a bond at par value. Shortly thereafter, interest rates fall. If you calculate the coupon rate, coupon yield, and yield to maturity for this bond after the decline in interest rates, which of the three values is highest and which is lowest? Explain.

Q4-6 Twenty-five years ago, the US government issued 30-year bonds with a coupon rate of about 8 per cent. Five years ago, the US government sold ten-year bonds with a coupon rate of about 5 per cent. Suppose that the current coupon rate on newly issued five-year Treasury bonds is 2.5 per cent. For an investor seeking a low-risk investment maturing in five years, do the bonds issued 25 years ago with a much higher coupon rate provide a more attractive return than the new five-year bonds? What about the ten-year bonds issued five years ago?

Q4-7 Describe how and why a bond's interest rate risk is related to its maturity.

Q4-8 Explain why municipal bonds can offer lower interest rates than equally risky corporate bonds.

Q4-9 Explain why the yield to maturity on a junk bond is not a particularly good measure of the return you can expect if you buy it and hold it until maturity.

Q4-10 Under the expectations theory, what does the slope of the yield curve reveal about the future path of interest rates?

Q4-11 If the yield curve typically slopes upward, what does this imply about the long-term path of interest rates if the expectations theory is true?

Q4-12 Go to http://www.stockcharts.com/charts/YieldCurve.html and click on the animated yield curve graph (be sure Java is enabled on your browser). Answer the following questions:

   a Is the yield curve typically upward-sloping, downward-sloping, or flat?

   b Notice the behaviour of the yield curve and the stock market between 28 July 1998 and 19 October 1998. In August 1998, Russia defaulted on billions of dollars of foreign debt. Then, in late September came the news that at the behest of the Federal Reserve, 15 financial institutions would infuse $3.5 billion in new capital into hedge fund Long-Term Capital Management, which had lost nearly $2 billion in the previous month. Comment on these events as they relate to movements in the yield curve and the stock markets that you see in the animation.

Q4-13 At http://www.nber.org/cycles.html, you can find the official beginning and ending dates for US business cycles, according to the National Bureau of Economic Research (NBER). For example, the NBER indicates that the US economy was in recession from January 1980 to July 1980, from July 1981 to November 1982 and from July 1990 to March 1991. Next, go to http://www.smartmoney.com/onebond/index. cfm?story=yieldcurve and click on the animation of the Living Yield Curve. Pause the animation at November 1978. Then, click one frame at a time until May 1980. Pause again at November 1981, and click one frame at a time until August 1982. Let the animation play again until you reach March 1989. What association do you notice between the shape of the yield curve and the NBER's dates for recessions?

Q4-14 Look again at the yield curve animation found at the SmartMoney website, http://www.smartmoney.com/onebond/index. cfm?story=yieldcurve. Make a note of the overall level of the yield curve from about mid-1979 to mid-1982. Compare that with the level of the curve for most of the 1990s. What accounts for the differences in yield curve levels in these two periods?

PROBLEMS

Valuation fundamentals

P4-1 A best-selling author decides to cash in on her latest novel by selling the rights to the book's royalties for the next six years to an investor. Royalty payments arrive once per year, starting one year from now. In the first year, the author expects €400 000 in royalties, followed by €300 000, then €100 000, then €10 000 in

the three subsequent years. If the investor purchasing the rights to royalties requires a return of 7 per cent per year, what should the investor pay?

P4-2 An oil well produces 20 000 barrels of oil per year. Suppose the price of oil is €20 per barrel. You want to purchase the right to the oil produced by this well for the next five years. At a discount rate of 10 per cent, what is the value of the oil rights? (You can assume that the cash flows from selling oil arrive at annual intervals.)

Bond prices and interest rates

P4-3 A €1000 par value bond makes two interest payments each year of €45 each. What is the bond's coupon rate?

P4-4 A €1000 par value bond has a coupon rate of 8 per cent and a coupon yield of 9 per cent. What is the bond's market price?

P4-5 A bond sells for €900 and offers a coupon yield of 7.2 per cent. What is the bond's annual coupon payment?

P4-6 A bond offers a coupon rate of 5 per cent. If the par value is €1000 and the bond sells for €1250, what is the coupon yield?

P4-7 A bond makes two €45 interest payments each year. Given that the bond's par value is €1000 and its price is €1050, calculate the bond's coupon rate and coupon yield.

P4-8 Calculate the price of a five-year, €1000 par value bond that makes semi-annual payments, has a coupon rate of 8 per cent and offers a yield to maturity of 7 per cent. Recalculate the price assuming a 9 per cent YTM. What is the general relationship that this problem illustrates?

> **SMART SOLUTIONS**
> See the problem and solution explained step-by-step at **Smart Finance**

P4-9 A €1000 par value bond makes annual interest payments of €75. If it offers a yield to maturity of 7.5 per cent, what is the price of the bond?

P4-10 A €1000 par value bond pays a coupon rate of 8.2 per cent. The bond makes semi-annual payments and it matures in four years. If investors require a 10 per cent return on this investment, what is the bond's price?

P4-11 Griswold Travel Company has issued six-year bonds that pay €30 in interest twice each year. The par value of these bonds is €1000 and they offer a yield to maturity of 5.5 per cent. How much are the bonds worth?

P4-12 Bennifer Jewellers recently issued ten-year bonds that make annual interest payments of €50. Suppose you purchased one of these bonds at par value when it was issued. Right away, market interest rates jumped, and the YTM on your bond rose to 6 per cent. What happened to the price of your bond?

P4-13 You are evaluating two similar bonds. Both mature in four years, both have a €1000 par value and both pay a coupon rate of 10 per cent. However, one bond pays that coupon in annual instalments, whereas the other makes semi-annual payments. Suppose you require a 10 per cent return on either bond. Should these bonds sell at identical prices or should one be worth more than the other? Use Equations 4.2 and 4.3, and let $r = 10$ per cent. What prices do you obtain for these bonds? Can you explain the apparent paradox?

P4-14 A bond makes annual interest payments of €75. The bond matures in four years, has a par value of €1000 and sells for €975.30. What is the bond's yield to maturity (YTM)?

P4-15 Johanson VI Advisers issued €1000 par value bonds a few years ago with a coupon rate of 7 per cent, paid semi-annually. After the bonds were issued, interest rates fell. Now with three years remaining before they mature, the bonds sell for €1055.08. What YTM do these bonds offer?

P4-16 A bond offers a 6 per cent coupon rate and sells at par. What is the bond's yield to maturity?

Types of bonds

P4-17 The nominal interest rate is 9 per cent and the inflation rate is 7 per cent. What is the real interest rate?

P4-18 The rate of inflation is 5 per cent and the real interest rate is 3 per cent. What is the nominal interest rate?

P4-19 Suppose investors face a tax rate of 40 per cent on interest paid by corporate bonds.

Suppose AAA-rated corporate bonds currently offer yields of about 7 per cent. Approximately what yield would AAA-rated municipal bonds need to offer to be competitive?

SMART SOLUTIONS
See the problems and solution explained step-by-step at **www.cengage.co.uk/ megginson**

P4-20 Investors face a tax rate of 33 per cent on interest paid by corporate bonds. If municipal bonds currently offer yields of 6 per cent, what yield would equally risky corporate bonds need to offer to be competitive?

P4-21 You purchase a US Treasury inflation-indexed bond at par value of $1000. The bond offers a coupon rate of 6 per cent paid semi-annually. During the first six months that you hold the bond, prices in the United States rise by 2 per cent. What is the new par value of the bond, and what is the amount of your first coupon payment?

P4-22 What is the price of a zero-coupon bond that has a par value of €1000? The bond matures in 30 years and offers a yield to maturity of 4.5 per cent. Calculate the price one year later, when the bond has 29 years left before it matures (assume the yield remains at 4.5 per cent). What is the return that an investor earns who buys the bond with 30 years remaining and sells it one year later?

Bond markets

P4-23 A Treasury bond's price is quoted as 98.11. What is the price of the bond if its par value is $1000?

P4-24 A corporate bond's price is quoted as 102.312. If the bond's par value is €1000, what is its market price?

Advanced bond valuation

P4-25 A one-year government security offers a 4 per cent yield to maturity (YTM). A two-year government security offers a 4.25 per cent YTM. According to the expectations hypothesis, what is the expected interest rate on a one-year security next year?

P4-26 A one-year Treasury bill offers a 6 per cent yield to maturity. The market's consensus forecast is that one-year T-bills will offer 6.25 per cent next year. What is the current yield on a two-year T-bill if the expectations hypothesis holds?

THOMSON ONE Business School Edition

Access financial information from the Thomson ONE – Business School Edition website for the following problem(s). Go to http://tobsefin.swlearning.com/. If you have already registered your access serial number and have a username and password, click **Enter**. Otherwise, click **Register** and follow the instructions to create a username and password. Register your access serial number and then click **Enter** on the aforementioned website. When you click Enter, you will be prompted for your username and password (please remember that the password is case sensitive). Enter them in the respective boxes and then click **OK** (or hit **Enter**). From the ensuing page, click **Click Here to Access Thomson ONE – Business School Edition Now!** This opens up a new window that gives you access to the Thomson ONE – Business School Edition database. You can retrieve a company's financial information by entering its ticker symbol (provided for each company in the problem(s)) in the box below 'Name/Symbol/Key.' For further instructions on using the Thomson ONE – Business School Edition database, please refer to *A Guide for Using Thomson ONE – Business School Edition*.

P4-27 Bond rating agencies, such as Standard and Poor's, Moody's and Fitch, investigate, among other things, a company's debt and profitability ratios (see Chapter 2 for these ratios) in order to rate its bonds. Examine these ratios for two sets of companies, Ryanair and British Airways and for CRH and Holcim, and explain which company's bonds are likely to have a higher rating and why. Does the industry matter more than the company, in your opinion?

MINICASE *Valuing bonds*

Y ou open your *Wall Street Journal* (WSJ) on the morning of 16 February 2005, and see the following bond quote for General Mills, Incorporated. Based on this WSJ information, answer the following questions.

Company (ticker)	Coupon	Maturity	Last price	Last yield	Est spread	UST	Est $ Vol (000s)
General Mills (GIS)	6.000	15 Feb. 2012	109.305	???	60	10	45 040

Assignment

1 What is the YTM for this General Mills corporate bond?

2 What is the coupon yield of this bond over the next year?

3 What is the expected capital gain or loss of this bond over the next year?

4 If your required rate of return for a bond of this risk class is 4.7 per cent, what

value do you place on this General Mills, Inc. bond?

5 At this required rate of return of 4.7 per cent are you interested in purchasing this bond?

6 If you purchased this General Mills, Inc. bond for $1093.05 yesterday and the market rate of interest for this bond dropped to 4.5 per cent today, do you have a gain or loss? How much is that gain or loss in dollars?

Chapter 5
Valuing Shares

OPENING FOCUS

Bidding wars

Bidding wars refer to situations where companies are being subject to takeover approaches. While we will discuss the financial aspects of takeovers later in the text, bidding wars by their very nature reflect on the issue we will discuss in this chapter. Consider London Stock Exchange Ltd, the listed company that owns and runs the London Stock Exchange (LSE, of which more later). What is the value of this company? Although the stock market is immensely complex in some respects, the business model is reasonably simple for an exchange. Fees from listing, data services and trading make up the bulk of the income. Expenditure is mostly on ensuring that the technology, human and IS, are as up to date as possible. Therefore one might think that the valuation of this sort of company is reasonably straightforward.

However, it is clearly not! In December 2005 the Australian company Macquarie Bank launched a bid for the LSE at 580p per share. This was rejected out of hand by the company which described it as 'derisory'. In March 2006 the LSE then received a bid from NASDAQ, again rejected, at 980p per share. In April 2006, NASDAQ took a large stake in the LSE through purchases from large existing shareholders, at an average price of 1175p per share and in November increased the bid again to 1243p. So, the fair value of the company, as reflected in how much sophisticated investors were willing to pay, more than doubled in a four-month period.

Another example is the Irish Airline, Aer Lingus. In October 2006 it floated on the Dublin and London exchanges, valued at €1.13 billion. One week later, Ryanair launched a bid that valued the company at €1.48 billion. Could that much really have changed over the week so as to add €300 million to the value of the company?

The purpose of this chapter is to introduce simple models for valuing shares. The first section describes the contractual features of shares. Understanding these features is the first step. The second section describes how firms work with investment bankers to issue new securities. Investment banking is one of the most exciting, demanding and lucrative career opportunities in finance, so this part of the chapter may help you decide whether that career path appeals to you. The third section explains how investors trade securities in the secondary market, and it gives an overview of the major trading venues in the world.

The technical part of valuing shares begins in the fourth section. We continue the theme from earlier: the price of any financial asset equals the present value of future cash flows distributed to owners of that asset. Before we delve into the technical aspects of valuing shares, we begin with a description of the features that distinguish debt from equity, and preference shares from shares. In the case of both ordinary and preference shares, the most obvious source of cash flow is dividends. Therefore, this chapter offers a discussion of several models that calculate the price of a share by estimating and discounting the dividends that the share pays over a very long horizon. Next, we discuss how firms, with the help of their investment bankers, sell new securities to the public and how investors trade those securities with each other. Following our discussion of valuation models that calculate share prices based on discounted dividends, the final two sections examine alternative valuation models that do not focus exclusively on dividend payments.

LEARNING OBJECTIVES

After studying this chapter you should be able to:

- Describe the differences between preference and ordinary shares.
- Understand how investment bankers help firms issue equity securities in the primary market.
- List the major secondary markets in which investors trade shares.
- Calculate the estimated value of shares using zero, constant and variable growth models.
- Value an entire company using the free cash flow approach.
- List alternative approaches for pricing shares that do not rely on discounted cash flow analysis.

SMART FINANCE
Use the learning tools at www.cengage.co.uk/megginson

This chapter focuses on valuing shares. We begin by describing the essential features of these instruments, comparing and contrasting them with the features of bonds that we covered in the previous chapter. Then, we explain how firms, with the assistance of investment bankers, issue these securities to investors and how trades between investors occur on an ongoing basis once the securities have been issued. Next, we apply the information from this chapter's first two sections to the basic discounted cash flow valuation framework from Chapter 4 in order to develop a method for pricing shares. We introduce three simple approaches – the zero, constant and variable growth models – for valuing shares based on the dividend streams they pay over time. We also present the free cash flow approach for valuing the entire enterprise. Finally, we review some other popular share valuation measures, including book value, liquidation value and multiples.

5.1 THE ESSENTIAL FEATURES OF SHARES

Debt versus equity

Periodically, firms issue new securities to investors to raise capital by selling either of two broad types of securities to investors – debt or equity. Debt securities, such as bonds, generally offer investors a legally enforceable claim with cash flows that are either fixed or vary according to a predetermined formula. Debt holders typically have little say in how a firm conducts its business. Instead, the investors who purchase a firm's debt securities can force the firm into bankruptcy if it does not make scheduled interest and principal payments on time.

Equity securities, such as shares, are quite different. Firms issuing shares make no specific promises to investors about how much cash they will receive, or when. Loosely speaking, a firm distributes cash to shareholders if it is generating enough cash from its operations to pay expenses and to undertake new profitable investment opportunities. In other words, whether investors in shares receive any cash at all depends on how well the firm performs. Lacking a solid commitment from the firm to distribute cash, holders of shares cannot push a firm into bankruptcy simply because they are unhappy with the outcome of their investment. However, unlike bondholders, shareholders collectively own the company. Their shares entitle them to vote on important matters ranging from electing a board of directors that monitors senior management to restructuring the firm through mergers and acquisitions. When equity investors become dissatisfied with the returns they have earned on their shares, they may exercise their voting rights to oust incumbent management, or they may seek to influence how executives manage the firm in other ways.

The preceding two paragraphs should give you a sense that debt and equity are associated with very different marginal benefits and costs for investors. They differ in terms of both the risks they require investors to take and the potential rewards for taking those risks. Comparatively, debt securities offer investors a relatively safe and predictable return. But safety comes at a price. Bond returns are rarely high enough to generate a lot of wealth quickly, and bondholders exercise almost no direct influence on corporate decisions. Shareholders accept more risk than bondholders. We discuss this phenomenon of very different risk versus return experiences in Chapter 6. Because shareholders are asked to take large risks, they have the opportunity to exercise some control over corporate decisions through their voting rights, and they tend to earn higher returns (at least on average) than accrue to bond investors.

Whereas the last chapter focused on debt, in this chapter we turn our attention to equity. As a starting point, we look at a security that is a bit of a hybrid, having some resemblance to bonds and some to shares. That security is preference shares.

Preference shares

Some features of preference shares resemble those of debt. When a firm issues preference shares, it promises investors a fixed periodic cash payment, called a **dividend**, much like the semi-annual interest payments made to bondholders. Firms usually pay preference dividends on a quarterly basis. Like bondholders, preference shareholders do not have the right to vote on important corporate decisions, so they exercise almost no direct control over management. Preference shares are a claim that, in many respects, is senior to ordinary shares, meaning that preference shareholders have a higher priority claim on a firm's cash flows. For instance, most companies that issue preference shares are required to pay the promised dividend on those shares before they can pay a dividend on their ordinary shares. Similarly, most preference shares have a feature known as cumulative dividends, meaning that if a firm misses any preference dividend payments, it must catch up and pay preference shareholders for all the dividends they missed (along with the current dividend) before it can pay dividends on ordinary shares. In all these instances, a preference share seems more like debt than equity.

In other respects, a preference share looks more like equity than debt. From a tax perspective, preference dividends are treated like ordinary share dividends; neither can be treated as a tax-deductible expense for the firm. Interest payments on debt are tax deductible. Though preference shares are senior to ordinary shares in many ways, they hold a claim that is junior to bonds, meaning that preference shareholders hold a lower priority claim than bondholders. In particular, preference shareholders cannot take a firm to court for failure to pay dividends as bondholders can do if a firm misses interest or principal payments. Finally, most preference shares do not have a specific maturity date and can remain outstanding indefinitely, similar to ordinary shares.

In the United States, most recent issuance of preference shares has been by public utilities such as water and electricity companies. This arises from the regulatory controls on the return that these companies can provide to shareholders. In Europe, relatively few companies have significant amounts of preference shares. Using the Thomson ONE database, we see (from the report writer tool) that in Europe and Africa only some 300 or so companies (out of over 72 000) have preference shares with, on average, this representing less than €130 million per company. So, while preference shares are not unknown in Europe, they are neither very common nor very significant.

dividend
A periodic cash payment that firms make to investors who hold the firms' preference or ordinary shares.

Real World

While preference shares are not very common, they are used. Consider the sale in December 2006 of Pearson Government Solutions (PGS). The company, part of the Pearson Group, which publishes among other titles the *Financial Times*, restructured, and part of this involved the sale of non-core assets. PGS designs and runs call services, and was sold to Veritas Capital, a New York-based private equity firm, which purchased the company for $560 million in cash, $40 million in preference shares and a 10 per cent equity stake in the ongoing business.

Ordinary shares

Shareholders as residual claimants Because shareholders own the firm, they generally retain all the important decision rights concerning what the firm does and how it is governed. However, shareholders cannot receive cash distributions from the company unless the firm first pays what it owes to its creditors and preference shareholders. Because ordinary shareholders hold the right to receive only the cash flow that remains after all other claims against the firm have been satisfied, they are sometimes called **residual claimants**. Obviously, holding the most junior claim on a firm's assets and cash flows is very risky. For this reason, shareholders generally expect to earn a higher, though more variable, return on their investment than do bondholders or preference shareholders.

residual claimants
Investors who have the right to receive cash flows only after all other claimants have been satisfied. Shareholders are typically the residual claimants of corporations.

majority voting system
System that allows each shareholder to cast one vote per share for each open position on the board of directors.

Shareholder voting rights As residual claimants, shareholders receive several important rights. The most important is the right to vote at any shareholders' meeting. Most corporations have a single class of shares outstanding, and every shareholder has the same rights and responsibilities. Most corporations also have a **majority voting system**, which allows each shareholder to cast one vote per share for each open position on the board of directors. It stands to reason that the owners (or owner) of 50.1 per cent of the firm's shares can decide every contested issue and can elect the people they want to become directors. In practice, an investor or group of investors can control a corporation even if they own less than a majority of the outstanding shares. All the controlling group needs is a *majority of the votes cast* on a ballot issue, and in most corporate elections, many shareholders do not vote at all.

Companies occasionally have two or more outstanding classes of shares, usually with different voting rights for each class. In these cases, corporate insiders generally concentrate their holdings in the superior voting-share class. Ordinary investors hold relatively more of the inferior voting-share class. This dual-class share structure is more common in many other countries than it is in the United States, at least partly because both the New York Stock Exchange (NYSE) and the Securities and Exchange Commission (SEC) have at times discouraged American companies from adopting such structures. The internet search engine company Google is the most prominent recent example of a US firm choosing the dual-class structure. In its initial public offering, Google sold shares to outside investors who had one vote per share, while certain Google insiders received a special class of shares entitled to ten votes per share. A dual-class structure allows insiders to raise the capital they need to finance growth, without losing voting control.

The disparity between ownership of cash flow and ownership of voting which these dual class shares can induce is sometimes very large. A paper by Faccio and Lang in the *Journal of Financial Economics* in 2002 showed that for the Italian company, Unichem, the Agnelli family owned nearly 48 per cent of the votes but were entitled to under 10 per cent of the cash flows. Similarly, in Swedish companies the use of multiple share classes and pyramidal ownership can result in the effective ownership of companies vesting in a small number of shareholders. In general, dual-class shares are most common in Denmark, Finland, Germany, Italy, Norway, Sweden and Switzerland. We should not, however, necessarily conclude that dual-class share structures are inefficient or reduce firm value. Research by the European Central Bank (ECB *Discussion Paper 465*) shows that while there is a boost in a firm's value if it moves from a dual-class to a single class of share, there are no clear differences in terms of growth opportunities. The research suggests that firms that wish to raise equity capital are much more likely to adopt a single class of share, and, because of this, dual-class share structures will disappear over time.

Source: 'Moving the Market: Taubmans Give Up Control of
Sotheby's', *Wall Street Journal*, 9 September 2005.

Real World

Sotheby's, along with Christie's, dominate the world of fine art and antiques auctioneering. Sotheby's, however, were often seen to suffer due to the existence of a dual-share structure. In 2005 this was resolved, when the Taubman family and affiliates reduced their stake in Sotheby's from almost 22 per cent of total shares outstanding and 62 per cent of the votes to 12.4 per cent of both. This was achieved via their exchanging 14 million of their special Class B shares for 7.1 million in shares and $168 million in cash from the auction house. Chief executive officer, William Ruprecht, summed up the move as being one that enhanced flexibility and liquidity, saying: 'There are a lot more investors who will consider investing in Sotheby's when you have a single class of stock.'

Proxies and proxy contests Because most investors who own a few shares do not attend annual meetings to vote, they may sign **proxy statements** giving their votes to another party. The firm's current managers generally receive most of the shareholders' proxies, partly because managers can solicit them at company expense. Occasionally, when the ownership of the firm is widely dispersed, outsiders may try to gain control by waging a **proxy fight**, an attempt to solicit a sufficient number of votes to unseat existing directors.

A significant fraction of shareholders routinely fail to exercise their right to vote. In some cases, brokers and banks that hold shares in 'street name' are allowed to vote on behalf of their clients, and they almost always side with management. Recent studies have found that when managers submit proposals for shareholder votes and believe the votes will be close, they craft the proposal in a way that maximizes the votes cast by brokers and banks. Therefore, managers have a limited ability to manipulate the proxy process to obtain outcomes favourable to their own interests.

proxy statement
A document mailed to shareholders that describes the matters to be decided by a shareholder vote in a forthcoming annual meeting. Shareholders can sign their proxy statements and grant their voting rights to other parties.

proxy fight
A ploy used by outsiders to attempt to gain control of a firm by soliciting a sufficient number of votes to unseat existing directors.

Winning Seats on Heinz Board', *Financial Times*,
9 September 2006.

Real World

One of the largest and most bitter proxy fights in recent years took place over the future direction of Heinz, the manufacturer of baby food, ketchup and tinned foods. Throughout 2006 Nelson Peltz, who held just under 6 per cent of the shares of the company, promoted a plan for the future of the giant that was at radical odds with that of management. This proxy fight ultimately revolved around control of the board of directors, who could implement either plan. In the end, neither side was a clear winner: the management nominees were not all elected at the AGM, while Peltz and an ally gained seats. However, the control of the company remained in the hands of the incumbents.

Rights to dividends and other distributions A firm's board of directors decides whether to pay dividends or not. Most US corporations that pay dividends pay them quarterly, whereas the common practice in other developed countries is to pay dividends semi-annually or annually. Firms usually pay dividends in cash, but they may also make dividend payments using shares or (on rare occasions) merchandise.

Shareholders have no guarantee that the firm will pay dividends, but they nevertheless come to expect certain payments based on the historical dividend pattern of the firm. The dividend decision and its effect on firm valuation have perplexed researchers for decades, and we examine it in detail in Chapter 13.

Just as shareholders have no guarantee that they will receive dividends, they have no assurance they will receive any cash settlement in the event that the firm is liquidated. Because of limited liability, however, shareholders cannot lose more than they invest in the firm. Moreover, shareholders can receive unlimited returns through dividends and through the appreciation in the value of their holdings. In other words, although nothing is guaranteed, the *possible* rewards for providing equity capital can be considerable.

The equity section of the balance sheet Table 5.1 details the shareholders' equity accounts of Anglo European Beauty Corporation (ABC). As of 31 December 2006, ABC had only ordinary shares outstanding. During 2006, the company paid off the €247 million of preference shares that it had outstanding at the end of 2005 and did not issue any new preference shares in replacement. Several terms that appear in these accounts require an explanation, beginning with 'par value'. As discussed in Chapter 2, shares can be sold with or without **par value**, which in most developed countries is a rather archaic term having little real economic significance. However, laws in many countries prohibit firms from selling shares at a price below par value, and therefore there is a clear incentive to set this value low. For this reason, ABC follows a standard convention of setting par value quite low, at €0.20 per share, so that such laws are unlikely ever to prove a binding constraint.

At the end of 2006, ABC had 4 687 500 000 **shares authorized**, meaning that the firm's shareholders had given the ABC board of directors the right to sell up to this number of shares without further shareholder approval. At that time, there were 1 913 513 218 **shares issued** and outstanding (compared with 1 893 940 595 at year-end 2005), with a total par value of €382 702 644 (€0.20/share × 1 913 513 218 shares). The total book value of shares equals €14 248 million, so we calculate the amount of **additional paid-in capital**, or capital in excess of par value, that ABC received for these shares as €13 865 million (€7.25 per share). This equals the

par value (shares)
An arbitrary value assigned to shares on a firm's balance sheet.

shares authorized
The amount of a company's shares that shareholders and the board authorize the firm to sell to the public.

shares issued
Shares that have been issued or sold to the public.

additional paid-in capital
The difference between the price the company received when it sold shares in the primary market and the par value of the shares, multiplied by the number of shares sold. This represents the amount of money the firm received from selling shares, above and beyond the share's par value.

TABLE 5.1

Shareholders' equity accounts for ABC, at 31 December 2006 and 2005 (€ millions)

	2006	2005

Preference shares, par value €0.01 per share
  Shares authorized: 150 000 000
  Shares issued: (2005) 2 546 011
	–	€ 247

Shares, par value €0.20 per share
  Shares authorized: 4 687 500 000
  Shares issued: (2006: 1 913 513 218; 2005: 1 893 940 595)
	€14 248	12 400

Retained earnings	30 142	23 784
Less: Treasury shares, at cost Shares: (2006: 190 319 489; 2005: 131 041 411)	20 114	13 800
Less: Employee benefits trust, at cost (shares, 2005: 20 000 000)	–	1712
Less: Accumulated gains and losses not affecting retained earnings	662	295
Total shareholders' equity	**€23 614**	**€20 624**

difference between the €14 248 million book value and the €383 million par value. Since ABC's shares price was €126.39 per share at the end of December 2006, we determine that ABC's **market capitalization** on that date was €241.86 billion (€126.39/share × 1 914 000 000 shares outstanding).

In addition to the shares outstanding at the end of 2006, ABC has been aggressively repurchasing its shares in the open market for several years. The company repurchased 59.3 million shares worth €6.3 billion in 2006. The shares repurchased during 2006 was held as **treasury shares**, with a book value of €20 114 million on 31 December 2006. ABC holds these shares as part of its employee shares purchase plan.

Finally, ABC's accounts show that the firm has retained earnings of €30 142 million at year-end 2006. This represents the cumulative amount of profits that the firm has reinvested over the years. Don't be fooled by the €30.1 billion balance of this account. Retained earnings do not represent a pool of cash that the firm can use should a need for cash arise. Retained earnings simply reflect earnings that ABC reinvested in previous years.

market capitalization
The value of a company's shares that are owned by the shareholders: the total number of shares issued multiplied by the current price per share.

treasury shares
Ordinary shares that have been issued but are no longer outstanding because the firm repurchased them.

---

1 Why are shareholders viewed as 'residual owners'? What rights do they get in exchange for taking more risk than creditors and preference shareholders take?

2 Most large Japanese corporations hold their annual shareholders' meeting on the same day and require voting in person. Therefore, it is impossible for a shareholder who owns shares in more than one company to go to more than one annual meeting. What does this practice say about the importance and clout of individual shareholders in Japanese corporate governance?

3 Why would companies issue dual classes of shares with different voting rights?

CONCEPT REVIEW QUESTIONS

5.2 PRIMARY MARKETS AND ISSUING NEW SECURITIES

Before we turn to a discussion about how investors trade and price preference and ordinary shares, we offer a brief overview of how firms issue equity securities to investors. As previously noted, the primary market refers to the market in which firms originally issue new securities. Once the securities have been issued in the primary market, investors can trade them in the secondary market. In this section, we examine the primary market and how investment bankers help firms sell new securities. Section 5.3 looks at the secondary market.

Investment banks play an important role in helping firms raise long-term debt and equity financing in the world's capital markets. **investment banks** sell new security issues and assist and advise corporations about major financial transactions, such as mergers and acquisitions, in exchange for fees and commissions. During the past 20 years, and especially since 1990, the global investment banking industry has grown dramatically in scale and in the variety of services it provides to corporations. Furthermore, with the recent repeal in the United States of the Glass-Steagall Act, commercial banks formerly excluded from providing investment banking services can now enter that business. Investment banks headquartered in the United States dominate the top ranks of global in this sector firms. The US pre-eminence is at least partly a result of the US investment banking industry being deregulated much earlier than Europe's. In particular, the SEC forced US investment banks to end fixed share trading commissions in May 1975, which prompted both a competitive free-for-all and rapid growth in share trading volume and securities issuance. In contrast, British capital markets were not significantly deregulated until the 'Big Bang' reforms were

SMART PRACTICES VIDEO

Pierangelo Franzoni, Chief Investment Officer, MPS Asset Management, Ireland

How the market allocates capital via shares and bonds.

See the entire interview at
www.cengage.co.uk/megginson

investment banks
Financial institutions that assist firms in the process of issuing securities to investors. Investment banks also advise firms engaged in mergers and acquisitions, and they are active in the business of selling and trading securities in secondary markets.

implemented in 1986. Continental European (and Japanese) markets were opened fully only during the 1990s.

JP Morgan Chase, Morgan Stanley, Goldman Sachs, Citigroup and Merrill Lynch are the five US banks having the highest market share. Here we briefly review the key services provided by investment banks before, during and after security offerings. (We discuss this in greater detail in Chapter 11.)

Key investment banking activities

Investment banks provide a broad range of services to corporations. The three principal lines of business are:

- corporate finance
- trading
- asset management.

Of the three business lines, corporate finance enjoys the highest visibility and includes activities such as new security issues and merger and acquisitions (M&A) advisory work. Corporate finance tends to be the most profitable line of business, especially for more prestigious banks that can charge the highest underwriting and advisory fees. However, corporate finance generates less than one-quarter of the typical investment bank's revenues, and it is often much less.

Investment banks earn revenue from trading debt and equity securities in two important ways. First, they act as dealers, facilitating trade between unrelated parties and earning fees in return. Secondly, they hold inventories of securities and may make or lose money as inventory values fluctuate. Revenues generated from trading activities, on average, account for one-quarter of large banks' revenues.

Finally, asset management encompasses several different activities, including managing money for individuals with high net worth, operating and advising mutual funds, and managing pension funds. Although unglamorous, revenues from asset management exceed those from the other primary investment banking services.

The investment banker's role in equity issues

initial public offering (IPO)
A corporation offers its shares for sale to the public for the first time; the first public sale of company shares to outside investors.

seasoned equity offering (SEO)
An equity issue by a firm that already has shares outstanding.

negotiated offer
The issuing firm negotiates the terms of the offer directly with one investment bank.

competitively bid offer
The firm announces the terms of its intended equity sale, and investment banks bid for the business.

We now turn to the services which investment banks provide to companies issuing new securities. We focus on ordinary share issues, though the procedures for selling bonds and preference shares are essentially similar. Investment banks play several different roles throughout the securities offering process. For shares offerings, the complexity of the investment banker's job depends on (1) whether a firm is selling equity for the first time, and in the process, converting from private to public ownership, or (2) whether the firm has previously issued shares and is simply going back to the equity market to raise money. The first type of transaction is much more complex and is called an **initial public offering (IPO)**. The second type is known as a **seasoned (or secondary) equity offering (SEO)**, implying that the shares offered for sale have previously been 'seasoned' in the market. Below, we describe the investment banker's role in an IPO, though the description would change little for an SEO.

Although it is possible for firms to issue securities without the assistance of investment bankers, in practice, almost all firms enlist investment banks when they issue equity. Broadly speaking, firms can choose an investment banker in one of two ways. The most common approach is a **negotiated offer**, where, as the name implies, the issuing firm negotiates the terms of the offer directly with one investment bank. In the other approach, a **competitively bid offer**, the firm announces the terms of its intended equity sale, and investment banks bid for the business. The vast majority of equity sales are negotiated offerings rather than competitive offers. Firms issuing securities often enlist the services of more than one investment bank. In these cases, it is typical for one of the banks to be named the **lead underwriter**, and the other participating banks are known as co-managers.

Investment bankers sell equity under two types of contracts. In a **best efforts** arrangement, the investment bank makes no guarantee about the ultimate success of the offering. Instead, it promises to give its best effort to sell the firm's securities at the agreed-upon price, but if insufficient demand emerges for the issue, the firm withdraws it from the market. Best efforts offerings are most common for very small, high-risk companies. The investment bank receives a commission based on the number of shares sold in a best efforts deal.

By contrast, in a **firm-commitment** offering, the investment bank agrees to **underwrite** the issue, meaning that the bank actually purchases the shares from the company and resells them to investors. In theory, this arrangement requires the investment bank to bear the risk of inadequate demand for the firm's shares. Bankers mitigate this risk in two ways. First, the lead underwriter forms an **underwriting syndicate** consisting of many investment banks. These banks collectively purchase the firm's shares and market them, thereby spreading the risk exposure across the syndicate. Secondly, underwriters go to great lengths to determine whether sufficient demand for a new issue exists before it comes to market. They generally set the issue's offer price and take possession of the securities no more than a day or two before the issue date. With such research efforts before sale, the risk that the investment bank might not be able to sell the shares that it underwrites is small.

In firm-commitment offerings, investment banks receive compensation for their services via the **underwriting spread**, the difference between the price at which the banks purchase shares from firms (the net price) and the price at which they sell the shares to institutional and individual investors (the offer price). In some offerings, the underwriters receive additional compensation in the form of warrants that grant underwriters the right to buy shares of the issuing company at a fixed price. Underwriting fees can be quite substantial, especially for firms issuing equity for the first time. The vast majority of US initial public offerings have underwriting spreads of 7 per cent, although lower spreads are common in very large IPOs. For example, if a firm conducting an IPO wants to sell shares worth $100 million, it will receive $93 million in proceeds from the offer. The underwriter earns the gross spread of $7 million. At the other extreme, large debt offerings of well-known issuers have underwriting spreads of around 0.5 per cent.

lead underwriter
The investment bank that takes the primary role in assisting a firm in a public offering of securities.

best efforts
The investment bank promises to give its best effort to sell the firm's securities at the agreed-upon price; but if there is insufficient demand for the issue, then the firm withdraws it from the market.

firm-commitment
An offering in which the investment bank underwrites the company's securities and thereby guarantees that the company will successfully complete its sale of securities.

underwrite
The investment banker purchases shares from a firm and resells them to investors.

underwriting syndicate
Consists of many investment banks that collectively purchase the firm's shares and market them, thereby spreading the risk exposure across the syndicate.

underwriting spread
The difference between the net price and the offer price.

Real World

Even if a company arranges an underwritten share offering, things can still go wrong. Consider JAL, Japanese Airlines. In June 2006 they moved to place ¥147 trillion (nearly €1 billion) in a share offering. This represented nearly 40 per cent of the existing shares of the company. The monies were needed, among other things, to meet the payments on maturing hybrid securities, and an underwriting syndicate was set up led by Mizuho Securities and Goldman Sachs. However, in early July a main player in the syndicate pulled out. Nikko Citigroup refused to comment, but speculation was rife that demand for the shares would be low, forcing the underwriters to take the shares themselves. Controversy was also generated by the fact that the issue was announced the day after the AGM, where no mention of this issue had been made. The shares were eventually issued, but the price slumped 7 per cent between the time of announcement and the issue date.

Just what do investment banks do to earn their fees? Investment banks perform a wide variety of services, ranging from carrying out the analytical work required to price a new security offering, to assisting the firm with regulatory compliance, marketing the new issue, and developing an orderly market for the firm's securities once they begin trading. The chronology of a typical equity offering provides a useful framework for describing these services.

Services provided before the offering

Early in the process of preparing for an equity offering, an investment bank helps the firm file the necessary documents with regulators. These documents in essence provide the regulators with a great deal of information about the securities being offered, as well as the firm selling them. Preparing this document may sound like a rather trivial undertaking, but, in fact, it is one of the most time-consuming parts of the capital-raising process, especially for IPOs. When a firm files these documents, it must take great pains to be sure that the information provided is timely and accurate. Firms typically spend weeks with their bankers putting this document together. The investment bankers also prepare a **prospectus**, a document containing extensive details about the firm and the security it intends to offer. The investment bank circulates the prospectus among potential investors as a starting point for marketing the new issue.

prospectus
A document that describes the securities being offered for sale and the company offering them.

While it is preparing the necessary legal documents, the investment bank must also begin to estimate the value of the securities the firm intends to sell. Generally speaking, this task is simpler for debt than for equity, and of course, it is easier to value the equity of a company that already has shares trading on the market than to value shares in an IPO. Investment banks use a variety of methods to value IPO shares, including discounted cash flow models and market 'comparables', both of which are described later in this chapter. In the latter case, an investment bank compares the firm issuing equity with similar publicly traded firms, often estimating the value of the new shares issued by applying a price/earnings multiple to the issuing firm's current or projected per-share earnings or cash flow.

road show
A tour of major cities taken by a firm and its bankers several weeks before a scheduled offering.

Several weeks before the scheduled offering, the firm and its bankers tour major cities to solicit demand for the offering from investors. Called the **road show**, this gruelling process usually lasts a week or two. It gives managers the opportunity to pitch their business plan to prospective investors. The investment banker's goal in this process is to build a book of orders for shares that is greater (often many times greater) than the amount of shares the firm intends to sell. The expressions of interest by investors during the road show are not legally binding purchase agreements, and the investment bank typically does not commit to an offer price at this point. Instead, bankers give investors a range of prices at which they expect to sell the offer, based on their assessment of demand. Given the tentative nature of the demand expressed on the road show, the banker seeks to **oversubscribe** the offering to minimize the bank's underwriting risk. Naturally, one way to create excess demand for an offering is to set the offer price below a level that would have resulted in all investors being satisfied. The vast majority of IPOs are underpriced, meaning that once IPO shares begin trading, they do so at a price that is above the original offer price set by the firm and its bankers.

oversubscribe
When the investment banker builds a book of orders for shares that is greater than the amount of shares the firm intends to sell.

Services provided during and after the offering

The lead underwriter conducts the security offering, ensuring that, on the issue date, participating investors receive their shares as well as copies of the final prospectus. The lead underwriter exercises some discretion over the distribution of shares among syndicate members and the

selling group (investment banks that may assist in selling shares but are not formal members of the syndicate). In oversubscribed offerings, the lead underwriter may exercise a **Green Shoe option** (or overallotment option), which is essentially an option to sell as much as 15 per cent more shares than originally planned.

Once a firm's securities begin trading, the underwriter may engage in **price stabilization**. The reputation of an underwriter suffers if investors buy shares in an offering only to find that, once trading begins, the share price falls below the offer price. Because investment banks repeatedly approach investors with new share issues, it is very costly for them if investors lose confidence in the banks' ability to price new issues. Therefore, if a new issue begins to falter in the market, the investment bank may buy shares on its own account, keeping the market price at or slightly above the offer price for an indefinite period. With limited capital, investment banks do not want to take large positions in the shares they underwrite, so the threat of having to stabilize the market gives underwriters an additional incentive to underprice new issues at the outset.

After a share offering is successfully sold, the lead underwriter often serves as the principal market-maker for trading in the firm's shares. A market-maker maintains an inventory of the firm's shares and continuously quotes bid and ask prices at which it is willing to buy or sell to investors. In this role, the lead underwriter purchases shares from investors wishing to sell, and sells shares to investors wishing to buy, thus 'making a market' in the new issue. The lead underwriter also assigns one or more research analysts to cover the issuing firm. The research reports these analysts write (which naturally tend to be flattering) help generate additional interest in trading the firm's securities. In fact, some firms choose their investment bankers largely based on the reputation of the analyst who will cover the shares once it goes public. Table 5.2 summarizes the chronology of an investment bank's activities through the IPO process.

To conclude this section, we want to highlight the conflicts that investment bankers may face. Firms issuing securities, on the one hand, want to obtain the highest possible price for their shares (or bonds). Firms also want favourable coverage from securities analysts employed by their investment bankers. Investors, on the other hand, want to purchase securities at prices low enough to ensure that they will earn a high return on their investments. Investors also value dispassionate, unbiased advice from analysts. Investment bankers must therefore walk a thin line, both ethically and economically, to please their constituents. Firms issuing securities are wise to remember this. Investment bankers deal with investors, especially large institutional investors, on a repeated basis. They must approach this group each time a new offering comes to the market. In contrast, over its entire life, a firm conducts just a single IPO.[1]

selling group
Consists of investment banks that may assist in selling shares but are not formal members of the underwriting syndicate.

green Shoe option
An option to sell more shares than originally planned.

price stabilization
Purchase of shares by an investment bank when a new issue begins to falter in the market, keeping the market price at, or slightly above, the offer price.

SMART ETHICS VIDEO

Jay Ritter, University of Florida
'Lots of buyers were willing to give things to the underwriters in terms of, for instance, generating extra commissions business.'

See the entire interview at **www.cengage.co.uk/megginson**

---

4 What is the difference between a primary market and a secondary market?

5 What do firms and their investment bankers hope to learn on the road show?

6 How are underwriters compensated?

CONCEPT
REVIEW
QUESTIONS

---

[1] A chief executive officer of a company that conducted an IPO during the 1990s told us: 'You have two friends in an IPO: your lawyer and your accountant.' Notice that the investment banker didn't make the list.

TABLE 5.2
AUS IPO

Source: Katrina Ellis, Roni Michaely and Maureen O'Hara (June 2000) 'When the Underwriter is the Market Maker: An Examination of Trading in the IPO Aftermarket', *Journal of Finance* 55:1039–1074.

MAJOR STEPS AND MAIN EVENTS	ROLE OF THE UNDERWRITER
1 Initial step Select book-running manager and co-manager	Book-running manager's role includes forming the syndicate and overseeing the entire process
Letter of intent	Letter specifies gross spread and Green Shoe (overallotment) option, and protects underwriter from unexpected expenses. Does not guarantee price or number of shares to be issued.
2 Registration process Registration statement and due diligence	After conducting due diligence, underwriter files necessary registration statement with SEC.
Red herring	Once registration statement is filed with SEC, it is transformed into a preliminary prospectus (red herring).
3 Marketing Distribute prospectus; road show	Red herring is sent to salespeople and institutional investors around the country. Concurrently, company and underwriter conduct a road show, and the investment bank builds a book based on expressed demand – but not legally binding.
4 Pricing and allocation Pricing; allocation	Once registration statement has SEC approval, underwriter asks the SEC to accelerate the date on which the issue becomes effective. Firm and underwriter meet the day before the offer to determine price, number of shares and allocation of shares.
5 Aftermarket activities Stabilization; overallotment	Underwriter supports the shares price by purchasing option shares if price declines. If shares price goes up, underwriter uses overallotment option to cover short position. If price goes down, underwriter covers overallotment by buying shares in open market.
Research coverage	Final stage of IPO process begins 25 calendar days after IPO, when the 'quiet period' ends. Only after this can underwriter and other syndicate members comment on the value of the firm and provide earnings estimates.

5.3 SECONDARY MARKETS FOR EQUITY SECURITIES

The secondary market permits investors to execute transactions among themselves – it's the market-place where investors can easily sell their holdings to others. Helping investors facilitate these trades are brokers and dealers. Brokers help bring buyers and sellers together. Dealers maintain an inventory of shares and stand ready to buy and sell shares with investors at any time. Dealers are also called market-makers because of the important role they play in bringing about a smoothly functioning secondary market. Included among the secondary markets are the various securities exchanges, in which orders from buyers and sellers come together in one physical location for the purpose of executing trades.

In addition, there is the over-the-counter (OTC) market, made up of a network of brokers and dealers who execute transactions in securities that are not listed on any exchanges. The securities exchanges typically handle securities of larger, better-known companies, and the over-the-counter market handles many of the smaller, lesser-known firms. There are many exceptions to that rule, however. The exchanges are well-structured institutions that bring together the market forces of supply and demand. The OTC market is basically a mass telecommunications network linking buyers and sellers.

brokers
Agents who facilitate secondary market trading by bringing buyers and sellers together.

dealers
Also called market-makers, dealers facilitate secondary market trading by standing ready to buy and sell securities with other investors.

Securities exchanges

The market forces of supply and demand come together in the major stock exchanges. So-called listed securities trade on these exchanges and account for about 60 per cent of the total monetary volume of all shares traded in major markets. Much of the world trading in listed securities is carried out in these places and under a broad set of rules by people who are members of the exchange. Only the securities of companies that have met established listing requirements are traded on the exchange. Those firms must comply with various regulations to ensure that they do not make financial or legal misrepresentations to their shareholders. Trading takes place in an auction format that brings together buyers and sellers and allows them to make transactions at competitive prices. Firms must not only comply with the rules of the specific exchange, but also fulfil certain requirements as established by the relevant regulatory bodies.

The New York Stock Exchange and the London Stock Exchange are the largest and most prestigious in the world. Table 5.3 lists the 13 stock markets whose aggregate market capitalization each exceeded $1 trillion at the end of 2006.

listed securities
Securities that trade on major stock exchanges.

EXCHANGE	MARKET CAPITALIZATION OF DOMESTIC COMPANIES ($ MN)	NUMBER OF COMPANIES LISTED	RANK BY MARKET CAPITALIZATION	RANK BY NUMBER OF COMPANIES
New York	15 421 168	2 281	1	6
Tokyo	4 614 069	2 416	2	5
NASDAQ	3 865 004	3 133	3	4
London	3 794 310	3 256	4	3
Euronext	3 708 150	1 210	5	9
Osaka	3 121 590	1 074	6	12

TABLE 5.3

The largest stock exchanges by market capitalization at end-2006

Source: World Federation of Stock Exchanges.

TABLE 5.3 (cont.)

EXCHANGE	MARKET CAPITALIZATION OF DOMESTIC COMPANIES ($ mn)	NUMBER OF COMPANIES LISTED	RANK BY MARKET CAPITALIZATION	RANK BY NUMBER OF COMPANIES
Hong Kong	1 714 953	1 173	7	10
Toronto	1 700 708	3 842	8	2
Deutsche Börse	1 637 610	760	9	16
Swiss Exchange	1 212 308	348	10	26
OMX	1 123 042	794	11	15
Australian SE	1 095 858	1 829	12	7
Borsa Italiana	1 026 504	311	13	31

COMPARATIVE CORPORATE FINANCE
Pssst . . . Want to buy a stock (exchange)?

International investors have long been able to purchase the shares of many different types of companies that are listed on global stock markets. Recently, however, these same investors have been offered the opportunity to purchase shares in many of the stock exchanges themselves. Since the mid-1990s, no fewer than 15 of the 56 exchanges that are members of the World Federation of Exchanges have sold shares to investors and listed these shares for trading, usually on the exchange itself. Five of the largest non-US stock exchanges (London Stock Exchange, Euronext, Deutsche Börse, TSX Toronto Stock Exchange and Hong Kong Exchanges and Clearing) are listed companies, and several other exchanges are considering a public listing. In the United States, the New York Stock Exchange was listed in March 2006, and the Chicago Mercantile Exchange (where investors can trade a wide range of financial products, including commodities and foreign currencies) went public during 2003.

Although the idea of buying shares in a stock exchange may seem odd at first, there are strong business reasons for exchanges to become fully private, profit-making companies with their own boards of directors and publicly traded shares. Exchanges have traditionally been either mutual associations, owned by individuals and brokerage firms, or member-owned limited companies. Unfortunately, these structures have proven to be cumbersome in today's rapidly changing global financial markets, where the ability to make quick decisions and exploit fleeting opportunities is crucial. An additional problem was that exchanges wanting to undertake acquisitions had to pay for their targets with cash. Exchanges did not have publicly traded shares to use for payment. By setting themselves up as full-fledged corporations with listed shares, stock exchanges can make decisions quickly and use their shares as a currency for acquisitions. They can also adopt shares-based employee renumeration programmes.

No company has been a more enthusiastic advocate of public listing than Euronext NV, Europe's second-largest exchange (as measured by market capitalization). Formed by the merger of the Paris Bourse, the Amsterdam Stock Exchange and the Brussels Stock Exchange in September 2000, this company executed an initial public offering and listed shares (on Euronext) in July 2001. In early 2002, Euronext acquired the London International Financial Futures and Options Exchange and merged with the Lisbon Stock Exchange, bringing the total number of exchanges in the group to five. Throughout 2006 Euronext engaged in discussions with Deutsche Börse and NYSE to form a merged entity, NYSE eventually winning out subject to regulatory approval. The Italian exchange is also likely to join in the merged group. As the accompanying chart makes clear, Euronext shareholders also have reason to cheer the group's efforts. Their shares have retained their value far better since July 2001 than have other European shares.

How are the shares of exchange shares valued? Just like any other company's shares: investors forecast the per-share cash flows that the company will generate in the future, and then use an appropriate risk-adjusted discount rate to determine the present value of those cash flows. Based on the share price performance of Euronext, Deutsche Börse and other listed exchanges, we expect to see continued growth in the number of stock exchanges that sell their own services to public investors.

Share price performance of Euronext versus the CAC40, Eurostoxx50 and FTSE100, 2001-2006

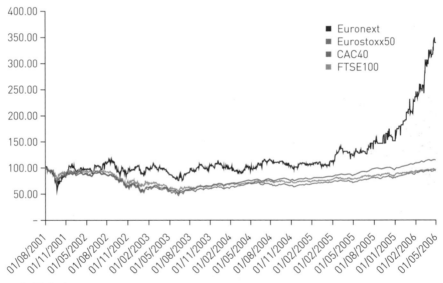

Source: EcoWin Database.

In addition to the NYSE, the USA has also seen the survival of a handful of smaller regional exchanges. The best known of these are the Midwest, Pacific, Philadelphia, Boston and Cincinnati exchanges. These exchanges deal primarily in securities with local and regional appeal. Most are modelled after the NYSE, but their membership and listing requirements are considerably more lenient. By contrast, there are no regional exchanges left in the UK – in 1973 the 11 remaining regional exchanges in Britain and Ireland merged into the London Stock Exchange. Regional exchanges still exist in Germany, Russia, Greece and other European countries, but in general the trend is towards consolidation and merger.

A recent study reported that 103 countries around the world had active stock markets at the turn of the century. As the Comparative Corporate Finance feature explains, more and more of these exchanges are converting to public ownership and making their shares available for public trading. Over 200 stock exchanges now have active trading status.

The over-the-counter (OTC) market

Unlike an exchange with a centralized location where trading occurs, the OTC market does not have a single, physical location. Instead, it exists as an intangible relationship between buyers and sellers of securities. Securities traded in this market are sometimes called unlisted securities. The market is linked by a mass telecommunications network. Unlike transactions in the physical securities exchanges, trade in the OTC market represents direct transactions between investors and securities dealers. That is, the investors buy from and sell to the securities dealers, whereas on the listed securities exchanges the brokers act as an intermediaries between buyers and sellers. More shares trade in the OTC market than on the exchanges. Dealers make markets in certain OTC securities by offering to either buy or sell them at stated prices.

National Association of Securities Dealers Automated Quotation (NASDAQ) System
An electronic system that facilitates trading in OTC shares.

In the USA a major part of the OTC market is made up of a select list of shares that trade on the **National Association of Securities Dealers Automated Quotation (NASDAQ) System**, which provides up-to-the-minute prices on thousands of shares. About 7000 issues actively trade in the NASDAQ portion of the OTC market, and about 2700 of these are part of the National Market System (NMS). The NMS is reserved for the biggest and most actively traded shares – those that generally have a national following. These securities are widely quoted, and trades are executed here about as quickly and inexpensively as on the floor of the NYSE. A number of large, well-known firms trade on the NASDAQ NMS, such as Intel, Oracle and Microsoft.

In the UK, OTC trading is also possible. One of the main players in this market is Plus Group (previously OFEX). Other systems also exist, relying on electronic communications networks to provide liquidity and tradability to smaller shares.

CONCEPT
REVIEW
QUESTIONS

7 When you buy shares in the secondary market, does the firm that issued the shares receive cash?

8 List several differences between the NYSE and the NASDAQ.

5.4 SHARE VALUATION

Pricing shares is much more difficult than valuing bonds. Unlike bonds, shares generally do not promise a fixed cash flow stream over time. The cash flows that accrue to shareholders are variable and uncertain. Because ordinary shares have no specific expiration date (as bonds do), estimates of the cash flows accruing to shareholders must necessarily take a long-term view. Whereas investors can easily calculate a bond's yield to maturity for an estimate of the return that the market requires on that bond, no mechanical calculation can provide an equally accurate picture of the market's required rate of return on a share.

Despite these difficulties, the principles involved in valuing shares mirror those we adopted to determine bond prices in Chapter 4. First, we estimate the cash flows that a shareholder receives over time. Secondly, we determine a discount rate that reflects the risk of those cash flows. Thirdly, we estimate the share price by calculating the present value. In other words, valuing shares is simply another application of Equation 4.1.

Preference share valuation

In Section 5.1, we noted that preference shares represent a hybrid security with some features of both debt and equity. Preference shares typically offer a fixed stream of cash flows with no specific maturity date. For that reason, we treat preference shares as a security with an infinite life in our valuation formulas.

In Chapter 3, you learned a shortcut for valuing a perpetuity – an annuity with an infinite life. For a perpetuity that makes annual cash payments, with the first payment arriving in one year, the present value equals the next payment divided by the discount rate. We have already met this model in Chapter 3, now the difference is that the value is that of a share. To find today's value of a preference share, PS_0, we use the equation for the present value of a perpetuity, dividing the preference dividend, D_p, by the required rate of return on the preference share, r_p:

$$PS_0 = \frac{Div_p}{r_p}$$

EQUATION 5.1

Applying the Model

Suppose that a particular preference share pays an annual dividend of €8. If the next dividend payment occurs in one year and the market's required return on this shares is 10 per cent, then its price will be €80 (€8 ÷ 0.10). If you know the price of a preference share, you can easily determine its yield by dividing the dividend by the price.

Equation 5.1 is valid if dividend payments arrive annually and if the next dividend payment comes in one year. However, simple modifications to the equation can handle dividend payments at other frequencies. For instance, for a preference share that pays quarterly dividends, simply divide the quarterly payment by a quarterly discount rate to calculate the price per share.

The basic share valuation equation

Like the value of bonds and preference shares, the value of an ordinary share equals the present value of all future benefits that investors expect it to provide. Unlike bonds, which have contractual cash flows, shares have cash flows that are non-contractual and unspecified. What are the benefits expected from a share? When you buy shares, you may expect to receive a periodic dividend payment from the firm, and you probably hope to sell the shares at a future date for more than their purchase price. But when you sell the shares, you are simply passing the rights to future benefits to the buyer. The buyer purchases the shares from you in the belief that the future benefits – dividends and capital gains – justify the purchase price. This logic extends to the next investor who buys the shares from the person who bought them from you, and so on, forever. Simply put, the value of a share equals the present value of all future dividends that investors expect the company to distribute. Firms can of course distribute cash directly to shareholders in forms other than dividends, and we discuss this in more detail in Chapter 13. For instance, firms may buy back their own shares. Also, when an acquiring firm buys a target, it may distribute cash to the target's shareholders. In this discussion, we assume for simplicity that cash payments always come in the form of dividends, but the logic of the argument does not change even if we allow for other forms of cash payments.

The easiest way to understand this argument is as follows. Suppose that an investor buys a share today for price P_0, receives a dividend equal to D_1 at the end of one year, and immediately sells the stock for price P_1. The return on this investment is easy to calculate:

$$r = \frac{D_1 + P_1 - P_0}{P_0}$$

The numerator of this expression equals the monetary profit or loss. Dividing that by the purchase price converts the return into percentage form. Rearranging this equation to solve for the current share price we get:

EQUATION 5.2

$$P_1 = \frac{D_1 + P_1}{(1 + r)}$$

This equation indicates that the value of a share today equals the present value of cash that the investor receives in one year. But what determines P_1, the selling price at the end of the year? Use Equation 5.2 again, changing the time subscripts to reflect that the price next year will equal the present value of the dividend and selling price received two years from now:

$$P_1 = \frac{D_2 + P_2}{(1 + r)}$$

Now, take this expression for P_1 and substitute it back into Equation 5.2:

$$P_0 = \frac{D_1 + \dfrac{D_2 + P_2}{(1 + r)}}{(1 + r)} = \frac{D_1}{(1 + r)} + \frac{D_2 + P_2}{(1 + r)}$$

We have an expression that says that the price of a share today equals the present value of the dividends it will pay over the next two years, plus the present value of the selling price in two years. Again we could ask, what determines the selling price in two years, P_2? By repeating the last two steps over and over, we can determine the price of a share today, as shown in Equation 5.3:

EQUATION 5.3

$$P_0 = \frac{D_1}{(1 + r)^1} + \frac{D_1}{(1 + r)^2} + \frac{D_1}{(1 + r)^3} + \dots$$

The price today equals the present value of the entire dividend stream that the shares will pay in the future. Now consider the problem that an investor faces if she tries to determine whether a particular share is overvalued or undervalued. In deciding whether to buy the shares, the investor must weigh the marginal benefits of owning the shares (the future dividend stream) against the marginal cost of acquiring it (the market price). As we will see in Chapter 7, finding shares or other financial assets with marginal benefits that exceed their marginal costs is very difficult.

To calculate the share price using Equation 5.3, an analyst must have two inputs: the future dividend amounts and the appropriate discount rate. Neither input is easy to estimate! The discount rate, or the rate of return required by the market on this share, depends on the share's risk. We defer a full discussion of how to measure risk and how to translate that into a required rate of return until Chapters 6 and 7. Here, we focus on the problem of estimating dividends. In most cases, analysts can formulate reasonably accurate estimates of dividends one year into the future. The real trick is to determine how quickly dividends will grow over time. Our discussion of share valuation centres on three possible scenarios for dividend growth – zero growth, constant growth and variable growth.

Zero growth

The simplest approach to dividend valuation, the **zero growth model**, assumes a constant dividend stream. If dividends do not grow, the dividend in each year is the same, D.

Plugging the constant value D for each dividend payment into Equation 5.3, you can see that the valuation formula simply reduces to the equation for the present value of a perpetuity:

$$P_0 = \frac{D}{r}$$

In this special case, the formula for valuing ordinary shares is essentially identical to that for valuing preference shares.

zero growth model
The simplest approach to share valuation that assumes a constant dividend stream.

Real World

One company that might appear to fit the zero growth model is the hamburger company, Wendy's International. Wendy's paid an uninterrupted string of $0.06 per share quarterly dividends from 1985 through 2003. After 18 years of identical dividends, investors might have reason to believe Wendy's will continue to pay the same dividend, $0.24 per year, forever. What price would they have be willing to pay for Wendy's shares?

The answer depends on Wendy's required rate of return. If investors demand a 10 per cent return on Wendy's shares, the shares should be worth $0.24 ÷ 0.10 = €2.40. In fact, in late 2003 and early 2004, Wendy's shares traded for just under $40 per share. This implies one of two things: either investors require a rate of return on Wendy's shares that is much less than 10 per cent, or they expect to receive higher cash distributions in the future than they have received in the past. As it turns out, investors who held Wendy's shares at the end of 2003 did not have to wait long to receive higher dividends, because the company doubled its payout in February 2004, to $0.12, increased it again in 2005 to $0.135 and then to $0.17 in 2006.

Source: Thomson ONE site and authors' own calculations.

Constant growth

Of all the relatively simple share valuation models that we consider in this chapter, the constant growth model probably sees the most use in practice. The model assumes that dividends will grow at a constant rate, g. If dividends grow at a constant rate forever, we calculate the value of that cash flow stream by using the formula for a growing perpetuity, given in Chapter 3. Denoting next year's dividend as D_1, we determine the value today of a share that pays a dividend growing at a constant rate:

$$P_0 = \frac{D_1}{r-g}$$

EQUATION 5.4

Gordon growth model
Values a share under the assumption that dividends grow at a constant rate forever.

The constant growth model in Equation 5.4 is commonly called the **Gordon growth model**, after Myron Gordon, who popularized this formula during the 1960s and 1970s.

Applying the Model

An example of a company that has seen stable dividend growth over the years is Arriva PLC, the UK-based operator of bus and train services. In general over the past ten years both its annual and interim dividends have grown by approximately 5 per cent. Suppose that investors expect Arriva to pay a dividend next year of £0.1995 per share, and they expect that dividend to continue growing at 5 per cent per year indefinitely. What would they pay for Arriva shares?

We can find out that the average return over the last three years on similar shares to Arriva is approximately 9 per cent. Given that, and substituting into the constant growth model, Equation 5.4, the result suggests that Arriva's share price in pence should be the following:

$$P_0 = \frac{D}{r-g} = \frac{0.1995}{0.09 - 0.05} = 498.75$$

In fact, at the ex-dividend date (the date when a shareholder has to be on the record to receive the dividend), Arriva shares traded at approximately £6.30, so the growth model appears to do a fairly good job of predicting price. Clearly, however, it is not a perfect model.

We do not want to overstate the accuracy of the constant growth model. We based our calculations on a reasonable set of assumptions, using the long-run growth rate in dividends for g and an estimate of the required rate of return on utility shares for r. By making small adjustments to the dividend, the required rate of return or the growth rate, we could easily obtain an estimate for Arriva's shares that matches the market price. But we could also obtain a very different price with an equally reasonable set of assumptions. For instance, increasing the required rate of return from 9 per cent to 9.5 per cent and decreasing the dividend growth rate from 5 per cent to 4 per cent decreases the price to £3.62! Obviously, analysts want to estimate the inputs for Equation 5.4 as precisely as possible, but the amount of uncertainty inherent in estimating required rates of return and growth rates makes obtaining precise valuations very difficult.

Nevertheless, the constant growth model provides a useful way to frame share valuation problems, highlighting the important inputs and, in some cases, providing price estimates that seem fairly reasonable. But the model should not be applied blindly to all types of firms – especially not to those enjoying rapid, albeit temporary, growth.

Variable growth

variable growth model
Assumes that the dividend growth rate will vary during different periods of time, when calculating the value of a firm's shares.

The zero and constant growth share valuation models just presented do not allow for any shift in expected growth rates. Many firms go through periods of relatively fast growth, followed by a period of more stable growth. Valuing the shares of such a firm requires a **variable growth model**, one in which the dividend growth rate can vary. Using our earlier notation, let D_0 equal the last or most recent per-share dividend paid, g_1 equal the initial (fast) growth rate of dividends, g_2 equal the subsequent (stable) growth rate of dividends and n equal the number of years in the initial growth period. We can write the general equation for the variable growth model as follows:

$$P_0 = \left\{ \frac{D_0(1+g_1)^1}{(1+r)^1} + \frac{D_0(1+g_1)^2}{(1+r)^2} + \dots + \frac{D_0(1+g_1)^n}{(1+r)^n} \right\}$$
$$+ \left\{ \frac{1}{(1+r)^n} \times \frac{D_{n+1}}{r-g_2} \right\}$$

EQUATION 5.5

The first part of the equation calculates the present value of the dividends expected during the initial fast-growth period. The last term, $D_{N+1} \div (r-g_2)$, equals the value, *as of the end of the fast-growth stage*, of all dividends that arrive after year N. To calculate the *present value* of this growing perpetuity, we must multiply the last term by $1 \div (1+r)^N$.

SMART CONCEPTS

See the concept explained step-by-step at **www.cengage.co.uk/ megginson**

Applying the Model

Imagine that a food company develops a new carbohydrate-free ice cream. As the popularity of this product increases, the firm (unlike its customers) grows quite rapidly, perhaps 20 per cent per year. Over time, as the market share of this new food increases, the firm's growth rate will reach a steady state. At that point, the firm may grow at the same rate as the overall economy, perhaps 5 per cent per year. Assume that the market's required rate of return on this share is 14 per cent.

To value this firm's shares, you need to break the future stream of cash flows into two parts. The first consists of the period of rapid growth, and the second is the constant-growth phase. Suppose that the firm's most recent (Year 0) dividend was €2 per share. You anticipate that the firm will increase the dividend by 20 per cent per year for the next three years. After that period the dividend will grow at 5 per cent per year indefinitely. The expected dividend stream over the next seven years looks like this:

FAST GROWTH PHASE (g_1 = 20%)		STABLE GROWTH PHASE (g_2 = 5%)	
Year 0	€2.00	Year 4	€3.63
Year 1	2.40	Year 5	3.81
Year 2	2.88	Year 6	4.00
Year 3	3.46	Year 7	4.20

The value of the dividends during the fast growth phase is calculated as follows:

$$PVfast = \left\{ \frac{2.40}{(1.14)^1} + \frac{2.88}{(1.14)^2} + \frac{3.46}{(1.14)^3} \right\}$$
$$= €6.66$$

The stable growth phase begins with the dividend paid four years from now. The final term of Equation 5.5 is similar to Equation 5.4, which indicates that the value of a constant-growth share at time t equals the dividend a year later, at time $t + 1$, divided by the difference between the required rate of return and the growth rate. Applying that formula here means valuing the shares at the end of Year 3, just before the constant-growth phase begins:

$$PV3 = \frac{3.63}{0.14 - 0.05}$$

$$= €40.33$$

Don't forget that €40.33 is the estimated price of the share *three years from now*. Today's present value equals €40.33 ÷ $(1.14)^3$ = €27.22. This represents the value today of all dividends that occur in Year 4 and beyond. Putting the two pieces together, we get the following:

$$PV0 = 6.66 + \frac{40.33}{(1.14)^3} = 6.66 + 27.22 = €33.88$$

Figure 5.1 depicts a time line for this calculation. The following single algebraic expression shows the same information in a more compact form:

$$P_0 = \left\{ \frac{2.40}{(1.14)^1} + \frac{2.88}{(1.14)^2} + \frac{3.46 + 40.33}{(1.14)^3} \right\} = €33.88$$

The numerator of the last term contains both the final dividend payment of the fast-growth phase, €3.46, and the present value *as of the end of Year 3* of all future dividends, €40.33. The value of the firm's shares using the variable growth model is €33.88.

FIGURE 5.1

Valuing a share using the variable growth model

The share's value consists of (1) the present value of dividends during the three-year rapid-growth phase and (2) the present value of the constant-growth perpetuity which begins in four years.

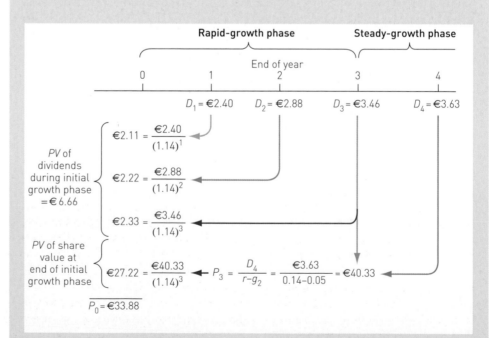

How to estimate growth

By now it should be apparent that a central component in many share pricing models is the growth rate. Unfortunately, analysts face a tremendous challenge in estimating a firm's growth rate, whether that growth rate refers to dividends, earnings, sales or almost any other measure of financial performance. A firm's rate of growth depends on several factors. Among the most important, however, are the size of the investments it makes in new and existing projects and the rate of return those investments earn.

A simple, but rather naïve method for estimating how fast a firm will grow uses information from financial statements. This approach acknowledges the importance of new investments in driving future growth. First, calculate the magnitude of new investments that the firm can make by determining its retention rate, *rr*, the fraction of the firm's earnings that it retains. Secondly, calculate the firm's return on equity, ROE (see Chapter 2), to estimate the rate of return that new investments will generate. The product of those two values is the firm's growth rate, *g*.

$$g = rr \times ROE$$

EQUATION 5.6

Applying the Model

Simon Manufacturing traditionally retains 75 per cent of its earnings to finance new investments and pays out 25 per cent as dividends. Last year, Simon's earnings available for shareholders were €44.6 million. The book value of its share equity was €297.33 million, resulting in a return on equity of 15 per cent. Substituting into Equation 5.6 and multiplying the retention rate by the return on equity, we estimate Simon's growth rate:

$$G = 0.75 \times 0.15 = 0.1125$$

The resulting estimate of Simon Manufacturing's growth rate is 11.25 per cent.

An alternative approach to estimating growth rates makes use of historical data. Analysts track a firm's sales, earnings and dividends over several years in an attempt to identify growth trends. But how well do growth rates from the past predict growth rates in the future? Unfortunately, the relationship between past and future growth rates for most firms is surprisingly weak. The fact that growth rates are largely unpredictable should not come as a great surprise. One of the most fundamental ideas in economics is that competition limits the ability of a firm to generate abnormally high profits for a sustained period. When one firm identifies a profitable business opportunity, people notice, and entrepreneurs (or other companies) attempt to enter the same business. As more and more firms enter, profits (or the growth rate in profits) fall. At some point, if the industry becomes sufficiently competitive, profits fall to such a low level that some firms exit. As firms exit, profits for the remaining firms rise again. The constant pressure created by these competitive forces means that it is rare to observe a firm with a consistent, long-term growth trend. Perhaps one reason that companies such as Microsoft and Intel are so well known is that their histories of exceptional long-run growth are so uncommon. Ultimately no company can grow, in the long run, at a rate that exceeds the real rate of world GNP: if it were to do so then the result would be that the value of the company would exceed that of the entire planet!

What if there are no dividends?

After seeing the different versions of the dividend growth model, students usually ask, 'What about firms that don't pay dividends?' Though many large, well-established firms pay regular dividends, the majority of firms do not pay dividends at all. Of the more than 5000 US companies listed on the NYSE, AMEX and NASDAQ, as many as 80 per cent pay no cash dividends in a given year. The percentage is different in Europe, with typically over 30 per cent paying dividends. Younger firms with excellent growth prospects are less likely to pay dividends than are more mature firms, and recent decades have seen tremendous growth in the number of young, high-growth companies.

Can we apply the share valuation models covered thus far to firms that pay no dividends? Yes and no. On the yes side, firms that do not currently pay dividends will begin paying them in the future. In fact, it is arguable that companies will always have to pay dividends, as from an economic and strategy perspective companies cannot keep reinvesting cash in projects. This will be discussed in more detail in the chapter on dividends. In that case, we simply modify the equations presented earlier to reflect that the firm pays its first dividend, not in one year, but several years in the future. However, from an entirely practical standpoint, predicting when firms will begin paying dividends and what the dollar value of those far-off dividends will be is extremely difficult.

What happens if a company never plans to pay a dividend or otherwise to distribute cash to investors? Our answer to this question is that for a share to have value, there must be an expectation that the firm will distribute cash in some form to investors at some point in the future. That cash could come in the form of dividends or share repurchases. If the firm is acquired by another company for cash, the cash payment comes when the acquiring firm purchases the shares of the target. Investors must believe that they will receive cash at some point in the future.

Real World

Source: *Financial Times*, multiple issues.

The pressure to pay dividends eventually can become intense. For many years Microsoft did not pay a dividend, arguing instead that the company was better off retaining the cash for future investment and as a buffer. Bill Gates for many years stated that he was 'proud of our conservatism'. Other attitudes are stronger: in 2003 Michael O'Leary, the CEO of Ryanair stated: 'We are never paying a dividend as long as I live and breathe and as long as I'm the largest individual shareholder.' Yet, even these iconic companies with strong leaders have submitted to the desire of shareholders to pay dividends – Microsoft paid a dividend in 2003 and Ryanair began discussions on paying one in 2007. It's hard to buck the market.

CONCEPT REVIEW QUESTIONS

9 Why is it appropriate to use the perpetuity formula from Chapter 3 to estimate the value of preference shares?

10 When a shareholder sells shares, what is being sold? What gives a share value?

11 What would happen to the price of Arriva if the market's required return on its shares increased?

5.5 VALUING THE ENTERPRISE: THE FREE CASH FLOW APPROACH

One way to deal with the valuation challenges presented by a firm that does not pay dividends is to value the firm's ability to generate cash rather than try to value only the firm's shares. The advantage of this procedure is that it requires no assumptions about when the firm distributes cash dividends to shareholders. Instead, when using the free cash flow approach, we begin by asking, what is the total operating cash flow generated by a firm? Next, we subtract from the firm's operating cash flow the amount needed to fund new investments in both fixed assets and current assets. The difference is total **free cash flow (FCF)**. Free cash flow, as noted in Chapter 2, represents the cash amount that a firm could distribute to investors after meeting all its other obligations. Note that we used the word 'investors' in the previous sentence. Total free cash flow is the amount that the firm could distribute to all types of investors, including bondholders, preference shareholders and ordinary shareholders. Once we have estimates of the FCFs that a firm will generate over time, we can discount them at an appropriate rate to obtain an estimate of the total enterprise value.

But what do we mean by 'an appropriate discount rate'? This is a subtle issue that we discuss in much greater detail in Chapter 10. To understand the main idea, recall that FCF represents the total cash available for all investors. We suspect that debt is not as risky as preference shares, and that these are not as risky as ordinary shares. This means that bondholders, preference shareholders and ordinary shareholders each have a different required return in mind when they buy a firm's securities. Somehow we have to capture these varying required rates of return to come up with a single discount rate to apply to free cash flow, the aggregate amount available for all three types of investors. The solution to this problem is known as the **weighted average cost of capital (WACC)**. The WACC is the after-tax, weighted average required return on all types of securities issued by the firm, where the weights equal the percentage of each type of financing in the firm's overall capital structure. For example, suppose that a firm finances its operation with 50 per cent debt and 50 per cent equity. Suppose it pays an after-tax return of 8 per cent on its outstanding debt and that investors require a 16 per cent return on the firm's shares. The WACC for this firm would be calculated as follows:

$$\text{WACC} = (0.5 \times 8\%) + (0.5 \times 16\%) = 12\%$$

If we obtain forecasts of the FCFs, and if we discount those cash flows at a 12 per cent rate, the resulting present value is an estimate of the total value of the firm, which we denote V_F.

When analysts value free cash flows, they use some of the same types of models that we have used to value other kinds of income. We could assume that a firm's free cash flows will experience zero, constant or variable growth. In each instance, the procedures and equations would be the same as those introduced earlier for dividends, except we would now substitute FCF for dividends.

Remember, our goal in using the free cash flow approach is to develop a method for valuing a firm's shares without making assumptions about its dividends. The free cash flow approach begins by estimating the total value of the firm. To find out what the firm's shares are worth, V_S, we subtract from the total enterprise value, V_F, the value of the firm's debt, V_D, and the value of the firm's preference shares, V_P. Equation 5.7 depicts this relationship:

$$V_s = V_f - V_d \times V_p$$

We already know how to value bonds and preferred shares, so this step is relatively straightforward. Once we subtract the value of debt and preference shares from the total

free cash flow (FCF)
The net amount of cash flow remaining after the firm has met all operating needs and paid for investments, both long-term (fixed) and short-term (current). Represents the cash amount that a firm could distribute to investors after meeting all its other obligations.

weighted average cost of capital (WACC)
The after-tax, weighted average required return on all types of securities issued by a firm, in which the weights equal the percentage of each type of financing in a firm's overall capital structure.

SMART EXCEL

See this problem explained in Excel at www.cengage.co.uk/megginson

EQUATION 5.7

enterprise value, the remainder equals the total value of the firm's shares. Simply divide this total by the number of shares outstanding to calculate the value per share, P_0.

Applying the Model

Had a good steak lately? One of the better-known purveyors of high-quality steak in the USA is Morton's of Chicago, operated by Morton's Restaurant Group (MRG). Its shares traded in the $20–$25 range in the first quarter of 2001. At the end of 2000, Morton's had debt with a market value, V_D, of about $66 million, no preference shares ($V_P = 0$) and 4 148 002 shares outstanding. Its year-2000 free cash flow, calculated using the techniques presented in Chapter 2, was about $4.8 million. Its revenues and operating profits both grew at compound annual rates of about 14 per cent between 1998 and 2000. Indeed, many consumers were returning to beef during that period. At the same time the steak-house market was growing, competition was beginning to heat up. We assume that Morton's will experience about 14 per cent annual growth in FCF from 2000 to 2004, followed by 7 per cent annual growth thereafter, because of increasing competition as well as changing consumer tastes and preferences. A rough estimate of Morton's WACC of 11 per cent is deemed applicable in this valuation.

Morton's forecast free cash flow for the fast growth period, 2000 to 2004, and for the year 2005, which begins the infinite-lived period of stable growth, are calculated in the following table:

END OF YEAR	GROWTH STATUS	GROWTH RATE [%]	FCF CALCULATION	FCF
2000	Historic	Given	€4 800 000	
2001	Fast	14	€4 800 000 × (1.14)^1 = €5 472 000	
2002	Fast	14	€4 800 000 × (1.14)^2 = €6 238 080	
2003	Fast	14	€4 800 000 × (1.14)^3 = €7 111 411	
2004	Fast	14	€4 800 000 × (1.14)^4 = €8 107 009	
2005	Stable	7	€8 107 009 × (1.07)^1 = €8 674 499	

Replacing dividends with free cash flow in Equation 5.5, and substituting $N = 4$, $r = 0.11$, and $g_2 = 0.07$, we can now estimate Morton's enterprise value at the beginning of 2001, V_F:

$$Vf = \frac{5472000}{(1.11)} + \frac{6238080}{(1.11)^2} + \frac{7111411}{(1.11)^3} + \frac{8107009}{(1.11)^4}$$
$$+ \left[\frac{1}{(1.11)^4} \times \frac{8674499}{(0.11 - 0.07)} \right]$$
$$= \$163\ 386\ 865$$

Substituting Morton's enterprise value of $163 386 865, its debt value, V_D, of $66 million and its preference share value, V_P, of $0 into Equation 5.7, we derive its total share value, V_S:

$$Vs = 163386865 - 66000000 - 0 = \$97\ 386\ 865$$

Dividing the total share value by the 4 148 002 shares outstanding at the beginning of 2001, we get the per-share value of Morton's shares, P_{2001}.

$$\frac{97386865}{4148002} = \$23.48$$

Our estimate of Morton's total share value at the beginning of 2001 of $97 386 865, or $23.48 per share, is within its actual trading range of $20–25 per share during the first quarter of 2001.[2]

The free cash flow approach offers an alternative to the dividend discount model that is especially useful when valuing shares that pay no dividends. Security analysts also estimate share values using several models that do not rely on the discounted cash flow methods we have studied so far. We next take a look at some of those alternatives.

CONCEPT REVIEW QUESTIONS

12 How can the free cash flow approach to valuing an enterprise be used to resolve the valuation challenge presented by firms that do not pay dividends? Compare and contrast this model with the dividend valuation model.

13 Can we use any of the models above when the company is neither paying dividends nor has positive cash flow? What assumptions would we need to make to apply some of these models?

5.6 OTHER APPROACHES TO SHARE VALUATION

Practitioners employ many different approaches to valuing shares. The more popular include the use of book value, liquidation value and some type of price/earnings multiple.

Book value

Book value refers to the value of a firm's equity shown on its balance sheet. Calculated using generally accepted accounting principles (GAAP), the book value of equity reflects the historical cost of the firm's assets, adjusted for depreciation, net of the firm's liabilities. Because of its backward-looking emphasis on historical cost figures,

book value
The value of a firm's equity as recorded on the firm's balance sheet.

---

[2] Here's an interesting postscript for this example. As it was for many businesses, 2001 was a tough year for Morton's. The company experienced significant declines in revenues, earnings and cash flows, highlighting the difficulties we mentioned earlier in predicting how fast a firm will grow over time. By the first quarter of 2002, Morton's stock had fallen by roughly 75 per cent, trading at times for less than $10 per share. However, some rather important investors thought Morton's was a bargain at that price. The company received a number of acquisition bids from private investors. Morton's board accepted an offer of $17 per share from the private equity group Castle Harlan, Inc. The board had rejected an earlier $17 per share offer from Carl Icahn after Castle responded by increasing its offer from $16 to $17. In fact, Castle raised its bid four times in response to bids from Icahn. The total offer was $71.2 million for 66 restaurants that generated revenues of $233 million in 2001.

book value usually provides a conservative estimate of true market value. Book value is usually less than market value in part because book value does not incorporate information about a firm's potential to generate cash flows in the future. An exception to this general rule occurs when firms experience financial distress. In some cases, such as when a firm's earnings prospects are very poor, the book value of equity may actually exceed its market value.

Liquidation value

To calculate liquidation value, analysts estimate the amount of cash that remains if the firm's assets are sold and all liabilities paid. Liquidation value may be more or less than book value, depending on the marketability of the firm's assets and the depreciation charges that have been assessed against fixed assets. For example, an important asset on many corporate balance sheets is real estate. The value of raw land appears on the balance sheet at historical cost, but, in many cases, its market value is much higher. In that instance, liquidation value exceeds book value. In contrast,

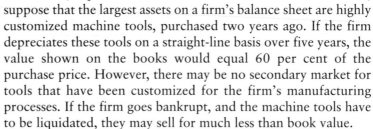

suppose that the largest assets on a firm's balance sheet are highly customized machine tools, purchased two years ago. If the firm depreciates these tools on a straight-line basis over five years, the value shown on the books would equal 60 per cent of the purchase price. However, there may be no secondary market for tools that have been customized for the firm's manufacturing processes. If the firm goes bankrupt, and the machine tools have to be liquidated, they may sell for much less than book value.

Price/earnings multiples

As noted in Chapter 2, the price/earnings (P/E) ratio reflects the amount investors are willing to pay for each euro of earnings. The P/E simply equals the current share price divided by annual earnings per share (EPS). The EPS used in the denominator of the P/E ratio may reflect either the earnings that analysts expect a firm to generate over the next year or earnings from the previous year. Analysts refer to 'leading' or 'trailing' P/E ratios, depending on whether the earnings number in the denominator is a forecast or historical value. An analyst using this method to value a share might proceed as follows. First, the analyst forecasts what the firm's EPS will be in the next quarter or year. Secondly, the analyst calculates the average P/E ratio for a group of 'comparable firms' in the same industry. Thirdly, the analyst obtains an estimate of the share price by multiplying the earnings forecast by the average or median P/E ratio for comparable firms.

Source: Adapted from 'Adecco offers €636m for DIS', *Financial Times*, 10 January 2006.

Real World

What is the value of a company that has next to no staff? In the world of temporary staffing, companies typically operate with very small head offices compared to the number of staff that they place with client firms. In 2006 two large European companies in this area merged. Adecco and DIS were both based in Germany, with Adecco trading at a P/E ratio of 20. In January 2006 Adecco offered over €600 million for DIS. Analysts however were concerned, noting that the valuation placed DIS on a P/E ratio of 31. One analyst stated that 'What investors have to decide is whether the DIS management can make a real difference to Adecco'.

Though P/E ratios are widely quoted in the financial press, interpreting them can be difficult. Stock analysts frequently tie a firm's P/E ratio to its growth prospects, using logic similar to the following. Suppose one firm has a P/E ratio of 50, and another has a P/E of 20. Why would investors willingly pay €50 per euro of earnings for the first company and only €20 per euro of earnings for the second? One possibility is that investors expect the first firm's earnings to grow more rapidly than those of the second firm.

To see this relationship more clearly, look again at Equation 5.4, which indicates that the price of a share depends on three variables – the dividend next period, the dividend growth rate and the required rate of return on the share. We can modify this formula by assuming that a firm pays out a constant percentage of its earnings as dividends. If we denote this payout percentage as d and next year's earnings per share as E_1, we can rewrite Equation 5.4 as follows:

$$P_0 = \frac{dE_1}{r - g}$$

where we replace the dividend next year in the numerator with the payout ratio times earnings next year. Now, divide both sides of this equation by E_1 to obtain the following:

$$\frac{P_0}{E_1} = \frac{d}{r - g}$$

On the left-hand side is the P/E ratio using next period's earnings. Notice that if the value of g increases, so does the P/E ratio. That provides some justification for the common notion that shares with high P/E ratios have high growth potential. However, the equation illustrates that either an increase in the dividend payout or a decrease in the required rate of return also increases the P/E ratio. Therefore, when comparing P/E ratios of different firms, we cannot conclude that the firm with the higher P/E ratio necessarily has better growth prospects. In addition, interpreting a P/E ratio is virtually impossible when the firm's earnings are negative or close to zero.

SMART IDEAS VIDEO

Robert Shiller, Yale University
'When the P/E ratio is high it's typically justified by an argument that earnings will go up in the future.'

See the entire interview at **www.cengage.co.uk/megginson**

Despite the difficulties associated with P/E ratios, analysts frequently use them to make rough value assessments. For instance, an analyst might calculate the average P/E ratio in a particular industry and then compare that average with the P/E ratio for a specific firm. If a particular share's P/E ratio falls substantially above (below) the industry average, the analyst might suspect that the share is overvalued (undervalued). In the same way, analysts sometimes look at the aggregate P/E ratio for the entire stock market to make judgements about whether shares generally are overvalued or undervalued.

Real World

A good instance of the interaction of markets and companies' P/E ratios was discussed in the *Financial Times* at the end of January 2007.

The article dissected the spectacular growth of the Shanghai Stock Exchange, and noted that much of the growth in share values was a reasonable response to future earnings potential. However, a worrying trend has emerged in the relationship between the P/E ratios of companies with dual listings. Companies that are dual listed typically have a P/E ratio on the Hong Kong Stock Exchange of around 18, while the exact same companies typically have a P/E ratio of 33 on the Shanghai Stock Exchange. The author of the article concluded that this is a classic case of unjustified share price growth. The previous collapse of the Shanghai exchange values in 2001 was shortly after a similar gap in values opened up.

And indeed, in late February and early March 2007, the Chinese market 'wobbled' and precipitated global market jitters.

CONCEPT REVIEW QUESTIONS

14 Why might the terms 'book value' and 'liquidation value', used to determine the value of a firm, be characterized as viewing it as 'dead rather than alive'? Explain why those views are inconsistent with the discounted cash flow valuation models.

15 Why is it dangerous to conclude that a firm with a high P/E ratio will probably grow faster than a firm with a lower P/E ratio?

5.7 SUMMARY AND CONCLUSIONS

- Preference shares have both debt and equity-like features and do not convey an ownership position in the firm.

- Ordinary shares represent a residual claim on a firm's cash flows, and shareholders have the right to vote on corporate matters.

- Stock markets can be classified as either primary or secondary. Shares are sold for the first time in the primary market, but after that, trading occurs in the secondary market.

- Investment bankers play an important role in helping firms issue new securities.

- Shares trade both on organized exchanges and in electronic over-the-counter markets.

- The same principles apply to the valuation of preference and ordinary shares. The value of a share depends on the cash flow that the share pays to its owner over time.

- Because preference shares pay a constant dividend with no specific expiration date, they can be valued using the perpetuity formula from Chapter 3.

- The approach used to valuing shares depends on investors' expectations of dividend growth. Zero dividend growth, constant dividend growth and variable dividend growth can all be incorporated into the basic valuation approach.

- Estimating dividend growth is very difficult. A starting point is to multiply the retention rate times the return on equity.

- Analysts use the free cash flow approach to value the entire enterprise. From that they derive a price per share.

- Other approaches to valuation rely on book value, liquidation value or price/earnings multiples.

INTERNET RESOURCES

For updates to links in this section and elsewhere in the book, please go to the books website at
www.cengage.co.uk/megginson.

http://www.nyse.com; http://www.nasdaq.com; http://www.londonstockexchange.com; http://www.
euronext.com
At the exchange sites you can learn about listing requirements, gather statistics on listed shares and
trading volume, and stay abreast of current market events.

http://www.mergent.com/Dividend_Achievers.asp
Mergent's site collects data on 'dividend achievers' – firms that have increased their dividend
payments for ten or more consecutive years.

http://www.dividenddiscountmodel.com
Here is a website devoted to the dividend discount model for valuing shares.

http://www.world-exchanges.org
The site of the World Federation of Stock Exchanges, a great source of comparative information.

KEY TERMS

additional paid-in capital
best efforts
book value
brokers
competitively bid offer
dealers
dividend
firm-commitment
free cash flow (FCF)
Gordon growth model
Green Shoe option
initial public offering (IPO)
investment banks
lead underwriter
listed securities

majority voting
  system
market capitalization
National Association of
  Securities Dealers
  Automated Quotation
  (NASDAQ) System
negotiated offer
oversubscribe
par value (shares)
price stabilization
prospectus
proxy fight
proxy statements
residual claimants

road show
seasoned equity offering (SEO)
selling group
shares authorized
shares issued
treasury shares
underwrite
underwriting spread
underwriting syndicate
variable growth model
weighted average cost of capital
  (WACC)
zero growth model

SELF-TEST PROBLEMS

ST5-1 Omega Healthcare Investors (ticker symbol, OHI) pays a dividend on its Series B preference shares of $0.539 per quarter. If the price of Series B preference shares is $25 per share, what quarterly rate of return does the market require on this share, and what is the effective annual required return?

ST5-2 The restaurant chain Applebee's International, Inc. (ticker symbol, APPB) announced an increase of their quarterly dividend from $0.06 to $0.07 per share in December 2003. This continued a long string of dividend increases. Applebee's was one of a few companies that had managed to increase its dividend at a double-digit clip for more than a decade. Suppose you want to use the dividend growth model to value Applebee's shares. You believe that dividends will keep growing at 10 per cent per year indefinitely, and you think the market's required return on this share is 11 per cent. Let's assume that Applebee's pays dividends annually and that the next dividend is expected to be $0.31 per share. The dividend will arrive in exactly one year. What would you pay for Applebee's shares right now? Suppose you buy the shares today, hold them just long enough to receive the next dividend, and then sell them. What rate of return will you earn on that investment?

QUESTIONS

Q5-1 How are preference and ordinary shares different?

Q5-2 What is a prospectus?

Q5-3 Describe the role of the underwriting syndicate in a firm-commitment offering.

Q5-4 Why is the relationship between an investment banker and a firm selling its securities somewhat adversarial?

Q5-5 Does secondary market trading generate capital for the company whose shares are trading?

Q5-6 How do you estimate the required rate of return on a preference share if you know its market price and its dividend?

Q5-7 The value of shares cannot be tied to the present value of future dividends because most firms do not pay dividends. Comment on the validity, or lack thereof, of this statement.

Q5-8 A common fallacy in stock market investing is assuming that a good company makes a good investment. Suppose we define a good company as one that has experienced rapid growth (in sales, earnings or dividends) in the recent past. Explain the reasons why shares of good companies may or may not turn out to be good investments.

Q5-9 Why is it not surprising to learn that growth rates rarely show predictable trends?

Q5-10 The book value of a firm's equity is usually lower than the market value of the shares. Why? Can you describe a situation in which the liquidation value of a firm's equity could exceed its market value?

PROBLEMS

The essential features of shares

P5-1 The equity section of the balance sheet for Hilton Web-Cams looks like this:

Shares, €0.25 par	€ 400 000
Paid-in capital surplus	€4 500 000
Retained earnings	€1 100 000

a How many shares has the company issued?

b What is the book value per share?

c Suppose that Hilton Web-Cams has made only one offering of shares. At what price did it sell shares to the market?

P5-2 The equity section of the balance sheet for SuperMega Entertainment appears below:

Shares, €0.60 par value	€_____
Paid-in capital surplus	€10 000 000
Retained earnings	€22 000 000

If the company originally raised €11 000 000 in its shares issue, how many shares did it sell and at what price?

Primary markets and issuing new securities

P5-3 Owners of the internet bargain site FROOGLE.com have decided to take their company public by conducting an initial public offering of shares. They have agreed with their investment banker to sell 3.3 million shares to investors at an offer price of €14 per share. The underwriting spread is 7 per cent.

a What is the net price that FROOGLE.com will receive for its shares?

b How much money will FROOGLE.com raise in the offering?

c What do FROOGLE.com's investment bankers make on this transaction?

Secondary markets for equity securities

P5-4 The following share quotes were taken from a recent issue of *The Wall Street Journal*:

YTD % chg	52-week HI	LO	Stock (SYM)	DIV
12.7	46.8	33.0	Smucker SJM	0.92
211.8	44.3	31.1	Verizon VZ	1.54

Yld (%)	PE	Vol 100s	Close	Net chg
2.1	20	1349	44.86	0.05
4.5	15	61517	34.17	0.04

a Which company had higher earnings per share over the last year?

b What was the closing price of Verizon as reported in the paper?

c Which company's shares earned a higher percentage return on the day as reported here?

P5-5 Fill in the missing figures in the table.

YTD % chg	52-week HI	LO	Stock (SYM)	DIV
19.7	94.5	73.17	IBM IBM	0.64
216.4	60.1	40.57	Merck MRK	

Yld (%)	PE	Vol 100s	Close	Net chg
	28	35964	92.79	20.60
3.3	14	66805	44.77	0.56

Share valuation

P5-6 Argaiv Towers has outstanding an issue of preference shares with a par value of €100. It pays an annual dividend equal to 8 per cent of par value. If the required return on Argaiv preference shares is 6 per cent, and if Argaiv pays its next dividend in one year, what is the market price of the preference shares today?

P5-7 Artivel Mining Corp.'s preference shares pays a dividend of €5 each year. If the shares sells for €40 and the next dividend will be paid in one year, what return do investors require on Artivel preference shares?

P5-8 Silaic Tools has issued preference shares that offer investors a 10 per cent annual return. The shares currently sell for €80, and the next dividend will be paid in one year. How much is the dividend?

P5-9 Suppose a preference share pays a quarterly dividend of €2 per share. The next dividend comes in exactly one-fourth of a year. If the price of the shares is €80, what is the effective annual rate of return that the shares offer investors?

P5-10 A particular preference share pays a €1 quarterly dividend and offers investors an effective annual rate of return of 12.55 per cent. What is the price per share?

P5-11 The C. Alice Stone Company's shares have paid a €3 dividend for so long that investors are now convinced that the shares will continue to pay that annual dividend forever. If the next dividend is due in one year and investors require an 8 per cent return on the shares, what is the current market price? What will the price be immediately after the next dividend payment?

P5-12 Propulsion Science's (PS) share dividend has grown at 10 per cent per year for many years. Investors believe that a year from now the company will pay a dividend of €3 and that dividends will continue their 10 per cent growth indefinitely. If the market's required return on PS shares is 12 per cent, what do the shares sell for today? How much will they sell for a year from today after the shareholders receive their dividend?

P5-13 Investors believe that a certain share will pay a €4 dividend next year. The market price of the share is €66.67, and investors expect a 12 per cent return on the share. What long-run growth rate in dividends is consistent with the current price of the share?

P5-14 Gail Dribble is analysing the shares of Petscan Radiology. Petscan's shares pay a dividend once each year, and it just distributed this year's €0.85 dividend. The market price of the shares is €12.14. Gail estimates that Petscan will increase its dividends by 7 per cent per year forever. After contemplating the risk of Petscan shares, Gail is willing to hold the shares only if they provide an annual expected return of at least 13 per cent. Should she buy Petscan shares or not?

P5-15 Carbohydrates Anonymous (CA) operates a chain of weight-loss centres for carb lovers. Its services have been in great demand in recent years, and its profits have soared. CA recently paid an annual dividend of €1.35 per share. Investors expect that the company will increase the dividend by 20 per cent in each of the next three years, and after that they anticipate that dividends will grow by about 5 per cent per year. If the market requires an 11 per cent return on CA shares, what should the shares sell for today?

P5-16 Hill Propane Distributors sells propane gas throughout eastern Europe. Because of population growth and a construction boom in recent years, the company has prospered and expects to continue to do well in the near term. The company will pay a €0.75 per-share dividend to investors one year from now. Investors believe that Hill Propane will increase that dividend at 15 per cent per year for the subsequent five years, before settling down to a long-run dividend growth rate of 3 per cent. Investors expect an 8 per cent return on Hill Propane shares. What is the current selling price of the shares?

P5-17 Yesterday, 22 September 2006, Wireless Logic Corporation (WLC) paid its annual dividend of €1.25 per share. Because WLC's financial prospects are particularly bright,

investors believe the company will increase its dividend by 20 per cent per year for the next four years. After that, investors believe WLC will increase the dividend at a modest annual rate of 4 per cent. Investors require a 16 per cent return on WLC shares, and WLC always makes its dividend payment on 22 September of each year.

a What is the price of WLC shares on 23 September 2006?

b What is the price of WLC shares on 23 September 2007?

c Calculate the percentage change in price of WLC shares from 23 September 2006 to 23 September 2007.

d For an investor who purchased WLC shares on 23 September 2006, received a dividend on 22 September 2007, and sold the shares on 23 September 2007, what was the total rate of return on the investment? How much of this return came from the dividend, and how much came from the capital gain?

e What is the price of WLC shares on 23 September 2010?

f What is the price of WLC shares on 23 September 2011?

g For an investor who purchased WLC shares on 23 September 2010, received a dividend on 22 September 2011, and sold the shares on 23 September 2011, what was the total rate of return on the investment? How much of this return came from the dividend, and how much came from the capital gain? Comment on the differences between your answers to this question and your answers to part (d).

P5-18 Today's date is 30 March 2006. E-Pay shares pays a dividend every year on 29 March. The most recent dividend was €1.50 per share. You expect the company's dividends to increase at a rate of 25 per cent per year through 29 March 2009. After that, you expect that dividends will increase at 5 per cent a year. Investors require a 14 per cent return on E-Pay shares. Calculate the price of the shares on the following dates: 30 March 2006; 30 March 2010; and 30 September 2007.

P5-19 One year from today, investors anticipate that Groningen Distilleries shares will pay a dividend of €3.25 per share. After that, investors believe that the dividend will grow at 20 per cent per year for three years before settling down to a long-run growth rate of 4 per cent. The required rate of return on Groningen shares is 15 per cent. What is the current shares price?

P5-20 Investors expect the following series of dividends from a particular share:

Year One	€1.10
2nd year	€1.25
3rd year	€1.45
4th year	€1.60
5th year	€1.75

After the fifth year, dividends will grow at a constant rate. If the required rate of return on this shares is 9 per cent and the current market price is €45.64, what is the long-term rate of dividend growth expected by the market?

P5-21 In the constant-growth model we can apply the equation $P = D/(r - g)$, only under the assumption that $r > g$. Suppose someone tries to argue with you that for a certain share, $r < g$, forever, not just during a temporary growth spurt. Why can't this be the case? What would happen to the share price if this were true? If you try to answer simply by looking at the formula, you will almost certainly get the wrong answer. Think it through.

P5-22 Stephenson Technologies (ST) produces the world's greatest single-lens-reflex (SLR) camera. The camera has been a favourite of professional photographers and serious amateurs for several years. Unfortunately, the camera uses old film technology and does not take digital pictures. Ron Stephenson, owner and chief executive officer of the company, has decided to let the business continue for as long as it can without making any new research-and-development investments to develop digital cameras. Accordingly, investors expect ST shares to pay a €4 dividend next year and that the dividend will then shrink by 10 per cent per year indefinitely. What is the market price of ST shares if investors require a 12 per cent return?

Valuing the enterprise: The free cash flow approach

P5-23 Roban Corporation is considering going public but is unsure of a fair offering price for the company. Before hiring an investment banker to assist in making the public offering, managers at Roban decide to make their own estimate of the firm's value. The firm's chief financial officer gathers data for performing the valuation using the free cash flow valuation model.

The firm's weighted average cost of capital is 12 per cent. It has €1 400 000 of debt at market value and €500 000 of preference shares at its assumed market value. The estimated free cash flows over the next five years, 2007 to 2011, are given below. Beyond 2011 to infinity, the firm expects its free cash flow to grow by 4 per cent annually.

YEAR	FREE CASH FLOW
2007	€250 000
2008	290 000
2009	320 000
2010	360 000
2011	400 000

a Estimate the value of Roban Corporation's entire company by using the free cash flow approach.

b Use your finding in part (a), along with the data provided above, to find Roban Corporation's shares value.

c If the firm plans to issue 220 000 shares, what is its estimated value per share?

P5-24 Dean and Edwards (D&E) is a firm that provides temporary employees to businesses. D&E's client base has grown rapidly in recent years, and the firm has been quite profitable. The firm's co-founders, Mr Dean and Mr Edwards, believe in a conservative approach to financial management and therefore have not borrowed any money to finance their business. A larger company in the industry has approached D&E about buying them out. In the most recent year, 2006, D&E generated free cash flow of €1.4 million. Suppose that D&E projects that these cash flows will grow at 15 per cent per year for the next four years, and then will settle down to a long-run growth rate of 7 per cent per year.

The co-founders want a 14 per cent return on their investment. What should be their minimum asking price from the potential acquirer?

Other approaches to share valuation

P5-25 Dauterive Barber Shops (DBS) specializes in providing quick and inexpensive haircuts for middle-aged men. The company retains about half of its earnings each year and pays the rest out as a dividend. Recently, the company paid a €3.25 dividend. Investors expect the company's dividends to grow modestly in the future, at about 4 per cent per year, and they require a 9 per cent return on DBS shares. Based on next year's earnings forecast, what is DBS's price/earnings ratio? How would the price/earnings ratio change if investors believed that DBS's long-term growth rate was 6 per cent rather than 4 per cent? Retaining the original assumption of 4 per cent growth, how would the price/earnings ratio change if investors became convinced that DBS was not very risky and were willing to accept a 7 per cent return on their shares going forward?

THOMSON ONE Business School Edition

Access financial information from the Thomson ONE – Business School Edition website for the following problem(s). Go to http://tobsefin.swlearning.com/. If you have already registered your access serial number and have a username and password, click **Enter**. Otherwise, click **Register** and follow the instructions to create a username and password. Register your access serial number and then click **Enter** on the aforementioned website. When you click Enter, you will be prompted for your username and password (please remember that the password is case sensitive). Enter them in the respective boxes and then click **OK** (or hit **Enter**). From the ensuing page, click **Click Here to Access Thomson ONE – Business School Edition Now!** This opens up a new window that gives you access to the Thomson ONE – Business School Edition database. You can retrieve a company's financial information by entering its ticker symbol (provided for each company in the problem(s)) in the box below 'Name/Symbol/Key'. For further instructions on using the Thomson ONE – Business School Edition database, please refer to *A Guide for Using Thomson ONE – Business School Edition*.

P5-26 What rate of return do investors require on Cement Roadstone Holdings shares? Use the annual dividends per share reported for the last five years to determine the compound annual growth rate in dividends. Assume that Cement Roadstone Holdings maintains this growth rate forever and has just paid a dividend. Use the latest available closing price as the current share price. How does this required rate of return compare with the compound annual share return over the last five years? Have investors been compensated sufficiently?

P5-27 Are shares of Interbrew currently underpriced or overpriced? Calculate the average P/E ratio over the last five fiscal years. Assuming that Interbrew maintains this average P/E into the future, determine the price per share using the average EPS estimate for the next fiscal year end. Is this estimate higher or lower than the latest closing price for Interbrew?

MINICASE *Valuing shares*

Your investment adviser has sent you three analyst reports for a young, growing company named VC Chips. These reports depict the company as speculative, but each one poses different projections of the company's future growth rate in earnings and dividends. All three reports show that VC Chips earned €1.20 per share in its most recent trading year. There is consensus that a fair rate of return to investors for this share is 14 per cent, and that management expects to consistently earn a 15 per cent return on the book value of equity (ROE = 15 per cent).

Assignment

1 The analyst who produced report A makes the assumption that VC Chips will remain a small, regional company that, although profitable, is not expected to grow. In this case, VC Chips' management is expected to elect to pay out 100 per cent of earnings as dividends. Based on this report, what model can you use to value shares in VC Chips? Using this model, what is the value?

2 The analyst who produced report B makes the assumption that VC Chips will enter the national market and grow at a steady, constant rate. In this case, VC Chips' management is expected to elect to pay out 40 per cent of earnings as dividends. This analyst discloses news that this dividend has just been committed to current shareholders. Based on this report, what model can you use to value shares in VC Chips? Using this model, what is the value?

3 The analyst who produced report C also makes the assumption that VC Chips will enter the national market, but expects a high level of initial excitement for the product that is then followed by growth at a constant rate. Earnings and dividends are expected to grow at a rate of 50 per cent over the next year, 20 per cent for the following two years and then revert back to a constant growth rate of 9 per cent thereafter. This analyst also discloses that VC Chips' management has just announced the payout of 40 per cent of the recently reported earnings to current shareholders. Based on this report, what model can you use to value shares in VC Chips? Using this model, what is the value?

4 Discuss the feature(s) that drives the differing valuations of VC Chips. What additional information do you need to garner confidence in the projections of each analyst's report?

Chapter 6

The Trade-Off Between Risk and Return

OPENING FOCUS

Eat well or sleep well . . .

Often in life we find ourselves concerned about risk: what is the risk of taking a medical treatment, or if one decides to park illegally, or to go surfing on a stormy sea. Intuitively human beings weigh up the perceived risks of an activity against the returns that they will get from it: a cure for the disease, less time carrying shopping, or the admiration of friends for surfing well in difficult conditions. In finance, as we will see, risk is all pervasive. However, just as in life there is a pay-off for risk. In general, lower risk means lower returns.

Consider Close Fund Management. Founded in 1995 by Marc Gordon, it is a boutique fund manager with a small staff and approximately €1.6 billion under management. Gordon believes in making it clear to customers the risk/return relationship, and considers that this is the key to ensuring that customers maintain respect for the fund management industry, regardless of their monetary experience. Close makes extensive use of derivatives to manage the risk profile of investments, but also focuses the work of the fund on short time horizons. This is in contrast to the traditional 'with profits' funds, where the minimum time horizon is usually five to seven years. The structuring of the funds are such that the investor is guaranteed a maximum loss (no loss even), is exposed to reduced variability (volatility) in the rates of return and does not gain all of any potential upside movements.

These trade-offs are very common in finance. Consider the electricity business. A report in 2005 noted that with deregulation and moves to a wider mix of generation methods (wind, nuclear, etc.), utility companies were fining it difficult to attract adequate funding. In particular, the effect on nuclear plants was noted, with enhanced safety regulations all making rates of return on new nuclear plants very low. However, while returns on utility investments in the 1970s were typically around 5–6 per cent, the study noted that this was too low now for the level of risk that companies faced. The overall implication was that companies would need to restructure their finances to reflect the fact that as risks have increased so too has the required return that investors seek.

Source: Adapted from 'Boutique With a Mission to Sell Products That Do Exactly What They Say', *Financial Times*, 8 January 2007. 'Risky Business', *Petroleum Economist*, April 2005.

LEARNING OBJECTIVES

After studying this chapter you should be able to:

- Calculate an investment's total return in money or percentage terms, identify the components of the total return and explain why total return is a key metric for assessing an investment's performance.

- Describe the historical performance of asset classes such as bills, bonds and shares, and articulate the important lessons that history provides.

- Calculate the standard deviation from a series of historical returns.

- Distinguish between systematic and unsystematic risk, explain why systematic risk is more closely linked to returns than is unsystematic risk and illustrate how diversification reduces volatility.

SMART FINANCE

Use the learning tools at www.cengage.co.uk/megginson

Finance teaches that investment returns are related to risk. From a purely theoretical perspective, it seems logical that risk and return should be linked, but the notion that an unavoidable trade-off between the two exists is grounded in fact. In countries around the world, historical capital market data offer compelling evidence of a positive relationship between risk and return. That evidence is a major focus of this chapter.

Naturally, most of us like to earn high returns on the money we save and invest. The returns we earn (and therefore the additional consumption we can undertake later in life) represent the marginal benefit of investing. At the same time, most investors would rather avoid dramatic swings in their wealth. Unfortunately, the higher the return that investors desire, the greater the risk they must bear. Risk represents the marginal cost of investing. Therefore, when individuals decide how to invest their money, they have to weigh the marginal benefit of a higher return against the marginal cost of additional risk. Not everyone will strike this balance in exactly the same way, but the historical data on risk and return that we study in this chapter provides evidence that markets present investors with an unavoidable trade-off between risk and reward.

In Chapters 4 and 5, we argued that corporate bonds are more risky than government securities and that shares are riskier than either corporate or government bonds. Based on that assessment, we should expect a relationship like that shown in Figure 6.1. If we arrange these assets from least to most risky, we expect returns to rise, as we move from left to right in the figure. Soon we will see that this is exactly the pattern revealed by historical data.

What is it worth? – perhaps the most important question in finance. For an investor contemplating a share purchase or for a corporate manager weighing a new plant construction proposal, placing a value on risky assets is fundamental to the decision-making process. The procedure for valuing a risky asset involves three basic steps:

1 determining the asset's expected cash flows

2 choosing a discount rate that reflects the asset's risk

3 calculating the present value.

FIGURE 6.1

The trade-off between risk and return

Intuitively, we expect that investors seeking higher returns must be willing to accept higher risk. Moving along the line from safe assets such as government debt to much riskier investments such as shares, returns should rise.

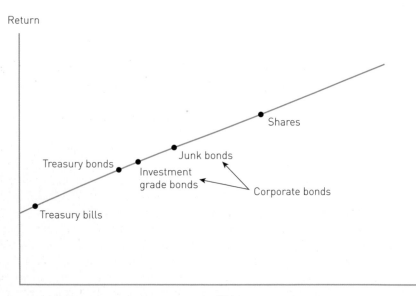

Finance professionals apply these three steps, known as discounted cash flow (DCF) analysis, to value a wide range of real and financial assets. Chapter 3 introduced you to the rather mechanical third step of this process – converting a sequence of future cash flows into a single number reflecting an asset's present value. Chapters 4 and 5 focused more on the first step in the process – projecting future cash flows. In this chapter and in Chapter 7, we will emphasize the second step in DCF valuation – determining an appropriate discount rate.

We begin by establishing a precise measure of an investment's performance called the total return. An asset's total return captures any income that the asset pays as well as any changes in the asset's price, which we call the capital gain. With the definition of total return in hand, we proceed to study the historical performance of broad asset classes such as shares. Because inflation gradually erodes the value of money, we focus on the real returns offered by various asset classes, not just their nominal returns. When people save their money and invest it, they do so in the hope of living more comfortably in the future. Their objective is not just to accumulate a large sum of money but to be able to spend that money to buy the necessities (and the luxuries) of life. Real returns matter because they measure the increase in purchasing power that a given investment provides over time. Moreover, although we do not dwell on it, the pattern of relative returns across asset classes that we will discuss holds, especially over the long term, in both real and nominal returns.

From a corporate finance perspective, all these concerns affect whether the managers' decisions to build a new plant, to launch a new product line, or to upgrade machinery provide a return that meets or beats investor's expectations. Firms have to assess each investment project's risk and then choose a discount rate that reflects the return that investors could obtain on similar investments elsewhere in the market. Matching a discount rate to a specific asset requires answers to two critical questions. First, how risky is the asset, investment or project that we want to value? Secondly, how much return should the project offer, given its risk? This chapter addresses the first question, showing how different ways of defining and measuring risk apply to individual assets as compared with portfolios (collections of different assets).

Real World

Companies with a social conscience are very much in the news. But what is the risk related to investing in such companies? Is the cost of ethical investment a lower return than could be earned in a company that doesn't profess to be so squeaky clean? Recent research suggests that this is indeed the case. A group of UK academics have produced the first large-scale research project in the UK that examines the share returns generated by a sample of over 450 companies listed on the FTSE All-Shares index. The shares performing worst on a corporate social responsibility basis correlated strongly to the best performers on returns. The low returns could not be explained by a preponderance of low-risk shares in the socially responsible companies. Indeed the differences between the two seemed not to be explainable by standard risk models. More-likely explanations are behavioural – investors are possibly accepting a lower return on ethical investments for moral reasons, or ethical operation has a bottom line cost that is punished by the financial markets.

Building on this foundation, Chapter 7 provides an answer to the second question. The capital asset pricing model (CAPM) proposes a specific way to measure risk and to determine what compensation the market expects in exchange for that risk. By quantifying the relationship between risk and return, the CAPM supplies finance professionals with a powerful tool for determining the value of financial assets such as shares, as well as real assets such as new factories and equipment.

6.1 UNDERSTANDING RETURNS

total return
A measure of the performance of an investment that captures both the income it pays and its capital gain or loss over a stated period of time.

Probably the first question that enters the mind of investors when they decide whether to undertake an investment is, 'How much money will this investment earn?' In finance, we refer to the total gain or loss on an investment as the total return. The total return, expressed either in monetary terms or on a percentage basis, measures the increase (or decrease) in wealth that an investor experiences from holding a particular asset such as a share or a bond.

The components of total return

An investment's total return consists of two components. The first part is the income stream the investment produces. For bonds, the income stream comes in the form of interest. For shares, dividends provide the income stream. As we learned in Chapters 4 and 5, the financial press regularly provides investment performance measures that primarily focus on an asset's income stream. For example, the coupon yield, which equals the coupon payment divided by the bond's market price, describes how much money the bondholder earns in interest as a percentage of the price of the bond. Similarly, the dividend yield, equal to a share's annual dividend payment divided by the share price, highlights the income component of share returns.

capital gain
The increase in the price of an asset that occurs over a period of time.

capital loss
The decrease in the price of an asset that occurs over a period of time.

Measures such as the coupon yield and dividend yield may provide investors with useful information, but any performance measure that focuses entirely on an investment's income stream misses the second, and often the most important, component of total returns. That component is the change in the asset's price, called the capital gain or capital loss. For some investments, such as zero-coupon bonds and shares that do not pay dividends, the capital gain or loss is the only component of total return because there is no income. For other investments, the price change may be more or less important than the income stream in determining the investment's total return.

For example, suppose that an investor spends €1000 to purchase a newly issued ten-year corporate bond that pays an annual coupon of €60. In this case, the coupon rate and the coupon yield are both 6 per cent (€60 ÷ €1000). Because this bond sells at par value, we know that the market requires a 6 per cent return on the bond. Suppose we want to assess the performance of this investment after one year. To do that, we need to add up both the income paid by the bond and any price change that occurs during the year. At the end of the year, the investor receives a €60 coupon payment, but what is her bond worth? We know from Chapter 4 that the answer to that question depends on what happens to market interest rates during the year. Suppose that the market's required return on this bond has risen from 6 per cent to 8 per cent. At the end of the first year, the bond has nine years left until maturity. Discounting the remaining cash flows at 8 per cent, we find that the bond's market price equals just €875.06. The investor's total return is considerably less than the 6 per cent coupon yield. In fact, the capital loss caused by rising interest rates results in a negative total return. The investor earns income of €60, but she also experiences a capital loss of €124.94 (€1000 − €875.06). That loss more than offsets the interest payment, and our investor ends the year with less wealth than when she started.

Note that the investor's total return this year does not depend on whether she sells the bond or continues to hold it. Selling or not selling the bond determines whether the capital loss in this example is realized or unrealized, but it has no effect on the investor's wealth (ignoring for the moment the issue of taxes that may be levied on such unrealized gains or losses). At the end of the year, the investor has €60 in cash plus a bond worth €875.06. That is equivalent to owning €935.06 in cash, which would be the investor's position if she sells the bond.[1] In any case, this example illustrates that both the income and capital gain or loss components influence an investor's wealth. The important lesson to remember is that one must focus on the total return when assessing an investment's performance.

Monetary returns and percentage returns

We can describe an investment's total return either in money terms or in percentage terms. Consider again the bond example in the previous two paragraphs. To calculate the total return on this investment, we simply add the income component to the capital gain or loss:

$$\text{Total return} = \text{Capital gain or loss} + \text{Income}$$ EQUATION 6.1

Earlier we defined an investment's total return as the change in wealth that it generates for the investor. In the present example, the investor begins with €1000. A year later, she receives €60 and she owns a bond worth €875.06. Therefore, end-of-year wealth equals €935.06. The change in wealth during the year equals −€64.94 (€935.06 − €1000):

$$\text{Total return} = 60 + (1000 - 875.06) = -€64.96$$

Money returns tell us, in an absolute sense, how much wealth an investment generates over time. Other things being equal, investors prefer assets that provide higher monetary returns. However, comparing the money returns of two different investments can be treacherous, as the following example illustrates.

Applying the Model

Terrell purchases 100 shares of Micro-Orb for €25 per share. A year later, the shares pay a dividend of €1 per share and sell for €30. Terrell's total money return is:

$$\text{Total return} = 100 \times (1 + 5) = €600$$

Meanwhile, Owen purchases 50 shares of Garcia Transportation for €15 per share. Garcia shares pay no dividends, but at the end of the year the shares sell for €25. Owen's total money return equals:

$$\text{Total return} = 50 \times (10) = €500$$

Based on these figures, it appears that Terrell had a better year than Owen did. But before we reach that conclusion, we ought to recognize that at the beginning of the year Terrell's investment was much larger than Owen's.

[1] Unrealized losses are sometimes called paper losses. This term simply means that the value of the paper that an investor holds, a bond or share certificate, has gone down. Some investors believe that paper losses are irrelevant and that losses only matter when they are realized because an investor sells.

The preceding example illustrates a problem we encounter when comparing money returns on different investments. Terrell's money return exceeds Owen's by €100, but that does not necessarily mean that Terrell's shares performed better. Terrell spent €2500 to purchase 100 Micro-Orb shares, while Owen devoted just €750 to his investment in Garcia Transportation. Intuitively, we might expect Terrell to earn a higher money return than Owen because he invested so much more than Owen did.

Another way to compare outcomes is to calculate the percentage return on each investment. The total percentage return equals the total money return divided by the initial investment.

Applying the Model

Given that Terrell initially invested €2500, while Owen invested just €750, we can calculate their total returns on a percentage basis as:

$$\text{Terrell} = 600/2500 = 0.24 \text{ or } 24\%$$
$$\text{Owen} = 500/750 = 0.67 = 67\%$$

On a percentage basis, Owen's investment performed better than Terrell's, but on a total money return basis the opposite is true. The conflict arises here because the initial amount invested by Terrell is so much larger than Owen's up-front investment. Which investment would you rather have, one that makes you €600 richer or one that increases your initial stake by 67 per cent? Comparing the returns on investments that involve different amounts of money is a fundamental problem to which we will return in Chapter 8. For now, we only say that money returns and percentage returns can lead to different relative rankings of investment alternatives.

Just as the total money return was the sum of an investment's income and its capital gain or loss, the total percentage return equals the sum of the investment's yield and its percentage capital gain or loss. Recall that the dividend yield equals a share's dividend divided by its market price. Using the beginning-of-year price of Micro-Orb shares to calculate its dividend yield, we have:

$$1/25 = 0.04 \text{ or } 4\%$$

Similarly, the percentage capital gain equals:

$$5/25 = 0.2 \text{ or } 20\%$$

Therefore, the total percentage return on Micro-Orb equals the sum of the dividend yield and the percentage capital gain (i.e. 24 per cent).

To summarize the important points from this section:

● Measuring an investment's performance requires a focus on total return.

● The total return consists of two components – income and capital gain or loss.

● We can express total returns either in total money terms or in percentage terms.

● When ranking the performance of two or more investments relative to each other, it is important to be careful that the amount of money initially invested in each asset is the same.

- If one asset requires a much larger up-front monetary commitment than the other, then money returns and percentage returns may lead to different performance rankings.

1   In Chapter 4 we defined several bond return measures, including the coupon, the coupon rate, the coupon yield and the yield to maturity. Indicate whether each of these measures (a) focuses on the total return or just one of the components of total return and (b) focuses on money returns or percentage returns.

2   You buy a share for €40. During the next year it pays a dividend of €2 and its price increases to €44. Calculate the total euro return and total percentage return and show that each of these is the sum of the dividend and capital gain components.

3   When might an investor be more concerned with total money return and when with percentage return?

6.2 THE HISTORY OF RETURNS (OR GETTING RICH SLOWLY)

British writer Aldous Huxley once said: 'That men do not learn very much from the lessons of history is the most important of all lessons that history has to teach.' We are more optimistic. Certainly, what we can learn from the history of financial markets benefits investors who study that history. Perhaps the most important lesson is this: an unavoidable trade-off exists between risk and return, so investors seeking higher returns almost always have to accept higher risk.

Nominal and real returns on shares, bonds and bills

How do different types of assets perform over time? Surprisingly, this question is not that simple to answer. Part of the problem is that it is only in the last 40 or so years that data are available for a wide variety of assets in a manner that is comparable. Part of the problem is that over the very long term many events occur that distort returns. Consider for example the returns to the equity market in the G7 countries (the UK, USA, Canada, Italy, Germany, France and Japan). If we wish to consider the history of these over a 100 year period we run into the problem that for a number of these countries there are two periods of equity market collapse during the two World Wars. Even over a shorter period, say 20 years, issues such as the reunification of Germany are sufficiently disruptive to make easy comparison not a trivial task.

The most authoritative datasets on comparable long-term data available are from two sources. The first is the dataset created by the London Business School, the DMS Dataset, available through Ibbotson Associates. This data originates in a book titled *Triumph of the Optimists: 101 Years of Global Investment Returns*, by Elroy Dimson, Paul Marsh and Mike Staunton (Princeton University Press, 2001). A second set of comparable data, which is more generally available, is that generated by Barclays Bank in their annual *Equity Gilt Study*. The *Equity Gilt Study* has been published annually since 1956. The study provides data and analysis of the annual returns on equities, government bonds (called 'gilts' in the UK) and cash from the end of 1899 for the UK, and from the end of 1925 for the US. Note that these data are not 'headline' indices, but instead are computed by Barclays. Consequently, although they show the same general pattern as may be achieved by looking at other indices, the particular figures from year to year can and do differ.

A paper presented at the Financial Management Association Meeting in Stockholm in 2006 ('The Worldwide Equity Risk Premium: A Smaller Puzzle' by Dimson, Marsh and Staunton) showed data for equity returns over the long term as set out in Table 6.1. The message from this is fairly clear; in the long run the return to equities is on average approximately 7 per cent. This would imply that an equity investment would double every ten years or so. This is a good return, but looking at equities alone is not sufficient. What is missing from the above data are two elements. First, we do not know how equities have performed relative to other assets. Secondly, we do not know how risky equities are relative to time or to other assets. We will look at these in turn.

Looking at the 2006 *Equity Gilt Study* we find some useful comparable figures. A graph (Figure 6.2) of the historical nominal returns for the two main classes, bills

TABLE 6.1

World equity returns (US$ terms, annual average percentage total money returns)

	2000 TO 2005	1990 TO 1999	1900 TO 2005	MEAN
Australia	7.78	8.98	7.7	9.21
Belgium	3.99	9.13	2.4	4.58
Canada	4.32	8.28	6.24	7.56
Denmark	9.41	7.52	5.25	6.91
France	−1.64	12.5	3.6	6.08
Germany	−4.08	9.89	3.09	8.21
Ireland	5.14	11.8	4.79	7.02
Italy	−0.73	6.42	2.46	6.49
Japan	0.64	−5.23	4.51	9.26
Netherlands	−5.41	17.8	5.26	7.22
Norway	10.9	8.25	4.28	7.08
South Africa	11.1	4.61	7.25	9.46
Spain	2.48	12.2	3.74	5.9
Sweden	−0.7	15	7.8	10.1
Switzerland	1.11	14	4.48	6.28
United Kingdom	−1.34	11.2	5.5	7.36
United States	−2.74	14.2	6.52	8.5
World (US$)	−1.25	7.87	5.75	7.16
World ex-US (US$)	0.11	3.41	5.23	7.02

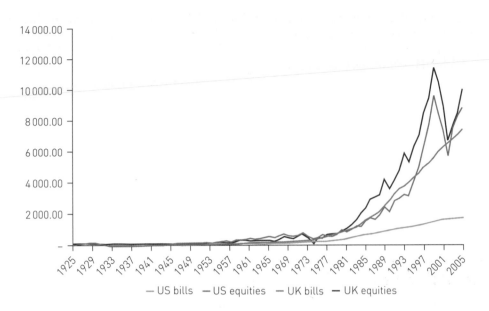

FIGURE 6.2

Nominal value of 100 invested in December 1925

Source: Authors' own calculations based on Barclays *Equity Gilt Study,* various years.

— US bills — US equities — UK bills — UK equities

(short-term government bonds) and equities, shows that there is a consistent, but not universal, rule: claims on the income of firms outperform claims on the income of governments. In short, shares do better.

If we look at this data in real terms, the relative ranking would be the same. Over the period we have the following averages:

PERIOD	UK BONDS	UK EQUITIES	US BONDS	US EQUITIES
Overall (106 years UK, 80 years USA)	1.2%	5.2%	2.3%	7.0%
10 years	5.6%	5.0%	4.9%	6.8%
20 years	6.2%	7.4%	6.4%	8.6%
50 years	2.1%	6.6%	2.4%	6.4%

Clearly the pattern of equities having a premium – an average return over that of gilts – holds good in the long term as well as in most time periods. Our analysis of past data above is presented with the geometric rather than the arithmetic average. Arithmetic averages can provide a misleading picture. For example, suppose equities rose from a base of 100 to 200 over one year and then fell back to 100 over the next year. The return for year one would have been 100 per cent and for year two minus 50 per cent. The arithmetic average return would be 25 per cent even though equities are actually unchanged in value over the two years. The geometric average return in this example would be zero. Over long periods of time the geometric average for total returns is the rate at which a sum invested at the beginning of the period will grow to by the end of the period, assuming all income is reinvested. The calculation of geometric averages depends only on the initial and final values for the investment, not particular values at any other point in time. For periods of one year, arithmetic and geometric averages will be the same. But over longer periods the geometric average is always less than the arithmetic average except when all the individual yearly returns are the same. Confusingly, although geometric returns are appropriate to analyse the past, arithmetic returns should be used to provide forecasts. The arithmetical average nominal return on US equities over the 80 years analysed by Barclays was 5.6 per cent, for UK equities 5.8 per cent, while the figures for bonds were 3.6 per cent and 5.4 per cent respectively.

The risk dimension

Another point is evident from the data shown above. The returns on government bonds are smoother than those on equities. This implies that although a portfolio invested entirely in shares grows more rapidly than a portfolio invested in government debt, the share portfolio displays more dramatic ups and downs from year to year. In the long run, share investors may grow wealthier than bond investors do, but their path to riches is a bumpy one. Some investors may be willing to pass up higher returns on shares in exchange for the additional security of bonds or bills. This is evident if we plot the year-on-year change in the indices discussed above (see Figure 6.3).

FIGURE 6.3

Year-on-year changes in asset class returns

Source: Authors' own calculations based on Barclays *Equity Gilt Study*, various years.

The most important lesson of capital market history is clear: *there is a positive relationship between risk and return.* Asset classes that experience more ups and downs offer investors higher returns, on average, than investments that provide more stable returns. As yet, we have not precisely defined the term risk, but you probably expect that 'risk' must capture the uncertainty surrounding an investment's performance.

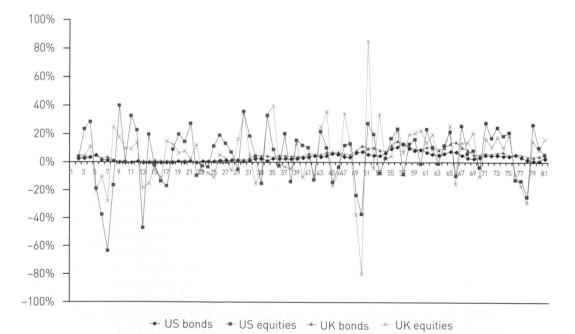

◆ US bonds   ■ US equities   ▲ UK bonds   ✕ UK equities

The trade-off between risk and return leads us to an important concept known as a risk premium. The risk premium is the additional return offered by a more risky investment relative to a safer one.

Keep in mind that the relationship between risk and return suggests that riskier assets pay higher returns *on average*, but not necessarily every single year. As stock markets decline and show negative returns, such as in the early part of the 21st century, the returns on bonds generally do not decline. But if it is true, on average, that riskier investments pay higher returns than safer ones, then we can use historical risk premiums as a starting point to determine what returns we might expect in the future on alternative investments. Perhaps the most important reason to study the lessons of history in financial markets is to make better guesses about what the future holds.

Dimson, Marsh and Staunton in their 2006 paper also showed some historical risk premia for countries. These are reproduced in Table 6.2.

risk premium
The additional return that an investment must offer, relative to some alternative, because it is more risky than the alternative.

	GEOMETRIC AVERAGE (%)	ARITHMETIC AVERAGE (%)
Australia	7.08	8.49
Belgium	2.80	4.99
Canada	4.54	5.88
Denmark	2.87	4.51
France	6.79	9.27
Germany	3.83	9.07
Ireland	4.09	5.98
Italy	6.55	10.46
Japan	6.67	9.84
Netherlands	4.55	6.61
Norway	3.07	5.70
South Africa	6.20	8.25
Spain	3.40	5.46
Sweden	5.73	7.98
Switzerland	3.63	5.29
UK	4.43	6.14
US	5.51	7.41
Average	4.81	7.14
World-ex US	4.23	5.93
World	4.74	6.07

TABLE 6.2
Annual equity risk premium versus short-term government debt, 1900–2005

Applying the Model

Suppose you want to construct a forecast for the return on Dutch shares for the next year. One approach is to use the average historical growth, which we have seen earlier to be 7.22 per cent over the very long run. A problem with this method is that this represents inflation. Similarly, in some past years, interest rates on bonds and bills were relatively high; in other years, rates were much lower. You can make use of current market information to construct a better forecast than the average historical return.

For example, suppose you look at short-term Dutch government bonds trading in the market at the time that you want to develop a forecast for equity returns At that time, you find that these offer a yield to maturity of about 3 per cent. From our discussion you see that the arithmetic average risk premium on Dutch equities relative to short-term government debt is 6.61 per cent. Add that premium to the current short-term bond yield to arrive at a forecast for equity returns of 9.61 per cent (3 + 6.61). This should be a superior forecast compared to the simple historical average because the estimate of 9.61 per cent reflects current market conditions (such as expected inflation rates and required returns on low-risk investments).

Analysts use data on risk premiums for many different purposes. In Chapter 4, we saw that bonds receiving lower ratings from bond rating agencies must pay higher yields. Bond traders know this and use data on the risk premium between relatively safe bonds and riskier bonds to price complex financial instruments. As we will see in future chapters, corporate executives use the risk premium on equities relative to government securities to estimate the rate of return that their investors expect on major capital expenditures. We will return to the subject of the equity risk premium several times in this book, but next we need to explore the meaning of the word 'risk' in more depth.

CONCEPT REVIEW QUESTIONS

4 Why do investors need to pay attention to real returns as well as nominal returns?

5 If the realized risk premium is negative in any year, what does that imply?

6 Is it always true that an asset's nominal return is higher than its real return? When would that not be the case?

6.3 VOLATILITY AND RISK

The distribution of historical equity returns

We begin our analysis of risk with one more historical illustration. Figure 6.4 shows a histogram of US and UK share returns since 1925. The shape of this histogram is probably familiar to you because it is somewhat reminiscent of a bell curve, also known as a 'normal distribution'.

FIGURE 6.4

The empirical distribution of equity returns, 1925–2005

Source: Authors' own calculations based on Barclays *Equity Gilt Study*, various years.

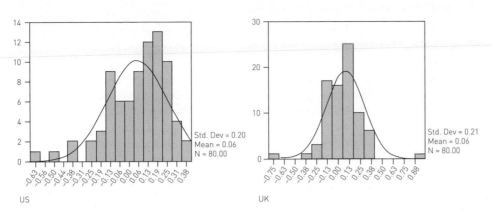

US   UK

Figure 6.4 gives us a sense that share returns can be quite volatile, and it tells us something about the relative frequencies of different outcomes in the stock market. We are interested in these frequencies not only for their historical significance but also for what they may tell us about future stock market returns. For example, a question that investors may want to ask is, 'What is the probability that a portfolio of shares will lose money in any given year?' Without a crystal ball, no one can answer that question precisely, but a close inspection of Figure 6.4 shows that returns were negative in 28 out of the last 104 years, or about 27 per cent of the time. At least as a starting point, we can estimate a 27 per cent probability that shares will lose money in a particular year.

If we could list every possible outcome that might occur in the stock market and attach an exact probability to each outcome, then we would have a 'probability distribution'. Some probability distributions are easy to describe. For example, the probability distribution that governs outcomes of a coin toss is as follows:

Outcome	Probability
Heads	50%
Tails	50%

Unfortunately, the probability distribution for future share returns is unknown. We rely on Figure 6.4 to give us clues about the characteristics of this distribution. A normal distribution is symmetric, so there is an equal chance of experiencing an above-average and a below-average outcome. For both the US and UK, the 'split' between above-average and below-average years in the stock market is 37 to 43. This suggests that our assumption of an underlying normal distribution may be a reasonable approximation to reality. However, a normal curve is superimposed on the empirical histogram, and this indicates that the fit is only approximate.[2]

---

[2] Extensive research on the distribution of equity returns teaches us that the normal distribution is only a rough approximation of the actual returns distribution. For example, equity returns do not appear to be distributed symmetrically around the mean. This makes sense in the light of the limited liability feature of modern company law. A fortunate shareholder might earn a return in excess of 100 per cent in any given year, but no investors can experience a loss greater than 100 per cent (unless they are buying shares using borrowed money). When we examine historical equity returns, we do observe outcomes that are far above the mean more frequently than we see outcomes well below the mean.

The variability of equity returns

standard deviation
A measure of volatility
equal to the square root
of variance.

Every normal distribution has two key characteristics – its mean and its variance. As you may recall from statistics, the variance measures the dispersion of observations around the mean of the distribution. To be more precise, the variance is the expected value (or the average value) of squared deviations from the mean. In equations, variance is usually noted by the Greek symbol σ^2. The **standard deviation** is just another measure of dispersion around the mean, but in the case of investment returns, it is easier to interpret because it is expressed in percentage terms.

Table 6.3 shows the average annual return and the standard deviation of returns for shares, and the excess return of shares over bills and bonds in the period 1900 to 2003. We saw the average returns previously but now we have a specific measure of risk to couple with the mean returns. Once again, we see evidence that risk and return are positively linked, at least if we define risk to mean volatility (as captured by standard deviation). Asset classes that display greater volatility pay higher returns on average.

Figure 6.5 plots this relationship between average returns and standard deviation for US shares, bonds and bills over the same period. In the figure, we chose to plot nominal returns, but switching to real returns would make very little difference. The figure also includes a trend line through the three data points. Notice that the relationship shown in the figure is almost perfectly linear, meaning that the dots fall very close to the trend line.

TABLE 6.3

Average returns and standard deviation for world equities, bonds and bills, 1900–2003

Source: Elroy Dimson, Paul Marsh and Mike Staunton ©2002. *Triumph of the Optimists: 101 Years of Global Investment Returns.* Published by Princeton University Press. Reproduced by permission of Princeton University Press

	ANNUAL AVERAGE RETURN	STANDARD DEVIATION
Equities	7.16	17.23
Excess over bonds	5.15	14.96
Excess over bills	6.07	16.65

FIGURE 6.5

The relationship between average (nominal) return and standard deviation for shares, Treasury bonds and bills, USA 1900–2003

The figure indicates that a positive relationship exists between the average returns offered by an asset class and the standard deviation of returns.

Source: Elroy Dimson, Paul Marsh and Mike Staunton ©2002. *Triumph of the Optimists: 101 Years of Global Investment Returns.* Published by Princeton University Press. Reproduced by permission of Princeton University Press

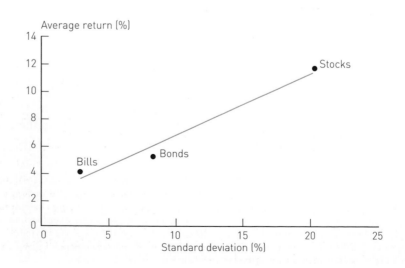

This is not the last time that we will see evidence of a straight-line relationship between risk and return. What are the implications of such a relationship? The most important implications are that (1) investors who want higher returns have to take more risk, and (2) the incremental reward from accepting more risk is constant. In other words, if an investor wants to increase his return from 5 per cent to 10 per cent, the additional risk that he has to accept is the same as the additional risk that another investor has to accept to increase her returns from 10 per cent to 15 per cent. In economics, we frequently see evidence of diminishing returns. This evidence shows up in graphs as a curve with a decreasing slope. For example, a factory can produce more output if there are more workers present, but at some point the incremental output produced by an additional worker (i.e. the marginal product) begins to fall as diminishing returns set in. With respect to risk and return, Figure 6.5 shows no similar evidence of diminishing returns to risk taking.

Thus far, we have seen that a trade-off between risk and return exists for major asset classes including shares, Treasury bonds and bills. Suppose we want to compare the investment performance of two specific assets such as a share of SAP and a share of Nokia. Does this same trade-off appear when we examine individual securities? As we will see in the next section, the answer is, 'it depends'.

7 Suppose nominal bond returns approximately follow a normal distribution. Using the information in this section, construct a range that should contain 95 per cent of historical bond returns. (*Hint*: Use the mean and standard deviation of bond returns to calculate the endpoints of this range.)

8 Suppose there is an asset class with a standard deviation that lies about halfway between the standard deviations of shares and bonds. Based on this section, what would you expect the average return on this asset class to be?

6.4 THE POWER OF DIVERSIFICATION

Systematic and unsystematic risk

In this section, our objective is to take the lessons we've learned about risk and return for major asset classes and apply those lessons to individual securities. As a starting point, examine Table 6.4, which shows the average annual return and the standard deviation of returns for several well-known shares. All these shares are components of the Dow Jones EuroStoxx 50 Index, an index designed to reflect the movements in very large eurozone-based companies. The average return and the average standard deviation for this group of shares appear at the bottom of the table.

First, the average return for this group of shares is higher than the average return for all shares in the last ten years. Secondly, and more important, most of these individual shares have a much higher standard deviation than the relevant benchmark index. In fact however, the shares listed in this table are not unusually volatile. These firms are corporate giants – household names because of their past success. The truth is that these companies are *less volatile* than the average firm with publicly traded shares. That raises an interesting question: how can the standard deviation of the market be less than that of average shares?

TABLE 6.4

Average returns and standard deviation for selected equity securities, 1995–2005

Source: Thomson ONE database.

YEAR	TOTAL GROUP	BANCO SANTANDER	NOKIA	SIEMENS	UNILEVER	EUROSTOXX 50
2005	0.26	0.20	0.20	0.07	0.20	0.20
2004	0.18	0.04	−0.19	0.02	−0.06	0.12
2003	0.01	0.30	−0.14	0.32	−0.19	0.08
2002	−0.11	−0.39	−0.40	−0.33	−0.01	−0.36
2001	−0.08	−0.19	−0.65	−0.43	−0.03	−0.29
2000	0.26	0.06	0.40	0.36	0.09	0.17
1999	0.27	0.31	1.15	0.62	−0.22	0.35
1998	0.00	0.17	0.77	−0.05	0.22	0.21
1997	0.44	0.64	0.63	0.36	0.49	0.35
1996	0.29	0.25	0.02	0.01	0.27	0.23
Average	0.15	0.14	0.18	0.09	0.08	0.11
Standard deviation	0.17	0.27	0.53	0.31	0.21	0.23

diversification
The act of investing in many different assets rather than just a few.

This is a key point. Individual shares generally display much higher volatility than do portfolios of shares.[3] **Diversification**, the act of investing in many different assets rather than just one or two, explains why a portfolio usually has a lower standard deviation than the individual shares that make up that portfolio. We can offer some simple intuition to explain this. In any given year, some shares in a portfolio will have high returns, while other shares in the portfolio will earn lower returns. Each year, the ups and downs of individual shares at least partially cancel each other out, so the standard deviation of the portfolio is less than the standard deviations of the individual shares. The diversification principle works not only for individual shares but also for broad classes of investments such as shares trading in different countries.

Figure 6.6 demonstrates the impact of diversification with just two shares, Siemens and Unilever. In each year from 1996 to 2005 we plot the return on these two shares. Recall from Table 6.4 that both Siemens and Unilever have an average return of around 8 per cent, so we have drawn a horizontal line across the bar chart to highlight the average performance for these firms. Notice that in the years 1996, 1997, 2000–2002 and 2005 the returns were moving together in the sense that both shares displayed positive performance in the same year. However, in other years, one share had a positive year, while the other had a negative year. We also find years when the shares both are similar in terms of above or below-average returns. What then would happen if we formed a portfolio by investing some of our money in Siemens and the rest in Unilever?

---

[3] The same statement could be made for other types of assets (e.g. individual bonds are more volatile than a portfolio of bonds).

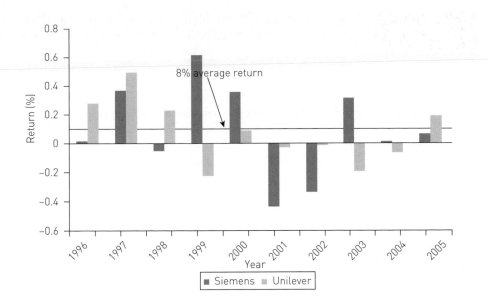

FIGURE 6.6

Annual returns on Siemens and Unilever, 1996–2005

Source: Authors' computations using data from Thomson ONE Banker.

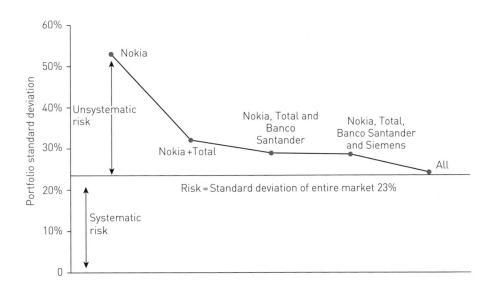

FIGURE 6.7

The relationship between portfolio standard deviation and the number of shares in the portfolio

Source: Authors' computations using data from Thomson ONE Banker.

In the years in which Siemens and Unilever move together, our portfolio return would be quite volatile, just as the individual share returns are volatile. For example, our portfolio return in 1997 would be very high because both shares did well that year, and in 2001 the portfolio would perform poorly because both shares did. However, in some other years the excellent performance of one shares will be largely offset by the sub-par performance of the other, and the portfolio's results will be close to the average return. In other words, the portfolio's return does not deviate as far or as often from the average as the individual share returns do. As a result, the standard deviation for the portfolio will be less than the standard deviation of either Siemens or Unilever.

Now extend that logic to portfolios containing more than two shares. Figure 6.7 indicates that the standard deviation of a portfolio falls as the number of shares in the portfolio rises. The dot in the upper-left corner of the graph represents a portfolio invested entirely in Nokia, the share with the highest average return. As Table 6.4 indicates, this share had a standard deviation of 53 per cent. Next, move down and to the right to the dot which represents a portfolio containing an equal share of Nokia and Total shares. We continue adding shares (keeping each in equal proportions) as we move down the line. Finally, the last dot on the far right shows what happens when we invest an equal amount in each of the five shares shown in Table 6.4. In this case, the portfolio's standard deviation is 22 per cent, just a little below the standard deviation of the overall market.

As you can see, there are diminishing returns to diversification. Adding more shares to this portfolio would lower the portfolio's volatility. But even if the portfolio contains every available shares in the market, the standard deviation will not drop below 21 per cent.[4] *Diversification lowers volatility, but only up to a point.* No matter how diversified the portfolio is, there will still be some volatility remaining. In finance, the risk that remains even in a well-diversified portfolio is called systematic risk. Another term for systematic risk is 'market' risk or 'undiversifiable' risk. The term 'systematic risk' refers to a risk that occurs systematically across many different shares. Examples of systematic risks would include the recession/expansion phases of the macroeconomy, as well as changes in inflation, interest rates and exchange rates.

systematic risk
Risk that cannot be eliminated through diversification.

Look again at the dot in Figure 6.7 showing the standard deviation of a portfolio containing nothing but Nokia shares. The standard deviation here is almost 60 per cent, but the standard deviation of a portfolio containing Nokia (and many other assets) is only 24 per cent. This suggests that most of Nokia's risk disappears once we put it inside a portfolio. What is true for Nokia is true for most shares. A substantial fraction of the volatility of an individual share vanishes when investors hold the share as part of a diversified portfolio. The risk of an individual share that disappears when one diversifies is called unsystematic risk. As the name implies, unsystematic risks are those risks that are not common to many securities. Instead, unsystematic risks affect just a few shares at a time. Unsystematic risk is sometimes called diversifiable risk, unique risk, firm-specific risk or idiosyncratic risk. Each of these terms implies that we are talking about risks that apply to a single firm or a few firms, not to many firms simultaneously.

unsystematic risk
Risk that can be eliminated through diversification.

To understand the difference between systematic and unsystematic risk, consider the defence industry. Suppose a government announces that it will spend billions of euros on a new high-tech weapons system. Several defence contractors submit bids to obtain the contract for this system. Investors know that each of these contracts has some chance of winning the bid, but they don't know which firm will prevail in the end. Before the government awards the contract, investors will bid up the price of every defence share, anticipating that for each firm there is some chance of winning the bid. However, once the government announces the winning bidder, that firm's share price will rise even more, while the prices of other defence shares will fall.

An investor who places an all-or-nothing bet by buying shares in only one defence contractor takes on a lot of risk. Either the investor will guess the outcome of the bidding process successfully, and the investment will pay off handsomely, or the investor will bet on the wrong firm and lose money. Instead, suppose the investor diversifies and holds a position in each defence firm. That way, no matter which firm wins the contract, the investor will be sure to have at least a small claim on the value of that deal. By

---

[4] Of course it is possible to construct some portfolio of stocks with a standard deviation below 21 per cent. To do this we would have to buy stocks that are less riskly than average. Such a portfolio would generate lower returns than one more broadly diversified.

diversifying, the investor eliminates the unsystematic risk in this situation. However, suppose there is a chance that the defence department will cancel its plans to build the weapons system. When that announcement is made, all defence shares will fall, and diversifying across all of these firms will not help an investor avoid that loss.

Risk and return revisited

Remember that our goal in this section is to be able to say something useful about the relationship between risk and return for individual assets. We already know that asset classes that pay higher returns have higher standard deviations. Is the same thing true for securities within a particular asset class? Do individual shares with higher standard deviations earn higher returns over time?

Figure 6.8 plots the average return and standard deviation for the shares analysed earlier. A broad pattern again emerges – the riskier the shares the higher the return. More formally, risk and return are related. As the trend line shows, this is by no means a perfect relationship, the R^2 of a simple regression of returns on standard deviation being less than one-third. However, think on this for a moment – fully one-third of the movements of a set of large shares can be explained simply by reference to their risk.

Why does the relationship between risk and return observed for asset classes seem to weaken when we focus on specific securities? The horizontal axis offers a clue. Remember that the standard deviation of a single share contains both systematic and unsystematic components. If investors are wise enough to diversify, then the unsystematic component of risk is irrelevant because diversification eliminates unsystematic risks. How difficult is it for investors to remove exposure to unsystematic risk? In fact, it is very easy for them to do so. The mutual fund industry is built on the idea of allowing many investors to pool their money so that even people with relatively little money to invest can buy a stake in a well-diversified portfolio. This chapter's Comparative Corporate Finance panel shows that it is possible to eliminate some unsystematic risk by diversifying globally.

If diversification is easy, and if it eliminates unsystematic risk, then what reward should investors expect if they choose not to diversify and to bear systematic risk? Just

SMART CONCEPTS

See the concept explained step-by-step at **www.cengage. co.uk/megginson**

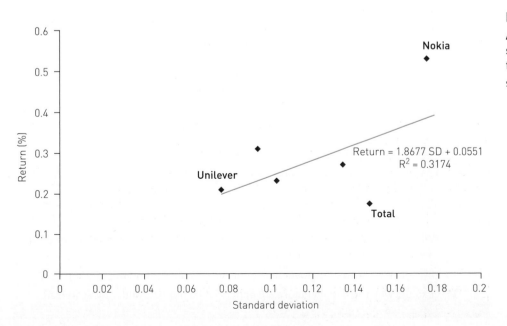

FIGURE 6.8

Average return and standard deviation for five shares

Source: Authors' calculations.

by equating marginal costs and benefits, we can predict that *bearing unsystematic risk offers no incremental reward*. The market rewards investors for bearing systematic risk but not unsystematic risk. Investors can eliminate their exposure to unsystematic risk at almost no cost by diversifying, so the marginal benefit of bearing unsystematic risk equals zero. The market offers higher returns only for investments that have higher systematic risk.

In Figure 6.5, we observed an almost linear relation between standard deviation and average return for three asset classes. In Figure 6.8, the relationship between standard deviation and return is not as clear. The difference between the figures is that in one case (Figure 6.5) we are looking at portfolios of assets, and in the other case (Figure 6.8) we are looking at individual assets. A well-diversified portfolio contains very little unsystematic risk. This is why the standard deviation of a portfolio of shares is typically so much lower than the standard deviation of a single share. For a portfolio, the standard deviation of returns consists almost entirely of systematic risk. For an individual asset, the standard deviation contains both types of risk. Therefore, if the market rewards systematic risk only, then in Figure 6.5 we see a nice linear relationship between portfolio standard deviation (systematic risk) and average returns, but in Figure 6.8 standard deviation (systematic + unsystematic risk) seems almost unrelated to average returns.

To conclude this chapter, let us take a step back and think about our original objective. The fundamental goal of finance is to value things. Usually, valuation involves projecting an asset's future cash flows, choosing a discount rate that is appropriate, given the asset's risk, and then calculating the present value. In this chapter, we have made some progress in understanding the second step of the valuation process. We know that what really matters is an investment's total return, and we want to know how that return relates to risk. Not all risks are equal, however, so we need to focus on an asset's systematic risk because that is what should drive the asset's return in the market. Diversified portfolios contain very little unsystematic risk; thus a measure like the standard deviation of the portfolio's return provides a good measure of the portfolio's systematic risk. As expected, a portfolio's standard deviation and its return are closely linked.

But complications arise for individual assets because their fluctuations reflect both systematic and unsystematic factors. Therefore, the standard deviation of returns for a single share does not focus exclusively on the share's systematic risk. As a result, when we compare standard deviations and average returns across many different shares, we do not see a reliable pattern between those two variables.

This is an important problem because both managers and investors have to assess the risk of individual investments, not just portfolios. They need a way to measure the systematic risk, and only the systematic risk, of each and every asset. If it is possible to quantify an individual asset's systematic risk, then we should expect that measure of risk to be reliably related to returns. This is precisely our focus in Chapter 7.

<table>
<tr><td>CONCEPT
REVIEW
QUESTIONS</td><td>**9**   Why is the standard deviation of a portfolio usually smaller than the standard deviations of the assets that comprise the portfolio?

10   In Figure 6.7, why does the line decline steeply at first and then flatten out?

11   Explain why the dots in Figure 6.8 appear to be almost randomly scattered.</td></tr>
</table>

COMPARATIVE CORPORATE FINANCE
Risk premiums around the world

The tendency for shares to outperform safer investments like government debt is not a phenomenon confined to the larger countries. As the table shows, the premium on equities relative to short-term government debt was in fact positive in 15 other countries from 1900–2005. The relative performance of equities versus short-term government debt was highest in Italy and lowest in Denmark, but in all countries equities earned higher returns than such debt. The US has a slightly higher risk premium, the UK a lower risk premium.

	ARITHMETIC AVERAGE REAL RISK PREMIUM AGAINST SHORT-TERM GOVERNMENT DEBT	STANDARD DEVIATION OF REAL RETURNS
Denmark	4.51	19.85
Belgium	4.99	23.06
Switzerland	5.29	18.79
Spain	5.46	21.45
Norway	5.7	25.90
Canada	5.88	16.71
Ireland	5.98	20.33
UK	6.14	19.84
Netherlands	6.61	22.36
Average	**7.14**	**22.8**
US	7.41	19.64
Sweden	7.98	22.09
South Africa	8.25	22.09
Australia	8.49	17.00
Germany	9.07	33.49
France	9.27	24.19
Japan	9.84	27.82
Italy	10.46	32.09
World-ex US	**5.93**	**19.30**
World	**6.07**	**16.72**

The second column of numbers shows the historical standard deviation of shares in each country. Germany, Japan and Italy had the most volatile stock markets over the period (what do these countries have in common historically?), but notice how many markets around the world had a standard deviation very close to that of the US market. Even more important, look at the bottom row of the table, which calculates the standard deviation and equity risk premium for a portfolio containing shares from all 16 countries. The world portfolio's standard deviation was just 16.7 per cent. Only the Canadian stock market was less volatile than the world market as a whole. Here again we see the power of diversification. The equity risk premium on the world portfolio fell in the middle of the pack relative to the individual countries, but it managed to achieve those average returns with very low volatility.

Source: Adapted from Elroy Dimson, Paul Marsh and Mike Staunton (2006). *The Equity Risk Premium: A Smaller Puzzle*. Working Paper.

6.5 SUMMARY AND CONCLUSIONS

- An important measure of an investment's performance is its total return. The total return is the sum of the income that the investment pays, plus any change in the price of the investment.

- Total returns can be expressed either in monetary or percentage terms.

- Historically, shares have earned higher average returns than long- and medium-term government debt, and such debt has earned higher returns than short-term government bonds. However, higher returns come at the price of higher volatility.

- Real returns measure the change in purchasing power over time, whereas nominal returns measure the change in money accumulated. Investors who care about what they can consume with their wealth should focus on real returns.

- Historically, share returns are only approximately normally distributed.

- One measure of risk is standard deviation, which captures deviations from the average outcome. For broad asset classes, the relationship between average returns and standard deviation is nearly linear.

- The volatility (standard deviation) of individual shares is generally higher than the volatility of a portfolio. This suggests that diversification lowers risk.

- There is a point beyond which additional diversification does not reduce risk. The risk that cannot be eliminated through diversification is called systematic risk, whereas the risk that disappears in a well-diversified portfolio is called unsystematic risk. The variance or standard deviation of any investment equals the sum of the systematic and unsystematic components of risk.

- Because investors can easily eliminate unsystematic risk by diversifying, the market should only reward investors based on the systematic risk that they bear.

- For individual investments, there is no strong linear relationship between average returns and standard deviation. This is the case, because standard deviation includes both systematic and unsystematic risk, and returns should only be linked to systematic risk.

INTERNET RESOURCES

For updates to links in this section and elsewhere in the book, please go to the book's website at www.cengage.co.uk/megginson.

http://www.globalfindata.com
This is an excellent resource for free historical data on share returns, bond returns and inflation.

http://www.morningstar.com
Use this site to obtain historical returns and estimates of volatility such as standard deviation for mutual funds.

http://www.firstactive.ie/sav_inv_pip_risk_return.asp
A site that gives a solid overview of the risk–return relationship in the context of funds management.

http://www.angelahennessey.co.uk/information.htm
A company in the UK that has interesting papers on the equity risk premium and unquoted shares.

KEY TERMS

capital gain
capital loss
diversification

risk premium
standard deviation
systematic risk

total return
unsystematic risk

SELF-TEST PROBLEMS

ST6-1 Download from Thomson ONE the data for the five shares analysed over the 1986–2006 period. Calculate the standard deviation of these share returns over the four five-year periods. Have these shares become more or less volatile over time?

ST6-2 Suppose that short-term government debt returns follow a normal distribution with a mean of 4.1 per cent and a standard deviation of 2.8 per cent. This implies that, 68 per cent of the time, short-term government debt returns should fall within what range?

QUESTIONS

Q6-1 Why is it important to focus on total returns when measuring an investment's performance?

Q6-2 Why do real returns matter more than nominal returns?

Q6-3 Under what conditions will the components of a bond's return have the opposite sign?

Q6-4 Explain why money returns and percentage returns can sometimes send conflicting signals when comparing two different investments.

Q6-5 Do the rankings of investment alternatives depend on whether we rank based on nominal returns or real returns?

Q6-6 Classify each of the following events as a source of systematic or unsystematic risk.

a The chairman of the ECB resigns and Michael Schumacher is appointed to take his place.

b An OPEC embargo raises the world market price of oil.

c A major consumer products firm loses a product liability case.

d The French parliament gives freedom to employers to hire and fire at will.

PROBLEMS

Understanding returns

P6-1 You purchase 1000 shares of Spears Grinders for €45 per share. A year later, a dividend of €1.25 per share is paid, and the share sells for €49.

a Calculate your total euro return.

b Calculate your total percentage return.

c Do the answers to parts (a) and (b) depend on whether you sell the shares after one year or continue to hold them?

P6-2 A financial adviser claims that a particular share earned a total return of 10 per cent last year. During the year the share price rose from €30 to €32.50. What dividend did the share pay?

P6-3 DS Trucking Company shares pay a €1.50 dividend every year without fail. A year ago, the shares sold for €25 per share, and their total return during the past year was 20 per cent. What do the shares sell for today?

P6-4 Nano-Motors Corporation has equity outstanding that sells for €10 per share.

Macro-Motors shares cost €50 each. Neither shares pay dividends at present.

a An investor buys 100 shares of Nano-Motors. A year later, the shares sell for €15. Calculate the total return in euro terms and in percentage terms.

b Another investor buys 100 shares of Macro-Motors. A year later, the shares are worth €56. Calculate the total return in euro terms and in percentage terms.

c Why is it difficult to say which investor had a better year?

SMART SOLUTIONS

See the problem and solution explained step-by-step at www.cengage.co.uk/ megginson

P6-5 David Rawlings pays €1000 to buy a five-year government bond that pays a 6 per cent coupon rate (for simplicity, assume annual coupon payments). One year later, the market's required return on this bond has increased from 6 per cent to 7 per cent. What is Rawlings total return (in euro and percentage terms) on the bond?

P6-6 G. Welch purchases a corporate bond that was originally issued for €1000 several years ago. The bond has four years remaining until it matures, the market price now is €1054.45 and the yield to maturity (YTM) is 4 per cent. The bond pays an annual coupon of €55, with the next payment due in one year.

a What is the bond's coupon rate? Its coupon yield?

b Suppose Welch holds this bond for one year and the YTM does not change. What is the total percentage return on the bond? Show that on a percentage basis, the total return is the sum of the interest and capital gain/loss components.

c If the yield to maturity decreases during the first year from 4 per cent to 3.5 per cent, what is the total percentage return that year?

P6-7 In this advanced problem, let's look at the behaviour of ordinary Treasury bonds and inflation-indexed bonds, or TIPS. We will simplify by assuming annual interest payments rather than semi-annual. Suppose over the next five years investors expect 3 per cent inflation each year. The Treasury issues a five-year ordinary bond that pays $55 interest each year. The Treasury issues a five-year TIPS that pays a coupon rate of 2 per cent. With TIPS, the coupon payment is determined by multiplying the coupon rate times the inflation-adjusted principal value. Like ordinary bonds, TIPS begin with a par value or principal value of $1000. However, that principal increases over time as inflation occurs. Assuming that inflation is in fact equal to 3 per cent in each of the next five years, then the cash flows associated with each bond would look like the table below. In the last row of the table, notice the final TIPS payment includes the return of the inflation-adjusted principal ($1159.27), plus the final coupon payment.

a Calculate the yield to maturity (YTM) of each bond. Why is one higher than the other? Show that the TIPS YTM equals the product of the real interest rate and the inflation rate.

b What is the real return on the T-bond?

c Suppose the real return on the T-bond stays constant, but investors expect 4 per cent inflation rather than 3 per cent. What happens to the required return on the T-bond in nominal terms?

d Imagine that during the first year, the inflation that actually occurred was 3 per cent, as expected. However, suppose that by the end of the first year, investors had come to expect 4 per cent inflation for the next four years. Fill out the remaining cash flows for each bond in the table at the top of page 215.

YEAR	T-BOND PAYS	TIPS PAYS	INFLATION-ADJUSTED PRINCIPAL (TIPS)	COUPON PYMT CALCULATION
0 (cost)	−1 000.00	−1 000.00	−1 000.00	NA
1	55.00	20.60	1 030.00	1 000.00(1.03) × 2%
2	55.00	21.22	1 060.90	1 030.00(1.03) × 2%
3	55.00	21.85	1 092.73	1 060.90(1.03) × 2%
4	55.00	22.51	1 125.51	1 092.73(1.03) × 2%
5	1 055.00	1 182.46	1 159.27	1 125.51(1.03) × 2%

YEAR	T-BOND PAYS	TIPS PAYS	INFLATION-ADJUSTED PRINCIPAL (TIPS)	COUPON PYMT CALCULATION
0 (cost)	−1 000.00	−1 000.00	−1 000.00	NA
1	55.00	20.60	1 030.00	1 000.00(1.03) × 2%
2				
3				
4				
5				

e Now calculate the market price of the Treasury bond as of the end of the first year. Remember to discount the bond's remaining cash flows, using the nominal required return that you calculated in part (c). Given this new market price, what is the total return offered by the T-bond the first year?

f Next, calculate the market price of the TIPS bond. Remember, at the end of the first year, the YTM on the TIPS will equal the product of one plus the real return (2 per cent) and one plus the inflation rate (4 per cent). What is the total nominal return offered by TIPS the first year?

The history of returns (or how to get rich slowly)

P6-8 The nominal return on a particular investment is 11 per cent and the inflation rate is 2 per cent. What is the real return?

P6-9 A bond offers a real return of 5 per cent. If investors expect 3 per cent inflation, what is the nominal rate of return on the bond?

P6-10 If an investment promises a nominal return of 6 per cent and the inflation rate is 1 per cent, what is the real return?

P6-11 The following data show the rate of return on a portfolio of shares and bonds. Calculate the risk premium on equities versus bonds each year and then calculate the average risk premium. Do you think, at the beginning of 2003, investors expected the outcomes we observe in this table?

YEAR	2003	2004	2005	2006
Return on shares (%)	−10.9	−11.0	−20.9	31.6
Return on bonds (%)	21.5	3.7	17.8	1.4
Risk premium (%)				

P6-12 The table below shows the average return on US shares and bonds for 25-year periods ending in 1925, 1950, 1975 and 2000. Calculate the equity risk premium for each quarter century. What lesson emerges from your calculations?

AVE. RETURN	1925	1950	1975	2000
Stocks	9.7%	10.2%	11.4%	16.2%
Bonds	3.5%	4.1%	2.4%	10.6%
Risk premium				

Source: Elroy Dimson, Paul Marsh and Mike Staunton (2001) *The Triumph of the Optimists: 101 Years of Global Investment Returns*, Princeton University Press. Reprinted with permission.

P6-13 The current yield to maturity on a one-year government stock is 2 per cent. You believe that the expected risk premium on shares versus short-term government stocks equals 7.6 per cent.

a Estimate the expected return on the stock market next year.

b Explain why the estimate in part (a) may be better than simply assuming that next year's stock market return will equal the long-term average return.

Volatility and risk

P6-14 Using data in this chapter, how would you estimate the probability that the return on the stock market will exceed 30 per cent in any given year?

P6-15 Here are the nominal returns on shares, bonds and bills for the 1920s and 1930s. For each decade, calculate the standard deviation of returns for each asset class. How do those figures compare with more recent numbers.

SMART SOLUTIONS
See the problem and solution explained step-by-step at www.cengage.co.uk/ megginson

NOMINAL RETURNS (%) ON STOCKS, BONDS AND BILLS

	1920s				1930s		
	STOCKS	BONDS	BILLS		STOCKS	BONDS	BILLS
1920	−17.9	5.8	7.6	1930	−28.3	4.7	2.4
1921	11.6	12.7	7.0	1931	−43.9	−5.3	1.1
1922	30.6	3.5	4.7	1932	−9.8	16.8	1.0
1923	3.0	5.7	5.2	1933	57.6	−0.1	0.3
1924	27.0	6.4	4.1	1934	4.4	10.0	0.2
1925	28.3	5.7	4.1	1935	44.0	5.0	0.2
1926	9.5	7.8	3.3	1936	32.3	7.5	0.2
1927	33.1	8.9	3.1	1937	−34.6	0.2	0.3
1928	38.7	0.1	3.6	1938	28.2	5.5	0.0
1929	−14.5	3.4	4.7	1939	2.9	5.5	0.0

Source: Elroy Dimson, Paul Marsh and Mike Staunton (2001) *The Triumph of the Optimists: 101 Years of Global Investment Returns*, Princeton University Press. Reprinted with permission.

P6-16 Use the data below to calculate the standard deviation of nominal and real Treasury bill returns from 1972–1982. Do you think that when they purchased T-bills, investors expected to earn negative real returns as often as they did during this period? If not, what happened that took investors by surprise?

YEAR	NOMINAL RETURN (%)	REAL RETURN (%)
1972	3.8	0.4
1973	6.9	−1.7
1974	8.0	−3.7
1975	5.8	−1.1
1976	5.1	0.3
1977	5.1	−1.5
1978	7.2	−1.7
1979	10.4	−2.6
1980	11.2	−1.0
1981	14.7	5.3
1982	10.5	6.4

Source: Elroy Dimson, Paul Marsh and Mike Staunton (2001) *The Triumph of the Optimists: 101 Years of Global Investment Returns*, Princeton University Press. Reprinted with permission.

P6-17 Based on Figure 6.5, about what rate of return would a truly risk-free investment (i.e. one with a standard deviation of zero) offer investors?

The power of diversification

P6-18 Troy McClain wants to form a portfolio of four different shares. Summary data on the four shares appear below. First, calculate the average standard deviation across the four shares and then answer this question. If Troy forms a portfolio by investing 25 per cent of his money in each of the shares in the table, it is very likely that the standard deviation of this portfolio's return will be (more than, less than, equal to) 43.5 per cent. Explain your answer.

SHARE	RETURN	STD. DEV.
no. 1	14%	71%
no. 2	10%	46%
no. 3	9%	32%
no. 4	11%	25%

P6-19 The table at the top of page 217 annual returns on chip maker Advanced Micro Devices and the pharmaceutical producer Merck. The last column of the table shows the annual return that a portfolio invested 50 per cent in AMD and 50 per cent in Merck would have earned each year. The portfolio's return is simply a weighted average of the returns of AMD and Merck. An example portfolio return calculation for 1994 is given at the top of the table.

SMART EXCEL

See this problem explained in Excel at **www.cengage.co.uk/ megginson**

YEAR	AMD	MERCK	50–50 PORTFOLIO
1994	40.1%	14.9%	27.5% (0.5 × 40.1% + 0.5 × 14.9%)
1995	−33.7%	76.4%	
1996	56.1%	24.0%	
1997	−31.1%	35.5%	
1998	63.4%	41.2%	
1999	−0.2%	−7.4%	
2000	−4.5%	41.7%	
2001	14.8%	−35.9%	
2002	−59.3%	−1.1%	
2003	130.7%	−11.2%	
Std. Dev.			

a Plot a graph similar to Figure 6.6 showing the returns on AMD and Merck each year.

b Fill in the blanks in the table above by calculating the 50–50 portfolio's return each year from 1995–2003 and then plot this on the graph you created for part (a). How does the portfolio return compare to the returns of the individual shares in the portfolio?

c Calculate the standard deviation of AMD, Merck and the portfolio, and comment on what you find.

P6-20 The table below shows annual prices for Clarins and one of its major competitors, Elizabeth Arden. The final column shows the annual return on a portfolio invested 50 per cent in Elizabeth Arden and 50 per cent in Clarins. The portfolio's return is simply a weighted average of the returns of the shares in the portfolio, as shown in the example calculation at the top of the table.

DATE	ANNUAL PRICE CLARINS	ANNUAL % CHANGE CLARINS	ANNUAL PRICE ELIZABETH ARDEN	ANNUAL % CHANGE ELIZABETH ARDEN	50–50 PORTFOLIO
30/12/2005	46.85		20.06		
31/12/2004	37.11		23.74		
31/12/2003	33.12		19.92		
31/12/2002	27.32		14.80		
31/12/2001	40.76		15.27		
29/12/2000	49.71		12.06		
31/12/1999	55.20		6.44		
31/12/1998	26.15		7.25		
31/12/1997	25.15		9.13		
31/12/1996	37.29		7.75		

(P6-20 continued)

a Fill in the blanks in the table above by calculating the 50–50 portfolio's return each year and then plot this on the graph. How does the portfolio return compare to the returns of the individual shares in the portfolio?

b Calculate the standard deviation for each share and the portfolio, and comment on what you find.

P6-21 The table below shows the standard deviation for various portfolios of shares. Plot the relationship between the number of shares in the portfolio and the portfolio's standard deviation. Comment on how the resulting graph is similar to and different from Figure 6.7.

SHARES IN THE PORTFOLIO	STD. DEVIATION (%)
Nokia	16.1
Nokia + Total	15.9
Nokia + Total + Banco Santanders	15.1
Nokia + Total + Banco Santanders + Airbus	13.6
Nokia + Total + Banco Santanders + Airbus + Fiat	13.1
Nokia + Total + Banco Santanders + Airbus + Fiat + Ricard	14.7

THOMSON ONE Business School Edition

Access financial information from the Thomson ONE – Business School Edition website for the following problem(s). Go to http://tobsefin.swlearning.com/. If you have already registered your access serial number and have a username and password, click Enter. Otherwise, click Register and follow the instructions to create a username and password. Register your access serial number and then click Enter on the aforementioned website. When you click Enter, you will be prompted for your username and password (please remember that the password is case sensitive). Enter them in the respective boxes and then click OK (or hit Enter). From the ensuing page, click Click Here to Access Thomson ONE – Business School Edition Now! This opens up a new window that gives you access to the Thomson ONE – Business School Edition database. You can retrieve a company's financial information by entering its ticker symbol (provided for each company in the problem(s)) in the box below 'Name/Symbol/Key'. For further instructions on using the Thomson ONE – Business School Edition database, please refer to *A Guide for Using Thomson ONE – Business School Edition*.

P6-22 Compare the average annual returns and standard deviations of annual returns of Cement Roadstone Holdings, Banco Santander and SAP to those of a portfolio containing the three companies' shares. Calculate the average and standard deviation of annual returns for each company. Now assume that you form a portfolio by investing equal amounts of money in each share. Determine the annual returns for this portfolio. To calculate the portfolio's return in each year, simply calculate a weighted-average of the returns of the shares in the portfolio. The weight given to each shares is one-third.

After calculating the portfolio's return in each year, then calculate the average and standard deviation of the portfolio's annual returns.

How do these compare to the average and standard deviation of annual returns of the three firms taken separately? What can you infer about the risk and return of the portfolio compared to those of the individual firms? Does your answer change if you invest 40 per cent of your capital in Banco Santander, 35 per cent in SAP and the remaining funds in CRH?

P6-23 Compare the nominal and real annual returns for SAP. Determine the annual nominal rate of return for SAP over the last ten years. Calculate the real annual rates of return for SAP – inflation rates for the eurozone can be found at http://www.ecb.int/stats/prices/hicp/html/index.en.html. Is the real rate of return less than the nominal rate of return every year? Why? What do you think will happen to this relationship if inflation in any given year were negative?

MINICASE *The trade-off between risk and return*

Assignment

Use the following information to compare the recent performance of the FTSE Index, the FTSE Small Cap Index, the UK Government Bond Index and UK inflation. Each of these index numbers is calculated in a way that assumes that investors reinvest any income they receive, so the total return equals the percentage change in the index value each year.

For the FTSE, the FTSE Small Cap Index and the UK Government Bond Index, calculate (a) the cumulative return over 20 years, (b) the average annual return in nominal terms, (c) the average annual return in real terms and (d) the standard deviation of the nominal return. Based on these calculations, discuss the risk/return relationship between these indexes. Which asset class earned the highest average return? For which asset class were returns most volatile? Plot your results on a graph with the standard deviation of each asset class on the horizontal axis and the average return on the vertical axis.

	FTSE INDEX	FTSE SMALL CAP INDEX	GOVERNMENT BOND INDEX	CONSUMER PRICES
30/12/1988	1 770.07	1 466.68	105.45	80.10
29/12/1989	2 358.87	1 568.06	114.59	84.10
31/12/1990	2 163.36	1 192.22	130.67	89.60
31/12/1991	2 408.12	1 351.59	147.29	94.90
31/12/1992	2 782.31	1 296.18	169.86	96.10
31/12/1993	3 322.26	1 805.45	185.72	97.30
30/12/1994	3 031.78	1 744.32	189.89	98.80
29/12/1995	3 650.83	1 944.61	212.32	101.60
31/12/1996	4 043.76	2 153.19	225.60	103.20
31/12/1997	5 081.13	2 295.49	241.29	103.70
31/12/1998	5 710.53	2 031.31	264.50	104.10
31/12/1999	6 735.59	3 003.19	273.08	103.90
29/12/2000	6 229.26	3 208.81	294.46	102.90
31/12/2001	5 180.91	2 598.10	314.54	101.70
31/12/2002	3 948.37	1 856.78	333.65	100.50
31/12/2003	4 396.89	2 453.79	345.80	100.40
31/12/2004	4 750.87	2 713.22	362.47	100.30
30/12/2005	5 551.62	3 252.60	379.70	100.60
29/12/2006	6 173.32	3 804.74	392.10	103.00

Chapter 7

Risk, Return and the Capital Asset Pricing Model

High beta impacts IPO

Over the ten years from 1995 the business of airline travel in Europe was transformed. Low-cost carriers such as Ryanair and easyJet adopted a business model that allowed them to radically undercut existing rivals. The success of these companies naturally induced a large number of competitors, and also forced existing carriers to cut costs and generate efficiencies. One of the more successful new entrants was Air Berlin, which rose by end 2005 to be the third largest low-cost carrier in Europe. In May 2006 Air Berlin was on course for flotation. However, on the eve of the IPO the company stalled the flotation for a further week. Analysts cited higher oil prices and enhanced competition, as well as concerns about the cyclical nature of the airline market. Financial analysts call shares like Air Berlin – that move very sharply in response to movements in the broader stock market – high-beta shares. Airlines generally have very high beta coefficients. Rather than issuing shares at an unfavourable price, Air Berlin executives decided to take a wait-and-see approach. This paid off because, after a week, the IPO ran successfully, although with lower take-up and lower monies raised than had been anticipated.

Sources: Business Week; Financial Times.

LEARNING OBJECTIVES

After studying this chapter you should be able to:

- Illustrate three different approaches for estimating an asset's expected return.
- Calculate a portfolio's expected return and its beta.
- Show how the capital asset pricing model (CAPM) links an asset's beta to its expected return.
- Describe the concept of market efficiency and its important lessons for investors.

SMART FINANCE
Use the learning tools at www.cengage.co.uk/megginson

In this chapter, we continue our study of the relationship between risk and return. We will see that a share's beta, a measure of how much a share's returns vary in response to variations in overall market returns, is an important determinant of its expected return. This is the central insight of the capital asset pricing model (CAPM), one of the most important ideas in modern finance. The scholars who developed the model earned a Nobel Prize in Economics in 1990 for their research. The CAPM is useful not only for investors in financial markets but also for managers who need to understand what returns shareholders expect on the money they contribute to corporate ventures.

7.1 EXPECTED RETURNS

expected return
A forecast of the return that an asset will earn over some period of time.

Ultimately, people want to know what return they can expect from an investment. Investors and corporate managers decide upon investments based on their best judgements about what the future will hold. In finance, when we use the term **expected return**, we have in mind a 'best guess' estimate of how an investment will perform in the future. For example, in Chapter 6 we saw ample evidence that investors should expect higher returns on shares than on bonds. Intuitively, such an expectation makes sense because shares are riskier than bonds, and investors should expect a reward for bearing risk. However, the claim that expected returns on shares exceed expected returns on bonds does not imply that shares will actually outperform bonds in any given year. Rather, it means that it is more reasonable to expect that shares will outperform bonds as opposed to bonds outperforming shares.

In Chapter 6 we noted that the benefit that an investment provides is its return, but the associated cost is the investment's risk. In this chapter we develop an explicit link between risk and return, and therefore between marginal costs and benefits of investing. To establish that link, we have to deal with a major challenge. *Expected returns are inherently unobservable.* More particularly, we are always looking at the past (ex post analysis) to determine what we expect in the future (ex ante analysis). Analysts have many techniques at their disposal to form estimates of expected returns, but it is important to remember that the numbers produced by these models are just estimates. As a starting point, let's see how analysts might use historical data to make educated guesses about the future.

The historical approach

The first method relies on historical data and assumes that the future and the past share much in common. Recall from Chapter 6 that we saw various long-term equity risk premia for a range of countries. This of course is from the market as a whole. Can we apply that logic to an individual share to estimate its expected return? First, remember that we saw at the end of Chapter 6 that pooling shares together changes the risk profile. So we would need to be certain that the share we are examining is very similar to the market. However, as a *first approximation* to the return to be expected from a share, the use of the historical approach has the advantage of being simple to construct. What is important, however, is to consider the share as itself, not as a proxy for the market.

Consider the case of three shares – Phillips Electronics, Boots the Chemist and Michelin. All of these have been trading for many years. Over the last 20 years we find that the long-run arithmetic average return for these shares was 6.28 per cent, 11.22 per cent and 6.98 per cent. Suppose also that over the same time period the shareholders have enjoyed an historical risk premium of 3 per cent, 5 per cent and 3.5 per cent. Given that the present day short-term government bond rates for the eurozone are 3.5 per cent and for the UK are 4 per cent, we might then estimate the expected returns as

Current short-term rate + Historical risk premium = 6.5% (Phillips),
9% (Boots the Chemist) and 6.5% (Michelin)

Although simple and intuitively appealing, this approach suffers from several drawbacks. First, over its long history, any company will have experienced many changes, ranging from executive turnover to technological breakthroughs, to increased competition from domestic and foreign rivals. Presumably, shareholders earned returns year by year and decade by decade that compensated them for the risks associated with holding these shares, but those risks vary over time. Calculating an historical risk premium over the last 20 years blends all these changes into a single number, and that number may or may not reflect the company's current status. Thus, the historical approach yields merely a naïve estimate of the expected return in any given year. Investors need to know whether shares today are more risky, less risky or just as risky as the long-term premium indicates.

A second flaw in applying this approach broadly is that most shares in the market do not have a long history. The average lifespan of companies on markets is less than 30 years.

The probabilistic approach

Another method for estimating expected returns uses statistical concepts. When statisticians want to estimate the expected value of some unknown quantity, they first list all possible values that the variable of interest might take, as well as the probability that each outcome will occur. In principle, analysts can use the same approach to calculate the expected return on shares and other financial assets. A potential advantage of this approach is that it does not require an analyst to assume that the future will look just like the past. Professional judgement plays a larger role here.

Consider the case of DaimlerChrylser, the German-US auto giant. DaimlerChrylser falls into a category of shares that traders call 'cyclicals', because these shares' fortunes rise and fall dramatically with the business cycle. The sectors that are considered cyclical include basic materials, capital goods, communications, consumer cyclical, energy, financial, healthcare and technology. To project the expected return on Daimler Chrysler shares, an analyst can estimate the probabilities associated with different states of the overall economy. Table 7.1 illustrates how this can work. The analyst assumes that the economy will be in one of three possible states next year – boom, expansion or recession. The current climate presents a 20 per cent chance that the economy will experience a recession, and the probabilities of a normal expansion or a boom are 70 per cent and 10 per cent, respectively. Next, the analyst projects that if the economy slips into recession, DaimlerChrylser shareholders will experience a 30 per cent loss. If the economy continues to expand normally, then the DaimlerChrylser share return will be 15 per cent. If the economy booms, GM shares will do very well, earning a total return of 55 per cent.

OUTCOME	PROBABILITY	DAIMLERCHRYLSER RETURN
Recession	20%	–30%
Expansion	70%	15%
Boom	10%	55%

TABLE 7.1

How returns change across the economic cycle

To calculate the expected return on DaimlerChrylser shares, multiply each possible return by the probability that it will occur and then add up the returns across all three possible outcomes:

$$0.20 \times (-0.30) + 0.70 \times 0.15 + 0.10 \times 0.55 = 10\%$$

With an estimate of the expected return in place, the analyst can use the same basic model to estimate the variance and standard deviation of DaimlerChrylser shares. To do so, subtract the 10 per cent expected return from the actual return on DaimlerChrylser shares in each state of the economy. Then, square that difference and multiply it by the probability of recession, expansion or boom. Table 7.2 illustrates the calculation.

TABLE 7.2

How risks change across the economic cycle

OUTCOME	PROBABILITY	DAIMLERCHRYLSER RETURN	RETURN − 10%	(RETURN − 10%)²
Recession	20%	−30%	−40%	1 600%²
Expansion	70%	15%	5%	25%²
Boom	10%	55%	45%	2 025%²

Variance = (0.20)(1600%²)+(0.70)(25%²)+(0.10)(2025%²) = 540%²
Standard deviation = √540%² = 23.2%

The analyst can apply the same model to any shares with returns tied to the business cycle. For example, purchases of chocolate do not vary over the business cycle as much as car purchases do, so Cadbury shares should be less sensitive to economic conditions than DaimlerChrylser shares. Perhaps when the economy is booming, Cadbury shareholders earn 36 per cent. Under normal economic conditions, Cadbury shares earns 12 per cent, but during an economic slump, the return on Cadbury shares equals −15 per cent. Maintaining the same assumptions about the probabilities of recession, expansion and boom, estimates of Cadbury's expected return, variance and standard deviation can be constructed as follows:

TABLE 7.3

How risk changes across the economic cycle: the case of Cadbury

OUTCOME	PROBABILITY	CADBURY RETURN	RETURN − 9%	(RETURN − 9%)²
Recession	20%	−15%	−24%	576%²
Expansion	70%	12%	3%	9%²
Boom	10%	36%	27%	729%²

Expected return = (0.20)(−15%) + (0.70)(12%) + (0.10)(36%) = 9%
Variance = (0.20)(576%²)+(0.70)(9%²)+(0.10)(729%²) = 194.4%²
Standard deviation = √194.4%² = 13.9%

But the probabilistic approach has its own drawbacks. To calculate expected returns for DaimlerChrysler, we started with a simplifying assumption that only three possible outcomes or scenarios were possible. Clearly, the range of potential outcomes is much broader than this. Similarly, we assumed that we could know the probability of each scenario in advance. Where did those probabilities come from? Analysts can draw from historical experience – for example, by estimating the probability of a recession by studying the frequencies of recessions in the past. If history shows that recessions occur in roughly one year out of every five, then 20 per cent might be a reasonable estimate of the probability of a recession in the future; then again, it might be well off the mark. In any case, the probabilistic approach involves a high degree of subjectivity. It requires analysts to specify possible future outcomes for share returns and to attach a probability to each outcome. Once again, these assumptions about possible states of the economy can be somewhat naïve if the assumptions are based on historical data.

The risk-based approach

A third approach to estimating an asset's expected return is more theoretically sound and is used in practice by most corporate finance professionals. It requires an analyst to first measure the risk of the asset and then to translate that risk measure into an expected return estimate. This approach involves a two-step process. The first step is to define what we mean by risk and to measure it, and the second step is to quantify how much return we should expect on an asset with a given amount of risk.

Measuring the risk of a single asset Recall that Chapter 6 introduced the notions of systematic and unsystematic risk. Recall these concepts:

- Systematic risks simultaneously affect many different securities, whereas unsystematic risks affect just a few securities at a time. Systematic risk refers to events, such as unexpected changes in the overall health of the economy, interest rate movements or changes in inflation. Events that we classify as examples of unsystematic risk include the failure of a firm's new product to gain market share, a scandal involving top management at a particular company or the loss of a key employee.

- Investors can eliminate unsystematic risk by diversifying, but diversification cannot eradicate systematic (or market) risk. We know that there is a general relationship between risk and the reward to an asset. Because it is easy for investors to shed one type of risk but not the other, the market rewards investors for bearing systematic risk. That is, assets with more exposure to systematic risk generally offer investors higher returns than assets with less exposure to systematic risk.

- The standard deviation of an asset's returns measures how much returns fluctuate around the average. Standard deviation makes no distinction between a movement in returns caused by systematic factors, such as an increase in the price of oil, and movements associated with unsystematic factors, such as the outcome of a product liability lawsuit filed against one firm. In other words, the standard deviation measures an asset's total risk, equal to the sum of its systematic and unsystematic components. Because only the systematic component of risk influences an asset's expected return, an asset's standard deviation is an unreliable guide to its expected return.

If systematic risk means risk that affects the entire market, then for an individual share, we need to know the extent to which the share moves when the market moves. We need a measure that captures *only* the systematic component of a share's volatility, because *only* that component should be related to the asset's expected return. When an event having a positive (or negative) effect on the overall market also has a pronounced positive (or negative) effect on a particular share, then that share has a high degree of systematic risk and should also have a high expected return.

For a visual explanation of this idea, examine Figures 7.1A and 7.1B. The figures show scatter plots of weekly share returns over the period 1995–2005 for two companies – LVMH, the French-based luxury goods company, and National Grid, the UK power distributor. For the example, each dot shows the return on the shares and the return on the MSCI Index for the relevant market in a particular week. MSCI indices are calculated by Morgan Stanley and are designed for comparability across different markets – something that is not always easy. Through each scatter plot we have drawn a trend line, estimated by using the method of linear regression. This trend line shows the average tendency for each share to move with the market.

These two shares respond differently, on average, to market movements. The slope of the trend line for LVMH equals 1.17. Thus, on average, if the market's return in a

FIGURE 7.1a

LVMH versus MSCI-France Index

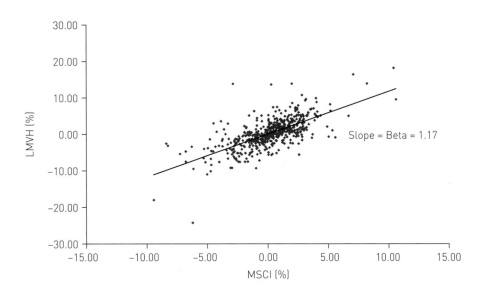

FIGURE 7.1b

National Grid versus MSCI-UK Index

The figure shows a scatter plot of weekly returns on LMVH shares (Figure 7.1a) and National Grid shares (Figure 7.1b) versus the weekly return on the MSCI index for each country. The scatter plots reveal a strong association between movements in the overall market return and movements in LMVH. The link between market movements and National Grid is much weaker.

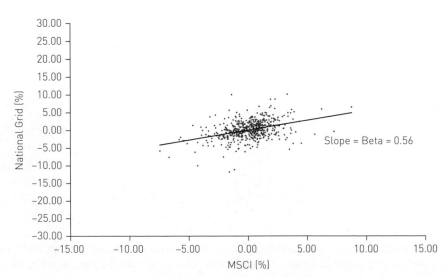

particular week moves by 1 per cent, then LVMH return moves in the same direction by 1.17 per cent. National Grid shares behave quite differently, displaying almost no tendency to move in conjunction with the market. With a slope of 0.56, the trend line for National Grid tells us that if the market return moves up or down 1 per cent, National Grid's return moves just 0.56 per cent in response. These differences in responsiveness lead to an important conclusion. Because returns on LVMH are more sensitive to overall market movements, LVMH shares show a higher degree of systematic risk than National Grid shares. In other words, when a macroeconomic event such as an unexpected shift in interest rates or inflation causes the entire stock market to move, LVMH shares respond more sharply to that event than National Grid shares do.

The slopes of the trend lines in Figures 7.1A and 7.1B have a special designation in finance, known as the **beta**. A share's beta measures the sensitivity of its return to movements in the overall market return. Thus, beta is a measure of systematic risk for a particular security. The return on a high-beta share like LVMH experiences dramatic up-and-down swings when the market return moves. Because LVMH's beta equals 1.17, we can say that the return on LVMH shares moves, on average, 1.17 times as much as does the market return. In contrast, with a beta of just 0.56, the return on National Grid shares barely responds at all when the overall stock market fluctuates. This is not the same thing as saying that National Grid shares do not fluctuate at all. Figure 7.1B shows that weekly returns on National Grid fall in a range roughly between positive and negative 10 per cent. Clearly, a share that can gain or lose 10 per cent in a week is volatile, but National Grid volatility is only weakly related to fluctuations in the overall market. Hence, most of National Grid risk is unsystematic and can be eliminated through diversification.

beta
A standardized measure of the risk of an individual asset, one that captures only the systematic component of its volatility.

Think a little about the businesses that these shares engage in, and the reason for the wide disparity between their betas may become clear. National Grid is a utility, and people use electricity in good times and bad. Energy consumption varies little with the ups and downs of the economy and the stock market, so the share return is not very sensitive to market movements. National Grid shares are affected more by factors – like weather, international commodity prices and government policies – that would not perhaps affect the wider stock market a great deal. On the other hand, LVMH sells luxury goods. People buy these products much more in good times than in bad. Consequently, the return on LVMH shares moves sharply up and down in response to changing macroeconomic conditions.

Risk and expected returns The risk-based approach to calculating expected returns involves two steps. The first step is to develop a measure of a particular asset's systematic risk. In beta we have such a measure. The second step involves translating the asset's beta into an estimate of expected return. To see how that process works, examine Figure 7.2.

In Figure 7.2 we plot the beta against the expected return for two important assets. First, suppose an asset is available that pays a return equal to 4 per cent with certainty. We designate this as the risk-free asset because it pays 4 per cent no matter what the market return may be. In reality, no asset can promise a completely risk-free return, but short-term government debt from a developed country comes very close. Therefore, think of, say, a US government T-bill or a German short-term government bond each time we refer to a risk-free asset. By definition, a risk-free asset has no systematic risk, and so its beta equals zero. We also say that 4 per cent is the risk-free rate.

The second asset plotted in Figure 7.2 is an average share. The term 'average share' means that this security's sensitivity to market movements is neither especially high, like LVMH, nor especially low, like National Grid. By definition, the beta of the average share equals 1.0. On average, its return goes up or down by 1 per cent when

FIGURE 7.2

Beta and expected returns

An investor willing to accept an average level of systematic risk, by holding a share with a beta of 1.0, expects a return of 10 per cent. By holding only the risk-free asset, an investor can earn 4 per cent without having to accept any systematic risk at all.

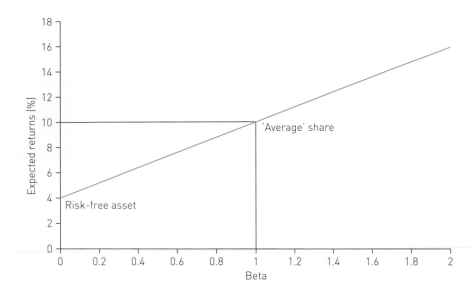

the market return goes up or down by 1 per cent. Assume for a moment that the expected return on this share equals 10 per cent.

By drawing a straight line connecting the two points in Figure 7.2, we gain some insight into the relationship between beta and expected returns. An investor who is unwilling to accept any systematic risk at all can hold the risk-free asset and earn 4 per cent. An investor who is willing to bear an average degree of systematic risk, by investing in a share with a beta equal to 1.0, expects to earn 10 per cent. But how about an investor who wants to take an intermediate level of risk, by holding a share with a beta of 0.5? Or an investor who has a high tolerance for risk and prefers to hold a share with a beta of 1.5?

As you might guess, we can simply find the desired beta along the horizontal axis and then go up to the line to find that asset's expected return. For example, a share with a beta of 0.5 has an expected return of 7 per cent, while a share with a beta of 1.5 has an expected return of 13 per cent. The line in Figure 7.2 plays a very important role in finance, and we will return to it later in this chapter. For now, the important lesson is that beta measures an asset's systematic risk and risk that has a direct relationship with expected returns.

Source: Adapted from 'Time to Dispel a Few Market Myths', *Financial Times*, 8 January 2007.

Real World

The prediction of risk premia is clearly not a trivial or simple task. In reality, it is immensely complex. Sometimes the complexity can be such that fund managers tend to ignore the problem. Take the case of the provocative book by noted US money manger Ken Fisher. Fisher, quoted in the *Financial Times* about his new book *Only Three Questions*, suggests that forecasts of risk premia are so wide in their margins as to be not of any practical use.

CONCEPT
REVIEW
QUESTIONS

1   What is the difference between an asset's expected return and its actual return? Why are expected returns so important to investors and managers?

2   Contrast the historical approach to estimating expected returns with the probabilistic approach.

3   Why should a share's beta and expected return be related, while no such relationship exists between a share's standard deviation and expected return?

4   Why is the risk-based approach the best method for estimating a share's expected return?

7.2 RISK AND RETURN FOR PORTFOLIOS

In Chapter 6 we saw that investors can reduce risk dramatically by holding diversified portfolios rather than individual shares. An investor who chooses to diversify will be more concerned with how her portfolio performs than with the performance of each individual security in the portfolio. Therefore, we need a way to measure risk and return for portfolios.

Portfolio expected return

Suppose an individual has €10 000 to invest, and she decides to divide that money between two different assets. Asset 1 has an expected return of 8 per cent, and Asset 2 has an expected return of 12 per cent. Our investor puts €4000 in Asset 1 and €6000 in Asset 2. What is the expected return on the portfolio?

To begin, we must calculate the fraction of the individual's wealth invested in each asset, known as the **portfolio weights**. The fraction invested in Asset 1 equals 0.40 (€4000/€10 000), and the fraction invested in Asset 2 equals 0.60 (€6000/€10 000). Notice that the portfolio weights add up to 1.0.

The portfolio's expected return equals the weighted average of the expected returns of the securities in the portfolio. In this case, the expected return equals:

$$0.40 \times 8\% + 0.60 \times 12\% = 10.4\%$$

We can write down a more general expression describing a portfolio's expected return. Suppose a portfolio contains N different securities. The expected returns on these securities are $E(R_1), E(R_2), \ldots, E(R_N)$. Finally, the portfolio weights are $w_1, w_2, \ldots, w_N$. The portfolio expected return $E(R_p)$ is given by the following equation:

$$E(R_p) = w_1 E(R_1) + w_2 E(R_2) + \cdots + w_N E(R_N)$$

EQUATION 7.1

portfolio weights
The percentage invested in each of several securities in a portfolio. Portfolio weights must sum to 1.0 (or 100 per cent).

Applying the Model

Calculate the expected return on the portfolio described in the following table:

STOCK	E (R)	€ INVESTED
L'Oreal	10%	2 500
French Connection	12%	5 000
Carrefour	8%	2 500
Danone	14%	10 000

First, calculate the portfolio weights. The total value of the portfolio is €20 000. The weights for the investments in Carrefour and L'Oreal are 0.125 (€2500/€20 000). The fraction invested in French Connection is 0.25, and the weight associated with Danone is 0.50. We therefore multiply those weights by the expected return for each share and add up:

$$E(Rp) = 0.125 \times 10\% + 0.125 \times 8\% + 0.25 \times 12\% + 0.50 \times 14\% = €12.25$$

SMART CONCEPTS

See the concept explained step-by-step at **Smart Finance**

selling short
Borrowing a security and selling it for cash at the current market price. An investor who sells short must eventually return the security to the lender by purchasing it at the then-current market price. Therefore, a short seller hopes that either (1) the price of the security sold short will fall, or (2) the return on the security sold short will be lower than the return on the asset in which the proceeds from the short sale were invested.

Short selling We noted that the portfolio weights have to add up to one. It is natural to assume that these weights also fall in a range between zero and one, meaning that an investor can invest nothing or everything in any particular asset.

However, a more exotic arrangement is possible – one that results in a negative portfolio weight for a particular asset. A negative portfolio weight means that rather than investing in the given asset, an individual is borrowing that asset, selling it, and using the proceeds to invest more in something else. When investors borrow a security and sell it to raise money to invest in something else, they are said to be **selling short**. Here's how that works.

Consider two assets in the market, Rocket.com and BricksNMortar Ltd. Both shares currently sell for €10 and pay no dividends. You are optimistic about Rocket.com's prospects, and you expect its return next year to be 25 per cent. In contrast, you believe that BricksNMortar will earn just 5 per cent. You have €1000 to invest, but you'd like to invest more than that in Rocket.com. To do this, you phone a friend who owns 50 shares of BricksNMortar and persuade him to let you borrow the shares, by promising that you'll return them in one year. Once you receive the shares, you sell them in the market, immediately raising €500. Next, you combine those funds with your own money and purchase €1500 (150 shares) of Rocket.com. In this situation, the weight invested in Rocket.com equals 1.5 (€1500 ÷ €1000), or 150 per cent of your total wealth. You can invest more than 100 per cent of your wealth (i.e. more than €1000) because you borrowed from someone else. The weight invested in BricksNMortar equals –0.5 because you took out a €500 loan equivalent to half your wealth. If you are right and BricksNMortar shares go up from €10 to €10.50 during the year (an increase of 5 per cent), then you will effectively pay your friend 5 per cent interest when you repurchase the BricksNMortar shares and return them next year. This loan will be very profitable if Rocket.com shares increases as rapidly as you expect. For example, in one year's time, if BricksNMortar sells for €10.50 and Rocket.com sells for €12.50 (up 25 per cent), your position will look like this:

TABLE 7.4

The effect of short selling

	BEGINNING OF YEAR
Initial investment	€1 000
Borrowed funds	€ 500 (50 shares @ €10)
Rocket shares	€1 500 (150 shares @ €10)

Source: Adapted from 'Short Selling Sells Long-term Investors Short', *Financial Times*, 27 November 2006.

TABLE 7.4 (cont.)

	END OF YEAR
Sell Rocket shares	€1 875 (150 shares @ €12.50)
Return borrowed shares	−€ 525 (50 shares @ €10.50)
Net cash earned	€1 350

Rate of return = (€1350 − €1000) / €1,000 = 0.35 = 35%

Notice that the expected return on this portfolio exceeds the expected return of either share in the portfolio. When investors take a short position in one asset to invest more in another asset, they are using 'financial leverage'. As we will see in a later chapter, leverage magnifies expected returns, but it also increases risk. Much short selling is associated with hedge funds.

Real World

Short-selling is not a miracle cure for portfolios. Much short-selling, as we note, is associated with hedge finds. However, short-only funds (funds where the only strategy the fund adopts is that of selling shares short) perform very poorly compared to other funds that take a mixture of approaches. In the late 1990s Warren Buffet, perhaps the 20th century's greatest investor, was widely reported as noting that while he was confident that technology shares were overvalued he was not engaging in short selling as he was unsure as to when the correction to the 'proper' price would occur. Perhaps the greatest problem is the asymmetric nature of the returns versus the risk. Shorts can only return less than 100 per cent (the shares can only drop to zero, less the cost of the monies invested) while the losses can be multiples as the price is unbounded upwards.

Portfolio risk

Based on the calculation of a portfolio's expected return, we might expect that a portfolio's risk is equal to a weighted average of the risks of the assets that comprise the portfolio. That statement is partly right and partly wrong. When we shift our focus from expected return to risk, we have to be very careful about the measure of risk that we use in our calculations.

For instance, suppose we estimated the standard deviation of returns for Advanced Micro Devices to be 56.4 per cent and the standard deviation for American Airlines (AMR) to be 47.8 per cent. Suppose we form a portfolio invested equally in AMD and AMR shares. With portfolio weights of 0.50, you might guess that the standard deviation of this portfolio equals:

$$0.5 \times 56.4\% + 0.5 \times 47.8\% = 52.1\%$$

As reasonable as that guess seems, it is wrong. As a general rule, the standard deviation of a portfolio is almost always less than the weighted average of the standard deviations of the shares in the portfolio. This is diversification at work. Combining securities together eliminates some of their unsystematic risk, so the portfolio is less volatile than the average shares in the portfolio.

However, diversification does not eliminate systematic risk. Therefore, if we redefine portfolio risk and focus on systematic risk only, not on standard deviation, which includes both systematic and unsystematic risk, then the simple weighted average formula works. For example, suppose AMD shares have a beta of 1.8 and AMR's beta equals 1.4. The beta of a portfolio with equal investments in each shares is a simple weighted average, in this case:

$$0.5 \times 1.8 + 0.5 \times 1.4 = 1.6$$

Applying the Model

Calculate the beta of the portfolio described in the following table.

STOCK	BETA	€ INVESTED
L'Oreal	1.00	2 500
French Connection	1.33	5 000
Carrefour	0.67	2 500
Danone	1.67	10 000

The portfolio weights here are the same as in the previous 'Applying the Model' section, so the portfolio beta equals:

$$E(Rp) = 0.125 \times 1 + 0.125 \times 0.67 + 0.25 \times 1.33 + 0.50 \times 1.67 = €12.25$$

The Comparative Corporate Finance panel illustrates why distinguishing between systematic and unsystematic risk is important, not just for investors who buy shares and bonds, but also for corporations that build factories, invest in distribution networks and make other kinds of investments in physical assets.

CONCEPT REVIEW QUESTIONS

5   How can the weight given to a particular share in a portfolio exceed 100 per cent?

6   Why is the standard deviation of a portfolio typically less than the weighted average of the standard deviations of the assets in the portfolio, while a portfolio's beta equals the weighted average of the betas of the shares in the portfolio?

COMPARATIVE CORPORATE FINANCE
How risky are emerging markets?

Over the past 25 years, many developing countries around the world adopted market-oriented reforms and opened their economies to inflows of foreign capital. Despite the success these countries have enjoyed in attracting new investors, a recent report by the consulting firm McKinsey & Company argues that most multinational corporations dramatically overestimate the risk of investing in these 'emerging markets'. According to McKinsey, these companies routinely assign a risk premium to projects in emerging markets that is more than double the risk premium that the same companies assign to similar projects in the United States and Europe. By overstating the risks, multinational firms understate the value of investments in emerging markets. McKinsey & Company believes that this leads firms to pass up profitable investment opportunities in these countries.

If it is true that firms overstate the risks of investing in emerging markets, what is the cause of that error? McKinsey proposes that firms do not take the proper portfolio view of the businesses they engage in around the world. Rather than looking at each business unit's contribution to overall firm risk (i.e. the contribution of each unit to the firm's portfolio of businesses), companies place too much emphasis on the unsystematic risks associated with individual countries.

To show how a portfolio view might change a firm's perception of the risk of investing in particular countries, McKinsey offers several pieces of evidence. The first graph shows the year-to-year variation in returns on investments in five separate countries. Clearly these investments display a great deal of volatility. However, for a multinational firm that holds each of these investments in a portfolio the picture changes considerably. The second graph contains two lines, one showing the performance of the portfolio of investments in five emerging markets and the other showing the performance of investments in developed markets. In the second picture, the emerging market portfolio does not appear to be much more volatile than the portfolio invested in assets in the more developed markets of the United States and Europe. (Note: the returns shown here are returns on physical investments like manufacturing plants, not share returns).

McKinsey provides a second kind of evidence to buttress its argument. For each emerging market, McKinsey calculates that market's beta relative to a world market index. By definition, the world market's beta equals 1.0. Especially risky countries should have

▶

betas much greater than 1.0, while supposedly 'safe' countries like the United States should have betas below 1.0. The bar chart shows betas for the United States, Europe and 22 emerging markets. Ten emerging markets have a beta below that of the US market, and in only one country, Russia, does the market beta justify a risk premium double that of the United States. The three charts here tell a common story. Investments that seem to be very risky when considered in isolation look much less risky as part of a portfolio. That's a lesson that applies to individual investors as well as to multinational corporations.

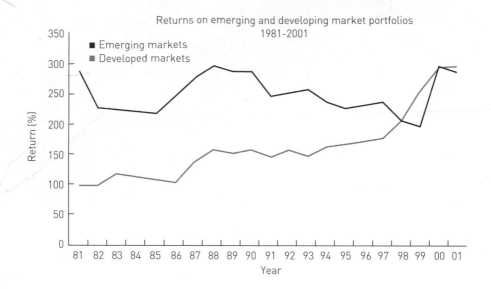

Returns on emerging and developing market portfolios 1981–2001

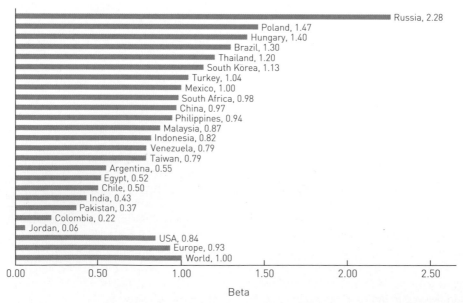

Betas of markets around the world

Source: Adapted from Marc H. Goedhart and Peter Haden, 'Are Emerging Markets as Risky as You Think?' *McKinsey on Finance*, Spring 2003.

7.3 THE SECURITY MARKET LINE AND THE CAPM

Now we are ready to tie together the concepts of risk and return for portfolios as well as for individual securities. Once again we will begin by considering a portfolio consisting of just two assets. One asset pays a risk-free return equal to R_f. We already know that the beta of the risk-free asset equals zero. The other asset is a broadly diversified portfolio. Imagine a portfolio that is so diversified that it contains at least some of every available risky asset in the economy. Because such a portfolio represents the overall market, we refer to it as the **market portfolio**. Designate the expected return on the market portfolio as $E(R_m)$.

> **market portfolio**
> A portfolio that contains some of every asset in the economy.

The beta of the market portfolio must equal 1.0. To see why, reconsider the definition of beta. An asset's beta describes how the asset moves in relation to the overall market. The market portfolio will mimic the overall market perfectly. Because the portfolio's return moves exactly in sync with the market, its beta must be 1.0. Figure 7.3 plots the beta and the expected return of the risk-free asset and the market portfolio.

Suppose we combine the risk-free asset, let's call it a T-bill, and the market portfolio to create a new portfolio. We know that the expected return on this new portfolio must be a weighted average of the expected returns of the assets in the portfolio. Similarly, we know that the beta of the portfolio must be a weighted average of the betas of a T-bill and the market. This implies that the new portfolio we've created must lie along the line connecting the risk-free asset and the market portfolio in Figure 7.3. What are the properties of this line?

With two points identified on the line, the T-bill and the market portfolio, we can calculate the line's slope by taking the rise over the run:

$$\text{Slope} = \frac{E(R_m) - R_f}{1 - 0}$$

This expression should be familiar. The difference in returns between a portfolio of risky securities and a risk-free asset is the **market risk premium**. The market risk premium indicates the reward that investors receive if they hold the market portfolio.

> **market risk premium**
> The additional return earned (or expected) on the market portfolio over and above the risk-free rate.

The intercept of the line in Figure 7.3 equals R_f. From elementary algebra we know that the equation for a straight line is $y = b + mx$ where b is the intercept and m is

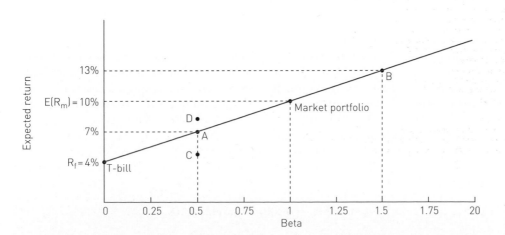

FIGURE 7.3

The security market line

The security market line plots the relationship between an asset's beta and its expected return. The line shows how an investor can construct a portfolio of short-term government debt, assumed to be risk-free, and the market portfolio to achieve the desired level of risk and return. One investor might choose a relatively conservative portfolio, mixing short-term government securities and the market portfolio in equal proportions. Another investor could construct a very risky portfolio by investing his own money and borrowing more to invest in the market.

the slope. In Figure 7.3, the variable we measure on the y-axis is the expected return on some portfolio of T-bills and the market portfolio. The variable we measure on the x-axis is the beta of this portfolio. Therefore, the equation of the line plotted in this figure is

$$E(R_p) = R_f + \beta(E(R_m) - R_f)$$

The equation says that the expected return on any portfolio consisting of T-bills and the market portfolio depends on three things: the risk-free rate, the portfolio beta and the market risk premium. It's easy to verify that this equation works with a numerical illustration.

Applying the Model

Suppose the risk-free rate is 4 per cent, and the expected return on the market portfolio is 10 per cent. This implies that the market risk premium is 6 per cent. What is the expected return on a portfolio invested equally in T-bills and shares? There are actually several ways to get the answer. First, we know that the expected return on the portfolio is simply the weighted average of the expected returns of the assets in the portfolio, so we have:

$$E(R_p) = 0.5 \times 4\% + 0.5 \times 10\% = 7\%$$

Alternatively, we could begin by calculating the beta of this portfolio. The portfolio beta is a weighted average of the betas of T-bills and the market portfolio, so we obtain:

$$\beta p = 0.5(\text{T-bill } \beta) + 0.5[10\% - 4\%] = 0.5$$

Now, using the equation of the line in Figure 7.3, we calculate the portfolio's expected return as follows:

$$E(R_p) = 4\% + 0.5 [10\% - 4\%] = 7\%$$

The position of this portfolio appears as point A in Figure 7.3.

What if an investor is willing to hold a position that is even more risky that the market portfolio? One option is to borrow money. When investors buy government debt, they are essentially loaning money to the government. Suppose investors also borrow money at the risk-free rate. To be more precise, suppose a certain investor has €10 000 to invest, but he raises an additional €5000 by borrowing. The investor then puts all €15 000 in the market portfolio. The portfolio weight on government debt becomes −0.50, and the weight invested in the market portfolio increases to 1.50. The investor now holds a portfolio with a beta greater than one and an expected return greater than 10 per cent, as confirmed in the following calculations:

$$\beta p = -0.5(0) + 1.5[1] = 1.5$$

$$E(R_p) = 4\% + 1.5 [10\% - 4\%] = 13\%$$

In Figure 7.3, the investor's portfolio lies up and to the right from the market portfolio at point B.

At this stage, we must stop and make a crucial observation. If it is true, as the preceding 'Applying the Model' section shows, that a portfolio with a beta of 0.5 offers an expected return of 7 per cent, then in equilibrium it must also be true that any individual security with a beta of 0.5 offers the same return. To understand this claim, examine point C in Figure 7.3. This point represents a share with a beta of 0.5 and an expected return of less than 7 per cent. Rational investors who own C will sell it, because they can create an equally risky portfolio that offers a higher return, by combining T-bills and the market portfolio. As investors sell asset C, its price will fall. We know that prices and returns of financial assets move in opposite directions, so as the price of C falls, its expected return rises until it reaches 7 per cent.

Similarly, consider point D in the figure. Point D represents an asset with a beta of 0.5 but an expected return greater than 7 per cent. This asset is a true bargain because it offers investors a higher rate of return than they can earn on a 50–50 portfolio of T-bills and shares, without requiring them to take on extra risk. Investors will rush to buy share D, and their buying pressure will drive up the price and push down the return of share D. As soon as the expected return on D reaches 7 per cent, the market once again reaches equilibrium.

Figure 7.3 therefore plots the relationship between betas and expected returns for individual securities as well as for portfolios. This relationship is called the 'security market line', and the equation of this line is the fundamental risk and return relationship predicted by the **capital asset pricing model (CAPM)**. The CAPM says that the expected return on any asset i, denoted by $E(R_i)$, depends on the risk-free rate, the security's beta and the market risk premium:

$$E(R_i) = R_f + \beta_i(E(R_m) - R_f)$$

The capital asset pricing model stands as one of the most important ideas in all of finance. Financial managers in nearly all large corporations know the model's key predictions, and they use the CAPM to establish required rates of return on all types of investment projects. The CAPM helps managers understand what returns the market requires on projects having different risk levels. That knowledge improves the quality of corporate investment decisions. As useful as it is, however, the CAPM is not a crystal ball. Remember that the CAPM is a theory, not a talisman. Like all theories it is an abstraction from reality. It gives us some insights about expected returns, but that is not the same thing as predicting how the future will unfold. In the next section, we explore the extent to which actual share returns, rather than expected returns, may be predictable.

capital asset pricing model (CAPM)
States that the expected return on a specific asset equals the risk-free rate plus a premium that depends on the asset's beta and the expected risk premium on the market portfolio.

EQUATION 7.2

SMART CONCEPTS

See the concept explained step-by-step at **www.cengage.co.uk/megginson**

CONCEPT REVIEW QUESTIONS

7 List the three factors that influence a share's expected return according to the CAPM.

8 If a particular share had no systematic risk, only unsystematic risk, what would be its expected return?

7.4 ARE SHARE RETURNS PREDICTABLE?

Microsoft Corporation debuted as a public company with its initial public offering (IPO) on 13 March 1986. On that day, one Microsoft share sold for $21. In the years that followed, shares splits turned a single share purchased at the IPO into 288 shares, worth an amazing $8326 by March 2007. That represents a compound annual return of more than 33 per cent per year! The purpose of this section is to investigate whether such a spectacular outcome could have been anticipated by smart investors.

Suppose upon graduating from business school you decide to forsake a career in the corporate world and open your own business. The question is, what kind of business should you start? A friend suggests opening a pizza restaurant. Having learned a few valuable lessons in school, you respond that the pizza business is a terrible place to begin. Most communities are already saturated with pizza outlets. Most of those offer similar varieties of pizza with a similar ambience, or lack thereof. You want to find a niche that is less competitive. You reason that getting rich selling pizzas is nearly impossible.

As competitive as the pizza business is, it hardly compares with the competitive environment of modern financial markets. The sheer size and transparency of financial markets make them more competitive than most markets for goods and services. Financial asset prices are set by open auction in arenas that are typically governed by rules designed to make the auction process as fair and open as possible. Each day, thousands of professional financial analysts (to say nothing of the tens of thousands of amateurs) worldwide scrutinize all available information about high-profile shares such as Microsoft, hoping to find any bit of information overlooked by the crowd that might lead to an advantage in determining the fair value of Microsoft shares. The rapid growth of electronic media during the past two decades, especially the internet, has caused an explosion in the total volume of financial information available to investors and has accelerated the speed with which that information arrives. All of this means that being a better-than-average share prognosticator is probably more difficult than building a better pizza.

In finance, the idea that competition in financial markets creates an equilibrium in which it is exceedingly difficult to identify undervalued or overvalued shares is called the **efficient markets hypothesis (EMH)**. The EMH says that financial asset prices rapidly and fully incorporate new information. An interesting implication of this prediction is that asset prices move almost randomly over time. We have to use the qualifier, 'almost' in the previous sentence because there is a kind of baseline predictability to asset returns that is related to risk. For example, over time, we expect shares to earn higher returns than bonds, because shares are riskier. Indeed, the historical record confirms this prediction. But in any given year, shares may do very well or very poorly relative to bonds. The efficient markets hypothesis says that it is nearly impossible to predict exactly when shares will do well relative to bonds or when the opposite outcome will occur.

The seemingly random changes in share prices occur because prices respond only to new information, and new information is almost by definition unpredictable. A few examples will illustrate this point.

Unconvinced that market efficiency makes share prices nearly unpredictable, you dig through the archives of historical share returns searching for trading strategies that, with the benefit of hindsight, would have been extraordinarily profitable. Your benchmark for success is the average annual return that an investor who bought shares and held them every year would have earned over the past century, 11.7 per cent.

efficient markets hypothesis (EMH)
Asserts that financial asset prices fully reflect all available information (as formally presented by Eugene Fama in 1970).

Of course, there is no end to the number of trading rules that can be tested using the historical data. In the vast majority of cases, these trading strategies do not generate significantly higher returns than a simple buy-and-hold approach. This suggests that share prices are indeed nearly unpredictable.

The most compelling evidence that markets are efficient is a comparison of passively managed versus actively managed mutual funds. A mutual fund that adopts a passive management style is called an index fund. Index fund managers make no attempt to analyse shares to determine which ones will perform well and which ones will do poorly. Instead, these managers try to mimic the performance of a market index, by buying the shares that make up the index. In contrast, fund managers adopting an active management style do extensive analysis to identify mispriced shares. Active managers trade more frequently than passive managers do and, in the process, generate higher expenses for their shareholders. Though there are notable exceptions (such as legendary managers Peter Lynch, Warren Buffet and Bill Gross), most research indicates that active funds earn lower returns, after expenses, than passive funds do. Buy-and-hold wins again.

If this section concludes with the statement that share returns are essentially unpredictable, then it is fair to ask why we place so much emphasis on the CAPM. After all, the CAPM's purpose is to provide an estimate of how a share will perform in the future. If share returns move essentially at random, then does the CAPM have any place in the practice of corporate finance?

It is true that the CAPM provides only an estimate of a share's expected return and that actual outcomes deviate considerably (and unpredictably) from that estimate in any given year. Even so, the CAPM gives analysts a tool for measuring the systematic risk of any particular asset. Because assets with high systematic risk should, on average, earn higher returns than assets with low systematic risk, the CAPM offers a framework for making educated guesses about the risk and return of investment alternatives. Though it is hardly infallible, that framework enjoys widespread use in corporate finance, as we will see in subsequent chapters.

SMART CONCEPTS
See the concept explained step-by-step at **www.cengage.co.uk/ megginson**

passively managed
An approach to running a mutual fund in which the fund manager makes no attempt to identify overvalued or undervalued shares, but instead holds a diversified portfolio and attempts to minimize the costs of operating the fund.

actively managed
An approach to running a mutual fund in which the fund manager does research to identify undervalued and overvalued shares.

index fund
A passively managed fund that tries to mimic the performance of a market index such as the FTSE 100.

---

9 If the stock market is efficient, what makes it efficient?

10 If prices move almost at random, then why should we place any value on the CAPM, which makes predictions about expected asset returns?

CONCEPT
REVIEW
QUESTIONS

7.5 SUMMARY AND CONCLUSIONS

- Investors and managers must make decisions based on expected returns.

- Estimates of expected returns may be obtained from historical data, from probabilistic calculations or from a risk-based approach.

- An asset's beta measures its systematic risk, and it is this risk that should be linked to expected returns.

- The expected return of a portfolio equals a weighted average of the expected returns of the assets in the portfolio. The same can be said of the portfolio's beta.

- The standard deviation of a portfolio usually does not equal the weighted average of the standard deviation of the shares in the portfolio. This is because some of the unsystematic fluctuations of individual shares cancel each other out in a portfolio. A fully diversified portfolio contains only systematic risk.

- The CAPM predicts that the expected return on a share depends on the share's beta, the risk-free rate and the market risk premium.

- In an efficient market, competition for information makes asset prices nearly unpredictable.

INTERNET RESOURCES

For updates to links in this section and elsewhere in the book, please go to the book's website at www.cengage.co.uk/megginson.

http://www.finportfolio.com/education/education.html
Part of a commercial site, this provides a good introduction to portfolio management.

http://viking.som.yale.edu/will/finman540/classnotes/notes.html
Online textbook introducing the foundations of portfolio theory – risk versus return, CAPM, beta, SML, APT and more.

http://www.stanford.edu/~wfsharpe/
Link to the work of the Nobel laureate who developed the capital asset pricing model.

http://perso.orange.fr/pgreenfinch/e7stkmng.htm
A slightly different view on portfolio formation and selection.

http://www.centralbank.ie/frame_main.asp?pg=fmo_inve.asp&nv=fmo_nav.asp
The view of a central bank on the components of risk in the management of a portfolio.

KEY TERMS

actively managed
beta
capital asset pricing model
    (CAPM)

efficient markets hypothesis (EMH)
expected return
index fund
market portfolio

market risk premium
passively managed
portfolio weights
selling short

SELF-TEST PROBLEMS

ST7-1 Calculate the arithmetic mean, variance and standard deviations for a share with the probability distribution outlined in the accompanying table:

OUTCOME	PROBABILITY	SHARE RETURN
Recession	10%	−40%
Expansion	60%	20%
Boom	30%	50%

ST7-2 You invest €25000 in T-bills and €50000 in the market portfolio. If the risk-free rate equals 2 per cent and the expected market risk premium is 6 per cent, what is the expected return on your portfolio?

ST7-3 The risk-free rate equals 4 per cent, and the expected return on the market is 10 per cent. If a share's expected return is 13 per cent, what is the share's beta?

QUESTIONS

Q7-1 The table below shows the expected return and standard deviation for two shares. Is the pattern shown in the table possible? Explain your answer.

SHARE	BETA	STD. DEV.
no. 1	1.5	22%
no. 2	0.9	35%

Q7-2 Which type of company do you think will have a higher beta: a fast-food chain or a cruise-ship firm? Why?

Q7-3 Is the data in the following table believable? Explain your answer.

SHARE	STD. DEV.
no. 1	40%
no. 2	60%
50–50	Portfolio 50%

Q7-4 How can investors hold a portfolio with a weight of more than 100 per cent in a particular asset?

Q7-5 According to the capital asset pricing model, is the following data possible? Explain your answer.

ASSET	RETURN	STD. DEV.
no. 1	4%	0%
no. 2	2%	20%

Q7-6 Share A has a beta of 1.5, and Share B has a beta of 1.0. Determine whether each statement below is true or false.

a Share A must have a higher standard deviation than Share B.

b Share A has a higher expected return than Share B.

c The expected return on Share A is 50 per cent higher than the expected return on B.

Q7-7 If an asset lies above the security market line, is it overpriced or underpriced? Explain why.

Q7-8 A share has a beta equal to 1.0. Is the standard deviation of the share equal to the standard deviation of the market? Explain your answer.

Q7-9 If share prices move unpredictably, does this mean that investing in shares is just gambling? Why or why not?

Q7-10 Explain why the efficient markets hypothesis implies that a well-run company is not necessarily a good investment?

PROBLEMS

Expected returns

P7-1 The table below shows the difference in returns between shares and Treasury bills in the USA and the difference between shares and Treasury bonds at ten year intervals.

YEARS	SHARES VERSUS T-BONDS	SHARES VERSUS T-BILLS
1964–73	3.7%	8.3%
1974–83	0.2%	8.6%
1984–93	7.5%	5.4%
1994–2003	4.8%	2.1%

a At the end of 1973, the yield on Treasury bonds was 6.6 per cent and the yield on T-bills was 7.2 per cent. Using these figures and the historical data above from 1964–1973, construct two estimates of the expected return on equities as of December 1973.

b At the end of 1983, the yield on Treasury bonds was 6.6 per cent and the yield on T-bills was 7.2 per cent. Using these figures and the historical data above from 1974–1983, construct two estimates of the expected return on equities as of December 1983.

c At the end of 1993, the yield on Treasury bonds was 6.6 per cent and the yield on T-bills was 2.8 per cent. Using these figures and the historical data above from 1984–1993, construct two estimates of the expected return on equities as of December 1993.

d At the end of 2003, the yield on Treasury bonds was 5.0 per cent and the yield on T-bills was 1.0 per cent. Using these figures and the historical data above from 1994–2003, construct two estimates of the expected return on equities as of December 2003.

e What lessons do you learn from this exercise? How much do your estimates of the expected return on equities vary over time, and why do they vary?

P7-2 Use the information below to estimate the expected return on the share of W.M. Hung Corporation.

Long-run average share return = 10%

Long-run average T-bill return = 4%

Current T-bill return = 2%

P7-3 Calculate the expected return, variance, and standard deviation for the shares in the table below.

PRODUCT DEMAND	PROBABILITY	SHARE RETURNS IN EACH SCENARIO		
		SHARE 1	SHARE 2	SHARE 3
High	20%	30%	20%	15%
Medium	60%	12%	14%	10%
Low	20%	−10%	−5%	−2%

P7-4 Calculate the expected return, variance and standard deviation for each share listed below.

STATE OF THE ECONOMY	PROBABILITY	SHARE RETURNS IN EACH STATE		
		SHARE A	SHARE B	SHARE C
Recession	15%	−20%	−10%	−5
Normal growth	65%	18%	13%	10%
Boom	20%	40%	28%	20%

P7-5 Refer to Figure 7.2 and answer the following questions.

a What return would you expect on a share with a beta of 2.0?

b What return would you expect on a share with a beta of 0.66?

c What determines the slope of the line in Figure 7.2?

Risk and return for portfolios

P7-6 Calculate the portfolio weights implied by the euro investments in each of the asset classes below.

ASSET	€ INVESTED
Shares	10 000
Bonds	10 000
T-bills	5 000

P7-7 Kevin Federline recently inherited €1 million and has decided to invest it. His portfolio consists of the following positions in several shares. Calculate the portfolio weights to fill in the bottom row of the table.

	BNP-PARIBAS	FIAT	P&G	RYANAIR
Shares	7 280	5 700	5 300	6 000
Price per share	€25	€45	€55	€45
Portfolio weights				

P7-8 Victoria Beckham is a financial adviser who manages money for high-net-worth individuals.

For a particular client, Victoria recommends the following portfolio of shares.

	GLOBAL RECORDING ARTISTS (GRA)	SOCCER INTL. (SI)	LIQUID OXYGEN CORP. (LO)	VIVA MFG. (VM)	WANNABE TRAVEL (WT)
Shares	8 000	9 000	7 000	10 500	4 000
Price per share	€40	€36	€45	€30	€60
Portfolio weights					

a Calculate the portfolio weights implied by Ms Beckham's recommendations. What fraction of the portfolio is invested in GRA and SI combined?

b Suppose that the client purchases the shares suggested by Ms Beckham, and a year later the prices of the five shares are as follows: GRA(€60), SI(€50), LO(€38), VM(€20), WT(€50). Calculate the portfolio weights at the end of the year. Now what fraction of the portfolio is held in GRA and SI combined?

P7-9 Calculate the expected return, variance and standard deviation for the shares in the table below. Next, form an equally weighted portfolio of all three shares and calculate its mean, variance, and standard deviation.

STATE OF THE ECONOMY	RETURNS IN EACH STATE OF THE ECONOMY			
	PROBABILITY	CYCLI-CAL LTD	HOME GROWN CROP	PHARMA-CEL
Boom	20%	40%	20%	20%
Expansion	50%	10%	10%	40%
Recession	30%	−20%	−10%	−30%

P7-10 You analyse the prospects of several companies and come to the following conclusions about the expected return on each:

SHARE	EXPECTED RETURN
SAP	18%
Nike	8%
Manchester United	16%
Unicredito	12%

You decide to invest €4000 in SAP, €6000 in Nike, €12 000 in Manchester United and €3000 in Unicredito Brands. What is the expected return on your portfolio?

P7-11 Calculate the expected return of the portfolio described in the accompanying table.

SHARE	€ INVESTED	EXPECTED RETURN
A	€40 000	10%
B	€20 000	14%
C	€25 000	12%

P7-12 Calculate the portfolio weights based on the euro investments in the table below. Interpret the negative sign on one investment. What is the size of the initial investment on which an investor's rate of return calculation should be based?

SHARE	€ INVESTED
1	€10 000
2	−€ 5 000
3	€ 5 000

P7-13 Pete Pablo has €20 000 to invest. He is very optimistic about the prospects of two companies, 919 Brands Ltd. and Diaries.com. However, Pete has a very pessimistic view of one firm, a financial institution known as Lloyd Bank. The current market price of each share and Pete's assessment of the expected return for each share appear below.

SHARE	PRICE	EXPECTED RETURN
919 Brands	€60	10%
Diaries.com	€80	14%
Lloyd Bank	€70	−8%

a Pete decides to purchase 210 shares of 919 Brands and 180 shares of Diaries.com. What is the expected return on this portfolio? Can Pete construct this portfolio with the amount of money he has to invest?

b If Pete buys 210 shares of 919 Brands and 180 shares of Diaries.com, and he simultaneously sells short 100 shares of Lloyd Bank, what are the resulting portfolio weights in each share? (*Hint:* the weights must sum to one, but they need not all be positive.)

P7-14 Shares in Springfield Nuclear Power currently sell for €25. You believe that the shares will be worth €30 in one year, and this implies that the return you expect on these

shares is 20 per cent (the company pays no dividends).

a If you invest €10 000 by purchasing 400 shares, what the expected value of your holdings next year?

b Now suppose that you buy 400 shares of SNP, but you finance this purchase with €5000 of your own funds and €5000 that you raise by selling short 100 shares of Nader Insurance Ltd. Nader Insurance shares currently sell for €50, but next year you expect them to be worth €52. This implies an expected return of 4 per cent. If both shares perform as you expect, how much money will you have at the end of the year after you repurchase 100 Nader shares at the market price and return them to your broker? What rate of return on your €5000 investment does this represent?

c Suppose you buy 400 shares of SNP and finance them as described in part (b). However, at the end of the year SNP shares are worth €31 each. What was the percentage increase in SNP shares? What is the rate of return on your portfolio (again, after you repurchase Nader shares and return them to your broker)?

d Finally, assume that at the end of one year, SNP shares have fallen to €24. What was the rate of return on SNP shares for the year? What is the rate of return on your portfolio?

e What is the general lesson illustrated here? What is the impact of short selling on the expected return and risk of your portfolio?

P7-15 You are given the following data on several shares:

STATE OF THE ECONOMY AUTOMOTIVE	RETURNS IN EACH STATE OF ECONOMY			
	PROBABILITY	GERE MINING	REUBENFELD FILMS	DELOREAN
Boom	25%	40%	24%	−20%
Expansion	50%	12%	10%	12%
Recession	25%	−20%	−12%	40%

a Calculate the expected return and standard deviation for each share.

b Calculate the expected return and standard deviation for a portfolio invested equally in Gere Mining and Reubenfeld Films. How does the standard deviation of this portfolio compare to a simple 50–50 weighted average of the standard deviations of the two shares?

c Calculate the expected return and standard deviation for a portfolio invested equally in Gere Mining and DeLorean Automotive. How does the standard deviation of this portfolio compare to a simple 50–50 weighted average of the standard deviations of the two shares?

d Explain why your answers regarding the portfolio standard deviations are so different in parts (b) and (c).

P7-16 In an odd twist of fate, the return on the stock market has been exactly 1 per cent in each of the last eight months. The return on Simon Entertainment shares in the past eight months has been as follows: 8%, 4%, 16%, −10%, 26%, 22%, 1%, −55%. From this information, estimate the beta of Simon shares.

P7-17 Petro-Chem Ltd shares have a beta equal to 0.9. Digi-Media Corp.'s share beta is 2.0. What is the beta of a portfolio invested equally in these two shares?

The security market line and the CAPM

P7-18 The risk-free rate is currently 5 per cent, and the expected risk premium on the market portfolio is 7 per cent. What is the expected return on a share with a beta of 1.2?

P7-19 The expected return on the market portfolio equals 12 per cent. The current risk-free rate is 6 per cent. What is the expected return on a share with a beta of 0.66?

P7-20 The expected return on a particular share is 14 per cent. The share's beta is 1.5. What is the risk-free rate if the expected return on the market portfolio equals 10 per cent?

P7-21 If the risk-free rate equals 4 per cent and a share with a beta of 0.75 has an expected return of 10 per cent, what is the expected return on the market portfolio?

P7-22 You believe that a particular share has an expected return of 15 per cent. The share's beta is 1.2, the risk-free rate is 3 per cent and the expected market risk premium is 6 per cent. Based on this, is your view that the share is overvalued or undervalued?

P7-23 A particular share sells for €30. The share's beta is 1.25, the risk-free rate is 4 per cent and the expected return on the market portfolio is 10 per cent. If you forecast that the share will be worth €33 next year (assume no dividends), should you buy the share or not?

P7-24 Currently the risk-free rate equals 5 per cent and the expected return on the market portfolio equals 11 per cent. An investment analyst provides you with the following information:

SHARE	BETA	EXPECTED RETURN
A	1.33	12%
B	0.7	10%
C	1.5	14%
D	0.66	9%

a Indicate whether each share is overpriced, underpriced or correctly priced.

b For each share, subtract the risk-free rate from the share's expected return and divide the result by the share's beta. For example, for share A this calculation is (12% − 5%) ÷ 1.33. Provide an interpretation for these ratios. Which share has the highest ratio and which has the lowest?

c Show how a smart investor could construct a portfolio of shares C and D that would outperform share A.

d Construct a portfolio consisting of some combination of the market portfolio and the risk-free asset such that the portfolio's expected return equals 9 per cent. What is the beta of this portfolio? What does this say about share D?

e Divide the risk premium on share C by the risk premium on share D. Next, divide the beta of share C by the beta of share D. Comment on what you find.

THOMSON ONE Business School Edition

For instructions on using Thomson ONE, refer to the introductory text provided with the Thomson ONE problems at the end of Chapters 1–6, or in *A Guide for Using Thomson ONE – Business School Edition*.

P7-25 Determine the beta of a portfolio consisting of Juventus Football Club, Aston Villa PLC, Newcastle United PLC and Southampton Leisure Holdings. You invest equal amounts of capital in each share. How does the beta of this portfolio compare with the individual betas? Explain. Instead of investing equal amounts of capital in each share, you decide to short shares worth €1000 in each of the two least risky shares (of the above four shares) and invest €2000 each in the two most risky shares. How do you think the beta of this new portfolio will compare with the individual share betas? Calculate the beta of this new portfolio and check if it matches your expectations. Consider another alternate portfolio. Do you think this portfolio will ever be profitable? If so, when?

P7-26 Determine whether the shares of Newcastle United PLC were mispriced (either underpriced or overpriced) at any time over the last five years. Assume that the beta for Newcastle United PLC stayed constant over the last five years and use the latest available beta. Further, assume that FTSE-350 proxies for the market portfolio and calculate the annual returns for the index over the last five years. Use the capital asset pricing model (CAPM) to estimate the expected annual stock returns for Newcastle United PLC for each year. Compare the expected share returns to the actual annual returns for each year and determine if the shares were mispriced.

MINICASE *Risk, return and the capital asset pricing model*

As a first-day trainee at Tri-Star Management Ltd the CEO asks you to analyse the following information pertaining to two share investments, Tech.com and Sam's Grocery Ltd. You are told that a short-term government stock will have a rate of return of 5 per cent over the next year. Also, information from an investment advising service lists the current beta for Tech.com as 1.68 and for Sam's Grocery as 0.52. You are provided with a series of questions to guide your analysis.

ECONOMY	PROBABILITY	ESTIMATED RATE OF RETURN		
		TECH.COM	SAM'S GROCERY	S&P 500
Recession	30%	−20%	5%	−4%
Average	20%	15%	6%	11%
Expansion	35%	30%	8%	17%
Boom	15%	50%	10%	27%

Assignment

1 Calculate the expected rate of return for Tech.com, Sam's Grocery and the FTSE-100 Index.

2 Calculate the standard deviations in estimated rates of return for Tech.com, Sam's Grocery and the FTSE-100 Index.

3 Which is a better measure of risk for the shares of Tech.com and Sam's Grocery – the standard deviation you calculated in Question 2 or the beta?

4 Based on the beta provided, what is the expected rate of return for Tech.com and Sam's Grocery for the next year?

5 If you form a two-share portfolio by investing €30 000 in Tech.com and €70 000 in Sam's Grocery, what is the portfolio beta and expected rate of return?

6 If you form a two-share portfolio by investing €70 000 in Tech.com and €30 000 in Sam's Grocery, what is the portfolio beta and expected rate of return?

7 Which of these two-share portfolios do you prefer? Why?

PART 3

Capital Budgeting

Overview

The long-run success or failure of most businesses depends more on the quality of their investment decisions than on any other factor. For many firms, the most important investment decisions are those that involve the acquisition of fixed assets like land or plant and equipment. In finance, we refer to the process of making these investment decisions as 'capital budgeting'. This part of the text focuses exclusively on capital budgeting.

Chapter 8 describes some of the methods that firms use to evaluate investment opportunities. Several methods are used widely, but from a purely theoretical perspective, one method dominates the others. The preferred approach is the net present value (or NPV) method. In an NPV analysis, a financial manager compares the incremental cash outflows and inflows (marginal costs and marginal benefits, again) associated with a particular investment and discounts those cash flows at a rate that reflects the investment's risk. The investment rule is to invest when the NPV is positive, because only then do the investment's marginal benefits exceed its marginal costs.

Chapter 9 goes deeper into NPV analysis by showing how analysts derive the cash flow estimates necessary to calculate a project's NPV. Experienced analysts know that certain types of cash flows occur in almost any investment project, so Chapter 9 lists several categories of cash flows and explains how to treat them properly in an NPV calculation.

Chapter 10 focuses on the second step in calculating NPV – choosing an interest rate at which the investment's cash flows will be discounted. Conceptually, the discount rate that a manager chooses should reflect the risk of the investment being analysed. Analysts should use higher discount rates when they evaluate riskier investment projects. Furthermore, managers should 'look to the market' to decide what rate of return investors expect the firm to achieve. Because every firm's assets are financed by some combination of debt and equity, it is possible for managers to discern the underlying required return on the assets they invest in by calculating the weighted average cost of capital (or WACC). The WACC establishes an important 'hurdle rate' for firms. On average, if the firm purchases assets that generate returns higher than the firm's WACC, then the firm makes its investors very happy, and it creates wealth for shareholders.

Chapter 8

Capital Budgeting Process and Techniques

OPENING FOCUS

Investment makes you rich . . . probably

Does it matter very much what a company does in terms of capital projects? After all, the stock market is populated by very smart people who can quickly apply the tools and techniques of corporate finance to determine the worth of a project. These tools are the very ones we are examining in the next few chapters? A number of studies have shown that in fact the share price of a company can receive a 'bounce' from the very announcement of a project. A 2004 study by European academics looked at the reaction of the shares of 500 (mainly UK-based) companies during the 1990s. They found that companies that announced new capital investments received what they called 'abnormal' returns, meaning returns over and above the share price change of comparable firms that had not announced such investments. Interestingly, the larger returns were for projects that were designed to facilitate future strategic growth, and the smaller returns for projects that were exercising existing opportunities.

This issue of share prices reacting to project announcements, particularly when these are perceived to create value, is well illustrated in the following example. On 20 June 2006 a small mining company, European Nickel PLC released its half-year report. In this they stated: ' . . . increases in the Caldag [Caldag is the mine in Turkey that the company recently opened] project IRR and NPV announced in April based on the same long-term nickel and cobalt prices used in the original study, giving an estimated internal rate of return of approximately 31.6% and a geared real net present value of approximately $175 million at a 10% discount rate'. The share price of the company rose by 3 per cent on the next trading day.

Source: Edwards Jones, Jo Danbolt and Ian Hirst (2004) 'Company Investment Announcements and the Market Value of the Firm', *The European Journal of Finance* 10(5):437–452. European Nickel PLC Interim Report, 20 June 2006, available at http://www.enickel.co.uk/.

LEARNING OBJECTIVES

After studying this chapter you should be able to:

- Understand capital budgeting procedures and the characteristics that management desires in a capital budgeting technique.

- Evaluate the use of the accounting rate of return, the payback period and the discounted payback to evaluate proposed capital expenditures.

- Discuss the logic, calculation, and pros and cons of using net present value (NPV) to evaluate proposed capital expenditures.

- Describe the logic, calculation, advantages and problems associated with the use of internal rate of return (IRR) to evaluate proposed capital expenditures.

- Differentiate between the NPV and IRR techniques by focusing on the scale and timing problems associated with mutually exclusive capital budgeting projects.

- Discuss the profitability index and recent findings with regard to the actual use of NPV and IRR in business practice.

On a daily basis, firms make decisions that have financial consequences. Some decisions, such as extending credit to a customer or ordering stock (inventory), have consequences that are short-lived. Moreover, managers can reverse these short-term actions with relative ease. In contrast, some decisions that managers face have a long-term impact on the firm and can be very difficult to unwind once started. Major investments in plant and equipment fit this description, but so might spending on advertising designed to build brand awareness and loyalty among consumers. The terms **capital investment** and **capital spending** refer to investments in these kinds of long-lived assets, and the term **capital budgeting** refers to the process of identifying which of these investment projects a firm should undertake.

The capital budgeting process involves three basic steps:

1 Identifying potential investments.

2 Analysing the set of investment opportunities, identifying and perhaps prioritizing those that will create shareholder value.

3 Implementing and monitoring the investment projects selected in Step 2.

So the capital budgeting process begins with an idea and ends with implementation and monitoring. Ideas for investment projects can come from virtually anywhere within the firm. Marketing may propose that the firm spend money to reach a new class of customers. Operations may want to modernize equipment to realize production efficiencies. Engineering may seek resources to engage in research and development designed to improve existing products or create new ones. Information Systems may want to upgrade the firm's computer network to enable more efficient information-sharing across functional areas and physical locations. Each group will undoubtedly have a compelling story to justify spending money on its pet project. The firm will analyse each proposal, considering its risk and return, and their combined effect on its value; some projects will be approved and others rejected.

Once a project gains approval, the attention of financial managers turns to implementation. They devote a significant fraction of their time to Step 3, implementing and monitoring investments that the firm has decided to make. When firms undertake a capital investment, they almost always do so with a specific budget, outlining the financial objectives and constraints of that investment. Financial managers work to ensure that project managers adhere to budget guidelines, and they help track a project's success over time to determine whether an investment's initial promises were realized.

Without understating the importance of Step 1 (which we discuss in Chapter 9) and Step 3, our focus in this chapter is on the second stage of the process, evaluating the merits of investment proposals. Here we ignore risk and assume that projects are equally risky; in Chapter 10, we relax this assumption and develop techniques that are consistent with Chapters 6 and 7, which recognize differences in project risk. In practice, firms use many different techniques to justify their capital investments, ranging from simple to sophisticated. In this chapter, we describe several of these techniques, highlighting their strengths and weaknesses. In the end, the preferred technique for evaluating most capital investments is the one called 'net present value'.

capital investment
Investments in long-lived assets such as plant, equipment and advertising.

capital spending
Investments in long-lived assets such as plant, equipment and advertising.

capital budgeting
The process of identifying which long-lived investment projects a firm should undertake.

8.1 INTRODUCTION TO CAPITAL BUDGETING

What do managers really want?

Firms use a variety of techniques to evaluate capital investments. Some techniques involve very simple calculations and are intuitively easy to grasp. Financial managers prefer (1) an easily applied technique that (2) considers cash flow, (3) recognizes the time value of money, (4) fully accounts for expected risk and return and (5) when applied, leads to higher share prices. Easy application accounts for the popularity of some simple capital budgeting methods such as accounting rate of return and the payback period (both defined later).

Unfortunately, when comparing simple capital budgeting methods with more complex ones, other things are decidedly not equal. Other methods, generally preferred by theoreticians but seen as more complex exist. These include methods such as net present value (NPV), internal rate of return (IRR) or the profitability index (PI), which it is accepted generally lead to better decision making because they take into account issues such as cash flow, the time value of money, the expected risk and return, and the effect on share value – factors that are neglected or ignored by simpler methods. Moreover, we will learn that the net present value approach provides a direct estimate of the increase or decrease in shareholder value resulting from a particular investment. Managers who seek to maximize shareholder value must understand not only how to use the more complex techniques but also the logic that explains why some methods are better than others. As challenging as that sounds, there is no reason to worry. We have already seen these tools at work in valuing bonds and shares, and now we will apply the discounted cash flow apparatus to real assets such as plant and equipment.

A capital budgeting problem

We apply each of the decision-making techniques in this chapter to a single, simplified business problem currently facing WireVid!, a (fictitious) worldwide provider of video download services to 3g mobile phones. These comprise highly profitable snippets of football, music video or cartoon programming. The growing sophistication of the technology and the increased penetration of mobile phones now makes the provision of these pay per segment offerings attractive.

Against this backdrop, WireVid! is contemplating a major expansion of its business in two different regions. Figure 8.1 depicts the projected cash inflows and outflows

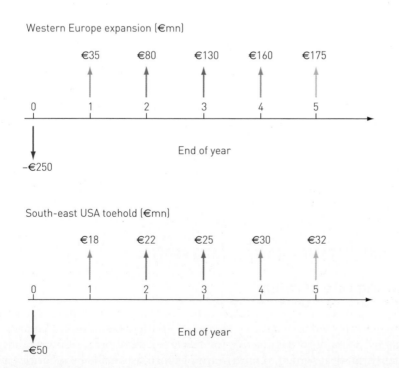

FIGURE 8.1

WireVid! investment proposals

The figure depicts on time lines the cash flows for WireVid!'s major Western European expansion and the south-east USA toehold.

of each project over the next five years. By investing €250 million, WireVid! could enter into an agreement with the main mobile telephony companies in Western Europe. Company analysts project that this investment could generate year-end net after-tax cash inflows that could grow over the next five years, as outlined below:

Initial outlay	−€250 million
Year 1 inflow	€ 35 million
Year 2 inflow	€ 80 million
Year 3 inflow	€130 million
Year 4 inflow	€160 million
Year 5 inflow	€175 million

Alternatively, WireVid! could make a much smaller investment to establish a toehold in a new market in the south-east United States. The US market is less technologically sophisticated and the costs greater given the lower penetration of phones and the need for more infrastructure in the larger geographic area. Nonetheless, the overall size of the market is potentially very attractive. For an initial investment of €50 million, WireVid! believes it can create a test programme based in the major metro areas of the south-east, centred on Atlanta, Georgia. The projected end-of-year cash flows associated with this project are as follows:

Initial outlay	−€50 million
Year 1 inflow	€18 million
Year 2 inflow	€22 million
Year 3 inflow	€25 million
Year 4 inflow	€30 million
Year 5 inflow	€32 million

From a business perspective the two projects are attractive and make sense. However, which investment should WireVid! make? If the company can undertake both investments, should it do so? If it can make only one investment, which one is better for shareholders? We will see how different capital budgeting techniques lead to different investment decisions, starting with the simplest, least-sophisticated approach – the accounting rate of return.

CONCEPT
REVIEW
QUESTION

1 What characteristics does management desire in a capital budgeting technique? Why?

8.2 ACCOUNTING-BASED METHODS

Accounting rate of return

For better or worse, managers in many firms focus as much on how a given project will influence reported earnings as on how it will affect cash flows. Managers justify this focus by pointing to the positive (or negative) share price response that occurs when their firms beat (or fail to meet) earnings forecasts made by securities analysts. There is ample research indicating that the stock market pays very close attention to reported earnings, and especially to the difference between forecast earnings and reported earnings of companies. A paper[1] by Narasimhan Jegadeesh of Emory University and Joshua Livnat of NYU in 2006 found that share prices respond very strongly to unexpected earnings, even when other factors are taken into account. A 1 per cent change in unexpected earnings reported can lead to a 2 per cent change in the share price. When you recall that earnings may be reported as pennies per share the room for small changes is very large! This phenomenon is not US only, as other studies[2] have shown that it persists across countries and accounting regimes. Managers may also pay more attention to the accounting-based earnings of a project than they pay to its cash flows because their compensation is based on meeting accounting-based performance measures such as earnings-per-share or return-on-total-assets targets. Consequently, many firms decide whether to invest in a given project based on the rate of return the investment will earn on an accounting basis.

Companies have many different ways of defining a 'hurdle rate' for their investment in terms of accounting rates of return. Almost all these metrics involve two steps: (1) to identify the net income associated with the project in each year of its life, and (2) to measure the amount of invested capital, as shown on the balance sheet, devoted to the project in each year. Given these two figures, a firm may calculate an **accounting rate of return** by dividing net income by the book value of assets, either on a year-by-year basis or by taking an average over the project's life. Note that this measure is comparable to return on total assets (ROA), also called return on investment (ROI), introduced in Chapter 2, for measuring a firm's overall effectiveness in generating returns with its available assets. Companies will usually establish some minimum accounting rate of return that projects must earn before they can be funded. When more than one project exceeds the minimum standard, firms prioritize projects, based on their accounting rates of return, and invest in projects with higher returns first.

accounting rate of return
Calculation of a hurdle rate by dividing net income by the book value of assets, either on a year-by-year basis or by taking an average over the project's life.

Applying the Model

Suppose that the practice at WireVid! is to calculate a project's accounting rate of return by taking the project's average contribution to net income and dividing by its average book value. WireVid! ranks projects based on this measure and accepts those that offer an accounting rate of return of at least 25 per cent. As noted earlier, so far we have been given the cash flows from each of the two projects that WireVid! is evaluating. Chapter 9 discusses in more depth the differences between cash flow and net income, but for now we will assume that we can determine each project's contribution to net income by subtracting depreciation from cash flow each year. We will assume that the company depreciates fixed assets on a straight-line basis over five years. Therefore, the Western Europe project will have an annual depreciation charge of €50 million (one-fifth of €250 million), and the south-east US project will have an annual depreciation charge

[1] Narasimhan Jegadeesh and Joshua Livnat (2006) 'Revenue Surprises and Stock Returns', *Journal of Accounting and Economics*, 41(1–2):147–171.
[2] Mark Myring (2006) 'The Relationship Between Returns and Unexpected Earnings: A Global Analysis by Accounting Regimes', *Journal of International Accounting, Auditing and Taxation*, 15(1):92–108.

of €10 million (one-fifth of €50 million). These assumptions yield the following net income figures for the next five years:

YEAR	WESTERN EUROPE PROJECT (€mn)	SOUTH-EAST US PROJECT (€mn)
1	−15	8
2	30	12
3	80	15
4	110	20
5	125	22

The Western Europe project begins with a book value of €250 million. After five years of depreciation it has a book value of €0. Therefore, the average book value of that project is €125 million [(€250 − €0) ÷ 2]. The project's average net income equals €66 million [(−€15 + €30 + €80 + €110 + €125) ÷ 5], so its average accounting rate of return is an impressive 52.8 per cent (€66 ÷ €125). The same steps applied to the south-east US project yield an average book value of €25 million [(€50 − €0) ÷ 2], an average net income of €15.4 million [(€8 + €12 + €15 + €20 + €22) ÷ 5], and an accounting rate of return of 61.6 per cent (€15.4 ÷ €25). On the basis of this analysis, WireVid! should be willing to invest in either project, but it would rank the south-east US investment above the Western Europe expansion.

Pros and cons of the accounting rate of return Because of their convenience, ease of calculation and ease of interpretation, accounting-based measures are used by many firms to evaluate capital investments. However, these techniques have serious flaws. First, as the preceding 'Applying the Model' section demonstrates, the decision about what depreciation method to use has a large effect on both the numerator and the denominator of the accounting rate of return formula. Secondly, this method makes no adjustment for the time value of money or project risk. Thirdly, investors should be more concerned with the market value than the book value of the assets that a firm holds. After five years, the book value of WireVid!'s investment (in either project) is zero, but the market value will almost certainly be positive and may be even greater than the initial amount invested. Fourthly, as explained in Chapter 2, finance theory teaches that investors should focus on a company's ability to generate cash rather than on its net income. Fifthly, the choice of the 25 per cent accounting return hurdle rate is essentially arbitrary. This rate is not based on rates available on similar investments in the market, but reflects a purely subjective judgement on the part of management.

CONCEPT REVIEW QUESTIONS

2 Why might managers focus on the effect that an investment will have on reported earnings rather than on the investment's cash flow consequences?

3 What factors determine whether the annual accounting rate of return on a given project will be high or low in the early years of the investment's life? In the latter years?

8.3 PAYBACK METHODS

The payback decision rule

The payback method is the simplest of all capital budgeting decision-making tools. It enjoys widespread use, particularly in small and cash-constrained firms. Firms using the payback approach typically define a minimum acceptable payback period. The **payback period** is the amount of time it takes for a given project's cumulative net cash inflows to recoup the initial investment. If a firm decides that it wants to avoid any investment that does not 'pay for itself' in three years or less, then the payback decision rule is to accept projects with a payback period of three years or less and reject all other investments. If several projects satisfy this condition, then firms may prioritize investments, based on which ones achieve payback more rapidly. The decision to use three years as the cut-off point is arbitrary, and there are no hard-and-fast guidelines that establish what the 'optimal' payback period should be. Nevertheless, suppose that WireVid! uses 2.75 years as its cut-off when doing payback analysis. What investment decision would it make?

payback period
The amount of time it takes for a given project's cumulative net cash inflows to recoup the initial investment.

Applying the Model

The investment to expand in Western Europe requires an initial outlay of €250 million. According to the firm's cash flow projections, this project will bring in just €245 million in its first three years (€35 million in year 1 + €80 million in year 2 + €130 million in year 3) and €405 million after four years (€245 million in the first 3 years + €160 million in year 4). So the firm will fully recover its €250 million initial outlay sometime between years 3 and 4. Because the firm only needs to recover €5 million (€250 million initial outlay − €245 million recovered in the first 3 years) in year 4, assuming cash flow occurs at a constant rate throughout the year, we can estimate the fraction of year 4 as 0.03, by dividing the €5 million that needs to be recovered in year 4 by the €160 million expected to be recovered in that year. The payback period for Western Europe is therefore 3.03 years, so WireVid! would reject the investment because this payback period is longer than the firm's maximum 2.75-year payback period.

The toehold investment in the south-east USA project requires just €50 million. In its first two years this investment generates €40 million in cash flow (€18 million in year 1 + €22 million in year 2). By the end of year 3 it produces a cumulative cash flow of €65 million (€40 million in the first 2 years + €25 million in year 3). Thus, the project earns back the initial €50 million at some point between years 2 and 3. It needs to recover €10 million (€50 million initial outlay −€40 million recovered in the first 2 years) in year 3. We can estimate the fraction of year 3 as 0.40, by dividing the €10 million that needs to be recovered in year 3 by the €25 million expected to be recovered that year. The payback for the south-east US project is therefore 2.40 years. WireVid! would undertake the investment because this payback period is shorter than the firm's maximum 2.75-year payback period.

Pros and cons of the payback method

Simplicity is the main virtue of the payback approach. Once a firm estimates a project's cash flows, it is a simple matter of addition to determine when the cumulative net cash inflows equal the initial outlay. The intuitive appeal of the payback method is strong.

It sounds reasonable to expect a good investment to pay for itself in a fairly short period of time. Furthermore, by requiring projects to earn back the initial cash outlay within a few short years, the payback approach recognizes the time value of money, although it fails to explicitly consider it. Some managers say that establishing a short payback period is one way to account for a project's risk exposure. Projects that take longer to pay off are intrinsically riskier than those that recoup the initial investment more quickly. Because of its ability to measure the project's exposure to the risk of not recovering the initial outlay, the payback period is a very popular decision-making technique in highly uncertain situations. It is popular for international investments made in unstable economic/political environments and in risky domestic investments such as oil drilling and new business ventures. In these situations, it is frequently used as the primary decision-making technique.

The payback period is an effective criterion when management has to worry about financing constraints, because it indicates how quickly the firm can recover cash flows for use in debt repayment or for financing other attractive investment opportunities. Career concerns may also lead managers to prefer the payback rule. Particularly in large companies, managers rotate quite often from one job to another. To obtain promotions and to enhance their reputations, managers want to make investments that enable them to point to success stories at each stage of their careers. A manager who expects to stay in a particular position in the firm for just two or three years may prefer to undertake investments that recover costs quickly rather than projects that have pay-offs far into the future. In that case, selecting projects based on how quickly they meet the payback requirement offers considerable appeal to someone trying to build a career. This is viewed as a disadvantage when it results in an agency problem – achievement of managers' career goals is not always in the best interests of shareholders. The use of payback as a mechanism to discipline managers by locking them into shorter-term projects that are inherently more controllable is one that several authors[3] have proposed as a solution to the popularity of payback processes.

Source: Adapted from 'LEX: Singapore Gambling', *Financial Times*, 11 October 2006.

Real World

As you read this chapter and the next you may be excused sometimes for thinking that trying to evaluate the likely return on a project is akin to rolling dice. But what if your business is just that – gambling? Consider the emerging battle between Singapore and Macau to become the gambling hub of South Asia. Both countries are striving to attract casinos. However, they have very different approaches. Macau is akin to Hong Kong, a special zone of the People's Republic of China, with an economy that is essentially dependent on gambling. Singapore is a much larger more diversified economy. As will become clear later, the higher a risk in a project the lower the payback period needed. It is not surprising therefore that the casino operators look for a payback period of five to eight years in Singapore and half that in Macau.

Despite these apparent virtues, the payback method suffers from several serious problems. First, the payback cut-off period is simply a judgemental choice with little or no connection to shareholder value maximization. How can we be sure that accepting projects that pay back within 2.75 years will maximize shareholder wealth

---

[3] R. McDonald (1998) 'Real Options and Rules of Thumb in Capital Budgeting', in Brennan, M.J. and Trigeorgis, L., (eds) *Innovation, Infrastructure, and Strategic Options*, London: Oxford University Press.

rather than accepting projects that pay back within two years or four years? Secondly, the way that the payback method accounts for the time value of money is crude in the extreme. The payback method assigns a 0 per cent discount rate to cash flows that occur before the cut-off point. That is, if the payback period is three years, then cash flows that occur in years 1, 2, and 3 receive equal weight in the payback calculation. Beyond the cut-off point, the payback method implicitly assigns an infinite discount rate to all future cash flows, thereby ignoring them. In other words, cash flows in year 4 and beyond receive zero weight (or have zero present value) in today's decision to invest or not to invest.[4] Thirdly, using the payback period as a way to control for project risk is equally crude. Finance teaches that riskier investments should offer higher returns. If it is true, as managers sometimes argue, that riskier projects have longer payback periods, then the payback rule simply rejects all such investments, whether or not they offer higher returns in the long run. Managers who naïvely follow the payback rule tend to underinvest in long-term projects that could offer substantial rewards for shareholders. Fourthly, if career concerns lead managers to favour projects with very quick payoffs, then firms should adjust the way that they evaluate employees. Firms could reduce incentives for managers to focus on short-term successes by rewarding them for their efforts in meeting the short-term goals of long-term projects (e.g. staying on budget, meeting revenue forecasts), as well as for long-term results.

SMART PRACTICES VIDEO

Dan Carter, Executive Vice President, Chief Financial Officer, Charlotte Russe
'It's a metric that frankly most of our operators can truly appreciate.'

See the entire interview at **www.cengage.co.uk/megginson**

Real World

Payback as a method of course suffers from problems. But sometimes it can give a good idea of the profitability of a project. *The Guardian* newspaper notes that while many hotels offer free broadband access in rooms, others charge significant amounts. A leading company involved in the business, Hotel Broadband, notes: 'If you don't want to allocate capital upfront . . . our solutions can cost as little as 11p per room, per day . . . . Some of our hotels are looking at a one-year payback period – so you could make the installation pay for itself.' Sometimes payback can be useful!

Discounted payback

The **discounted payback** rule is essentially the same as the payback rule except that in calculating the payback period, managers discount cash flows first. In other words, the discounted payback method calculates how long it takes for a project's discounted cash flows to recover the initial outlay. This represents a minor improvement over the simple payback method in that it does a better job of accounting for the time value of cash flows that occur within the payback cut-off period. As with the ordinary payback rule, discounted payback totally ignores cash flows that occur beyond the cut-off point.

discounted payback
The amount of time it takes for a project's discounted cash flows to recover the initial investment.

---

[4] We know that the present value of a future cash flow becomes smaller and smaller as we discount at higher and higher interest rates. Discounting at an infinite interest rate results in a future cash flow having zero present value.

Applying the Model

Suppose that WireVid! uses the discounted payback method, with a discount rate of 18 per cent and a cut off period of 2.75 years. The following schedule shows the present values of each project's cash flows during the first three years. For example, €29.7 million is the present value of the €35 million that the Western Europe investment is expected to earn in its first year, €57.4 million is the present value of the €80 million that the project is expected to earn in its second year, and so on.

PRESENT VALUE	WESTERN EUROPE PROJECT (€mn)	SOUTH-EAST US PROJECT (€mn)
PV of year 1 inflow	29.7	15.2
PV of year 2 inflow	57.4	15.8
PV of year 3 inflow	79.1	15.2
Cumulative PV years 1–3	166.2	46.2

Recall that the initial outlay for the Western Europe expansion project is €250 million, whereas it is €50 million for the south-east US toehold project. Because, after three years, neither project's cumulative present value of cash flows exceeds its initial outlay (Western Europe: Cumulative PV years 1–3 = €166.2 million <€250 million initial outlay and Southeast US: Cumulative PV years 1–3 = €46.2 million <€50 million initial outlay), it is clear that neither investment satisfies the condition that the discounted cash flows recoup the initial investment in 2.75 years or less. Therefore, WireVid! would reject both projects.

Pros and cons of discounted payback

The discounted payback rule offers essentially the same set of advantages and disadvantages as ordinary payback analysis. The primary advantage is its relative simplicity. Discounted payback does correct the payback rule's problem of implicitly applying a 0 per cent discount rate to all cash flows that occur before the cut-off point. However, like the ordinary payback rule, the discounted payback approach ignores cash flows beyond the cut-off point, in essence, applying an infinite discount rate to these cash flows. In the final analysis, even though it represents a marginal improvement over the simplest version of the payback rule, discounted payback analysis is likely to lead managers to underinvest in profitable projects with long-run pay-offs.

By now you may have noticed some common themes in our discussion of the pros and cons of different approaches to capital budgeting. None of the methods discussed thus far factor all the cash flows of a project into the decision-making process. Each of these methods fails to properly account for the time value of money, and none of them deal adequately with differences in risk from one investment to another. We now turn our attention to a method that solves all these difficulties and therefore enjoys widespread support from both academics and businesspeople.

CONCEPT
REVIEW
QUESTIONS

4 What factors account for the popularity of the payback method? In what situations is it often used as the primary decision-making technique? Why?

5 What are the major flaws of the payback period and discounted payback approaches?

8.4 NET PRESENT VALUE

Net present value calculations

The **net present value (NPV)** of a project is the sum of the present value of *all* its cash flows, both inflows and outflows, discounted at a rate consistent with the project's risk. Calculating the NPV of an investment project is relatively straightforward. First, write down the net cash flows that the investment will generate over its life. Secondly, discount these cash flows at an interest rate that reflects the degree of risk inherent in the project. (Note: The development of this rate is discussed in Chapter 10.) The resulting sum of discounted cash flows equals the project's net present value. The NPV decision rule says to invest in projects when the net present value is greater than zero.

$$NPV_0 = CF_0 + \frac{CF_1}{(1+r)^1} + \frac{CF_2}{(1+r)^2} + \cdots + \frac{CF_n}{(1+r)^n}$$

In this expression, CF_t represents net cash flow in year t, r is the discount rate, and n represents the life of the project. The cash flows in each year may be positive or negative, though we usually expect projects to generate cash outflows initially and cash inflows later on. For example, suppose that the initial cash flow, CF_0, is a negative number representing the outlay necessary to get the project started, and suppose that all subsequent cash flows are positive. In this case, the NPV can be defined as the present value of future cash inflows minus the initial outlay. The NPV decision rule says that firms should invest when the sum of the present values of future cash inflows exceeds the initial project outlay. That is, NPV $>$€0, when the following occurs:

$$-CF_0 < \frac{CF_1}{(1+r)^1} + \frac{CF_2}{(1+r)^2} + \cdots + \frac{CF_n}{(1+r)^n}$$

Simply stated, the NPV decision rules are:

NPV $>$€0   Invest
NPV $<$€0   Do not invest

Why does the NPV rule generally lead to good investment decisions? Remember that the firm's goal in choosing investment projects is to maximize shareholder wealth. Conceptually, the discount rate, r, in the NPV equation represents an opportunity cost, the highest rate of return that investors can obtain in the market-place on an investment with risk equal to the risk of the specific project. When the NPV of a cash flow stream equals zero, that stream of cash flows provides a rate of return exactly equal to shareholders' required return. Therefore, when a firm finds a project with a positive NPV, the project offers a return that exceeds shareholders' expectations. A firm that consistently finds positive NPV investments will consistently surpass shareholders' expectations and enjoy a rising share price. The NPV, in effect, represents the amount of additional value created by the investment. Clearly, the acceptance of positive NPV projects is consistent with the firm's value-creation goal. Conversely, if the firm makes an investment with a negative NPV, the investment will destroy value and disappoint shareholders. A firm that regularly makes negative NPV investments will see its share price lag as it persists in generating lower-than-required returns for shareholders.

We can develop an analogy, drawing on what we already know about valuing bonds, to drive home the point about the relationship between share prices and the NPV rule. Suppose that, at a given point in time, investors require a 5 per cent return on five-year government bonds. Of course, this means that if the government issues

net present value (NPV)
The sum of the present value of all of a given project's cash flows, both inflows and outflows, discounted at a rate consistent with the project's risk. Also, a method for valuing capital investments.

EQUATION 8.1

five-year, €1000 par value bonds paying an annual coupon of €50, the market price of these bonds will be €1000, exactly equal to par value.

$$1000 = \frac{50}{(1.05)^1} + \frac{50}{(1.05)^2} + \cdots + \frac{1050}{(1.05)^5}$$

Now apply NPV logic. If an investor purchases one of these bonds for €1000, the NPV equals zero because the bond's cash flows precisely satisfy the investor's expectation of a 5 per cent return.

$$NPV = 0 = -1000 + \frac{50}{(1.05)^1} + \frac{50}{(1.05)^2} + \cdots + \frac{1050}{(1.05)^5}$$

Next, imagine that in a fit of election-year largesse, the government decrees that the coupon payments on all government bonds will double, so this bond now pays €100 in interest per year. If the bond's price remains fixed at €1000, this investment's NPV will suddenly switch from zero to positive:

$$NPV = 216.47 = -1000 + \frac{100}{(1.05)^1} + \frac{100}{(1.05)^2} + \cdots + \frac{1100}{(1.05)^5}$$

Of course, the bond's price will not remain at €1000. Investors will quickly recognize that at a price of €1000 and with a coupon of €100, the return offered by these bonds substantially exceeds the required rate of 5 per cent. Investors will flock to buy the bonds, rapidly driving up bond values until prices reach the point at which buying bonds becomes a zero NPV investment once again. In the new equilibrium, the bond's price will rise by €216.47, exactly the amount of the NPV that was created when the government doubled the coupon payments:

$$NPV = 0 = -1216.47 + \frac{100}{(1.05)^1} + \frac{100}{(1.05)^2} + \cdots + \frac{100}{(1.05)^5}$$

The same forces drive up a firm's share price when it makes a positive NPV investment, as shown in Figure 8.2. In the figure we depict a firm that investors believe will pay an annual dividend of €4 in perpetuity. If investors require a 10 per cent return on this firm's shares, the price will be €40. What happens if the firm makes a new investment? If the return on this investment is greater than 10 per cent, it will have a positive NPV. Investors will recognize that the firm has made an investment that exceeds their expectations, and investors will raise their forecast of future dividends, perhaps to €4.10 per year. At that level, the new share price will be €41. The same thing happens in reverse if the firm makes an investment that earns a return below 10 per cent. At that rate, the project has a negative NPV. Shareholders recognize that this investment's cash flows fall below their expectations, so they lower their estimates of future dividends to €3.90 per year. As a consequence, the share price falls to €39.

Now apply this thought process to WireVid!. Suppose that its shareholders demand an 18 per cent return on their shares. According to the principles we discussed in Chapter 5, the price of WireVid! shares will reflect the value of all future cash distributions that investors expect from the company, discounted at a rate of 18 per cent. But what if Wire-Vid! discovers that it can make an investment that offers a return substantially above 18 per cent? By definition, such an investment has a positive NPV, and by undertaking it WireVid! will increase the price of its shares as investors come to realize that the company is able to distribute higher-than-anticipated cash flows as a result of the investment opportunity. How far will the share price rise? Simply divide the project's NPV (which represents the amount of wealth the project creates) by the number of outstanding shares. The result is the amount by which the WireVid! share price should increase.

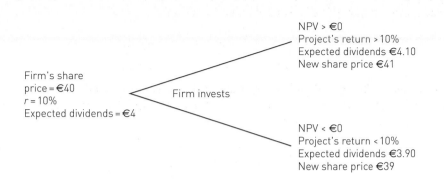

FIGURE 8.2

The NPV rule and shareholder wealth

If a firm invests in a project that earns more than its required return, its expected dividends and share price are expected to rise. If the project earns less than the required return, the expected dividends and share price are expected to fall.

Applying the Model

What are the NPVs of each of the investment opportunities now facing WireVid!? Time lines depicting the NPV calculations for WireVid!'s projects are given in Figure 8.3. Discounting each project's cash flows at 18 per cent yields the following results:

$$NPV_{Western\ Europe} = 75.3$$

$$= -250 + \frac{35}{(1.18)^1} + \frac{80}{(1.18)^2} + \frac{130}{(1.18)^3} + \frac{160}{(1.18)^4} + \frac{175}{(1.18)^5}$$

$$NPV_{South-east\ US} = 25.7$$

$$= -50 + \frac{18}{(1.18)^1} + \frac{22}{(1.18)^2} + \frac{25}{(1.18)^3} + \frac{30}{(1.18)^4} + \frac{32}{(1.18)^5}$$

Both projects increase shareholder wealth, so both are worth undertaking. One could say that 'both projects outrun the firm's 18 per cent required return and are therefore acceptable'. However, if the company can make only one investment, it should choose to expand its presence in Western Europe. That investment increases shareholder wealth by €75.3 million, whereas the south-east US investment increases wealth by only about one-third as much. If WireVid! has 100 million ordinary shares outstanding, then accepting the Western Europe project should increase the share price by about €0.75 (€75.3 million ÷ 100 million shares). Accepting the south-east US investment would increase the share price by almost €0.26 (€25.7 million ÷ 100 million shares).

Pros and cons of NPV

The net-present-value method solves all the problems we have identified with the payback and discounted payback rules, as well as the problems associated with decision rules that are based on the accounting rate of return. First, the NPV rule focuses on cash flow, not accounting earnings. Secondly, when properly applied, the net-present-value method makes appropriate adjustments for the time value of money. Thirdly, the decision rule to invest when NPVs are positive and to refrain from investing when NPVs are negative reflects the firm's need to compete for funds in the market-place rather than an arbitrary judgement of management. Fourthly, the NPV approach offers

FIGURE 8.3a

NPV of WireVid!'s projects at 18 per cent (€mn)

Western Europe project

The net present value (NPV) of WireVid!'s Western Europe project is €75.3 million, which means that it is acceptable (NPV > €0) and therefore creates wealth for its shareholders. This project would be preferred over the south-east US project which has a lower NPV, as shown in Figure 8.3b.

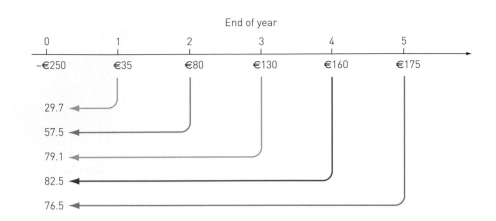

NPV=€75.3

Spreadsheet

Row \ Column	A	B
1	Cash flow 0	−250
2	Cash flow 1	35
3	Cash flow 2	80
4	Cash flow 3	130
5	Cash flow 4	160
6	Cash flow 5	175
7	Interest	18%
8	Number of periods	5
9	**Net present value**	**€75.3**
10	*Formula B9:* NPV(B7,B1,B2,B3,B4,B5,B6)	

Calculator

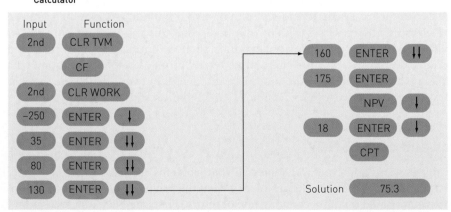

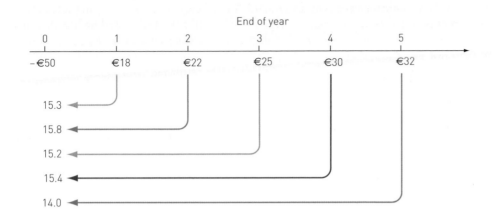

FIGURE 8.3b

NPV of WireVid!'s projects at 18 per cent (€mn)

South-east US project

The net present value (NPV) of Global Wireless's south-east US Project is €25.7 million, which means that it is acceptable (NPV >€0) and therefore creates value for shareholders. This project is inferior to the Western Europe project, which has a higher NPV as shown in Figure 8.3a.

NPV = €25.7

Spreadsheet

Row \ Column	A	B
1	Cash flow 0	–50
2	Cash flow 1	18
3	Cash flow 2	22
4	Cash flow 3	25
5	Cash flow 4	30
6	Cash flow 5	32
7	Interest	18%
8	Number of periods	5
9	**Net present value**	**€25.7**
10	*Formula B9:* NPV(B7,B1,B2,B3,B4,B5,B6)	

Calculator

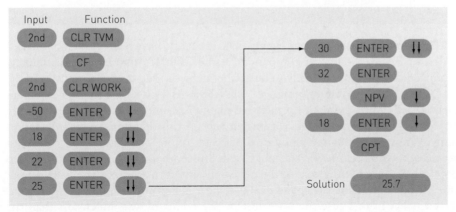

a relatively straightforward way to control for differences in risk among alternative investments. Cash flows on riskier investments should be discounted at higher rates. Fifthly, the NPV method incorporates all the cash flows that a project generates over its life, not just those that occur in the project's early years. Sixthly, the NPV gives a direct estimate of the change in shareholder wealth resulting from a given investment.

Although we are enthusiastic supporters of the NPV approach, especially when compared with the other decision methods examined thus far, we must acknowledge that the NPV rule suffers from a few weaknesses. Relative to alternative capital budgeting tools, the NPV rule seems less intuitive to many users. When you hear that WireVid!'s south-east US project has an NPV of €25.7 million, does that seem more or less intuitive than learning that the investment pays back its initial cost in 2.4 years or that it earns an accounting rate of return of 61.6 per cent? Though the mathematics of an NPV calculation can hardly be called sophisticated, it is still easier to calculate a project's payback period than its NPV. It is also easier to communicate to managers that the project pays for itself in three years than to state that, given the required rate of return, the NPV of the project, etc.

Whereas most large corporations apply the NPV method, perhaps in conjunction with other capital budgeting tools, to make major investment decisions, the NPV rule has a close cousin known as the 'internal rate of return', which is perhaps even more widely used. The internal rate of return uses essentially the same mathematics as NPV for evaluating a project's merits. The output of internal rate of return analysis is a single, intuitively appealing number representing the return that an investment earns over its life. In most cases, the internal rate of return yields investment recommendations that are in agreement with the NPV rule, although important differences between the two approaches arise when ranking alternative projects.

CONCEPT REVIEW QUESTIONS

6 What does it mean if a project has an NPV of €1 million?

7 Why might the discount rates used to calculate the NPVs of two competing projects differ at a given point in time?

Real World

Sometimes markets overreact to events that, in reality, have a small NPV. Consider the case of EADS, the parent company of Airbus. On 13 June 2006 the company announced that there were likely to be further delays, of up to seven months, in the final launch of its new super-jumbo jet, the A380. As we will see in the next chapters, this vastly complex type of project has many risks, and complex calculations are involved. The markets reacted very negatively to this announcement, the shares falling by more than €4, wiping over 25 per cent off the value of the company. But this was an overreaction. On 16 June Credit Suisse, the investment bank, released a note calculating that the cost of the delay amounted to approximately €1.40 per share. Although outside the scope of this text, it is not uncommon for markets to overreact, but in this case the NPV lost by the company was much less than the value lost by shareholders. What is interesting is that the increase in value of shares in the main rival, Boeing, was almost that lost by EADS. Clearly investors shifted from a company that was announcing negative NPV news to a company that was not doing so.

8.5 INTERNAL RATE OF RETURN

Finding a project's IRR

All methods used for evaluating investment projects – accounting rate of return, payback and discounted payback – suffer from common problems, namely the complete or partial failure to make adjustments for the time value of money and for risk. Alternative methods exist that correct these shortcomings. Perhaps the most popular and most intuitive of these alternatives is known as the **internal rate of return (IRR)** method. An investment's internal rate of return is analogous to a bond's yield to maturity (YTM), a concept we introduced in Chapter 4. Recall that the YTM of a bond is the discount rate that equates the present value of the bond's future cash flows to its market price. The YTM measures the compound annual return that an investor earns by purchasing a bond and holding it until maturity (provided that all payments are made as promised and that interest payments can be reinvested at the same rate). In a similar vein, the IRR of an investment project is the compound annual rate of return on the project, given its up-front costs and subsequent cash flows.

internal rate of return (IRR)
The compound annual rate of return on a project, given its up-front costs and subsequent cash flows.

A project's IRR is the discount rate that makes the net present value of all project cash flows equal to zero:

$$NPV_0 = 0 = CF_0 + \frac{CF_1}{(1+r)^1} + \frac{CF_2}{(1+r)^2} + \cdots + \frac{CF_n}{(1+r)^n}$$

EQUATION 8.2

To find a project's IRR, we must begin by specifying the project's cash flows. Next, using a financial calculator, a spreadsheet, or even trial and error, we find the discount rate that equates the present value of cash flows to zero. Once we have the IRR in hand, we compare it with a prespecified hurdle rate established by the firm. The hurdle rate represents the firm's minimum acceptable return for a given project, so the decision rule is to invest only if the project's IRR exceeds the hurdle rate.

But where does the hurdle rate come from? How do firms decide whether to require projects to exceed a 10 per cent hurdle or a 20 per cent hurdle? The answer to this question provides insight into another advantage of IRR over capital budgeting methods that focus on a project's accounting rate of return or payback period. A company should set the hurdle rate at a level that reflects market returns on investments that are just as risky as the project under consideration. For example, if the project at hand involves expanding a chain of fast-food restaurants, then the hurdle rate should reflect the returns that other fast-food businesses offer investors in the market-place. Therefore, the IRR method, like the NPV method, establishes a hurdle rate or a decision criterion that is *market-based*, unlike the accounting-based and payback approaches that establish arbitrary thresholds for investment approval. In fact, for a given project, the hurdle rate used in IRR analysis should be the discount rate used in NPV analysis.

Figure 8.4 is a **net present value (NPV) profile**, which plots a project's NPV (on the y-axis) against various discount rates (on the x-axis). The NPV profile can be used to illustrate the relationship between the NPV and the IRR for a typical project. By 'typical', we mean a project with cash flows that begin with an initial outflow, followed by a series of inflows. In this case, the NPV declines as the discount rate used to calculate the NPV increases. Not all projects have this feature, as we will soon see. The line in Figure 8.4 plots the NPV of a project at various discount rates. When the discount rate is relatively low, the project has a positive NPV. When the discount rate is high, the project has a negative NPV. At some discount rate, the NPV of the project will equal zero, and that rate is the project's IRR. It is important to note that the IRR of a project is *not* some rate that the analyst or manager imposes. It does not come from outside the project, but from inside, and emerges from the cash flows over time.

net present value (NPV) profile
A plot of a project's NPV (on the y-axis) against various discount rates (on the x-axis). It is used to illustrate the relationship between the NPV and the IRR for the typical project.

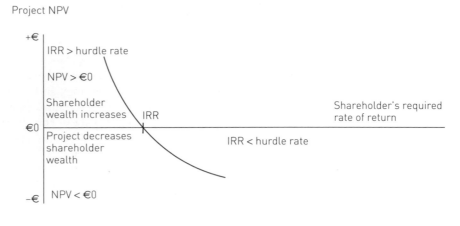

FIGURE 8.4

NPV profile and shareholder wealth

The NPV profile for the 'typical' project, which begins with an initial outflow followed by a series of inflows, shows that the NPV declines as the discount rate used to calculate the NPV increases. The project's IRR is the discount rate that causes the NPV to equal zero.

Thus, unlike the payback methods, there is no subjectivity in the calculation of the IRR, and that is a major advantage of it as a method of appraisal.

Applying the Model

Suppose that WireVid! requires its analysts to calculate the IRR of all proposed investments, and the company agrees to undertake only those investments that offer an IRR exceeding 18 per cent, a rate that WireVid! believes to be an industry standard. Figure 8.5 presents a time line depicting the IRR calculation procedure for WireVid!'s two projects. Calculating the IRR for each of WireVid!'s potential investments involves solving these two equations:

$$IRR_{WE}: 0 = -250 + \frac{35}{(1 + r_{WE})^1} + \frac{80}{(1 + r_{WE})^2} + \frac{130}{(1 + r_{WE})^3} + \frac{160}{(1 + r_{WE})^4} + \frac{175}{(1 + r_{WE})^5}$$

$$IRR_{US}: 0 = -50 + \frac{18}{(1 + r_{US})^1} + \frac{22}{(1 + r_{US})^2} + \frac{25}{(1 + r_{US})^3} + \frac{30}{(1 + r_{US})^4} + \frac{32}{(1 + r_{US})^5}$$

The numerical values in these equations come from each project's cash flow estimates, and the terms r_{WE} and r_{US} represent the IRR for the Western Europe and south-east US investments, respectively. Solving these expressions yields the following:

$$r_{WE} = 27.8\%$$

$$r_{SE} = 36.7\%$$

Because both investments exceed the hurdle rate of 18 per cent, WireVid! would like to undertake both projects. But what if it can invest in only one project or the other? Should the company invest in the south-east US project because it offers a higher IRR than the alternative? The simple IRR approach doesn't give us a straightforward method.

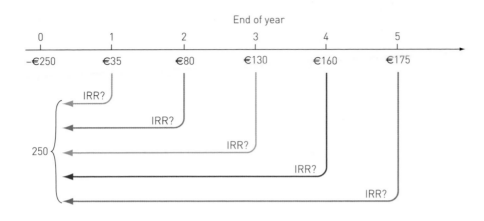

NPV = €0
IRR = 27.8%

FIGURE 8.5a

IRR of WireVid!'s projects (€mn)

Western Europe project

The internal rate of return (IRR) for WireVid!'s Western Europe project is 27.8 per cent, which is the discount rate that causes the project's cash flows to have an NPV of €0. The project is acceptable because its NPV is greater than the firm's 18 per cent hurdle rate. Because the IRR for the Western Europe project is less than the 36.7 per cent IRR for the south-east US project shown in Figure 8.5b, the south-east US project is preferred.

Spreadsheet

Row \ Column	A	B
1	Cash flow 0	−250
2	Cash flow 1	35
3	Cash flow 2	80
4	Cash flow 3	130
5	Cash flow 4	160
6	Cash flow 5	175
7	**IRR**	**27.8%**
8	*Formula B7:* IRR(B1:B6)	

Calculator

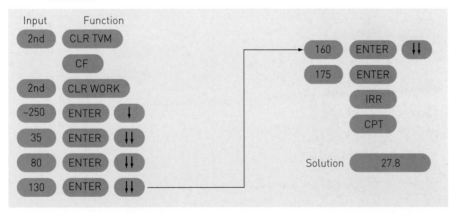

FIGURE 8.5b

IRR of WireVid!'s projects (€mn)

South-east US project

The internal rate of return (IRR) for WireVid!'s south-east US project is 36.7 per cent, which is the discount rate that causes the project's cash flow to have an NPV of €0. Because the IRR for this project is above the 27.8 per cent IRR for the Western Europe project, this project is preferred.

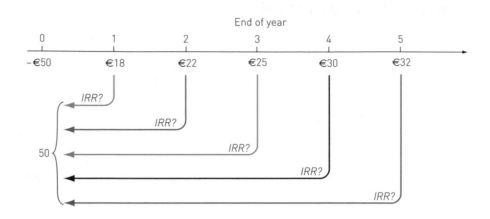

NPV = €0
IRR = 36.7%

Spreadsheet

Column / Row	A	B
1	Cash flow 0	−50
2	Cash flow 1	18
3	Cash flow 2	22
4	Cash flow 3	25
5	Cash flow 4	30
6	Cash flow 5	32
7	**IRR**	**36.7%**
8	*Formula B7:* IRR(B1:B6)	

Calculator

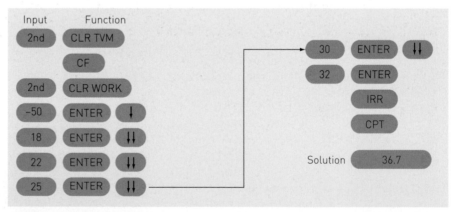

Source: Adapted from 'UraMin Raises $60 Million For Mine At Trekkopj', *The Namibian*, 16 May 2006, 'Russians Hit Shell With Extra Bill Over Sakhalin', *Financial Times*, 29 December 2006.

Advantages of the IRR method

The question of how to rank investments that offer different IRRs points to an important weakness of this method. However, before considering the problems associated with IRR analysis, let us discuss the advantages that make it one of the most widely used methods for evaluating capital investments.

First, the IRR makes an appropriate adjustment for the time value of money. The value of a euro received in the first year is greater than the value of a euro received in the second year. Even cash flows that arrive several years in the future receive some weight in the analysis (unlike payback, which totally ignores distant cash flows). Secondly, the hurdle rate itself can be based on market returns obtainable on similar investments. This takes away some of the subjectivity that creeps into other analytical methods, like the arbitrary threshold decisions that must be made when using accounting rate of return or payback, and it allows managers to make explicit, quantitative adjustments for differences in risk across projects. Thirdly, because the 'answer' that comes out of an IRR analysis is a rate of return, its meaning is easy for both financial and non-financial managers to grasp intuitively. They can easily compare a project's IRR with objective as well as subjective hurdle rates to assess its economic viability. As we will see, however, the intuitive appeal of the IRR approach has its drawbacks, particularly when ranking investments with different IRRs. Fourthly, the IRR technique focuses on cash flow rather than on accounting measures of income.

Though it represents a substantial improvement over accounting rate of return or payback analysis, the IRR technique has some quirks and problems that in certain situations should concern analysts. Some of these problems arise from the mathematics of the IRR calculation, but other difficulties come into play only when companies must discriminate between **mutually exclusive projects**. If the IRRs of several projects exceed the hurdle rate (or NPVs exceed €0), but only a subset of those projects can be undertaken at the given time, how does the firm choose? It turns out that the intuitive approach, selecting those projects with the highest IRRs, can lead to bad decisions in certain cases.

mutually exclusive projects
The situation that occurs when the IRRs of several projects exceed the hurdle rate (or the NPVs exceed €0), but only a subset of those projects can be undertaken at the given time.

Real World

Companies can and do use the IRR to justify projects. In May 2006 a company UraMin Inc., with access to potential uranium resources of 112 million kg of uranium oxide in Namibia and South Africa, raised N$380 million (N = Namibian dollars) to provide funds to further exploit the mine. The company stated that, based on then prevailing uranium prices, and at the projected recovery rates and operating costs, it expected a 44 per cent project internal rate of return (at the then uranium price).

Or consider the issue of the giant gas and oil field development at Sakhalin Island in Russia. The development of the project has been beset by arguments between the main developers and the Russian government over who pays what proportion of what costs. The complex negotiations concluded in December 2006. Commenting on this, Jonathan Wright of Citigroup said: 'It depends on what you expect for oil and gas prices, but my figures suggest an internal rate of return for the project of 11 per cent. That's above the cost of capital, but not sufficiently above it, given the region and the risks involved, to be able to say this is an attractive project.' This perfectly encapsulates a proper use of IRR, to monitor and evaluate a project in conjunction with other methods.

Problems with the internal rate of return

There are two classes of problems that analysts encounter when evaluating investments using the IRR technique. The first class can be described as 'mathematical problems', which are difficulties in interpreting the numbers that one obtains from solving an IRR equation. Theoretically when one is solving for an IRR one is getting the roots of a quadratic equation of order n. In both the above cases we have a quadratic in order 5, as there were 5 years of data. However, we know that there are as many *potential* roots to such an equation as there are sign changes in it. We are lucky above in that there is only one sign change in each situation: from the negative outflow in year zero to positive in year 1 and each year thereafter. However, what if this was not the case?

Multiple IRRs As an example, consider a project with the following stream of cash flows:

YEAR	CF (€mn)
0	+100
1	−460
2	+791
3	−602.6
4	+171.6

Admittedly, this project has a rather strange sequence of alternating net cash inflows and outflows, but it is not hard to think of real-world investments that generate cash flow streams that flip back and forth like this. For example, think about high-technology products. A new product costs money to develop. It generates plenty of cash for a year or two, but it quickly becomes obsolete. Obsolescence necessitates more spending to develop an upgraded version of the product, which then generates cash again. The cycle continues indefinitely.

Figure 8.6 presents the NPV profile for a project with the cash flows shown above at various discount rates. Notice that there are several points on the graph at which the project NPV equals zero. In other words, there are several IRRs for this project,

FIGURE 8.6

NPV profile for a project with multiple IRRs

This project with alternating cash inflows and outflows has an NPV profile that reflects multiple IRRs. At each discount rate for which the NPV = €0, there is an IRR. In this case, IRRs occur at 0 per cent, 10 per cent, 20 per cent and 30 per cent.

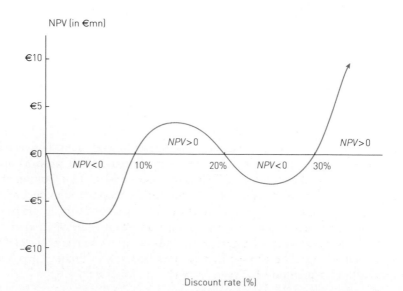

including 0 per cent, 10 per cent, 20 per cent, and 30 per cent. How does one apply the IRR decision rule in a situation such as this? Suppose that the hurdle rate for this project is 15 per cent. Two of the four IRRs on this project exceed the hurdle rate, and two fall below the hurdle rate. Should the firm invest or not? The only way to know for sure is to check the NPV. On the graph, we see that at a discount rate of 15 per cent, the project's NPV is positive, so the firm should invest.

We know that the maximum number of IRRs that a project can have equals the number of sign changes in the cash flow stream. Therefore, in the typical project with cash outflows up front and cash inflows later on, there is just one sign change, and there will be at most one IRR. In the previous example, there are four sign changes in the cash flow stream and four different IRRs. In the event that you have to evaluate a project with more than one sign change in the cash flows, beware of the multiple IRR problem. In this situation, the NPV profile must be analysed because use of the IRR typically does not result in the correct decision.

No real solution Occasionally, when you enter the cash flows from a particular investment into a calculator or a spreadsheet, you may receive an error message indicating that there is no solution to the problem. For some cash flow patterns, it is possible that there is no real discount rate that equates the project's NPV to zero. In these cases, the only solution to the IRR equation involves imaginary numbers – hardly something that we can compare with a firm's hurdle rate.

Applying the Model

When we first looked at the WireVid! Western Europe expansion project, we examined cash flows over a five-year project life. Let's modify the example a little. Suppose that the project life is six years rather than five, and in the sixth year the firm must incur a large negative cash outflow. The modified cash flow projections look like this:

YEAR	WESTERN EUROPE PROJECT (€mn)
0	−250
1	35
2	80
3	130
4	160
5	175
6	−355

When we attempt to calculate the IRR for this stream of cash flows, we find that our financial calculator (or Excel) returns an error code. The problem is that for this stream of cash flows, there is no real solution to the IRR equation. That is, there is no (real) interest rate at which the present value of cash flows equals zero. If we cannot determine the IRR of this project, how can we determine whether the project meets the firm's hurdle rate of 18 per cent? In this particular example, the magnitudes of the cash outflows at the beginning and end of the modified project are such that intuition suggests that WireVid! should not invest.

However, it is possible to generate scenarios in which no solution to the IRR equation exists. The pattern of cash flows over time is sufficiently complex, so it is difficult to decide whether to invest, based on intuition.

The last two examples illustrate various problems that analysts may encounter when using the IRR decision rule. These problems are mathematical in nature in the sense that they involve difficulties in getting a solution to the IRR equation. Although we do not want to diminish the importance of watching out for these mathematical problems, we suspect that, in practice, they are of secondary importance. We mean that most investment projects that you will evaluate using the IRR method will probably have a unique solution with little ambiguity (because most projects involve cash outflows up front, followed by cash inflows). However, two additional problems may arise when analysts use the IRR method to prioritize projects or to choose between mutually exclusive projects.

IRR, NPV and mutually exclusive projects

The scale problem Suppose that a friend promises to pay you €2 tomorrow if you lend him €1 today. If you make the loan and your friend fulfils his end of the bargain, you will have made an investment with a 100 per cent IRR.[5] Now consider a different case. Your friend asks you to lend him €100 today in exchange for €150 tomorrow. The IRR on that investment is 50 per cent, exactly half the IRR of the first example. Both of these loans offer very high rates of return. Assuming that you trust the friend to repay you in either case, which investment would you choose if you could choose only one? The first investment increases your wealth by €1, and the second increases your wealth by €50. Even though the rate of return is lower on the second investment, most people would prefer to lend the larger amount because of its substantially greater pay-off.

The point of these examples is not to tempt you to enter the loan-shark business, but rather to illustrate the scale problem inherent in IRR analysis. When choosing between mutually exclusive investments, we cannot conclude that the one offering the highest IRR necessarily provides the greatest wealth-creation opportunity. When several alternative investments offer IRRs that exceed a firm's hurdle rate, choosing the investment that maximizes shareholder wealth involves more than picking the project with the highest *IRR*. For example, take another look at the investment opportunities faced by WireVid! – opportunities that vary dramatically in scale.

Applying the Model

Here again are the NPV and IRR figures for the two investment alternatives.

PROJECT	IRR	NPV (@18%)
Western Europe	27.8%	€75.3 million
South-east US	36.7%	€25.7 million

If we had to choose just one project, and we ranked them based on their IRRs, we would choose to invest in the south-east US project. But we have also seen that the Western Europe project generates a much higher NPV, meaning that it creates more wealth for WireVid! shareholders. The NPV criterion tells us to expand in Western Europe rather than in the south-east United States. Why the conflict? The scale of the Western Europe expansion is roughly five times that of the south-east US project. Even though the south-east US investment provides a higher rate of return, the opportunity to make the much larger Western Europe investment (an investment that also offers a return well above the firm's hurdle rate) is more attractive.

---

[5] The IRR is 100 per cent per day in this example, which is not a bad return if you annualize it.

Fortunately for analysts who prefer to use the IRR method, there is a resolution to the scale problem. Discussion of this procedure is beyond the scope of this introductory text. Suffice it to say that the methodology allows one to use the IRR technique to find precisely the same solution that would result using NPV.

The timing problem Managers of public corporations often receive criticism for neglecting long-term investment opportunities for the sake of meeting short-term financial performance goals. We prefer to remain non-committal on whether corporate managers, as a rule, put too much emphasis on short-term performance. However, we agree with the proposition that a naïve reliance on the IRR method can lead to investment decisions that sometimes favour investments with short-term pay-offs over those that offer returns over a longer horizon. The next 'Applying the Model' section illustrates the problem we have in mind.

Real World

Mutually exclusive projects are not that uncommon. Consider the report in *Flight International*, the respected aviation trade magazine, on Bombardier, the Canadian airliner manufacturer. The report noted that the company, which is one of the smaller airliner manufacturers, was considering its options in regard to two new aircraft. The company's Aerospace vice president for strategy and business development was quoted as stating: 'The two projects are not mutually exclusive . . . but you have to ask yourself if in terms of resources we'd want to do both? . . . We don't have unlimited technical and financial resources.'

Applying the Model

A company wants to evaluate two investment proposals. The first involves a major effort in new product development. The initial cost is €1 billion, and the company expects the project to generate relatively meagre cash flows in the first four years, followed by a big pay-off in year 5. The second investment is a significant marketing campaign to attract new customers. It too has an initial outlay of €1 billion, but it generates significant cash flows almost immediately and lower levels of cash in the later years. A financial analyst prepares cash flow projections and calculates each project's IRR and NPV as shown in the following table (the firm uses 10 per cent as its hurdle rate):

CASH FLOW	PRODUCT DEVELOPMENT (€mn)	MARKETING CAMPAIGN (€mn)
Initial outlay	−1 000	− 1 000
Year 1	0	450
Year 2	50	350
Year 3	100	300
Year 4	200	200
Year 5	1 500	100

Technique		
IRR	14.1%	15.9%
NPV (@10%)	€184.44	€122.44

The analyst observes that the first project generates a higher NPV, whereas the second offers a higher IRR. Bewildered, he wonders which project to recommend to senior management.

Even though both projects require the same initial investment and both last for five years, the marketing campaign generates more cash flow in the early years than the product development proposal. Therefore, in a relative sense, the pay-off from product development occurs later than the pay-off from marketing. We know from our discussion of interest rate risk in Chapter 4 that when interest rates change, long-term bond prices move more than short-term bond prices do. The same phenomenon is at work here. Figure 8.7 plots the NPV profiles for the two projects on the same set of axes. Notice that one line, the line plotting NPVs for the product development idea, is much steeper than the other. In simple terms, this means that the NPV of that investment is much more sensitive to the discount rate than is the NPV of the marketing campaign.

Each investment's IRR appears in Figure 8.7 where the NPV lines cross the x-axis. Figure 8.7 shows that both IRRs exceed the hurdle rate of 10 per cent and that the marketing campaign has the higher IRR. The two lines intersect at a discount rate of 12.5 per cent. At that discount rate, the NPVs of the projects are equal. At discount rates below 12.5 per cent, product development, which has a longer-term pay-off, has the higher NPV. At discount rates above 12.5 per cent, the investment in the marketing campaign offers a larger NPV. Given that the required rate of return on investments for this particular firm is 10 per cent, the firm should choose to spend the €1 billion on product development. However, if the firm bases its investment decision solely on achieving the highest IRR, it will choose the marketing campaign proposal instead.

In summary, we can say that when the timing of cash flows is very different from one project to another, the project with the highest IRR may or may not have the highest NPV. As in the case of the scale problem, the timing problem can lead firms to reject

FIGURE 8.7

NPV profiles demonstrating the timing problem

Because of the differences in the timing of the two projects' cash flows, the marketing campaign has a higher IRR than the product development proposal, and both IRRs exceed the 10 per cent hurdle rate. But the NPV for the product development proposal at 10 per cent exceeds the NPV for the marketing campaign.

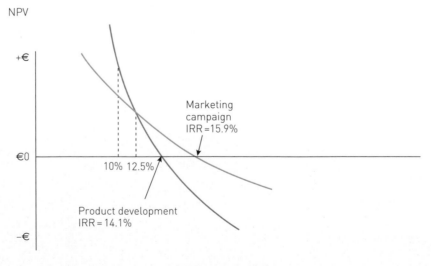

investments that they should accept. We want to emphasize that this problem (and the scale problem) occurs only when firms must choose between mutually exclusive projects. In the previous example, if the firm could invest in both projects, it should.

When firms must prioritize projects, leaving some acceptable projects on the table, there are two ways they can avoid falling into the timing trap. First, using NPV will lead to the correct decision when evaluating projects with very different cash flow patterns over time. Secondly, analysts can use mathematical techniques that are beyond the scope of this introductory text to resolve the timing problem. The methodology allows one to use the IRR technique to find precisely the same solution that would result using NPV. Clearly, the most straightforward and, theoretically, the best decision technique is net present value.

SMART CONCEPTS

See the concept explained step-by-step at **www.cengage.co.uk/ megginson**

8 Describe how the IRR and NPV approaches are related.

9 If the IRR for a given project exceeds a firm's hurdle rate, does that mean that the project necessarily has a positive NPV? Explain.

10 Describe the 'scale problem' and the 'timing problem' and explain the potential effects of these problems on the choice of mutually exclusive projects, using IRR versus NPV.

CONCEPT
REVIEW
QUESTIONS

8.6 PROFITABILITY INDEX

A final capital budgeting tool that we discuss is the **profitability index (PI)**. Like the IRR, the profitability index is a close cousin of the NPV approach. Mathematically, for simple projects that have an initial cash outflow (CF_0) followed by a series of inflows (CF_1, CF_2, ...,CF_N), the PI equals the present value of a project's cash inflows divided by the initial cash outflow.

profitability index (PI)
A capital budgeting tool, defined as the present value of a project's cash inflows divided by its initial cash outflow.

$$PI = \frac{\dfrac{CF_1}{(1+r)^1} + \dfrac{CF_2}{(1+r)^2} + \dfrac{CF_3}{(1+r)^3} + \cdots + \dfrac{CF_n}{(1+r)^n}}{CF_0}$$

EQUATION 8.3

The decision rule to follow when evaluating investment projects using the PI is to invest when the PI is greater than 1.0 (i.e. when the present value of cash inflows exceeds the initial cash outflow) and to refrain from investing when the PI is less than 1.0. Notice that if the PI is above 1.0, the NPV must be greater than zero. That means that the NPV and PI decision rules will always yield the same investment recommendation when we are simply trying to decide whether to accept or reject a single project.

Applying the Model

To calculate the PI for each of WireVid!'s investment projects, calculate the present value of its cash inflows from years 1–5 and then divide by the initial cash outflow to obtain the following result:

PROJECT	PV OF CF (1–5) (€mn)	INITIAL OUTLAY (€mn)	PI
Western Europe	325.3	250	1.3
South-east US	75.7	50	1.5

Because both projects have a PI greater than 1.0, both are worthwhile. However, notice that if we rank projects based on the PI, the south-east US project looks better.

Because the NPV, IRR and PI methods are so closely related, they share many of the same advantages relative to accounting rate of return or payback analysis, and there is no need to reiterate those advantages here. However, it is worth pointing out that the PI and the IRR share an important flaw. Both suffer from the scale problem described earlier. Recall that our NPV calculations suggested that the Western Europe project created more value for WireVid! shareholders than the south-east US endeavour, whereas the IRR and PI comparisons suggest just the opposite project ranking. The reason that the IRR and PI analyses identify the south-east US project as the superior investment is that they do not take into account the differences in scale between the two projects. For the south-east US project, the PI indicates that project cash inflows exceed the initial cash outflow by 50 per cent on a present-value basis. The present value of cash inflows for the Western Europe investment exceeds the initial cash outflow by just 30 per cent. But the Western Europe project is much larger, and as our NPV figures reveal, it generates considerably more wealth for WireVid! shareholders.

CONCEPT REVIEW QUESTIONS

11 How are the NPV, IRR and PI approaches related?

12 What important flaw do both the IRR and PI share? Explain.

8.7 WHICH TECHNIQUES DO FIRMS ACTUALLY USE?

The techniques above are not simply dry academic theories. They are used in the largest companies in the word. In a survey of 392 chief financial officers (CFOs), Graham and Harvey (2001)[6] studied the capital budgeting methods that companies use to make real investment decisions. They asked CFOs to indicate how frequently they used several capital budgeting methods by ranking them on a scale ranging from 0 (never) to 4 (always). The techniques CFOs use most often are NPV (score = 3.08) and IRR (score = 3.09), with roughly 75 per cent of CFOs indicating that they always or almost always use these techniques. A 30-year-old study by Gitman and Forrester (1977)[7] found that only 9.8 per cent of large firms used NPV as a primary capital budgeting tool, so Graham and Harvey's results clearly illustrate that the popularity of the NPV approach has grown over time. Interestingly, the popularity of the NPV approach is correlated both with the size of the firm and the educational background of its CFO. Large, publicly traded firms run by CFOs with MBAs are much more likely to rely on the NPV method than are small, private firms headed by CFOs without MBAs.

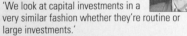

SMART PRACTICES VIDEO

Beth Acton, former Vice President and Treasurer of Ford Motor Co.
'We look at capital investments in a very similar fashion whether they're routine or large investments.'

See the entire interview at **www.cengage.co.uk/megginson**

---

[6] J. Graham and R.C. Harvey (2001) 'Theory and Practice of Corporate Finance: Evidence From the Field', *Journal of Financial Economics* 60(2–3):187–243.

[7] L.J. Gitman and J.R. Forrester, Jr. (1977) 'A Survey of Capital Budgeting Techniques Used by Major U.S. Firms', *Financial Management* Fall:66–71.

Third on the list of most frequently used capital budgeting tools is the payback method. Small firms, in particular, use the payback approach almost as often as they use NPV and IRR. Older CFOs and those without MBA degrees also tend to make decisions based on payback analysis much more frequently than do other CFOs. Most CFOs reported that they rarely used accounting rate of return, discounted payback or the profitability index when making investment decisions. The Comparative Corporate Finance panel compares Graham and Harvey's results to similar studies conducted in other countries All these papers point to the pre-eminence of discounted cash flow analysis techniques in making investment decisions around the world.

COMPARATIVE CORPORATE FINANCE
Capital budgeting in Sweden, South Africa and the United Kingdom

We have seen that managers of publicly traded US firms use discounted cash flow techniques in capital budgeting far more today than in the past. But what of managers in other countries? Recent academic studies present survey evidence of how frequently discounted cash flow techniques are used by managers of Swedish, South African, British and European companies. The results are somewhat encouraging. Sandahl and Sjögren (2003) find that 64.8 per cent of the 128 responding Swedish companies use either NPV (52.3 per cent) or IRR (22.7 per cent), or both, with larger firms more likely to use one of these methods than smaller companies. On the other hand, 78.1 per cent of the responding companies use the payback period. This is by far the most commonly employed tool for companies that use only one capital budgeting decision rule, with 58.3 per cent using payback versus 12.5 per cent for both NPV and IRR.

In a survey of companies listed on the Industrial Sector of the Johannesburg Stock Exchange, Hall (2000) finds that two-thirds of responding South African firms use discounted cash flow techniques to make capital budgeting decisions. Specifically, 32.3 per cent of these firms report that they believe that the IRR method is the best tool for evaluating capital investments, while 16.9 per cent say that NPV is their preferred tool,

and 16.9 per cent rely on discounted payback. Moreover, the importance of these techniques in the investment decision process rises with the size of the firm. Among the smallest South African firms in the survey, just over 14 per cent calculate the NPV or IRR of their investment projects, but 75 per cent of the largest firms do. Finally, a study published in Lumby (1991) reports similar patterns among UK firms, with 54 per cent using discounted cash flow techniques. The same positive relationship between a firm's size and its tendency to use discounted cash flow analysis that exists in South Africa also emerges in the United Kingdom. In the case of European companies, a major survey by Brounen *et al.* (2004) found a greater reliance on IRR when they examined the per centage of companies that frequently used it (Germany 42 per cent, France 44 per cent, UK 53 per cent and the Netherlands 56 per cent) in evaluating capital investment decisions. NPV was the second most popular (Germany 46 per cent, France 35 per cent, UK 47 per cent and the Netherlands 70 per cent). There was still a high reliance, however, on the payback methods (Germany 50 per cent, France 51 per cent, UK 69 per cent and the Netherlands 54 per cent). As found previously, the chances are that the larger the firm the more likely it is to use the NPV approaches.

Sources: Gert Sandahl and Stefan Sjögren (2003) 'Capital Budgeting Methods Among Sweden's Largest Groups of Companies: The State of the Art and a Comparison with Earlier Studies', *International Journal of Production Economics* 84:51–69; J. H. Hall (2000) 'An Empirical Investigation of the Capital Budgeting Process', *University of Pretoria Working Paper*; L. Lumby (1991) *Investment Appraisal and Investment Decisions*, 4th ed., London: Chapman & Hall; Dirk Brounen, Abe de Jong and Kees C.G. Koedijk (2004) 'Corporate Finance in Europe: Confronting Theory with Practice', *Financial Management*, 33(4).

8.8 SUMMARY AND CONCLUSIONS

- The capital budgeting process involves generating, reviewing, analysing, selecting and implementing long-term investment proposals that are consistent with the firm's strategic goals.

- Other things being equal, managers would prefer an easily applied capital budgeting technique that considers cash flow, recognizes the time value of money, fully accounts for expected risk and return, and, when applied, leads to higher share prices.

- Though simplicity is a virtue, the simplest approaches to capital budgeting do not always lead firms to make the best investment decisions.

- Capital budgeting techniques include the accounting rate of return, the payback period and the discounted payback period, which are less sophisticated techniques because they do not explicitly deal with the time value of money and are not tied to the firm's wealth-maximization goal. More sophisticated techniques include net present value (NPV), internal rate of return (IRR) and profitability index (PI). These methods often give the same

- accept or reject decisions but do not necessarily rank projects the same.

- Table 8.1 summarizes the definitions, advantages and disadvantages of each of the capital budgeting techniques presented in this chapter.

- Using the IRR approach can lead to poor investment decisions when projects have cash flow streams alternating between net inflows and outflows. The IRR technique may provide suboptimal project rankings when different investments have very different scales or when the timing of cash flows varies dramatically from one project to another.

- Although the NPV and IRR techniques give the same accept or reject decisions, these techniques do not necessarily agree in ranking mutually exclusive projects. Because of its lack of mathematical, scale and timing problems, the most straightforward and, theoretically, the best decision technique is net present value (NPV).

- The profitability index is a close cousin of the NPV approach, but it suffers from the same scale problem as the IRR approach.

TABLE 8.1

Analysis of capital budgeting techniques

TECHNIQUE	DEFINITION	ADVANTAGES	DISADVANTAGES
Accounting rate of return	Net income divided by the book value of assets, either on a year-to-year basis or averaged over the project's life.	• Convenience • Ease of calculation • Ease of interpretation	• Significantly effected by the depreciation method used by the firm • Makes no adjustment for project's risk or the time value of money • Considers book values, not market values, of firm's assets • Focuses on income rather than cash flow • Relies on an arbitrary hurdle rate
Payback period	Amount of time for cumulative net cash inflow to recoup initial investment.	• Simple to calculate • Intuitively appealing • Gives some consideration to the time value of money • Accounts for project risk exposure	• Relies on an arbitrary cut-off period • Method of accounting for time value of money is crude in the extreme • Ignores cash flows after the payback period

TABLE 8.1 (cont.)

TECHNIQUE	DEFINITION	ADVANTAGES	DISADVANTAGES
			• Crude method of controlling for project risk • Career concerns may cause managers to incorrectly favour projects with short paybacks
Discounted payback	Same as payback except that cash flows are discounted and then the payback is calculated	• Same as for the payback period except it explicitly considers time value of money in the cash flows that occur before the payback period	• Same as for the payback period except it does recognize time value for the payback period
Net present value (NPV)	The sum of the present values of all of a project's cash flows, both inflows and outflows, discounted at a rate consistent with the project's risk	• Focuses on cash flows not accounting values • Makes appropriate adjustments for the time value of money • Reflects the firm's need to compete for funds in the market-place rather than arbitrary judgement • Provides a convenient way to control for differences in risk among investment alternatives through discount rate adjustments • Incorporates all cash flows the project will generate over its life, not just those in the early years • Gives a direct estimate of the change in shareholder wealth resulting from a given investment	• NPV is less intuitive than payback or a rate of return measure • More difficult to compute than is the payback period
Internal rate of return (IRR)	The compound annual rate of return on a project, given its up-front costs and subsequent cash flows	• Makes an appropriate adjustment for the time value of money • Hurdle rate can be based on market returns obtainable on similar investments • Because it is a rate of return, it is easy for both financial and non-financial managers to grasp it intuitively • Focuses on cash flow rather than accounting measures of income	• Can have multiple IRRs when a project's cash flows alternate between inflows and outflows • For some cash flow patterns, there is no real discount rate that equates a project's NPV to zero, and therefore, there is no real IRR • For mutually exclusive projects, due to the 'scale problem' the project with the highest IRR may not provide the greatest wealth creation opportunity • For mutually exclusive projects, IRR can lead to investment decisions that sometimes favour investments with short-term pay-offs over those that offer returns over a longer horizon
Profitability index (PI)	The ratio present value of a project's cash inflows divided by its initial cash outflow	• Same as NPV	• Same as NPV except suffers from the same 'scale problem' as IRR – i.e. the project with the highest PI may not provide the greatest wealth-creation opportunity

INTERNET RESOURCES

For updates to links in this section and elsewhere in the book, please go to the book's website at www.cengage.co.uk/megginson.

http://www.teachmefinance.com/
A site that has definitions and examples of many finance concepts, including most of the capital budgeting tools discussed in this chapter.

http://clinton3.nara.gov/pcscb/
Contains a report by the President's Commission to Study Capital Budgeting, a group created in 1997 to evaluate capital budgeting techniques used by other governments and the private sector.

http://www.swlearning.com/finance/finance_news/fin_capital_budgeting.html/
A site maintained by South Western Publishing Company that summarizes news events relating to capital budgeting and investment evaluation techniques.

http://www.cimaglobal.com/cps/rde/xchg/SID-0AAAC544–3EFD6D9E/live/root.xsl/
document_broker.htm?filename=tech_resrep_management_accounting_practices_in_uk_food_and_
drink_industry_2006.pdf
A report on capital budgeting processes in a major industry.

KEY TERMS

accounting rate of return	discounted payback	net present value (NPV) profile
capital budgeting	internal rate of return (IRR)	payback period
capital investment	mutually exclusive projects	profitability index (PI)
capital spending	net present value (NPV)	

SELF-TEST PROBLEMS

ST8-1 Nader International is considering investing in two assets – A and B. The initial outlay, annual cash flows and annual depreciation for each asset is shown in the table below for the assets' assumed five-year lives. As can be seen, Nader will use straight-line depreciation over each asset's five-year life. The firm requires a 12 per cent return on each of those equally risky assets. Nader's maximum payback period is 2.5 years, its maximum discounted payback period is 3.25 years and its minimum accounting rate of return is 30 per cent.

	ASSET A		ASSET B	
INITIAL OUTLAY (CF_0)	€200 000		€180 000	
YEAR (t)	CASH FLOW (CF_t)	DEPRECIATION	CASH FLOW (CF_t)	DEPRECIATION
1	€ 70 000	€40 000	€80 000	€36 000
2	80 000	40 000	90 000	36 000
3	90 000	40 000	30 000	36 000
4	90 000	40 000	40 000	36 000
5	100 000	40 000	40 000	36 000

a Calculate the accounting rate of return from each asset, assess its acceptability and indicate which asset is best, using the accounting rate of return.

b Calculate the payback period for each asset, assess its acceptability, and indicate which asset is best, using the payback period.

c Calculate the discounted payback for each asset, assess its acceptability and indicate which asset is best, using the discounted payback.

d Compute and contrast your findings in parts (a), (b) and (c). Which asset would you recommend to Nader, assuming that they are mutually exclusive? Why?

ST8-2 JK Products is considering investing in either of two competing projects that will allow the firm to eliminate a production bottleneck and meet the growing demand for its products. The firm's engineering department narrowed the alternatives down to two – Status Quo (SQ) and High Tech (HT). Working with the accounting and finance personnel, the firm's CFO developed the following estimates of the cash flows for SQ and HT over the relevant six-year time horizon. The firm has an 11 per cent required return and views these projects as equally risky.

	PROJECT SQ	PROJECT HT
INITIAL OUTFLOW (CF_0)	€670 000	€940 000
YEAR (t)	CASH INFLOWS (CF_t)	
1	€250 000	€170 000
2	200 000	180 000
3	170 000	200 000
4	150 000	250 000
5	130 000	300 000
6	130 000	550 000

a Calculate the net present value (NPV) of each project, assess its acceptability and indicate which project is best, using NPV.

b Calculate the internal rate of return (IRR) of each project, assess its acceptability and indicate which project is best, using IRR.

c Calculate the profitability index (PI) of each project, assess its acceptability and indicate which project is best, using PI.

d Draw the NPV profile for project SQ and HT on the same set of axes and use this diagram to explain why the NPV and the IRR show different preferences for these two mutually exclusive projects. Discuss this difference in terms of both the 'scale problem' and the 'timing problem'.

e Which of the two mutually exclusive projects would you recommend that JK Products undertake? Why?

QUESTIONS

Q8-1 Can you name some industries where the payback period is unavoidably long?

Q8-2 In statistics, you learn about Type I and Type II errors. A Type I error occurs when a statistical test rejects a hypothesis when the hypothesis is actually true. A Type II error occurs when a test fails to reject a hypothesis that is actually false. We can apply this type of thinking to capital budgeting. A Type I error occurs when a firm rejects an investment project that would actually enhance shareholder wealth. A Type II error occurs when a firm accepts a value-decreasing investment, which should have been rejected.

a Describe the features of the payback rule that could lead to Type I errors.

b Describe the features of the payback rule that could lead to Type II errors.

c Which error do you think is more likely to occur when firms use payback analysis? Does your answer depend on the length of the cut-off payback period? You can assume a 'typical' project cash flow stream, meaning that most cash outflows occur in the early years of a project.

Q8-3 Holding the cut-off period fixed, which method has a more severe bias against long-lived projects – payback or discounted payback?

Q8-4 For a firm that uses the NPV rule to make investment decisions, what consequences result if the firm misestimates shareholders' required returns and consistently applies a discount rate that is 'too high'?

Q8-5 'Cash flow projections more than a few years out are not worth the paper they're written on. Therefore, using payback analysis, which ignores long-term cash flows, is more reasonable than making wild guesses as one has to do in the NPV approach.' Respond to this comment.

Q8-6 'Smart analysts can massage the numbers in NPV analysis to make any project's NPV look positive. It is better to use a simpler approach like payback or accounting rate of return that gives analysts fewer degrees of freedom to manipulate the numbers.' Respond to this comment.

Q8-7 In what way is the NPV consistent with the principle of shareholder wealth maximization? What happens to the value of a firm if a positive NPV project is accepted? If a negative NPV project is accepted?

Q8-8 A particular firm's shareholders demand a 15 per cent return on their investment, given the firm's risk. However, this firm has historically generated returns in excess of shareholder expectations, with an average return on its portfolio of investments of 25 per cent.

a Looking back, what kind of share price performance would you expect to see for this firm?

b A new investment opportunity arises, and the firm's financial analysts estimate that the project's return will be 18 per cent. The CEO wants to reject the project because it would lower the firm's average return and therefore lower the firm's share price. How do you respond?

Q8-9 What are the potential faults in using the IRR as a capital budgeting technique? Given these faults, why is this technique so popular among corporate managers?

Q8-10 Why is the NPV considered to be theoretically superior to all other capital budgeting techniques? Reconcile this result with the prevalence of the use of IRR in practice. How would you respond to your CFO if she instructed you to use the IRR technique to make capital budgeting decisions on projects with cash flow streams that alternate between inflows and outflows?

Q8-11 Outline the differences between NPV, IRR and PI. What are the advantages and disadvantages of each technique? Do they agree with regard to simple accept or reject decisions?

Q8-12 Under what circumstances will the NPV, IRR and PI techniques provide different capital budgeting decisions? What are the underlying causes of the differences often found in the ranking of mutually exclusive projects using NPV and IRR?

PROBLEMS

Accounting-based methods

P8-1 Kenneth Gould is the general manager at a small-town newspaper that is part of a national media chain. He is seeking approval from corporate headquarters (HQ) to spend €20 000 to buy some Macintosh computers and a laser printer to use in designing the layout of his daily paper. This equipment will be depreciated using the straight-line method over four years. These computers will replace outmoded equipment that will be kept on hand for emergency use.

HQ requires Kenneth to estimate the cash flows associated with the purchase of new equipment over a four-year horizon. The impact of the project on net income is derived by subtracting depreciation from cash flow each year. The project's average accounting rate of return equals the average contribution to net income divided by the average book value of the investment. HQ accepts any project that (1) has an average accounting rate of return that exceeds the cost of capital of 15 per cent, and (2) returns the initial investment within four years (on a cash flow basis). The following are Kenneth's estimates of cash flows:

	YEAR 1	YEAR 2	YEAR 3	YEAR 4
Cost savings	€7500	€9100	€9100	€9100

a What is the average contribution to net income across all four years?

b What is the average book value of the investment?

c What is the average accounting rate of return?

d What is the payback period of this investment?

e Critique the company's method for evaluating investment proposals.

CASH FLOWS	ALPHA (€mn)	BETA (€mn)	GAMMA (€mn)
Initial outflow	−1.5	−0.4	−7.5
Year 1	0.3	0.1	2.0
Year 2	0.5	0.2	3.0
Year 3	0.5	0.2	2.0
Year 4	0.4	0.1	1.5
Year 5	0.3	−0.2	5.5

a Calculate the payback period of each investment.

b Which investments does the firm accept if the cut-off payback period is three years? Four years?

c If the firm invests by choosing projects with the shortest payback period, which project would it invest in?

d If the firm uses discounted payback with a 15 per cent discount rate and a four-year cut-off period, which projects will it accept?

e One of these almost certainly should be rejected, but may be accepted if the firm uses payback analysis. Which one?

f One of these projects almost certainly should be accepted (unless the firm's opportunity cost of capital is very high), but may be rejected if the firm uses payback analysis. Which one?

Net present value

P8-4 Calculate the net present value (NPV) for the following 20-year projects. Comment on the

Payback methods

P8-2 Suppose that a 30-year Greek government bond offers a 4 per cent coupon rate, paid semi-annually. The market price of the bond is $1000, equal to its par value.

a What is the payback period for this bond?

b With such a long payback period, is the bond a bad investment?

c What is the discounted payback period for the bond, assuming its 4 per cent coupon rate is the required return? What general principle does this example illustrate regarding a project's life, its discounted payback period and its NPV?

P8-3 The cash flows associated with three different projects are as follows:

acceptability of each. Assume that the firm has an opportunity cost of 14 per cent.

a Initial cash outlay is €15 000; cash inflows are €13 000 per year.

b Initial cash outlay is €32 000; cash inflows are €4000 per year.

c Initial cash outlay is €50 000; cash inflows are €8500 per year.

P8-5 Michael's Bakery is evaluating a new electronic oven. The oven requires an initial cash outlay of €19 000 and will generate after-tax cash inflows of €4000 per year for eight years. For each of the costs of capital listed, (1) calculate the NPV, (2) indicate whether to accept or reject the machine and (3) explain your decision.

a The cost of capital is 10 per cent

b The cost of capital is 12 per cent.

c The cost of capital is 14 per cent.

P8-6 Using a 14 per cent cost of capital, calculate the NPV for each of the projects shown in the following table and indicate whether or not each is acceptable.

	PROJECT A	PROJECT B	PROJECT C	PROJECT D	PROJECT E
Initial cash outflow (CF_o)	€20 000	€600 000	€150 000	€760 000	€100 000
YEAR (t)	**CASH INFLOWS (CF_t)**				
1	€ 3 000	€120 000	€ 18 000	€185 000	€ 0
2	3 000	145 000	17 000	185 000	0
3	3 000	170 000	16 000	185 000	0
4	3 000	190 000	15 000	185 000	25 000
5	3 000	220 000	15 000	185 000	36 000
6	3 000	240 000	14 000	185 000	0
7	3 000		13 000	185 000	60 000
8	3 000		12 000	185 000	72 000
9	3 000		11 000		84 000
10	3 000		10 000		

P8-7 Scotty Manufacturing is considering the replacement of one of its machine tools. Three alternative replacement tools – A, B and C – are under consideration. The cash flows associated with each are shown in the following table. The firm's cost of capital is 15 per cent.

	A	B	C
Initial cash outflow (CF_o)	€95 000	€50 000	€150 000
YEAR (t)	**CASH INFLOWS (CF_t)**		
1	€20 000	€10 000	€ 58 000
2	20 000	12 000	35 000
3	20 000	13 000	23 000
4	20 000	15 000	23 000
5	20 000	17 000	23 000
6	20 000	21 000	35 000
7	20 000	–	46 000
8	20 000	–	58 000

a Calculate the NPV of each alternative tool.

b Using NPV, evaluate the acceptability of each tool.

c Rank the tools from best to worst, using NPV.

P8-8 Erwin Enterprises has 10 million shares outstanding with a current market price of €10 per share. There is one investment available to Erwin, and its cash flows are provided below. Erwin has a cost of capital of 10 per cent. Given this information, determine the impact on Erwin's share price and firm value if capital markets fully reflect the value of undertaking the project.

Initial cash outflow = €10 000 000

SMART SOLUTIONS

See the problem and solution explained step-by-step at **www.cengage. co.uk/ megginson**

YEAR	CASH INFLOW
1	€3 000 000
2	€4 000 000
3	€5 000 000
4	€6 000 000
5	€9 800 000

Internal rate of return

P8-9 For each of the projects shown in the following table, calculate the internal rate of return (IRR).

	PROJECT A	PROJECT B	PROJECT C	PROJECT D
Initial cash outflow (CF_0)	€72 000	€440 000	€18 000	€215 000
YEAR (t)	CASH INFLOWS (CF_t)			
1	€16 000	€135 000	€ 7 000	€108 000
2	20 000	135 000	7 000	90 000
3	24 000	135 000	7 000	72 000
4	28 000	135 000	7 000	54 000
5	32 000	—	7 000	—

P8-10 William Industries is attempting to choose the better of two mutually exclusive projects for expanding the firm's production capacity. The relevant cash flows for the projects are shown in the following table. The firm's cost of capital is 15 per cent.

	PROJECT A	PROJECT B
Initial cash outflow (CF_0)	€550 000	€358 000
YEAR (t)	CASH INFLOWS (CF_t)	
1	€110 000	€154 000
2	132 000	132 000
3	165 000	105 000
4	209 000	77 000
5	275 000	55 000

a Calculate the IRR for each of the projects.

b Assess the acceptability of each project based on the IRRs found in part (a).

c Which project is preferred, based on the IRRs found in part (a)?

P8-11 Contract Manufacturing is considering two alternative investment proposals. The first proposal calls for a major renovation of the company's manufacturing facility. The second involves replacing just a few obsolete pieces of equipment in the facility. The company will choose one project or the other this year, but it will not do both. The cash flows associated with each project appear below, and the firm discounts project cash flows at 15 per cent.

YEAR	RENOVATE	REPLACE
0	−€9 000 000	−€1 000 000
1	3 500 000	600 000
2	3 000 000	500 000
3	3 000 000	400 000
4	2 800 000	300 000
5	2 500 000	200 000

a Rank these investments based on their NPVs.

b Rank these investments based on their IRRs.

c Why do these rankings yield mixed signals?

P8-12 Consider a project with the following cash flows and a firm with a 15 per cent cost of capital.

END OF YEAR	CASH FLOW
0	−€20 000
1	50 000
2	−10 000

a What are the two IRRs associated with this cash flow stream?

b If the firm's cost of capital falls between the two IRR values calculated in part (a), should it accept or reject the project?

P8-13 A certain project has the following stream of cash flows:

YEAR	CASH FLOW
0	€ 17 500
1	−80 500
2	138 425
3	−105 455
4	30 030

a Fill in the following table:

COST OF CAPITAL (%)	PROJECT NPV
0	___
5	___
10	___
15	___
20	___
25	___
30	___
35	___
50	___

b Use the values developed in part (a) to draw an NPV profile for the project.

c What is this project's IRR?

d Describe the conditions under which the firm should accept this project.

Profitability index

P8-14 Evaluate the following three projects, using the profitability index. Assume a cost of capital of 15 per cent.

	PROJECT		
CASH FLOWS	LIQUIDATE	RECONDITION	REPLACE
Initial cash outflow	−€100 000	−€500 000	−€1 000 000
Year 1 cash inflow	50 000	100 000	500 000
Year 2 cash inflow	60 000	200 000	500 000
Year 3 cash inflow	75 000	250 000	500 000

a Rank these projects by their PIs.

b If the projects are independent, which would you accept according to the PI criterion?

c If these projects are mutually exclusive, which would you accept according to the PI criterion?

d Apply the NPV criterion to the projects, rank them according to their NPVs, and indicate which you would accept if they are independent and mutually exclusive.

e Compare and contrast your answer from part (c) with your answer to part (d) for the mutually exclusive case. Explain this result.

P8-15 You have a €10 million capital budget and must make the decision about which investments your firm should accept for the coming year. Use the information in the table at the bottom of the page on three mutually exclusive projects to determine which investment your firm should accept. The firm's cost of capital is 12 per cent.

a Which project do you accept on the basis of NPV?

b Which project do you accept on the basis of PI?

c If these are the only investments available, which one do you select?

Which techniques do firms actually use?

P8-16 Both Old Line Industries and New Tech Ltd use the IRR to make investment decisions. Both firms are considering investing in a more efficient €4.5 million mail-order processor. This machine could generate after-tax savings of €2 million per year over the next three years for both firms. However, due to the risky nature of its business, New Tech has a much higher cost of capital (20 per cent) than does Old Line (10 per cent). Given this information, answer parts (a)–(c).

a Should Old Line invest in this processor?

b Should New Tech invest in this processor?

CASH FLOWS	PROJECT 1	PROJECT 2	PROJECT 3
Initial cash outflow	−€4 000 000	−€5 000 000	−€10 000 000
Year 1 cash inflow	1 000 000	2 000 000	4 000 000
Year 2 cash inflow	2 000 000	3 000 000	6 000 000
Year 3 cash inflow	3 000 000	3 000 000	5 000 000

c Based on your answers in parts (a) and (b), what can you infer about the acceptability of projects across firms with different costs of capital?

P8-17 Butler Products has prepared the following estimates for an investment it is considering. The initial cash outflow is €20 000, and the project is expected to yield cash inflows of €4400 per year for seven years. The firm has a 10 per cent cost of capital.

a Determine the NPV for the project.

b Determine the IRR for the project.

c Would you recommend that the firm accept or reject the project? Explain your answer.

P8-18 Reynolds Enterprises is attempting to evaluate the feasibility of investing €85 000, CF_0, in a machine having a five-year life. The firm has estimated the cash inflows associated with the proposal as shown below. The firm has a 12 per cent cost of capital.

END OF YEAR (t)	CASH INFLOWS (CF_t)
1	€18 000
2	22 500
3	27 000
4	31 500
5	36 000

a Calculate the payback period for the proposed investment.

b Calculate the NPV for the proposed investment.

c Calculate the IRR for the proposed investment.

d Evaluate the acceptability of the proposed investment using NPV and IRR. What recommendation would you make relative to implementation of the project? Why?

P8-19 Sharpe Manufacturing is attempting to select the best of three mutually exclusive projects. The initial cash outflow and after-tax cash inflows associated with each project are shown in the following table.

CASH FLOWS	PROJECT X	PROJECT Y	PROJECT Z
Initial cash outflow (CF_0)	€80 000	€130 000	€145 000
Cash inflows (CF_t), Years (t) = 1–5	27 000	41 000	43 000

a Calculate the payback period for each project.

b Calculate the NPV of each project, assuming that the firm has a cost of capital equal to 13 per cent.

c Calculate the IRR for each project.

d Summarize the preferences dictated by each measure and indicate which project you would recommend. Explain why.

P8-20 Wilkes Ltd must invest in a pollution-control programme in order to meet EU regulations to stay in business. There are two programmes available to Wilkes: an all-at-once programme that will be immediately funded and implemented, and a gradual programme that will be phased in over the next three years. The immediate programme costs €5 million, whereas the phase-in programme will cost €1 million today and €2 million per year for the following three years. If the cost of capital for Wilkes is 15 per cent, which pollution-control programme should Wilkes select?

P8-21 A consumer product firm finds that its brand of laundry detergent is losing market share, so it decides that it needs to 'freshen' the product. One strategy is to maintain the current detergent formula but to repackage the product. The other strategy involves a complete reformulation of the product in a way that will appeal to environmentally conscious consumers. The firm will pursue one strategy or the other but not both. Cash flows from each proposal appear below, and the firm discounts cash flows at 13 per cent.

SMART SOLUTIONS

See the problem and solution explained step-by-step at **www.cengage. co.uk/ megginson**

YEAR	REPACKAGE	REFORMULATE
0	–€3 000 000	–€25 000 000
1	2 000 000	10 000 000
2	1 250 000	9 000 000
3	500 000	7 000 000
4	250 000	4 000 000
5	250 000	3 500 000

a Rank these investments based on their NPVs.
b Rank these investments based on their IRRs.
c Rank these investments based on their PIs.
d Draw NPV profiles for the two projects on the same set of axes and discuss these profiles.
e Do these investment rankings yield mixed signals?

P8-22 Lundblad Construction Co. recently acquired ten acres of land and is weighing two options for developing the land. The first proposal is to build ten single-family homes on the site. This project would generate a quick cash pay-off as the homes are sold over the next two years. Specifically, Lundblad estimates that it would spend €2.5 million on construction costs immediately, and it would receive €1.6 million as cash inflows in each of the next two years.

The second proposal is to build a strip shopping mall. This project calls for Lundblad to retain ownership of the property and to lease space for retail businesses that would serve the neighbourhood. Construction costs for the strip mall are also about €2.5 million, and the company expects to receive €350 000 annually (for each of 50 years, starting one year from now) in net cash inflows from leasing the property. Lundblad's cost of capital is 10 per cent.

a Rank these projects based on their NPVs.

b Rank these projects based on their IRRs.

c Rank these projects based on their PIs. Do these rankings agree with those based on NPV or IRR?

d Draw NPV profiles for these projects on the same set of axes. Use this graph to explain why, in this case, the NPV and IRR methods yield mixed signals.

e Which project should Lundblad choose?

f Which project should Lundblad choose if its cost of capital is 13.5 per cent? 16 per cent? 20 per cent?

THOMSON ONE **Business School Edition**

For instructions on using Thomson ONE, refer to the introductory text provided with the Thomson ONE problems at the end of Chapters 1–6, or in *A Guide for Using Thomson ONE – Business School Edition*.

P8–23 Select two companies operating in the same industry segment from the Thomson ONE database. Bond rating agencies investigate, among other things, a company's debt and profitability ratios to rate its bonds. Examine these ratios for the two companies and explain which company's bonds are likely to have a higher bond rating and why.

MINICASE *Capital budgeting process and techniques*

Contact Manufacturing is considering two alternative investment proposals. The first proposal calls for a major renovation of the company's manufacturing facility. The second involves replacing just a few obsolete pieces of equipment in the facility. The company will choose one project or the other this year, but it will not do both. The cash flows associated with each project appear below and the firm discounts project cash flows at 15 per cent.

YEAR	RENOVATE	REPLACE
0	–€9 000 000	–€2 400 000
1	3 000 000	2 000 000
2	3 000 000	800 000
3	3 000 000	200 000
4	3 000 000	200 000
5	3 000 000	200 000

Assignment

1 Calculate the payback period of each project and, based on this criteria, for which project would you recommend acceptance?

2 Calculate the net present value (NPV) of each project and, based on this criteria, for which project would you recommend acceptance?

3 Calculate the internal rate of return (IRR) of each project and, based on this criteria, for which project would you recommend acceptance?

4 Calculate the profitability index (PI) of each project and, based on this criteria, for which project would you recommend acceptance?

5 Overall, you should find conflicting recommendations based on the various criteria. Why is this occurring?

6 Chart the NPV profiles of these projects. Label the intersection points on the X and Y axes and the crossover point.

7 Based on this NPV profile analysis and assuming the WACC is 15 per cent, which project is recommended? Why?

8 Based on this NPV profile analysis and assuming the WACC is 25 per cent, which project is recommended? Why?

9 Discuss the important elements to consider when deciding between these two projects.

Chapter 9
Cash Flow and Capital Budgeting

OPENING FOCUS

Betting the company . . . across the Atlantic

Capital budgeting decisions are very important for most firms, but usually do not involve 'betting the company' on a single investment project. This issue comes up with more frequency than might be imagined, however, especially in the airliner manufacturing industry. The decision the board of directors of the Boeing Company faced in December 2003 was stark, because the directors had to decide whether to commit up to $12 billion to develop and market an entirely new 200-passenger commercial aircraft, the 7E7 'Dreamliner'. Not only were the financial stakes enormous, but also the organizational challenges: Boeing had not launched a new aircraft in over a decade. It was saddled with an ageing product line that left it reeling from the competitive onslaught represented by its only rival Airbus's modern fleet of fuel-efficient aircraft. Airbus had successfully launched a string of new planes, most recently the 550-passenger A380. If Boeing did not develop a winning new plane, it faced the real prospect of eventually being swept out of the commercial aircraft manufacturing business.

This chapter will describe the processes involved in generating estimates of the initial investment required to launch a capital investment project, the net cash flows that this project will generate over its economic life, and the final-period cash flows that result at the project's termination date. Boeing's managers and directors performed precisely this exercise in deciding whether to launch the Dreamliner. Their task was almost unimaginably complex because of the scale of the project and the uncertainty involved in estimating the different cash flows. To generate estimates of the initial investment required, Boeing had to account for three special circumstances that few other manufacturers had to address. First, Dreamliner would employ brand new assembly techniques. Boeing had to account for an unusually high level of technological risk during the

plane's development stage. The other two factors complicating their estimation of the initial investment required would actually benefit Boeing by reducing the company's own financial exposure. Boeing would be able to count on the suppliers of jet engines and other major sub-assemblies to incur up to half of the Dreamliner's overall development costs. Additionally, by shrewdly causing several American states to compete with each other to attract the assembly plant for the 7E7, Boeing was able to entice the state of Washington to offer tax and other incentives worth $3.2 billion over 20 years and to raise the state's gasoline tax by 5 cents per gallon to fund a $4.2 billion Seattle-area transportation plan that Boeing wanted. Finally, Boeing faced a major strategic challenge from Airbus, who were simultaneously developing a very large airliner, the A380. These two models represented very different concepts of how passenger movements were expected to develop. Boeing were in effect betting that passengers would increasingly wish to travel from point to point, which would necessitate a fuel-efficient, long-range, medium-sized aircraft. Airbus, by contrast, were expecting the hub-and-spoke model, where passengers travel via a very large airport to and from their origins and destinations, to continue. In this case the premium would be on numbers of passengers moved. We deal in Chapter 10 with how to consider tackling these risks and uncertainties.

As you might expect, generating these long-term, after-tax cash flow estimates for the Dreamliner was also very challenging for Boeing's managers and directors. The company estimates that between 2000 and 3000 aircraft in the 7E7's market segment will be purchased by the world's airlines over the next 20 years. The total value of these sales will be about $1.9 trillion. If Boeing could count on dominating this market over the coming two decades as thoroughly

Sources: 'Boeing May Count on New Dreamliner to Regain Lead from Airbus', Bloomberg.com (3 October 2003); Caroline Daniel (2003) 'Boeing to Offer Mid-sized 7E7 Jet Next Year', Financial Times, 17 December; and Jack Lyne (2003) 'Boeing's €900-Million 7E7 Plant Nearing Touchdown', Site Selection

as it had traditionally dominated other aircraft markets, the 7E7 project would likely prove extremely profitable. However, 2003 marked the first year in history in which Airbus sold more planes than Boeing, so even if Boeing's 20-year sales forecast proved accurate, there was no guarantee that the company would be able to grab a large share of these sales. Therefore, Boeing faced great uncertainty in forecasting the cash inflows that would result from launching the Dreamliner. Finally, in the commercial aircraft industry, the price of success is a never-ending requirement to make ever larger capital investments to stay competitive. To that end, Boeing had to project how the possibility of a successful Dreamliner launch would affect its future capital budgeting plans.

So what did Boeing's board decide to do? On 17 December 2003 the company announced that the board had given the go-ahead to launch the 7E7. The Dreamliner was to become a reality, and, in April 2004, All Nippon Airways placed the first firm order for 50 Dreamliners (worth $6 billion), thus becoming the plane's all-important launch partner. Airbus had already achieved this with its orders from Emirates Airlines.

As we saw in Chapter 8 the Airbus project has been beset by problems, resulting in massive delays in the launch of the A380. By the end of 2006 Boeing had orders for over 450 Dreamliners, while Airbus had orders for 166 A380s.

LEARNING OBJECTIVES

After studying this chapter you should be able to:

- Differentiate between cash flow and accounting profit with regard to incremental cash flow, financing costs, taxes and non-cash expenses.

- Discuss depreciation, fixed asset expenditures, working capital expenditures and terminal value.

- Understand the importance of focusing on relevant cash flows and the effects on these of sunk costs, opportunity costs and cannibalization.

- Demonstrate the procedures for determining the relevant cash flows for a capital budgeting problem.

- Understand how to analyse capital rationing decisions, competing replacement projects with unequal lives and excess capacity utilization projects.

Chapter 8 described various capital budgeting techniques that analysts use to evaluate and rank investment proposals. Each of the examples in Chapter 8 began with a sequence of cash flows, although we did not discuss the origins of those cash flow figures. This chapter describes procedures for determining a project's relevant cash flows, the inputs for the capital budgeting decision tools from Chapter 8. We begin with an overview of the kinds of cash flows that may appear in almost any type of investment. Then, we consider the relevant cash flows and some challenges in estimating them. Next, an extended capital budgeting example is presented and we discuss special problems and situations that frequently arise in the capital budgeting process.

9.1 TYPES OF CASH FLOWS

Cash flow versus accounting profit

When accountants prepare financial statements for external reporting, to shareholders or to regulators, they have a very different purpose in mind than financial analysts have when they evaluate the merits of an investment. Accountants need to produce financial statements that fairly and accurately represent the state of a business at any given time, as well as over a period of time. Given this purpose, accountants typically measure the inflows and outflows of a business's operations on an accrual basis rather than on a cash basis. For example, accountants typically credit a firm for earning revenue once a sale is made, even though customers may not pay cash for their purchases for several weeks or months. Similarly, accountants typically will not record the full cost of an asset as an expense if they expect the asset to confer benefits to the firm over a long period of time. The best example of this approach is depreciation. If a firm spends €1 billion on an asset that it plans to use over ten years, accountants may count only one tenth of the purchase price, or €100 million, as a current-year depreciation expense. However, in cash terms the monies are spent and this is taken as the appropriate basis by analysts.

Simply stated, financial analysts focus solely on cash flows when evaluating potential investments. In doing this, they estimate the 'relevant cash flows' by focusing on the incremental cash flows, ignoring financing costs, considering taxes, and adjusting for any non-cash expenses such as depreciation. Here, we briefly consider the effect of each of these items on cash flow.

Focusing on incremental cash flows For capital budgeting purposes, financial analysts focus on incremental cash inflows and outflows, emphasizing that no matter what earnings a firm may show on an accrual basis, it cannot survive for long unless it generates cash to pay its bills. Cash is the lifeblood of a company. If a firm purchases an asset for €500 million, with a purchase contract requiring an immediate payment, then the firm must come up with €500 million in cash, even if it plans to deduct only a portion of the purchase price each year as depreciation expense. The importance placed on cash flow in capital budgeting also reflects the time value of money. If a firm sells a product for €1000, the value of that sale is greater if the customer pays immediately, rather than 30 or 90 days in the future. To develop the relevant cash flows, the financial analyst must determine the **incremental cash flows**, which are the cash flows that directly result from the proposed investment. These cash flows effectively represent the marginal costs (MC) and the marginal benefits (MB) expected to result from undertaking the proposed investment. Once these MCs and MBs are estimated, capital budgeting techniques (described in Chapter 8) can be applied to them to account for the time value of money and risk. These procedures

incremental cash flows Cash flows that directly result from a proposed investment. They effectively represent the marginal costs (MC) and marginal benefits (MB) expected to result from undertaking a proposed investment.

allow the analyst to choose only those projects that increase shareholder value. The procedures for estimating incremental cash flows are demonstrated later in this chapter. As we shall see later, it is not always totally clear which costs are truly incremental and which are not.

Ignoring financing costs Much of this chapter focuses on which cash flows to include in calculating a project's NPV. We should also mention an important category of cash flows that should be excluded – financing cash flows. This may seem perverse – surely a company has to return to its shareholders and debtholders sums of money that are relevant to the project. If they did not take on the project then there would be no increased dividend payments or debt servicing, and thus the incremental cash flows change? However, this is not the case. When calculating a project's NPV, analysts should ignore the costs of raising the money to finance the project, whether those costs are in the form of interest expense from debt financing or dividend payments to equity investors. It may seem counterintuitive to ignore an item, such as interest expense, which appears on the income statement, but it is necessary to do so because financing costs are fully captured in the process of discounting a project's future cash flows to the present. In previous chapters, we have seen that the discounted present value of a cash flow is less than its future value. When analysts discount a project's future cash flows, they take into account the opportunity that investors have to invest in other firms. Therefore, if an analyst deducted cash outflows to investors, such as interest and dividend payments, the analyst would, in effect, double-count the financing costs of the investment. The relevant discount rate we use for the calculation of the NPV takes into account the financing costs.

In an operational sense, when using the income statement to develop an investment's relevant cash flows, we ignore financing costs by focusing on earnings before interest rather than earnings after deduction of interest expense. Given the structure of an income statement, earnings before interest excludes all dividends paid to preference and/or ordinary shareholders as well. The deduction of interest expense and dividends would double-charge the firm for its financing costs – once in the cash flows and again in the discount rate used to find present value. As we demonstrate later in this chapter, both interest and dividends are ignored when developing an investment's relevant cash flows.

Considering taxes Analysts should measure all cash flows of a project on an after-tax basis. Remember, when deciding whether an investment is worth making, we must determine whether the cash flows of the project are sufficient to meet or exceed shareholders' expectations. The firm can only distribute after-tax cash flows to investors, and thus, only after-tax cash flows are relevant in the decision process. The tax consequences associated with a particular investment can be very complex, in part because cash flows from a single investment may fall under several tax jurisdictions (local, state, national, international, etc.) and may be subject to both ordinary and capital gains taxes. It is important to note that because the discount rate (required return) is an after-tax value, we can ignore the tax shield resulting from the pre-tax deduction of interest, which, as noted above, does not enter into the calculation of an investment's cash flows. Simply stated, an after-tax point of view is consistent with ignoring financing costs when determining relevant cash flows.

An examination of all the nuances of the tax code is well beyond the scope of this book, but we offer simplified illustrations of the principles involved in measuring after-tax cash flows. The most important of these principles is that financial managers should measure the after-tax cash flows of a given investment by using the firm's **marginal tax rate**, which, as noted in Chapter 2, equals the tax rate applicable to the next item of income. For convenience, throughout this chapter we assume that the

marginal tax rate
The percentage of taxes owed on the next euro of income.

marginal tax rate equals 40 per cent. However, note again that tax elements are exceptionally complex, are local and are liable to change.

Adjusting for non-cash expenses Another tax-related principle relevant to measuring pertinent cash flows is that analysts cannot entirely ignore **non-cash expenses** (tax-deductible expenses for which there is no corresponding cash outflow) when projecting cash flows. Non-cash expenses include depreciation, amortization and depletion. We focus here solely on depreciation, which is the most common non-cash expense involved in making capital investments. Depreciation plays a key role when projecting cash flows. As a non-cash expense, it reduces not only taxable income but also the cash outflows associated with tax payments. There are two ways to calculate cash flows that take this effect into account. First, we can add non-cash expenses back to net income before interest and after taxes. Secondly, we can ignore non-cash expenses when calculating net income before interest and after taxes, and then add back the tax savings created by non-cash deductions.[1]

non-cash expenses
Tax-deductible expenses for which there is no corresponding cash outflow. They include depreciation, amortization and depletion.

Applying the Model

Let's examine two ways to treat non-cash expenses to obtain cash flow numbers for a simple project. Suppose a firm spends €30 000 in cash to purchase a fixed asset today that it plans to fully depreciate on a straight-line basis over three years. This means that it can take depreciation in each year equal to one-third of the value, or €10 0000. Acquiring this machine, the firm can now produce 10 000 units of some product each year. The product costs €1 to make and sells for €3. The following is a simple income statement (that ignores any financing costs) for a typical year of this project:

Sales	€30 000
Less: Cost of goods	€10 000
Gross profit	€20 000
Less: Depreciation	€10 000
Pre-tax income	€10 000
Less: Taxes (40%)	€ 4 000
Net income after taxes	€ 6 000

How much cash flow does this project generate in a typical year? There are two ways to arrive at the answer. First, take net income after taxes and add back depreciation, for which there was no cash outlay:

$$\text{Cash flow} = \text{Net income after taxes} + \text{Depreciation}$$

$$= €6000 + €10000 = \underline{€16000}$$

---

[1] Deriving accurate cash flow numbers from real financial statements issued by real companies is considerably more complex than the following simple example may lead you to believe, primarily due to the need to measure cash flows *before interest and after taxes*.

> Second, calculate net income after taxes, ignoring depreciation expense, and then add back the tax savings generated by the depreciation deduction:
>
> | | | |
> |---|---|---|
> | Sales | €30 000 | |
> | Less:Cost of goods | €10 000 | |
> | Pre-tax income | €20 000 | |
> | Less: Taxes (40%) | € 8 000 | |
> | After-tax income | €12 000 | |
> | Plus: Depreciation tax savings | €4 000 | (40% × €10 000) |
> | Total cash flow | €16 000 | |

Depreciation

The largest non-cash item for most investment projects is depreciation. Analysts must know the magnitude and timing of depreciation deductions for a given project because these deductions affect the amount of taxes that the firm will pay. Treating depreciation properly is complicated because the law allows firms to use several different depreciation methods. For example, in the United States and the United Kingdom, firms can (and do) keep separate sets of books, one for tax purposes and one for financial reporting purposes, using different depreciation methods for each set. Their goal is to show low taxable income to the taxing authorities and stable, growing income to investors. As a result, most US and UK firms use accelerated depreciation methods for tax purposes and straight-line depreciation for financial reporting. In contrast, in nations such as Japan, Sweden and Germany, the law requires that the income firms report to the tax authorities be substantially the same as the income they report to investors. Naturally, firms in these countries want to enjoy the tax benefits of accelerated depreciation, so they depreciate assets using methods such as double-declining balance or sum-of-the-years' digits almost exclusively.[2] Because we are interested in the cash flow consequences of investments, and because depreciation only affects cash flow through taxes, we consider only the depreciation method that a firm uses for tax purposes when determining project cash flows.

Fixed asset expenditures

Many capital budgeting decisions involve the acquisition of a fixed asset. The cost of this investment often appears as the initial cash outflow for a project (assuming that the firm pays the full purchase price in one cash payment). Additional factors that influence the cash consequences of fixed asset acquisitions include installation costs and proceeds from sales of any existing fixed assets that are being replaced.

In many cases, the cost of installing new equipment can be a significant part of a project's initial outlay. For tax purposes, firms must combine the asset's purchase price and its installation cost to arrive at the asset's 'depreciable basis'. Though depreciation itself is not a cash outflow, we have seen that depreciation deductions affect future

---

[2] The International Forum on Accountancy Development (IFAD) maintains a website where you can find a brief overview of accounting standards in 62 different countries, all benchmarked against international accounting standards (IAS).

cash flows by lowering taxes. Depreciation deductions influence taxes through another channel when firms sell old fixed assets. Specifically, when a firm sells an old piece of equipment, there is a tax consequence if the selling price exceeds or falls below the old equipment's book value. If the firm sells an asset for more than its book value, the firm must pay taxes on the difference. If a firm sells an asset for less than its book value, then it can treat the difference as a tax-deductible expense.

Applying the Model

Electrocom Manufacturing purchased €100 000 worth of new computers three years ago. Now it is replacing these machines with newer, faster computers. The firm has a 40 per cent tax rate. Electrocom classes its computers as having a five-year lifespan so they write off 20 per cent (€20 000) in depreciation each year. After three years then the company has depreciated 60 per cent of the old machines' cost, leaving a book value of €40 000. Electrocom sells its old computers to another firm for €10 000. This allows Electrocom to report a loss on the sale of €30 000 (€40 000 book value − €10 000 sale price). Assuming that Electrocom's business is otherwise profitable, it can deduct this loss from other pre-tax income, resulting in a tax savings of €12 000 (0.40 × €30 000).

Working capital expenditures

Consider a retail firm evaluating the opportunity to open a new store. Part of the cash outflow of this investment involves expenditures on fixed assets such as shelving, cash registers and merchandise displays, but stocking the store constitutes another important cash outflow. A portion of this cash outflow may be deferred if the firm can purchase stock (inventory) from suppliers on credit. By the same token, cash inflows from selling the inventory may be delayed if the firm sells to customers on credit.

net working capital
The difference between a firm's current assets and its current liabilities. Often used as a measure of liquidity.

working capital
Refers to what is more correctly known as net working capital.

Just as a firm must account for cash flows on fixed assets, it must also weigh the cash inflows and outflows associated with *changes* in **net working capital**, which equals the difference between current assets and current liabilities. Frequently, the term **working capital** is used to refer to what is more correctly known as 'net working capital'. An increase in net working capital represents a cash outflow. Notice that, assuming all other current accounts remain unchanged, net working capital increases if current assets rise (e.g. if the firm buys more inventory) or if current liabilities fall (e.g. if the firm pays down accounts payable). As noted in Chapter 2, any increase (decrease) in a current asset account or any decrease (increase) in a current liability account results in a cash outflow (inflow). Net working capital decreases when current assets fall (as when a firm sells inventory) or when current liabilities increase (as when the firm borrows from suppliers). Therefore, a decrease in net working capital represents a cash inflow.

Applying the Model

Have you ever noticed the cottage industries that temporarily spring up around certain big events? Think about the booths that open in shopping centres near the end of each year and sell nothing but calendars? Or think about the sellers of scary masks and rubber fangs at Halloween, or retailers of Christmas paraphernalia?

Suppose you are evaluating the opportunity to operate one of these Christmas calendar booths from November to January. You begin by ordering (on credit) €15 000 worth of calendars. Your suppliers require a €5000 payment on the first day of each month, starting in December. You anticipate that you will sell (entirely on a cash basis) 30 per cent of your inventory in November, 60 per cent in December and 10 per cent in January. You plan to keep €500 in the cash register until you close the booth on 1 February. Your balance sheet at the beginning of each month looks like this:

	1 Oct	1 Nov	1 Dec	1 Jan	1 Feb
Cash	€0	€ 500	€ 500	€ 500	€ 0
Inventory	0	15 000	10 500	1 500	0
Accounts payable	0	15 000	10 000	5 000	0
Net working capital	0	500	1 000	–3 000	0
Monthly net working capital *change*	NA	+500	+500	–4 000	+3 000

The cash flows associated with *changes* in net working capital are as follows:

€500 cash outflow from October to November
€500 cash outflow from November to December
€4000 cash inflow from December to January
€3000 cash outflow from January to February

Notice that at the start of November, purchases of inventory are entirely on credit, so the increase in inventory is exactly offset by an increase in accounts payable. The only working capital cash outflow occurs because you must raise €500 to put in the cash register. During November, sales reduce your inventory by €4500 (inflow), but you pay suppliers €5000 (outflow). You still have the same amount in the cash register as before, €500, so on net you have an outflow of €500, exactly equal to the increase in net working capital from the prior month. During the month of December, sales reduce your inventory by €9000 (inflow), and you pay €5000 to suppliers (outflow). That leaves you with cash inflow of €4000, equal to the decrease in net working capital during the month. By 1 February, sales reduce your inventory by the remaining €1500 in calendars (inflow), you empty €500 from the cash register (inflow) and you pay the last €5000 to suppliers (outflow). The net effect is a €3000 cash outflow during January.[3]

Terminal value

Some investments have a well-defined lifespan. The lifespan may be determined by the physical life of a piece of equipment, by the length of time until a patent expires, or by the period of time covered by a leasing or licensing agreement. Often, however,

---

[3] Notice that we are only looking at the working capital cash flows associated with this project. We have not considered any fixed asset investment up front. We are not considering the profits from selling calendars at a mark-up, nor the labour costs of operating the booth.

investments have an indefinite life. For example, when a company acquires another company as a going concern, as noted in the stock valuation discussion in Chapter 5, it generally expects the acquired company's assets to continue to generate cash flow for a very long period of time.

When managers invest in an asset with a long lifespan, they typically do not construct cash flow forecasts more than five to ten years into the future. These long-term forecasts are so inaccurate that the fine detail in an item-by-item cash flow projection is not very meaningful. Instead, managers project detailed cash flow estimates for five to ten years, then calculate a project's **terminal value**, the value of a project at a given future date. There are a number of ways to calculate terminal value.

terminal value
The value of a project at a given future date.

Perhaps the most common approach to calculating terminal value is to take the final year of cash flow projections and make an assumption that all future cash flows from the project will grow at a constant rate. For example, in valuing a large acquisition, many acquiring firms project the target company's cash flows for five to ten years in the future. After that, they assume that cash flows will grow at a rate equal to the growth rate in gross domestic product (GDP) for the economy.[4]

Real World

Source: Adapted from Lex column, *Financial Times*, 5 November 2005.

When you purchase sportswear, two major brands dominate in Europe – Puma and Adidas. Both are branches of the same parent firm, and both are owned and controlled by members of the Dassler family. Puma has higher margins, and a more fashion-driven management. However, it was noted in 2005 by the influential Lex column in the *Financial Times* that Puma had become a massive machine for the creation of free cash flow. And, even allowing for a WACC of 10 per cent this would, the columnist reported, give a value to Puma of 2.5 times its market capitalization, without allowing for any terminal value. The company shares rose by 5p, or just under 2.5 per cent the next trading day, reflecting perhaps some traders recognizing the value of a terminal value.

Applying the Model

Suppose that analysts at JDS Ltd were analysing the potential acquisition of SDL Ltd. They projected that the acquisition of SDL would generate the following new stream of cash flows:

Year 1	€0.50 billion
Year 2	1.00 billion
Year 3	1.75 billion
Year 4	2.50 billion
Year 5	3.25 billion

---

[4] We emphasize that when companies assume that an investment's cash flows will grow at some rate in perpetuity, the rate of growth in GDP, either in the local economy or the world economy, serves as a maximum potential long-run growth rate. Why? If an investment generates cash flows that grow forever at a rate that exceeds the growth of GDP, then mathematically, that one investment eventually attains a value greater than the entire economy.

In year 6 and beyond, analysts believed that cash flows would continue to grow at 5 per cent per year. What is the terminal value of this investment? Recall that in Chapters 3 and 5 we learned that we can determine the present value, at a discount rate r, of a stream of cash flows growing at a perpetual rate, g, by using the following formula:

$$PV_t = \frac{CF_{t+1}}{r - g}$$

We know that the year 6 cash flow is 5 per cent more than in year 5, or €3.41 billion (1.05 × €3.25 billion). Put that figure in the numerator of the equation. We also know that g = 5 per cent. Suppose that JDS discounted the cash flows of this investment at 10 per cent. Using the formula above, we can determine that the present value, *as of year 5*, of cash flows in year 6 and beyond equals the following:

$$PV_t = \frac{3.41}{0.1 - 0.5} = 68.20$$

This means that the terminal value, the value of the project at the end of year 5, equals €68.20 billion. To determine the entire value of the project, discount this figure along with all the other cash flows at 10 per cent to obtain a total value of €48.67 billion. Notice that this is the gross present value, not the NPV, because we are not deducting any up-front costs incurred to acquire SDL.

$$\frac{0.5}{(1.1)^1} + \frac{1}{(1.1)^2} + \frac{1.75}{(1.1)^3} + \frac{2.5}{(1.1)^4} + \frac{3.25}{(1.1)^5} + \frac{68.2}{(1.1)^5} = 48.67$$

Given this set of assumptions, the most JDS should pay to acquire SDL is about €48.67 billion.

Notice in the preceding example that the terminal value was very large relative to all the other cash flows. If we discount the terminal value for five years at 10 per cent, we find that €42.35 billion of the project's total €48.67 billion present value comes from the terminal value assumptions. Those proportions are not uncommon for long-lived investments, illustrating just how important estimates of terminal value can be in assessing an investment's merit. Analysts must think very carefully about the assumptions they make when calculating terminal value. For example, the growth rate used to calculate a project's terminal value does not always equal the long-run growth rate of the economy. A factory with fixed capacity might offer zero growth in cash flows, or growth that just keeps pace with inflation, once the firm hits the capacity constraint.

Several other methods maintain widespread application in terminal value calculations. One method calculates terminal value by multiplying the final year's cash flow estimate by a market multiple such as a price-to-cash-flow ratio for publicly traded firms with characteristics similar to those of the investment. For example, the last specific cash flow estimate for the SDL Ltd acquisition was €3.25 billion in year 5. JDS Ltd may observe that the average price-to-cash-flow ratio for companies in this industry is 20. Multiplying €3.25 billion by 20 results in a terminal value estimate of €65 billion, quite close to the estimate obtained from the perpetual growth model. One hazard in using this approach is that market multiples fluctuate through time, which means that when year 5 finally arrives, even if SDL generates €3.25 billion in cash flow as anticipated, the market may place a much lower value on that cash flow than it did when the acquisition originally took place.

Other approaches to this problem use an investment's book value or its expected liquidation value to estimate the terminal value figure. Using book value is most common when the investment involves physical plant and equipment with a limited useful life. In such a case, firms may plausibly assume that after a number of years of depreciation deductions, the asset's book value will be zero. Depending on whether the asset has fairly standard characteristics that would enable other firms to use it, its liquidation value may be positive or it may be zero.[5] Finding liquidation value often involves inclusion of the tax cash flows that result from selling the asset for a price that differs from its book value at the time of sale. Some assets may even have negative terminal values if disposing of them entails substantial costs. Projects that involve the use of substances hazardous to the environment fit this description. When an investment has a fixed lifespan, part of the terminal value or terminal cash flow may also include recovery of working capital investments. When a retail store closes, for example, the firm realizes a cash inflow from liquidating inventory.

<table>
<tr><td>

CONCEPT
REVIEW
QUESTIONS

</td><td>

1 Why is it important for the financial analyst to (a) focus on incremental cash flows, (b) ignore financing costs, (c) consider taxes and (d) adjust for non-cash expenses when estimating a project's relevant cash flows?

2 Why do we consider changes in net working capital associated with a project to be cash inflows or outflows rather than consider the absolute level of net working capital?

3 For what kinds of investments does terminal value account for a substantial fraction of the total project NPV, and for what kinds of investments is terminal value relatively unimportant?

</td></tr>
</table>

9.2 THE RELEVANT CASH FLOWS

relevant cash flows
All of the incremental, after-tax cash flows (initial outlay, operating cash flow and terminal value) associated with a proposed investment.

The **relevant cash flows** for an investment are all the incremental, after-tax, cash flows (initial outlay, operating cash flow and terminal value) associated with a proposed investment. As noted in Section 9.1, these cash flows ignore financing costs, include working capital outlays and recovery, and reflect adjustments for any non-cash expenses, typically depreciation. Here we consider incremental cash flows in greater detail and discuss sunk costs, opportunity costs and cannibalization – a few challenges to correctly measuring relevant cash flows. An understanding of these challenges allows you to more accurately estimate a proposed investment's relevant cash flows.

Incremental cash flow

We have seen that many investment problems have similar types of cash flows that analysts must estimate: initial outlays on fixed assets and working capital, operating

---

[5] It has been estimated that firms can expect to recover no more than 20–50 per cent of the original purchase cost of a new machine, once it has been installed. This finding is applicable even for assets with reasonably active secondary markets.

cash flow and terminal value. But, in a broader sense, there is only one type of cash flow that matters in capital budgeting analysis – incremental cash flow. To rephrase the oath that witnesses take in television courtroom dramas, analysts must focus on 'all incremental cash flow and nothing but incremental cash flow'. Determining which cash flows are incremental and which are not for a given project can become complicated at times.

Consider, for example, the incremental cash flows associated with the decision of an employed person with a bachelor's degree to leave his job and return to university or business school to pursue an MBA degree. Many of the incremental outflows are fairly obvious, such as tuition and fees, the cost of textbooks and possibly relocation expenses. What about expenditures on room and board? Whether or not a student decides to pursue an MBA, he or she still has to eat and have a place to sleep at night. Therefore, room and board expenditures are not incremental to the decision to go back to school.[6]

The cash inflows associated with an investment in an MBA degree are more difficult to estimate. For most students, obtaining an MBA degree offers the opportunity to earn higher pay after graduation than they earned before returning to university or business school. Furthermore, most students hope that, after obtaining an MBA, their salary will increase at a much faster rate than it otherwise would have. The net cash flow equals the difference in the salary that a student earns with an MBA versus the salary earned without an MBA, after taxes, of course.

Applying the Model

Norm Paul earns €60 000 per year working as a designer, and he pays taxes at a flat rate of 35 per cent. He expects salary increases each year of about 5 per cent. Lately, Norm has been thinking about going back to school to earn an MBA. A few months ago, he spent €1000 to enrol in a Graduate Management Admission Test (GMAT) study course. He also spent €2000 visiting various MBA programmes. From his research on MBA programmes, Norm has learned a great deal about the costs and benefits of the degree. At the beginning of each of the next two years, his out-of-pocket costs for tuition, fees and textbooks will be €35 000. He expects to spend roughly the same amount on room and board in business school that he spends now. At the end of two years, he anticipates that he will receive a job offer with a salary of €90 000, and he expects that his pay will increase by 8 per cent per year over his career (about the next 30 years). The schedule of incremental cash flows for the next few periods, excluding the salary that Norm gives up if he goes back to school (more on that later), looks like this:

Year 0	−€35 000
Year 1	−35 000
Year 2	+15 503
Year 3	+18 032

---

[6] Of course, there may be a difference between money spent on housing and food, depending on whether the person is a student or a working professional. The difference in spending would be an incremental cash flow, but it could be an incremental inflow (if these costs are lower at university or business school) or an outflow (if the MBA programme is located in a city with a high cost of living).

The cash outflows at time zero and for year 1 are obvious. The cash inflow figures for years 2 and 3 require some explanation. Had Norm stayed at his current job for the next two years, rather than go back to school, his pay would have increased to €66 150 [€60 000 × (1 + 0.05)^2]. Therefore, the difference between that figure and his €90 000 post-MBA salary represents a net cash inflow of €23 850. Assuming that Norm pays about 35 per cent of his earnings in taxes, the after-tax inflow would be €15 503 [€23 850 × (1.00 − 0.35)]. In year 3, Norm expects to earn 8 per cent more, or €97 200, compared with what he would have earned at his old job, €69 458 [€66 150 × (1 + 0.05)]. The after-tax cash inflow in year 3 equals €18 032 [(€97 200 − €69 458) × (1.00 − 0.35)]. If you carry these steps out for 30 years, you will quickly see that the MBA has a substantial positive NPV at almost any reasonable discount rate.

Sunk costs

sunk costs
Costs that have already been paid and are therefore not recoverable.

A **sunk cost** is a cost that has already been paid and is therefore not recoverable; thus, it is irrelevant to the investment decision. For instance, in the preceding 'Applying the model' example, Norm's cash outflows did not include the money he had already spent on the GMAT review and on visits to MBA programmes. Clearly, these costs are not recoverable as a result of his decision on whether to give up his job and return to school. The money has already been spent and therefore has no bearing on his investment decision. Simply stated, sunk costs are irrelevant and therefore should be ignored when determining an investment's relevant cash flows. Note, however, that there is a sting in the tail here: sunk costs still have to be paid for, although they are not relevant to the project under analysis.

Opportunity costs

opportunity costs
Lost cash flows on an alternative investment that the firm or individual decides not to make.

We made a number of simplifying assumptions in the preceding 'Applying the model' example. For instance, we assumed that Norm received his pay in a lump sum each year and that he faced a flat tax rate. Of course, the incremental salary that Norm earns arrives monthly, and his higher earnings may be taxed at a higher rate. All these effects are easy to account for, although the calculations become a bit more tedious.

However, there is one major error in our analysis of Norm's investment problem. We ignored a significant opportunity cost. Undertaking one investment frequently means passing on an alternative. In capital budgeting, the **opportunity costs** of an investment are the cash flows that the firm (or in this case, the individual) will not receive from other investments (or actions) as a result of undertaking the proposed investment. If Norm did not attend school, he would earn €60 000 [€39 000 after taxes (€60 000 × (1.00 − 0.35))] the first year and €63 000 [€40 950 after taxes (€63 000 × (1.00 − 0.35))] the second year. This is Norm's opportunity cost of getting an MBA, and it is just as important in the overall calculation as his out-of-pocket expenses for tuition, fees and books. Though it is still true, given the assumptions of our example, that the NPV of an MBA is positive, the value of the degree falls substantially once we recognize opportunity costs. As every MBA student knows, opportunity costs are real, not just hypothetical numbers from a textbook. Directors of MBA programmes all over the world know that MBA applications are counter-cyclical. That is, the number of students applying to MBA programmes rises during economic downturns and falls during booms. The most plausible explanation of this phenomenon is that potential MBA students face higher opportunity costs when the economy is strong.

What kinds of opportunity costs do businesses encounter in capital budgeting problems? Assume that JDS Ltd, introduced in an earlier 'Applying the model' example, acquired SDL Ltd by issuing €41 billion worth of stock to acquire the shares of SDL. (Note that this transaction was made at a price well below the €48.67 billion maximum price we calculated earlier.) Assume that at the time of this acquisition some 'experts' indicated that the cash flow consequence of this transaction was nil, because 'the firms just traded pieces of paper, and no one paid or received cash'. This view ignores JDS's opportunity cost. Though it may be true that JDS could not have raised €41 billion in cash had it attempted to sell the same number of shares that it gave to SDL shareholders in the acquisition, JDS certainly could have raised a substantial amount of cash from a stock sale. The amount of cash that JDS gave up by issuing shares to pay for the acquisition, rather than selling them, is the opportunity cost of the acquisition.

Probably the most common type of opportunity cost encountered in capital budgeting problems involves the alternative use of an asset owned by a firm. Suppose that a company owns raw land that it purchased some years ago in anticipation of an expansion opportunity. Now the firm is ready to expand by building new facilities on the raw land. Even though the firm may have paid for the land many years ago, using the land for expansion entails an incremental opportunity cost. The opportunity cost is the cash that could be raised if the firm sold the land or leased it for another purpose. That cost (the revenue given up) should be factored into the NPV calculation for the firm's expansion plans. Recall the Boeing-Airbus investment at the start of the chapter. If the companies were to forego the investments in the Dreamliner and the A380 they could invest in other projects or use the assets in another manner.

> **SMART CONCEPTS**
> See the concept explained step-by-step at **www.cengage.co.uk/ megginson**

Cannibalization

Incremental cash flows show up in surprising forms. One type of incremental cash outflow that firms must be careful to measure when launching a new product is called **cannibalization**. This involves the 'substitution effect' that frequently occurs when a firm introduces a new product. Typically, some of the new product's sales come at the expense of the firm's existing products. In the food products industry, sales of a low-fat version of a popular product may reduce sales of the original (presumably, high-fat) version. Consider when a football club issues a new home or away strip: sales of the existing club replica shirts fall off as fans desire to have the new replica. Some consumers may effectively substitute purchase of the new 'improved' product for purchase of the original product. Firms must be careful to consider the incremental cash outflows from existing product sales that are cannibalized by a newer product.

> **cannibalization**
> Loss of sales of an existing product when a new product is introduced.

Real World

New Look is a company that owns and operates clothing chain stores across Europe. One if its strategic drivers, according to its chief executive Phil Wrigley, is to avoid cannibalization. It operates 73 stores in the UK and also has a foothold in France where it operates several hundred Mim stores. In 2006 it began to open New Look stores in France and Belgium, where it sees both a gap in the market and also the potential to achieve synergies with its Mim stores. However, it feels that with its present product line it cannot expand further in the UK without cannibalization of existing stores.

French Foray', Datamonitor CommentWire, 18 April 2006.

In the next section, we work through an extended example of a capital budgeting project, illustrating how to apply the principles from this section to calculate the project's cash flows each year. Before getting into the details, we want to remind you of the overall picture. Cash flows are important because they are necessary to calculate a project's NPV. Estimating the NPV is important because it provides an estimate of the increase or decrease in shareholder value that will occur if the firm invests. Research has demonstrated the connection between capital investment decisions and shareholder value by showing that share prices rise on average when firms publicly announce significant new capital investment programmes. This suggests that, on average, firms invest in positive NPV projects. The Comparative Corporate Finance panel offers evidence supporting the overall picture – what matters is not just the amount of investment that firms undertake but how efficiently they invest.

CONCEPT REVIEW QUESTIONS

4 What is meant by a potential investment's relevant cash flows? What are sunk costs and cannibalization, and do they affect the process of determining a proposed investment's incremental cash flows?

5 A property development firm owns a fully leased 40-floor office building. A tenant recently moved its offices out of two storeys of the building, leaving the space temporarily vacant. If the property firm considers moving its own offices into this 40-storey office building, what cost should it assign for the space? Is the cost of the vacant space zero because the firm paid for the building long ago, a cost that is sunk, or is there an incremental opportunity cost?

6 Suppose that an analyst makes a mistake and calculates the NPV of an investment project by discounting the project's contribution to net income each year rather than by discounting its relevant cash flows. Would you expect the NPV based on net income to be higher or lower than the NPV calculated using the relevant cash flows?

COMPARATIVE CORPORATE FINANCE

Is a high investment rate good for a nation's economic health?

Most people accept as a given that a high investment rate, measured as capital investment spending as a percentage of GDP, is strongly correlated with rapid growth in industrial production and overall employment. However, as the table below makes clear, no such strong relationship exists for industrialized countries over the period 1990 to 2002. The industrialized country with the highest investment rate, Japan, saw industrial production fall by 8 per cent and total

employment decline by 17 per cent between 1990 and 2002. Similarly, the large continental European economies of France, Germany and Italy had above-average investment rates throughout the period from 1990 to 2002, but industrial production grew more slowly than the average for all industrial countries. All three nations experienced large net employment declines over these 12 years. Country-specific factors help explain the exceptional performance of two of the smaller countries in the table, Ireland and Norway. Ireland adopted an explicit open market strategy during the 1980s and attracted large net inflows of foreign direct investment thereafter – with a spectacular pay-off in industrial production, plus a more muted, but still significant, increase in employment. Norway benefited from an investment boom resulting from exploration and development of massive North Sea petroleum deposits.

However, by far the best-performing large economy was the United States. Despite having a below-average investment rate throughout this period, industrial production increased by 43 per cent and employment by 19.5 per cent between 1990 and 2002. The moral is clear: how efficiently capital is invested is far more important to a nation's economic health than is the absolute level of investment.

COUNTRY	CAPITAL INVESTMENT SPENDING (As a % OF GDP)		INDUSTRIAL PRODUCTION INDEX (1995 = 100)		TOTAL EMPLOYMENT (1995 = 100)	
	1990	2002[a]	1990	2002[a]	1990	2002[a]
United States	18.0%	18.4%	86.5	123.6	93.4	111.6
Canada	20.7	19.9	88.8	119.8	112.6	117.4
Japan	32.8	25.5	105.3	96.4	101.7	84.3
France	23.4	19.3	100.4	115.9	113.6	97.1
Germany	24.6	23.2	103.2	111.8	100.0[b]	85.9[b]
Ireland	21.0	22.0	62.1	255.3	90.7	112.3
Italy	22.2	19.9	93.5	108.2	107.7	102.3
Spain	25.4	26.0	96.9	118.1	104.5	120.2
Norway	23.3	18.9	86.5	110.3	97.7	102.8
Sweden	21.3	17.2	87.8	124.9	124.7	93.1
Switzerland	28.3	17.2	97.0	121.4	119.4	93.3
United Kingdom	20.2	16.0	94.1	100.0	102.5	109.8
Industrial country average	**22.6%**	**19.9%**	**95.2**	**111.0**	**102.4**	**99.2**

[a] Or most recent year, usually 2001.
[b] Employment index for Germany, 1990 = 100 and data ends 1994.

Source: International Monetary Fund, *International Financial Statistics Yearbook 2003*, Washington, DC: IMF.

9.3 CASH FLOWS FOR GAMEBUZZ.TV

GameBuzz.TV is a company that provides online gaming sites, through an agreement with satellite television broadcasters. The company is considering a proposal to expand its games selection to include online gambling for real money, as its 'Play-Casino' games suite has proved very popular. Management has surveyed the client base and believes that the company has a built-in clientele for the new gaming product. If the company decides to undertake this project, it will begin selling memberships in the new television-based casino products in a couple of month's time, when its new fiscal year begins. GameBuzz.TV has to offer membership in order to circumvent local regulations in several of the countries where it broadcasts, which do not permit casinos. The company would therefore make the required investment before the end of the current fiscal year (year 0). The company has a policy that it accepts projects with positive NPVs, and it uses a 10 per cent discount rate to calculate NPV.

Up-front costs associated with the investment include €50 000 in computer equipment (which the company depreciates on a straight-line basis over five years) and €4500 in inventory (€2500 of which is purchased on credit). For transactions purposes, the firm plans to increase its cash balance by €1000 immediately. The firm does not expect to begin selling memberships until the new fiscal year begins. Currently, the average selling price of GameBuzz.TV's casino membership is €13.50, and company executives believe that this price will increase over time at a 2 per cent annual rate. GameBuzz.TV knows that some of its resellers will sell memberships to individuals on credit. In addition to relying on this trade credit, the firm expects to finance this investment using cash flow generated from its existing game cash flows.

Like most new business ventures, this one will not be profitable immediately. Managers expect unit sales volume to increase rapidly in the first few years before reaching a long-run stable growth rate. As sales volume increases, the firm expects gross profit margins to widen slightly. The firm does allow credit sales to customers with excellent payment histories. Expanding sales volume will require increases in current assets, as well as additional spending on fixed assets. GameBuzz.TV pays taxes at a 40 per cent rate.

Table 9.1 shows various projections for the online casino project. The top two lines list anticipated selling prices (rounded to the nearest €0.01) and unit volumes in each of the next six years. Below that appears a series of projected income statements for

TABLE 9.1

The online casino project

	SETUP	YEAR 1	YEAR 2	YEAR 3	YEAR 4	YEAR 5	YEAR 6
Sales price per unit	€ 14	€ 14	€ 14	€ 14	€ 15	€ 15	€ 15
Units sold	€ —	€ 4 000	€ 10 000	€ 16 000	€ 22 000	€ 24 000	€ 25 000
Projected income statement							
Revenues	€ —	€55 080	€140 454	€229 221	€321 482	€357 722	€380 080
COGS	€ —	€41 861	€105 341	€169 623	€234 682	€259 349	€273 657
Gross profit	€ —	€13 219	€ 35 113	€ 59 598	€ 86 800	€ 98 373	€106 423
SG&A	€ —	€ 8 262	€ 19 664	€ 29 799	€ 35 363	€ 35 772	€ 38 008
Depreciation		€10 000	€ 12 000	€ 13 000	€ 18 000	€ 26 000	€ 19 000
Pre-tax profit	€ —	−€ 5,043	€ 5 449	€ 19 799	€ 41 437	€ 52 601	€ 68 415
Projected balance sheet							
Cash	€ 1 000	€ 2 000	€ 2 500	€ 3 000	€ 3 200	€ 3 300	€ 3 500
Accounts receivable	€ —	€ 4 590	€ 11 705	€ 19 102	€ 26 790	€ 29 810	€ 31 673
Inventory	€ 4 500	€ 7 344	€ 18 727	€ 30 563	€ 42 864	€ 47 696	€ 50 677
Current assets	€ 5 500	€13 934	€ 32 932	€ 52 665	€ 72 854	€ 80 806	€ 85 850
Gross PP&E	€50 000	€60 000	€ 65 000	€ 90 000	€130 000	€145 000	€155 000
Accumulated depreciation	0	€10 000	€ 22 000	€ 35 000	€ 53 000	€ 79 000	€ 98 000
Net PP&E	€50 000	€50 000	€ 43 000	€ 55 000	€ 77 000	€ 66 000	€ 57 000
Total assets	€55 500	€63 934	€ 77 932	€112 665	€162 854	€175 806	€190 850

the next six years. Top-line revenue equals the product of expected selling price (unrounded) and unit volume each year. The figures for cost of goods sold and selling, general and administrative expenses (SG&A) reflect management's belief that costs as a per centage of sales will fall slightly as volume increases. Depreciation expense each year is determined by spending on fixed assets all of which are depreciated on a five-year basis. Thus the depreciation in each year is a reflection of the past investment in fixed assets stretching back across the previous five years.

Beneath the income statement appears a series of abbreviated projected balance sheets. Each shows the project's total asset requirements (including both current and fixed assets) as well as the financing available from suppliers in the form of accounts payable. As mentioned previously, any additional financing the project requires will come from internally generated funds from existing game cash flows.

To determine whether this is an investment opportunity worth taking, we need to determine the project's cash flows through time and discount them at 10 per cent to calculate the project's NPV. As part of this calculation, we have to estimate the value of the endeavour beyond the sixth year. In other words, we have to estimate the project's terminal value.

Year 0 cash flow

The firm will have cash outlays of €50 000 for computer equipment immediately. Because the company has no other expenses or revenues, the project's incremental pre-tax profits this year are zero. The firm sets up a cash account with an initial balance of €1000 and purchases €4500 in inventory. Accounts payable totalling €2500 are used to finance a portion of these outlays, resulting in an initial net working capital investment of €3000 (€1000 cash + €4500 inventory − €2500 payables). Therefore, the net cash flow for year 0 is shown as follows:

Increase in gross fixed assets	−€50 000
Initial working capital investment	−3 000
Net cash flow	−€53 000

Year 1 cash flow

Notice above that gross plant and equipment (P&E) increases by €10 000 in year 1. This means that GameBuzz.TV has purchased €10 000 in additional computer equipment or other fixed assets. Depreciation in the first full year of operation equals €10 000, which is one-fifth of the total investment in fixed assets of €50 000 in the previous year.

With sales volume increasing, the firm also makes additional investments in working capital. Cash balances increase by €1000 (€2000 − €1000), receivables rise by €4590 (€4590 − €0), and inventories go up by €2844 (€7344 − €4500), partially offsetting the increase in current assets is an increase in accounts payable of €1820 (€4320 − €2500). Therefore, net working capital increases by €6614 (€1000 cash + €4590 receivables + €2844 inventory − €1820 payables), a net cash outflow for the firm.

At a sales volume of 4000 units in its first year of operation, the casino business earns a pre-tax loss of €5043. Before we can convert this figure into cash flow, we must make two adjustments. First, if GameBuzz.TV can charge this loss against profits in its other operations, then the loss will generate tax savings of €2017 (40% × €5043). Second, we need to add depreciation expense back into the pre-tax loss because depreciation involves no cash outlay. Together, these adjustments result in a net operating cash inflow of €6974 (−€5043 + €2017 + €10 000).

Combining each source of cash flow, we can determine the net cash flow for the project's first full year:

Increase in working capital	−€ 6 614
Increase in fixed assets	−€10 000
Operating cash flow	−€ 3 026
Depreciation	€10 000
Total project cash flow	−€ 9 640

Year 2 cash flow

We can simply repeat the steps we followed in year 1 to determine cash flow for year 2. First, gross fixed assets increase by €5000. Depreciation for year 2 is €12 000 – again, the difference between accumulated depreciation in year 2 and year 1. The depreciation in year 2 equals the sum of allowable depreciation on assets purchased up front, €10 000 and year 2, €2000.

Sales continue to rise in year 2, requiring a large investment in working capital. Total current assets increase by €18 998 (€500 cash + €7115 receivables + €11 383 inventory), but accounts payable rise by €6696 (€11 016 − €4320). The increase in net working capital equals €12 302 (€18 998 increase in current assets − €6696 increase in payables) and results in a cash outflow.

In year 2, the firm earns a small pre-tax profit of €3449. After taxes are deducted, the net earnings amount to €2069. Add to that figure the depreciation expense of €12 000 to arrive at operating cash inflow of €14 069. Thus, the following are the total net cash flows in year 2:

Increase in working capital	−€12 302
Increase in fixed assets	−€ 5 000
Operating cash flow	€ 2 069
Depreciation	€12 000
Total project cash flow	−€ 3 233

Table 9.2 illustrates the annual net cash flows for the online casino project all the way through the sixth year. As you can see, project cash flows do not turn from negative to positive until the fifth year. If we calculate the NPV (using the 10 per cent discount rate) of the stream of cash flows shown in Table 9.2, it is not surprising that the project generates a negative NPV, of nearly €50 000. However, just because the year-by-year cash flow projections end in year 6 does not mean that the project ends at that time. To complete our analysis, we must estimate the project's terminal value.

	SETUP	YEAR 1	YEAR 2	YEAR 3	YEAR 4	YEAR 5	YEAR 6
Increase in working capital	−€ 3 000	−€ 6 614	−€12 302	−€12 771	−€12 953	−€ 5 109	−€ 3 291
Increase in fixed assets	−€50 000	−€10 000	−€ 5 000	−€25 000	−€40 000	−€15 000	−€10 000
Operating cash flow	€ —	−€ 3 026	€ 2 069	€10 079	€20 062	€21 961	€29 649
Depreciation	€ —	€10 000	€12 000	€13 000	€18 000	€26 000	€19 000
Total project cash flow	−€53 000	−€ 9 640	−€ 3 233	−€14 692	−€14 891	€27 852	€35 358

TABLE 9.2

Online casino annual net cash flows

Terminal value

We produce two different terminal value estimates for this project. In the first, we assume that by year 6 the project has reached a steady state, meaning that cash flows continue to grow at 2 per cent per year indefinitely. In the second, we assume that the firm sells its investment at the end of year 6 and receives a cash payment equal to the project's book value.

In year 6, the project generates a net cash inflow of €35 358. Assuming that cash flows beyond the sixth year grow at 2 per cent per year, and discounting those cash flows at 10 per cent, we can use the equation for a growing perpetuity (Equation 3.11) to determine the terminal value of the project *as at the end of year 6*, as follows:

$$TV = \frac{36065}{0.1 - 0.02} = 450814$$

Notice that the numerator in the expression above is 2 per cent greater than the cash flow in year 6 (i.e. 1.02 × €35 358 = €36 065). Remember (from Chapter 3, Equation 3.11, and Chapter 5, Equation 5.4), when valuing a stream of cash flows that grows at a perpetual rate, the value today equals next year's cash flow divided by the difference between the discount rate and the growth rate. Thus, to determine the terminal value in year 6, we must use the cash flow in year 7 in the numerator.

As a second approach, assume that the terminal value of the project simply equals the book value at the end of year 6. At that time, the firm owns fixed assets worth €57 000 (see Table 9.1 Net P&E for year 6). In this case, because the project is assumed to be terminated and liquidated at the end of year 6, the firm will recover its net working capital investment (i.e. liquidate its current assets and pay off outstanding trade credit), which will generate an additional €56 041 (from Table 9.1 for year 6: €85 851 current assets −€29 810 accounts payable) in cash. The terminal value equals the sum of these two items, €113 041 (€57 000 net fixed assets + €56 041 net working capital recovery). Notice that this value is much less than the value we obtained using the perpetual growth model. The magnitude of that difference should not surprise us too much. In general, as noted in Chapter 5, a profitable, growing business will have a market value that exceeds its book value.

TABLE 9.3

Online casino annual net cash flows

	SETUP	YEAR 1	YEAR 2	YEAR 3	YEAR 4	YEAR 5	YEAR 6
Using stable cash flows							
Cash flow	−€ 53 000	−€9 640	−€3 233	−€14 692	−€14 891	€27 852	€486 172
Discount factor	1.00	1.10	1.21	1.33	1.46	1.61	1.77
PV	−€ 53 000	−€8 763	−€2 672	−€11 038	−€10 170	€17 294	€274 431
NPV	€ 206 082						
Using book value							
Cash flow	−€ 53 000	−€9 640	−€3 233	−€14 692	−€14 891	€27 852	€148 399
Discount factor	1.00	1.10	1.21	1.33	1.46	1.61	1.77
PV	−€ 53 000	−€8 763	−€2 672	−€11 038	−€10 170	€17 294	€83 767
NPV	€ 15 417						

Online casino project NPV

Putting all this together, we arrive at two different estimates of the project's NPV, depending on which estimate of terminal value we use (see Table 9.3).

In this example, the project yields a positive NPV, no matter which terminal value estimate we choose, so investing in the project will increase shareholder wealth. However, in many real-world situations, especially those involving long-lived investments, the 'go' or 'no-go' decision will depend critically on terminal value assumptions. It is not at all uncommon for the perpetual growth approach to yield a positive NPV, while the book value approach shows a negative NPV. In that case, managers have to think more deeply about the long-run value of their enterprise.

SMART PRACTICES VIDEO

David Nickel, Controller for Intel Communications Group, Intel Corporation
'Capital budgeting is the key theme for deciding which programmes get funded.'

See the entire interview at **www.cengage.co.uk/megginson**

CONCEPT REVIEW QUESTIONS

7 Embedded in the analysis of the proposal is an assumption about how GameBuzz.TV's customers will behave when they are able to choose from an expanded set of offerings. What is that assumption?

8 What other ways might GameBuzz.TV estimate the terminal value of this project?

9 Suppose that management decide to reclassify computers as three-year equipment rather than five-year equipment. In general, what impact would this have on the project's NPV?

10 Given that a company can in certain circumstances produce one set of accounts for taxation and the other for shareholders, and that depreciation schedules are a matter of both accounting policy and tax law, can we ever really be sure that a project is worth taking on?

9.4 SPECIAL PROBLEMS IN CAPITAL BUDGETING

Though our objective in writing this book has been to give it the most real-world focus possible, real business situations are more complex and occur in more varieties than any textbook can reasonably convey. In this section, we examine common business decisions with special characteristics that make them a little more difficult to analyse than the examples we have covered thus far. We will see that whereas the analysis may require a little more thinking, the principles involved are the same ones discussed throughout this chapter and Chapter 8.

Capital rationing

In Chapter 8 we asked the following question: If a firm must choose between several investment opportunities, all worth taking, how does it prioritize projects? We learned that the IRR and PI methods sometimes rank projects differently than the NPV does, although all three techniques generate the same accept or reject decisions.

The fundamental question There is a fundamental question that we have avoided until now. If the firm has many projects with positive NPVs (or investments with acceptable IRRs), why not accept all of them? One possibility is that the company may be constrained by the availability of trained and reliable personnel – especially managers. This prevents the firm from growing extremely rapidly, especially because adding a new product or project would require managerial talent of the highest order. Another possibility is that the firm simply does not have enough money to finance all its attractive investment opportunities. But surely couldn't a large, publicly traded firm raise money by issuing new shares to investors and using the proceeds to undertake any and all appealing investments?

If you watch firms closely over a period of time, you notice that most do not often issue new shares. As Chapter 11 discusses more fully, firms seem to prefer to finance investments with internally generated cash flow and will only infrequently raise money in the external capital markets by issuing new equity. There are several possible reasons for this apparent reluctance to issue new equity. First, when firms announce their intention to raise new equity capital, they may send an unintended negative signal to the market. Perhaps investors may interpret the announcement as a sign that the firm's existing investments are not generating acceptable levels of cash flow. Perhaps investors may see the decision to issue new shares as an indication that managers believe the firm's shares are overvalued. In either case, investors may react negatively to this announcement, causing the share price to fall. Undoubtedly, managers try to persuade investors that the funds being raised will be invested in profitable projects, but convincing investors that this is the true motive for the issue is an uphill struggle.

A second reason why managers may avoid issuing new equity is that, by doing so, they dilute their ownership stake in the firm (unless they participate in the offering by purchasing some of the new shares). A smaller ownership stake means that managers control a shrinking block of votes, raising the potential for a corporate takeover or other threat to their control of the firm.

In conversations with senior executives, we often hear a third reason why firms do not fund every investment project that looks promising. Behind every idea for a new investment is a person, someone who may have an emotional attachment to the idea, or a career-building motivation for proposing the idea in the first place. Upper-level managers are wise to be a little sceptical of the cash flow forecasts they see on projects with favourable NPVs or IRRs. It is a given that every cash flow forecast will prove to be wrong. If the forecasting process is unbiased, half the time forecasts will be too pessimistic, and half the time they will be too optimistic. Which half is likely to surface on the radar screen of a CFO or CEO in a large corporation? Establishing an annual budget constraint on capital expenditures to ration capital is one mechanism by which senior managers impose discipline on the capital budgeting process. By doing so, they hope to weed out some of the investment proposals with an optimistic bias built into the cash flow projections. We will return to this issue later.

Selecting the best projects under rationing Regardless of their motivation, managers cannot always invest in every project that offers a positive NPV. In such an environment, **capital rationing** occurs. Given a set of attractive investment opportunities, managers must choose a combination of projects that maximizes shareholder wealth, subject to the constraint of limited funds. In this environment, ranking projects using the profitability index (PI) can be very useful. Once managers rank projects, they select the investment with the highest PI. If the total amount of capital available has not been fully exhausted, then managers invest in the project with the second-highest PI, and so on, until no more capital remains to invest. By following this routine, managers select a portfolio of projects that in aggregate generates a higher NPV than any other combination of projects.[7] The following example demonstrates the application of this approach for selecting investments under capital rationing.

capital rationing
The situation where a firm has more positive NPV projects than its available budget can fund. It must choose a combination of those projects that maximizes shareholder wealth.

Applying the Model

Assume that a particular firm has five projects to choose from as shown in Table 9.4. Note that all of the projects require an initial cash outflow in year 0 that is followed by four years of cash inflows. All of the projects have positive NPVs, IRRs that exceed the firm's 12 per cent required return, and PIs greater than 1.0. Notice that the first project has the highest IRR and the highest PI, but project 5 has the largest NPV. This is again the familiar 'scale problem' discussed in Chapter 8. Suppose that this firm can invest no more than €300 million this year. What portfolio of investments maximizes shareholder wealth?

Notice that there are several combinations of projects that satisfy the constraint of investing no more than €300 million. If we begin by accepting the project with the highest PI, then continue to accept additional projects until we bump into the €300 million capital constraint, we will invest in projects 1, 2 and 3. With these three projects, we have invested just €250 million, but that does not leave us with enough capital to fund either project 4 or 5. The total NPV obtainable from the first three projects is €170.8 (€59.2 + €52.0 + €59.6) million. No other combination of projects that satisfies the capital constraint yields a higher aggregate NPV. For example,

---

[7] We are simplifying a bit here. Sorting projects according to the PI and selecting from that list until capital runs out may not maximize shareholder wealth when capital is rationed, not only at the beginning of an investment's life but also in all subsequent periods. This method can also lead to suboptimal decisions when projects are interdependent – that is, when one investment is contingent on another. In these situations, more complex decision tools, such as integer programming, may be required.

TABLE 9.4

Capital rationing and the profitability index (12 per cent required return)

YEAR	PROJECTS				
	1	2	3	4	5
0	−€70	−€80	−€100	−€150	−€200
1	30	30	40	50	90
2	40	35	50	55	80
3	50	55	60	60	80
4	55	60	65	90	110
NPV	€59.2	€52.0	€59.6	€38.4	€71.0
IRR	44%	36%	36%	23%	28%
PI	1.8	1.6	1.6	1.3	1.4

investing in projects 3 and 5, thereby using up the full allotment of €300 million in capital, generates a total NPV of just €130.6 (€59.6 + €71.0) million. Likewise, investing in projects 1, 2 and 4, another combination that utilizes all €300 million in capital, generates an aggregate NPV of €149.6 (€59.2 + €52.0 + €38.4) million.[8]

Equipment replacement and equivalent annual cost

Assume that a firm must purchase an electronic control device to monitor its assembly line. Two types of devices are available. Both meet the firm's minimum quality standards, but they differ in three dimensions. First, one device is less costly than the other. Secondly, the cheaper device requires higher maintenance expenditures. Thirdly, the less expensive device (three-year life) does not last as long as the more expensive one (four-year life), so it will have to be replaced sooner. The sequence of expected cash outflows (we have omitted the negative signs for convenience) for each device are as follows:

DEVICE	END OF YEAR (ALL VALUES ARE OUTFLOWS)				
	0	1	2	3	4
A	€12 000	€1 500	€1 500	€1 500	
B	14 000	1 200	1 200	1 200	1 200

Notice that the maintenance costs do not rise over time. This means either that the expected rate of inflation equals zero or that we have ignored inflation in making the projections. Suppose this firm uses a discount rate of 7 per cent. Following is the NPV of each stream of cash outflows:

DEVICE	NPV
A	€15 936
B	18 065

---

[8] Reviewing Table 9.4, we see that the IRR and PI result in identical project rankings. Therefore, had we used the IRR rather than the PI we would have selected the same set of projects. These two decision techniques generally result in similar, but not necessarily identical, project rankings. We favour the PI because of its close link to NPV.

Purchasing and operating device A seems to be much cheaper than using device B (remember that we are looking for a lower NPV, because these are cash outflows). But this calculation ignores the fact that using device A will necessitate a large replacement expenditure in year 4, one year earlier than device B must be replaced. We need a way to capture the value of replacing device B less frequently than device A.

One way to do this is to look at both machines over a 12-year time horizon. Over the next 12 years, the firm will replace device A four times (4×3 years = 12 years) and device B three times (3×4 years = 12 years). At the end of the twelfth year, both machines have to be replaced, and thus begins another 12-year cycle. Table 9.5 shows the streams of cash flows over the cycle, assuming that when either control device wears out it can be replaced and maintained at the same costs that initially applied (i.e. all future costs remain the same). Notice that in the replacement years, the firm must pay both the maintenance cost on the old device (to keep it running through the year) and the purchase price of the new device. The present value (using a 7 per cent discount rate) of the cash outflows for the devices over the entire 12-year period follows:

DEVICE	NPV
A	€48 233
B	42 360

TABLE 9.5

Operating and replacement cash flows for two devices (all values are outflows)

Note: At the end of 12 years, the firm has to replace equipment, regardless of whether it chooses device A or B; thus, a new 12-year cycle begins.

YEAR	DEVICE A	DEVICE B
0	€12 000	€14 000
1	1 500	1 200
2	1 500	1 200
3	13 500	1 200
4	1 500	15 200
5	1 500	1 200
6	13 500	1 200
7	1 500	1 200
8	1 500	15 200
9	13 500	1 200
10	1 500	1 200
11	1 500	1 200
12	1 500	1 200
NPV (@7%)	€48 233	€42 360

Taking into account the greater longevity of device B, it is the better choice. Remember, our objective is to find the minimum-cost alternative, which, in this case, is device B.

An alternative approach to this problem is called the **equivalent annual cost (EAC) method**. The EAC method begins by calculating the present value of cash flows for each device over its lifetime. We have already seen that the NPV for operating device A for three years is €15 936, and the NPV for operating device B for four years is €18 065. Next, the EAC method asks, what annual expenditure over the life of each machine would have the same present value? That is, the EAC solves each expression as follows:

equivalent annual cost (EAC) method Represents the annual expenditure over the life of each asset that has a present value equal to the present value of the asset's annual cash flows over its lifetime.

$$15936 = \frac{X}{1.07^1} + \frac{X}{1.07^2} + \frac{X}{1.07^3}; X = 6072$$

$$18065 = \frac{X}{1.07^1} + \frac{X}{1.07^2} + \frac{X}{1.07^3} + \frac{X}{1.07^4}; X = 5333$$

In the first equation, the variable X represents the annual cash flow from a three-year annuity that has the same present value as the actual purchase and operating costs of device A. If the firm purchases device A and keeps replacing it every three years for the indefinite future, the firm will incur a sequence of cash flows over time with the same present value as a perpetuity of €6072. In other words, €6072 is the equivalent annual cost (EAC) of device A. Likewise, in the second equation, X represents the annual cash flow from a four-year annuity with the same present value as the purchase and operating costs of device B. If the firm buys device B and replaces it every four years, then the firm will incur a sequence of cash flows having the same present value as a perpetuity of €5333. The firm should choose the alternative with the lower EAC, which is device B.

Our approaches for solving the problem of choosing between equipment with unequal lives both assume that the firm will continue to replace worn-out equipment with similar machines for a long period of time. That may not be a bad assumption in some cases, but new technology often makes old equipment obsolete. For example, suppose that the firm in our example believes that in three years a new electronic device will be available that is more reliable, less costly to operate and longer-lived. If this new device becomes available in three years, the firm will replace whatever device it is using at the time with the newer model. Furthermore, the superior attributes of the new model imply that the salvage value for the old device will be zero. How should the firm proceed? Knowing that it will replace the old device with the improved device in three years, the firm can simply discount cash flows for three years:

$$NPV(a) = 12000 + \frac{1500}{1.07^1} + \frac{1500}{1.07^2} + \frac{1500}{1.07^3}; = 15936$$

$$NPV(b) = 14000 + \frac{1200}{1.07^1} + \frac{1200}{1.07^2} + \frac{1200}{1.07^3}; = 17149$$

In this case, the best device to purchase is A rather than B. Remember that B's primary advantage was its longevity. In an environment in which technological developments make old machines obsolete, longevity is not much of an advantage.

Source: 'More Support Needed For Marine and Offshore Wind', *Power UK*, 21 July 2005.

Real World

The equivalent annual cost concept is well illustrated in the July 2005 edition of *Power UK*. In that trade journal there is a discussion of the need for governments, in this case the UK government, to further subsidize alternative energy sources. The point is made explicitly that as the costs and revenues of these sources are very different and the lifetimes of the projects also, the EAC method gives some idea of how to consider the options.

Excess capacity

Firms often operate at less than full capacity. In such situations, managers encourage alternative uses of the excess capacity because they view it as a free asset. Although it may be true that the marginal cost of using excess capacity is zero in the very short run, using excess capacity today may accelerate the need for more capacity in the future. When that is so, managers should charge the cost of accelerating new capacity development against the current proposal for using excess capacity. This procedure can be demonstrated by the following example.

Applying the Model

Imagine a central European discount clothing store chain with a regional distribution centre in northern Italy. At the moment, the distribution centre is not fully utilized. Managers know that in two years, as new stores are built in the new member states of the EU, the firm will have to invest €2 million (cash outflow) to expand the distribution centre's warehouse.

A proposal surfaces to lease all the excess space in the warehouse for the next two years at a price that would generate beginning-of-year cash inflow of €125 000 per year. If the firm accepts this proposal, it will have no excess capacity. In order to hold inventory for new stores coming on line in the next few months, the firm will have to begin expansion immediately. The incremental investment in this expansion is the difference between investing €2 million now versus investing €2 million two years from today. The incremental cash inflow is, of course, the €125 000 lease cash flows that are received today and one year from today. Should the firm accept this offer? Assuming a 10 per cent discount rate, the NPV of the project is shown as follows:

$$\text{NPV} = 125000 - 2000000 + \frac{125000}{1.1^1} + \frac{2000000}{1.1^2} = -108471$$

Notice that we treat the €2 million investment in the second year as a cash inflow in this expression. By building the warehouse today, the firm avoids having to spend the money two years later. Even so, the NPV of leasing excess capacity is negative. However, a clever analyst could propose a counter-offer derived from the follow equation:

$$\text{NPV} = X - 2000000 + \frac{X}{1.1^1} + \frac{2000000}{1.1^2} = 0$$

The value of X represents the amount of the lease cash inflows (one received today and the other received in one year) that would make the firm indifferent to the proposal. Solving the equation, we see that if the lease cash inflows are €181 818, the project NPV equals zero. Therefore, if the firm can lease its capacity for a price above €181 818, it should do so.

11 When a firm is faced with capital rationing, how can the profitability index (PI) be used to select the best projects? Why does choosing projects with the highest PI not always lead to the best decision?

12 Under what circumstance is the use of the equivalent annual cost (EAC) method to compare substitutable projects with different lives clearly more efficient computationally than using multiple investments over a common period where both projects terminate in the same year?

13 In almost every example so far, firms must decide to invest in a project immediately or not at all. But suppose that a firm could invest in a project today or it could wait one year before investing. How could you use NPV analysis to decide whether to invest now or later?

14 Can you articulate circumstances under which the cost of excess capacity is zero? Think about why the cost of excess capacity normally is not zero.

15 In the situation above when we examined the equivalent annual cost, we worked the solution out 'manually'. Is there an algebraic formulation that allows us to consider any given question of that type?

9.5 SUMMARY AND CONCLUSIONS

- To estimate an investment's relevant cash flows, the analyst focuses on incremental cash flows, ignores financing costs, considers taxes and adjusts for any non-cash expenses such as depreciation.

- The costs of financing an investment, such as interest paid to lenders and dividends paid to shareholders, should not be counted as part of a project's cash outflows. The discount rate captures the financing costs, so deducting interest expense and dividends from a project's cash flows would be double counting.

- Certain types of cash flow are common to many different kinds of investments. These include fixed asset cash flow, working capital cash flow, operating cash flow and terminal cash flow.

- To find working capital cash flow, calculate the change in net working capital from one period to the next. Increases in net working capital represent cash outflows, whereas decreases in net working capital represent cash inflows.

- To find operating cash flow, calculate after-tax net income and add back any non-cash expenses.

- To find terminal value, or terminal cash flow, employ one of several methods, including the perpetual growth model and the use of book value.

- Only the incremental cash flows (marginal benefits and marginal costs) associated with a project should be included in NPV analysis. The analyst should avoid including

- sunk costs in estimates of incremental cash flows.

- Opportunity costs and any cannibalization should be reflected in an investment's cash flow projections.

- The profitability index (PI) is useful in making investment decisions that maximize NPV when capital rationing exists.

- When evaluating alternative equipment purchases with unequal lives, determine the equivalent annual cost (*EAC*) of each type of equipment and choose the one that is least expensive.

- When confronted with proposals to use excess capacity, think carefully about the true cost of that capacity. It is rarely zero.

INTERNET RESOURCES

For updates to links in this section and elsewhere in the book, please go to the book's website at www.cengage.co.uk/megginson.

http://www.ifad.net/content/ie/ie_f_gaap_frameset.htm
An excellent comparison of accounting standards for different countries.

http://clinton3.nara.gov/pcscb/
An interesting report, prepared in 1999 for President Clinton, outlining capital budgeting trends and practices in both the public and private sectors.

http://www.quicken.com/taxes/investing/marginal/yahoo
Site can be used for personal investment decisions by calculating your own marginal tax rate.

http://www.secondarymarket.com
Site can be searched by registered users for used equipment in many different industrial sectors; can use market prices of used equipment to form estimates of salvage value or terminal value for a long-lived project.

http://www.exinfm.com/free_spreadsheets.html
Free capital budgeting-related spreadsheets.

KEY TERMS

cannibalization	marginal tax rate	relevant cash flows
capital rationing	net working capital	sunk costs
equivalent annual cost (EAC) method	non-cash expenses	terminal value
incremental cash flows	opportunity costs	working capital

SELF-TEST PROBLEMS

ST9-1 Claross Ltd wants to determine the relevant operating cash flows associated with the proposed purchase of a new piece of equipment that has an installed cost of €10 million and is depreciated over five years. The firm's financial analyst estimated that the relevant time horizon for analysis is six years. She expects the revenues attributable to the equipment to be €15.8 million in the first year and to increase at 5 per cent per year through year 6. Similarly, she estimates all expenses, other than depreciation attributable to the equipment, to total €12.2 million in the first year and to increase by 4 per cent per year through year 6. She plans to ignore any cash flows after year 6. The firm has a marginal tax rate of 40 per cent and its required return on the equipment investment is 13 per cent. (Note: round all cash flow calculations to the nearest €0.01 million.)

a Find the relevant incremental cash flows for years 0 through 6.

b Using the cash flows found in part (a), determine the NPV and IRR for the proposed equipment purchase.

c Based on your findings in part (b), would you recommend that Claross Ltd purchase the equipment? Why?

ST9-2 Atech Industries wants to determine whether it would be advisable for it to replace an existing, fully depreciated machine with a new one. The new machine will have an after-tax installed cost of €300 000 and will be depreciated under a three-year schedule. The old machine can be sold today for €80 000, after taxes. The firm is in the 40 per cent marginal tax bracket and requires a minimum return on the replacement decision of 15 per cent. The firm's estimates of its revenues and expenses (excluding depreciation) for both the new and the old machine (in € thousands) over the next four years are given below.

YEAR	NEW MACHINE		OLD MACHINE	
	REVENUE	EXPENSES (EXCLUDING DEPRECIATION)	REVENUE	EXPENSES (EXCLUDING DEPRECIATION)
1	€925	€740	€625	€580
2	990	780	645	595
3	1 000	825	670	610
4	1 100	875	695	630

Atech also estimates the values of various current accounts that could be impacted by the proposed replacement. They are shown below for both the new and the old machine over the next four years. Currently (at time 0), the firm's net investment in these current accounts is assumed to be €110 000 with the new machine and €75 000 with the old machine.

NEW MACHINE	YEAR			
	1	2	3	4
Cash	€20 000	€25 000	€ 30 000	€ 36 000
Accounts receivable	90 000	95 000	110 000	120 000
Inventory	80 000	90 000	100 000	105 000
Accounts payable	60 000	65 000	70 000	72 000

OLD MACHINE	YEAR			
	1	2	3	4
Cash	€15 000	€15 000	€15 000	€15 000
Accounts receivable	60 000	64 000	68 000	70 000
Inventory	45 000	48 000	52 000	55 000
Accounts payable	33 000	35 000	38 000	40 000

Atech estimates that after four years of detailed cash flow development, it will assume, in analysing this replacement decision, that the year 4 incremental cash flows of the new machine over the old machine will grow at a compound annual rate of 2 per cent from the end of year 4 to infinity.

a Find the incremental operating cash flows (including any working capital investment) for years 1 to 4, for Atech's proposed machine replacement decision.

b Calculate the terminal value of Atech's proposed machine replacement at the end of year 4.

c Show the relevant cash flows (initial outlay, operating cash flows and terminal cash flow) for years 1 to 4, for Atech's proposed machine replacement.

d Using the relevant cash flows from part (c), find the NPV and IRR for Atech's proposed machine replacement.

e Based on your findings in part (d), what recommendation would you make to Atech regarding its proposed machine replacement?

ST9-3 Performance Ltd is faced with choosing between two mutually exclusive projects with differing lives. It requires a return of 12 per cent on these projects. Project A requires an initial outlay at time 0 of €5 000 000 and is expected to require annual maintenance cash outflows of €3 100 000 per year over its two-year life. Project B requires an initial outlay at time 0 of €6 000 000 and is expected to require annual maintenance cash outflows of €2 600 000 per year over its three-year life. Both projects are acceptable investments and provide equal quality service. The firm assumes that the replacement and maintenance

costs for both projects will remain unchanged over time.

a Find the NPV of each project over its life.

b Which project would you recommend, based on your finding in part (a)? What is wrong with choosing the best project based on its NPV?

c Use the equivalent annual cost (EAC) method to compare the two projects.

d Which project would you recommend, based on your finding in part (c)? Compare and contrast this recommendation with the one you gave in part (b).

QUESTIONS

Q9-1 In capital budgeting analysis, why do we focus on cash flow rather than accounting profit?

Q9-2 To finance a certain project, a company must borrow money at 10 per cent interest. How should it treat interest payments when it analyses the project's cash flows?

Q9-3 Does depreciation affect cash flow in a positive or negative manner? From a net present value perspective, why is accelerated depreciation preferable? Is it acceptable to utilize one depreciation method for tax purposes and another for financial reporting purposes? Which method is relevant for determining project cash flows?

Q9-4 In what sense does an increase in accounts payable represent a cash inflow?

Q9-5 List several ways to estimate a project's terminal value.

Q9-6 What are the tax consequences of selling an investment asset for more than its book value? Does this have an effect on project cash flows that must be accounted for in relevant cash flows? What is the effect if the asset is sold for less than its book value?

Q9-7 Why must incremental, after-tax cash flows, rather than total cash flows, be evaluated in project analysis?

Q9-8 Differentiate between sunk costs and opportunity costs. Which of these costs should be included in incremental cash flows and which should be excluded?

Q9-9 Why is it important to consider cannibalization in situations where a company is considering adding substitute products to its product line?

Q9-10 Before entering business school, a student estimated the value of earning an MBA at €300 000. Based on that analysis, the student decided to enter business school. After completing the first year, the student ran the NPV calculations again. How would you expect the NPV to look after the student has completed one year of the programme? Specifically, what portion of the analysis must be different from it was the year before?

Q9-11 Total Taxidermy Group (TTG) operates a chain of taxidermy shops across northern England, with a handful of locations in the south. A rival firm, Heads Up Ltd, has a few northern locations, but most of its shops are located in the south. TTG and Heads Up decide to consolidate their operations by trading ownership of a few locations. TTG will acquire four Heads Up locations in the north, and will relinquish control of its southern locations in exchange. No cash changes hands up front. Does this mean that an analyst working for either company can evaluate the merits of this deal by assuming that the project has no initial cash outlay? Explain.

Q9-12 What is the only relevant decision for independent projects if an unlimited capital budget exists? How does your response change if the projects are mutually exclusive? How does your response change if the firm faces capital rationing?

Q9-13 Explain why the equivalent annual cost (EAC) method helps firms evaluate alternative investments with unequal lives.

Q9-14 Why isn't excess capacity free?

PROBLEMS

Types of cash flows

P9-1 A certain piece of equipment costs €32 million, plus an additional €2 million to instal. The percentage of this equipment's basis that is depreciable each year is 20 per cent in year 1, 32 per cent in year 2, 19.20 per cent in year 3, 11.52 per cent in year 4, 11.52 per cent in year 5 and 5.76 per cent in year 6. For a firm that discounts cash flows at 12 per cent and faces a tax rate of 34 per cent, what is the present value of the depreciation tax savings associated with this equipment? By how much would that number change if the firm could treat the €2 million installation cost as a deductible expense rather than include it as part of the depreciable cost of the asset?

P9-2 The government is considering a proposal to allow even greater accelerated depreciation deductions than those already in existence.

a For which type of company would this change be more valuable, a company facing a 10 per cent tax rate or one facing a 30 per cent tax rate?

b If companies take larger depreciation deductions in the early years of an investment, what will be the effect on reported earnings? On cash flows? On project NPVs? How do you think the stock market might respond if the tax law changes to allow greater accelerated depreciation?

P9-3 Taylor United is considering overhauling its equipment to meet increased demand for its product. The cost of equipment overhaul is €3.8 million, plus €200 000 in installation costs. The firm will depreciate the equipment modifications using a five-year recovery period. Additional sales revenue from the overhaul should amount to €2.2 million per year, and additional operating expenses and other costs (excluding depreciation) will amount to 35 per cent of the additional sales. The firm has an ordinary tax rate of 40 per cent. Answer the following questions about Taylor United, for each of the next six years.

a What additional earnings, before depreciation and taxes, will result from the overhaul?

b What additional earnings after taxes will result from the overhaul?

c What incremental operating cash flows will result from the overhaul?

P9-4 Wilbur Corporation is considering replacing a machine. The replacement will cut operating expenses by €24 000 per year for each of the five years that the new machine is expected to last. Although the old machine has a zero book value, it has a remaining useful life of five years. The depreciable value of the new machine is €72 000. Wilbur will depreciate the machine using a five-year recovery period, and is subject to a 40 per cent tax rate on ordinary income. Estimate the incremental operating cash flows attributable to the replacement. Be sure to consider the depreciation in year 6.

P9-5 Advanced Electronics is considering purchasing a new packaging machine to replace a fully depreciated packaging machine that will last five more years. The new machine is expected to have a five-year life and depreciation charges of €4000 in year 1; €6400 in year 2; €3800 in year 3; €2400 in both year 4 and year 5; and €1000 in year 6. The firm's estimates of revenues and expenses (excluding depreciation) for the new and the old packaging machines are shown in the following table. Advanced Electronics is subject to a 40 per cent tax rate on ordinary income.

YEAR	NEW PACKAGING MACHINE		OLD PACKAGING MACHINE	
	REVENUE	EXPENSES (EXCLUDING DEPRECIATION)	REVENUE	EXPENSES (EXCLUDING DEPRECIATION)
1	€50 000	€40 000	€45 000	€35 000
2	€51 000	€40 000	€45 000	€35 000
3	€52 000	€40 000	€45 000	€35 000
4	€53 000	€40 000	€45 000	€35 000
5	€54 000	€40 000	€45 000	€35 000

a Calculate the operating cash flows associated with each packaging machine. Be sure to consider the depreciation in year 6.

b Calculate the incremental operating cash flows resulting from the proposed packaging machine replacement.

c Depict on a time line the incremental operating cash flows found in part (b).

P9-6 Premium Wines, a producer of medium-quality wines, has maintained stable sales and profits over the past eight years. Although the market for medium-quality wines has been growing by 4 per cent per year, Premium Wines has been unsuccessful in sharing this growth. To increase its sales, the firm is considering an aggressive marketing campaign that centres on regularly running ads in major food and wine magazines and airing TV commercials in large metropolitan areas. The campaign is expected to require an annual tax-deductible expenditure of €3 million over the next five years. Sales revenue, as noted in the following income statement for 2006, totalled €80 million. If the proposed marketing campaign is not initiated,

sales are expected to remain at this level in each of the next five years, 2007–2011. With the marketing campaign, sales are expected to rise to the levels, shown in the sales forecast table, for each of the next five years. The cost of goods sold is expected to remain at 75 per cent of sales; general and administrative expense (exclusive of any marketing campaign outlays) is expected to remain at 15 per cent of sales; and annual depreciation expense is expected to remain at €2 million. Assuming a 40 per cent tax rate, find the relevant cash flows over the next five years associated with Premium Wines' proposed marketing campaign.

Premium Wines Income Statement for the Year Ended 31 December 2006

Sales revenue		€80 000 000
Less: Cost of goods sold (75%)		60 000 000
Gross profits		€20 000 000
Less: Operating expenses		
General and administrative expense (15%)	€12 000 000	
Depreciation expense	2 000 000	
Total operating expense		14 000 000

Net profits before taxes	€ 6 000 000
Less: Taxes (rate = 40%)	2 400 000
Net profits after taxes	€ 3 600 000

Premium Wines sales forecast

Year	Sales revenue
2007	€82 000 000
2008	€84 000 000
2009	€86 000 000
2010	€90 000 000
2011	€94 000 000

The relevant cash flows

P9-7 Identify each of the following situations as involving sunk costs, opportunity costs, and/or cannibalization. Indicate what amount, if any, of these items would be relevant to the given investment decision.

a The investment requires use of additional computer storage capacity to create a data warehouse containing information on all your customers. The storage space you will use is currently leased to another firm for €37 500 per year, under a lease that can be cancelled without penalty by you at any time.

b An investment that will result in producing a new lighter-weight version of one of the firm's best-selling products. The new product will sell for 40 per cent more than the current product. Because of its high price, the firm expects the old product's sales to decline by about 10 per cent from its current level of €27 million.

c An investment of €8 million in a new venture that is expected to grow sales and profits. To date, you have spent €135 000 researching the venture and performing feasibility studies.

d Subleasing 100 parking spaces in your firm's car park to the tenants in an adjacent building that has inadequate off-street parking. You pay €20 per month for each space under a non-cancelable 50-year lease. The sublessee will pay you €15 per month for each space. You have advertised the spaces for over a year with no other takers, and you do not anticipate needing the 100 spaces for many years.

e The firm is considering launching a completely new product that can be sold by your existing salesforce, which is already overburdened with a large catalogue of products to sell. On average, each sales rep sells about €2.1 million per year. You expect that, given the extra time involved in selling the new product, your sales reps will likely devote less time to selling existing products. Although you forecast that the average sales rep will sell about €300 000 of the new product annually, you project a decline of about 7 per cent per year in existing product sales.

P9-8 Barans Manufacturing is developing the incremental cash flows associated with the proposed replacement of an existing stamping machine with a new, technologically advanced one. Given the following costs related to the proposed project, explain whether each would be treated as a sunk cost or an opportunity cost in developing the incremental cash flows associated with the proposed replacement decision.

a Barans could use the same dies and other tools (with a book value of €40 000) on the new stamping machine that it used on the old one.

b Barans could link the new machine to its existing computer system to control its operations. The old stamping machine did not have a computer control system. The firm's excess computer capacity could be leased to another firm for an annual fee of €17 000.

c Barans needs to obtain additional floor space to accommodate the new, larger stamping machine. The space required is currently being leased to another company for €10 000 per year.

d Barans can use a small storage facility, built by Barans at a cost of €120 000 three years earlier, to store the increased output of the new stamping machine. Because of its unique configuration and location, it is currently of no use to either Barans or any other firm.

e Barans can retain an existing overhead crane, which it had planned to sell for its €180 000 market value. Although the crane was not needed with the old stamping machine, it can be used to position raw materials on the new stamping machine.

P9-9 Blueberry Electronics is exploring the possibility of producing a new handheld device that will serve both as a basic PC, with internet access, and as a mobile phone. Which of the following items are relevant for the project's analysis?

a Research and development funds that the company has spent while working on a prototype of the new product.

b The company's current-generation product has no mobile phone capability. The new product may therefore make the old one obsolete in the eyes of many consumers. However, Blueberry expects that other companies will soon bring to market products combining mobile phone and PC features, which will also reduce sales of Blueberry's existing products.

c Costs of ramping up production of the new device.

d Increases in receivables and inventory that will occur as production increases.

Cash flows for GameBuzz.TV

P9-10 Corleone Pizza Company is considering replacing an existing oven with a new, more sophisticated oven. The old oven was purchased three years ago at a cost of €20 000, and this amount was being depreciated using a five-year recovery period. The oven has five years of usable life remaining. The new oven being considered costs €30 500, requires €1500 in installation costs, and would be depreciated using a five-year recovery period. The old oven can currently be sold for €22 000 without incurring any removal or clean-up costs. The firm pays taxes at a rate of 40 per cent on both ordinary income and capital gains. The revenues and expenses (excluding depreciation) associated with the new and the old machines for the next five years are given in the following table.

YEAR	NEW OVEN		OLD OVEN	
	REVENUE	EXPENSES (EXCLUDING DEPRECIATION)	REVENUE	EXPENSES (EXCLUDING DEPRECIATION)
1	€300 000	€288 000	€270 000	€264 000
2	300 000	288 000	270 000	264 000
3	300 000	288 000	270 000	264 000
4	300 000	288 000	270 000	264 000
5	300 000	288 000	270 000	264 000

a Calculate the initial cash outflow associated with replacement of the old oven by the new one.

b Determine the incremental cash flows associated with the proposed replacement. Be sure to consider the depreciation in year 6.

c Depict on a time line the relevant cash flows found in parts (a) and (b), associated with the proposed replacement decision.

P9-11 Speedy Auto Wash is contemplating the purchase of a new high-speed washer to replace the existing washer. The existing washer was purchased two years ago at an installed cost of €120 000; it was being depreciated using a

five-year recovery period. The existing washer is expected to have a usable life of five more years. The new washer costs €210 000 and requires €10 000 in installation costs; it has a five-year usable life and would be depreciated using a five-year recovery period. The existing washer can currently be sold for €140 000, without incurring any removal or clean-up costs. To support the increased business resulting from purchase of the new washer, accounts receivable would increase by €80 000, inventories by €60 000, and accounts payable by €116 000. At the end of five years the existing washer is expected to have a market value of zero; the new washer would be sold to net €58 000 after removal and clean-up costs, and before taxes. The firm pays taxes at a rate of 40 per cent on both ordinary income and capital gains. The estimated profits before depreciation and taxes over the five years for both the new and the existing washer are shown in the following table.

YEAR	PROFITS BEFORE DEPRECIATION AND TAXES	
	NEW WASHER	**EXISTING WASHER**
1	€86 000	€52 000
2	86 000	48 000
3	86 000	44 000
4	86 000	40 000
5	86 000	36 000

a Calculate the initial cash outflow associated with the replacement of the existing washer with the new one.

b Determine the incremental cash flows associated with the proposed washer replacement. Be sure to consider the depreciation in year 6.

c Determine the terminal cash flow expected at the end of year 5 from the proposed washer replacement.

d Depict on a time line the relevant cash flows associated with the proposed washer replacement decision.

P9-12 TransBaltica Shipping Lines is considering replacing an existing ship with one of two newer, more efficient ones. The existing ship is three years old, cost €32 million and is being depreciated using a five-year recovery period. Although the existing ship has only three years (years 4, 5, and 6) of depreciation remaining, it has a remaining usable life of five years. Ship A, one of the two possible replacement ships, costs €40 million to purchase and €8 million to outfit for service. It has a five-year usable life and will be depreciated using a five-year recovery period. Ship B costs €54 million to purchase and €6 million to outfit. It also has a five-year usable life and will be depreciated using a five-year recovery period. Increased investments in net working capital will accompany the decision to acquire ship A or ship B. Purchase of ship A would result in a €4 million increase in net working capital; ship B would result in a €6 million increase in net working capital. The projected profits before depreciation and taxes for each alternative ship and the existing ship are given in the following table.

YEAR	PROFITS BEFORE DEPRECIATION AND TAXES		
	SHIP A	**SHIP B**	**EXISTING SHIP**
1	€21 000 000	€22 000 000	€14 000 000
2	21 000 000	24 000 000	14 000 000
3	21 000 000	26 000 000	14 000 000
4	21 000 000	26 000 000	14 000 000
5	21 000 000	26 000 000	14 000 000

The existing ship can currently be sold for €18 million and will not incur any removal or clean-up costs. At the end of five years, the existing ship can be sold to net €1 million before taxes. Ships A and B can be sold to net €12 million and €20 million before taxes, respectively, at the end of the five-year period. The firm is subject to a 40 per cent tax rate on both ordinary income and capital gains.

a Calculate the initial outlay associated with each alternative.

b Calculate the operating cash flows associated with each alternative. Be sure to consider the depreciation in year 6.

c Calculate the terminal cash flow at the end of year 5, associated with each alternative.

d Depict on a time line the relevant cash flows associated with each alternative.

P9-13 The management of Kimco is evaluating replacing their large mainframe computer with a modern network system that requires much less office space. The network would cost

€500 000 (including installation costs) and, due to efficiency gains, would generate €125 000 per year in operating cash flows (accounting for taxes and depreciation) over the next five years. The mainframe has a remaining book value of €50 000 and would be immediately donated to a charity for the tax benefit. Kimco's cost of capital is 10 per cent and the tax rate is 40 per cent. On the basis of NPV, should management instal the network system?

P9-14 Pointless Luxuries Ltd (PLL) produces unusual gifts targeted at wealthy consumers. The company is analysing the possibility of introducing a new device designed to attach to the collar of a cat or dog. This device emits sonic waves that neutralize airplane engine noise, so that pets travelling with their owners can enjoy a more peaceful ride. PLL estimates that developing this product will require up-front capital expenditures of €10 million. These costs will be depreciated on a straight-line basis for five years. PLL believes that it can sell the product initially for €250. The selling price will increase to €260 in years 2 and 3, before falling to €245 and €240 in years 4 and 5, respectively. After five years the company will withdraw the product from the market and replace it with something else. Variable costs are €135 per unit. PLL forecasts sales volume of 20 000 units the first year, with subsequent increases of 25 per cent (year 2), 20 per cent (year 3), 20 per cent (year 4) and 15 per cent (year 5). Offering this product will force PLL to make additional investments in receivables and inventory. Projected end-of-year balances appear in the following table.

	YEAR 0	YEAR 1	YEAR 2	YEAR 3	YEAR 4	YEAR 5
Accounts receivable	€0	€200 000	€250 000	€300 000	€150 000	€0
Inventory	0	500 000	650 000	780 000	600 000	0

The firm faces a tax rate of 34 per cent. Assume that cash flows arrive at the end of each year, except for the initial €10 million outlay.

a Calculate the project's contribution to net income each year.

b Calculate the project's cash flows each year.

c Calculate two NPVs, one using a 10 per cent discount rate and the other using a 15 per cent discount rate.

d A PLL financial analyst reasons as follows: 'With the exception of the initial outlay, the cash flows from this project arrive in more or less a continuous stream rather than at the end of each year. Therefore, by discounting each year's cash flow for a full year, we are understating the true NPV. A better approximation is to move the discounting six months forward (e.g. discount year 1 cash flows for six months, year 2 cash flows for 18 months and so on), as if all the cash flows arrive in the middle of each year rather than at the end.' Recalculate the NPV (at 10 per cent and 15 per cent) maintaining this assumption. How much difference does it make?

P9-15 TechGiant International (TGI) is evaluating a proposal to acquire Fusion Chips, a young company with an interesting new chip technology. This technology, when integrated into existing TGI silicon wafers, will enable TGI to offer chips with new capabilities to companies with automated manufacturing systems. TGI analysts have projected income statements for Fusion five years into the future. These projections appear in the income statements below, along with estimates of Fusion's asset requirements and accounts payable balances each year. These statements are designed assuming that Fusion remains an independent, stand-alone company. If TGI acquires Fusion, analysts believe that the following changes will occur.

1 TGI's superior manufacturing capabilities will enable Fusion to increase its gross margin on its existing products to 45 per cent.

2 TGI's massive salesforce will enable Fusion to increase sales of its existing products by

10 per cent above current projections (for example, if acquired, Fusion will sell €110 million, rather than €100 million, in 2007). This increase will occur as a consequence of regularly scheduled conversations between TGI salespeople and existing customers and will not require added marketing expenditures. Operating expenses as a per centage of sales will be the same each year as currently forecasted (ranges from 10 per cent to 12 per cent). The fixed asset increases currently projected through 2011 will be sufficient to sustain the 10 per cent increase in sales volume each year.

3 TGI's more efficient receivables and inventory management systems will allow Fusion to increase its sales as previously described, without making investments in receivables and inventory beyond those already reflected in the financial projection. TGI also enjoys a higher credit rating than Fusion, so after the acquisition, Fusion will obtain credit from suppliers on more favourable terms. Specifically, Fusion's accounts payable balance will be

30 per cent higher each year than the level currently forecast.

4 TGI's current cash reserves are more than sufficient for the combined company, so Fusion's existing cash balances will be reduced to €0.

5 Immediately after the acquisition, TGI will invest €50 million in fixed assets to manufacture a new chip that integrates Fusion's technology into one of TGI's best-selling products. These assets will be depreciated on a straight-line basis for eight years. After five years, the new chip will be obsolete, and no additional sales will occur. The equipment will be sold at the end of year 5 for €1 million. Before depreciation and taxes, this new product will generate €20 million in (incremental) profits the first year, €30 million the second year and €15 million in each of the next three years. TGI will have to invest €3 million in net working capital up front, all of which it will recover at the end of the project's life.

6 Both companies face a tax rate of 34 per cent.

Fusion Chips income statements (€000 for years ended 31 December)

	2007	2008	2009	2010	2011
Sales	€100 000	€150 000	€200 000	€240 000	€270 000
– Cost of goods sold	60 000	90 000	120 000	144 000	162 000
Gross profit	€ 40 000	€ 60 000	€ 80 000	€ 96 000	€108 000
– Operating expenses	12 000	17 250	22 000	25 200	27 000
– Depreciation	12 000	18 000	24 000	28 800	32 400
Pre-tax income	€ 16 000	€ 24 750	€ 34 000	€ 42 000	€ 48 600
– Taxes	5 440	8 415	11 560	14 280	16 524
Net income	€ 10 560	€ 16 335	€ 22 440	€ 27 720	€ 32 076

Fusion Chips assets and accounts payable (€000 on 31 December)

	2006	2007	2008	2009	2010	2011
Cash	€ 400	€ 400	€ 525	€ 600	€ 600	€ 600
Accounts receivable	6 000	7 000	10 500	14 000	16 800	18 900
Inventory	10 000	12 500	18 750	25 000	30 000	33 750
Total current assets	€16 400	€ 19 900	€ 29 775	€ 39 600	€ 47 400	€ 53 250
Plant and equipment						
Gross	€80 000	€113 000	€166 500	€226 000	€283 200	€336 900
Net	€50 000	€ 71 000	€106 500	€142 000	€170 400	€191 700
Total assets	€66 400	€ 90 900	€136 275	€181 600	€217 800	€244 950
Accounts payable	€ 7 500	€ 13 500	€ 20 250	€ 27 000	€ 32 400	€ 36 450

Note: The 2006 figures represent the balances currently on Fusion's balance sheet.

a Calculate the cash flows generated by Fusion as a stand-alone entity in each year from 2007 to 2011.

b Assume that by 2011 Fusion reaches a 'steady state', which means that its cash flows will grow by 5 per cent per year in perpetuity. If Fusion discounts cash flows at 15 per cent, what is the present value as at the end of 2011 of all cash flows that Fusion will generate from 2012 forward?

c Calculate the present value, as of 2006, of Fusion's cash flows from 2007 forward. What does this NPV represent?

d Suppose TGI acquires Fusion. Recalculate Fusion's cash flows from 2007 to 2011, making all the changes previously described in items 1–4 and 6.

e Assume that after 2011 Fusion's cash flows will grow at a steady 5 per cent per year. Calculate the present value of these cash flows, as of 2011, if the discount rate is 15 per cent.

f Ignoring item 5 in the list of changes, what is the PV, as of 2006, of Fusion's cash flows from 2007 forward? Use a discount rate of 15 per cent.

g Finally, calculate the NPV of TGI's investment to integrate its technology with Fusion's. Considering this in combination with your answer to part (f), what is the maximum price that TGI should pay for Fusion? Assume a discount rate of 15 per cent.

P9-16 A project generates the following sequence of cash flows over six years:

YEAR	CASH FLOW (€mn)
0	−59.00
1	4.00
2	5.00
3	6.00
4	7.33
5	8.00
6	8.25

a Calculate the NPV over the six years. The discount rate is 11 per cent.

b This project does not end after the sixth year, but instead will generate cash flows far into the future. Estimate the terminal value, assuming that cash flows after year 6 will continue at €8.25 million per year in perpetuity, and then recalculate the investment's NPV.

c Calculate the terminal value, assuming that cash flows after the sixth year grow at 2 per cent annually in perpetuity, and then recalculate the NPV.

d Using market multiples, calculate the terminal value by estimating the project's market value at the end of year 6. Specifically, calculate the terminal value under the assumption that at the end of year 6 the project's market value will be 10 times greater than its most recent annual cash flow. Recalculate the NPV.

Special problems in capital budgeting

P9-17 You have a €10 million capital budget and must make the decision about which investments your firm should accept for the coming year. Projects 1, 2 and 3 in the table below are mutually exclusive and Project 4 is independent of all three. The firm's cost of capital is 12 per cent.

a Use the information on the three mutually exclusive projects to determine which of those three investments your firm should accept on the basis of NPV?

b Which of the three mutually exclusive projects should the firm accept on the basis of PI?

c If the three mutually exclusive projects are the only investments available, which one do you select?

	PROJECT 1	PROJECT 2	PROJECT 3	PROJECT 4
Initial cash outflow	−€4 000 000	−€5 000 000	−€10 000 000	−€5 000 000
Year 1 cash inflow	1 000 000	2 000 000	4 000 000	2 700 000
Year 2 cash inflow	2 000 000	3 000 000	6 000 000	2 700 000
Year 3 cash inflow	3 000 000	3 000 000	5 000 000	2 700 000

d Now given the availability of Project 4, the independent project, which of the mutually exclusive projects do you accept? (Note: Remember, there is a €10 million budget constraint.) Is the better technique in this situation the NPV or the PI? Why?

P9-18 Semper Mortgage wishes to select the best of three possible computers, each expected to meet the firm's growing need for computational and storage capacity. The three computers – A, B, and C – are equally risky. The firm plans to use a 12 per cent cost of capital to evaluate each of them. The initial outlay and the annual cash outflows over the life of each computer are shown in the following table.

	COMPUTER A	COMPUTER B	COMPUTER C
Initial outlay (CF_0)	€50 000	€35 000	€60 000
YEAR (t)		**CASH OUTFLOWS** (CF_t)	
1	€ 7 000	€ 5 500	€18 000
2	7 000	12 000	18 000
3	7 000	16 000	18 000
4	7 000	23 000	18 000
5	7 000	–	18 000
6	7 000	–	18 000

a Calculate the NPV for each computer over its life. Rank the computers in descending order, based on NPV.

b Use the equivalent annual cost (EAC) method to evaluate and rank the computers in descending order, based on the EAC.

c Compare and contrast your findings in parts (a) and (b). Which computer would you recommend that the firm acquire? Why?

P9-19 Kalin Manufacturing is considering the purchase of one of three mutually exclusive projects for improving its assembly line. The firm plans to use a 14 per cent cost of capital to evaluate these equal-risk projects. The initial outlay and the annual cash outflows over the life of each project are shown in the following table.

	PROJECT X	PROJECT Y	PROJECT Z
Initial outlay (CF_0)	€156 000	€104 000	€132 000
YEAR (t)		**CASH OUTFLOWS** (CF_t)	
1	€ 34 000	€ 56 000	€ 30 000
2	50 000	56 000	30 000
3	66 000	–	30 000
4	82 000	–	30 000
5	–	–	30 000
6	–	–	30 000
7	–	–	30 000

a Calculate the NPV for each project over its life. Rank the projects in descending order based on NPV.

b Use the equivalent annual cost (EAC) method to evaluate and rank the projects in descending order based on the EAC.

c Compare and contrast your findings in parts (a) and (b). Which project would you recommend that the firm purchase? Why?

SMART SOLUTIONS

See the problem and solution explained step-by-step at **www.cengage.co.uk/megginson**

P9-20 As part of a hotel renovation programme, a company must choose between two grades of carpet to instal. One grade costs €22 per square metre, and the other, €28. The costs of cleaning and maintaining the carpets are identical, but the less expensive carpet must be replaced after six years, whereas the more expensive one will last nine years before it must be replaced. The relevant discount rate is 13 per cent. Which grade should the company choose?

P9-21 Gail Dribble is a financial analyst at Hill Propane Distributors. Gail must provide a financial analysis of the decision to replace a truck used to deliver propane gas to residential customers. Given its age, the truck will require increasing maintenance expenditures if the company keeps it in service. Similarly, the market value of the truck declines as it ages. The current market value of the truck, as well as the market value and the required maintenance expenditures for each of the next four years, appears below.

YEAR	MARKET VALUE	MAINTENANCE COST
Current	€7 000	€0
1	5 500	2 500
2	3 700	3 600
3	0	4 500
4	0	7 500

The company can purchase a new truck for €40 000. The truck will last 15 years and will require end-of-year maintenance expenditures of €1500. At the end of 15 years the new truck's salvage value will be €3500.

a Calculate the equivalent annual cost (EAC) of the new truck. Use a discount rate of 9 per cent.

b Suppose the firm keeps the old truck one more year and sells it then rather than now.

What is the opportunity cost associated with this decision? What is the present value of the cost of this decision as of today? Restate this cost in terms of year-1 euros.

c Based on your answers to (a) and (b), is it optimal for the company to replace the old truck immediately?

d Suppose the firm decides to keep the truck for another year. Gail must analyse whether replacing the old truck after one year makes sense or whether the truck should stay in use another year. As at the end of year 1, what is the present value of the cost of using the truck and selling it at the end of year 2? Restate this answer in year-2 euros. Should the firm replace the truck after two years?

e Suppose the firm keeps the old truck in service for two years. Should it replace it rather than keep it in service for the third year?

P9-22 A firm that manufactures and sells ball bearings currently has excess capacity. The firm expects that it will exhaust its excess capacity in three years. At that time, it will spend €5 million, which represents the cost of equipment as well as the value of depreciation tax shields on that equipment, to build new capacity. Suppose that this firm can accept additional manufacturing work as a subcontractor for another company. By doing so, the firm will receive net cash inflows of €250 000 immediately, and in each of the next two years. However, the firm will also have to spend €5 million two years earlier than originally planned to bring new capacity on line. Should the firm take on the subcontracting job? The discount rate is 12 per cent. What is the minimum cash inflow that the firm would require (per year) to accept this job?

THOMSON ONE Business School Edition

For instructions on using Thomson ONE, refer to the introductory text provided with the Thomson ONE problems at the end of Chapters 1–6, or in *A Guide for Using Thomson ONE – Business School Edition*.

P9-23 Compute the annual depreciation tax savings for BASF (ticker: D:BAS) over the last five years. Use an average tax rate (income taxes divided by pre-tax income from the income statement) for each year. How have depreciation tax savings changed for BASF over these years?

P9-24 Calculate changes in net working capital for Circuit City Stores, Inc. (ticker: CC) over the last five years. For each year, determine if the change represents a cash inflow or a cash outflow for the company. From the balance sheet, identify source(s) for this change.

MINICASE *Cash flow and capital budgeting*

ACE Rental Cars (ACE) is analysing whether to enter the discount second-hand rental car market. This project would involve the purchase of 100 used, late-model, mid-sized cars at the price of €9500 each. In order to reduce their insurance costs, ACE will have a LoJack Stolen Vehicle Recovery System installed in each automobile at a cost of €1000 per vehicle. ACE will also utilize one of their abandoned parking lots to store the vehicles. If ACE does not undertake this project they could sublease this lot to an car repair company for €80 000 per year. The €20 000 annual maintenance cost on this lot will be paid by ACE whether the lot is subleased or used for this project. In addition, if this project is undertaken, net working capital will increase by €50 000.

The percentage of this equipment's basis that is depreciable each year is 33.33 per cent in year 1, 44.45 per cent in year 2, 14.81 per cent in year 3 and 7.41 per cent in year 4. Each car is expected to generate €4800 a year in revenue and have operating costs of €1000 per year. Starting four years from now, one-quarter of the fleet is expected to be replaced every year with a similar fleet of second-hand cars. This is expected to result in a net cash flow (including acquisition costs) of €100 000 per year continuing indefinitely. This discount rental car business is expected to have a minimal impact on ACE's regular rental car business where the net cash flow is expected to fall by only €25 000 per year. ACE expects to have a marginal tax rate of 32 per cent.

Based on this information, answer the following questions.

Assignment

1 What is the initial cash flow (fixed asset expenditure) for this discount used rental car project?

2 Is the cost of installing the LoJack System relevant to this analysis?

3 Are the maintenance costs relevant?

4 Should you consider the change in net working capital?

5 Estimate the depreciation costs incurred for each of the next four years.

6 Estimate the net cash flow for each of the next four years.

7 How are possible cannibalization costs considered in this analysis?

8 How does the opportunity to sublease the lot affect this analysis?

9 What do you estimate as the terminal value of this project at the end of year four (use a 12 per cent discount rate for this calculation)?

10 Using the standard discount rate of 12 per cent that ACE uses for capital budgeting, what is the NPV of this project? If ACE adjusts the discount rate to 14 per cent to reflect higher project risk, what is the NPV?

Chapter 10
Capital Cost and Capital Budgeting

Opening Focus

What's the cost of capital?

Since the largest firms routinely finance massive capital investment programmes by raising money through public issues of debt and equity securities, virtually all public companies have a 'weighted average cost of capital' that their managers use in deciding whether to accept specific investment projects. Historically, very few of these companies have publicly stated their cost of capital. In recent years, however, this has changed. Consider BASF, the German-based chemicals company. Not only does it disclose its cost of capital, it discusses the role of this in its annual reports. The after-tax cost of capital, as at the end of 2005, was stated by BASF to be 6 per cent. The company also discloses that it has a pre-tax cost of capital of 10 per cent and that it has an internal target of ensuring that earnings before interest and taxes are at least at 10 per cent to cover this cost of capital. Further on it makes clear that its aim is to make a premium on the (pre-tax) cost of capital by improving its cost structure, disciplining capital expenditure and seeking superior growth opportunities.

Another very large company that discloses its policies on the cost of capital is Alcoa Inc. For example, not only did this company specify that its cost of capital was 9 per cent in early 2004, it also went to great lengths to measure how efficiently it employs its capital by benchmarking its own return on capital against the return earned by the most profitable 100 members of the Standard & Poor's 500 Industrial Stock Index. Alcoa's publicly stated goal is to meet the return on capital performance of these top S&P 500 companies.

But how did Alcoa come up with a 9 per cent cost of capital? How did BASF come up with 6 per cent? As we discuss in this chapter, a company should determine a weighted average cost of capital (WACC) by finding the after-tax cost of each major source of financing it plans to tap for funds, and then by computing an average cost based on the fraction of total funding it wants to draw from each source. Though neither Alcoa nor BASF described in detail how they computed their WACC, they do outline in brief how they calculate the basis cost of equity and debt. The cost of equity is related to the market value of shares outstanding, while the cost of debt is determined by the loans the company has outstanding.

LEARNING OBJECTIVES

After studying this chapter you should be able to:

- Differentiate between operating and financial leverage, and the potential effect each of them has on a firm's cost of capital.

- Estimate the firm's weighted average cost of capital, both with and without the allowed tax-deductibility of interest payments to bondholders.

- Review the roles of breakeven analysis and sensitivity analysis in evaluating investment opportunities.

- Explain how scenario analysis, Monte Carlo simulation and decision trees can be used to assess an investment's risk.

- Discuss the human aspects of capital budgeting.

SMART FINANCE
Use the learning tools at www.cengage.co.uk/megginson

This chapter concludes our coverage of capital budgeting. Chapter 8 preached the virtues of NPV analysis and Chapter 9 showed how to generate cash flow estimates required to calculate a project's NPV. This chapter focuses on the risk dimension of project analysis. Remember, that to accurately measure marginal costs (MCs) and marginal benefits (MBs) in financial decision making, we must incorporate risk factors into the analysis. To achieve this objective with regard to NPV, an analyst must evaluate the risk of a project and decide what discount rate adequately reflects the opportunity costs of investors who are willing to invest in the project. In many cases, the best place to discover clues for solving this problem is the market for the firm's securities.

The chapter begins with a discussion of how managers can look to the market to calculate a discount rate that properly reflects the risk of firms' investment projects. Even when managers are confident that they have estimated project cash flows carefully and have chosen a proper discount rate, they want to perform additional analysis to understand the sources of a project's risk. Such tools include breakeven analysis, sensitivity analysis, scenario analysis, simulation and decision trees, all covered in the middle part of this chapter.

10.1 CHOOSING THE RIGHT DISCOUNT RATE

Cost of equity

What discount rate should managers use to calculate a project's NPV? This is a very difficult question indeed, and undoubtedly the source of heated discussions when firms evaluate capital investment proposals. Conceptually, when a firm establishes a project's discount rate, the rate should reflect the opportunity costs of investors who can choose to invest either in the firm's project or in similar projects undertaken by other firms. This is a rather roundabout way of saying that a project's discount rate must be high enough to compensate investors for the project's risk. One implication of this statement is that if a firm undertakes many different kinds of investment projects, each of which may have a different degree of risk, managers go astray if they apply a single, firm-wide discount rate to each investment. In principle, the appropriate discount rate to use in NPV calculations can vary from one investment to another as long as risks vary across investments.

To simplify things a little, consider a firm that finances its operations using only equity and invests in only one industry. Because the firm has no debt, its investments must provide returns sufficient to satisfy just one type of investor, ordinary shareholders. Because the firm invests in only one industry, we may assume that all its investments are equally risky. Therefore, when calculating the NPV of any project that this firm might undertake, its managers can use the required return on equity, often called the cost of equity, as the discount rate. If the firm uses the cost of equity as its discount rate, by definition, any project with a positive NPV will generate returns that exceed shareholders' required returns.

To quantify shareholders' expectations, managers must look to the market. Recall from Chapter 7 that, according to the CAPM, the expected or required return on any security equals the risk-free rate plus the security's beta times the expected market risk premium:

EQUATION 10.1

$$E(R_p) = R_f + \beta[E(R_m) - R_f]$$

Managers can estimate the return that shareholders require if they know (1) their firm's stock beta, (2) the risk-free rate and (3) the expected market risk premium. Research has shown that managers actually do use the CAPM to compute their firm's cost of equity this way.

Applying the Model

Carbonlite manufactures bicycle frames that are both extremely strong and very light. Carbonlite, which finances its operations 100 per cent with equity, is evaluating a proposal to build a new manufacturing facility that will enable the firm to double its frame output within three years. Because Carbonlite sells a luxury good, its fortunes are very sensitive to macroeconomic conditions, and its stock has a beta of 1.5. Carbonlite's financial managers observe that the current interest rate on risk-free government bonds is 5 per cent, and they believe that the expected return on the overall stock market will be about 11 per cent per year in the future. Substituting this information into the CAPM, we find that Carbonlite should calculate the NPV of the expansion proposal using a discount rate of 14 per cent:

$$E(R_p) = 5\% + 1.5[11\% - 5\%] = 14\%$$

To reiterate, Carbonlite can use its cost of equity capital, 14 per cent, to discount cash flows because we have assumed that (1) the company has no debt on its balance sheet and (2) undertaking any of Carbonlite's investment proposals will not alter the firm's risk. If either assumption is invalid, then the cost of equity is not the appropriate discount rate.

In the preceding example, Carbonlite's share beta is 1.5 because sales of premium bicycle frames are highly correlated with the state of the economy. Carbonlite's investment in new capacity is therefore riskier than an investment in new capacity by a firm that produces a product with sales that are relatively insensitive to economic conditions. For example, managers of a food-processing company may apply a lower discount rate to an expansion project than Carbonlite's managers would because the share of a food processor would have a lower beta. The general lesson is that the same type of capital investment project (such as capacity expansion, equipment replacement or new product development) may require different discount rates in different industries. The level of systematic (non-diversifiable) risk varies from one industry to another, and so too should the discount rate used in capital budgeting analysis.

Cost structure and operating leverage Several other factors affect betas, which, in turn, affect project discount rates. One of the most important factors is a firm's cost structure, specifically its mix of fixed and variable costs. In general, holding all other factors constant, the greater the importance of fixed costs in a firm's overall cost structure, the more volatile will be its cash flows and the higher will be its share beta. **Operating leverage** measures the effect of fixed operating costs on the responsiveness of the firm's earnings before interest and taxes (EBIT) to changes in the level of sales. Mathematically, the definition of operating leverage can be expressed as follows:

operating leverage
Measures the tendency of the volatility of operating cash flows to increase with fixed operating costs.

EQUATION 10.2

$$OL = \frac{\Delta EBIT}{EBIT} \bigg/ \frac{\Delta Sales}{Sales}$$

where the symbol Δ means 'change in'. In accounting, operating profits typically equal the firm's EBIT. Operating leverage equals the percentage change in earnings before interest and taxes, divided by the percentage change in sales. When a small percentage increase (decrease) in sales leads to a large percentage increase (decrease) in EBIT, the firm has high operating leverage. The connection between operating leverage and the relative importance of fixed and variable costs is easy to see in the following example.

Applying the Model

Carbonlite uses robotic technology to paint its finished bicycle frames, whereas its main competitor, Fibrespeed Corporation, offers customized, hand-painted finishes to its customers. Robots represent a significant fixed cost for Carbonlite, but its variable costs are quite low. Fibrespeed has very low fixed costs, but it has high variable costs due to the time and effort that is expended painting frames by hand. Both firms sell their bike frames at an average price of €1000 apiece. Last year each firm made a profit of €1 million on sales of 10 000 bicycle frames, as shown in Table 10.1. Suppose next year both firms experience a 10 per cent increase in sales volume to 11 000 frames, holding constant all the other figures. Carbonlite's fixed costs do not change, and its EBIT increases by €600 (€1000 price minus €400 variable costs) per additional frame sold. Carbonlite's total EBIT increases by €600 000 (1000 additional frames × EBIT of €600 per frame), or 60 per cent (from €1 million to €1.6 million), whereas Fibrespeed's total EBIT increases by €300 000 [1000 additional frames × (€1000 price minus €700 variable cost)], or just 30 per cent (from €1 million to €1.3 million).

Because Carbonlite has higher fixed costs and lower variable costs, its EBIT increases more rapidly in response to a given increase in sales than does Fibrespeed's EBIT. Of course, this works both ways: Carbonlite's EBIT will decrease

TABLE 10.1

Financial data for Carbonlite and Fibrespeed

ITEM	CARBONLITE	FIBRESPEED
Fixed cost per year	€5 million	€2 million
Variable cost per bike frame	€400	€700
Sale price per bike frame	€1000	€1000
Contribution margin[a] per bike frame	€600	€300
Last year's sales volume	10 000 frames	10 000 frames
EBIT[b]	€1 million	€1 million

[a] Contribution margin is the sale price per unit minus the variable cost per unit. In this case:
  Carbonlite: €1000 − €400 = €600 per bike
  Fibrespeed: €1000 − €700 = €300 per bike

[b] EBIT equals sales volume times the contribution margin minus fixed costs. In this case:
  Carbonlite: (10 000 × €600) − €5 000 000 = €1 000 000
  Fibrespeed: (10 000 × €300) − €2 000 000 = €1 000 000

more rapidly in response to a given decrease in sales than will Fibrespeed's EBIT. The magnification of changes in sales on EBIT occurs equally in both directions. In short, Carbonlite has more operating leverage. Figure 10.1 shows this graphically. The figure shows two lines, one line tracing out the relationship between sales growth (from the base of 10 000 bicycles per year) and EBIT growth (from the €1 million EBIT base) for Carbonlite, and the other line illustrating the same linkage for Fibrespeed.[1] Because of its higher operating leverage, Carbonlite has a much steeper line than Fibrespeed does. Even though Carbonlite and Fibrespeed compete in the same industry, they may use different discount rates in their capital budgeting analysis because its greater operating leverage increases the risk of Carbonlite's cash flows relative to Fibrespeed's.

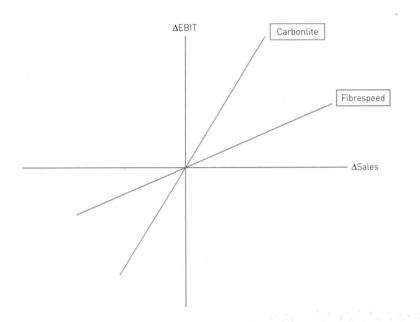

FIGURE 10.1

Operating leverage for Carbonlite and Fibrespeed

The higher operating leverage of Carbonlite is reflected in its steeper slope, demonstrating that its EBIT is more responsive to changes in sales than is the EBIT of Fibrespeed.

Real World

As we have seen already, stock exchanges have the ability like all firms to float on exchanges (including themselves). The consolidation of exchanges however is not just driven by management desires. In 2006 the chief executive of the NYSE, John Thain, stated: 'Exchanges have a lot of operating leverage. If you can consolidate the trading platforms and cut down on the overall technology spend, you can make them much more profitable.' Operating leverage can make a significant contribution to a company's 'bottom line'. Consider online retailer Amazon. Amazon's third quarter 2006 results were excellent, and the market reacted favourably. While part of the improved profitability came from Amazon's ever increasing range of goods sold, Jeff Bezos the CEO also noted the part played by 'significant sequential improvement in operating leverage'.

18 June 2006; 'Groceries, Fashion Rack Up Sales for Amazon', *Financial Times*, 1 February 2007.

---

[1] These comparisons are based on a reference point of 10 000 bikes per year sold at a price of €1000 per bike and EBIT of €1 million. All changes described and shown in Figure 10.1 assume these points of reference in each case. Clearly, the sensitivity of these values to change will vary depending on the point of reference utilized.

Financial structure and financial leverage We have seen that Carbonlite's sales are very sensitive to the business cycle because the firm produces a luxury item. We have also observed that Carbonlite's EBIT is quite sensitive to sales changes due to high operating leverage. Both of these factors contribute to Carbonlite's relatively high share beta of 1.5 and its correspondingly high cost of equity of 14 per cent. One other factor looms large in determining whether firms have high or low share betas. Remember that Carbonlite's financial structure is 100 per cent equity. In practice, it is much more common to see both debt and equity on the right-hand side of a firm's balance sheet. When firms finance their operations with debt and equity, the presence of debt creates **financial leverage**, which leads to a higher share beta. The effect of financial leverage on share betas is much the same as the effect of operating leverage. When a firm borrows money, it creates a fixed cost that it must repay whether sales are high or low.[2] As was the case with operating leverage, an increase (decrease) in sales will lead to sharper increases (decreases) in earnings for a firm with financial leverage compared with a firm that has only equity on its balance sheet.

Table 10.2 illustrates the effect of financial leverage on the volatility of a firm's cash flows, and hence on its beta. The table compares two firms, A and B, which are identical in every respect except that Firm A finances its operations with 100 per cent equity, and Firm B uses 50 per cent long-term debt with an interest rate of 8 per cent, and 50 per cent equity. For simplicity, we assume that neither firm pays taxes. Firms A and B sell identical products at the same price, they both have €100 million in total assets and they face the same operating cost structure. Suppose over the next year both firms generate EBIT equal to 20 per cent of total assets, or €20 million. Firm A pays no interest, so it can distribute all €20 million to its shareholders, a 20 per cent return on their €100 million investment. Firm B pays 8 per cent interest on €50 million for a total interest cost of €4 million (0.08 × €50 million). After paying interest, Firm B can distribute €16 million to shareholders, but that represents a 32 per cent return on their investment of €50 million. Conversely, now suppose that the firms earn EBIT equal to just 5 per cent of assets, or €5 million. Firm A pays out all €5 million to its shareholders, a return of 5 per cent. Firm B pays €4 million in interest, leaving just €1 million to pay out to its shareholders, a return of only 2 per cent. Therefore, in periods when business is very good, shareholders of Firm B earn higher returns than shareholders of Firm A, and the opposite happens when business is bad.

The inclusion of debt as part of a firm's capital structure complicates discount rate selection in two ways. First, as just shown, debt creates financial leverage, which increases a firm's share beta relative to the value that it would be if the firm financed investments only with equity. Secondly, when a firm issues debt, it must satisfy two groups of investors rather than one. Cash flows generated from capital investment projects must be sufficient to meet the return requirements of both bondholders and shareholders. Therefore, a firm that issues debt cannot discount project cash flows using only its cost of equity capital. It must choose a discount rate that reflects the expectations of both investor groups. Fortunately, finance theory offers a way to find that discount rate.

financial leverage
Using debt to magnify both the risk and expected return on a firm's investments. Also, the result of the presence of debt when firms finance their operations with debt and equity, leading to a higher share beta.

---

[2] Note that if the firm enters into a loan arrangement where it pays variable-rate interest this is very unlikely to vary with the level of sales. So we can consider a floating-rate loan as fixed expenses with regard to sales.

TABLE 10.2

The effect of financial leverage on shareholder returns

ACCOUNT	FIRM A	FIRM B
Assets	€100 million	€ 100 million
Debt (interest rate = 8%)	€ 0 (0%)	€ 50 million (50%)
Equity	€100 million (100%)	€ 50 million (50%)
When return on assets equals 20%		
EBIT	€ 20 million	€ 20 million
Less: Interest	0	4 million (0.08 × €50 million)
Cash to equity	€ 20 million	€ 16 million
ROE	€ 20 million/€100 million = 20%	€ 16 million/€50 million = 32%
When return on assets equals 5%		
EBIT	€ 5 million	€ 5 million
Less: Interest	0	4 million (0.08 × €50 million)
Cash to equity	€ 5 million	€ 1 million
ROE	€ 5 million/€100 million = 5%	€ 1 million/€50 million = 2%

Weighted average cost of capital (WACC)

In Chapter 7 we learned that the expected return on a portfolio of two assets equalled the weighted average of the expected returns of each asset in the portfolio. We can apply that idea to the problem of selecting an appropriate discount rate for a firm that has both debt and equity in its capital structure. Imagine that Alpha AFC, a soccer club, has outstanding €100 million worth of ordinary shares on which investors require a return of 15 per cent. In addition, the firm has outstanding €50 million in bonds that offer a 9 per cent return.[3] To simplify our discussion, we hold the firm's overall risk constant by assuming that the investments being considered do not change either the firm's cost structure or financial structure. Using this information, we can answer the question: What rate of return must the firm earn on its investments to satisfy both groups of investors?

The basic formula The answer lies in a concept known as the **weighted average cost of capital (WACC)**. Let the letters D and E represent the market value of the firm's debt and equity securities, respectively, and let r_d and r_e represent the rate of return that investors require on bonds and shares. The WACC is the simple weighted average of the required rates of return on debt and equity, where the weights equal the percentage of each type of financing in the firm's overall financial structure.

$$WACC = \left(\frac{D}{D+E} \right) r_d + \left(\frac{E}{D+E} \right) r_e$$

weighted average cost of capital (WACC)
The after-tax weighted average required return on all types of securities issued by a firm, in which the weights equal the percentage of each type of financing in a firm's overall financial structure.

EQUATION 10.3

[3] The return we have in mind here is the yield to maturity (YTM) – developed in Chapter 4 – on the firm's bonds. Unless the bonds sell at par, the coupon rate and the YTM will be different, but the YTM provides a better measure of the return that investors who purchase the firm's debt can expect.

Plugging in the values from our example, we find that the WACC for Alpha AFC equals 13 per cent:

$$WACC = \left(\frac{50}{50 + 100}\right)9\% + \left(\frac{100}{50 + 100}\right)15\% = 13\%$$

How can Alpha's managers be sure that a 13 per cent return on its investments will satisfy the expectations of both bondholders and shareholders? There are two ways to see the answer. First, imagine that a wealthy US-based investor in sports clubs decides to purchase all the outstanding debt and equity securities of Alpha. One-third of the portfolio would contain the firm's bonds, with an expected return of 9 per cent, and two-thirds of the investor's portfolio would consist of Alpha shares, with an expected return of 15 per cent. Relying on the portfolio theory concepts covered in Chapter 7, we can conclude that the expected return on this wealthy investor's portfolio would be 13 per cent. If the firm invests (1) only in projects that do not alter the firm's overall risk and (2) in projects that have positive NPVs (i.e. projects offering returns in excess of 13 per cent), it will generate returns that exceed the investor's expectations.

Here's a second way to verify that the WACC is the proper hurdle rate for Alpha. Suppose the company invests in iSpike, a professional ice-hockey team. It is used to owning, managing and running top-notch sports and so the project does not alter the firm's overall risk. Let's further assume that iSpike earns exactly 13 per cent. It therefore has a zero NPV if the company uses the WACC as its hurdle rate. Alpha has €150 million in assets. A project that offers a 13 per cent return will generate €19.5 million in cash flow each year (13% × €150 million). Suppose that the company distributes this cash flow to its investors. Will they be satisfied? Table 10.3 illustrates that the cash flow the company generates is just enough to meet the expectations of bondholders and shareholders. Bondholders receive €4.5 million, or exactly the 9 per cent return they expected when they purchased bonds. Shareholders receive €15 million, representing a 15 per cent return on their €100 million investment in the firm's shares.

The WACC is a figure of critical importance to almost all firms. Firms that use the WACC to value real investments know that a higher WACC means that investments have to pass a higher hurdle before they generate shareholder wealth. If an event beyond the firm's control increases the firm's WACC, both its existing assets and its prospective investment opportunities become less valuable. The Comparative Corporate Finance panel describes what happens to the corporate cost of capital when a nation that has been closed to inflows of foreign investment from abroad decides to open up to foreign investors.

COMPARATIVE CORPORATE FINANCE

Does opening up to the world reduce the corporate cost of capital?

What happens to the corporate cost of capital when a nation that has been closed to inflows of financial investment from abroad decides to open up to foreign investors? Finance theory suggests that capital account liberalization – the process of allowing in foreign capital – should reduce the overall cost of external financing for the country's publicly traded companies by increasing the supply of potential lenders and equity investors from whom domestic firms can obtain external financing. Empirical evidence now strongly supports this idea.

A recent academic study by Peter Blair Henry found that three economically important things happen when emerging economies open their stock markets to foreign investors. First, the average cost of equity capital, as measured by the aggregate dividend yield on publicly traded stocks, falls by 240 basis points (2.4 per cent) over the five years after liberalization. Secondly, the nation's overall stock of capital increases by an average of 1.1 percentage point per year, meaning that companies invest more in productive assets. Thirdly, the growth rate of output per worker rises by 2.3 percentage points per year. Because the cost of capital falls, the amount of investment increases sharply, and the productivity of workers rises rapidly when countries open their stock markets.

This result has been confirmed more recently in the work of Patro. Unlike Henry, who looked at aggregate stock market index level data, Patro and Wald looked at individual firms (nearly 2000 of them) in the same 18 countries as Blair. Their findings were of a slightly lower drop in mean dividend yield, by on average 137 basis points (1.37 per cent) in the six years after liberalization. However, this average masked some very large changes, the country with the greatest fall being Turkey, where dividend yields fell by 387 basis points! Finally, Collins and Abrahamson examined the cost of equity for African companies over the 1990s. They found in their study of six African markets that the cost of equity fell very significantly in all sectors and in all markets (except Morocco) over the 1990s, a period of significant liberalization and opening up of markets.

Sources: Peter Blair Henry (2003) 'Capital Account Liberalization: The Cost of Capital, and Economic Growth', *American Economic Review, Papers and Proceedings* 93:91–96. Dilip K. Patro and John K. Wald (2005) 'Firm Characteristics and the Impact of Emerging Market Liberalizations', *Journal of Banking & Finance*, 29(7):1671–1695; Daryl Collins and Mark Abrahamson (2006) 'Measuring the Cost of Equity in African Financial Markets', *Emerging Markets Review*, 7(1):67–81.

Modifying the basic WACC formula Firms can modify the WACC formula to accommodate more than two sources of financing. The weighted average is simply that – a weighted average where the weights are the percentage of the capital structure that each element accounts for. In general therefore, letting i stand for each individual source of capital (ordinary shares, preference shares, bonds, bank loans, etc.), v for the value of any capital source and K for the total capital, made up of the sum of the market values of all these individual capital sources, we have:

$$WACC = \sum_{i=bond,\ etc}^{n} \frac{v_i}{K} r_i$$

Source: Adapted from 'The Nuclear Liabilities', *Financial Times* Lex column, 8 March 2005.

Real World

Lest we think that the discount rate issue is a mechanical one, remember that it underlies the calculation of NPV. In 2005 the influential Lex column in the *Financial Times* noted a recent analyst's report on two energy companies, E.ON and RWE. A report by an investment bank had stated that the companies were overly cautious in valuation of the costs of decommissioning nuclear plants. The report noted that, in some cases the companies were using a zero per cent discount rate, ignoring the time value of money and thus massively overstating the net present value of the costs of the clean-ups. For the companies this meant that their market value was reduced by several billion euro.

ITEM	DISTRIBUTION
Total cash flow available to distribute (13% × €150 million)	€19.5 million
Less: Interest owed on bonds (9% × €50 million)	4.5 million
Cash available to shareholders (€19.5 million − €4.5 million)	€15.0 million

Rate of return earned by shareholders (€15 million ÷ €100 million) 15%

TABLE 10.3

Cash distributions to Alpha investors

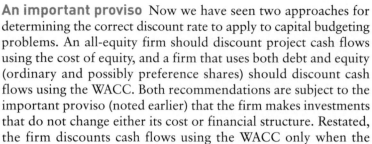

An important proviso Now we have seen two approaches for determining the correct discount rate to apply to capital budgeting problems. An all-equity firm should discount project cash flows using the cost of equity, and a firm that uses both debt and equity (ordinary and possibly preference shares) should discount cash flows using the WACC. Both recommendations are subject to the important proviso (noted earlier) that the firm makes investments that do not change either its cost or financial structure. Restated, the firm discounts cash flows using the WACC only when the project under consideration is very similar to the firm's existing assets, and the firm's financing mix remains unchanged. For example, assuming an unchanged financing mix, if managers at Alpha AFC believe that the firm should vertically integrate its merchandising by investing in a cotton mill, they should not discount cash flows from that investment at the firm's WACC. The risks of running a cotton mill hardly resemble those of running a sports team, and it is the latter that is reflected in the firm's WACC. Evaluating investments that deviate significantly from a firm's existing investments requires a different approach. To understand this approach, we need to revisit the CAPM to see how it is related to the WACC.

The WACC, CAPM and taxes

The CAPM states that the required return on any asset is directly linked to the asset's beta. By now we are used to thinking about betas of ordinary shares, but there is nothing about the CAPM that restricts its predictions to shares. When a firm issues preference shares and bonds, the required returns on those securities should reflect their systematic risks (i.e. their betas) just as the required returns on the firm's ordinary shares do. Because both preference shares and bonds generally make fixed, predictable cash payments over time, measuring the rate of return that investors require on these securities is relatively easy, even without knowing their betas. For preference shares, the dividend yield (annual dividend divided by price) provides a good measure of required returns, and for debt, the yield to maturity (YTM) does the same. However, this does not rule out the possibility that we could estimate the beta of a preference shares or of a bond in much the same manner as we do for ordinary shares. But we will save that discussion for a more advanced course.

The main lessons Summarizing the main lessons we have learned thus far, we offer the following rules about finding the right discount rate for an investment project:

1 When an all-equity firm invests in an asset similar to its existing assets (i.e. its cost structure remains unchanged), the cost of equity is the appropriate discount rate to use in NPV calculations.

2 When a firm with both debt and equity invests in an asset similar to its existing assets, the WACC is the appropriate discount rate to use in NPV calculations, as long as its financial structure remains unchanged.

3 The WACC reflects the return that the firm must earn on average across all its assets to satisfy investors, but using the WACC to discount cash flows of a particular investment can lead to mistakes. The reason for this is that a particular investment may be more or less risky than the firm's average investment, requiring a higher or lower discount rate than the WACC, assuming an unchanged financial structure.

Considering taxes Nothing in the real world is as simple as it is portrayed in textbooks. One important item that we have neglected thus far is the effect of taxes on project discount rates. In many countries, corporations must pay taxes on their earnings, but interest payments to bondholders are tax deductible. Thus the costs of debt and equity above should be the *after-tax* costs. In the case of equity the cost is the same pre and post tax, but the cost of debt should be calculated as $r_d(1 - T_c)$, where T_c is the marginal corporate tax rate. The WACC formula becomes:

$$WACC = \left(\frac{D}{D + E} \right)(1 - T_c)r_d + \left(\frac{E}{D + E} \right)r_e$$

EQUATION 10.4

Fortunately, the three main lessons listed previously do not change when we add taxes to the picture. Only the calculations change. When a firm is making an 'ordinary' investment, it can use Equation 10.4 to determine its after-tax WACC, which serves as the discount rate in NPV calculations.

Source: Adapted from 'Vodafone Wins Essar', *Financial Times*, 12 February 2007; 'Danish Tax Plan for Company Borrowing Comes Under Fire', *Financial Times*, 3 February 2007.

Real World

Vodafone provides us with an interesting insight into the interaction of taxes and the cost of capital. In 2007 the company acquired a 67 per cent stake in Essar, the fourth largest Indian mobile phone company, spending £11 billion. The company stated that it expected the return to be in excess of the cost of capital by 2011. However, commentators noted that the predicted cost of capital for the company was based on a forecast by Vodafone of continuing low tax rates.

The interaction of tax rates and capital costs is thus perhaps surprising: as the tax rate falls the cost of capital rises. This lay at the heart of the debate in Denmark in 2007 over the country's tax rates. The government wished to reduce both the corporate tax rate and the extent to which debt can be used to offset taxes. Part of the debate involved a political fear that private equity funds were gaining too much dominance in Denmark. Private equity funds are companies who have very high leverage and who purchase companies and (sometimes very aggressively) restructure them. On the Danish proposals, one private equity executive said: 'It would stop private equity, real estate, infrastructure funds from investing in Denmark and increase the cost of capital for Danish companies to the extent they use leverage.' So while it's unusual to see companies seeking higher tax rates, such rates can sometimes work in their favour.

1 Why is using the cost of equity to discount project cash flows inappropriate when a firm uses both debt and equity in its capital structure?

2 Two firms in the same industry have very different equity betas. Offer two reasons why this could occur.

3 For a firm considering expansion of its existing line of business, why is the WACC, rather than the cost of equity, the preferred discount rate if the firm has both debt and equity in its capital structure?

4 The cost of debt, r_d, is generally less than the cost of equity, r_e, because debt is a less risky security. A naïve application of the WACC formula may suggest that a firm could lower its cost of capital (thereby raising the NPV of its current and future investments) by using more debt and less equity in its capital structure. Give one reason why using more debt may not lower a firm's WACC, even if $r_d < r_e$.

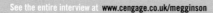
10.2 A CLOSER LOOK AT RISK

Thus far, the only consideration we have given to risk when performing capital budgeting analysis is selecting the right discount rate. But it would be simplistic to say that, given a set of project cash flows, once an analyst has discounted those cash flows using a risk-adjusted discount rate to determine the NPV, the analyst's work is done. Managers generally want to know more about a project than just its NPV. They want to know the sources of uncertainty in the project as well as the quantitative importance of each source. Managers need this information to decide whether a project requires additional analysis, such as market research or product testing. Managers also want to identify a project's key value drivers, so they can closely monitor them after an investment is made. In this section, we explore several techniques that give managers deeper insights into the uncertainty structure of capital investments.

Breakeven analysis

breakeven analysis
The study of what is required for a project's profits and losses to balance out.

When firms make investments, they do so with the objective of making a profit. But another objective that sometimes enters the decision process is avoiding losses. Managers often want to know what is required for a project to break even. **Breakeven analysis** can be formulated in many different ways. For instance, when a firm introduces a new product, it may want to know the level of sales at which incremental net income turns from negative to positive. Evaluating a new product launch over several years, managers may ask what growth rate in sales the firm must achieve to reach a project NPV of zero. When considering a decision to replace old production equipment, a firm may calculate the level of production volume needed to generate cost savings equal to the cost of the new equipment. The standard equation for the **breakeven point (BEP)** is found by dividing the fixed costs (FC) by the **contribution margin**, which is the sale price per unit (SP) minus variable cost per unit (VC).

breakeven point (BEP)
The level of sales or production that a firm must achieve in order to avoid losses by fully covering all costs. Calculated by dividing total fixed costs (FC) by the contribution margin.

contribution margin
The sale price per unit (SP) minus variable cost per unit (VC).

EQUATION 10.5

$$BEP = \frac{Fixed\ costs}{Contribution\ margin} = \frac{FC}{SP - VC}$$

Applying the Model

Take another look at Table 10.1, which shows price and cost information for two companies – Carbonlite and Fibrespeed. How many bicycle frames must each firm sell to achieve a breakeven point with EBIT equal to zero? We can obtain the answer by substituting the data for each firm into Equation 10.5.

Carbonlite breakeven point = €5 000 000 ÷ (€1000 − €400)
= 8333 frames

Fibrespeed breakeven point = €2 000 000 ÷ (€1000 − €700)
= 6667 frames

Figures 10.2a and 10.2b illustrate the breakeven point (BEP) for each firm. Despite its €600 contribution margin, Carbonlite's high fixed costs result in a breakeven point at higher sales volume than Fibrespeed's breakeven point. This should not surprise us, as we already know that Carbonlite's production process results in higher operating leverage than Fibrespeed's.

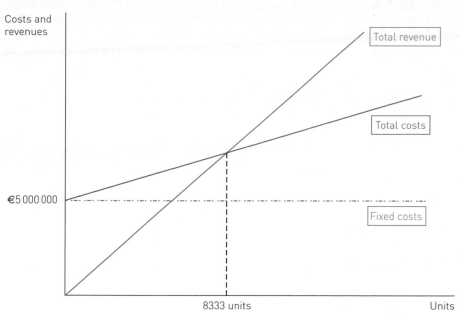

Carbonlite has high fixed costs (€5 000 000), and also a high contribution margin (€ 600/bike). High BEP, but profits grow rapidly after FC are covered.

FIGURE 10.2a

Breakeven point for Carbonlite

The breakeven point (BEP) for Carbonlite is 8333 units, which occurs at the point where its total costs equal its total revenue.

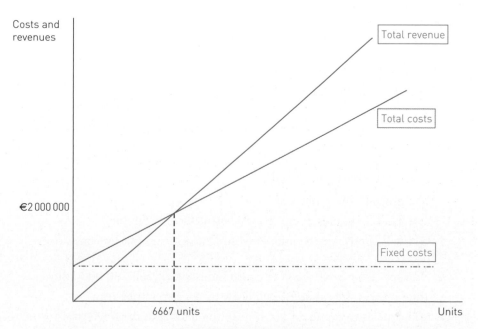

Fibrespeed has low fixed costs (€2 000 000), and also a high contribution margin (€ 300/bike). Low BEP, but profits grow slowly after FC are covered.

FIGURE 10.2b

Breakeven point for Fibrespeed

The breakeven point (BEP) for Fibrespeed is 6667 units, which occurs at the point where its total costs equal its total revenue.

The popularity of breakeven analysis among practitioners arises, in part, because it gives managers very clear targets. From breakeven calculations, managers can derive specific targets for different functional areas in the firm (e.g. produce at least 10 000 units, gain at least a 5 per cent market share, hold variable costs to no more than 65 per cent of the selling price). As always, we encourage managers to use breakeven analysis in the context of net present values rather than earnings. A project that reaches the breakeven point in terms of net income may destroy shareholder value because it does not recover the firm's cost of capital.

Source: 'Next Delay for A380: A Decade Before Break Even', *International Herald Tribune*, 19 October 2006.

Real World

Recall in an earlier chapter that we spoke about the battle between Airbus and Boeing over the future of the airliner. Both companies provide breakeven analyses. Boeing analysts estimate breakeven at 250, while Airbus, after the delays and problems, raised its breakeven number to 420 A380s.

Sensitivity analysis

sensitivity analysis A tool that allows exploration of the impact of individual assumptions on a decision variable, such as a project's net present value, by determining the effect of changing one variable while holding all others fixed.

Most capital budgeting problems require analysts to make many different assumptions before arriving at a final NPV. For instance, forecasting project cash flows may require assumptions about the selling price of output, costs of raw materials, market share and many other unknown quantities. In **sensitivity analysis**, managers have a tool that allows them to explore the impact of each individual assumption, holding all other assumptions fixed, on the project's NPV. To conduct a sensitivity analysis, firms establish a 'base-case' set of assumptions for a particular project and calculate the NPV based on those assumptions. Next, managers allow one variable to change while holding all others fixed, and they recalculate the NPV based on that change. By repeating this process for all the uncertain variables in an NPV calculation, managers can see how sensitive the NPV is to changes in base-case assumptions. An example can be used to illustrate this procedure.

Applying the Model

Imagine that Greene Transportation International (GTI) has developed a new skateboard equipped with a gyroscope for improved balance. GTI's estimates indicate that this project has a positive NPV of €236 000, under the following base-case assumptions:

1 The project's life is five years.
2 The project requires an up-front investment of €7 million.
3 GTI will depreciate the initial investment on a straight-line basis over five years.
4 One year from now, the skateboard industry will sell 500 000 units.
5 Total market size (in units) will grow by 5 per cent per year.
6 GTI expects to capture 5 per cent of the market in the first year.
7 GTI expects to increase its market share by one percentage point each year after year 1.

8 The selling price will be €200 in year 1.

9 The selling price will decline by 10 per cent per year after year 1.

10 All production costs are variable and will equal 60 per cent of the selling price.

11 GTI's marginal tax rate is 30 per cent.

12 The appropriate discount rate is 14 per cent.

Under the base-case assumptions, the project's positive NVP of €236 000 is small relative to the €7 million investment. GTI's managers want to explore how sensitive the NPV is to changes in the assumptions. Analysts often begin a sensitivity analysis by developing both pessimistic and optimistic forecasts for each of the model's important assumptions. These forecasts may be based on subjective judgements about the range of possible outcomes or on historical data drawn from the firm's past investments. For example, a firm with historical data available on output prices may set the pessimistic and optimistic forecasts at one standard deviation below and above their expected price.

Table 10.4 shows pessimistic and optimistic forecasts for several of the NPV model's key assumptions. Next to each assumption is the project NPV that results from changing one, and only one, assumption from the base-case scenario. For example, if GTI can sell its product for €225 rather than €200 per unit the first year, the project NPV increases to €960 000. If, however, the selling price is less than expected, at €175 per unit, the project NPV declines to −€488 000. A glance at Table 10.4 reveals that changes in market share assumptions generate very large NPV changes, whereas similar changes in market-size figures have less impact on NPVs.

Real World

Companies do use these sensitivity analysis methods to evaluate projects. Consider the Irish telecoms company, Eircom. In their financial statements for the year ended March 2006 they discuss the value of goodwill in their operations. The values given on the balance sheet are tested against a number of scenarios. For the fixed line business they normally use a WACC of 8.5 per cent but also tested a value of 9.5 per cent. For the mobile business they tested the normal rate of 11.5 per cent against a value of 12.5 per cent. In addition, the DCF calculations assumed a certain growth rate in the terminal value of the cash flows, and these were tested against a zero growth rate.

Source: Eircom PLC Annual Report, 2006.

NPV	PESSIMISTIC	ASSUMPTION	OPTIMISTIC	NPV
−€ 558	€8 000	Initial investment	€6 000	€1 030
−€ 343	450 000 units	Market size in year 1	550 000 units	€ 815
−€ 73	2% per year	Growth in market size	8% per year	€ 563
−€1 512	3%	Initial market share	7%	€1 984
−€1 189	0%	Growth in market share	2% per year	€1 661
−€ 488	€175	Initial selling price	€225	€ 960
−€ 54	62% of sales	Variable costs	58% of sales	€ 526
−€ 873	−20% per year	Annual price change	0% per year	€1 612
−€ 115	16%	Discount rate	12%	€ 617

TABLE 10.4

Sensitivity analysis of the gyroscope skateboard project (base-case NPV = €236 000) (euro values in thousands, except price)

Scenario analysis and Monte Carlo simulation

scenario analysis
A more complex form of
sensitivity analysis that
provides for calculating
the decision variable,
such as net present
value, when a whole
set of assumptions
changes in a
particular way.

Scenario analysis is just a more complex form of sensitivity analysis. Rather than adjust one assumption up or down, analysts conduct scenario analysis by calculating the project NPV when a whole set of assumptions changes in a particular way. For example, if consumer interest in GTI's new skateboard is low, the project may achieve a lower market share and a lower selling price than originally anticipated. If production volume falls short of expectations, cost as a percentage of sales may also be higher than expected.

Developing realistic scenarios requires a great deal of thinking about how an NPV model's assumptions are related to each other. Analysts must ask questions such as, if the market doesn't grow as fast as we expect, which other of our assumptions will also probably be wrong? As with sensitivity analysis, firms often construct a base-case scenario along with more pessimistic and optimistic ones. For instance, consider a worst-case scenario for GTI's new skateboard. Suppose Murphy's Law is manifested, and every pessimistic assumption from Table 10.4 becomes a reality. In that case, the project NPV is a disastrous negative €4.9 million. On the other hand, if all the optimistic assumptions turn out to be correct, then the NPV rises to €11.7 million. Neither of these outcomes is particularly surprising. If everything goes wrong, the company should expect an extremely negative NPV, and it should expect just the opposite if the project does better than predicted in every possible way. These scenarios are still useful because they illustrate the range of possible NPVs.

Monte Carlo simulation
A sophisticated risk
assessment technique
that provides for
calculating the decision
variable, such as net
present value, using a
range or probability
distribution of potential
outcomes for each of a
model's assumptions.

An even more sophisticated variation on this theme is Monte Carlo simulation. In a simulation, analysts specify a range or a probability distribution of potential outcomes for each of the model's assumptions. For example, a simulation could specify that GTI's skateboard price is a random variable drawn from a normal distribution with a mean of €200 and a standard deviation of €30. Similarly, the analyst could dictate that the skateboard could achieve an initial market share anywhere between 1 per cent and 10 per cent, with each outcome being equally likely (i.e. a uniform distribution). It is even possible to specify the degree of correlation between key variables. The model could be structured in such a way that when the demand for skateboards is unusually high, the likelihood of obtaining a high price increases.

Analysts enter all the assumptions about distributions of possible outcomes into a spreadsheet. Next, a simulation software package begins to take random 'draws' from these distributions, calculating the project's cash flows (and perhaps its NPV) over and over again, perhaps thousands or tens of thousands of times. After completing these calculations, the software package produces a large amount of statistical output, including the probability distribution of project cash flows (and NPVs) as well as sensitivity figures for each of the model's assumptions.

The use of Monte Carlo simulation has grown dramatically in the last decade because of steep declines in the costs of computer power and simulation software. The bottom line is that simulation is a powerful, effective tool when used properly. Its fundamental appeal is that it provides decision makers with a probability distribution of NPVs rather than a single point estimate of the *expected* NPV. This improves the information available to decision makers by allowing them to consider the risk (probability distribution) as well as the expected value of NPV. Using simulation to explore the distribution of a project's cash flows and NPVs, and the major sources of uncertainty driving that distribution, is very sensible, and is expected to result in better investment decisions.

Decision trees

Most important investment decisions involve much more complexity than simply forecasting cash flows, discounting at the appropriate rate and investing if the NPV exceeds zero. In the real world, managers face a sequence of future decisions that influence an investment's value. These decisions may include whether to expand or abandon a project, whether to alter a marketing programme, when to upgrade manufacturing equipment, and, most important, how to respond to actions of competitors. A **decision tree** is a visual representation of the sequential choices that managers face over time with regard to a particular investment. Sketching out a decision tree is somewhat like thinking several moves ahead in a game of chess. The value of decision trees is that they force analysts to think through a series of 'if–then' statements that describe how they will react as the future unfolds. The following example illustrates the use of decision trees.

decision tree
A visual representation of the sequential choices that managers face over time with regard to a particular investment.

Applying the Model

Imagine that Arom, an independent cosmetics company, has invented a new ultraviolet sensitive foundation, branded Tattu, which it is aiming at the younger teenage market. The company is trying to decide whether to spend €5 million to test-market in Germany. Depending on the outcome of that test, Arom may spend an additional €50 million one year later to launch a full line of similar products across Europe. If consumer acceptance in Germany is high, the company predicts that its full product line will generate net cash inflows of €12 million per year for ten years.[4] If consumers in Germany respond less favourably, Arom expects cash inflows from a nationwide launch to be just €2 million per year for ten years. Arom's cost of capital equals 15 per cent.

Figure 10.3 shows the decision tree for this problem. Initially, the firm can choose to spend the €5 million on test-marketing or not. If Arom goes

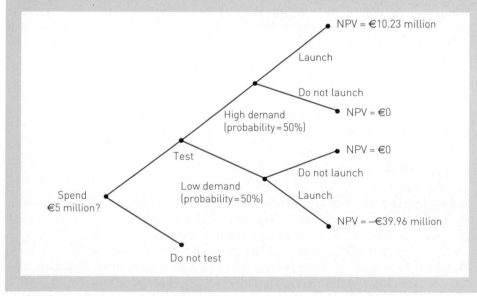

FIGURE 10.3

Decision tree for Tattu investment

The decision tree depicts the sequence of decisions affecting Arom's decision whether to spend €5 million to test market Tattu. If the test market is successful, the NPV of launching the product is €10.23 million; if the initial test results are negative, and it launches the product, it will have an NPV of −€39.96 million.

---

[4] Note that the test begins immediately, the €50-million investment starts one year later, and the stream of €12-million annual cash inflows begins one year after that.

ahead with the market test, it estimates the probability of high-and low consumer acceptance to be 50 per cent. Once the company sees the test results, it can decide whether to invest €50 million for a major product launch.

The proper way to work through a decision tree is to begin at the end and work backward to the initial decision. Suppose one year from now, Arom learns that the German market test was successful. At that point, the NPV of launching the product can be determined as follows:

$$NPV = -50 + \frac{12}{1.15^1} + \frac{12}{1.15^2} + \cdots + \frac{12}{1.15^{10}} = 10.23$$

Clearly, Arom will invest if it winds up in this part of the decision tree, but what if initial test results are unfavourable and it launches the product? In that situation, the following NPV results:

$$NPV = -50 + \frac{12}{1.15^1} + \frac{12}{1.15^2} + \cdots + \frac{12}{1.15^{10}} = -39.96$$

The best decision to make if the initial test does not go well is to walk away. After the test has been done, its cost is a sunk cost. Therefore, as of time 1, the NPV of doing nothing is zero.

Now we have a set of simple 'if–then' decision rules that come from the decision tree. If initial test results indicate high consumer acceptance of Tattu, Arom should go ahead with the full product launch to capture a positive NPV of €10.23 million. On the other hand, if initial results show that consumers do not particularly want Tattu, Arom should not invest the additional €50 million.

Finally, with this information in hand, we can evaluate today's decision about whether to spend the €5 million on testing. Recall that we calculated the NPVs in terms of year-1 euros – that is, as of the date of the decision whether or not to launch the product nationwide. In terms of today's money the expected NPV of conducting the market test is determined as follows:

$$NPV = -5 + 0.5\left(\frac{10.23}{1.15}\right) + 0.5\left(\frac{0}{1.15}\right) = -0.55$$

Spending the money for market testing does not appear to be worthwhile.

Evaluating the role of decision trees There is a very subtle flaw in the preceding analysis of Arom's proposed Tattu investment. Can you spot it? At the present time, when Arom must decide whether to invest in test-marketing, it does not know what the results of the test will be. One year later, when the firm chooses whether to invest €50 million for a major product launch, it knows a great deal more. If Tattu is a big success in Germany, the risk that it will flop elsewhere in Europe may be very low. If so, does it make sense to use a discount rate of 15 per cent when calculating the NPV of the product launch decision? Even a one-point reduction in the discount rate, from 15 per cent to 14 per cent, would be sufficient to change Arom's decision about test-marketing.

Though decision trees are useful tools for sharpening strategic thinking, the previous example illustrates their most serious flaw. The risk of many investments changes as you move from one point in the decision tree to another. Worse, analysts have no obvious way to make adjustments to the discount rate to reflect these risk changes. That makes it very difficult to know whether the final NPV obtained from a decision tree is the correct one.

Another practical difficulty in using decision trees is determining the probabilities for each branch of the tree. Unless firms have a great deal of experience making similar 'bets' over and over again, estimating these probabilities is more an art than a science. How does Arom know that the probability of a successful Germany market test equals 50 per cent? Why not 80 per cent, or 10 per cent? The only way to form even remotely reliable estimates of these probabilities is to rely on experience – your experience or the experience of others. For example, large pharmaceutical companies have enough experience investing in potential drug compounds to make reasonable estimates of the odds that any particular drug will make it to market.

CONCEPT
REVIEW
QUESTIONS

5 Why would a project that reaches the breakeven point (BEP) in terms of net income be potentially bad for shareholders?

6 Which variable do you think would be more valuable to examine in a project sensitivity analysis – the growth rate of sales or the allowable depreciation deductions each year? Explain.

7 You work for an airline that is considering a proposal to offer a new, non-stop flight between Madrid and Tokyo. Senior management asks a team of analysts to run a Monte Carlo simulation of the project. Your job is to advise the group on what assumptions they should put in the simulation regarding the distribution of the ticket price your airline will be able to charge. How would you go about this task?

8 Why might the discount rate vary as you move through a decision tree?

10.3 THE HUMAN FACE OF CAPITAL BUDGETING

We have been examining capital budgeting as though it was a cut-and-dried method. In general, however, it is not. There are relatively simple rules of thumb that guide managers in this task, but executing these rules in practice is an obvious challenge. Deciding which costs are incremental and which are not, incorporating the myriad of tax factors that influence cash flows, and measuring opportunity costs properly are much more complex manoeuvres than we or anyone else can convey in a textbook. The nuances of capital budgeting are best learned through practice.

There is another factor that makes real-world capital budgeting more complicated than textbook examples – the *human element*. Neither the ideas for capital investments nor the financial analysis used to evaluate them occur in a vacuum. Almost any investment proposal important enough to warrant a thorough financial analysis has a champion behind it – someone who believes that the project is a good idea and perhaps will advance the individual's own career. When companies allocate investment capital across projects or divisions, they must recognize the potential for an optimistic bias to creep into the numbers. This bias can arise through intentional manipulation of the cash flows to make an investment look more attractive, or it may simply arise if

**SMART
ETHICS
VIDEO**

**Jon Olson,
Vice President of
Finance, Intel Corp.**

'Our job at the company is to test the limit, not just create financial analysis that ratifies people's intuition.'

See the entire interview at
www.cengage.co.uk/ megginson

the analyst calculating the NPV is also the cheerleader advocating the project in the first place.

One way that companies attempt to control this bias is by putting responsibility for analysing an investment proposal under an authority independent from the individual or group proposing the investment. For example, it is common in large firms for a particular group to have the responsibility of conducting the financial analysis required to value any potential acquisition targets. In this role, financial analysts play a gatekeeper role, protecting shareholders' interests by steering the firm away from large, negative NPV investments. Naturally, these independent analysts face intense pressure from the advocates of each project to portray the investment proposal in its best possible light. Consequently, financial experts need to know more than just which cash flows count in the NPV calculation. They also need to have a sense of what is reasonable when forecasting a project's profit margin and its growth potential. Analysts must also prepare to defend their assumptions, explaining why their (often more conservative) projections do not line up with those offered by the managers advocating a given investment.

Many experienced managers say that they have never seen an investment with a negative NPV. They do not mean that all investments are good investments, but rather that all analysts know enough about NPV analysis to recognize how to make any investment look attractive. Small adjustments to cash flow projections and discount rates can often sway a project's NPV from negative to positive. In this environment, another skill comes into play in determining which project receives funding. We refer to this skill as storytelling, as opposed to number crunching. Most good investments have a compelling story behind them – a reason, based on sound economic logic, that the investment's NPV should be positive. The best financial analysts not only provide the numbers to highlight the value of a good investment but also explain why the investment makes sense, highlighting the competitive opportunity that makes one investment's NPV positive and another one's negative.

SMART IDEAS VIDEO

Professor Abe de Jong, RSM Erasmus University, Rotterdam

European capital structure practices.

See the entire interview at www.cengage.co.uk/megginson

Finally, there is the issue that the models of risk management presented here are only part of what managers want. A study of 370 managers reported in June 2006[5] indicated that, by and large, there was a potential disconnect between what academics and managers considered the best use of risk management tools. All agreed that the tools noted above were essential for the correct running of a company. However, while in general finance academics tend to focus on the use of risk management skills to make better decisions, the managers had a subtle but important distinction. They saw risk management tools as enabling them to make better business decisions, which sometimes required disregarding the finance prescription. After all, managers are paid to take risks in order to reap rewards, not to avoid all risks.

CONCEPT REVIEW QUESTIONS

9 What role does the human element play in the capital budgeting decision process? Could it cause a negative NPV project to be accepted?

10 Why must manager intuition be part of the investment decision process regardless of a project's NPV or IRR?

[5] Henri Servales and Peter Tufano (2006): 'Ranking Risk and Finance', *Financial Times*, 9 June 2006.

10.4 SUMMARY AND CONCLUSIONS

- All-equity firms can discount their 'standard' investment projects at the cost of equity. Managers can estimate the cost of equity using the CAPM.

- The cost of equity is influenced by a firm's cost structure (operating leverage) as well as by its financial structure (financial leverage).

- Firms with both debt and equity in their capital structures can use the weighted average cost of capital, or WACC, to discount the cash flows of investments that do not change the firm's cost structure or financial structure.

- The WACC equals the weighted average of the cost of each source of financing used by a firm, with the weights equal to the proportion of the market value of each source of financing.

- The WACC and the CAPM are connected in that the cost of debt and equity (and any other financing source) are driven by the betas of the firm's debt and equity. Rather than calculate betas for preference shares and debt, we can estimate their returns using dividend yield for preference shares and yield to maturity (YTM) for debt.

- The WACC can be calculated on both a pre-tax and an after-tax basis. Because typically interest payments to bondholders are tax deductible, we usually focus on the after-tax WACC formula.

- A variety of tools exist to assist managers in understanding the sources of uncertainty in a project's cash flows. These tools include breakeven analysis, sensitivity analysis, scenario analysis, Monte Carlo simulation and decision trees.

- In making capital budgeting decisions we must realize that it is not mechanistic but involves persuasion and judgement. We cannot underestimate the importance of the human factor.

INTERNET RESOURCES

For updates to links in this section and elsewhere in the book, please go to the book's website at www.cengage.co.uk/megginson.

http://www.quicken.com
Contains information relevant to calculating the WACC, including equity betas, total market value of equity and debt-to-equity ratios.

http://valuation.ibbotson.com
A fee-based site with cost-of-capital estimates for more than 300 industries.

http://www.stern.nyu.edu/~adamodar
Website of NYU professor Aswath Damodaran; contains downloadable data sets with levered and unlevered industry betas, as well as industry-level estimates of the cost of capital.

http://www.expectationsinvesting.com/tutorial8.shtml
A worked-through example of the calculation of the cost of capital for a company.

http://www.bankofengland.co.uk/publications/quarterlybulletin/qb050303.pdf
An evaluation of how the factors that determine the cost of capital for UK companies have changed over time.

KEY TERMS

breakeven analysis
breakeven point (BEP)
contribution margin
decision tree

financial leverage
Monte Carlo simulation
operating leverage
scenario analysis

sensitivity analysis
weighted average cost of capital
(WACC)

SELF-TEST PROBLEMS

ST10-1 A financial analyst for Quality Investments, a diversified investment fund, has gathered the following information for the years 2005 and 2006 on two firms – A and B – that it is considering adding to its portfolio. Of particular concern are the operating and financial risks of each firm.

	2005		2006	
	FIRM A	**FIRM B**	**FIRM A**	**FIRM B**
Sales (€mn)	10.7	13.9	11.6	14.6
EBIT (€mn)	5.7	7.4	6.2	8.1
Assets (€mn)			10.7	15.6
Debt (€mn)			5.8	9.3
Interest (€mn)			0.6	1.0
Equity (€mn)			4.9	6.3

a   Use the data provided to assess the operating leverage of each firm (using 2005 as the point of reference). Which firm has more operating leverage?

b   Use the data provided to assess each firm's ROE (cash to equity/equity), assuming the firm's return on assets is 10 per cent and 20 per cent in each case. Which firm has more financial leverage?

c   Use your findings in parts (a) and (b) to compare and contrast the operating and financial risks of Firms A and B. Which firm is more risky? Explain.

ST10-2 Sierra Vista Industries (SVI) wishes to estimate its cost of capital for use in analysing projects that are similar to those that already exist. The firm's current capital structure, in terms of market value, includes 40 per cent debt,

10 per cent preference shares and 50 per cent ordinary shares. The firm's debt has an average yield to maturity of 8.3 per cent. Its preference shares have a €70 par value, an 8 per cent dividend and are currently selling for €76 per share. SVI's beta is 1.05, the risk-free rate is 4 per cent and the return on the Bolsa de Madrid (the market proxy) is 11.4 per cent. SVI is in the 40 per cent marginal tax bracket.

a   What are SVI's pre-tax costs of debt, preference shares and ordinary shares?

b   Calculate SVI's weighted average cost of capital (WACC) on both a pre-tax and an after-tax basis. Which WACC should SVI use when making investment decisions?

c   SVI is contemplating a major investment that is expected to increase both its operating and financial leverage. Its new capital structure will contain 50 per cent debt, 10 per cent preference shares and 40 per cent ordinary shares. As a result of the proposed investment, the firm's average yield to maturity on debt is expected to increase to 9 per cent, the market value of preference shares is expected to fall to their €70 par value and its beta is expected to rise to 1.15. What effect will this investment have on SVI's WACC? Explain your finding.

QUESTIONS

Q10-1 Explain when firms should discount projects using the cost of equity. When should they use the WACC instead? When should they use neither?

Q10-2 If a firm takes actions that increase its operating leverage, we can expect to see an increase in its equity beta. Why?

Q10-3 Firm A and Firm B plan to raise €1 million to finance identical projects. Firm A finances the project with 100 per cent equity, whereas firm B uses a 50–50 mix of debt and equity. The interest rate on the debt equals 7 per cent. At what rate of return on the investment (i.e. assets) will the rate of return on equity be the same for Firms A and B? (*Hint*: think through Table 10.2.)

Q10-4 Why do you think it is important to use the market values of debt and equity, rather than book values, to calculate a firm's WACC?

Q10-5 Assuming that there are no corporate income taxes, how can the costs of preference shares and debt be estimated without finding a preference share and a bond beta?

Q10-6 What are the three main lessons learned about choosing the right discount rate for use in evaluating capital budgeting projects?

Q10-7 How does the calculation of the after-tax WACC differ from that of the before-tax WACC?

Q10-8 In what sense could one argue that if managers make decisions using breakeven analysis, they are not maximizing shareholder wealth? How can breakeven analysis be modified to solve this problem?

Q10-9 Explain the differences between sensitivity analysis and scenario analysis. Offer an argument for the proposition that scenario analysis offers a more realistic picture of a project's risk than sensitivity analysis does.

Q10-10 In Chapter 9 we discussed how one can calculate the NPV of earning an MBA. Suppose that you are asked to do a sensitivity analysis on the MBA decision. Which of the following factors do you think would have a larger impact on the degree's NPV?

a The ranking of the business school you choose to attend.

b Your choice of a subject area.

c Your marks.

d The state of the job market when you graduate.

Q10-11 Suppose you want to use a decision tree to model, based on economic considerations, the decision on whether to pursue an MBA degree. What would such a decision tree look like?

PROBLEMS

Choosing the right discount rate

P10-1 Krispy Kreme Doughnuts (KKD) has a capital structure consisting almost entirely of equity.

a If the beta of KKD ordinary shares equals 1.6, the risk-free rate equals 6 per cent and the expected return on the market portfolio equals 11 per cent, what is KKD's cost of equity?

b Suppose that a 1 per cent increase in expected inflation causes a 1 per cent increase in the risk-free rate. Holding all other factors constant, what will this do to the firm's cost of equity? Is it reasonable to hold all other factors constant? What other part of the calculation of the cost of equity is likely to change if expected inflation rises?

P10-2 Fournier Industries, a publicly traded waste disposal company, is a highly leveraged firm with 70 per cent debt, 0 per cent preference shares and 30 per cent common equity financing. Currently the risk-free rate is about 4.5 per cent, and the return on the CAC 40 (the market proxy) is 12.7 per cent. The firm's beta is currently estimated to be 1.65.

a What is Fournier's current cost of equity?

b If the firm shifts its capital structure to a less highly leveraged position by selling preference shares and using the proceeds to retire debt, it expects its beta to drop to 1.20. What is its cost of equity in this case?

c If the firm shifts its capital structure to a less highly leveraged position by selling additional ordinary shares and using the proceeds to retire debt, it expects its beta to drop to 0.95. What is its cost of equity in this case?

d Discuss the potential impact of the two strategies discussed in parts (b) and (c) above on Fournier's weighted average cost of capital (WACC).

P10-3 In its 2001 annual report, The Coca-Cola Company reported sales of $20.09 billion for fiscal year 2001 and $19.89 billion for fiscal year 2000. The company also reported operating income (roughly equivalent to EBIT) of $5.35 billion, and $3.69 billion in 2001 and 2000,

SMART SOLUTIONS

See the problem and solution explained step-by-step at **www.cengage.co.uk/ megginson**

respectively. Meanwhile, arch-rival PepsiCo, Inc. reported sales of $26.94 billion in 2001 and $25.48 billion in 2000. PepsiCo's operating profit was $4.03 billion in 2001 and $3.82 billion in 2000. Based on these figures, which company had higher operating leverage?

P10-4 Gail and Company had the following sales and EBIT during the years 2004 through 2006.

	2004	2005	2006
Sales (€mn)	75.2	82.7	95.1
EBIT (€mn)	26.3	30.5	36.0

a Use the data provided to assess Gail and Company's operating leverage over the following periods

(1) 2004–2005
(2) 2005–2006
(3) 2004–2006

b Compare, contrast and discuss the firm's operating leverage between the 2004–2005 period and the 2005–2006 period. Explain any differences.

c Compare the operating leverage for the entire 2004–2006 period to the values found for the 2004–2005 and 2005–2006 periods and explain the differences.

P10-5 Firm 1 has a capital structure with 20 per cent debt and 80 per cent equity. Firm 2's capital structure consists of 50 per cent debt and 50 per cent equity. Both firms pay 7 per cent annual interest on their debt. Finally, suppose both firms have invested in assets worth €100 million. Calculate the return on equity (ROE) for each firm, assuming the following:

a The return on assets is 3 per cent.

b The return on assets is 7 per cent.

c The return on assets is 11 per cent.

What general pattern do you observe?

P10-6 Firm A's capital structure contains 20 per cent debt and 80 per cent equity. Firm B's capital structure contains 50 per cent debt and 50 per cent equity. Both firms pay 7 per cent annual interest on their debt. Firm A's shares have a beta of 1.0, and Firm B's a beta of 1.375. The risk-free rate of interest equals 4 per cent, and the expected return on the market portfolio equals 12 per cent.

a Calculate the WACC for each firm, assuming there are no taxes.

b Recalculate the WACC figures, assuming that the firms face a marginal tax rate of 34 per cent.

c Explain how taking taxes into account in part (b) changes your answer found in part (a).

P10-7 A firm has a capital structure containing 60 per cent debt and 40 per cent ordinary shares. Its outstanding bonds offer investors a 6.5 per cent yield to maturity. The risk-free rate currently equals 5 per cent, and the expected risk premium on the market portfolio equals 6 per cent. The firm's ordinary shares' beta is 1.20.

a What is the firm's required return on equity?

b Ignoring taxes, use your finding in part (a) to calculate the firm's WACC.

c Assuming a 40 per cent marginal tax rate, recalculate the firm's WACC found in part (b).

d Compare and contrast the values for the firm's WACC found in parts (b) and (c).

P10-8 Dingel International is attempting to evaluate three alternative capital structures – A, B and C. The following table shows the three structures along with relevant cost data. The firm is subject to a 40 per cent marginal tax rate. The risk-free rate is 5.3 per cent and the market return is currently 10.7 per cent.

CAPITAL STRUCTURE

ITEM	A	B	C
Debt (€mn)	35	45	55
Preference shares (€mn)	0	10	10
Ordinary shares (€mn)	65	45	35
Total capital (€mn)	100	100	100
Debt (yield to maturity)	7.0%	7.5%	8.5%
Annual preference share dividend	—	€2.80	€2.20
Preference share (market price)	—	€30.00	€21.00
Ordinary share beta	0.95	1.10	1.25

a Calculate the after-tax cost of debt for each capital structure.

b Calculate the cost of preference shares for each capital structure.

c Calculate the cost of ordinary shares for each capital structure.

d Calculate the weighted average cost of capital (WACC) for each capital structure.

e Compare the WACCs calculated in part (d) and discuss the impact of the firm's financial leverage on its WACC and its related risk.

P10-9 A firm has a capital structure containing 40 per cent debt, 20 per cent preference shares and 40 per cent ordinary shares. The firm's debt has a yield to maturity of 8.1 per cent, its annual preference share dividend is €3.10 and the preference share's current market price is €50.00 per share. The firm's ordinary shares have a beta of 0.90, and the risk-free rate and the market return are currently 4.0 per cent and 13.5 per cent, respectively. The firm is subject to a 40 per cent marginal tax rate.

a What is the firm's cost of preference shares?

b What is the firm's cost of ordinary shares?

c Calculate the firm's after-tax WACC.

d Recalculate the firm's WACC, assuming that its capital structure is deleveraged to contain 20 per cent debt, 20 per cent preference shares and 60 per cent ordinary shares.

e Compare, contrast and discuss your findings from parts (c) and (d).

A closer look at risk

P10-10 Alliance Pneumatic Manufacturing, a specialty machine-tool producer, has fixed costs of €200 million per year. Across all the firm's products, the average contribution margin equals €1200. What is Alliance's breakeven point in terms of units sold?

P10-11 Turn to the values in Table 10.4 on page 349. Determine which of the following has the greater effect on the NPV of the gyroscope skateboard project – an increase in the selling price of 12.5 per cent (compared to the base case) or an increase in the size of the market of 10 per cent in year 1.

P10-12 JK Manufacturing is considering a new product and is unsure about its price as well as the variable cost associated with it. JK's marketing department believes that the firm can sell the product for €500 per unit, but feel that if the initial market response is weak, the price may have to be 20 per cent lower in order to be competitive with existing products. The firm's best estimates of its costs are fixed costs of €3.6 million and variable cost of €325 per unit. Concern exists with regard to the variable cost per unit due to currently volatile raw material and labour costs. Although the firm expects this cost to be about €325 per unit, it could be as much as 8 per cent above that value. The firm expects to sell about 50 000 units per year.

a Calculate the firm's breakeven point (BEP) assuming its initial estimates are accurate.

b Perform a sensitivity analysis by calculating the breakeven point for all combinations of the sale price per unit and variable cost per unit. (*Hint*: there are four combinations.)

c In the best case, how many units will the firm need to sell to break even?

d In the worst case, how many units will the firm need to sell to break even?

e If each of the possible price/variable cost combinations is equally probable, what is the firm's expected breakeven point?

f Based on your finding in part (e), should the firm go forward with the proposed new product? Explain why.

P10-13 Consumer Products International (CPI) is considering performing a feasibility study for a new product available from one of its foreign suppliers. Because CPI will have to make an initial investment of €20 million to obtain exclusive European marketing rights to the product, the firm is contemplating performing a feasibility study of the product's market potential. The cost of the study, which will take two years to complete, is an up-front fee of €2 million. Included in this cost is an exclusive option that gives CPI two years in which to make the decision to pay the foreign supplier the €20 million. If CPI performs the feasibility study, its preliminary estimates indicate that there is a 50 per cent chance of strong product demand, which will result in cash inflows of

€5.2 million per year for eight years; there is a 20 per cent chance of moderate product demand, which will result in cash inflows of €4.5 million per year for eight years; and there is a 30 per cent chance of weak demand, which will result in cash inflows of €4.0 million per year for eight years. Note that the €20 million would be paid at the end of year 2, immediately after the feasibility study is completed and that all outcomes will provide only eight years of cash inflows. CPI's cost of capital applicable to the proposed new product decision is 12 per cent.

a Draw the decision tree associated with CPI's proposed feasibility study.

b Calculate the NPV associated with each of the possible product demand outcomes – strong, moderate and weak.

c Find the expected NPV of performing the feasibility study.

d Based on your findings in part (c), what recommendation would you give CPI about the proposed feasibility study? Explain.

THOMSON ONE **Business School Edition**

For instructions on using Thomson ONE, refer to the introductory text provided with the Thomson ONE problems at the end of Chapters 1–6, or in *A Guide for Using Thomson ONE – Business School Edition*.

P10-14 Compare the operating leverage of Toyota Motor Corp. (ticker: J:TYMO) with that of Nissan Motor Company Limited (J:NR@N), using financial information from the last five years. Which company has the higher operating leverage and why? Which company do you expect will have the higher beta? Check the reported betas on Thomson ONE to see if they match your expectations.

P10-15 Conduct a similar analysis on financial leverage for the same two companies in Problem 10-14.

MINICASE *Capital cost and capital budgeting*

The CEO of Blankson Manufacturing asks to meet with you, the firm's Financial Analyst. The intention of this meeting is for you to answer her questions regarding how the firm assesses project risk. She will use this information when she presents some major capital budgeting recommendations to the board of directors for their approval. To assist you in preparing for this meeting your Management Assistant took it upon himself to ask for a list of possible questions. As a result, the CEO has submitted the following questions for you to answer.

Assignment

1 How do the concepts of marginal benefits (MB) and marginal costs (MC) relate to the evaluation of project risk and capital budgeting decisions?

2 In what case would the cost of equity be the appropriate discount rate to use to calculate a project's NPV?

3 How would managers estimate the cost of equity?

4 How would the mix of a company's fixed and variable costs (cost structure) affect the firm's beta?

5 How might managers assess or measure how the firm's cost structure affects its risk?

6 How would financial leverage affect company risk?

7 When a company adds debt to its capital structure, how does it affect its discount rate?

8 How do taxes affect the WACC?

9 What other techniques might managers use to gauge the risk associated with possible capital investments?

PART 4

Capital Structure and Dividend Policy

PART 4
Overview

The previous chapters provided a framework for deciding how a firm should invest its money. Next, we examine the opposite side of that question. How should managers finance the investments that they undertake? Should managers pay for new investments by using cash that the firm generates internally (which cash belongs ultimately to the shareholders, the owners of the company) or should external sources of funds be tapped? If the decision is to use external funds, is it better to finance with equity or with debt? If the firm's investments are successful, should the company reward its shareholders by paying a dividend or should it repurchase shares instead? To answer these questions, managers have to assess the marginal benefits and costs of alternative actions. Unfortunately, the advice we have to offer managers who are asking these questions is not as clear-cut as our advice on capital budgeting matters. No one solution is optimal – there is no capital structure equivalent to the NPV rule. Nevertheless, there are some important general principles to convey.

Chapter 11 describes some of the trade-offs firms face when they choose between internal or external financing or between debt and equity. The chapter explains how firms issue equity. Because investment bankers serve two masters – the firms that want to sell securities and the investors who must be persuaded to buy them – the investment banking business is fraught with potential conflict of interest problems. Chapter 11 describes some of the conflicts that arise in this industry and summarizes some of the recent scandals that have plagued it.

In Chapter 12 we explore the question of whether managers can increase the value of a firm by financing its operations with an optimal mix of debt and equity. A classic and important line of argument in finance suggests that finding an optimal capital structure may be impossible, but the chapter offers useful guidelines that managers can consult when deciding what type of funding to raise for their companies.

Chapter 13 examines the related question of how managers can affect the value of a firm through dividend policy. In Chapter 5, we presented a model that claimed that the value of any share should equal the present value of all dividends that the share will pay through time (or more broadly, the value of all cash payments that the share will make). The surprising message of Chapter 13 is that although dividends are clearly important, dividend policy may or may not affect the value of a firm.

SMART FINANCE
Use the learning tools at www.cengage.co.uk/megginson

Chapter 11
Raising Long-Term Equity Financing

OPENING FOCUS

China: Huge promise, huge IPO

Over the last decade the Chinese economy and financial system have been transformed. This is perhaps most evident when one looks at the 2006 IPO of Industrial and Commercial Bank of China (ICBC). Although not quite the largest ever IPO, it is one of the largest. In total the company raised just under $22 billion, or 17 per cent of its value before it was floated.

This was the culmination of a long transformation of the bank, which had included strategic purchases of stakes in 2005 by three other investment banks (Dresdner, Goldman Sachs and American Express). These and additional state injections were used to ensure a solid capital base. In total, since 1998 the company had absorbed over $160 billion in capital injections and loan write-offs. Since early 2006 the company had been preparing for the flotation, which was managed by a consortium led by Merrill Lynch, and including Credit Suisse, Deutsche Bank and two Chinese banks, CICC and ICEA.

On 27 October 2006 shares in ICBC were issued to the public on both the Shanghai and Hong Kong stock exchanges. The offering was mainly directed to international buyers via the Hong Kong market, where over $14 billion was raised. At the end of the first day of trading the company's shares had risen by 15 per cent. So popular was the offering and so high the demand that the underwriters exercised their option to release more shares during the day – the so-called 'green shoe' option.

ICBC was not just a large investment bank going public – in its roadshow it was portrayed and seen as 'buying China'. The roadshow is the name given to the process whereby the advisers and underwriters take to the road and present or pitch the shares to investors. This takes place via presentations and lectures. In ICBC's case there were two: the international roadshow in Singapore, Dubai, London and New York, and the domestic roadshow, which included a four-hour webcast and involved upwards of 100 million potential investors.

Source: Adapted from 'ICBC Surges on Completion of IPO', *Financial Times*, 28 October 2007.

LEARNING OBJECTIVES

After studying this chapter you should be able to:

- Discuss the basic choices that corporations face in raising long-term financing.
- Describe the costs and benefits of raising long-term funds by issuing securities on capital markets rather than by borrowing from a financial intermediary.
- Understand how investment banks help corporations issue securities, and describe the services investment banks provide before, during and after a security issue.
- Explain the basic issuance and pricing patterns observed in the initial public offering (IPO) and seasoned equity offering (SEO) market in the major financial centres.
- Explain what American depositary receipts (ADRs) are and discuss why these have proved to be so popular with US investors.

SMART FINANCE
Use the learning tools at www.cengage.co.uk/megginson

This chapter introduces the primary instruments that companies around the world use for long-term equity financing, and it examines key patterns observed in corporate financial systems. The basic instruments are similar worldwide and include ordinary and preference shares, and long-term debt. However, significant differences exist across countries in terms of how corporations use these instruments and in the degree to which firms rely on capital markets, rather than financial intermediaries, for funding. For example, countries such as Canada, the United States, the United Kingdom and Australia are characterized by large, highly liquid share and bond markets. Other industrialized countries, particularly those in continental Europe, have much smaller capital markets and rely primarily on commercial banks for corporate financing. Despite these differences in financial systems, corporations around the world display certain common tendencies. Perhaps the most important of these patterns is the near universal reliance on internally generated cash flow (retained earnings) as the dominant source of new financing.

Debt and equity constitute the two main sources of corporate long-term financing. The basic features of debt securities were described in Chapter 4, while the basics of shares were discussed in Chapter 5. Equity capital represents an ownership interest that is junior to debt, while debt capital represents a legally enforceable claim, with cash flows that are either fixed or varied, according to a predetermined formula. These basic financial instruments exist in most countries, and the rights and responsibilities of the holders of these instruments are very similar worldwide.

11.1 THE BASIC CHOICES IN LONG-TERM FINANCING

Companies around the world face the same basic financing problem – how to fund those projects and activities that firms need to undertake if they are to grow and prosper. This section examines the choices firms face in selecting among financing alternatives, particularly the choices regarding internal versus external financing. The section also surveys key issues related to the choice between financing via capital markets versus financial intermediaries.

The need to fund a financial deficit

financial deficit
More financial capital for investment and investor payments than is retained in profits by a corporation.

Corporations everywhere are net dissavers, which is an economic way of saying they demand more financial capital for investment than they supply in the form of retained profits. Corporations must close this **financial deficit** by borrowing or by issuing new equity securities. Every major firm confronts four key financing decisions on an ongoing basis:

1 How much capital must the company raise each year?

2 How much of this must be raised externally rather than through retained profits?

3 How much of the external funding should be raised through borrowing from a bank or another financial intermediary, and how much capital should be raised by selling securities directly to investors?

4 What proportion of the external funding should be structured as ordinary shares, preference shares or long-term debt?

The answer to the first question depends on the capital budgeting process of a particular firm, as discussed in Chapters 8–10. A company must raise enough capital to fund all its positive-NPV investment projects and to cover its working capital needs. The true financing decision begins with Question 2 – the choice between internal versus external financing.

The choice between internal versus external financing

At first glance, the internal/external choice seems to be a decision that firms can make mechanically. Managers may approximate external funding needs by subtracting cash dividend payments from their firms' **cash flow from operations** (net income plus depreciation and other non-cash charges). The difference between this internally generated funding and the firms' total financing needs equals the external financing requirement. The decision is not simple, however. Management may want to build up or reduce working capital stocks over time, and besides, dividend policy is not fixed, except in the very short term. Additionally, there are obviously higher legal and transaction costs to raising capital externally than by retaining internal cash flow. Managers should choose to raise capital externally whenever the benefits of doing so – such as the ability to raise greater sums of money, or to raise new capital in the form of debt – exceed the additional transaction and other costs of raising external funds. This is another practical application of the marginal benefits equals marginal costs decision rule. Not surprisingly, the residual nature of external funding needs implies that this figure will be highly variable from year to year for individual companies.

External funding is also a highly variable figure for the corporate sector as a whole. Internal cash flow is the dominant source of corporate funding in the United States, with businesses regularly financing two-thirds to three-quarters of all their capital spending needs internally. Over time, other countries have also moved in the same direction. While as recently as the 1970s European corporations relied heavily on external funding, the corporate sectors of Western European nations now meet the majority of their total funding needs internally. Japanese corporations still meet up to half of their total financing needs externally, primarily through bank borrowing. But even this level implies far lower dependence on external funding than was the case prior to the 1980s. In other words, even though we see ever increasing news programmes, publications and commentary on the capital markets, companies are increasingly funding themselves in a simple, old fashioned manner – by selling goods and services for a price that is greater than the cost of production.

> **cash flow from operations**
> Cash inflows and outflows directly related to the production and sale of a firm's products or services. Calculated as net income plus depreciation and other non-cash charges.

> **SMART CONCEPTS**
> See the concept explained step-by-step at **www.cengage.co.uk/ megginson**

Raising capital from financial intermediaries or on capital markets

Should a corporation care whether it raises capital by selling securities to investors in public capital markets or by dealing more directly with a financial intermediary such as a commercial bank? Before analysing this issue, we should formally define what a financial intermediary is and briefly describe what services it provides. A **financial intermediary (FI)** is an institution that raises capital by issuing liabilities against itself – for example, in the form of demand or savings deposits. The intermediary then pools the funds raised and uses these to make loans to borrowers or, where allowed, to make equity investments in non-financial firms. Borrowers repay the intermediary and have no direct contact with the individual savers who actually funded the loans. In other words, both borrowers and savers deal directly with the intermediary, which specializes in credit analysis and collection, while it offers financial products tailored to the specific needs of both borrowers and savers.

In many countries, intermediaries also play an extremely important corporate governance role, distinct from their activities in granting credit and monitoring loan repayment. Commercial banks, in particular, frequently help set operating and financial policies of firms they have invested in, by serving on corporate boards and monitoring the performance of senior managers. This has been particularly the position in continental Europe, where banks and other financial intermediaries will

> **financial intermediary (FI)**
> An institution that raises capital by issuing liabilities against itself. Also, a commercial bank or other entity that lends to corporations.

often play a major role. However, traditionally, banks in the United States have been prohibited from playing any meaningful corporate governance role.

In response to public opinion, US policymakers in the 1920s discouraged the growth of large intermediaries (especially commercial banks), in part, by imposing on them severe geographical restrictions. Existing restrictions were codified into national law when Congress passed the **McFadden Act** in 1927, which prohibited interstate banking. This was only overturned in July 1994. After numerous failed attempts to repeal the McFadden Act over the years, a bill allowing full interstate branch banking was finally approved by Congress in July 1994.

The second pivotal law affecting American FIs was the **Glass-Steagall Act**, which was passed in 1933 in response to perceived banking abuses during the Great Depression. This legislation mandated the separation of investment and commercial banking. Commercial banks were thereby prohibited from underwriting corporate security issues, providing security brokerage services to their customers, or even owning voting equity securities on their own account. Banking's corporate financing role was thus effectively restricted to making commercial loans and to providing closely related services, such as leasing.

As with the McFadden Act, there were repeated attempts to repeal Glass-Steagall, and these finally succeeded when Congress passed the **Gramm-Leach-Bailey Act** in November 1999. This Act allows commercial banks, securities firms and insurance companies to join together in a new financial holding company structure, also defined by the Act. However, the Act still prohibits non-financial companies from owning commercial banks. The Act also mandates 'functional regulation' for banks, insurance companies, securities firms and other financial companies. This means that regulation applies to specific financial services (i.e. brokerage services, deposit-taking) that are provided by all types of financial companies. Previously, regulators had been assigned based on institutional form. All the activities of commercial banks were regulated by the Federal Reserve Board. The activities of securities firms were regulated by the SEC. All the products and services offered by insurance companies were overseen by state insurance boards.

In markets outside the United States, commercial banks typically play much larger roles in corporate finance. In most countries, a relative handful of very large banks service most large firms, and the size and competence of these banks give them tremendous influence over corporate financial and operating policies. This power is further strengthened by the ability of most non-US banks to underwrite corporate security issues and to make direct equity investments in commercial firms. Most Western countries allow commercial banks to act as true **merchant banks**, capable of providing the full range of financial services. Compared to US banks, most non-US banking firms tend to have much more significant power over the business affairs of corporate borrowers. This is particularly evident in cases of financial distress or bankruptcy where the lender will often play a dominant role in relation to how and if the firm works itself out of this position.

McFadden Act
Congressional Act of 1927 that prohibited interstate banking.

Glass-Steagall Act
Congressional Act of 1933 mandating the separation of investment and commercial banking.

Gramm-Leach-Bailey Act
Act that allowed commercial banks, securities firms and insurance companies to join together.

merchant bank
A bank capable of providing a full range of financial services.

Real World

Not all merchant banks are old, established firms with histories dating back to Napoleonic times. One of the more innovative and aggressive and newest is the Australian bank Macquarie. In addition to operating as a traditional financial adviser and lender, Macquarie as we have seen in the battle for the London Stock Exchange is also not averse to taking the role of purchaser and manager. It has significant infrastructure holdings in the UK, Australia and North America, such as toll roads, gas suppliers and airport services. And it also offers loans.

Source: Authors' own research; *The Economist*, various issues.

The expanding role of securities markets in corporate finance

No trend in modern finance is as clear or as transforming as the worldwide shift towards corporate reliance on securities markets rather than intermediaries for external financing. Table 11.1 presents summary information from the Bank for International Settlements on **primary security issues**. Primary issues actually raise capital for firms and are thus distinct from **secondary offerings** in which investors

primary security issues
Security offerings that raise capital for firms.

secondary offering
An offering whose purpose is to allow an existing shareholder to sell a large block of shares to new investors. This kind of offering raises no new capital for the firm.

TABLE 11.1

Worldwide securities issues, 1990–2005

This table details the total value, in billions of US dollars, and the number (in parentheses) of securities issues worldwide for selected years in the period 1990–2005. The data are taken from early January issues of the Investment Dealers' Digest.

Source: *Investment Dealers' Digest*, early January issues.

TYPE OF SECURITY ISSUE	1990	1995	2000	2005
Worldwide offerings	$504	$1 066	$ 3 268	$6 514
[debt and equity]	(7 574)	(9 305)	(14 659)	(20 118)
Global debt	184	385	2 624	5 997
	(1 376)	(2 548)	(10 827)	(17 008)
Yankee bonds	13	45	47	92
	(81)	(237)	(112)	(248)
International shares (excl. US)[a]	7	21	335	520
	(132)	(242)	(2 662)	(3 122)
US issuers worldwide[b]	313	700	1 958	3 382
[debt and equity]	(6 141)	(6 807)	(15 686)	(11 130)
All debt[c]	—	—	1 726	3 640
			(7 824)	(10 290)
Straight corporate debt[d]	109	417	744	1 186
	(1 016)	(4 562)	(2 986)	(3 813)
High-yield corporate debt	1	28	43	97
	(7)	(153)	(196)	(355)
Collateralized securities	175	155	488	1 143
	(4 542)	(709)	(1 201)	(2 061)
Convertible debt and preference shares	5	9	56	68
	(43)	(57)	(161)	(208)
Ordinary shares[e]	14	82	223	142
	(362)	(1 159)	(955)	(720)
Initial public offerings[e]	5	30	60	40
	(174)	(572)	(386)	(230)

Notes:

[a] Capital-raising, private-sector offers; does not include privatization issues.

[b] For 2000 and 2003, all figures include Rule 144A offers on US markets.

[c] Includes mortgage-backed securities (MBS), asset-backed securities (ABS) and municipal bonds.

[d] Years 2000 and 2003 are long-term straight debt only. Before 1999, figures are for investment grade debt.

[e] Excludes closed-end funds. Data for 1990–2000 are not comparable to 2005 due to definition change.

securitization
The repackaging of loans and other traditional bank-based credit products into securities that can be sold to public investors.

sell their holdings of existing securities. Since the late 1980s the value of these external fundraising securities has increased more than ten-fold. This increase in the value of security market financing was not matched by a remotely comparable increase in world trade, investment or economic activity. Instead, it is a reflection of the power of the trend toward the 'securitization' of corporate finance. As we have seen in Chapter 4, **securitization** involves the repackaging of loans and other traditional bank-based credit products into securities that can be sold to public investors.

Besides rapid recent growth, another major trend that can be observed from these data is the relatively steady fraction of worldwide security offerings accounted for by US issuers. American issues represented 51 per cent of the worldwide total value of security offerings in 2005 ($3382 billion of $6514 billion). This is the lowest US percentage of issues in recent times. US issuers have generally sold between 62 per cent and 74 per cent of the global total every year since 1990, but the trend is for US issuers, while still the largest single source of issues by value, to decline as a percentage of the overall total.

Looking more closely at the statistics we can identify several other trends First, companies issue far more debt than equity each year. Secondly, the relative insignificance of new equity issues as a financing source for corporations is further emphasized considering that initial public offerings (IPOs) accounted for only a small proportion of shares issued by companies. Virtually all companies choose to list their stock on one of the organized exchanges so that investors can easily buy or sell the stock. America's IPO market is easily the world's largest and most liquid source of equity capital for small, rapidly growing firms. One of the more important types of bonds is the class known as **Eurobonds**, which are bonds issued by an international borrower and sold to investors in countries with currencies other than that in which the bond is denominated. Thus a South African rand-denominated bond issued in London would be classified as a Eurobond.

Eurobond
A bond issued by an international borrower and sold to investors in countries with currencies other than that in which the bond is denominated.

foreign bond
A bond issued in a host country's financial market, in the host country's currency, by a non-resident corporation.

Other bonds include a **foreign bond** (a bond issued in a host country's financial market, in the host country's currency, by a non-resident corporation).

To summarize, the growth in international security issues has kept pace with that in the United States, though this growth has probably affected non-US economies to a greater degree because it began from a much smaller base.

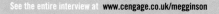

CONCEPT REVIEW QUESTIONS

1 What are financial intermediaries, and what role do these firms play in providing long-term capital to publicly traded non-financial corporations?

2 What patterns are observed in security issues each year?

11.2 INVESTMENT BANKING AND THE PUBLIC SALE OF SECURITIES

Although internal financing is the dominant source of funding for corporations around the world, many firms raise capital externally in any given year. Managers may or may not enlist the help of an **investment bank** to sell their firms' debt and equity securities. If they desire assistance from an investment bank, managers can negotiate privately with individual banks regarding the terms of the security sale, or they can solicit competitive bids for the business. Firms can issue securities to a small group of sophisticated investors in a private placement, or they can execute a public offering to the general population of investors. If companies want to sell new stock, they can issue shares to existing shareholders through a rights offering, or they can engage in a general cash offering open to all investors.

Table 11.2 presents a **league table** that ranks investment banks, based on the total value of securities they underwrote globally during 2005. The highest-ranked firms in 2005 generally occupied the top rankings in previous years, and these firms are perennial members of investment banking's prestigious **bulge bracket**. Bulge-bracket firms generally occupy the lead or co-lead manager's position in large, new security offerings, meaning that they take primary responsibility for the new offering (even though other banks participate as part of a syndicate). As a result, they earn higher fees. Investment banks are compensated with an underwriting spread, which is the difference between the offering price per share and the amount per share that the underwriter passes on to the issuing firms. You can readily identify the lead investment bank in a security offering by looking at the offering **prospectus**, the legal document that describes the terms of the offering. The lead bank's name appears on the front page, usually in larger, bolder print than the names of other participating banks.

As noted earlier, the USA remains the largest single market for the raising of capital. This is the case in IPOs as well as capital generally. Shown in Table 11.3 are some figures for the international equity market for 2002–05. What is striking is the volatility of the numbers, which is a persistent phenomenon in IPOs. Companies and advisers are reluctant to issue capital when the market is perceived to be weak

investment bank
A bank that helps firms acquire external capital.

league table
Ranks investment banks, based on the total value of securities they underwrote globally during a given year.

bulge bracket
Consists of firms that generally occupy the lead or co-lead manager's position in large, new security offerings, meaning that they take primary responsibility for the new offering (even though other banks participate as part of a syndicate), and as a result they earn higher fees.

prospectus
The first part of a registration statement; it is distributed to all prospective investors.

COMPANY	PROCEEDS ($m)	MARKET SHARE %	NUMBER OF ISSUES	DISCLOSED FEES ($m)
Citygroup	616 700	8.46	1849	1 619.3
JP Morgan	463 251	6.35	1469	907.8
Deutsche Bank	461 402	6.33	1338	510.5
Morgan Stanley	411 461	5.64	1225	1 091
Lehman Bros	406 186	5.57	1066	794.5
Merrill Lynch	406 150	5.57	1105	1 331.7
Goldman Sachs	356 987	4.90	833	1 370.2
Credit Suisse	353 054	4.84	1043	791.8
Barclays Capital	352 424	4.83	1007	139.6
UBS	316 654	4.34	1161	854.2
Industry Total	7 290 172	100.00	18 989	14 470.1

TABLE 11.2

Investment banking league tables, global debt and equity issues, 2006

Source: *Investment Dealers' Digest, January 2007.*

TABLE 11.3

Global equity issues by stock exchange ($m raised), 2002–2006

	2006		2004		2002	
	NEW COMPANIES	EXISTING COMPANIES	NEW COMPANIES	EXISTING COMPANIES	NEW COMPANIES	EXISTING COMPANIES
NASDAQ	17 374.9	NA	3 528.2	NA	5 113.7	NA
NYSE	37 130.1	66 040.1	26 874.5	39 071.6	8 645.8	14 454.1
Toronto	9 105.9	6 34 970.2	14 568.5	25 384.0	1 736.2	1 823.6
Australia	12 877.4	33 647.5	52.5	109.5	802.0	922.6
Hong Kong	42 972.8	24 465.0	2 186.8	8 369.5	1 549.7	3 384.5
Osaka	431.3	NA	971.4	2 375.4	307.0	1 513.8
Tokyo	NA	22 133.7	NA	671.4	NA	15 749.216
Shanghai	11 817.7	4 734.6	1 438.4	5 963.7	11 931.4	13 247.2
Spanish exchanges	14 663	13 568.1	851.7	851.7	504.8	542.8
London SE	55 807.4	38 560.7	3 982.6	5 179.4	27.2	712.4
Euronext	27 045	73 333.2	6 533.2	6 533.2	404.4	1 143.6
Deutsche Börse	11 700.6	NA	726.8	1 228.8	38.8	1 548.6

Source: World Federation of Stock Exchanges (www.world-exchanges.org).

unseasoned equity offering
An initial offering of shares by a company that does not currently have a public listing for trading its shares.

book-building
A process in which underwriters ask prospective investors to reveal information about their demand for the offering. Through conversations with investors, the underwriter tries to measure the demand curve for a given issue, and the investment bank sets the offer price after gathering all the information it can from investors.

or volatile. This of course further depresses the amount of capital raised and the cycle continues. Another striking element is the concentration of IPO issuance in the few leading exchanges. NASDAQ, the New York Stock Exchange, London and Tokyo account for a very significant percentage of both monies raised and companies floating.

Underwriting spreads vary considerably depending on the type of security being issued. Banks charge higher spreads on equity issues than on debt issues. They also charge higher spreads for **unseasoned equity offerings** (i.e. IPOs) than they do for seasoned equity offerings (SEOs), which are equity issues by firms that already have shares outstanding. In general, the riskier the security being offered, the higher the spread charged by the underwriter, so spreads on non-investment grade ('junk') bonds exceed those on investment grade bonds. Similarly, securities that have both debt and equity-like features, such as convertible bonds or preference shares, have spreads higher than those of ordinary debt but lower than those of shares.

Spreads on international IPOs are significantly lower than on US initial offers. In part, this reflects differences in underwriting practices across countries. US underwriters typically use a process, known as **book-building**, to assess demand for a company's shares and to set the offer price, in which underwriters ask prospective investors to reveal information about their demand for the offering. Through conversations with investors, called a roadshow, the underwriter tries to measure the demand curve for a given issue, and the investment bank can then set the offer price after gathering all the information it can from investors. In international markets, book-building is common, and greatly increasing, but so is a method called a fixed-price offer. In fixed-price offers, underwriters set the final offer price for a new issue weeks in advance. Since this imposes more risk on the underwriters, they would naturally charge higher spreads if offering prices were set the same as under book-building. To protect themselves, underwriters thus set share offering prices significantly lower in fixed-price offering, and observed spreads are therefore lower than in book-built offerings.

roadshow
The process whereby the analysts from the book-building syndicate make presentations to interested parties as part of the book-building process.

fixed-price offer
An offer in which the underwriters set the final offer price for a new issue weeks in advance.

Source: *Financial Times*, various issues, November 2005.

Real World

Book-building is becoming more common in European flotations, and can provide a useful buffer for companies that face potential turbulence in markets. Take the example of EDF, the French government-owned electricity and distribution utility. The flotation of the company was politically sensitive, and using a book-building approach, the government was able to ensure that the 15 per cent of the company that was to be floated was priced accurately and that the underwriters were in a position to actually place the shares accurately. Despite political concerns and equity market turbulence, the flotation in November 2005 was a great success with the shares being offered at the top of the expected price range.

Conflicts of interest facing investment banks

The institutional arrangements for selling securities to the public, as described above, confront investment banks with many potential conflicts of interest. Banks are providing advice and underwriting services to companies that want to issue securities and that are naturally eager to sell those securities for the highest possible price. On the other hand, investment banks are selling these securities to their own clients – retail and institutional investors – who naturally want to purchase securities at bargain prices. Furthermore, research analysts working for investment banks produce reports that are supposed to advise clients on whether securities are fairly priced. Banks cannot 'solve' these conflicts of interest; instead, they must price new security issues to strike a balance between the revenue maximization goal of the issuing firms and the profit maximization objective of their investing clients.

In recent years, various legal actions taken against investment banks suggest that the banks have failed to strike an appropriate balance between the competing interests that they serve. For example, in 2002, ten of the top US investment banking firms agreed to pay fines totalling $1.4 billion to settle an investigation by New York Attorney General Elliot Spitzer. Part of the settlement required investment banks to purchase independent research from third parties. The purpose of this provision is to try to remove any potential bias in investment banks' research that may arise if banks present

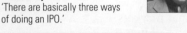

overly optimistic reports on companies with which they have an underwriting relationship.[1]

More recently, Morgan Stanley, Deutsche Bank and Bear, Stearns & Co. agreed to pay $15 million as part of an investigation by the National Association of Securities Dealers (NASD). The investigation alleged that these firms were engaged in a kickback scheme in which they would give large allocations of 'hot' IPO shares to clients, who, in turn, agreed to pay unusually high commissions to the banks for subsequent trades in other companies. In a hot IPO, the price of the issuing company's shares shoots up dramatically once trading begins in the secondary market. Because the demand for shares in a hot IPO far exceeds the supply, the investment bankers' right to control the initial allocation of shares is quite valuable. Banks may choose to 'reward' some of their best customers by giving them large share allocations in hot deals. Sometimes banks may cross an ethical line and use their power to allocate shares in hot IPOs to generate revenue, in addition to the fees paid by the issuing firm. In one such case, a customer of Bear Stearns received a large share allocation in a hot IPO and subsequently paid $2 per share to trade 50 000 shares of a different stock, when the customary commission for a trade of that size might be $0.06 per share. This represented a kind of kickback for Bear Stearns. Interestingly, Google structured its August 2004 IPO as an auction, open to all investors, rather than as an allocated offering specifically in order to prevent investment banks from favouring institutional investors over the ordinary investing public.

Lawmakers and regulators recognize that the investment banking business is fraught with conflict of interest problems, and so there is an extensive set of rules that impose constraints on how securities may be sold. Now we turn to a brief overview of the legal environment surrounding security issues.

CONCEPT REVIEW QUESTION	**3** What does the phrase 'bulge bracket' mean?

11.3 THE US MARKET FOR INITIAL PUBLIC OFFERINGS

Because the USA remains the pre-eminent market-place for companies sourcing funds, we examine first the process of issuing shares in the USA, and then turn our attention to the major international markets.

---

[1] The French luxury goods maker, LVMH, recently sued Morgan Stanley successfully in a French court and won a €30 million settlement. The suit alleged that Morgan Stanley's research on one of LVMH's competitors, Gucci, was overly optimistic because Morgan Stanley had other profitable business ties to Gucci. Because Morgan's biased research attracted investors away from LVMH and to Gucci, LVMH successfully persuaded the court that it had been harmed by the biased research reports.

All the US stock markets compete fiercely for IPO listings. The competition is particularly intense between the two largest, the New York Stock Exchange (NYSE) and the NASDAQ electronic market, which merged with the American Stock Exchange in 1998. Although the number of IPOs (usually a few hundred per year) and the total capital they have raised ($30–$75 billion) each year since the mid-1990s does not seem immense in a $10 trillion economy, IPOs generally represent 20–40 per cent of all new equity raised yearly by US corporations. In other words, IPOs collectively raise one-third as much external equity capital each year as do established giants such as IBM, Exxon and General Motors.

Patterns observed in the US IPO market

To the uninitiated, a quick survey of the US IPO market reveals some decidedly odd patterns. For example, it is one of the most highly cyclical securities markets imaginable. Aggregate IPO volume shows a very distinct pattern of boom and bust. Throughout most of the 1990s, the IPO market boomed. The year 1996 set a record for the number of IPOs (666), while 2000 set the record for total proceeds of $65.68 billion. However, as the prices of US stocks tumbled after March 2000, a chill subdued the market. The number of transactions in 2003 was only one-tenth of the 1996 total, and the 2003 IPOs raised barely $10 billion – only 15 per cent of 2000's proceeds. By 2005 this figure had risen again to $56 billion, from 380 IPOs.

Another interesting pattern observed in the IPO market is the tendency for firms going public in a certain industry to 'cluster' in time. It is common to see bursts of IPO activity in fairly narrow industry sectors, such as energy, biotechnology and communications, and, in the late 1990s, internet-related companies. Indeed, the latter half of the 1990s saw an incredible boom in both the number of internet companies going public and the valuations assigned to them by the market. Companies such as Netscape, Yahoo!, Amazon.com and eBay were able to raise hundreds of millions of dollars in equity, despite their relatively short operating histories and non-existent profits. Investors were so eager to purchase shares in these firms that their share prices often doubled the first day they began trading.

Applying the Model

The short-term share price increases for internet-related IPOs had financial experts scratching their heads in 1999, none more so than the 9 December 1999 debut of VA Linux. The company went public with an offer price of $30 per share, and after one trading day the closing price was almost $240 per share. For investors who bought shares at the offer price and sold them as soon as possible, the one-day return was an astronomical 700 per cent. Investors who held on for the long term did not fare as well. After the IPO, the shares closed above $240 only once. By June 2007, the company, now renamed SourceForge, saw its shares trading at just over $4.25.

As recently as the early 1980s, investment banks targeted initial offerings almost exclusively at individual investors, more particularly at retail customers of the brokerage firms involved in the underwriting syndicate. Over the past 25 years, however, institutional investors have grown in importance. Now they generally receive 50–75 per cent of the shares offered in typical IPOs and up to 90 per cent, or more, of the 'hot' issues.

Rule 144A offering
A special type of offer, first approved in April 1990, that allows issuing companies to waive some disclosure requirements by selling shares only to sophisticated institutional investors, who may then trade the shares among themselves.

A final pattern emerging in the US IPO market is its increasingly international flavour. The largest and most visible of the international IPOs are associated with privatizations of formerly state-owned enterprises. However, both established international companies and non-US entrepreneurial firms are also choosing to make initial share offerings to US investors, either publicly via a straight IPO or to institutional investors through a **Rule 144A offering**. This special type of offer, which was first approved in April 1990, allows issuing companies to waive some disclosure requirements by selling shares only to sophisticated institutional investors, who may then trade the shares among themselves.

Source: Adapted from *Financial Times*, 12 November 2005.

Real World

A good example of Rule 144a in action is the flotation of the Swiss investment bank EFG. In late 2005 the company floated, with an IPO in the Swiss market and a Rule 144a placement in the USA. The 144A placement was a private placement, which was fully subscribed.

equity carve-out
Occurs when a parent company sells shares of a subsidiary corporation to the public through an initial public offering. The parent company may sell some of the subsidiary shares that it already owns, or the subsidiary may issue new shares.

Specialized IPOs: Equity carve-outs, spin-offs, reverse LBOs and tracking stocks

The four special types of IPOs are equity carve-outs (ECOs), spin-offs, reverse LBOs and tracking stocks. An **equity carve-out** occurs when a parent company sells shares of a subsidiary corporation to the public through an initial public offering. The parent company may sell some of the subsidiary shares that it already owns, or the subsidiary may issue new shares. In any event, the parent company almost always retains a controlling stake in the newly public company.

Source: Adapted from the *Wall Street Journal* and the *Financial Times*, February–March 2000.

Real World

Perhaps one of the most famous carve-outs was 3Com's decision to carve out Palm. Palm, the makers of the popular handheld computer, was initially brought to the market via a sale of 5 per cent of its equity in early 2000. At the time, 3Com announced that it planned to spin off its remaining shares of Palm to 3Com's shareholders before the end of the year. 3Com shareholders would receive 1.5 shares of Palm for every share of 3Com. The conclusion was that the value of 3Com should have been 1.5 times the value of Palm. Investors could therefore buy shares of Palm directly or through buying shares embedded within shares of 3Com. Given 3Com's other profitable business assets, it was expected that 3Com's price would also be significantly greater than the 1.5 multiple of Palm. The day before the Palm IPO, the price of 3Com closed at \$104.13 per share. After the first day of trading, Palm closed at \$95.06 per share, implying that the price of 3Com should have jumped to at least \$145. Instead, 3Com fell to \$81.81.

spin-off
A parent company creates a new company with its own shares to form a division or subsidiary, and existing shareholders receive a pro rata distribution of shares in the new company.

A **spin-off** occurs when a public parent company 'spins off' a subsidiary to the parent's shareholders by distributing shares on a pro rata basis. Thus, after the spin-off, there are two public companies rather than one. Conceptually, the total share value of the parent should drop by approximately the same amount that the market values the shares of the newly public spin-off. Instead, however, academic research finds significantly positive price reactions for the shares of divesting parent companies at the time that spin-offs are announced, perhaps indicating that the market expects that the two independent companies will be managed more effectively than they would have been had they remained together.

Real World

Source: Adapted from the *Financial Times*, 10 February 2006.

In early 2006 Securitas, the world's leading provider of security and security staffing, announced that it was considering spinning off three of its divisions – its cash-handling division in Europe and the USA (Wells Fargo), its direct sales insurance business in Sweden and its security systems division. The company had been badly underperforming for many years, and was the subject of frequent speculation about being taken private or being subject to an LBO. On the announcement, the shares of the company rose by 10 per cent.

In a **reverse LBO (or second IPO)**, a formerly public company that has previously gone private, through a leveraged buyout, goes public again. Reverse LBOs are easier to price than traditional IPOs because information already exists about how the market valued the company when it was publicly traded. Empirical research indicates that the LBO partners earn very high returns on these transactions. One reason for this is obvious: only the most successful LBOs can subsequently go public again.

reverse LBO (or second IPO)
A formerly public company that has previously gone private through a leveraged buyout and then goes public again. Also called a second IPO.

Real World

Source: Adapted from the *Irish Times*, various editions.

Reverse LBOs are not that common. Take, however, the case of Eircom, the Irish telecommunications company. Initially a government monopoly, it was successfully floated on the Irish and London stock exchanges in 1999. With the collapse in telecoms shares and facing difficulties with major shareholders, the company eventually was broken up and sold to private investors. However, a restructured company, with the same core business was later refloated in 2003. As expected, the partners in the LBO had made significant gains. Having paid around €3 billion, over the two years of the LBO dividends of over €500 million were paid out. And the company had in effect been bought at near zero cost, as the LBO partners had financed the deal with debt. However, in 2006 this company in turn was taken private again. So we have an example of a company that has had two IPOs in less than a decade.

The final type of specialized equity offering, **tracking stocks**, is a very recent innovation. These are equity claims based on (and designed to mirror, or track) the earnings of wholly owned subsidiaries of diversified firms. They are hybrid securities, because the tracking stock 'firm' is not separated from the parent company in any way. Instead, it remains integrated with the parent, legally and operationally. In contrast, both carve-outs and spin-offs result in legally separate firms. AT&T conducted the largest common stock offering in US history, when it issued $10.6 billion in AT&T Wireless tracking stock in April 2000. As has been true for most other tracking stock offerings, AT&T's shares rose significantly when it announced the Wireless offering. Unfortunately, both parent and tracking stock performed abysmally during the months after the issue. Thus, in July 2001, AT&T spun off the Wireless division as a separate company. In March 2004, Sprint also announced plans to eliminate its tracking stock, which the company issued in 1998. However, tracking stocks are subject to fashion like IPOs, and come and go in popularity.

tracking stocks
Equity claims based on (and designed to mirror, or track) the earnings of wholly owned subsidiaries of diversified firms.

Source: Adapted from Liberty Media Corporation website and the *Financial Times*, various issues.

Real World

Liberty Media, the US diversified news, telecoms and IT company has created a number of tracking stocks that trade on NASDAQ. These include Liberty Capital and Liberty Interactive. Liberty Interactive is a stock designed to track the performance of the company's interests in Expedia and its subsidiary QVC (the home shopping channel). Liberty Media is structured to track the performance of Starz and OnCommand (US-based home and commercial on-command movie channels), and OpenTV (a provider of digital interactivity to television channels including Discovery, BBC and SkyItalia). The company created these as they believed that the capital structure of the overall company, Liberty Media, was overly complex and therefore the value of the stock was below the value of the company assets.

flip
To buy shares at the offer price and sell them on the first trading day. Also called staging.

IPO underpricing
Occurs when the offer price in the prospectus is consistently lower than what the market is willing to bear.

initial return
The gain when an allocation of shares from an investment banker is sold at the first opportunity because the offer price is consistently lower than what the market is willing to bear.

The investment performance of IPOs

Are IPOs good investments? The answer seems to depend on the investment horizon of the investor and whether the investor can purchase IPO shares at the offer price. If an investor can buy shares at the offer price and **flip** them (sell them on the first trading day), then the returns on IPOs are substantial. If, instead, the investor buys shares in the secondary market and holds them for the long term, the returns are much less rewarding.

Positive initial returns for IPO investors (underpricing) Year in and year out, in virtually every country around the world, the very short-term returns on IPOs are surprisingly high. In the United States, the share price in the typical IPO closes roughly 15 per cent above the offer price after just one day of trading. Researchers refer to this pattern as **IPO underpricing**, meaning that the offer price in the prospectus is consistently lower than what the market is willing to bear. To capture this **initial return**, an investor must be fortunate enough to receive an allocation of shares from the investment banker and to sell those shares at the first opportunity. Therein lies a problem. Not all investors are allowed to participate in the investment bank's allocations. Bankers discourage those investors who do participate from immediately selling (i.e. flipping) the shares they received on the open market. For investors who buy IPO shares when they begin trading in the open market, in the hope of making a quick profit, the rewards are much smaller, and the risks much greater, than those faced by investors who participate in the initial offering.

SMART PRACTICES VIDEO
Jay Ritter, University of Florida
'Every single country in the world has IPOs underpriced on average.'

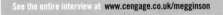
See the entire interview at **www.cengage.co.uk/megginson**

Applying the Model

On 19 February 2002, shares of the pioneer in internet payment methods, Paypal Inc. (ticker symbol, PYPL), began trading for the first time. According to the IPO prospectus, Paypal offered its shares for $13.00 to participating investors. At the close of the first day, Paypal shares were worth $18.20, for a one-day return of 40 per cent. However, for investors who could not buy shares from the syndicate but instead bought shares once trading began, the first-day results were not as good. Paypal shares opened the first day of trading at $19.29 before falling 5.7 per cent by the day's end. Seven months later, Paypal was acquired by eBay in a stock deal worth $1.37 billion, or $22.68 per share.

Clearly, underpricing is a pervasive phenomenon. However, the long-run performance of IPOs presents a different puzzle.

Negative long-term IPO returns US Research on the long-run performance of IPOs is not encouraging for investors. Typically this research indicates that investors will fare poorly if they buy IPO shares at the end of the first month of trading and then hold these shares for five years thereafter, compared to the returns these investors would have earned by purchasing the shares of comparable-sized firms. On average, investors' net returns are over 40 per cent below what they would have earned after five years on alternative equity investments. Other work has suggested that this phenomenon is global, and where companies issue large amounts of shares outside their home markets then the degree of long-term underperformance is greater.[2] This phenomenon of long-term underperformance holds across markets and is widespread. As we will see shortly, the phenomenon coexists with another relating to the first day of trading.

SMART PRACTICES VIDEO

Jay Ritter, University of Florida
'By the middle of 2001, 97 per cent of internet companies were trading below the offer price.'

See the entire interview at **www.cengage.co.uk/megginson**

Because these findings challenge the notions that investors are rational and that financial markets are efficient, they are quite controversial, and more recent research casts doubt on this long-run underperformance for IPO shares.[3] Given these conflicting findings, we cannot yet draw firm conclusions about the long-run return on IPO shares.

---

4 What patterns have been observed in the types of firms going public in the United States? Why do you think that certain industries become popular with investors at different times?

5 What does the term 'underpricing' refer to? If the average IPO is underpriced by about 15 per cent, how could an unsophisticated investor, who regularly invests in IPOs, earn an average return less than 15 per cent?

6 How does underpricing add to the cost of going public?

CONCEPT REVIEW QUESTIONS

11.4 SEASONED EQUITY OFFERINGS

Seasoned equity offerings (SEOs) are surprisingly rare for both US and non-US companies. In fact, the typical large corporation will not sell new shares, even as frequently as once per decade. Nevertheless, when an SEO is launched, it tends to be much larger than the typical IPO. Seasoned share issues must generally follow the same regulatory and underwriting procedures as unseasoned offerings. In the United States, the company must prepare a registration statement, including a preliminary prospectus, and file it with the SEC. After the SEC approves the registration statement, a final prospectus is printed and the securities can then be sold to investors.

---

[2] J.R. Ritter (1991) 'The Long-Run Performance of Initial Public Offerings', *Journal of Finance* 42: 365–394; C. Wu and C. Kwok (2006) 'Long-Run Performance of Global Versus Domestic Initial Public Offerings', *Journal of Banking and Finance* 3:609–627.

[3] See for example B.E. Eckbo and O. Norli (2005) 'Liquidity Risk, Leverage and Long-Term IPO Returns', *Journal of Corporate Finance* 11:1–35.

Besides its larger-than-average size, a seasoned offering is principally different from an unseasoned offering in that the seasoned securities have an observable market price when the offering is made. Obviously, this makes pricing seasoned offers much easier. Academic studies show that SEOs tend to be priced very near the current market price. However, ease of pricing does not mean that investors welcome new equity offering announcements, as we now discuss.

Share price reactions to seasoned equity offerings

One reason that corporations very rarely issue seasoned equity is that share prices usually fall when firms announce plans to conduct SEOs. On average, the price decline is about 3 per cent. Again, this holds across countries, with results documented in the USA, the UK and the Pacific Basin. Clearly, the announcement of seasoned equity issues conveys negative information to investors, though precisely what information is transmitted is not always clear. The message may be that management, which is presumably better informed about a company's true prospects than are outside investors, believes the firm's current share price is too high. Alternatively, the message may be that the firm's earnings will be lower than expected in the future, and management is issuing shares to make up for this internal cash flow shortfall.

There is also evidence that SEOs are bad news for shareholders not only at the time they are announced but also over longer holding periods of one to five years. As for IPOs, there is evidence that firms suffer negative long-run returns following seasoned equity offerings, although this does to an extent depend on the comparison benchmark.

Most equity sales fall under the category of **general cash offerings**, meaning that shares are offered for sale to any and all investors. However, there is a special type of seasoned equity offering that allows firms' existing owners to buy new shares at a bargain price or to sell that right to other investors. These **rights offerings/issues** are relatively scarce in the United States but are more common in other developed countries.

general cash offerings
Shares are offered for sale to any and all investors. Most equity sales fall under this category.

rights offering/rights issue
A special type of seasoned equity offering that allows the firm's existing owners to buy new shares at a bargain price or to sell that right to other investors.

Source: Adapted from the *Financial Times*, 22 November 2005.

Real World

In November 2005 Rhodia, the French chemicals company, launched a €600 million rights issue. The company stated that the proceeds would be used to pay down debt and finance development projects. Shareholders were to receive one preferential subscription right for each existing share held, and eight preferential subscription rights entitled them to subscribe to seven new shares at €1.10 per new share. At the time the company shares were trading at between €1.30 and €1.32.

Rights offerings

One of the basic tenets of English common law, and thus of commercial laws derived from it, is that shareholders have first claim on anything of value distributed by a corporation. These **pre-emptive rights** give shareholders the right to maintain their proportionate ownership in the corporation, by purchasing shares whenever the firm sells new equity. The laws of most American states grant shareholders the pre-emptive right to participate in new issues, unless this right is removed by shareholder consent. Most publicly traded US companies have removed pre-emptive rights from their corporate charters, with shareholder consent, so rights offerings by large American companies are quite rare today. However, rights offerings are still quite common in other countries, as the following 'Applying the model' section indicates.

pre-emptive rights
These hold that shareholders have first claim on anything of value distributed by a corporation.

Applying the Model

It is often said that 'the threat of disaster concentrates the mind', which was certainly true for the world's largest telecommunications firms during the bleak period after the steep decline in high-tech stocks in March 2000. After a decade of extremely rapid growth in capital spending, fuelled primarily by unprecedented borrowing from banks and bond markets, by late 2002 many telecoms companies found themselves teetering on the brink of bankruptcy. The slower-than-expected revenue growth, coupled with the higher-than-expected costs incurred, to roll out 'third-generation' mobile telephone networks, had left most of the large European operators with dangerously high debt levels. Without reducing their outstanding debts, firms risked seeing their credit ratings plummet.

To avert the prospect of financial meltdown, three of the largest European telecoms – British Telecom (BT), the Netherlands' KPN and France Telecom (FT) – took the highly unusual step of launching immense rights offerings of shares. BT raised £5.9 billion ($8.5 billion) in June 2001, and KPN issued €5 billion ($4.5 billion) six months later, briefly making these the two largest rights offerings in history. In March 2003, FT shattered all previous records with an enormous €15 billion ($15.8 billion) rights offering. Because this strategy keeps all the gains and losses on share issues 'within the family' of current shareholders, firms usually price rights offerings well below the current market price to assure that the offerings sell out, and firms raise the funds needed. All three companies followed this pattern. For example, BT priced its shares, which were selling for 435 pence ($7.54) each at the time of the rights issue, for 300 pence ($5.20) each. FT also priced its rights issue at about a 30 per cent discount to the share's pre-offer closing price, while KPN priced its new shares at a 4.5 per cent discount.

Though all three companies saw their share prices fall sharply when they announced their rights offerings, the rights issues themselves were successful, and all three issues met with excess demand (in investment banking terms, the issues were 'oversubscribed'). After the offerings, however, all three shares underperformed their national stock market indices, and, in the summer of 2004, all three shares were more than 75 per cent below their March 2000 peaks.

---

7 What happens to a company's share price when the firm announces plans for a seasoned equity offering? What are the long-term returns to investors following an SEO?

8 Why do you think that rights offerings have largely disappeared in the United States?

CONCEPT
REVIEW
QUESTIONS

11.5 IPOs INTERNATIONALLY

The international market for equity offerings can be broken down into two parts: each nation's market for domestic share offerings and the international, or cross-border, market for share offerings. We briefly look at each, beginning with an overview of national markets.

Non-US initial public offerings

Any nation with a well-functioning stock market must have some mechanism for taking private firms public. The total number of IPOs outside the United States each year usually exceeds the American total by a wide margin. However, far less money is raised in aggregate by private sector issuers on non-US markets, as these international IPOs are, on average, very much smaller than those on the NASDAQ or NYSE. Yet, many of the same anomalies documented in the United States are also observed internationally. First, non-US private sector IPOs also demonstrate significant first-day returns that are often much higher than for US IPOs. The Comparative Corporate Finance panel summarizes IPO underpricing studies from 38 different countries; all show significant underpricing, and many of these countries have mean initial returns greater than the US average.

A second empirical finding internationally is that seasoned equity offerings also seem to yield negative long-term returns. However, studies of non-US long-run returns are subject to all the methodological problems bedevilling US studies (perhaps even more), so it is unclear whether SEOs truly underperform or not. Thirdly, popular non-US issues also tend to be heavily oversubscribed, and the allocation rules mandated by national law or exchange regulations largely determine who captures the IPO initial returns. These rules and regulations differ across countries and as such make accurate comparison very difficult. Fourthly, hot-issue markets are as prevalent internationally as in the United States. Finally, taxation issues (particularly capital gains tax rules) significantly affect how issues are priced and which investors the offers target.

International IPO markets do, however, differ in important ways from US markets. For example, some governments impose social mandates on firms wanting to go public, requiring them to allocate minimum fractions of the issue to their employees or to other targeted groups. Furthermore, the net effect of pricing restrictions in many countries is to ensure that IPOs are severely underpriced; this is especially common in countries where shares must be priced on a par value basis and where minimum dividend payouts may be mandated. Some governments (for example, Japan's) routinely prohibit firms from making IPOs during periods when market conditions are 'unsettled'. They may require explicit permission to be obtained before an IPO can be launched. Many countries require that initial offering prices be set far in advance of the issue, which usually means that offerings that actually proceed tend to be significantly underpriced. Non-US entrepreneurs often have different motivations for taking firms public than do owner/managers of US private companies. Whereas the studies by Ritter and others have mainly found that US and UK companies go public to acquire the equity capital needed to finance rapid growth, continental European entrepreneurs go public mainly to rebalance their firms' capital structures and to achieve personal liquidity.[4] Most other countries place fewer restrictions on pre-offer marketing and discussion than do US regulators.

More recently, there has been a greater convergence of IPO market conditions and situations towards US practice. For example, there has been a growth of book-building as a procedure for pricing and allocating. On the other hand, in general in European IPOs gross spreads are lower and less clustered than in the US. Another striking feature of the European market is that, with the exception of the Alternative

---

[4] See M. Pagano, F. Panetta and L. Zingales (1998) 'Why Do Companies Go Public?', *Journal of Finance* 53(1):27–64 for the Italian evidence; and Kristian Rydqvist and Kenneth Högholm (1995) 'Going Public in the 1980s', *European Financial Management* 1(3):287–315 for the Swedish evidence.

Investment Market (AIM) in the UK, there has been a marked difficulty in sustaining interest in markets for smaller companies in Europe, with several initiatives failing in the last decade.

COMPARATIVE CORPORATE FINANCE
Average first-day returns on IPOs for 38 countries

Significantly positive returns on initial public offerings are observed in many other countries besides the United States. As this figure shows, IPO underpricing is observed in at least 38 countries, though the average level varies greatly – from less than 5 per cent in Denmark, to an amazing 250 per cent in China.

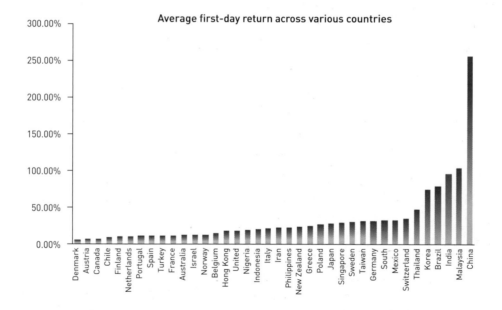

Source: Studies cited in Tim Loughran, Jay R. Ritter and Kristian Rydqvist (1994) 'Initial Public Offerings: International Insights', *Pacific-Basin Finance Journal* 2:165–199; plus updates at http://bear.cba.ufl.edu/ritter/ipodata.htm.

International share issues

Although the international market for shares is not, and probably never will be, as large as the international market for debt securities, cross-border trading and issuance of shares have increased dramatically during the past 15 years. Much of this increase can be accounted for by a growing desire on the part of institutional and individual investors to diversify their investment portfolios internationally. Because foreign shares currently account for a small fraction of US institutional holdings – as is true in other developed economies – this total will surely grow rapidly in the years ahead.

Corporations have discovered the benefits of issuing shares outside their home markets. Issuing shares internationally both broadens the ownership base and helps a company integrate itself into the local business scene. A share listing increases the local press coverage and also serves as effective corporate advertising. Having locally traded shares can also make corporate acquisitions easier because shares can then be used as an acceptable method of payment.

American and global depositary receipts[5] Many foreign corporations have discovered the benefits of trading their stock in advanced capital markets such as the United Kingdom or the United States, although they do so differently than do companies from the UK or the USA. For example, in the USA, the disclosure and reporting requirements mandated by the US Securities and Exchange Commission have historically discouraged all but the largest foreign firms from directly listing their shares on the New York or American stock exchanges. Thus, in mid-1993, Daimler Benz was the first large German company to seek such a listing. Instead, most foreign companies tap the US market through **American depositary receipts (ADRs)**. These dollar-denominated claims, issued by US banks, represent ownership of a foreign company's shares that are held on deposit by a US bank in the issuing firm's home country.

ADRs have proved to be very popular with US investors, partly because they allow investors to diversify internationally. However, because the shares are covered by American securities laws and pay dividends in dollars (dividends on the underlying shares are converted from the local currency into dollars before being paid out), US investors are able to diversify at very low cost.

The shares of over 1700 foreign companies were traded in the United States in the form of sponsored and unsponsored ADRs as at the end of 2006. A **sponsored ADR** is one for which the issuing (foreign) company absorbs the legal and financial costs of creating and trading the security. In this case, the companies pay a US depositary bank to create an ADR issue. An **unsponsored ADR** is one in which issuing firms are not involved with the issue at all, and may even oppose it. Historically, unsponsored ADRs typically resulted from US investor demand for shares of particular foreign companies. Since 1983, however, the SEC has required that all new ADR programmes be sponsored, so less than 200 unsponsored ADRs still exist. There are four different levels of ADR programmes, corresponding to different levels of required disclosure and tradability.

There are also now **global depositary receipts (GDRs)**. Companies in effect create a depositary receipt but instead of trading taking place on US exchanges the GDRs trade on other large and liquid exchanges. Most GDRs are issued in London or Luxembourg. Over the last ten years there has been a general decline in the number of ADRs, while GDRs have grown significantly. Of the 150 depositary receipts created in 2006, 100 were GDRs.

The two ADR programmes with the highest dollar-value trading volume during 2006 were BP with $60.6 billion traded and Petrobras (Brazil) with $57 billion traded. In London the largest programmes were two Russian energy companies, Lukoil ($70.6 billion) and Gazprom ($57.6 billion).

American depositary receipts (ADRs)
Dollar-denominated claims, issued by US banks, that represent ownership of shares of a foreign company held on deposit by the US bank in the issuing firm's home country.

sponsored ADR (or GDR)
A depositary receipt for which the issuing (foreign) company absorbs the legal and financial costs of creating and trading the security.

unsponsored ADR (or GDR)
A now rare type of a depositary receipt in which the issuing firm is not involved with the issue at all, and may even oppose it.

global depositary receipts (GDRs)
Local currency-denominated claims, issued by local banks, that represent ownership of shares of a foreign company held on deposit by that bank in the issuing firm's home country.

---

[5] Much of the data for this section is from the excellent Bank of New York ADR website (www.adrbny.com).

Applying the Model

To demonstrate how ADRs are created, assume that the Dutch Trading Company (DTC) wants to set up an ADR programme for its shares on the New York Stock Exchange. Suppose that DTC's shares are trading on Euronext Amsterdam at €21.00 per share, and the US dollar/euro exchange rate is $1.2500/€. If DTC wants to establish an ADR programme worth about $100 million, the firm could ask Bank of New York (ticker symbol, BK), one of the two leading ADR issuers, to handle the issue and could offer to pay all of BK's issuing and listing expenses – including underwriting fees. Assume further that BK believes the ideal price for shares to trade on the NYSE is about $50 per share. BK can implement this ADR programme by taking the following steps:

1. Purchase 4 million shares of DTC on Euronext Amsterdam at €21.00/share, paying €84 million. This represents an investment worth $105 000 000 by Bank of New York (€84 000 000 × $1.2500/€).

2. Create 2 million ADRs for listing on the NYSE, with each ADR representing ownership of two DTC shares.

3. Sell the 2 million ADRs to American investors at a price of $52.50 per ADR. This is the dollar price implied by DTC's price in euros, the current $/€ exchange rate, and considering that each ADR is worth two DTC shares (€21.00/share × 2 shares/ADR × $1.2500/€ = $52.50/ADR).

The total proceeds of this offering are $105 000 000, which is exactly equal to the amount BK paid for the shares originally. Holders of these ADRs have a security that is denominated in dollars, but which perfectly reflects both DTC's share price in euros and fluctuations in the dollar/euro exchange rate.

To demonstrate how ADRs reflect changes in DTC's share price, assume that DTC's shares increase by €1.00 per share in early-morning trading in the Netherlands. We can compute that the ADRs should rise by $2.50 each (€1.00/share × 2 shares/ADR × $1.2500/€) to $55.00 per share when they begin trading in New York later that day. To demonstrate how ADRs reflect exchange rate movements, assume that DTC's price remains unchanged at €21 per share, but that the euro appreciates from $1.2500/€ to $1.3095/€ immediately before trading begins in New York. The ADRs should begin trading at $55.00 per share (€21.00/share × 2 shares/ADR × $1.3095/€) when the NYSE opens. In other words, either an increase in DTC's share price from €21.00 to €22.00 per share, while holding exchange rates constant, or an appreciation of the euro from $1.2500/€ to $1.3095/€ (holding DTC's share price unchanged) can cause the price of each Dutch Trading Company ADR to rise by $2.50, from $52.50 to $55.00 per ADR.

Real World

Companies can sometimes issue shares in both an IPO and a GDR. Take the example of Cherkizovo Group, a family-owned Russian meat-producer, which raised over $300 million on the London exchange in April 2006. The company set a structure that had 150 GDRs representing one ordinary share, and raised half the capital via GDRs and half via a straight IPO process. Similarly, in July 2006 Rosneft, the Russian oil company, raised $6.1 billion using depositary receipts as part of its $10.4 billion initial public offering in London and Moscow. With Rosneft, each GDR traded in London represents one of the company's shares, which are traded in Moscow. GDRs are listed in London and Luxembourg, while the company also issued ADRs.

Cross listings

Cross listing is the process whereby a company issues (usually as an SEO but possibly as an IPO as we saw in the 'Opening focus' section) shares on more than one market. Cross listing is a natural alternative to depositary receipts in raising capital and in raising awareness of a company. However, the costs are higher and as such cross listings tend to be the province of larger companies. The evidence is fairly strong that cross listing brings benefits to a company in the form of lower cost of capital and greater liquidity in shares. There is also a share bounce from the announcement of a cross listing.

The extent of cross listing varies greatly across exchanges. Some exchanges have very few cross-listed companies, others many (see Table 11.4). A striking feature of the table is that many of the world's largest exchanges are not represented. Very few if any companies from outside China list on the Shanghai exchange for example. The general flow of companies cross listing is towards NYSE, London and NASDAQ, world poles of capital. However, note the regional poles – very large numbers of Latin American companies list on the Mexican exchange and Asian companies on the Singapore exchange.

Share issue privatizations

share issue privatization (SIP)
A government executing one of these will sell all or part of its ownership in a state-owned enterprise to private investors via a public share offering.

Anyone who examines international share offerings is soon struck by the size and importance of share issue privatizations in non-U.S. stock markets. A government executing a **share issue privatization (SIP)** sells all or part of its ownership in a state-owned enterprise to private investors, via a public share offering. The words public and private can become confusing in this context, because a SIP involves the sale of shares in a state-owned company to private investors, via a public capital market share offering. Since Britain's Thatcher government first popularized privatizations in the early 1980s, there have been more than 850 privatizing share offerings by almost 100 national governments. Prompted by the British success, governments around the world launched privatization programmes that have, to date, raised over $1.25 trillion. Virtually all this money flowed to the selling governments rather than to the firms being privatized.

For our purposes, the most important aspect of privatization programmes is the transforming role they have played in developing many national stock markets, in general, and IPO markets, in particular. Share issue privatizations are particularly important for market development because of their size (see Table 11.5) and the way their shares are allocated to potential investors. SIPs tend to be vastly larger than their private sector counterparts; in fact, the 11 largest (and 24 of the 25 largest) share offerings in history have all been either share issue privatizations or rights offerings by partially privatized companies. Almost without exception, SIPs have been the largest share offerings in the histories of individual countries. The first several large privatization IPOs generally yield a dramatic increase in a national stock market's

TABLE 11.4

Number of domestic and foreign companies by exchange

EXCHANGE	2005				2000				1995			
	TOTAL	DOMESTIC	FOREIGN	FOREIGN %	TOTAL	DOMESTIC	FOREIGN	FOREIGN %	TOTAL	DOMESTIC	FOREIGN	FOREIGN %
American	595	495	100	17%	649	598	51	8%	791	725	66	8%
Bermuda	56	19	37	66%	47	22	25	53%				
Buenos Aires	104	100	4	4%	125	122	3	2%	149	149	0	0%
Lima	224	193	31	14%	227	209	18	8%	243	242	1	0%
Mexico	326	150	176	54%	177	173	4	2%	185	185	0	0%
NASDAQ	3 164	2 832	332	10%	4 734	4 246	488	10%	5 127	4 766	361	7%
NYSE	2 270	1 818	452	20%	2 468	2 035	433	18%	2 242	1 996	246	11%
Sao Paulo	381	379	2	1%	467	464	3	1%	544	543	1	0%
TSX Group	3 758	3 719	39	1%	1 394	1 353	41	3%	1 258	1 196	62	5%
Australian	1 714	1 643	71	4%	1 406	1 330	76	5%	1 178	1 129	49	4%
Malaysia	1 019	1 015	4	0%	790	787	3	0%	526	523	3	1%
Hong Kong	1 135	1 126	9	1%	790	779	11	1%	542	518	24	4%
Jakarta	336	336	0	0%	286	286	0	0%	237	237	0	0%
Korea	1 616	1 616	0	0%	702	702	0	0%	721	721	0	0%
New Zealand	185	153	32	17%	203	147	56	28%	175	135	40	23%
Osaka	1 064	1 063	1	0%	1 310	1 310	0	0%	1 222	1 222	0	0%
Philippine	237	235	2	1%	230	228	2	1%	205	205	0	0%
Singapore	686	564	122	18%	480	417	63	13%	272	250	22	8%
Taiwan	696	691	5	1%	532	531	1	0%	347	347	0	0%
Thailand	504	504	0	0%	381	381	0	0%	416	416	0	0%
Tokyo	2 351	2 323	28	1%	2 096	2 055	41	2%	1 791	1 714	77	4%
Athens	304	302	2	1%	310	309	1	0%	186	186	0	0%
Borsa Italiana	282	275	7	2%	297	291	6	2%	254	250	4	2%
Deutsche Börse	764	648	116	15%	983	742	241	25%	1 622	678	944	58%
Euronext	1 259	966	293	23%	1 326	1 325	371	28%	1 698	1 213	485	29%
Irish	66	53	13	20%	96	76	20	21%	80	9		0%
JSE	373	348	25	7%	606	583	23	4%	638	612	26	4%
London	3 091	2 757	334	11%	2 374	1 926	448	19%	2 502	1 971	531	21%
OMX	678	656	22	3%	704	671	33	5%	548	527	21	4%
Oslo Børs	219	191	28	13%	214	191	23	11%	165	151	14	8%
Swiss	400	284	116	29%	416	252	164	39%	449	216	233	52%
Wiener Börse	111	92	19	17%	111	97	14	13%	148	109	39	26%

Source: World Federation of Stock Exchanges (www.world-exchanges.com).

trading volume and liquidity. In addition to size, SIPs differ from private sector share issues in being almost exclusively secondary offerings. In other words, the proceeds from SIPs go to the government rather than to the firm being privatized. The sole major exception to this rule to date has occurred in China; almost all Chinese SIPs have been primary offerings.

TABLE 11.5

The world's largest share offerings

With one exception (the AT&T Wireless tracking stock issue in April 2000), the 24 largest share offerings in history have either been share issue privatizations or share offerings by partially privatized companies.

DATE	COMPANY	COUNTRY	AMOUNT ($mn)	IPO/SEO
Nov 87	Nippon Telegraph & Telephone	Japan	$40 260	SEO
Oct 88	Nippon Telegraph & Telephone	Japan	22 400	SEO
Nov 99	ENEL	Italy	18 900	IPO
October 06	ICBC	China/Hong Kong	18 400	IPO
Oct 98	NTT DoCoMo	Japan	18 000	IPO
Mar 03	France Telecom	France	15 800	SEO[a]
Oct 97	Telecom Italia	Italy	15 500	SEO
Feb 87	Nippon Telegraph & Telephone	Japan	15 097	IPO
Nov 99	Nippon Telegraph & Telephone	Japan	15 000	SEO
Jun 00	Deutsche Telekom	Germany	14 760	SEO
Nov 96	Deutsche Telekom	Germany	13 300	IPO
Oct 87	British Petroleum	United Kingdom	12 430	SEO
Apr 00	ATT Wireless (tracking stock)	United States	10 600	IPO
Nov 98	France Telecom	France	10 500	SEO
Nov 97	Telstra	Australia	10 530	IPO
Oct 99	Telstra	Australia	10 400	SEO
Jun 99	Deutsche Telekom	Germany	10 200	SEO
Dec 90	Regional Electricity Companies[b]	United Kingdom	9 995	IPO
Dec 91	British Telecom	United Kingdom	9 927	SEO
May 06	Bank of China	China	9 700	IPO
Jun 00	Telia	Sweden	8 800	IPO
Dec 89	UK Water Authorities[b]	United Kingdom	8 679	IPO
Feb 01	NTT DoCoMo	Japan	8 200	SEO
Dec 86	British Gas	United Kingdom	8 012	IPO
Jun 98	Endesa	Spain	8 000	SEO
Jul 97	ENI	Italy	7 800	SEO

Notes:

[a] Rights offering, in which the French government participated proportionately, so not a SIP in the traditional sense. Though a share offering by a state-owned firm, government ownership did not decline.

[b] Indicates a group offering of multiple companies that trade separately after the IPO.

Source: Adapted from Table 12 of William L. Megginson and Jeffry M. Netter (2001) 'From State to Market: A Survey of Empirical Studies on Privatization', *Journal of Economic Literature* 39:321–389. Updated through June 2005 using data reported in the *Financial Times*.

The importance of SIPs in creating new shareholders derives from the way these issues are typically priced and allocated. Governments almost always set offer prices well below their expected open-market value (they deliberately underprice), thereby ensuring excess demand for shares in the offering. The issuing governments then tend to allocate shares in a way that ensures maximum political benefit. Invariably, governments favour employees and other small domestic investors (who typically have never purchased shares before) with relatively large share allocations, whereas domestic institutions and foreign investors are allocated far less than they desire. The net result of this strategy is to guarantee that most of the short-term capital gains of privatization IPOs are captured by the many citizen investors (who vote) rather than by institutional and foreign investors (who do not). Furthermore, the long-run excess returns to investors who purchase privatizing share issues are significantly positive. All these features help promote popular support for privatization and other economic reform measures that the government wants to enact. In all, privatization share offerings have done as much to promote the development of international stock markets during the last 25 years as any other single factor.

9 In what ways are non-US (private sector) initial public offerings similar to US IPOs, and in what ways are they different?

10 What are depositary receipts, and how are these created? Why do you think they have proved to be so popular?

11 In what key ways do share issue privatizations (SIPs) differ from private sector share offerings? Why do you think governments deliberately underprice SIPs?

CONCEPT
REVIEW
QUESTIONS

11.6 ADVANTAGES AND DISADVANTAGES OF AN IPO

The decision to convert from private to public ownership is not an easy one. The benefits of having publicly traded shares are numerous, but so too are the costs.

Benefits of going public

Chapter 2 of the accounting firm KPMG Peat Marwick's publication *Going Public: What the CEO Needs to Know* (1998) suggests the following advantages of an IPO to an entrepreneur.

1 **New capital for the company.** An initial public offering gives the typical private firm access to a larger pool of equity capital than is available from any other source. Whereas venture capitalists can provide perhaps $10–$40 million in funding throughout a company's life as a private firm, an IPO allows that same company to raise many times that amount in one offering. Recent academic studies find that the typical US IPO over the past 15 years raised about $110 million. An infusion of equity not only permits firms to pursue profitable investment opportunities but also improves their overall financial condition and provides additional borrowing capacity. Furthermore, if the stock of these firms performs well, the companies will be able to raise additional equity capital in the future.

2 **Publicly traded shares for use in acquisitions.** Unless a firm has publicly traded shares, the only way it can acquire another company is to pay in cash. After going public, a firm has the option of exchanging its own shares for that of the target firm. Not only does this minimize cash outflow for the acquiring firm, but such a payment method may be free from capital gains tax for the target firm's owners. This tax benefit may reduce the price that an acquirer must pay for a target company.

3 **Listed shares for use as remuneration.** Having publicly traded shares allows companies to attract, retain and provide incentives for talented managers by offering them share options and other equity-based remuneration. Going public also offers liquidity to managers who were awarded options while the firms were private.

4 **Personal wealth and liquidity.** Entrepreneurship almost always violates finance's basic dictum about diversification: real entrepreneurs generally have most of both their financial wealth and human capital tied up in their companies. Going public allows entrepreneurs to reallocate personal wealth away from their businesses and diversify their portfolios. Entrepreneurial families also frequently execute IPOs during times of transition, when, for example, the company founder wants to retire, and therefore provide a method of allocating family assets among those heirs who do and who do not desire to remain active in the business.

In addition to these benefits, the act of going public generally results in a blaze of media attention, which often helps promote a company's products and services. Being a public company also increases a firm's overall prestige. However, the obvious benefits of an IPO must be weighed against the often massive costs of such an offer.

Drawbacks to going public

KPMG Peat Marwick's listing also includes the drawbacks of an IPO for a firm's managers.

1 **The financial costs of an IPO.** Few entrepreneurs are truly prepared for just how costly the process of going public can be in terms of out-of-pocket cash expenses and opportunity costs. Total cash expenses of an IPO, such as printing, accounting and legal services, frequently are well over €1 million, and most of these must be paid even if the offering is postponed or cancelled. Additionally, the combined costs associated with the underwriter's discount (usually 7 per cent) and the initial underpricing of a firm's stock (roughly 15 per cent on average) represent a very large transfer of wealth from current owners to the underwriters and to the new shareholders.

2 **The managerial costs of an IPO.** As costly as an IPO is financially, many entrepreneurs find the unending claims made on their time during the IPO planning and execution process to be even more burdensome. Rarely, if ever, can CEOs and other top managers delegate these duties, which grow increasingly intense as the offering date approaches. There are also severe restrictions on what an executive can say or do during the immediate pre-offering period. Because the IPO process can take many months (or more) to complete, the cost of going public in terms of managerial distraction is very high. Top executives must also take time to meet with important potential shareholders before the IPO is completed, and forever thereafter.

3 **Share price emphasis.** Owners/managers of private companies frequently operate their firms in ways that balance competing personal and financial interests. This includes seeking profits, but frequently also includes employing family members in senior positions and other forms of personal consumption. Once a company goes public, however, external pressures build to maximize a firm's share price. Furthermore, as managerial shareholdings fall, managers become vulnerable to losing their jobs, either through takeover or through dismissal by the board of directors.

4 **Life in a fishbowl.** Public shareholders have the right to a great deal of information about a firm's internal affairs. Releasing this information to shareholders also implies releasing it to competitors and potential acquirers as well. Managers must disclose, especially in the IPO prospectus, how and in what markets they intend to compete – information that is obviously valuable to competitors. Additionally, managers who are also significant shareholders

are subject to binding disclosure requirements and face serious constraints on their ability to buy or sell company shares.

In spite of these drawbacks, we have seen that several hundred management teams each year decide that the benefits of going public outweigh the costs, and they begin the process of planning for an IPO.

---

12 What are the principal benefits of going public? What are the key drawbacks?

CONCEPT
REVIEW
QUESTION

11.7 SUMMARY AND CONCLUSIONS

- In almost all market economies, internally generated funds (primarily retained earnings) are the dominant source of funding for corporate investment. External financing is used only when needed, and then debt is almost always preferred to equity financing. The difference between a firm's total funding needs and its internally generated cash flow is referred to as its financial deficit.

- Financial intermediaries are institutions that raise funds by selling claims on themselves (often in the form of demand deposits or checking accounts) and then use those funds to purchase the debt and equity claims of corporate borrowers. They thus break – or intermediate – the direct link between final savers and borrowers that exists when companies fund their investment needs by selling securities directly to investors.

- The total volume of security issues has surged, and US corporate issuers routinely account for two-thirds of the worldwide total.

- Companies wanting to raise capital externally must make a series of decisions, beginning with whether to issue debt or equity, and whether to employ an investment bank to assist with the securities' sale. This chapter focuses on ordinary share offerings, but the decisions and issuing procedures are very similar for preference shares and debt securities.

- Firms wanting to raise new equity must decide whether to sell shares to public investors through a general cash offering, or to rely on sales to existing shareholders in a rights offering. Rights issues are now fairly rare in the United States, though they remain common in other developed countries.

- In the United States, shares can be sold through private placements to accredited investors, or to the public if the securities are registered with the SEC. A company's first public offering of shares is known as its initial public offering, or IPO. The typical American IPO is underpriced, on average, by about 15 per cent, and this has held true for several decades. International IPOs are also underpriced. It is unclear whether IPOs are poor long-term investments.

- Subsequent offerings of shares are known as seasoned equity offerings, or SEOs. The announcement of a seasoned equity issue tends to decrease a company's share price. There is strong evidence that firms issuing seasoned equity underperform over the long term.

- Investment banks assist companies in selling new securities by underwriting security offerings. Underwriting a security offering involves three tasks: (1) managing the offering, which includes advising companies about the type and amount of securities to sell, (2) underwriting the offering, by purchasing the securities from the issuer at a fixed price to shift the price risk from the issuer to the investment bank, and (3) selling the securities to investors.

● The largest share offerings in world history have all been share issue privatizations, or SIPs. Since 1981, governments have raised over $850 billion through these share offerings, and they have transformed stock market capitalization, trading volume and the number of citizens who own shares in many countries.

INTERNET RESOURCES

For updates to links in this section and elsewhere in the book, please go to the book's website at www.cengage.co.uk/megginson.

http://adrbny.com
The Bank of New York's ADR website provides detailed information about ADR listing and trading patterns. This site also makes available the bank's semi-annual *ADR Market Summary* report.

http://marketrac.nyse.com/mt/index.html
A portion of the NYSE site, offering a virtual tour of the exchange floor that shows which shares trade at each 'post' and gives numerous up-to-date trading statistics for each share.

http://www.investorhome.com/ipo.htm
A site linking to IPO data, research articles and other information.

http://www.ipohome.com
A site operated by Renaissance Capital, offering up-to-date information on venture capital, IPOs and seasoned equity offerings; has a calendar of upcoming financing events.

http://www.sec.gov/news/extra/handbook.htm
How to write clear, informative disclosure documents for investors, with a preface from Warren Buffet.

http://www.allipo.com
A UK-based company site that discusses IPO investment opportunities for individual investors.

KEY TERMS

American depositary receipts (ADRs)	financial deficit	global depositary receipts (GDRs)
book-building	financial intermediary (FI)	Gramm-Leach-Bliley Act
bulge bracket	fixed-price offer	initial return
cash flow from operations	flip	international shares
equity carve-out	foreign bond	investment bank
Eurobond	general cash offerings	IPO underpricing
	Glass-Steagall Act	league table

McFadden Act	rights offering/rights issue	spin-off
merchant bank	roadshow	sponsored ADR (or GDR)
pre-emptive rights	Rule 144A offering	tracking stocks
primary security issues	secondary offering	unseasoned equity offering
prospectus	securitization	unsponsored ADR (or GDR)
reverse LBO (or second IPO)	share issue privatization (SIP)	

SELF-TEST PROBLEMS

ST11-1 Last year Guaraldi Instruments conducted an IPO, issuing 2 million ordinary shares with a par value of €0.25 to investors, at a price of €15 per share. During its first year of operation, Guaraldi earned net income of €0.07 per share and paid a dividend of €0.005 per share. At the end of the year, the company's shares were selling for €20 each. Construct the equity account for Guaraldi at the end of its first year in business and calculate the firm's market capitalization.

ST11-2 The Bloomington Company needs to raise €20 million of new equity capital. Its share price is currently €42. The investment bankers require an underwriting spread of 7 per cent of the offering price. The company's legal, accounting and printing expenses associated with the seasoned offering are estimated to be €450 000. How many new shares must the company sell to net €20 million?

ST11-3 Assume that Zurich Semiconductor Company (ZSC) wants to create a sponsored ADR programme, worth $75 million, to trade its shares on the NASDAQ stock market. Assume that ZSC is currently selling on the SWX Swiss Exchange for SF25.00 per share, and the current dollar/Swiss franc exchange rate is $0.8000/SF. American Bank and Trust (ABT) is handling the ADR issue for ZSC and has advised the company that the ideal trading price for high-technology shares on the NASDAQ is about $60 per share (or per ADR).

a Describe the precise steps ABT must take to create an ADR issue that meets ZSC's preferences.

b Assume that ZSC's share price declines from SF25.00 to SF22.50. If the exchange rate does not also change, what will happen to ZSC's ADR price?

c If the Swiss franc depreciates from $0.8000/SF to $0.7500/SF, but the price of ZSC's shares remains unchanged in Swiss francs, how will ZSC's ADR price change?

QUESTIONS

Q11-1 How can a corporation estimate the amount of financing that must be raised externally during a given year? Once that amount is known, what other decision must be made?

Q11-2 Differentiate between a US commercial bank and the merchant banks found in other developed countries. How have these differences affected the securities markets in the United States versus those in other developed countries?

Q11-3 What do you think are the most important costs and benefits of becoming a publicly traded firm? If you were asked to advise an entrepreneur whether to take his or her firm public, what are the key questions you would ask before making your recommendation?

Q11-4 If you were an investment banker, how would you determine the offering price of an IPO?

Q11-5 Are the significantly positive short-run returns and the significantly negative long-run returns earned by IPO shareholders compatible with market efficiency? If not, why not?

Q11-6 List and briefly describe the key services that investment banks provide to firms that are issuing securities, before, during and after the offering.

Q11-7 What are American depositary receipts (ADRs), and why have they proved to be so popular with US investors?

Q11-8 How do you explain why the underwriting spread on IPOs averages about 7 per cent of the offering price, whereas the underwriting spread on a seasoned offering of shares averages less than 5 per cent?

Q11-9 Discuss the various points that must be considered in selecting an investment banker for an IPO. Which type of placement is usually preferred by the issuing firm?

Q11-10 In terms of IPO investing, what does it mean to 'flip' a stock? According to the empirical results regarding short- and long-term returns that follow equity offerings, is flipping a wise investment strategy?

Q11-11 What materials are presented in an IPO prospectus? In general, what result is documented regarding sales of shares by insiders and venture capitalists?

Q11-12 How do you explain the highly politicized nature of share issue privatization (SIP) pricing and share allocation policies? Are governments maximizing offering proceeds, or are they pursuing primarily political and economic objectives?

PROBLEMS

P11-1 Meltzer Electronics estimates that its total financing needs for the coming year will be €34.5 million. During the coming fiscal year, the firm's required financing payments on its debt and equity financing will total €12.9 million. The firm's financial manager estimates that operating cash flows for the coming year will total €33.7 million and that the following changes will occur in the accounts noted.

ACCOUNT	FORECAST CHANGE
Gross fixed assets	€8.9 million
Change in current assets	+2.3 million
Change in accounts payable	+1.3 million
Change in accrued liabilities	+0.8 million

a Use Equation 2.3 and the data provided to estimate Meltzer's free cash flow in the coming year.

b How much of the free cash flow will the firm have available as a source of new internal financing in the coming year?

c How much external financing will Meltzer require during the coming year to meet its total forecast financing need?

P11-2 West Coast Manufacturing Company (WCMC) is executing an initial public offering with the following characteristics. The company will sell 10 million shares at an offer price of €25 per share, the underwriter will charge a 7 per cent underwriting fee, and the shares are expected to sell for €32 each by the end of the first day's trading. Assuming this IPO is executed as expected, answer the following:

a Calculate the initial return earned by investors who are allocated shares in the IPO.

b How much will WCMC receive from this offering?

c What is the total cost (underwriting fee and underpricing) of this issue to WCMC?

P11-3 Suppose you purchase shares of a company that recently executed an IPO at the post-offering market price of €32 per share, and you hold the shares for one year. You then sell your shares for €35 per share. The company does not pay dividends, and you are not subject to capital gains taxation. During this year, the return on the overall stock market was 11 per cent. What net return did you earn on your share investment? Assess this return compared with the overall market return.

P11-4 Norman Internet Service Company (NISC) is interested in selling shares to raise capital for capacity expansion. The firm has consulted First Tulsa Company, a large underwriting firm, which believes that the stock can be sold for €50 per share. The underwriter's investigation found that its administrative costs will be 2.5 per cent of the sale price, and its selling costs will be 2.0 per cent of the sale price. If the underwriter requires a profit equal to 1 per cent of the sale price, how much, in euros, will the spread have to be to cover the underwriter's costs and profit?

P11-5 The Norman Company needs to raise €50 million of new equity capital. Its shares currently sell for €50 each. The investment bankers require an underwriting spread of 3 per cent of the offering price. The company's legal, accounting and printing expenses associated with the seasoned offering are estimated to be €750 000. How many new shares must the company sell to net €50 million?

P11-6 LaJolla Securities specializes in the underwriting of small companies. The terms of a recent offering were as follows:

Number of shares	2 million
Offering price	€25 per share
Net proceeds	€45 million

LaJolla Securities' expenses, associated with the offering, were €500 000. Determine LaJolla Securities' profit on the offering if, immediately after the offering began, the secondary market price of each share was as follows:

a €23 per share

b €25 per share

c €28 per share

P11-7 SMG Corporation sold 20 million shares in a seasoned offering. The market price of the company's shares, immediately before the offering, was €14.75. The shares were offered to the public at €14.50, and the underwriting spread was 4 percent. The company's expenses associated with the offering were €7.5 million. How much new cash did the company receive?

The market for initial public offerings

P11-8 Go to http://www.ipohome.com, and find (under IPO Marketwatch, then Pricings) information about firms that went public in the first few weeks of 2005. Write down the ticker symbols and offer prices for the firms you select; then go to Yahoo! and download daily

price quotes since the IPO date. For each firm, calculate the following:

a The first-day percentage return, measured from the offer price to the closing price.

b The first-day percentage return, measured from the opening price to the closing price.

P11-9 Four companies conducted IPOs last month: Hot.Com, Biotech Pipe Dreams Corp., Sleepy Tyme, and Bricks N Mortar International. All four companies went public at an offer price of €10 per share. The first-day performance of each share (measured as the percentage difference between the IPO offer price and the first-day closing price) appears below:

COMPANY	FIRST-DAY RETURN
Hot.Com	45%
Biotech Pipe Dreams	30%
Sleepy Tyme	5%
Bricks N Mortar	0%

a You submit a bid through your broker for 100 shares of each company. Your orders were filled completely, and you cashed out of each deal after one day. What was your average return on these investments?

b Next, suppose your orders were not all filled completely because of excess demand for 'hot' IPOs. After ordering 100 shares of each company, you were able to buy only 10 shares of Hot.Com, 20 shares of Biotech Pipe Dreams, 50 shares of Sleepy Tyme and 100 shares of Bricks N Mortar. Recalculate your average return, taking into account that your orders were only partially filled.

Seasoned equity offerings

P11-10 After a banner year of rising profits and positive equity market returns, the managers of Raptor Pharmaceuticals Corporation (RPC) decided to launch a seasoned equity offering to raise new equity capital. RPC currently has 10 million shares outstanding, and yesterday's closing market price was €75.00 per RPC share. The company plans to sell 1 million newly issued shares in its seasoned offering. The investment banking firm Robbum and Blindum (R&B) has agreed to underwrite the new share issue for a 2.5 per cent discount from the offering price, which RPC and R&B have agreed should be €0.75 per share lower than RPC's closing price the day before the offering is sold.

a What is likely to happen to RPC's share price when the plan for this seasoned offering is publicly announced?

b Assume that RPC's share price closes at €72.75 per share the day before the seasoned offering is launched. What net proceeds will RPC receive from this offering?

c Calculate the return earned by RPC's *existing* shareholders on their shares from the time preceding the announcement of the seasoned offering through the time it was actually sold for €72.75 per share.

d Calculate the total cost of the seasoned equity offering to RPC's existing shareholders as a percentage of the offering proceeds.

IPOs *internationally*

P11-11 The Rome Electricity Company (REC) wants to create a sponsored ADR programme, worth $300 million, to trade its shares on the New York Stock Exchange. Assume that REC is currently selling on the Borsa Italiana (the Italian Stock Exchange, in Milan) for €30.00 per share, and the current dollar/euro exchange rate is $1.2500/€. American Bank and Trust (ABT) is handling the ADR issue for REC and has advised REC that the ideal trading price for utility company shares on the NYSE is about $75 per share (or per ADR).

a Describe the precise steps ABT must take to create an ADR issue that meets REC's preferences.

b Suppose REC's share price rises from €30.00 to €33.00 per share. If the exchange rate does not change, what will happen to REC's ADR price?

c If the euro appreciates from $1.2500/€ to $1.2900/€, but the price of REC's shares remains unchanged in euros, what will happen to REC's ADR price?

P11-12 Nippon Computer Manufacturing Company (NCM) wants to create a sponsored ADR programme, worth $250 million, to trade its shares on NASDAQ. Assume that NCM is currently selling on the Tokyo Stock Exchange for ¥1550 per share, and the current dollar/yen exchange rate is $0.008089/¥ or, equivalently, ¥123.62/$. Metropolis Bank and Trust (MBT) is handling the ADR issue for NCM and has advised NCM that the ideal trading price for high-technology shares on the NASDAQ is about $20 per share (or per ADR).

a Describe the precise steps MBT must take to create an ADR issue that meets NCM's preferences.

b Suppose NCM's share price rises from ¥1550 to ¥1650 per share. If the exchange rate does not change, what will happen to NCM's ADR price?

c If the yen depreciates from $0.008089/¥ to $0.008050/¥, but the price of NCM's shares remains unchanged in yen, what will happen to NCM's ADR price?

THOMSON ONE **Business School Edition**

For instructions on using Thomson ONE, refer to the introductory text provided with the Thomson ONE problems at the end of Chapters 1–6, or in *A Guide for Using Thomson ONE – Business School Edition*.

P11-13 Determine the sources of capital for Canon Inc. (ticker: J:CN@N) in each of the last five years. How much capital was raised through internal sources, and how much was raised through external sources? Compare the sources of capital for Canon to those of Xerox Corp. (U:XRX). Does one company appear to depend more heavily on internal sources rather than external sources, or vice versa? What are some possible reasons for this?

 MINICASE *Raising long-term equity financing*

Since graduation from university, you have worked at Precision Manufacturing, as a financial analyst. You have recently been promoted to the position of Senior Financial Manager, with responsibilities that include capital budgeting decisions and the raising of long-term financing. Therefore, you decide to investigate the various alternatives for raising funds. You understand that your goal is to ascertain that the marginal benefits received from undertaking long-term projects should be greater than the marginal costs of raising the long-term funds needed to finance those projects. With this goal in mind, you decide to answer the following questions.

Assignment

1 What should managers consider when making the decision whether to finance internally or externally?

2 What services does an investment banker offer to corporations that choose to raise funds in the capital market?

3 What legal rules govern the issue of securities to the public in the United States?

4 What are the benefits to the corporation of going public?

5 What are the drawbacks to the corporation of going public?

6 What returns can investors in the shares expect on the first day of trading if they commit to purchase shares through the IPO issue? What factors may affect the relative amount of these first-day returns?

7 Describe the following offers: (a) seasoned equity offer; (b) rights offer; and (c) private placement. In what circumstances would a company use each of these offerings to raise funds?

8 Discuss international differences in public offerings.

Chapter 12
Capital Structure

OPENING FOCUS

How do the world's most admired companies fund themselves?

Each spring, *Fortune* magazine publishes a list of the most admired public companies worldwide. The data derive from a survey of executives in a wide range of large companies. For 2006, the top ten most admired worldwide companies were General Electric, Toyota Motor, Procter & Gamble, FedEx, Johnson & Johnson, Microsoft, Dell, Berkshire Hathaway, Apple Computer and Wal-Mart Stores.

What characteristics do these ten companies have in common that allow them to prosper and impress, year after year? All ten companies have achieved high sales growth rates, at least over the past decade, all are solidly profitable, and as a group, they have turned in impressive long-term share price performance. Most pay dividends, all have high price/earning ratios and the list includes the very largest companies in the world. Yet they have very different capital structures. Shown below are the ratios of long-term debt to total capital of these firms as at the end of 2005.

The purpose of this chapter is to help you understand why some firms use a great deal of debt, while other firms use very little. For some people, the strategies of firms like Starbucks, Juventus Football Club or Paddy Power plc, which issue almost no debt, are intuitively appealing. These firms have adopted a relatively conservative financing strategy and are simply following William Shakespeare's advice, 'neither a borrower nor a lender be'. On the other hand, readers who have a basic understanding of tax may see a benefit to the high-debt capital structure chosen by companies such as GE or Peugeot. The tax law treats interest payments as a tax-deductible business expense, but the same treatment does not apply to dividends. Therefore, by using a significant amount of debt, GE shelters more of the cash flow that it generates from taxation.

In each chapter of this text we have explained how managers weigh marginal benefits and costs to

Different capital structure types in the *Fortune* 'Global Most Admired Companies 2006'

COMPANY	LONG-TERM DEBT AS A PERCENTAGE OF TOTAL CAPITAL
General Electric	64.39
Toyota Motor	33.59
Procter & Gamble	36.38
FedEx	20.20
Johnson & Johnson	5.06
Microsoft	0.00
Dell	10.85
Berkshire Hathaway	11.95
Apple Computer	0.00
Wal-Mart Stores	35.58

Source: Companies taken from the *Fortune* 'Global Most Admired Companies 2006' and data sourced from the Thomson ONE site.

create value for shareholders. When it comes to financing decisions, our framework suggests that managers should trade off the benefits of debt (e.g. tax deductibility) with its costs (e.g. risk of default and bankruptcy) to arrive at an 'optimal' capital structure that maximizes the wealth of shareholders. However, if all the 'most admired companies' can prosper while taking such different approaches to financing their operations, then we may wonder whether the decision to use debt or equity has any influence at all on how they perform. Almost 50 years ago, Franco Modigliani and Merton Miller, two economists who later received the Nobel Prize, reached a controversial and counter-intuitive conclusion – a firm's decision to finance its operations with debt or with equity has no effect on its total market value. In this chapter, we explore the factors that determine whether managers can increase the values of their firms by choosing an optimal capital structure or whether they should focus their attention on something other than financing decisions.

LEARNING OBJECTIVES

After studying this chapter you should be able to:

- Explain how financial leverage increases both a firm's risk and its returns.

- Understand how the Modigliani-Miller model proves that capital structure is irrelevant in a world without taxes and other market frictions, but that the use of debt is favoured when companies are subject to corporate income taxes.

- Discuss how corporate and personal taxes affect capital structure.

- Explain how the costs of bankruptcy and financial distress affect capital structure decisions and explore the questions raised by the agency cost/tax shield trade-off model of corporate leverage.

- Describe the most important capital structure patterns observed around the world and explain what factors may be driving leverage choices.

SMART FINANCE
Use the learning tools at www.cengage.co.uk/megginson

The 'Opening Focus' poses a series of questions about capital structure decisions. The most important is: Why do some firms choose to issue large amounts of long-term debt, while other companies issue little or no debt? This question has transfixed financial economists for half a century. Although we still do not have a completely satisfactory answer, experience and research have taught us much about how companies set their leverage ratios. This chapter describes the key influences on managers' decisions to finance with debt or with equity. We begin by showing why firms may choose to substitute debt for equity capital, even in a world without corporate income taxes. We then show that the common practice of allowing companies to deduct interest payments from taxable income provides a strong incentive for corporations to substitute debt for equity.

12.1 WHAT IS FINANCIAL LEVERAGE AND WHY DO FIRMS USE IT?

When firms in the US have debt in their capital structures, we say that they are using financial leverage. In Britain, the common term for debt is gearing. Both terms imply that the effect of debt is to magnify or amplify a firm's financial performance in some way. In this section, we show how debt can dramatically affect the returns that firms can deliver to their shareholders. That effect can be either positive or negative, depending on the cash flow that firms can generate on their invested capital. A simple example illustrates this principle.

Consider the decision facing Susan Smith, chief financial officer of the High-Tech Manufacturing Company (HTMC), a publicly listed business that currently has no debt. HTMC has 200 000 shares outstanding, and shares trade in the market for €50 each. This implies that HTMC's total market capitalization is €10 000 000. Susan Smith agrees with this valuation, because she expects HTMC to generate total profits of €1 000 000 per year, for the foreseeable future. Financial analysts who follow the firm, state that HTMC's required return on assets (ROA) equals 10 per cent. Treating the €1 000 000 annual earnings stream as a perpetuity, then the HTMC's total value equals €10 000 000 (€1 000 000 ÷ 0.10 = €10 000 000). Note that because HTMC has no debt, the return on assets and the return on equity are equal.

Susan Smith is weighing a proposal that was presented to her by one of HTMC's largest and most important shareholders. The shareholder suggested that HTMC should issue €5 000 000 in long-term debt, at an interest rate of 6.0 per cent, and then use the proceeds of this debt issue to repurchase half the company's shares. That would leave HTMC with 100 000 shares. For now, let's assume that the shares remaining will still sell for €50 each. This **recapitalization** changes the mix of HTMC's debt and equity financing, but it does not change the total amount of financing available to the company. It would change HTMC's capital structure from being entirely equity (€10 000 000 worth of shares and no debt) to one that was 50 per cent debt and 50 per cent equity. In other words, this strategy would convert HTMC's debt-to-equity ratio from its current level of 0 to 1.0, after the recapitalization. Table 12.1 summarizes HTMC's current and proposed capital structures.

The shareholder suggests that this strategy will increase the expected return to HTMC's shareholders, as measured by earnings per share. Though initially dubious of this proposal, Susan Smith creates Tables 12.2 and 12.3 to test the shareholder's prediction. As noted, she thinks that HTMC's earnings, before interest and taxes (EBIT), will be €1 000 000 next year, if the economy continues to grow at a normal rate. For now, we assume that there are no taxes. Therefore, there is no difference between EBIT and net income for an unlevered company like HTMC. (We relax this no-tax assumption in Section 12.3.) However, if the country falls into a recession next

recapitalization
Alteration of a company's capital structure to change the relative mix of debt and equity financing, leaving total capitalization unchanged.

	CURRENT	PROPOSED
Assets	€10 000 000	€10 000 000
Equity	€10 000 000	€ 5 000 000
Debt	€ 0	€ 5 000 000
Debt-to-equity ratio	0	1.0
Shares outstanding	200 000	100 000
Share price	€ 50.00	€ 50.00
Interest rate on debt	—	6.0%

TABLE 12.1

The current and proposed capital structures for High-Tech Manufacturing Company

	CURRENT CAPITAL STRUCTURE: ALL-EQUITY FINANCING	PROPOSED CAPITAL STRUCTURE: 50% DEBT: 50% EQUITY
EBIT	€1 000 000	€1 000 000
– Interest (6.0%)	€ 0	(€ 300 000)
Net income	€1 000 000	€ 700 000
Shares outstanding	200 000	100 000
Earnings per share	€ 5.00	€ 7.00
Return on equity (P_0 = €50.00/share)	**10.0%**	**14.0%**

TABLE 12.2

Cash flows to shareholders and bondholders under the current and proposed capital structure for High-Tech Manufacturing Company

Assuming EBIT = €1 000 000

year, High-Tech's sales will fall, and EBIT will be only €500 000. On the other hand, if the economy booms, HTMC will enjoy rising sales, and EBIT will be €1 500 000. Ms Smith believes that the probability of each outcome is one-third, so the expected value of EBIT equals €1 000 000:

$$\text{Expected EBIT} = (1/3) \, €1\,500\,000 + (1/3) \, €1\,000\,000 + (1/3) \, €500\,000$$
$$= €1\,000\,000$$

Table 12.2 describes the pay-offs to HTMC, and to its security-holders, for the current and proposed capital structure, assuming that the economy grows at a normal rate and that EBIT equals €1 000 000. If the current capital structure is retained, earnings per share (EPS) will be €5.00. Because HTMC shares are currently worth €50 each, and the company pays out all net profits as dividends, HTMC's shareholders will earn a return on equity of 10 per cent (€5.00 ÷ €50.00) over the coming year. If HTMC instead adopts the proposed recapitalization, the firm will have to pay €300 000 interest on the €5 000 000 debt (0.06 × €5 000 000), leaving

TABLE 12.3

Expected cash flows to shareholders and bondholders under the current and proposed capital structure for High-Tech Manufacturing Company

For three equally likely economic outcomes.

EBIT	RECESSION €500 000		NORMAL GROWTH €1 000 000		BOOM €1 500 000	
	ALL-EQUITY FINANCING	50% DEBT: 50% EQUITY	ALL-EQUITY FINANCING	50% DEBT: 50% EQUITY	ALL-EQUITY FINANCING	50% DEBT: 50% EQUITY
– Interest (6.0%)	€ 0	(€300 000)	€ 0	(€300 000)	€ 0	(€ 300 000)
Net income	€500 000	€200 000	€1 000 000	€700 000	€1 500 000	€1 200 000
Shares outstanding	200 000	100 000	200 000	100 000	200 000	100 000
Earnings per share	€ 2.50	€ 2.00	€ 5.00	€ 7.00	€ 7.50	€ 12.00
% Return on shares (P_0 = €50.00/share)	5.0%	4.0%	10.0%	14.0%	15.0%	24.0%

€700 000 in net income (€1 000 000 EBIT − €300 000 interest). Only 100 000 shares remain outstanding after the recapitalization, so EPS will be €7.00. In this scenario, the return on equity enjoyed by shareholders is 14 per cent (€7 ÷ €50).

So far, the recapitalization plan looks rather attractive. But what happens if the economy either falls into a recession or booms? Clearly then the EBIT of the company will change, rising in the boom and decreasing in the recession. Table 12.3 demonstrates the pay-offs to HTMC's shareholders and bondholders in all three economic states next year – recession, normal growth and boom. If the economy booms, High-Tech's EBIT will be €1 500 000. With the existing capital structure, EPS will be €7.50 and ROE will be 15.0 per cent. HTMC's shareholders will truly benefit if the company recapitalizes and the economy booms. In this case, EPS will be €12.00 and ROE will be an impressive 24.0 per cent!

So what's the catch? What could possibly argue against HTMC adopting the recapitalization plan and increasing EPS and ROE? The answer is that the national economy may well fall into a recession next year, in which case High-Tech's EBIT will only be €500 000. With the existing all-equity capital structure, the company would achieve an EPS of €2.50, yielding a 5.0 per cent ROE for shareholders. However, if HTMC recapitalizes and the economy falls into a recession, net income will only be €200 000, after paying €300 000 in interest. Thus, EPS will be €2.00 and ROE only 4.0 per cent. In other words, whether the recapitalization plan generates a higher or a lower ROE for shareholders depends on the level of EBIT.

Recall that Susan Smith believes that each of the three economic scenarios is equally likely. Based on that view, we already calculated the expected level of EBIT. But what about expected EPS and expected ROE? As HTMC's major shareholder claimed, the expected return to shareholders rises if HTMC adds debt to its capital structure.

$$\text{Expected EPS (no debt)} = (1/3)\ 7.5 + (1/3)\ 5 + (1/3)\ 2.5 = €5$$

$$\text{Expected ROE (no debt)} = (1/3)\ 15 + (1/3)\ 10 + (1/3)\ 5 = 10\%$$

Expected EPS (with debt) = (1/3) 12 + (1/3) 7 + (1/3) 2 = €7

Expected ROE (with debt) = (1/3) 24 + (1/3) 14 + (1/3) 4 = 14%

How leverage increases the risk of expected earnings per share

Figure 12.1 graphically describes the relationship between EBIT and EPS for High-Tech's shareholders, under both the current and proposed capital structures. For both the normal growth and economic boom scenarios, with EBIT of €1 000 000 and €1 500 000, respectively, the company will have higher EPS with the proposed 50 per cent debt/50 per cent equity capital structure than with the current all-equity capitalization. In a recession, with EBIT of €500 000, High-Tech's shareholders will earn higher EPS with the current all-equity capitalization than with the proposed capital structure. In fact, for any EBIT above €600 000, HTMC's shareholders earn a higher EPS with the 50 per cent debt/50 per cent equity capitalization than they would with the current all-equity capital structure. For any EBIT below €600 000, the reverse is true – shareholders earn higher EPS with an all-equity capitalization than they would if debt is used.

The €600 000 level of EBIT is thus the breakeven level of operating profits for the proposed recapitalization. If the firm's EBIT is €600 000 and it has no debt, its return on equity will be 6 per cent. This is also the assumed interest rate HTMC would pay if it issued debt. Therefore, if the firm can issue debt at 6 per cent and earn more than

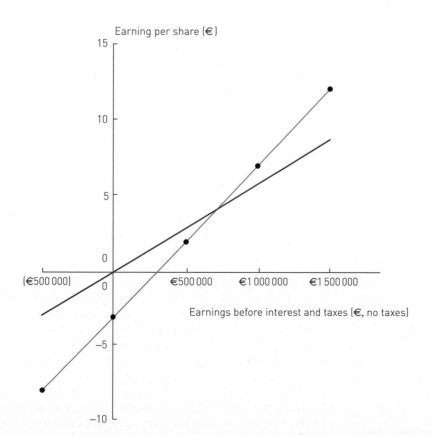

FIGURE 12.1

Using debt to increase expected earnings per share (red line) for High-Tech Manufacturing Company (HTMC), versus all-equity capital structure (blue line)

6 per cent with the money, then EPS goes up, relative to the all-equity case. If EBIT is less than €600 000, the firm's ROE is less than 6 per cent, and EPS goes down, relative to the all-equity case. Additionally, the proposed capital structure magnifies the effect on EPS of any change in EBIT away from €600 000. If EBIT increases by 25 per cent (from €600 000 to €750 000), then EPS increases by 50 per cent (from €3.00 to €4.50) under the proposed half-debt and half-equity capital structure. However, EPS increases by only 25 per cent (from €3.00 to €3.75) under the current all-equity capital structure. On the other hand, if EBIT declines by 25 per cent (from €600 000 to €450 000), the decline in EPS will be far greater under the proposed capital structure (−50 per cent) than under the existing all-equity structure (−25 per cent). If the economy falls into a truly deep recession next year, to the point where HTMC just breaks even on an operating basis (EBIT = 0), the shareholders will also break even (EPS = 0) under the current all-equity capitalization. But they will suffer losses of €3.00 per share under the proposed capital structure (−€300 000 net income ÷ 100 000 shares outstanding).

The fundamental principle of financial leverage

financial leverage
Using debt to magnify both the risk and expected return on a firm's investments. Also, the result of the presence of debt when firms finance their operations with debt and equity, leading to a higher share beta.

fundamental principle of financial leverage
States that substituting long-term debt for equity in a company's capital structure increases both the level of expected returns to shareholders – measured by earnings per share or ROE – and the risk (dispersion) of those expected returns.

The simple example using the High-Tech Manufacturing Company shows why employing long-term debt financing is called applying financial leverage. Just as a lever is used in the physical world to magnify the effect of a given force on an object, debt financing magnifies the impact of a change in EBIT on earnings per share. If High-Tech's realized EBIT comes in next year at €600 000, or higher, employing debt financing will increase earnings per share for the firm's shareholders. However, the reverse also holds true. If EBIT falls below €600 000, HTMC's earnings per share will be lower than they would have been with an all-equity capital structure. This yields a basic and important result, termed the fundamental principle of financial leverage, under which, substituting long-term debt for equity in a company's capital structure increases both the level of expected returns to shareholders – measured by earnings per share or ROE – and the risk (dispersion) of those expected returns.

Although the addition of debt to HTMC's balance sheet increases expected returns to shareholders, it also increases the risk that HTMC shareholders must bear. As a consequence, we should expect that HTMC shareholders will demand a higher return on their investment. Therefore, if the underlying question is whether the recapitalization is good for shareholders (i.e. whether it increases the total market value of HTMC), then we have to consider two offsetting effects. On average, the cash flows that HTMC can distribute to shareholders increase with debt, but so does the discount rate at which HTMC shareholders discount those cash flows.

Leverage increases expected return – but does it increase value?

Though we have demonstrated the effect that financial leverage should have on HTMC's shareholders, we haven't yet helped Susan Smith decide whether to adopt the 50 per cent debt/50 per cent equity recapitalization or to retain the company's existing all-equity capital structure. In Tables 12.1 and 12.2, and in Figure 12.1, she documents that employing debt can increase expected EPS and ROE for HTMC's shareholders, but the added risk associated with debt makes her uncertain about the net benefit of the recapitalization.

In creating Table 12.1, we assumed that immediately after HTMC's recapitalization the remaining shares would still sell for €50. If that assumption is valid, then the total market value of

HTMC equals €10 million, whether the firm finances with all equity, or with some debt and some equity. Recall that if HTMC recapitalizes, its expected EPS increases from €5 to €7. Likewise, expected ROE increases from 10 per cent to 14 per cent. Because of the added risk that they must bear, suppose HTMC shareholders increase their required return from 10 per cent to 14 per cent. If shareholders believe that HTMC's earnings will be €7 per share in perpetuity, then the stock price will remain at €50, and the recapitalization will have no net impact on HTMC's total value:

$$P = \frac{€7}{0.14} = €50$$

From this analysis, Susan Smith concludes that there is no unique, optimal capital structure for her company that maximizes firm value. There is a trade-off, and it is not clear, from the initial position, what the best policy is in regards to the mixture of debt and equity. Substituting debt for equity will increase expected EPS, but only at the cost of higher variability. With higher EPS volatility, shareholders will expect a higher return, meaning that they will discount future earnings at a higher rate. These two effects essentially cancel each other out, so shareholders are just as happy with a capital structure that includes no debt as they are with one that consists of equal proportions of debt and equity.[1]

Source: Adapted from the *Financial Times*, 16 August 2006.

Real World

Companies do clearly believe that the use of leverage can allow them to increase the value of their assets. Consider the following statement from the CEO of Cable & Wireless. Speaking of the need to increase their penetration in high-quality wireless businesses, he states: 'If you look at the size of the transactions we are targeting . . . and the use of leverage, we have got absolutely no financial constraints on our ability to grow this business.'

CONCEPT REVIEW QUESTIONS

1 What is a recapitalization? Why is this considered a pure capital structure change?

2 What is the fundamental principle of financial leverage? How does it pertain to the reasons why managers may choose to substitute debt for equity in their firm's capital structure?

12.2 THE MODIGLIANI AND MILLER CAPITAL STRUCTURE IRRELEVANCE PROPOSITIONS

Though she does not realize it yet, Susan Smith has reached the same capital structure irrelevance conclusion proposed by two economists almost half a century ago. In 1958, Franco Modigliani and Merton Miller showed that in a world with 'perfect capital

---

[1] This result holds for any other mix of debt and equity. The total market value of HTMC is the same whether the firm uses 100 per cent equity, 75 per cent equity and 25 per cent debt, or any other capital structure.

business risk
Refers to the variability of a firm's cash flows, as measured by the variability of EBIT.

financial risk
Refers to how a firm chooses to distribute the business risk affecting a firm's cash flows between shareholders and bondholders.

markets', capital structure cannot influence firm value and is thus irrelevant! In this context, perfect capital markets are those without frictions such as taxes, trading costs, or any problems transferring information between managers and investors. These two economists, subsequently referred to as M&M, made an important distinction between a firm's **business risk** and its **financial risk**. Business risk refers to the variability of a firm's cash flows, whereas financial risk refers to how a firm chooses to distribute that risk between shareholders and bondholders. HTMC's business risk is determined by how its earnings, before interest and taxes, fluctuate with the state of the economy. Notice that the volatility of EBIT is the same, whether HTMC recapitalizes or whether it finances with 100 per cent equity. In either case, EBIT will be €500 000, €1 000 000 or €1 500 000 depending on the state of the economy.

If HTMC retains its all-equity structure, then the financial risk that shareholders bear equals HTMC's underlying business risk. With no debt, the variations in EBIT translate directly into variations in EPS. However, under the 50-50 recapitalization, HTMC's leverage magnifies the financial risk borne by shareholders. With debt, HTMC issues a claim to bondholders that insulates them entirely from the firm's business risk. Whether the economy booms, grows normally or falls into a recession, bondholders receive the €300 000 interest payment they are promised. In this example, because bondholders bear no risk, even though HTMC's business risk has not changed, the shareholders remaining after the recapitalization have to shoulder even more risk than they did before.

Modigliani and Miller pointed out that leverage changes neither the total cash flows generated by a firm, nor the variability of those cash flows. Therefore, changing leverage cannot change the overall value of a firm. Leverage simply determines how firms divide their cash flows (and their risk) between shareholders and bondholders.

Proposition I: The capital structure irrelevance proposition

M&M's famous **Proposition I**, the 'irrelevance proposition', asserts that the market value of any firm is independent of its capital structure and is given by capitalizing its expected net operating income (EBIT) at the rate *r*. Equation 12.1 expresses this simple relationship mathematically.

EQUATION 12.1

$$V = (E + D) = \frac{EBIT}{r}$$

where V = total market value of the firm
E = market value of equity
D = market value of debt
$EBIT$ = earnings before interest and taxes
r = required return on a firm's assets

Proposition I
The famous 'irrelevance proposition', which imagines that a company is operating in a world of frictionless capital markets, and in a world where there is uncertainty about corporate revenues and earnings.

According to M&M, investors will generate an expectation about the long-run level of operating profits that a firm's assets will yield. They will capitalize this stream of profits by dividing EBIT by a discount rate *r*, appropriate to the business risk of the company. The discount rate *r* is the required return on assets and is based on the variability of expected EBIT. This is exactly what Susan Smith did for HTMC. She generated an expected level of operating profits for HTMC (€1 000 000 EBIT per year), and then discounted this stream of expected earnings, using a discount rate (*r* = 10 per cent), appropriate to the business risk that HTMC faces. Firm value is thus determined by the level of HTMC's operating profits and by the firm's degree of business risk, not by whether the EBIT stream is then allocated entirely to shareholders in the all-equity capital structure or split between debt and equity security-holders under the proposed capitalization.

Under HTMC's current, all-equity capital structure, the return on equity is the same as the return on the firm's assets. Both ROA and ROE are 10 per cent. But what happens if HTMC issues low-risk debt and uses the proceeds to repurchase half the firm's outstanding equity? The company's business risk (the variability of expected EBIT) is unchanged by this transaction, and all this risk is still borne by shareholders. However, the risk for shareholders is now magnified, because there is only half as much equity outstanding as before. By how much will the risk to HTMC's shareholders be magnified if the company adopts the proposed 50 per cent debt/50 per cent equity capital structure? It turns out that M&M also provided an answer to this question, with their Proposition II.

Proposition II: How increasing leverage affects the cost of equity

Modigliani and Miller's **Proposition II** states that if we hold the required return on assets (r) and the required return on debt (r_d) constant, the required return on levered equity (r_l) rises as the debt-to-equity ratio rises:

$$r_l = r + (r - r_d)\frac{D}{E}$$

EQUATION 12.2

Does this formula yield the same expected returns on equity for HTMC's shareholders that Susan Smith had calculated earlier under the current all-equity and the proposed 50 per cent debt/50 per cent equity capital structures? Remember that the firm's underlying business risk justifies a return, r, of 10 per cent and that its cost of debt, r_d, is 6 per cent. Clearly, under the current all-equity structure, there is no debt outstanding, and the D/E ratio is zero. Therefore, the term to the right of the plus sign is also zero. Equation 12.2 says that the return on equity equals the return on assets, or 10 per cent:

Proposition II Asserts that the expected return on a levered firm's equity is a linear function of that firm's debt-to-equity ratio.

$$r_l = 0.10 + (0.10 - 0.06)\frac{0}{10000000} = 0.10$$

The proposed 50 per cent debt/50 per cent equity capital structure yields a debt-to-equity ratio of 1.0. We can use Equation 12.2 to calculate that the return on levered equity must be 14 per cent, just as Susan Smith had calculated previously.

$$r_l = 0.10 + (0.10 - 0.06)\frac{5000000}{5000000} = 0.14$$

Proposition II has another important interpretation. Let's rearrange the equation so that r, the return on assets, appears by itself on the left-hand side. This results in the following expression:

$$r = r_l\left[\frac{E}{D+E}\right] + r_d\left[\frac{D}{D+E}\right]$$

Does this look familiar? It should. It's the expression for a firm's weighted average cost of capital (WACC) that we introduced in Chapter 10. We have already said the value of r depends on a firm's business risk and is independent of the firm's capital structure. This equation appears to contradict that claim because it seems that changing the values of E and D on the right-hand side might change r. But remember, Proposition II says that as leverage increases, so does the required return on equity. If a firm replaces equity with debt in its capital structure, the term $E/(D + E)$ falls and the term $D/(D + E)$ rises. However, r_l goes up because of the added financial risk

FIGURE 12.2

M&M Proposition II illustrated – the cost of equity, cost of debt and weighted average cost of capital for a firm in a world without taxes

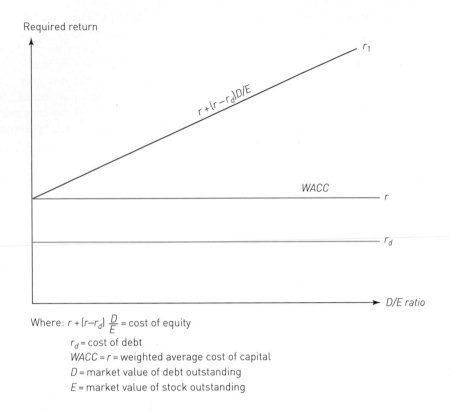

Where: $r + (r-r_d)\dfrac{D}{E}$ = cost of equity

r_d = cost of debt

$WACC = r$ = weighted average cost of capital

D = market value of debt outstanding

E = market value of stock outstanding

borne by shareholders. The net effect of all this is to leave the WACC unchanged. For example, when HTMC uses all debt, we know that the required return on equity is 10 per cent, so the WACC is 10 per cent too:

$$r = 0.10(1.0) + 0.06(0) = 0.10$$

If HTMC recapitalizes, then it pays 6 per cent to bondholders, shareholders demand a 14 per cent return and the WACC remains unchanged at 10 per cent:

$$r_l = 0.14(0.50) + 0.06(0.50) = 0.10$$

SMART CONCEPTS

See the concept explained step-by-step at **www.cengage.co.uk/ megginson**

If capital structure is irrelevant (if Proposition I holds), Proposition II tells us what the required return on levered equity must be to maintain the same total firm value (or the same WACC). As Figure 12.2 shows, the cost of equity will rise continuously as firms substitute debt for equity, but the weighted average cost of capital remains the same.

Remember that the value of a firm equals its cash flows discounted by its cost of capital. If managers could adjust capital structure to achieve a lower overall WACC (while leaving cash flows unchanged), then that would also increase the value of the firm. Propositions I and II illustrate why this cannot happen in perfect markets. Proposition I says that there is no capital structure that maximizes the value of a firm, while Proposition II says that there is no capital structure that minimizes the WACC.

CONCEPT REVIEW QUESTIONS

3 Explain how Propositions I and II are different and how they are similar.

4 What is the difference between levered and unlevered equity? What effect does substituting debt for equity have on the required return on (levered) equity?

12.3 THE M&M CAPITAL STRUCTURE MODEL WITH CORPORATE AND PERSONAL TAXES

You should now understand why capital structure choices are irrelevant in a world without market frictions, but that is not the world in which we live. One real-world market friction that could change the irrelevance result is corporate taxes. Because interest payments are generally tax-deductible, whereas dividend payments to shareholders generally are not, perhaps adding debt to the HTMC capital structure could increase the firm's value by reducing the government's tax claim on HTMC's cash flows?

The M&M model with corporate taxes

Let's begin our analysis by assuming, as before, that the High-Tech Manufacturing Company's EBIT will be €1 000 000 next year and that we are trying to decide whether to retain the firm's existing, all-equity capital structure or adopt a proposed 50 per cent debt/50 per cent equity capitalization. Assume that investors still require a 10 per cent return on the firm's assets, so $r = 0.10$, as before. However, we now propose that HTMC faces a 35 per cent corporate tax rate on earnings ($T_c = 0.35$). In computing taxable earnings, HTMC can deduct interest expense.

Table 12.4 shows the after-tax cash flows to HTMC's shareholders and debtholders under the current and proposed capital structure, if EBIT is €1 000 000, as expected. Corporate taxes reduce the amount of money that can be distributed to security-holders under either capital structure, but the effect is greater under the all-equity plan. In this case, HTMC pays taxes of €350 000, leaving only €650 000 available for distribution to shareholders. EPS thus drops to €3.25 from €5.00 under the no-tax scenario.

	CURRENT CAPITAL STRUCTURE: ALL-EQUITY FINANCING	PROPOSED CAPITAL STRUCTURE: 50% DEBT: 50% EQUITY
EBIT	€1 000 000	€1 000 000
– Interest (6.0%)	€ 0	(€ 300 000)
Taxable income	€1 000 000	€ 700 000
– Corporate taxes ($T_c = 0.35$)	(€ 350 000)	(245 000)
Net income	€ 650 000	€ 455 000
Shares outstanding	200 000	100 000
Earnings per share	€ 3.25	€ 4.55

TABLE 12.4

Cash flows to shareholders and bondholders under the current and proposed capital structure for HTMC – with corporate taxation

Assuming EBIT = €1 000 000 and $T_c = 0.35$

Under the proposed capital structure, tax-deductible interest payments of €300 000 reduce taxable profits to €700 000, and HTMC pays only €245 000 in corporate taxes. This leaves €455 000 in net income that can be distributed to shareholders, yielding an EPS of €4.55 from €7.00 under the no-tax scenario. Note that under the proposed capital structure, HTMC is able to distribute €755 000 to private investors (€300 000 interest to debtholders and €455 000 in dividends to shareholders). Under the all-equity capitalization, HTMC can distribute only €650 000 to private investors (dividends to shareholders).

We can now compute the value of both the unlevered and levered versions of HTMC, and define these values as V_U and V_L, respectively. The basic valuation formula (Equation 12.1) used in the absence of taxes to discount EBIT must now be modified to discount after-tax net income (*NI*), yielding the following formula for the value of an unlevered HTMC:

EQUATION 12.3

$$V_U = \frac{[EBIT(1 - T_c)]}{r} = \frac{NI}{r} = \frac{650000}{0.1} = €6500000$$

The introduction of a 35 per cent corporate profits tax causes an immediate €3 500 000 reduction (from €10 000 000 to €6 500 000) in the market value of the current all-equity version of HTMC.

Determining the present value of debt tax shields

Equation 12.3 reveals that corporate taxes cause a reduction in the value of an unlevered firm, compared with its value in a zero-tax environment. How can we modify this valuation formula to reflect the increase in firm value that results from adding leverage to HTMC's capital structure? If the new debt that HTMC will issue under the proposed 50 per cent debt/50 per cent equity plan, is assumed to be *permanent* – meaning that the firm will always reissue maturing debt – the interest deduction represents a perpetual tax shield of €105 000 per year. This is equal to the tax rate times the amount of interest paid

$$T_c \times r_d \times D = 0.35 \times 0.06 \times €5000000 = €105000$$

each year. To find the present value of this perpetuity, capitalize this stream of benefits at *rd*, the 6 per cent rate of interest charged on HTMC's debt. With these assumptions, the present value of HTMC's interest tax shields is:

EQUATION 12.4

$$PV = \frac{T_c(r_d D)}{r_d} = T_c D = 0.35(5000000) = €1750000$$

In other words, the present value of interest tax shields on (perpetual) debt is equal to the tax rate times the face value of the debt outstanding. Therefore, the value of the levered version of HTMC, V_l, is equal to the value of the unlevered company plus the present value of the interest tax shields:

EQUATION 12.5

$$V_L = V_U + PV(TaxShield) = V_U + T_d D$$
$$= 6500000 + 1750000 = €8250000$$

What a deal! In essence, the government has given HTMC's shareholders a €1 750 000 subsidy to employ debt financing rather than equity.

Figure 12.3 illustrates the effect of taxes on firm value by using a series of pie charts. Panel A represents the situation in the original M&M world of no taxes. In this case, capital structure is irrelevant, because no matter how you slice up the value of firms (the overall pie) between debt and equity claimants, their overall size (value) remains

FIGURE 12.3

Pie chart models of capital structure with and without corporate income taxes

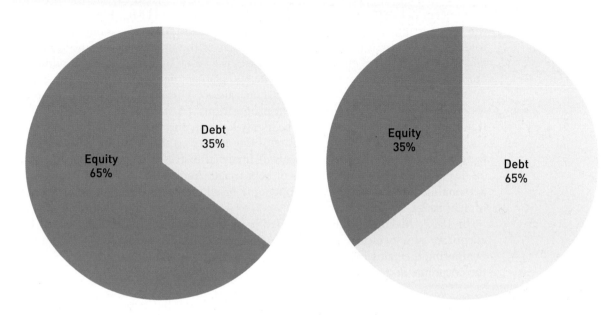

Panel A: No taxes, corresponding to the original M&M (1958) model. In this case, how the pie – representing the value of a firm's cash flows from operations – is divided between debt and equity does not affect the size of the pie, and thus capital structure is irrelevant.

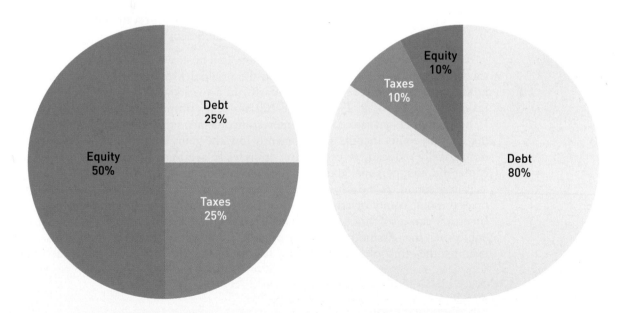

Panel B: Corporate income is subject to taxes at a constant rate T_c, corresponding to the M&M (1963) 'modified' model. In this case, the government's tax claim represents a deadweight drain on a firm's cash flows. By issuing debt and deducting interest payments from taxable income, firms minimize the tax claim and maximize the fraction of their cash flows that go to private investors. In this case, capital structure matters and the use of debt maximizes a firm's market value.

constant. When we introduce corporate income taxes into the M&M model, the value of firms to private investors is not independent of capital structure. The amount of debt that firms issue determines the size of the government's tax slice of the pie. The more firms borrow, the smaller is the government's claim, and therefore the larger are the claims held by private investors. Panel B of Figure 12.3 illustrates this point.

The M&M model with corporate and personal taxes

Clearly, accounting for corporate income taxes leads us to favour the proposed 50 per cent debt/50 per cent equity capital structure for HTMC. However, this isn't the best possible outcome. If a 50 per cent debt-to-capital ratio increases HTMC's total firm value by €1 750 000 more than that of the unlevered version of HTMC, and if each additional euro of debt increases the value by €0.35, then shouldn't the *optimal* leverage ratio for the company be 100 per cent debt? This is the result derived by M&M in 1963, though they never quite said so. This result, more than any other, lessened the initial acceptance of their propositions. How could the theory be correct if it predicted that all firms should be highly levered, and yet, in the real world, many companies use little or no debt? Part of the answer to this question is that non-tax factors, such as the debt-related costs of financial distress that we discuss in Section 12.4, partly offset the tax benefits of debt usage. Another part of the answer is that personal income taxes can cancel out some or all of the corporate-level tax benefits of debt usage.

In 1977, Merton Miller developed a valuation model that incorporated both corporate and personal taxes. From this model, Miller provided a formula for computing the gains from using leverage, G_L, both for individual companies and for the corporate sector as a whole:

EQUATION 12.6

$$G_L = \left[1 - \frac{(1 - T_c)(1 - T_{ps})}{(1 - T_{pd})} \right] D$$

where T_c = tax rate on corporate profits, as before
T_{ps} = personal tax rate on income from shares (capital gains and dividends)
T_{pd} = personal tax rate on income from debt (interest income)
D = market value of a firm's outstanding debt

This is, in fact, a very general formulation. In a no-tax world ($T_c = T_{ps} = T_{pd} = 0$), the gains from leverage equal zero, and the original M&M irrelevance proposition holds. (See if you can verify this yourself.) In a world with only corporate income taxes ($T_c = 0.35$; $T_{ps} = T_{pd} = 0$), the 100 per cent optimal debt result again obtains. If, however, personal tax rates on interest income are sufficiently high, and personal tax rates on equity income are sufficiently low, the gains to corporate leverage can be dramatically reduced, or even offset entirely. To see this, assume for a moment, as Miller did, that personal taxes on equity income are zero ($T_{ps} = 0$). This is not as wild as it may sound, as most investors pay capital gains taxes only upon realization, and taxes on some equity investments can be skipped entirely with careful estate planning. Investors can also choose non-dividend-paying stocks to avoid personal taxes on equity income. Assuming that personal taxes on equity income are zero, we can examine the effect of various country tax rates using the highest marginal tax rates:

TABLE 12.5

Is there a gain from leverage?

TAX RATE	USA	UK	GERMANY	IRELAND
T_{ps}	0%	0%	0%	0%
T_{pd}	40%	40%	45%	40%
T_c	35%	30%	25%	13%
Gain from leverage?	−8.33%	−16.67%	−36.36%	−45.83%

Using this set of tax rates, the 'gain' from leverage is typically negative! There is an actual discouragement for companies to use debt in the balance sheet. We can also work out the situation where for an individual case the effects of corporate and personal taxes may exactly offset each other. In the USA if the personal tax rate on equity income is 7.7 per cent, the gain from leverage is zero, and capital structure is again irrelevant. However, in the UK the rate would have to be 14 per cent and in Ireland the rate would have to be 31 per cent. In the latter case, this is almost impossible, as the tax rate on capital gains is at most 20 per cent.

CONCEPT REVIEW QUESTIONS

5 What effect does incorporating corporate income taxation have on the M&M capital structure irrelevance hypothesis? Why?

6 In 2003 the United States passed a law that, in effect, reduced the likely taxes that a US investor would pay on dividends received. What effect do you expect this Act to have on corporate incentive to use debt?

12.4 THE AGENCY COST/TAX SHIELD TRADE-OFF MODEL OF CORPORATE LEVERAGE

We have now seen that the corporate capital structure choice is irrelevant in a world without taxes or other market frictions. We have learned not only that corporate income taxes, by themselves, give corporations a strong incentive to employ financial leverage, but also that things are much less clear-cut when personal income taxes are considered. On balance, corporate and personal taxes seem to influence, but not solely explain, the variation in leverage ratios observed in modern economies. But if taxes do not explain why firms and investors pay attention to capital structure, then what does? One possibility is that the costs of bankruptcy and financial distress may discourage corporate managers from adopting 'maximum leverage' capital structures. This section considers the likely effect of bankruptcy and financial distress costs on capital structure choice.

Costs of bankruptcy and financial distress

The threat of bankruptcy may well discourage debt financing. High leverage makes it more likely that firms will be unable to make interest and principal payments when cash flows are low. This could cause companies to default on their debts, which, in turn, could force companies into bankruptcy. In general, when a firm goes bankrupt, the firm's original shareholders lose their entire investment and the ownership of the firm (or the firm's remaining assets) passes to bondholders and other creditors. **Bankruptcy costs** are the direct and indirect costs (defined below) of the bankruptcy process itself.

Direct costs of bankruptcy are out-of-pocket cash expenses directly related to bankruptcy filing and administration. Document printing and filing expenses, as well as professional fees paid to lawyers, accountants, investment bankers and court personnel are all examples of direct bankruptcy costs. These can run to several million euros per month for complex cases. However, empirical research indicates that direct costs are much too small, relative to the pre-bankruptcy market value of large firms, to truly discourage the use of debt financing. **Indirect bankruptcy costs**, as the name

bankruptcy costs
The direct and indirect costs of the bankruptcy process.

direct costs of bankruptcy
Out-of-pocket cash expenses directly related to bankruptcy filing and administration.

indirect bankruptcy costs
Expenses or economic losses that result from bankruptcy but are not cash outflows spent on the process itself.

implies, are economic losses that result from bankruptcy but are not cash outlays spent on the process itself. These include the diversion of management's time while bankruptcy is under way, lost sales during and after bankruptcy, constrained capital investment and R&D spending, and the loss of key employees after a firm declares bankruptcy. Even though indirect bankruptcy costs are inherently difficult to measure, empirical research clearly suggests they are significant – significant enough, in many cases, to lessen the incentive for corporate managers to employ financial leverage. This allows us to expand the basic valuation formula, first presented in Section 12.3, to express the value of a levered firm, V_L, relative to the value of an unlevered firm, V_U, the present value of the benefits from debt tax shields, and the present value of expected bankruptcy costs:

EQUATION 12.7

$$V_L = V_U + PV(TaxShields) - PV(bankruptcy)$$

Asset characteristics and bankruptcy costs Intuitively, it seems that certain firms should be able to weather financial distress better than others. As a general rule, producers of sophisticated products or services have an incentive to use less debt than firms producing simple goods or basic services. It is very important for producers of high-value, durable goods to assure customers that their firms are able to provide ongoing service, warranty and repair work, as well as product improvements. Based on this logic, it is not surprising that the 'Opening Focus' section shows that technology-based companies such as Dell and Microsoft use leverage very sparingly.

A firm's asset characteristics also influence its willingness to risk financial distress by using large amounts of debt. Companies with mostly tangible assets and well-established secondary markets should be more willing to use debt than companies with mostly intangible assets. Therefore, trucking companies, airlines, construction firms, pipeline companies and railways can all employ more debt than can companies with fewer tangible assets, such as pharmaceutical manufacturers, food distributors (what is the collateral value of week-old tomatoes?) and pure service companies. There is something to this if we examine the data: Toyota and General Electric have much higher leverage ratios than Johnson & Johnson or Microsoft.

There are two reasons why financial distress can be particularly damaging to firms that produce R&D-intensive goods and services. First, most of the expenses incurred in production are sunk costs, which have already been made and which can be recovered only with a long period of profitable sales. Secondly, a financially distressed company is unable to finance the R&D spending required to produce 'cutting-edge' goods and services. Further, intangible assets such as patents and trademarks are extremely valuable and are unlikely to survive financial distress or bankruptcy intact. Microsoft and Johnson & Johnson are classic examples of companies that invest massive sums in R&D in order to produce cutting-edge products and services. The Opening Focus shows that both of these firms are essentially debt free!

Another major problem associated with financial distress is that it provides otherwise trustworthy managers with perverse, but rational, incentives to play a variety of financial and operating 'games', mostly at bondholders' expense. Two such games, those of asset substitution and underinvestment, are particularly important and potentially damaging. Both typically begin when a company first encounters financial difficulties, and its managers realize that the firm will probably not fulfil its obligations to creditors.

million in Legal Costs', *Airfinance Journal*, April 2006.

Real World

Although not large in relative terms, the costs of bankruptcy and reorganization can run into hundreds of millions of euros. The United Airlines Chapter 11 (bankruptcy protection and reorganization) process is estimated to have cost it over $300 million in legal costs alone.

The asset substitution problem To illustrate how **asset substitution** works, assume that a firm has bonds with a face value of €10 million outstanding, which mature in 30 days. These bonds were issued years ago when the firm was prospering, but since then, the firm has fallen on hard times. In spite of its difficulties, the firm still has €8 million in cash on hand, and the company's managers still make the firm's investment decisions. The company can invest this cash in either of two available projects, both of which require a cash investment of €8 million. Otherwise, the firm can simply hold the cash in reserve to partially repay the bond issue in 30 days. The first investment opportunity is a low-risk project (called project 'ChingChing', by company insiders) that will return a near certain €8.15 million in 30 days. This is a monthly return of 1.88 per cent, or an annual return of almost 25 per cent. In other words, it is a positive-NPV project that will increase firm value, but it does not earn enough to fully pay off the maturing bonds.

The second investment opportunity (called project 'BlingBling') is basically a gamble. It offers a 40 per cent chance of a €12 million pay-off and a 60 per cent chance of a €4 million pay-off. Because its expected value is only €7.2 million (0.4 × €12 000 000 + 0.6 × €4 000 000), project BlingBling is a negative-NPV 'investment' that the firm's managers would reject if the firm did not have debt outstanding. However, if project BlingBling is successful, the project's €12 million pay-off will allow the company to fully pay off the bonds and pocket a €2 million profit.

Consider the incentives facing this company's managers. Clearly, bondholders want the managers to either select the low-risk project or retain the firm's cash in reserve. But because shareholders will lose control of the firm unless they can pay off the creditors' claims in full, when they mature, shareholders want the company's managers to accept project BlingBling. If successful, the project will yield enough for shareholders to pay off the creditors and to retain ownership of the firm. On the other hand, if project BlingBling is unsuccessful, the shareholders will simply hand over the firm and any remaining assets to bondholders, after defaulting on the maturing bonds. (Because of limited liability, the corporation's shareholders do not have to repay the bonds themselves.) This is also what will happen if the firm plays it safe by either retaining cash in the firm or accepting project ChingChing. Shareholders therefore have everything to gain and nothing to lose from accepting project BlingBling, and their agents (the managers) control the firm's investment policy until default actually occurs.

The underinvestment problem The second game set up by financial distress is **underinvestment**. To demonstrate this, assume that the firm described above gains access to a very profitable, but short-lived, investment opportunity. Specifically, a long-time supplier offers to sell its excess inventory to the company at a sharply discounted price, but only if the company will pay for the inventory immediately with cash. The additional supplies will cost €9 million today but will allow the firm to increase

asset substitution
An investment that will increase firm value but does not earn a return high enough to fully redeem the maturing bonds.

underinvestment
A situation of financial distress in which default is likely, yet a very profitable but short-lived investment opportunity exists.

production and profitability dramatically over the next 30 days. In fact, the firm will be able to sell the additional production so profitably that, in 30 days' time, it will build up the €10 million cash needed to pay off the maturing bond issue. However, because the firm has only €8 million in cash on hand today, the firm's shareholders must contribute the additional €1 million needed to buy the supplier's inventory. Accepting this project would maximize overall firm value and would clearly benefit the bondholders. But the shareholders would rationally choose *not* to accept the project because the shareholders would have to finance the investment, and all the investment's pay-off would accrue to the bondholders.

An all-equity firm is not vulnerable to either of these two games that are associated with financial distress. Managers, acting in the interests of shareholders, have the incentive to choose the project that maximizes firm value, in the first example, and the shareholders' incentive is to choose to contribute cash for positive-NPV projects, in the second example. Because these costs of financial distress are related to conflicts of interest between the two groups of security-holders, they are also referred to as 'agency costs' of the relationship between bondholders and shareholders.

Agency costs and capital structure

In addition to taxes and the costs of financial distress, several other forces influence the corporate capital structure choice. Some 30 years ago, Michael Jensen and William Meckling proposed an agency cost model of financial structure. Jensen and Meckling observed that when entrepreneurs own 100 per cent of the stock of a company, there is no separation between corporate ownership and control. Entrepreneurs bear all the costs and reap all the benefits of their actions. Once entrepreneurs sell a fraction of their stock to outside investors, they bear only a fraction of the cost of any actions they take that reduce the value of the firm. This gives entrepreneurs a clear incentive to, in Jensen and Meckling's tactful phrasing, 'consume perquisites' (goof off, purchase a corporate jet, frequently tour the firm's plant in Hawaii, become a regular 'business commentator' on television, etc.).

By selling off a stake in the company, entrepreneurs lower the cost of consuming perquisites (or perks), but this does not come free of charge. In an efficient market, investors expect entrepreneurs' performance to change after they sell stakes in their firms, so investors reduce the price they will pay for these shares. In other words, entrepreneurs are charged *in advance* for the perks they are expected to consume after the equity sale, so entrepreneurs bear the full costs of their actions. Society also suffers because these **agency costs of (outside) equity** reduce the market value of corporate assets. We are therefore at an impasse. Selling shares to outside investors creates agency costs of equity, which are borne solely by the entrepreneur, but which also harm society, by reducing the value of corporate assets and discouraging additional entrepreneurship. On the other hand, selling external equity is vital for entrepreneurs and for society at large, because this allows firms to pursue growth opportunities that would exhaust an entrepreneur's personal wealth.

Using debt to overcome the agency costs of outside equity Jensen and Meckling show how using debt financing can help overcome the agency costs of external equity, in two ways. First, using debt, by definition, means that less external equity will have to be sold to raise a given euro amount of external financing. Secondly, and more important, the effect of employing outside debt rather than equity financing is a reduction in the amount and value of perquisites that managers can consume. The burden of having to make regular debt-service payments serves as a very effective tool for disciplining corporate managers. With debt outstanding, the cost of excessive perk consumption may well include managers losing control of their

agency costs of (outside) equity
In an efficient market, informed investors only pay a price per share that fully reflects the perks an entrepreneur is expected to consume after the equity sale, so the entrepreneur bears the full costs of her or his actions.

companies following default. Because taking on debt shows a manager's willingness to risk losing control of her firm, if she fails to perform effectively, shareholders are willing to pay a higher price for a firm's shares.

Agency costs of outside debt If debt is such an effective disciplining device, then why don't firms use 'maximum debt' financing? The answer is that there are also **agency costs of debt**. To understand these, keep in mind that, as the fraction of debt in a firm's capital structure increases, bondholders begin taking on more of the company's business and operating risk. However, shareholders and managers still control the firm's investment and operating decisions. This gives managers a variety of incentives to effectively steal bondholder wealth for themselves and other shareholders. The easiest way to do this is to float a bond issue and then pay out the money raised to shareholders as a dividend. After default, the bondholders are left with an empty corporate shell, and limited liability prevents them from trying to collect directly from shareholders.

Bondholders are generally sophisticated enough to take steps to prevent managers from playing these games with their money. The most effective, preventive step that bond investors can take is to write very detailed covenants into bond contracts, which limit borrowers' ability to expropriate bondholder wealth. We discussed bond covenants in Chapter 4. The downside of covenants is that they make bond agreements costly to negotiate and to enforce. In any case, the agency costs of debt are real, and they become more important as a firm's leverage ratio increases.

The agency cost/tax shield trade-off model of corporate leverage

Our discussion thus far has shown that certain real-world factors – such as corporate income taxes and agency costs of outside equity – give corporate managers an incentive to substitute debt for equity in their firms' capital structure. Other factors such as personal income taxes, bankruptcy and agency costs of outside debt give managers an incentive to favour equity financing. We are now ready to tie together all these influences and present the **agency cost/tax shield trade-off model of corporate leverage**. This model expresses the value of a levered firm as the value of an unlevered firm, plus the present values of tax shields and the agency costs of outside equity, minus the present value of bankruptcy costs and the agency costs of debt, as follows:

$$V_L = V_U + PV(TaxShields) - PV(Bankruptcy) + PV(Equity\ agency)$$
$$- PV(Debt\ agency)$$

EQUATION 12.8

Figure 12.4 describes how agency costs bankruptcy costs and tax benefits of leverage interact to determine a typical firm's optimal debt level. Starting from a capital structure with no debt, managers can increase firm value by replacing equity with debt, thus shielding more cash flow from taxation. In the absence of bankruptcy costs and the agency costs of debt, managers would maximize firm value by borrowing as much as possible – a situation represented by the green line in Figure 12.4. The red line shows how bankruptcy and agency costs alter this conclusion. As a firm borrows more, it increases the probability that it will go bankrupt. Therefore, expected bankruptcy costs and agency costs of debt rise with leverage. At some point, the additional tax benefit from issuing more debt is exactly offset by the increase in expected bankruptcy and agency costs. When that occurs, the red line reaches a maximum, and managers have found the mix of debt and equity that maximizes the value of the firm.

FIGURE 12.4

The agency cost/tax shield trade-off model of corporate leverage

This model describes the optimal level of debt for a given firm as a trade-off between the tax benefits of corporate borrowing and the increasing agency and bankruptcy costs that come from additional borrowing.

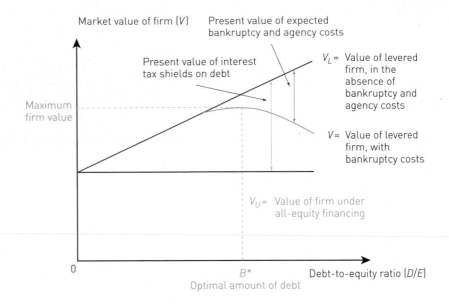

As we see in the next section, empirical research in finance offers much support for the agency cost/tax shield trade-off model. It explains many of the key patterns that are observed in corporate capital structures around the world.

CONCEPT REVIEW QUESTIONS

7 What are the important direct and indirect costs of bankruptcy? Which of these, do you think, are the most important for discouraging maximum debt use by corporate managers?

8 Suppose an individual borrows from a bank to buy a new car. Later on, the borrower realizes that in a few months he will have to default on this loan and the bank will repossess the car. What kind of underinvestment problem could occur here?

9 Suppose a commercial bank experiences losses on some of its loans. As a result, it approaches bankruptcy. What kinds of asset-substitution problems may arise?

10 Think of the corporate perks given to managers, such as a plush office, a company jet or luxury box seats at professional sporting events. How can managers justify these as value-maximizing corporate expenditures that benefit the shareholders?

12.5 PATTERNS OBSERVED IN CORPORATE CAPITAL STRUCTURES

Observers who study actual capital structure patterns quickly reach two important conclusions. First, they realize that there are several methods used to measure financial leverage for individual firms, and, for each specific financial ratio, there is both a 'book value' and a 'market value' measure of debt and equity. Secondly, they conclude that several strong patterns stand out in the capital structures of companies.

Book versus market value leverage ratios

By definition, measuring a firm's capital structure means determining the mix of long-term debt and equity on the right-hand side of a company's balance sheet. Thus, capital structure refers to long-term debt (LTD) and shareholders' equity (E), which itself consists of ordinary and preference shares. As described in Chapter 2, there are several financial ratios that can be used to measure leverage. The two most important are long-term debt-to-equity (LTD ÷ E), which is often referred to as the debt-to-equity ratio, and long-term debt to total capitalization [LTD ÷ (LTD + E)], or the debt-to-total capital ratio. Because these two ratios involve the same variables, arranged somewhat differently, they naturally both provide the same basic results. However, the debt-to-equity ratio must always be either greater than or equal to the debt-to-total capitalization ratio (can you see why?).

Yet, leverage ratios, which are computed by using either the book values of long-term debt and equity, or market values, often differ dramatically. Because the market value of a typical firm's ordinary share is usually much higher than its book value, market value debt ratios tend to be much *lower* than book value ratios. The debt-to-equity ratios of the admired companies, described in the 'Opening Focus' section, illustrate this point. The book value D/E ratios of those companies, with significant debt outstanding, are from two to seven times higher than the corresponding market value D/E ratios. Economists prefer using market value leverage ratios, because they measure how investors value corporate securities and so indicate on what terms companies can issue new securities. Corporate practitioners, however, tend to use book value leverage ratios because these are the measures specified in the contracts governing security issues (indentures) and in bank loan agreements.

Are capital structures randomly selected?

If capital structure choices have no effect on firm values, then we may not expect to see any predictable patterns in leverage ratios across companies. When we examine different firms in different industries, however, we can quickly conclude that capital structures are not randomly generated. Instead, they show a number of patterns discussed in the following subsections.

Capital structures show strong industry patterns In all developed countries, certain industries have high debt-to-equity ratios, whereas other industries employ little or no long-term debt financing. Highly leveraged industries include utilities, transportation companies (trucking, airlines, railways), property and many capital-intensive manufacturing sectors. Firms in the service, mining, oil and gas exploration, and high-technology industries generally use little or no debt. These patterns are observed in almost all countries, suggesting that an industry's asset mix and operating environment significantly influence the capital structures that are chosen by firms in that industry, worldwide. Table 12.6 presents median book value, debt-to-equity ratios and debt-to-total capital ratios for selected industries, in 2006. A glance at the table reveals a clear tendency for firms in industries that are technologically-rich, such as healthcare and telecoms, to use low debt, whereas firms in asset-rich industries, such as utilities and oil and gas, tend to have much higher leverage ratios.

Economy-wide average leverage ratios vary across countries Although the same industries have high and low leverage ratios in all countries, national average debt ratios also differ systematically from each other. Firms in Japan, France, Germany, Italy and South Korea tend to have higher book value debt ratios than do companies headquartered in the United States, Britain, Canada, Brazil, Mexico and

TABLE 12.6

Five-year average long-term debt as a % of equity for broad industrial groups

Source: Thomson ONE.

Industrials	82.35
Utilities	68.42
Oil and gas	54.33
Basic industries	51.73
Consumer goods	44.18
Technology	36.77
Telecoms	34.19
Consumer services	26.59
Healthcare	18.84

many other countries. If leverage is measured using market values, however, German companies typically use less long-term debt than firms in any other developed economy. Why leverage ratios vary so much across countries remains an unsolved puzzle. In part, differences in leverage may reflect differences in the industrial composition of national economies. Indeed, historical, institutional and even cultural factors all probably play a part, as does a nation's reliance on capital markets versus banks for corporate financing. In particular, market value leverage ratios tend to be low in those countries where creditors have the greatest power to seize assets and to force corporate borrowers to liquidate when they default on loans. Therefore, borrowing firm managers have a very strong incentive not to issue too much debt. Research points to the very strong influence that legal structures have on financial structures. Much of this work is associated with Rafael LaPorta, who in a series of papers since the late 1990s has shown this influence across a very long time period and a very large range of countries.

Leverage ratios are negatively related to the costs of financial distress
Across both industries and countries, the larger the perceived costs of bankruptcy and financial distress, the less debt firms use. For example, when the principal assets of a company are intangible (e.g. patents, brands, copyrights and other intellectual property), the costs of financial distress are much higher than when the principal assets are tangible structures and equipment. These can be pledged as collateral and easily sold by lenders if a borrower defaults. Companies with valuable intangible assets thus tend to use less debt than do tangible, asset-rich companies.

Within industries, the most profitable companies borrow the least Regardless of the industry in question, the most profitable companies have the lowest leverage ratios, suggesting that observed leverage ratios are partly the result of past decisions, made by managers, to retain high profits. This is a surprising (though robust) observation, since debt financing enjoys a tax advantage in most countries because firms can deduct interest payments before paying taxes. The implication is that, other things being equal, profitable firms should use *more* leverage than unprofitable firms should use. By borrowing money, profitable companies shelter a larger proportion of their cash flows from taxes.

Corporate and personal income taxes influence capital structures, but taxes alone cannot explain differences in leverage across firms, industries or countries Taxes certainly influence corporate leverage usage, but they are not decisive. American corporations apparently used no less debt prior to the introduction of the income tax in 1913 than they did either after its introduction or when corporate and personal income tax rates peaked during World War II. In general we see gradual changes in leverage, which seem at odds with the sudden changes in tax laws (and hence, sudden changes in the tax advantages of debt) that characterize modern economies. On the other hand, research has shown that increasing corporate income tax rates generally causes firms to issue more debt, and that decreasing personal tax rates on equity income, relative to those on interest income, prompts companies to issue less debt.

Shareholders consider leverage-increasing events to be 'good news' and leverage-decreasing events to be 'bad news' Almost every published empirical study shows that share prices rise when a company announces leverage-increasing events such as debt-for-equity exchange offers, debt-financed share repurchase programmes and debt-financed cash tender offers to acquire control of another company. On the other hand, leverage-decreasing events such as equity-for-debt exchange offers, new share offerings and acquisition offers involving payment with a firm's own shares almost always generate share price declines.

Is there a 'pecking order'? The observed behaviour of companies has led some theorists to suggest that there may be a 'pecking order' process at work. In brief, pecking order theory (POT) suggests that firms will prefer internal finance before external finance. If external finance is required, firms will issue the safest security first. That is, they start with bank debt, then external debt such as bonds, then perhaps hybrid securities such as convertible bonds, then new seasoned equity as a last resort. In this case, POT suggests that there is no well-defined target debt–equity mix, because there are two kinds of equity, internal and external, one at the top of the pecking order and one at the bottom. Each firm's observed debt ratio reflects its total historical requirements and desire for external and internal finance.

An implication of POT is that there should be a negative relationship between profitability and leverage. The more profitable is a firm the more internal funds it has to draw upon and therefore the less should it require external funds of any sort. Much empirical work indicates that the pecking order implications are carried through. However, underlying POT is the role of information asymmetries, and this is not generally found to be a significant driver of the decision to issue debt or equity. Thus the observations of POT and its supposed drivers are at variance.

SMART IDEAS VIDEO

Professor Abe de Jong, RSM Erasmus University, Rotterdam
European capital structure practices.

See the entire interview at
www.cengage.co.uk/ megginson

---

11 In most countries, firms in high-tech industries are almost all intangible asset-rich rather than fixed asset-rich. What effect do you think the continued growth of these industries will have on average leverage ratios in the future?

12 What happens to share prices when corporate managers announce leverage-increasing transactions such as debt-for-equity exchange offers? What happens to share prices in response to leverage-decreasing announcements? How do you interpret these findings?

CONCEPT
REVIEW
QUESTIONS

12.6 IS EUROPE DIFFERENT?

We know from the above that there exist distinct patterns in financing across industries and across countries. However, can we say in general if there is a distinct 'European' corporate financing pattern? Part of the difficulty in answering this question lies in data availability. For many years research on corporate finance was almost exclusively US-orientated. While this partially reflected the dominance of the US in the market it also reflected the existence of two high-quality databases. The CRSP (Center for Research in Securities Prices) and Compustat databases allowed researchers to delve deeply into the financing patterns of US corporations and to assess the effect of these patterns on the companies traded debt and equity. No such databases existed (or exist still) for Europe. In recent years, however, this research gap has been narrowed, mostly by survey analysis. However, this gap is unlikely to be fully closed as there still exist significant accounting and tax issues across European countries.

Nonetheless, some patterns can be observed in relation to capital structure. A recent study[2] of over 300 chief finance officers in four countries (the UK, Germany, France and the Netherlands) finds some interesting issues that contrast with the US evidence. In comparison with the USA, the respondents were much less concerned with agency and signalling issues. With the striking exception of Germany, respondents were more concerned with the costs of bankruptcy than applies in the US. With the exception of the Netherlands, the European respondents were conscious of and cautious about the effect of debt levels on shareholder/bondholder relative payouts. German and French firms are significantly less concerned about the effect on existing securities when they change their capital structure than are those in the Netherlands, the UK or the USA, which reflects a general split in terms of market orientation. However, in general the institutional and practical differences are not reflected in vastly different US and European capital structures or preferences for financing.

There is also the issue of the emerging 'law and finance' literature. Concentrating in its recent forms around the work of Rafale LaPorta in the middle 1990s, this study discipline concerns itself with the interaction of legal forms, organizational structures and the resultant financial decisions. Much of the work emphasises a distinct difference between what are called civil law and common law countries. Civil law countries tend to have greater codification and are generally more rule-orientated, while common law countries tend to permit greater discretion and allow courts to make law via precedent and appeal. Civil law countries include most of continental Europe and their ex colonies while common law countries include the USA, the UK and Australia. The findings of LaPorta and of those that follow his work are complex, including the finding that common law countries have firms that take on higher levels of debt as compared to their counterparts originating from civil law countries; the general explanation given is that common law tends to provide stronger investor protection and, as a consequence, the shareholders are happy to allow more debt, confident in their legal protection. An important element here is that civil law countries can themselves be divided into those that follow a Germanic and a French style. The level of bank debt is the highest of all groups in the Germanic system. So Europe seems not to be very different from other areas and the notion of a distinct European capital structure is not one that has strong empirical support.

---

[2] Dirk Brounen, Abe de Jong and Kees Koedijk (2006) 'Capital Structure Policies in Europe; Survey Evidence', *Journal of Banking & Finance,* 30(5):1409–1442.

12.7 SUMMARY AND CONCLUSIONS

- Financial leverage (or gearing) means using fixed-cost debt financing to increase expected earnings per share. Unfortunately, financial leverage also increases the dispersion of expected earnings per share.

- Franco Modigliani and Merton Miller showed that capital structure is irrelevant in a world of frictionless capital markets. This means that the leverage choice cannot affect firm valuation.

- In a world with only company-level taxation of operating profits and tax-deductible interest payments, the optimal corporate strategy is to use the maximum possible leverage. This minimizes the government's claim on profits, in the form of taxes, and maximizes the amount of income flowing to private investors.

- When corporate profits are taxed at both the corporate and personal levels (with taxes on interest and dividends received), the benefits of high levels of corporate leverage are much reduced and may be completely negated. In this more 'realistic' world of multiple taxes and other market imperfections, such as transactions cost in issuing securities, it is unclear whether an 'optimal' debt level exists for the average firm in any given nation.

- In addition to corporate and personal taxation of income, several characteristics of a firm's asset structure, operating environment, investment opportunities and ownership structure significantly influence the level of debt that the firm will choose to have.

- Firms with large amounts of tangible assets, such as buildings, transportation equipment and general-purpose machine tools, tend to use a large amount of debt in their capital structures. These assets can pass fairly easily through bankruptcy, with their values intact. In contrast, firms that rely more on intangible assets, such as brand names and R&D spending, tend to use very little financial leverage.

- Creditors know that corporate managers, who operate their firms in the interests of shareholders, have incentives to try to expropriate creditor wealth, by playing a series of 'games'

with their firms' investment policies. Asset substitution is one such game. It involves promising to purchase a safe investment asset to obtain an interest rate that reflects this risk, and then substituting a higher risk asset that promises a higher expected return. Creditors protect themselves from these games through a variety of techniques, especially by inserting covenants into loan agreements.

- There are several important agency costs inherent in the relationship between corporate managers and outside investors and creditors. In some cases, using financial leverage can help overcome these agency problems; in others, use of leverage exacerbates the problems. The modern trade-off theory of corporate leverage predicts that a firm's optimal debt level will be set by trading off the tax benefits of increasing leverage against the increasingly severe agency costs of heavy debt usage.

- Corporate debt ratios can be measured in various ways, but 'capital structure' ratios measure the ratio of a firm's long-term or permanent debt to its equity capital. More problematic is the need to express leverage ratios in terms of both book value and market value, because each type of measure is appropriate for some purposes, but not for others. We usually focus on market value capital structure ratios.

- Several patterns are observed in capital structure patterns around the world. In general, industries rich in fixed assets and those with assets that retain their value in bankruptcy, tend to have high leverage, whereas industries rich in intangible assets tend to have low levels of indebtedness. This is particularly true for industries in which R&D spending is important.

- Though firms in the same industries tend to exhibit similar debt levels in all countries, there are also significant differences in average leverage levels between countries. In those countries where bankruptcy laws favour creditors, especially Britain and Germany, market value leverage levels tend to be lower than in nations where debtors enjoy greater bankruptcy protection.

INTERNET RESOURCES

For updates to links in this section and elsewhere in the book, please go to the book's website at
www.cengage.co.uk/megginson.

http://www.investopedia.com/terms/m/modigliani-millertheorem.asp
Investopedia's take on the MM theorems.

http://www.quicken.com; http://www.yahoo.com; http://www.sec.gov
Three sites from which you can download leverage figures for specific companies and compare them
to figures for firms in the same industry as well as firms in other industries.

http://www.taxsites.com/international.html
A site that provides country-specific tax information for dozens of countries, as well as links to a
wide variety of tax-related sites.

http://www.standardandpoors.com
A site with information on bond ratings as well as the latest changes to ratings on outstanding bonds.

http://www.moneyinstructor.com/art/capitalstructure.asp
Useful concise site on capital structure choices.

http://www.cfoeurope.com/displayStory.cfm/8625989
Looks at the practical issues in the choice of capital for companies.

KEY TERMS

agency cost/tax shield trade-off model of corporate leverage	business risk	indirect bankruptcy costs
agency costs of (outside) equity	direct costs of bankruptcy	Proposition I
agency costs of debt	financial leverage	Proposition II
asset substitution	financial risk	recapitalization
bankruptcy costs	fundamental principle of financial leverage	underinvestment

SELF-TEST PROBLEMS

ST12-1 As financial director of the United Service Corporation (USC), you are considering a recapitalization plan that would convert USC from its current all-equity capital structure to one including substantial financial leverage. USC now has 150 000 shares outstanding, which are selling for €80.00 each. The recapitalization proposal is to issue €6 000 000 worth of long-term debt, at an interest rate of 7.0 per cent, and use the proceeds to repurchase 75 000 shares worth €6 000 000. USC's earnings in the next year will depend on the state of the economy. If there is normal growth, EBIT will be €1 200 000. EBIT will be €600 000 if there is a recession, and EBIT will be €1 800 000 if there is an economic boom. You believe that each economic outcome is equally likely. Assume there are no market frictions such as corporate or personal income taxes.

a If the proposed recapitalization is adopted, calculate the number of shares outstanding, the per-share price and the debt-to-equity ratio for USC.

b Calculate the earnings per share (EPS) and the return on equity for USC shareholders, under all three economic outcomes (recession, normal growth and boom), for both the current all-equity capitalization and the proposed mixed debt/equity capital structure.

c Calculate the breakeven level of EBIT, where earnings per share for USC shareholders are the same, under the current and proposed capital structures.

d At what level of EBIT will USC shareholders earn zero EPS, under the current and the proposed capital structures?

ST12-2 An unlevered company operates in perfect markets and has net operating income (EBIT) of €2 000 000. Assume that the required return on assets for firms in this industry is 8 per cent. The firm issues €10 million worth of debt, with a required return of 6.5 per cent, and uses the proceeds to repurchase outstanding shares. There are no corporate or personal taxes.

a What is the market value and required return of this firm's shares before the repurchase transaction, according to M&M Proposition I?

b What is the market value and required return of this firm's remaining shares after the repurchase transaction, according to M&M Proposition II?

ST12-3 Westside Manufacturing has EBIT of €10 million. There is €60 million of debt outstanding, with a required rate of return of 6.5 per cent. The required rate of return on the industry is 10 per cent. The corporate tax rate is 30 per cent. Assume there are corporate taxes but no personal taxes.

a Determine the present value of the interest tax shield of Westside Manufacturing, as well as the total value of the firm.

b Determine the gain from leverage, if personal taxes of 10 per cent on share income and 35 per cent on debt income exist.

ST12-4 You are the manager of a financially distressed company, with €10 million in debt outstanding, which will mature in one month. Your firm currently has €7 million cash on hand. Assume that you are offered the opportunity to invest in either of the two projects described below.

● **Project 1:** the opportunity to invest €7 million in risk-free government stock, with a 4 per cent annual interest rate (or a 0.333 per cent per month interest rate).

● **Project 2:** a high-risk gamble, which will pay off €12 million in one month, if it is successful (probability = 0.25), but will only pay €4 million if it is unsuccessful (probability = 0.75).

a Compute the expected pay-off for each project and state which one you would adopt if you were operating the firm in the shareholders' best interests? Why?

b Which project would you accept if the firm was unlevered? Why?

c Which project would you accept if the firm was organized as a partnership rather than a company? Why?

ST12-5 Run-and-Hide Detective Company currently has no debt and expects to earn €5 million in EBIT each year, for the foreseeable future. The required return on assets for detective companies of this type is 10.0 per cent, and the corporate tax rate is 35 per cent. There are no taxes on dividends or interest at the personal level. Run-and-Hide calculates that there is a 5 per cent chance that the firm will fall into bankruptcy in any given year. If bankruptcy does occur, it will impose direct and indirect costs, totalling €8 million. If necessary, they will use the industry required return for discounting bankruptcy costs.

a Compute the present value of bankruptcy costs for Run-and-Hide.

b Compute the overall value of the firm.

c Recalculate the value of the company assuming that the firm's shareholders face a 15 per cent personal tax rate on equity income.

QUESTIONS

Q12-1 Why is the use of long-term debt financing referred to as using financial leverage?

Q12-2 What is the fundamental principle of financial leverage?

Q12-3 What is the basic conclusion of the original Modigliani and Miller Proposition I?

Q12-4 Deriving from the conclusion of Proposition I, what is the crux of M&M Proposition II? What is the natural relationship between the required returns on debt and on equity that results from Proposition II?

Q12-5 In what way did M&M change their conclusion, regarding capital structure choice, with the additional assumption of corporate taxes? In this context, what comprises the difference in value between levered and unlevered firms?

Q12-6 By introducing personal taxes into the model for capital structure choice, how did Miller alter the previous M&M conclusion that 100 per cent debt is optimal? What happens to the gains from leverage if personal tax rates on interest income are significantly higher than those on share-related income?

Q12-7 Why do a firm's shareholders hold a valuable 'default option'? How could this option induce shareholders to employ high levels of financial leverage?

Q12-8 All else equal, which firm would face a greater level of financial distress, a software-development firm or a hotel chain? Why would financial distress costs affect the firms so differently?

Q12-9 Describe how managers whose firms have debt outstanding and face financial distress could jeopardize the investments of creditors with the 'games' of asset substitution and underinvestment.

Q12-10 Differentiate between direct and indirect costs of bankruptcy. Which of the two is generally more significant?

Q12-11 How can restrictive covenants in bonds be both an agency cost of debt and a way to prevent agency costs of debt?

Q12-12 What are the trade-offs in the agency cost/tax shield trade-off model? How is the firm's optimal capital structure determined under the assumptions of this model? Does empirical evidence support this model?

Q12-13 What industrial and national capital structure patterns are exhibited globally? What factors seem to be driving these patterns?

Q12-14 What is the observed relationship between debt ratios and profitability, and the perceived costs of financial distress? Why does the relationship between leverage and profitability imply that capital structure choice is residual in nature?

Q12-15 How influential are corporate and personal taxes on capital structure? Historically, have changes in US tax rates greatly affected debt ratios?

Q12-16 How do stock prices generally react to announcements of firms' changes in leverage? Why is this result perplexing and seemingly contradictory, given your answer to Question 12-2?

PROBLEMS

What is financial leverage and why do firms use it?

P12-1 As finance director of the Magnificent Electronics Corporation (MEC), you are considering a recapitalization plan that would convert MEC from its current all-equity capital structure to one including substantial financial leverage. MEC now has 500 000 shares outstanding, which are selling for €60 each, and you expect the firm's EBIT to be €2 400 000 per year for the foreseeable future. The recapitalization proposal is to issue €15 000 000 worth of long-term debt, at an interest rate of 6.0 per cent, and use the proceeds to repurchase 250 000 shares worth €15 000 000. Assuming there are no market frictions such as corporate or personal income taxes, calculate the expected return on equity for MEC shareholders under both the current all-equity capital structure and under the recapitalization plan.

P12-2 The All-Star Production Company (APC) is considering a recapitalization plan that would convert APC from its current all-equity capital structure to one including some financial leverage. APC now has 10 000 000 shares outstanding, which are selling for €40.00 each, and you expect the firm's EBIT to be €50 000 000 per year for the foreseeable future. The recapitalization proposal is to issue €100 000 000 worth of long-term debt, at an interest rate of 6.50 per cent, and use the proceeds to repurchase as many shares as possible, at a price of €40.00 per share. Assume there are no market frictions such as corporate or personal income taxes. Calculate the expected return on equity for APC shareholders, under both the current all-equity capital structure and under the recapitalization plan.

a Calculate the number of shares outstanding, the per-share price and the debt-to-equity ratio for APC if the proposed recapitalization is adopted.

b Calculate the earnings per share (EPS) and the return on equity for APC shareholders, under both the current all-equity capitalization and the proposed mixed debt/equity capital structure.

c Calculate the breakeven level of EBIT, where earnings per share for APC stockholders are the same, under the current and proposed capital structures.

d At what level of EBIT will APC shareholders earn zero EPS under the current and the proposed capital structures?

P12-3 As chief financial officer of the Clarion Supply Corporation (CSC), you are considering a recapitalization plan that would convert CSC from its current all-equity capital structure to one including substantial financial leverage. CSC now has 250 000 shares outstanding, which are selling for €60.00 each, and the recapitalization proposal is to issue €7 500 000 worth of long-term debt at an interest rate of 6.0 per cent and use the proceeds to repurchase 125 000 shares worth €7 500 000. CSC's earnings next year will depend on the state of the economy. If there is normal growth, EBIT will be €2 000 000; EBIT will be €1 000 000 if there is a recession and €3 000 000 if there is an economic boom. You believe that each economic outcome is equally likely. Assume there are no market frictions such as corporate or personal income taxes.

a Calculate the number of shares outstanding, the per-share price and the debt-to-equity ratio for CSC if the proposed recapitalization is adopted.

b Calculate the expected earnings per share (EPS) and return on equity for CSC shareholders under all three economic outcomes (recession, normal growth and boom), for both the current all-equity capitalization and the proposed mixed debt/equity capital structure.

c Calculate the breakeven level of EBIT where earnings per share for CSC shareholders are the same under the current and proposed capital structures.

d At what level of EBIT will CSC shareholders earn zero EPS under the current and the proposed capital structures?

The M&M *capital structure irrelevance propositions*

P12-4 An unlevered company operates in perfect markets and has a net operating income (EBIT) of €250 000. Assume that the required return on assets for firms in this industry is 12.5 per cent. The firm issues €1 million worth of debt, with a required return of 5 per cent, and uses the proceeds to repurchase outstanding shares.

a What is the market value and required return of this firm's shares before the repurchase transaction?

b What is the market value and required return of this firm's remaining shares after the repurchase transaction?

P12-5 Assume that capital markets are perfect. A firm finances its operations with €50 million in shares, with a required return of 15 per cent, and €40 million in bonds, with a required return of 9 per cent. Assume that the firm could issue €10 million in additional bonds, at 9 per cent. Using the proceeds to retire €10 million worth of equity, what would happen to the firm's WACC? What would happen to the required return on the company's shares?

P12-6 A firm operates in perfect capital markets. The required return on its outstanding debt is 6 per cent, the required return on its shares is 14 per cent, and its WACC is 10 per cent. What is the firm's debt-to-equity ratio?

P12-7 Assume that two firms, U and L, are identical, in all respects, except that Firm U is debt-free, and Firm L has a capital structure that is 50 per cent debt and 50 per cent equity, by market value. Further suppose that the assumptions of the Modigliani and Miller capital structure irrelevance proposition hold (no taxes or transaction costs, no bank-ruptcy costs, etc.) and that each firm will have net operating income (EBIT) of €800 000. If the required return on assets, r, for these firms is 12.5 per cent, and risk-free debt yields 5 per cent, calculate the following values for both Firm U and Firm L: (1) total firm value; (2) market value of debt and equity; and (3) required return on equity.

SMART SOLUTIONS
See the problem and solution explained step-by-step at www.cengage.co.uk/megginson

P12-8 Hearthstone Corporation and The Shaky Image Company are companies that compete in the luxury consumer goods market. The two companies are virtually identical, except that Hearthstone is financed entirely with equity, and The Shaky Image uses equal amounts of debt and equity. Suppose each firm has assets with a total market value of €100 million. Hearthstone has 4 million shares outstanding worth €25 each. Shaky has 2 million shares outstanding, and it also has publicly traded debt, with a market value of €50 million. Both companies operate in a world with perfect capital markets (no taxes, etc.). The WACC for each firm is 12 per cent. The cost of debt is 8 per cent.

a What is the price of Shaky stock?

b What is the cost of equity for Hearthstone? For Shaky?

P12-9 In the mid-1980s, Michael Milken and his firm, Drexel Burnham Lambert, made the term 'junk bonds' a household phrase. Many of Drexel's clients issued junk bonds (bonds with low credit ratings) to the public to raise money to conduct a leveraged buyout (LBO) of a target firm. After the LBO, the target firm would have an extremely high debt-to-equity ratio, with only a small portion of equity financing remaining. Many politicians and members of the financial press worried that the increase in junk bonds would bring about an increase in risk for the US economy because so many large firms had become highly leveraged. Merton Miller disagreed. See if you can follow his

argument by assessing whether each of the statements below is true or false:

a The junk bonds issued by acquiring firms were riskier than investment grade bonds.

b The remaining equity in highly leveraged firms was more risky than it had been before the LBO.

c After an LBO, the target firm's capital structure would consist of very risky junk bonds and very risky equity. Therefore, the risk of the firm would increase after the LBO.

d The junk bonds issued to conduct the LBO were less risky than the equity they replaced.

The M&M capital structure model with corporate and personal taxes

P12-10 Herculio Mining has net operating income of €5 million; there is €50 million of debt outstanding, with a required rate of return of 6 per cent; the required rate of return on the industry is 12 per cent; and the corporate tax rate is 40 per cent. Assume there are corporate taxes but no personal taxes.

a Determine the present value of the interest tax shield of Herculio Mining, as well as the total value of the firm.

b Determine the gain from leverage if personal taxes of 20 per cent on share income and 30 per cent on debt income exist.

P12-11 An all-equity firm is subject to a 30 per cent tax rate. Its total market value is initially €3 500 000. There are 175 000 shares outstanding. The firm announces a programme to issue €1 million worth of bonds at 10 per cent interest, and to use the proceeds to buy back shares. Assume that there is no change in costs of financial distress and that the debt is perpetual.

a What is the value of the tax shield that the firm acquires through the bond issue?

b According to Modigliani and Miller, what is the likely increase in the firm's market value per share after the announcement, assuming efficient markets?

c How many shares will the company be able to repurchase?

P12-12 Intel Corporation is a firm that uses almost no debt and had a total market capitalization of about $179 billion in April 2004. Assume that

Intel faces a 35 per cent tax rate on corporate earnings. Ignore all elements of the decision, except the corporate tax savings.

a By how much could Intel managers increase the value of the firm by issuing $50 billion in bonds (which would be rolled over in perpetuity) and simultaneously repurchasing $50 billion in shares? Why do you think that Intel has not taken advantage of this opportunity?

b Suppose the personal tax rate on equity income, faced by Intel shareholders, is 10 per cent, and the personal tax rate on interest income is 40 per cent. Recalculate the gains to Intel from replacing $50 billion of equity with debt.

P12-13 Soonerco has €15 million of shares outstanding, a net operating income of €2.5 million per year and €15 million of debt outstanding, with a required return (interest rate) of 8 per cent. The required rate of return on assets in this industry is 12.5 per cent and the corporate tax rate is 35 per cent. Within the M&M framework of corporate taxes but no personal taxes, determine the present value of the interest tax shield of Soonerco, as well as the total value of the firm. Finally, determine the gain from leverage if personal taxes are levied at the rates of 15 per cent on share income and 25 per cent on debt income.

Costs of bankruptcy and financial distress

P12-14 Assume that you are the manager of a financially distressed company with €1.5 million in debt outstanding that will mature in two months. Your firm currently has €1 million cash on hand. Assuming that you are operating the firm in the shareholders' best interests and that debt covenants prevent you from simply paying out the cash to shareholders as cash dividends, what should you do?

P12-15 You are the manager of a financially distressed company with €1.5 million in debt outstanding that will mature in three months. Your firm currently has €1 million cash on hand. Assume that you are offered the opportunity to invest in either of the two projects described below.

● **Project 1:** The opportunity to invest €1 million in risk-free government stock,

with a 4 per cent annual interest rate (a quarterly interest rate of 1 per cent = 4 per cent per year ÷ 4 quarters per year).

● **Project 2:** A high-risk gamble, which will pay off €1.6 million in two months, if it is successful (probability = 0.4), but will only pay €400 000 if it is unsuccessful (probability = 0.6).

a Compute the expected pay-off for each project and state which one you would adopt if you were operating the firm in the shareholders' best interests? Why?

b Which project would you accept if the firm was unlevered? Why?

c Which project would you accept if the firm was organized as a partnership rather than a company? Why?

P12-16 A firm has the choice of investing in one of two projects. Both projects last for one year. Project 1 requires an investment of €11 000 and yields €11 000 with a probability of 0.5, and €13 000 with a probability of 0.5. Project 2 also requires an investment of €11 000 and yields €5000 with a probability of 0.5, and €20 000 with a probability of 0.5. The firm is capable of raising €10 000 of the required investment through a bond issue that carries an annual interest rate of 10 per cent. Assuming that the investors are concerned only about expected returns, which project would shareholders prefer? Why? Which project would bondholders prefer? Why?

P12-17 An all-equity firm has 100 000 shares outstanding worth €10 each. The firm is considering a project that requires an investment of €400 000 and has an NPV of €50 000. The company is also considering financing this project with a new issue of equity.

a What is the price at which the firm needs to issue the new shares so that the existing shareholders are indifferent to whether the firm takes on the project with this equity financing or does not take on the project?

b What is the price at which the firm needs to issue the new shares so that the existing shareholders capture the full benefit associated with the new project?

P12-18 You are the manager of a financially distressed company that has €5 million in loans, which come due in 30 days. Your firm has €4 million cash on hand. Suppose that a long-time supplier of materials to your firm is planning to exit the business but has offered to sell your company a large supply of material at a bargain price of €4.5 million – but only if payment is made immediately in cash. If you choose not to acquire this material the supplier will offer it to a competitor. Your firm will then have to acquire the materials at market prices, totalling €5 million, over the next few months.

a Assuming that you are operating the firm in the shareholders' best interests, would you accept the project? Why or why not?

b Would you accept this project if the firm were unlevered? Why or why not?

c Would you accept this project if the company were organized as a partnership? Why or why not?

Agency costs and capital structure

P12-19 Magnum Enterprises has net operating income of €5 million. There is €50 million of debt outstanding, with a required rate of return of 6 per cent. The required rate of return on the industry is 12 per cent. The corporate tax rate is 40 per cent. There are corporate taxes but no personal taxes. Compute the value of Magnum, assuming that the present value of bankruptcy costs are €10 million.

P12-20 Slash and Burn Construction Company currently has no debt and expects to earn €10 million in net operating income each year for the foreseeable future. The required return on assets for construction companies of this type is 12.5 per cent, and the corporate tax rate is 40 per cent. There are no taxes on dividends or interest at the personal level. Slash and Burn calculates that there is a 10 per cent chance that the firm will fall into bankruptcy in any given year. If bankruptcy does occur, it will impose direct and indirect costs totalling €12 million. If necessary, use the industry required return for discounting bankruptcy costs.

a Compute the present value of bankruptcy costs for Slash and Burn.

b Compute the overall value of the firm.

c Recalculate the value of the company, assuming that the firm's shareholders face a 25 per cent personal tax rate on equity income.

P12-21 Slash and Burn Construction Company currently has no debt and expects to earn €10 million in net operating income each year for the foreseeable future. The required return on assets for construction companies of this type is 12.5 per cent, and the corporate tax rate is 40 per cent. There are no taxes on dividends or interest at the personal level. Slash and Burn calculates that there is a 10 per cent chance that the firm will fall into bankruptcy in any given year. If bankruptcy does occur, it will impose direct and indirect costs totalling €12 million. If necessary, use the industry required return for discounting bankruptcy costs. Assume that the managers of this company are weighing two capital structure alteration proposals.

● **Proposal 1** involves borrowing €20 million, at an interest rate of 6 per cent, and using the proceeds to repurchase an equal amount of outstanding shares. With this level of debt, the likelihood that Slash and Burn will fall into bankruptcy in any given year increases to 15 per cent. If bankruptcy occurs, it will impose direct and indirect costs totalling €12 million.

● **Proposal 2** involves borrowing €30 million at an interest rate of 8 per cent, and also using the proceeds to repurchase an equal amount of outstanding shares. With this level of debt, the likelihood of Slash and Burn falling into bankruptcy in any given year rises to 25 per cent. The associated direct and indirect costs of bankruptcy, if it occurs, increase to €20 million.

For each proposal, calculate both the present value of the interest tax shields and the overall value of the firm, assuming that there are no personal taxes on debt or on equity income.

Capital structure patterns observed worldwide – and is Europe different?

P12-22 Go to Yahoo! and download recent balance sheets for Microsoft, Holcim, Diageo and Oracle. Calculate several debt ratios for each company and comment on the differences that you observe in the use of leverage. What factors do you think account for these differences?

THOMSON ONE **Business School Edition**

For instructions on using Thomson ONE, refer to the introductory text provided with the Thomson ONE problems at the end of Chapters 1–6, or in *A Guide for Using Thomson ONE – Business School Edition*.

P12-23 How does the value of an unlevered firm change if it takes on debt in a perfect capital market? Abercrombie & Fitch (ticker: ANF) is an all-equity firm. Using the latest year's net operating income (EBIT) and its weighted average cost of capital (WACC), calculate the value of ANF. If the company decides to change its debt-to-equity ratio to 0.5, by issuing debt and by using the proceeds to repurchase shares, what will ANF's value be after the change in capital structure? Assume that its cost of debt is one quarter of its cost of equity and that markets are perfect. What happens to its cost of equity after the new debt is issued? What is likely to happen to ANF's equity beta after debt is issued?

P12-24 How does the value of an unlevered firm change if it takes on debt in the presence of corporate taxes? Repeat the analysis for ANF from the previous problem, after relaxing only the 'no corporate tax' assumption of perfect capital markets. Use the average tax rate (income taxes divided by pre-tax income from the income statement) for the latest available year. What is the value of ANF after it issues debt? What is the benefit of issuing debt when there are corporate taxes? How will the beta for a levered ANF in the presence of corporate taxes, compare to that of an all-equity ANF and that of a levered ANF in perfect capital markets? When capital markets are perfect, except for corporate taxes, what is the optimal level of debt the company should issue? In reality, do we observe firms that maintain this optimal level of debt? Why or why not?

MINICASE *Capital structure*

A few years after being appointed financial manager at Sedona Fabricators Limited, you are asked by your boss to prepare for your first presentation to the board of directors. This presentation will pertain to issues associated with capital structure. It is intended to ensure that some of the newly appointed, independent board members understand certain terminology and issues. As a guideline for your presentation, you are provided with the following outline of questions.

Assignment

1 What is capital structure?

2 What is financial leverage?

3 How does financial leverage relate to firm risk and expected returns?

4 Modigliani and Miller demonstrated that capital structure policy is irrelevant. What is the basis for their argument? What are their Propositions I and II?

5 How does the introduction of corporate taxes affect the M&M model?

6 How do the costs of bankruptcy and financial distress affect the M&M model?

7 What are agency costs? How can the use of debt reduce agency costs associated with equity?

Chapter 13
Dividend Policy

OPENING FOCUS

British Airways cuts dividend to preserve cash during airline crisis

To say that the period immediately following the 11 September 2001 terrorist attacks on the World Trade Center and the Pentagon was a difficult one for the world's airlines would be a serious understatement. Traffic on all the major airlines fell precipitously, and almost all were forced to cut both staff and schedules quite severely. Within weeks of the attack, two major European carriers – Swissair and Sabena – filed for bankruptcy protection, and several other international carriers appeared on the brink of following suit. The threat to the viability of the US airline industry was so severe, in fact, that the major carriers successfully lobbied the US Congress for an unprecedented $15 billion bailout package. Even with this financial lifeline, US carriers announced job cuts of more than 120 000 people in the weeks following 11 September.

British Airways (London Stock Exchange ticker symbol BAY) faced these same pressures, and more, during the autumn of 2001. Most of British Airways' scheduled flights were international rather than domestic, and these had suffered the largest decline in demand following the attacks. In early October 2001, in response to the financial pressures weighing on the firm, it took the unprecedented step of suspending its interim (semi-annual) dividend payment, which it normally paid in December. The company also announced that its full-year dividend payment for fiscal year 2002 was in serious jeopardy. This dividend suspension was very traumatic for the company because it had taken great pride in paying a dividend every six months since its privatization in 1987. Over the years, its dividend payment had

increased steadily and stood at 17.8 pence per share for fiscal year 2001. In line with industry norms, this payment represented over 57 per cent of the company's net profits for 2001. But with massive financial losses looming and job cuts of 7000 employees already announced, British Airways' managers felt there was no alternative but to eliminate dividend payments. The chief executive officer had already announced he would take a salary cut and the firm had told the British government it might need a bailout package, similar to the one given to the American airline industry. The firm was clearly fighting for financial survival.

Though traumatic for British Airways and its shareholders, the dividend cut allowed the company to retain £193 million, which it otherwise would have paid out each year. This, in turn, helped the company weather the next two turbulent years, during which the number of passengers it carried declined by 15 per cent, and revenue passenger kilometres fell by almost one-fifth. The company suffered a net loss of £142 million during the fiscal year that ended in March 2002, but was able to rebound to a net profit of £72 million for fiscal year 2003. The company's share price, which had been above 300 pence per share in August 2001, fell to less than 150 pence per share, immediately after the World Trade Center attacks. It then declined even further, to 95 pence per share, in March 2003. By early September 2004, British Airways' share price had more than doubled, to 237 pence, and the company was regaining its financial health – though its officials were not yet promising to resume dividend payments anytime soon.

Sources: Kevin Done and Cathy Newman (2001) 'BA's Dividend Warning Signals Trouble', *Financial Times* (7 October, p. 10); company information at the British Airways' website (http://www.britishairways.com); 9 September 2004 share price data from the *Financial Times* website (http://mwprices.ft.com/custom/ft-com/html-markets DataTools.asp).

LEARNING OBJECTIVES

After studying this chapter you should be able to:

- Discuss the fundamentals of dividends, including payment procedures, types of policies and other forms of dividends.
- Describe the observed patterns of dividend policies on a worldwide basis.
- Understand the agency cost model of dividends.
- Explain the argument for dividend irrelevance in a world with perfect capital markets.
- Review the real-world influences on dividend policy such as taxes, transaction costs and uncertainty.
- Summarize the predictions of the agency cost model regarding expected dividend payout.

SMART FINANCE

Use the learning tools at www.cengage.co.uk/megginson

A firm's 'dividend policy' refers to the choices the firm makes about whether to pay shareholders a cash dividend, about how large the cash dividend should be, and about how frequently it should be distributed. In a broader sense, dividend policy also encompasses decisions such as whether to distribute cash to investors via share repurchases or specially designated dividends, rather than regular dividends, and whether to rely on share or on cash distributions.

Though there are numerous elements in the dividend decision, modern corporations still struggle with the same issues that occupied managers in the 1950s. Managers must decide if firms should maintain their current dividends or change them. Managers tend to increase regular dividends only when they expect that future cash flow is sufficient to pay the dividends and to meet their firm's other financial needs. Firms must also weigh the stock market's reaction to changes in dividend policy. Influencing that reaction are factors such as the level of a firm's dividends, the volatility of the dividend stream over time, and the income taxes that investors must pay when they receive dividends. As you can see, the many dimensions of this problem make dividend policy decisions quite difficult, at least for some firms.

In addition to these firm-level issues regarding dividend policy, recent trends in the aggregate dividend decisions of companies are interesting. The first of these is the growth in both the number of firms implementing alternative approaches to delivering value to shareholders, typically using **share repurchase programmes** and in the total value of these programmes. Companies that announce a share repurchase programme state that they will buy some of their own shares over a period of time. In executing a repurchase programme, firms distribute some of the cash they have accumulated to investors who want to sell their shares. Therefore, dividends and share repurchases are alternative means by which firms distribute cash to investors. In fact, the annual value of share repurchases in the United States sometimes exceeds that of cash dividends.

share repurchase programme
A company announcing this kind of programme states that it will buy some of its own shares over a period of time.

The second dramatic trend in corporate dividend policy is the continued sharp decline in the percentage of publicly traded companies that pay any dividends at all. As Panel A of Figure 13.1 demonstrates, the percentage of all publicly traded US firms paying dividends was four times greater in the 1950s than it is today. Panel B breaks this down by exchange. Additionally, those firms that do pay dividends now pay out a lower fraction of their earnings than they did before. In other words, companies have a lower *propensity* to pay dividends today than they had in years past. This is not just a US phenomenon. A recent study of European Union member countries, the results of which are shown in Figure 13.2, indicates that over the 1990s the percentage of EU-based companies that paid out dividends also declined. In general, we can expect around one-third of companies to pay dividends.

Our objective in this chapter is to answer two basic questions. First, does dividend policy matter? Can managers increase or decrease the total market value of a firm's securities by changing its dividend payments? Secondly, if dividend policy does matter, what factors determine a firm's optimal dividend policy? Before attacking these questions, however, we provide a brief overview of the fundamentals of dividend payments, which defines the key terms and discusses the basic issues that corporate managers everywhere must face in setting dividend policies. Section 13.2 provides an overview of dividend payment patterns around the world. These are the patterns that a modern theory of dividend policy should be able to explain. Section 13.3 shows that dividends are irrelevant in a world of perfect (frictionless) capital markets, which suggests that dividends exist because of some flaw in markets or human nature. Section 13.4 describes various real-world market imperfections that affect actual dividend policy decisions. Finally, Section 13.5 presents both a summary of the

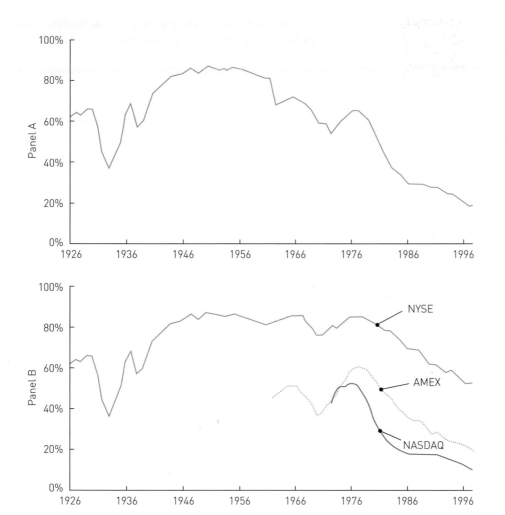

FIGURE 13.1

The fractions of publicly traded US firms paying cash dividends, 1926–1999

This figure details the percentage of all publicly traded firms in the United States that paid regular cash dividends over the period 1926–1999. Panel A shows this for all publicly traded firms, whereas Panel B breaks this down by exchange, from 1962 (AMEX) and 1972 (NASDAQ) onwards.

Source: Adapted from Eugene F. Fama and Kenneth R. French (2001) 'Disappearing Dividends: Changing Firm Characteristics or Lower Propensity to Pay?', *Journal of Applied Corporate Finance* 14:67–79. Reproduced with permission.

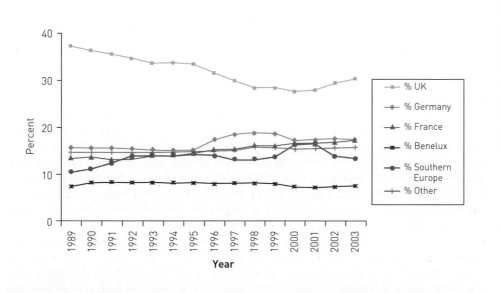

FIGURE 13.2

Percentage of European Firms paying dividends or engaging in share repurchases

Source: J. Henk von Eije and William L. Megginson (2006) 'Dividend Policy in the European Union'. Available at SSRN: http://ssrn.com/abstract 5 900749.

predictions of the current 'mainstream' model of dividend policy and a checklist that practising managers can use to set dividend policies for their firms.

13.1 DIVIDEND FUNDAMENTALS

In Chapter 4 we argued that the value of a share equals the present value of cash flows that the shareholder receives over time. Even though a company is not paying dividends today, its market value reflects the likelihood that the firm will either pay dividends in the future or be acquired by another company, at a price that reflects a higher stream of dividend payments. To provide an understanding of the fundamentals of dividend policy, we discuss the procedures for paying cash dividends and the factors affecting dividend policy. In essence, the payment of dividends, as we will see, is generally taken to indicate that the company cannot find a use for the cash it is returning such that that use would generate a return on equity equal or greater to the overall company average. In other words, dividend payment indicates that to a certain extent the company has come up against the limits to growth.

Cash dividend payment procedures

In most countries, shareholders do not have a legal right to receive dividends. Instead, a firm's board of directors must decide whether to pay dividends. The directors usually meet to evaluate the firm's recent financial performance and future outlook and to determine whether, and in what amount, dividends should be paid. The payment date of the cash dividend, if one is declared, must also be established.

Most US firms that pay cash dividends do so once every quarter, whereas corporations in other industrialized countries generally pay dividends annually or semi-annually. Firms adjust the size of their dividends periodically, but not necessarily every quarter. For example, among the roughly 1300 US firms that paid dividends continuously from 1999 to 2003, just over 36 per cent changed their dividend once per year, on average. About 14 per cent of these firms maintained a constant dividend during this five-year span, and about 23 per cent changed their dividend more frequently than once per year. Only five of the 1300 firms changed their dividend every quarter. These figures suggest that firms maintain a constant dividend until significant increases or decreases in earnings justify changing it. Companies also do not change their frequency of payment much. A recent study found that overall over 90 per cent of companies held the frequency of dividend payments constant during the 1990s.[1]

announcement date
The day a firm releases details of the dividend amount and the record and payment dates to the public.

date of record
The date on which the names of all persons who own shares in a company are recorded as shareholders and thus eligible to receive a dividend.

ex-dividend
A purchaser of a share does not receive the current dividend.

Relevant dates If a firm's directors declare a dividend, they also set the dividend record date and the payment dates. The day on which firms release this information to the public is the **announcement date**. All persons whose names are recorded as shareholders on the **date of record** receive the declared dividend at a specified future time. The shareholders who own shares on this record date are often referred to as shareholders of record. Because of the time it takes to make bookkeeping entries when a share is traded, the shares begins selling **ex-dividend** several business days prior to the date of record. Purchasers of a stock selling ex-dividend do not receive the current dividend. Ignoring normal market fluctuations, the share price should drop by

---

[1] Ferris, Noronha and Ulnu (2006) 'The More, the Merrier: An International Analysis of the Frequency of Dividend Payment', FMA Annual Meetings, October.

approximately the amount of the declared dividend on the ex-dividend date. For example, suppose a share that pays a €1 dividend sells for €51 just before going ex-dividend. Once the ex-dividend date passes, the price should drop to €50, in the absence of any other news affecting the stock. However, the average ex-dividend day price drop in most countries is significantly less than 100 per cent of the value of the dividend payment, partly due to what appears to be a personal tax effect. The **payment date** is generally set a few weeks after the record date. The payment date is the actual date on which the firm posts dividend payments to the holders of record.

payment date
The actual date on which a firm posts the dividend payment to the holders of record.

Real World

In a move that surprised almost all commentators, Microsoft Corporation announced on 16 January 2003 that it would pay a cash dividend to shareholders for the first time ever. The company declared an annual dividend of $0.08 per share, which would be out of earnings for fiscal year 2003, ending 30 June 2003. In contrast to standard practice for most US corporations, dividends would be paid only once per year rather than quarterly. Microsoft's earnings per share were $0.92 for fiscal year 2003, implying a payout ratio of 8.7 per cent. Though the total amount of the dividend, $870 million, would make only a small dent in Microsoft's holdings of cash and marketable securities (worth more than $56 billion in March 2004), investors generally applauded the company's announcement. In September 2003, Microsoft announced that fiscal year 2004 dividends per share would be doubled, to $0.16 per share. Ten months later, Microsoft shocked investors by announcing plans to pay a one-time $32 billion special cash dividend and also to once again double the annual dividend payment.

Real World

It's not just the very largest companies that pay dividends, but small companies paying dividends are rare. Consider the Alternative Investment Market in the UK, which has over 1500 companies quoted. Of these, only 270 are dividend payers, and only 37 have a yield of more than 5 per cent. More than two-thirds pay less than 3 per cent. Fewer than 50 companies per annum in the UK initiate dividend payments.

External factors affecting dividend policy

Before discussing the basic types of dividend policies, we should briefly consider some of the practical issues related to formulating a value-maximizing policy (theoretical issues are discussed in later sections). These include legal constraints, contractual constraints, internal constraints, the firm's growth prospects and owner considerations.

Most tax regimes prohibit companies from paying out in dividends a sum greater than the invested capital of the company. In other words, a firm cannot pay more in cash dividends than the sum of its most recent and historic retained earnings. However, laws do not prohibit a firm from paying more in dividends than its current earnings.

Source: Market reports, 2003, 2004.

Value in Inheritance Tax Planning, *Financial Times*, 1 September 2006.

dividend payout ratio
The percentage of current earnings available for ordinary shareholders paid out as dividends. Calculated by dividing the firm's cash dividend per share by its earnings per share.

constant payout ratio dividend policy
Used by a firm to establish that a certain percentage of earnings is paid to owners in each dividend period.

constant nominal payment policy
Based on the payment of a fixed euro dividend in each period.

target dividend payout ratio
Under this policy, the firm attempts to pay out a certain percentage of earnings, but rather than let dividends fluctuate, it pays a stated euro dividend and adjusts it towards the target payout slowly as proven earnings increases occur.

low-regular-and-extra policy
Policy of a firm paying a low regular dividend supplemented by an additional cash dividend when earnings warrant it.

extra dividend/special dividend
The additional dividend that a firm pays if earnings are higher than normal in a given period.

Source: Adapted from 'Drax to Pay a Special Dividend', *Financial Times*, 13 September 2006, and 'PT to Offer Special Dividend', *Financial Times*, 7 March 2006.

Types of dividend policies

The following sections describe three basic dividend policies, but bear in mind that the 'constant nominal dividend policy' predominates in every major economy. A particular firm's cash dividend policy may incorporate elements of each policy type.

Constant payout ratio policy One type of dividend policy that is rarely adopted by firms is a constant payout ratio. The **dividend payout ratio**, calculated by dividing the firm's cash dividend per share by its earnings per share, indicates the percentage of each euro earned that is distributed to the owners. With a **constant payout ratio dividend policy**, the firm establishes that a certain percentage of earnings is paid to owners in each dividend period. The problem with this policy is that if the firm's earnings drop, or if a loss occurs in a given period, the dividends may be low or even non-existent, making them as volatile as the firm's earnings.

Constant nominal payment policy Another type of dividend policy, the **constant nominal payment policy**, is based on the payment of a fixed euro dividend in each period. Using this policy, firms often increase the regular dividend once a *proven* increase in earnings has occurred. Under this policy, firms almost never cut dividends unless they face a true crisis.

Firms that pay a steady dividend may build their policy around a **target dividend payout ratio**. Under this policy, the firm attempts to pay out a certain percentage of earnings. Rather than let dividends fluctuate, however, it pays a stated euro dividend and slowly adjusts it towards the target payout, as proven earnings increases occur. This is known as a 'partial-adjustment strategy', and it implies that at any given time, firms may be in a transition between two dividend payment levels.

Low-regular-and-extra policy Some firms establish a **low-regular-and-extra policy** that pays a low regular dividend, supplemented by an additional cash dividend when earnings warrant it. If earnings are higher than normal in a given period, the firm may pay this additional dividend, which is designated an **extra dividend** or a **special dividend**. By designating the amount – by which the dividend exceeds the regular payment – as an extra dividend, the firm avoids giving shareholders false hopes. The use of the 'extra' or the 'special' designation is more common among companies that experience temporary shifts in earnings. For example, interest rates on residential mortgages declined to the lowest level in 35 years, during 2003. As a result, many homeowners refinanced their loans. The refinancing boom resulted in a sharp increase in fees earned by banks and other financial institutions that were active in the mortgage market. Many of these companies paid special dividends as a way of distributing some of this cash to investors.

Real World

Special dividends can be initiated for a variety of reasons. In September 2006 Drax, the UK quoted power generating company, announced a special dividend to return excess cash to its shareholders. The company announced an interim dividend of 4p per share, as well as the special dividend of 80p per share. The cost of the special dividend was some £326 million. That pales in comparison with the £5 billion that Unilever returned to shareholders in 1999, but represents a general policy that some companies adopt to boost shareholder returns.

Companies also sometimes offer special dividends to shareholders as part of heir defence against a takeover. Consider Portugal Telecom, which offered to pay shareholders €3 billion in dividends over three years as part of a defence against a hostile €11.2 billion bid from Sonae, the Portuguese conglomerate.

Other forms of dividends

In addition to paying cash dividends, firms often employ three other methods of distributing either cash or securities to investors: stock dividends; capitalization issues (or stock splits); and share repurchases.

Stock dividends A **stock dividend** is the payment to existing owners of a dividend in the form of stock. For example, if a firm declares a 20 per cent stock dividend, it will issue 20 new shares for every 100 shares that an investor owns. Often, firms pay stock dividends as a replacement for, or as a supplement to, cash dividends. Remember that a stock dividend does not necessarily increase the value of an investor's holdings. If a firm pays a 20 per cent stock dividend, and nothing else about the firm changes, then the number of outstanding shares increases by 20 per cent, and the stock price drops by 20 per cent. The net effect on shareholder wealth is neutral. Shareholders receiving stock dividends also maintain a constant proportional share in the firm's equity.

stock dividend
The payment to existing owners of a dividend in the form of stock.

Capitalization issues These have an effect on a firm's share price, similar to that of stock dividends. When a firm conducts a **capitalization issue** (termed a 'stock split' in the USA), its share price declines because the number of outstanding shares increases. For example, in a 2-for-1 issue or split, the firm doubles the number of shares outstanding. As in the case of a stock dividend, intuition suggests that capitalization issues should not create value for shareholders. After all, if someone offers to give you two €5 bills in exchange for one €10 bill, you are no better off. A capitalization issue also has no effect on the firm's capital structure; it simply increases the number of shares outstanding and reduces the per-share par value.

capitalization issue
Involves a company splitting the par value of its shares and issuing new shares to existing investors. For example, in a 2-for-1 issue, the firm doubles the number of shares outstanding.

We have often stated that managers should strive to increase share prices, not decrease them. In the case of a capitalization issue (or stock dividend), if the decrease in share price is proportional to the change in shares outstanding, the net effect on shareholder wealth is zero (ignoring the administrative costs of the exercise). Managers nevertheless decide to engage in capitalization issues because they believe that if the price per share gets too high, some investors (especially individual investors) will no longer wish to buy it.

Real World

Since going public in March 1986, Microsoft has split its stock nine times, most recently on 14 February 2003. An investor who purchased a single Microsoft share in its IPO in 1986 would own 288 Microsoft shares today. Look at this another way. Microsoft's stock price in mid-September 2006 was around $27. But that price reflected the cumulative 288-for-1 splits that took place since 1986. Taking Microsoft's stock performance since its IPO as a given, had Microsoft never split its stock, the price in June 2004 would have been about $7776 per share.

Other companies that have engaged in frequent stock splits are conglomerate GE and internet company Cisco with nine splits, retailing giant Wal-Mart with 11 splits and specialist retailer The Limited with 12. However, some companies never split stocks, most famously perhaps Berkshire Hathaway, the investment vehicle of Warren Buffet.

reverse stock split
Occurs when a firm replaces a certain number of outstanding shares with just one new share. This is done to increase the share price.

Firms sometimes conduct **reverse stock splits**, in which they replace a certain number of outstanding shares with just one new share. For example, in a 1-for-2 split, one new share replaces two old shares; in a 2-for-3 split, two new shares replace three old shares; and so on. Firms initiate reverse stock splits when their shares are selling at a very low price, possibly so low that the listing exchange threatens to remove them.

Share repurchases or buybacks US and UK firms have dramatically increased repurchases of their own outstanding shares in recent years. Figure 13.3 illustrates the dramatic growth in US company repurchases between 1972 and 2001, especially since 1982 when an important ruling by the SEC was made. (See also Figure 13.4.) The practical motives for share repurchases include obtaining shares to be used in acquisitions, having shares available for employee share option plans, and retiring shares. From a broader perspective, the rising importance of share repurchases implies that they enhance shareholder value, perhaps because they have traditionally been a tax-advantaged method of distributing cash. Though it is not clear exactly what managers are trying to achieve through repurchases, frequently mentioned rationales include sending a *positive signal* to investors in the market-place that management believes the shares are undervalued, thus reducing the number of shares outstanding and thereby raising earnings per share (EPS).

A recent study argues convincingly that share repurchases have grown rapidly since the early 1990s, largely to offset the dilution effects of the exercise of share options. As the number and the value of options, granted to (and exercised by) top executives, have increased in importance, companies have been buying back shares to keep the total number outstanding from rising too sharply, thus reducing earnings per share.

Source: Adapted from 'Statoil in Buyback Agreement with Government', *Financial Times*, 27 May 2006.

Real World

A nice example of share repurchase is the programme offered by Statoil. Statoil is 70 per cent owned by the Norwegian government, and the concern was that in offering a share buyback it would result in strengthened state control. However this runs counter to the wishes of both the state and the company, and so an agreement was reached to retire some of the existing state capital as the buyback rolls out.

There are several methods that companies use to repurchase shares. The most common approach is called an 'open-market share repurchase', in which, as the name implies, firms buy back their shares by transacting in the open market. A second share repurchase method is called a 'tender offer', or 'self-tender'. Firms using this approach announce their intentions to buy back a certain number of their outstanding shares at a premium above the current market price. The market reaction to self-tender announcements is generally quite positive.

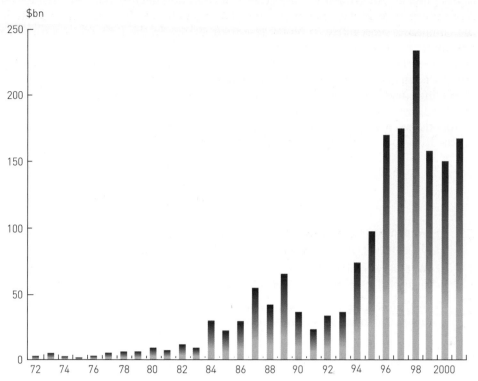

FIGURE 13.3

Market value of share repurchases by US corporations, 1972–2001

Source: Table B-90, Economic Report of the President (2002) and Thomson Financial Securities Data, as reported in Table 1 of J. Fed Weston and Juan A. Siu (2003) 'Changing Motives for Share Repurchases', *Finance Paper 3* (2003), Anderson Graduate School of Management, UCLA.

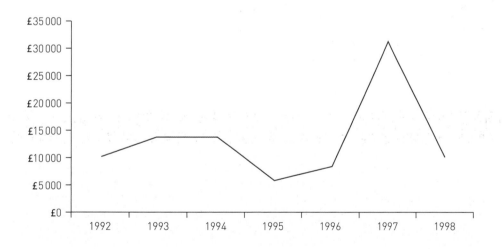

FIGURE 13.4

Aggregate value (£ mn) of share buybacks by UK companies

Source: Renneboog, Luc and Trojanowski, Grzegorz (2005) 'Patterns in Payout Policy and Payout Channel Choice of UK Firms in the 1990s', *ECGI – Finance Working Paper No. 70/2005; CentER Discussion Paper No.22/2005*; TILEC Discussion Paper 002/2005, Table 5.

The phenomenal recent growth in repurchases significantly complicates our discussion in this chapter, as it blurs exactly what we mean by 'dividend payout'. Repurchases today in the USA are equal to between one-third and one-half the total value of ordinary cash dividend payments. Therefore, we should probably talk about corporate payout policy as encompassing both dividends and share repurchases because both represent regular cash distributions from corporations to their shareholders.[2] Additionally, empirical research documents that dividends and repurchases are complements – companies paying high cash dividends also tend to be the companies most likely to repurchase their shares. In the following sections, we thus adopt the convention of referring to 'payout policy' when we are talking about both types of cash distributions; we use the narrower term 'dividend policy' when we are discussing just the payment of cash dividends.

Having surveyed the basic mechanics and issues surrounding dividend payments, we can now look more closely at the economically interesting questions about dividends, such as why firms pay dividends at all and how capital markets value dividends.

CONCEPT REVIEW QUESTIONS

1 What policies and payments comprise a firm's 'dividend policy'? Why is determining dividend policy more difficult today than in decades past?

2 What do you think the typical stock market reaction is to the announcement that a firm will increase its dividend payment? Why?

3 Why should we expect a firm's share price to decline by approximately the amount of the dividend payment on the ex-dividend date?

13.2 PATTERNS OBSERVED IN PAYOUT POLICIES WORLDWIDE

Similar to our discussion of capital structure, we find that observation of worldwide dividend payment and share repurchase patterns clarifies exactly what a robust theory of payout policy suggests. The following analysis facts reveal remarkable similarities in the dividend policies observed around the world, but there are equally fascinating differences as well.

Payout patterns observed

Payout policies show distinct national patterns As shown in Table 13.1, companies that are headquartered in countries with legal systems based on English common law generally have higher cash dividend payout ratios than do companies that are headquartered in countries with civil law systems. British, Australian,

---

[2] Professors Roni Michaely and Franklin Allen point out that an even broader definition of 'payout' encompasses cash payments for shares acquired by bidding firms in mergers and acquisitions. Because the acquired firm disappears as a separate entity after the merger, cash payments by the acquirer to the target's shareholders are effectively the same as a liquidating cash dividend. In recent years, cash payments in mergers have exceeded the combined value of share repurchases and ordinary cash dividends, which means that the total cash payout from the corporate sector significantly exceeds the total net profits of US companies every year. This 'excess payout' must be financed by new security issues (roughly one-third equity, two-thirds debt) and net borrowing from financial institutions. See Roni Michaely and Franklin Allen (2002) 'Payout Policy', in George Constantinides *et al.* (eds.) *Handbook of Economics* (North Holland).

COUNTRY	NUMBER OF FIRMS	DIVIDENDS TO CASH FLOW (%)	DIVIDENDS TO EARNINGS (%)	DIVIDENDS TO SALES (%)
Belgium	33	11.77%	39.38%	1.09%
Denmark	75	6.55	17.27	0.71
Finland	39	8.08	21.27	0.77
France	246	9.46	23.55	0.63
Germany	146	12.70	42.86	0.83
Italy	58	9.74	21.83	0.92
Japan	149	13.03	52.88	0.72
Netherlands	96	11.29	30.02	0.74
Norway	50	10.74	23.91	0.98
Spain	33	15.77	30.45	1.04
Sweden	81	5.59	18.33	0.78
Switzerland	70	10.38	25.30	0.98
Civil law median	**33**	**9.74%**	**25.11%**	**0.83%**
Australia	103	22.83%	42.82%	2.22%
Canada	236	8.00	19.78	0.78
Hong Kong	40	35.43	45.93	7.51
Malaysia	41	15.29	37.93	3.12
Singapore	27	22.28	41.04	2.14
South Africa	90	16.16	35.62	1.90
United Kingdom	799	16.67	36.91	1.89
United States	1 588	11.38	22.11	0.95
Common law median	**40**	**18.28%**	**37.42%**	**2.02%**
Sample median	**39**	**11.77%**	**30.02%**	**0.98%**

TABLE 13.1

Dividend payout measures for OECD and selected developing countries

This table classifies countries by legal origin (civil law versus common law) and presents three measures of average dividend payout for the firms from each country.

Source: Rafael LaPorta, Florencio Lopez-de-Silanes, Andrei Shleifer and Robert W. Vishny (2000) 'Agency Problems and Dividend Policies Around the World', *Journal of Finance* 55:1–33. Reproduced with permission.

Singaporean and South African firms have especially high payout ratios, whereas US firms are nearer the global average.[3] French and Italian firms tend to have lower payouts than do other Western companies. Companies that are headquartered in developing countries typically have very low dividend payouts, if they pay dividends at all. Many factors influence these patterns, but clearly the nation's legal system is an important factor. This factor also underlies other differences, such as differences in capital market size and efficiency. Common law countries that rely heavily on capital markets for corporate financing tend to observe higher dividend payments than do

---

[3] Having the United States fall in the mid-range of national payout policies actually represents a very significant change from the traditional pattern. American companies have historically ranked near the top of the dividend payout league, but this has changed over the past decade for three reasons. First, as noted above, share repurchases have grown dramatically in recent years. Secondly, as shown by Professors Eugene Fama and Ken French, a far lower fraction of publicly traded US firms pay dividends today than in the past – and those that do pay dividends pay out less than in previous eras. Thirdly, European and Japanese companies have significantly increased their payout ratios since the early 1990s. This picture is significantly different when one looks at payout policy (including share repurchases) rather than just dividends. Though these are now legal in most developed countries, only the United States has witnessed a dramatic surge in the total value of repurchases. When both dividends and repurchases are included, the United States once more becomes a high-payout country; in fact, by this definition the payout ratio of the US corporate sector has been increasing, rather than decreasing, since the early 1990s. See Eugene F. Fama and Kenneth R. French (2001) 'Disappearing Dividends: Changing Firm Characteristics or Lower Propensity to Pay?', *Journal of Financial Economics* 60:3–43.

continental European and other countries, which rely more on financing by banks and other financial intermediaries. Not surprisingly, countries with either a strong socialist tradition or a long history of state involvement in the economy are inclined to discourage dividend payments to private investors.

Payout policies show pronounced industry patterns, and these are the same worldwide In general, large, profitable firms, in mature industries, tend to pay out much larger fractions of their earnings than do firms in younger, rapidly growing industries. Utility companies have very high dividend payouts in almost every country. The most important influences on payout decisions appear to be industry growth rate, capital investment needs, profitability, earnings variability and asset characteristics (the mix between tangible and intangible assets). In the United States, an industry's average payout ratio (dividends plus repurchases) is negatively related to the richness of its investment opportunities and positively related to the degree to which the industry is regulated. Table 13.2 lists average dividend payout ratios for several industries and countries. Note that the highest dividends are in the asset rich industries of oil and gas and utilities, and the lowest in the technology and telecommunications sectors.

Asset-rich, regulated and slow-growing companies tend to have high dividend payout ratios Companies in which tangible assets make up a large fraction of total value tend to have higher dividend payouts, whereas companies in which intangible assets are more important tend to have low payouts. Furthermore, regulated companies (particularly utilities) pay out more of their earnings than do unregulated companies. The relationship between dividend payout and growth rate is equally clear. Rapidly growing firms hoard cash and select zero or very low dividend payouts. As these companies mature, dividend payouts typically increase. Table 13.3 reports dividend payout ratios and dividend yields for the largest companies by market capitalization as at end-2006. Dividend yield is computed by dividing a firm's annual dividend per share by its share price. Rapidly growing and/or high-technology companies pay little or no dividends; slower-growing, less high-technology firms have relatively high dividend yields.

Firms maintain constant nominal dividend payments per share for significant periods of time Put another way, companies everywhere tend to 'smooth' dividend payments. These payments show far less variability than do the corporate profits on which they ultimately are based. In the terminology introduced in Section 13.1, firms follow a policy of constant nominal dividend payments (regular dividends), with

TABLE 13.2

Average dividend payout ratio 2001–2006 by country and industry

Source: Thomson ONE

	GERMANY	UK	USA	THREE COUNTRIES
Basic industries	37.21	16.70	20.25	21.68
Consumer goods	30.79	32.88	12.13	17.31
Consumer services	12.79	23.72	6.31	10.70
Healthcare	16.86	9.88	2.57	4.10
Industrials	26.59	32.00	9.71	15.69
Oil and gas	53.01	9.94	9.65	10.07
Technology	9.87	7.18	1.84	3.15
Telecoms	0.00	17.17	12.24	12.45
Utilities	31.63	49.08	56.64	52.45
Total	21.61	22.68	8.43	11.81

TABLE 13.3

Dividend and PE ratios for the world's largest companies

This table presents the annual dividend payment, as well as dividend yield and payout ratios, for the 25 largest companies by market value, as ranked by *Business Week* magazine, for 2006.

COMPANY	COUNTRY	INDUSTRY	MARKET VALUE	DIVIDEND YIELD	PE RATIO	DIVIDEND PAYOUT RATIO
Royal Dutch Shell	Netherlands/UK	Petroleum	€158.48	71.0%	4.2%	16.8
BP	UK	Petroleum	153.24	120.7	3.7	32.7
Vodafone Group	UK	Telecommunications	147.99	29.1	1.3	22.4
HSBC Holdings	UK	Banking	126.97	63.5	4.5	14.1
GlaxoSmithKline	UK	Pharmaceuticals	118.96	50.8	3.3	15.4
Novartis	Switzerland	Pharmaceuticals	113.09	37.4	1.9	19.7
NTT DoCoMo	Japan	Telecommunications	105.31	11.9	0.2	59.3
Total	France	Petroleum	103.78	67.1	4.9	13.7
Toyota Motor	Japan	Automobiles	86.32	14.2	1.3	10.9
Nokia	Finland	Mobile phone mfrg	86.09	38.7	1.8	21.5
Nestlé	Switzerland	Food and beverages	83.00	38.0	2.6	14.6
Royal Bank of Scotland Group	UK	Banking	75.13	30.8	2.8	11.0
Roche Holdings	Switzerland	Pharmaceuticals	72.61	31.6	0.9	35.1
AstraZeneca	UK	Pharmaceuticals	69.67	36.7	1.7	21.6
UBS	Switzerland	Banking	67.64	53.9	2.9	18.6
Deutsche Telekom	Germany	Telecommunications	62.85	0	0	−2.0
Telecom Italia	Italy	Telecommunications	60.12	43.2	4	10.8
Unilever	Netherlands/UK	Consumer products	59.36	24.4	3.4	12.6
France Telecom	France	Telecommunications	57.45	0	0	−3.2
Telefonica	Spain	Telecommunications	56.80	0	0	25.2
Nippon Telegraph	Japan	Telecommunications	55.58	34.2	1.2	28.5
L'Oreal	France	Cosmetics and luxury goods	49.06	45.9	1.6	28.7
Sanofi-Synthelabo	France	Pharmaceuticals	46.81	18.7	2.3	22.6
Barclays	UK	Banking	46.19	44.8	4.3	10.5

Source: Authors' computations.

partial adjustments made as earnings change over time. Managers will not increase per-share dividends until they believe that 'permanent' earnings have increased enough to support a higher dividend level. Even then, managers will gradually increase dividend payments to reach a new equilibrium payment. Likewise, corporate managers will try to maintain constant per-share dividend payments, even in the face of temporary net losses, until it becomes clear that earnings will not revive. Managers will then reduce, but rarely eliminate, dividend payments, and they will make the full downward adjustment in one large cut.

Aggregate payout ratio increasing Whereas the number (and fraction) of publicly traded companies that pay dividends has been declining over the past three decades, the aggregate payout ratio of the corporate sector has been increasing. Figure 13.5 shows the aggregate dividend payout ratio for the US corporate sector from 1972 to 2001. This figure also shows the 'payout ratio' for share repurchases as a fraction of the total net income of the corporate sector. In other words, corporations have been steadily increasing their payout ratios over the past three decades. This seemingly contradictory finding can be rationalized by observing that relatively few very large companies account for the bulk of cash dividend payments each year. However, these companies account for a large fraction of the annual net profits earned by US businesses. Remember what we noted about dividends – that they indicated that companies were reaching the natural limit to growth. By that stage the company is probably quite large. In that case, even if it makes more money it probably cannot reinvest it as profitably as it could have done the difference will be paid out in dividends. For European companies, the picture is not as clear, due to a lack of long-run comparable data. However, some insight can be gained from recent research. Megginson, von Eije and Henk (in a 2006 paper titled 'Dividend Policy in the European Union', available at http://ssrn.com/abstract=900749) and Ferris, Sen and Yui (2006: 'Are Fewer Firms Paying More Dividends? The International Evidence', *Journal of Multinational Financial Management*, 16(4):333–362) examine UK dividend data over the 1990s. Note that, unlike the USA, there are no detailed aggregate series on share repurchases. What they find is very similar to the US findings: fewer firms pay dividends, but those that do pay out a higher percentage. This finding is also common for Japanese and other industrialized companies.

Investors react positively to dividend and share repurchase announcements, but react negatively to dividend decreases or eliminations When a company announces either its first regular cash dividend payment (an initiation) or an increase in its existing per-share dividend, that company's share price typically increases by 1 to 3 per cent. A similar response occurs when firms announce share repurchase programmes. Investors appear to believe that dividend increases imply that management expects higher earnings in the future. On the other hand, the markets punish firms that cut or eliminate their dividends, often shaving 25 per cent, or more, from the

FIGURE 13.5

Aggregate payout ratio (dividends and share repurchases as a percentage of total earnings) for the US corporate sector, 1972–2001

Source: Table B-90, Economic Report of the President (2002) and Thomson Financial Securities Data, as reported in Table 2 of J. Fed Weston and Juan A. Siu (2003) 'Changing Motives for Share Repurchases', *Finance* Paper 3 (2003), Anderson Graduate School of Management, UCLA. Reproduced with permission.

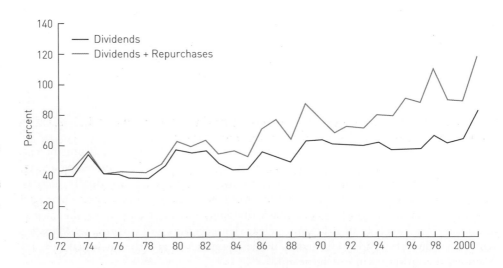

Real World

On 18 February 2003 the NorthWestern Corporation announced that it was suspending its shares dividend to free up $48 million to help pay down its $2.2 billion debt burden. NorthWestern thus became the eleventh publicly traded US electric utility to cut its dividend as a result of the industry-wide credit crunch that followed Enron Corporation's collapse in late 2001. The firm also announced plans to sell off non-core assets to raise cash. Following the news of the dividend cut, NorthWestern's shares fell by 7 per cent.

company's share price following the announcement. Because the market reaction is so spiteful, managers only cut dividends when a firm is in serious financial trouble.

Taxes influence payout policies, but taxes neither cause nor prevent companies from initiating dividend payments or share repurchases It appears obvious that levying income taxes on investors who receive dividend payments would reduce the demand for dividends and thus prompt corporations to retain a larger share of their profits. In the extreme, very high tax rates should cause corporations to stop paying dividends entirely. Plausible though these arguments may be, they are not supported by empirical evidence; in fact, some studies show that dividend payouts actually increase following tax increases. Furthermore, in the US corporations paid dividends long before the adoption of the personal income tax on dividends in 1936, and they continued paying dividends even when marginal tax rates increased to over 90 per cent. In the UK the 'imputed' tax system for dividends, where some of the ultimate recipients' tax burden is credited as being paid via the corporate tax payments of the company, results in regular changes in the effective tax rate on dividend income. However, again we see little in the way of matching changes in payouts. In general, tax changes appear to have had little effect on the dividend payout ratios of companies.

In spite of intensive research, it is unclear exactly how dividend payments affect the required return on a firm's shares Some asset pricing models predict that shares with high dividend yields must offer higher pre-tax returns than shares with lower dividend yields. The intuition behind this prediction is simple. Suppose two shares are identical, except that one pays a higher dividend than the other. Because dividends are taxed at a higher rate than capital gains, the after-tax return will be lower on the high-dividend share. In equilibrium, we could expect investors to require a higher pre-tax return on the high-dividend share to compensate them for the extra tax liability they incur. Although some empirical research supports this prediction, other studies contradict it, and the net effect of dividend taxes on the valuation of corporate equity remains an unsolved puzzle.

SMART PRACTICES VIDEO
Howard Millar, Ryanair
The decision to initiate dividends.

See the entire interview at
www.cengage.co.uk/megginson

Changes in transaction costs or in the technical efficiency of capital markets seem to have very little effect on dividend payments Some theories suggest that the presence of transaction costs causes investors to value dividends. Dividends put cash in investors' hands without requiring them to pay brokerage commissions or other transaction costs. If transaction costs do create an investor preference for dividends, the steep decline in transaction costs in recent years should have been accompanied by a steep decline in dividends. It is true that the percentage of companies paying dividends has recently declined, whereas aggregate dividend payments have not. If we broaden our focus to include all forms of cash payments to shareholders, then corporations today pay out an even higher fraction of total profits than in the past.

Ownership matters One of the most enduring myths about dividends is that private or closely held companies rarely pay any dividends at all. Yet publicly traded companies are likely to pay out substantial fractions of their earnings as dividends each year. In almost every country and every industry, firms with tight ownership structures, composed of a few controlling shareholders, tend to have very low dividend payouts; widely held companies with diffuse ownership tend to have higher payouts.

Introduction to the agency cost/contracting model of dividends

As was true for capital structure, it is hard to conceive of a single theoretical model that can explain all the empirical conclusions previously described. Nonetheless, several theoretical models have been developed, and each has garnered some empirical support. In this chapter we concentrate on one of these, the agency cost/contracting model of dividends (or simply, the agency cost model). We also briefly introduce the agency cost model's principal competitor, the signalling model of dividend payments.

agency cost/contracting model of dividends
A theoretical model that explains empirical regularities in dividend payment and share repurchase patterns, based on agency problems between managers and shareholders.

The agency cost model assumes that dividend payments arise as an attempt to overcome the agency problems that result when there is a separation of corporate ownership and control. In privately held companies with tight ownership coalitions, there is little or no separation between ownership and control. Because agency problems in these firms are minimal, dividends are unnecessary. Even after a company goes public, it rarely commences dividend payments immediately. Ownership tends to remain quite concentrated for a number of years after the IPO. Eventually, however, ownership becomes widely dispersed, as firms raise new equity capital and as original shareholders/owners diversify their holdings. As ownership becomes more dispersed, few investors have the incentive or the ability to monitor and control corporate managers. Agency problems become more important and especially severe in large, slowly growing firms that generate large quantities of free cash flow. The natural tendency of corporate managers is to spend this cash flow (calling it 'investment', of course) rather than to pay it out to shareholders. Investors understand these incentives and will pay a low price for manager-controlled firms that hoard cash. On the other hand, shareholders are willing to pay higher prices for shares in companies with more responsive management teams. Managers who want to maximize firm value will thus begin paying dividends, committing to paying out free cash flow. By doing this, managers overcome the agency costs related to retaining excess cash in the firm. This model thus explains why announcements of dividend initiations or increases are related to share price increases. Other aspects of the model help explain cross-sectional variations in dividend payments, based on industry growth rates, firm size or asset characteristics.

Applying the Model

The agency cost model predicts that dividend-paying firms are older and larger than firms that do not pay dividends. It also predicts that dividend payers have fewer growth opportunities. The data confirm these predictions. If we compare US and UK firms that pay dividends with firms that do not, we find that dividend payers are nearly seven times larger in size and grow more slowly than non-payers. The average age of dividend payers in the USA is more than twice the average age of non-payers.

Recent research shows that firms that increase dividends become less profitable and less risky, whereas the opposite happens to firms that cut dividends. Similarly, dividend-increasing firms cut back on capital spending after raising payouts, whereas dividend-decreasing firms increase capital expenditures. These results are broadly consistent with the agency cost model. When a firm has many profitable investment opportunities on hand, it reinvests more cash and distributes less to investors. When a firm's investment opportunities dim, it pays higher dividends, rather than reinvesting its cash in negative-NPV projects.

The competing **signalling model of dividends** assumes that managers use dividends to convey positive information to poorly informed shareholders. Cash dividend payments are costly, both to the paying firms, as this reduces the amount of money the firm can use for investment, and to shareholders receiving the dividends, as they will have to pay taxes on the dividends received. This means that only the 'best' (most profitable) firms can afford to pay dividends, in the sense that they can bear the cost of these payments. Weaker firms cannot mimic the dividend payments of strong firms, so dividends help investors solve an asymmetric information problem – distinguishing between high-quality and low-quality firms. Like the agency cost model, the signalling model predicts that share prices should rise (fall) in response to dividend increases (cuts). However, the signalling model also predicts that firms with high-growth opportunities will pay higher dividends, contrary to the empirical evidence. Finally, many observers think that the 'tax cost' of signalling with dividends is implausibly high. That is, when firms distribute cash by paying dividends rather than by repurchasing shares, they impose an additional tax burden on investors.

Before describing a model that explains why managers may choose to pay cash dividends – and why investors may demand them – we must ask whether dividends 'matter' in a world of perfect and frictionless capital markets. In other words, would investors demand and managers pay dividends if there were no taxes at the corporate and personal level, if there were no costs of trading or issuing securities and if managers and investors all had the same information? Our old friends from the capital structure chapter, Merton Miller and Franco Modigliani, examined this question in 1961, and they came to a similar conclusion – in a world of perfect markets, dividend policy is irrelevant.[4]

> **signalling model of dividends**
> Assumes that managers use dividends to convey positive information to poorly informed shareholders.

---

4 How do average dividend payout ratios for companies headquartered in English common law countries compare with those of companies headquartered in civil law countries? What explains this difference?

5 If high-dividend shares offer a higher expected (and required) return than low-dividend shares, due to the higher personal taxes levied on the former, why don't corporations simply reduce dividend payments and thus lower their cost of capital?

6 Which industries are characterized by relatively high dividend payout ratios? Are these same industry patterns observed in other industrialized countries? What explains these industry patterns?

7 What is the basis of the argument that transaction costs provide a reason for firms to pay dividends, and how has the steep decline in transaction costs in recent years affected this argument?

---

[4] See Merton Miller and Franco Modigliani (1961) 'Dividend Policy, Growth, and the Valuation of Shares', *Journal of Business* 34:411–433.

13.3 DIVIDEND IRRELEVANCE IN A WORLD WITH PERFECT CAPITAL MARKETS

In a world of frictionless capital markets, payout policy cannot affect the market value of the firm. Value derives solely from the inherent profitability of the firm's assets and the competence of its management team. Even though markets are not perfect, describing how dividend payments or share repurchases affect firm valuation in frictionless markets allows us to more conclusively say under what conditions dividend policy *will* matter in a world with frictions such as taxes, transaction costs, information asymmetries and other market imperfections. In a frictionless world, there is little difference between cash dividends and share repurchases. In the interest of simplicity, we analyse only cash dividend payments in this section.

The notion that dividends are irrelevant appears to be a contradiction. After all, we argued in Chapter 5 that the value of shares was equal to the present value of the dividends that the shares would pay over time. If cash dividends are the only source of value to market participants, how do we arrive at a dividend irrelevance result? As was the case for capital structure, the answer to this question is that the economic value of a firm is always derived solely from the operating profits that the firm is currently generating and will continue to generate in the future, as its investments unfold. As long as the firm accepts all positive-NPV investment projects and has *costless* access to capital markets, it can pay any level of dividends it desires each period. But if a firm pays out its earnings as dividends, it must issue new shares to raise the cash required to finance its ongoing investment projects. So a company can choose to retain all its profits and to finance its investments with internally generated cash flow, or that same company can pay out all its earnings as dividends and raise the cash needed for investment by selling new shares. As usual, this principle is best explained with an example.

Consider two firms, Retention and Payout, which are the same size today (1 January 2007), are in the same industry and have access to the same investment opportunities. Suppose both companies have assets worth €20 million, generating a net cash inflow of €2 million continuously during 2007, and thus providing a return on investment of 10 per cent. Furthermore, assume that the return required by investors, r, is 10 per cent per year for both companies and that each company is presented with the opportunity to invest €2 million in a positive-NPV project during 2007. Each firm currently has 1 million shares outstanding, implying that each firm's share price is €20 ($P_{\text{Jan06}} = €20$). The managers of firm Payout want to distribute all the firm's earnings as dividends, but they also intend to finance the company's €2 million investment opportunity by issuing as many new shares as necessary. The managers of firm Retention would rather not pay dividends, preferring instead to retain the firm's net cash inflow for use in funding the planned €2 million investment programme. Can each management team pursue its preferred strategy and still have identical market values at the end of the period?

Yes. To see how, we first examine Retention's strategy. Retention's managers decide to retain the €2 million (€2 per share) profit, which the firm earns during 2007, to internally finance the €2 million investment project. Therefore, the total dividends paid (and dividends per share) during 2007 are zero. The market value of the firm on 31 December 2007 is equal to the €20 million beginning value, plus the €2 million in reinvested earnings, plus the net present value of the investment opportunity. For simplicity, assume that the project's NPV is positive but small enough to be ignored. The value of Retention at year-end 2007 is therefore equal to €22 million (€20 million + €2 million), which is equal to €22 per share ($P_{\text{Dec07}} = €22$), because the firm did not have to issue any new shares to finance its investment opportunity. Plugging these values into our basic valuation equation (Chapter 5) verifies that

Retention shareholders indeed earn the 10 per cent return on investment that they expected:

$$r = \frac{D_{07} + P_{Dec07} - P_{Jan07}}{P_{Jan07}} = \frac{0 + 22 - 20}{20} = 0.10$$

We can extend this example indefinitely into the future. In each period, firm Retention commits to reinvesting all its annual profits (10 per cent return on assets) in new productive assets. Shareholders earn their return by seeing the value of their shares increase by 10 per cent each year. No new shares are ever issued, so the number of outstanding shares remains fixed at 1 million over time.

So far, so good, but what about firm Payout? This firm's managers decide to pay out, as dividends, the net cash flow of €2 million, as it is received during 2007, so they must raise the €2 million needed to finance the investment project by selling new shares today (1 January 2007). But how many shares must they sell? To answer that, we must reason through what the price of Payout's shares will be on 31 December 2007. After it distributes the dividend during 2007, Payout will have assets worth €20 million, exactly the amount that it started with on 1 January. With 1 million shares outstanding, the share price will still be €20, so Payout must issue 100 000 new shares, at €20 each, to raise the €2 million it needs to undertake its investment opportunity. After the company issues new shares and invests the proceeds, Payout's total market value will equal €22 million (€20 per share × 1.1 million shares outstanding). Therefore, on 31 December 2007, the market value of Payout, €22 million, is identical to the market value of Retention. Once again, we can verify that Payout's original shareholders earned exactly the rate of return that they expected, the same return earned by Retention's investors:

$$r = \frac{D_{07} + P_{Dec07} - P_{Jan07}}{P_{Jan07}} = \frac{2 + 20 - 20}{20} = 0.10$$

As was the case earlier, we can repeat this process indefinitely. Each year Payout distributes all of its net cash flow as a dividend, and the firm issues new shares to finance new investment opportunities.

We have shown that the market capitalization of Retention equals that of Payout on 31 December 2007, even though they follow radically different dividend policies. Retention has 1 000 000 shares outstanding, worth €22 each, while Payout has 1 100 000 shares outstanding, worth €20 each. Because both companies have an aggregate value of €22 million we can conclude that dividend policy is irrelevant in determining the value of a firm, at least when markets are frictionless. But what if investors in Retention prefer that the company pay out earnings rather than reinvest them, or what if shareholders in Payout prefer that the company reinvest earnings rather than issue new shares? We can reinforce the notion that dividend policy is irrelevant, by demonstrating that investors can 'unwind' the dividend policy decisions of firms. In the end, what is true for the firm, as a whole, is true for each investor: dividend policy is irrelevant.

SMART CONCEPTS
See the concept explained step-by-step at www.cengage.co.uk/megginson

Applying the Model

Consider two investors, Burt and Ernie. On 1 January 2007 Burt owns an 11 per cent (110 000 shares) stake in Retention, whereas Ernie holds an 11 per cent stake (also 110 000 shares) in Payout. By the end of 2007 Burt has received no dividend, but he still owns 11 per cent of Retention's outstanding shares, which are now worth €22 each. Ernie, however, receives a dividend payment of €220 000 during 2007, but because Payout issues 100 000 shares to finance its investment opportunity, the shares Ernie owns now represent only a 10 per cent ownership stake in Payout (110 000 ÷ 1 100 000).

If either Burt or Ernie is unhappy with the dividend policy of the firm in which he has invested, either can 'unwind' that policy. For example, suppose Burt would like to receive a dividend. At the end of 2007 Burt could sell 10 000 of his shares for €22 each, generating a cash inflow of €220 000, exactly equal to the dividend that Ernie received on his investment. After selling a portion of his shares, Burt would own just 10 per cent of the outstanding equity of Retention, exactly equal to the ownership stake that Ernie holds in Payout.

Conversely, suppose that Ernie prefers that Payout did not pay dividends. The solution to Ernie's problem is simple. As he receives the €220 000 dividend during 2007, he could simply reinvest the money by purchasing 11 000 new shares in Payout. That would bring his total ownership stake to 121 000, or 11 per cent, of Payout's outstanding shares (121 000 ÷ 1 100 000). In other words, Ernie's position is just like Burt's.

This may seem complex, but the essential points of these examples are really quite simple. Investors are indifferent about whether (1) the firm retains earnings to fund positive-NPV investments, or (2) the firm distributes cash dividends and sells new shares to finance new investments. In either case, shareholders' returns are determined by the cash flows generated by the firm's investments, not by how the firm distributes those cash flows. In the absence of taxes, transaction costs or any other market friction, investors do not care whether they earn returns in the form of dividends (as Payout's shareholders do) or capital gains (as Retention's shareholders do).

CONCEPT REVIEW QUESTIONS

8 What does it mean to say that dividends are 'irrelevant' in a world without taxes or other market frictions?

9 Managers of slow-growing, but profitable, firms (e.g. tobacco companies) *should* pay out these high earnings as dividends. What can they choose to do instead?

10 How do Miller and Modigliani arrive at their conclusion that dividend policy is irrelevant in a world of frictionless capital markets? Why is the assumption of fixed investment policy crucial to this conclusion?

13.4 REAL-WORLD INFLUENCES ON DIVIDEND POLICY

Few of us have ever traded in frictionless capital markets, so our next task is to examine whether dividend policy continues to be irrelevant when we account for 'real-world' factors such as taxes, trading costs and information differences between managers and investors. Our final goal for this section is to determine whether a given firm has an 'optimal' (value-maximizing) dividend policy and, if so, how that policy should be set. As we proceed, you may notice a puzzling fact: almost all the real-world issues we incorporate – such as taxes, transaction costs for issuing new securities and uncertainty about a firm's investment opportunities – argue *against* the payment of cash dividends. Yet, US corporations pay out over half their annual earnings in most years, and non-US firms also regularly pay out substantial fractions of their earnings. We show that accounting for agency costs and conflicts between managers and investors does a better job of explaining dividend policies than do arguments based on taxes or market frictions such as trading costs. In other words, dividends do not exist to overcome changing technical problems with markets and tax regimes; dividends exist to overcome unchanging human problems with trust, communication and commitment.

Personal income taxes

When the personal tax rate on dividends is higher than the tax rate on capital gains, we have a clear-cut result: firms should not pay any cash dividends. Instead, profitable companies should retain all their earnings, and shareholders should earn their investment returns by selling stock after it has increased in value. To see this, note that personal taxes reduce the after-tax value of dividends, relative to capital gains, so firms should not pay dividends as long as dividends are taxed at a higher rate. Any distribution from the firm should be through a share repurchase programme. This offers investors the choice of either receiving cash in a tax-favoured form (as a capital gain) or foregoing the cash altogether by not selling shares, and thus seeing their share values increase as their fractional ownership increases.

What if a large capital gains tax is imposed? Will that re-establish dividend policy irrelevance? (Before reading on, see if you can reason through to an answer.) Apparently, imposing a capital gains tax at a rate equal to the dividend tax rate will again make investors indifferent to whether they receive taxable dividends or taxable capital gains. But this will happen only if the tax on share appreciation is levied every period, regardless of whether the shares are sold or not. Such a levy is called a **wealth tax**. Although never used in the United States, such a tax has been tried in Norway and some other Western European countries. Capital gains taxes are almost always paid only at *realization*, when the shares are actually sold, and a tax payment delayed is a tax payment rendered less painful. Furthermore, in the United States and other countries, share-related capital gains taxes can often be avoided entirely if shares are bequeathed to an investor's heirs. Therefore, investors generally have a tax preference for capital gains over cash dividends, even if the nominal tax rates for both types of income are the same. Debt financing enjoys a tax advantage, relative to equity, in most industrialized countries, but retained earnings almost always enjoy a significant tax preference, relative to dividend payments. In summary, almost all real-world dividend taxation systems discourage the payment of cash dividends. We must look elsewhere for a reason for dividends to exist.

What is the empirical evidence regarding the effect of taxes on dividend payments? Researchers have employed two principal methodologies to study tax effects. The first method is to employ a variant of the capital asset pricing model (CAPM) to see whether investors demand a higher pre-tax return on high-dividend-paying shares than they do on shares paying a low dividend, as is expected if investors paid a higher effective tax rate on cash dividend income than on capital gains income. Studies using this approach show mixed results. Despite the empirical findings, proponents of a tax-effect model have great difficulty explaining why rational corporate managers would ever pay cash dividends when doing so results in a higher pre-tax required return. Apparently, managers could increase share prices and thus lower the firm's cost of capital simply by cutting dividend payouts. The survival of dividend payments in modern economies therefore suggests that the tax-effect model of dividend valuation must be missing something important.

wealth tax
A tax levied on share appreciation every period, regardless of whether the shares are sold or not.

The second method used to study tax effects is to examine the average change in a firm's share price on its ex-dividend day. Prior to this day, an investor who owns the share is entitled to receive the next dividend payment. If an investor buys the share after it goes ex-dividend, the dividend is paid to the former owner. Consider the problem faced by a taxable investor who holds a share and wants to sell it near an ex-dividend date. The investor faces a choice between selling the share before the ex-dividend date, at the higher 'cum-dividend' (with dividend) price, thus earning a return in the form of a capital gain, or waiting until the share goes ex-dividend, selling the share at a lower price, and receiving a return in the form of cash dividends. If share prices fall by the full amount of the dividend payment, the investor would prefer to sell shares before they go ex-dividend. By selling the shares and realizing a capital gain, rather than receiving a dividend, the investor earns a higher after-tax return. The only circumstances under which this investor would be indifferent about whether to take the dividend or the capital gain is if the ex-dividend price drop is less than the dividend payment. In that case, the higher pre-tax return from receiving the dividend offsets the tax disadvantage of dividends. The empirical observation that, on ex-dividend day, share prices fall by significantly less than the amount of the dividend has often been interpreted as evidence of a tax effect in dividend valuation.

Applying the Model

Three months ago, you purchased a share for €20. Today that share sells for €22, a gain of 10 per cent. The share will pay a €2 dividend in a few days, and the ex-dividend date is tomorrow. Suppose you want to sell the share, and you face a 33 per cent tax rate on dividend income and a 20 per cent tax rate on capital gains. If you sell today, you earn an after-tax profit of €1.60 (€2 capital gain minus €0.40 in taxes). That represents an 8 per cent return on your original €20 investment. If you sell tomorrow, your after-tax return depends on how far the price drops when the share goes ex-dividend. If the price drops by the full €2, then you earn no capital gain, and your after-tax profit equals €1.34 (€2 dividend minus €0.66 in taxes), or 6.7 per cent. Clearly, in this scenario, your after-tax return is higher if you sell the share before it goes ex-dividend. However, suppose the share price drops by just €1 when it goes ex-dividend. In that case, if you wait to sell the share, you receive a €1 capital gain (worth €0.80 after taxes) and a €2 dividend (worth €1.34 after taxes), for an after-tax return of €2.14, or 10.7 per cent. In that case, it pays to wait for the dividend. Only when the share price falls by €1.675 on the ex-dividend date would you be indifferent about whether to sell immediately or wait until the dividend is paid.

Although ex-dividend day studies show plausible average results, there is reason to be suspicious about whether these studies are definitive evidence of differential tax effects, particularly because transaction costs must be very high for a pure tax effect to occur. The reason is that tax-free traders have an incentive to buy shares just before they go ex-dividend, if the traders expect the price to decline by less than the dividend. For example, suppose the share described above is about to pay a €2 dividend, and traders expect the price to drop €1.675 on the ex-dividend date because of differential tax rates applied to capital gains and dividends. As the example demonstrated, a taxable investor, presented with these figures, would be indifferent between selling the share immediately or waiting until it goes ex-dividend. But a tax-free investor would be anything but indifferent. Such an investor could purchase the share at €22, receive the €2 dividend, and then resell the share immediately afterwards for €20.33, generating a one-day profit of €0.33. If the transaction costs associated with this strategy are greater than €0.33 per share, then 'dividend arbitrage' is not profitable. The differential tax treatment of capital gains and dividends determines the size of the ex-dividend day price decline. However, currently in US markets the per-share cost of a round-trip trade can be as low as a few pennies. In that case, the actions of tax-free investors should increase the ex-dividend day price decline to almost the full amount of the dividend.

Perhaps we may soon be able to determine, once and for all, if the ex-dividend day price effect is indeed a tax effect. The US government has given us a natural experiment. Since the Jobs and Growth Tax Relief Reconciliation Act of 2003 made the federal tax rate on cash dividends received by an individual equal to the investor's marginal capital gains tax rate, there is now little tax reason to forego dividends. If taxes were driving the effect historically, the average ex-dividend day share price drop should move closer to the nominal cash dividend. If the average ex-dividend day price drop continues to be significantly less than the amount of the dividend, then it will be clear that differential personal tax rates were never the key influence on ex-day price changes.

Why do we not see more companies substituting share repurchase programmes for cash dividend payments? There are three answers to this question. First, as we have seen, many US companies *have* been repurchasing their shares for several years. Increasing numbers of non-US companies are beginning to do so as their national laws allow. Secondly, the firms that initiate share repurchase programmes are the same companies that also make large cash dividend payments. In the language of economics, this means that firms seem to treat repurchases and cash dividends as 'complements' rather than 'substitutes'. Finally, the IRS has the power to rule that a given company's share repurchase programme is merely an attempt to avoid taxes. Under the programme, it can impose the higher personal income tax rates on all income received by investors. In other words, companies that adopt routine share repurchase programmes, in lieu of dividend payments, can theoretically be imposing large supplemental tax liabilities on their shareholders. The actual importance of this rule in deterring repurchases is questionable, however, because the IRS almost never invokes it.

On balance, incorporating personal taxes into our model does not help us understand why firms pay dividends. However, tax effects may account for some of the patterns we observe, such as the rise in share repurchase programmes worldwide.

Trading and other transaction costs

If personal taxes cannot explain observed dividend payments, what about transaction costs of issuing and trading shares? Positive trading costs affect expected dividend payouts in two potentially offsetting ways. First, if investors find it costly to sell just a few shares to generate cash (i.e. to create home-made dividends), then they could pay a premium for shares that habitually pay dividends. Regular cash dividend payments are a costless way to receive a cash return on an investor's share portfolio. This cash could be used either for consumption or for rebalancing the investor's portfolio. A serious flaw in this argument, however, is the suggestion that dividend payments should be highest in undeveloped markets with very high transaction costs. In reality, dividend payments are highest in countries with liquid, low-cost stock markets – such as the UK, Germany and Australia – and are lowest or non-existent in most developing countries. Furthermore, a transaction cost argument cannot easily explain why aggregate dividend payouts in the United States have remained fairly high, even as

US stock markets have become vastly more efficient, and the costs of trading have declined dramatically.

The second effect of transaction costs on dividend payments is completely negative. This relates to a corporation's need to replace cash paid out as dividends with cash obtained through new share sales. Remember that our dividend-irrelevance result depends critically on a company being able to fund its investment, either by retaining corporate profits or by paying out profits as dividends, and to replace this cash by issuing new shares. As long as share issues are costless, investors are indifferent about whether to receive returns in the form of capital gains (on non-dividend-paying shares) or as cash dividends on shares. If issuing securities entails large costs, however, all parties should prefer a full-retention strategy. No corporation should ever both pay dividends and raise funds for investment by issuing new shares. Because many large corporations do just that, it is obvious that transaction costs alone do not explain observed dividend policy.[5]

The residual theory of dividends

The previous discussion suggests another possible explanation of observed dividend payments. Might they simply be a residual – the cash left over after corporations have

funded all their positive-NPV investments? This would help explain why firms in rapidly growing industries retain almost all their profits, whereas firms in mature, slow-growing industries tend to have very high dividend payouts. It would also explain the 'life-cycle' pattern of dividend payments for individual firms, where young, fast-growing companies rarely pay any dividends. But those same companies typically change to a high-payout strategy once they mature and their growth rate slows.

The **residual theory of dividends** probably has some merit, but it suffers from one massive empirical problem. Dividend payments are not as variable as they would be if firms were viewing them as residuals from cash flow. In fact, dividend payments are the most stable of any cash flow, into or out of a firm. All available evidence suggests that corporate managers smooth dividends, and they are very cautious about changing established dividend-payout levels. Clearly, the residual theory is not the sole explanation of observed dividend payments.

residual theory of dividends
States that observed dividend payments will simply be a residual; the cash left over after corporations have funded all their positive-NPV investments.

Paying dividends as a means of communicating information

Sooner or later, many who study the dividend puzzle recognize that firms may pay dividends to convey information to investors. Managers, who have a better understanding of the firm's true financial condition than shareholders do, can convey this information to shareholders through the dividend policy that managers select. Dividend payments have what accountants call 'cash validity', meaning that these payments are believable and are harder for weaker firms to duplicate. Phrased in economic terms, in a world that is characterized by informational asymmetries between managers and investors, cash dividend payments serve as a credible conduit

---

[5] Interestingly, at least one academic researcher suggests that corporations pay dividends precisely because this forces them into the capital market for financing (rather than relying solely on internal financing), where investors have the incentive and the ability to monitor and discipline corporate management. See Frank H. Easterbrook (1984) 'Two Agency-Cost Explanations of Dividends', *American Economic Review* 74:650–659.

of information from corporate insiders (officers and directors) to the company's shareholders. Viewed this way, every aspect of a firm's dividend policy conveys significant new information.

What type of information is being communicated? When a company begins paying dividends (a dividend initiation), the company is conveying management's confidence that the firm is now profitable enough to both fund its investment projects and pay out cash. Investors and managers know that cutting or eliminating dividend payments, once they begin, results in a very negative market reaction. Therefore, dividend initiations send a strong signal to the market about management's assessment of the firm's long-term ability to generate cash.

The same logic applies to dividend increases. Because everyone understands that dividend cuts are to be avoided at almost all costs, management's willingness to increase dividend payments clearly implies confidence that its profits will remain high enough to support the new payment level. Dividend increases suggest a *permanent* increase in a firm's normal level of profitability. In other words, dividends change only when the level of permanent earnings changes. Unfortunately, this logic applies even more strongly to dividend decreases. Dividend cuts are viewed as very bad news. Managers reduce dividend payments only when they have no choice, such as when there is a cash flow crisis or when the financial health of the firm is declining, and no turnaround is in sight. Therefore, it is no surprise that when managers do cut dividends, the market reaction is often severe.

Dividend payments as solutions to agency problems

The free cash flow hypothesis offers yet another solution to the dividend puzzle. This hypothesis is based squarely on the agency problems that result from the separation of ownership and control, as observed in large public companies. When firms are small and growing rapidly, they not only have tight ownership structures but also tend to have many profitable investment opportunities. These growth firms can profitably use all the cash flow that they generate internally. Thus, they have no reason to pay cash dividends. In time, successful growth firms establish secure, often dominant, market positions. They begin to generate operating cash flows that are much larger than the remaining positive-NPV investment opportunities open to them. Michael Jensen defines free cash flow as any cash flow in excess of that needed to fund all positive-NPV projects.[6] Managers of firms with free cash flow *should* begin to pay dividends to ensure that they will not invest the free cash flow in negative-NPV projects. However, managers may prefer to retain cash and spend it, because of the increased status attained from running a larger (though not necessarily more valuable) company.

Jensen asserts that, if managers are given the proper incentives, they will initiate dividend payments as soon as the firm begins generating free cash flow. Managerial contracts that tie compensation to the firm's share price performance are designed to ensure that managers pay out free cash flow rather than invest it unwisely. The larger the free cash flow generated, the larger the dividend payout should be. This is the essential prediction of what is known as the agency cost/contracting model of dividend payments, which was introduced in Section 13.2. The central predictions of this model are three-fold. First, it predicts that dividend initiations and increases should be viewed as good news by investors and thus should lead to share price increases upon

SMART IDEAS VIDEO

Professor Abe de Jong, RSM Erasmus University, Rotterdam
European dividend and repurchase policies.

See the entire interview at **www.cengage.co.uk/ megginson**

---

[6] Michael C. Jensen (1986) 'Agency Costs of Free Cash Flow, Corporate Finance and Takeovers', *American Economic Review* 76:323–329.

announcement. Secondly, the agency cost model predicts that firms (and industries) that generate the largest amounts of free cash flow should also have the highest dividend payout ratios. Finally, this model predicts that managerial compensation contracts will not only be designed to entice managers to pursue a value-maximizing dividend policy but will also be effective. The empirical patterns observed in dividend payment policies worldwide, described in Section 13.2, are all consistent with these predictions.

CONCEPT REVIEW QUESTIONS

11 During the late 1960s, the top marginal personal income tax rate on dividends, received by British investors, reached 98 per cent, yet dividend payouts actually *increased.* How can you justify this empirical fact?

12 In what way can managers use dividends to convey pertinent information about their firms in a world of informational asymmetry? Why would a manager choose to convey information via a dividend policy? Does empirical evidence support or refute the informational role of dividends?

13 Why is it difficult for a firm with weaker cash flows to mimic a dividend increase undertaken by a firm with stronger cash flows?

14 According to the residual theory of dividends, how does a firm set its dividend? With which dividend policy is this theory most compatible? Does it appear to be empirically validated?

13.5 A CHECKLIST FOR DIVIDEND PAYMENTS

As we have seen, the agency cost model explains cash dividend payments as value-maximizing attempts by managers of certain companies to minimize the agency costs that result from the separation of ownership and control. The severity of these agency problems is, in turn, a function of (a) a firm's investment opportunity set and (b) its ownership structure. The investment opportunity set encompasses the industry in which the firm operates, the company's size, the capital intensity of the firm's production process, the free cash flow generated and the availability of positive-NPV investment opportunities to the firm. Ownership structure refers to the number of shareholders, the size of each investor's holdings, and the presence or absence of an active investor, willing and able to directly monitor corporate management. Other factors that influence dividend payments include transaction costs, taxes, and two characteristics of a firm's home country – its legal system and the importance of capital markets relative to financial intermediaries.

SMART IDEAS VIDEO

John Graham, Duke University
'Why do companies hesitate to initiate a dividend or to increase a dividend?'

See the entire interview at **www.cengage.co.uk/megginson**

Developing a checklist for dividend policy

In this section we summarize what managers need to know about dividends. The following tables provide the predictions of the agency cost model about the relationship between corporate-level variables and expected dividend payout. In Table 13.4, the second column shows the effect on dividend payout of an increase in each firm-level variable in the first column.

FIRM-LEVEL VARIABLE	EFFECT OF INCREASE ON DIVIDEND PAYOUT
Asset growth rate	Reduce
Positive-NPV investment opportunities	Reduce
Capital intensity of the production process	Increase
Free cash flow generated	Increase
Number of individual shareholders	Increase
Relative 'tightness' of ownership coalition	Reduce
Size of largest block holder	Reduce

TABLE 13.4
Firm-level variables that affect dividend policy

In addition to firm-level variables, macroeconomic and national financial variables also influence equilibrium dividend payments. The predictions of the agency cost/contracting model concerning these variables are detailed in Table 13.5. Again, the second column shows the effect on dividend payout of an increase in each macroeconomic variable in the first column.

MACROECONOMIC VARIABLE	EFFECT OF INCREASE ON DIVIDEND PAYOUT
Transaction costs of security issuance	Increase
Personal tax rates on dividend income	Reduce
Personal tax rates on capital gains income	Increase
Importance of institutional investors	Reduce
Corporate governance power of institutional investors	Reduce
Capital market, relative to intermediated (bank) financing	Increase

TABLE 13.5
Macroeconomic variables that affect dividend policy

13.6 SUMMARY AND CONCLUSIONS

- One of the most enduring features of corporate finance worldwide is that large publicly traded corporations almost invariably choose to pay regular cash dividends to their shareholders. Furthermore, these payments are generally a constant, absolute amount per period (e.g. €0.25 per share), rather than a constant fraction (say 20 per cent) of the firm's profits. In the United States, dividends are usually paid on a quarterly basis, but are paid annually or semi-annually in most other countries.

- There are striking similarities in the patterns of dividend payments, as observed across countries and industries. Among developed countries, dividend payout ratios (dividends as a fraction of corporate profits) tend to be highest in British Commonwealth countries, whereas payouts are much smaller in France and Italy. Payouts by US and other continental European companies tend to fall between these two extremes. However, the same industries (utilities, transportation firms) have high dividend payouts in all countries, and certain other industries (high-technology, health sciences) have low dividend payouts in all countries.

- Increasingly corporations frequently choose to repurchase shares on the open market rather than to pay (or in addition to paying) ordinary cash dividends, partly because repurchases are subject to lower effective tax rates for most individual investors. In recent years, repurchases by US corporations have exceeded $100 billion per year, and ordinary (cash) dividend payments have been around $250 billion annually.

- Capitalization issues (called stock splits in the USA) and stock dividends are used by companies that want to reduce the per-share price of their shares in the open market. In a 2-for-1 capitalization issue, for example, one new share is distributed for every existing share an investor holds, and the price of the share falls by roughly half.

- In a world without market imperfections, dividend policy is irrelevant, in the sense that it cannot affect the value of a firm. However, the fact that many firms pay dividends is something of a puzzle because most real market imperfections (such as taxes) argue against paying cash dividends.

- One theory of dividend policy assumes that dividend payments serve to reduce agency costs between corporate managers and external investors by committing the firm to pay out excess profits. Managers are prevented from consuming the profits as perquisites or wasting them on unwise capital investments (such as unrelated corporate acquisitions). Most of the empirical evidence supports this agency cost model of dividends over the competing signalling model, which predicts that managers use dividend payments to convey information to investors about the firm's expected future earnings.

- In addition to ownership considerations, several other aspects of a firm's operating and regulatory environment seem to influence dividend payouts. Other things being equal, closely held corporations, which operate in a high-growth industry where large ongoing capital investments are needed to compete, have lower dividend payouts than do widely held firms in slow-growing or highly regulated industries.

INTERNET RESOURCES

For updates to links in this section and elsewhere in the book, please go to the book's website at www.cengage.co.uk/megginson.

http://www.tenpercentdividends.com
Describes how to identify and to invest in companies with high dividend yields.

http://www.ex-dividend.com
Lists recent stock splits and dividend changes; includes record dates, ex-dividend dates and payment dates.

http://www.dripcentral.com
Describes what a dividend reinvestment plan (DRIP) is and how it works; lists the companies that offer these plans, which allow shareholders to automatically use the cash they receive in dividends to purchase additional shares.

http://www.directinvesting.com/; http://www.dripinvestor.com/
General information on dividend reinvestment plans (DRIPs).

http://www.revenue.ie/index.htm?/revguide/foreign_dividends.htm;
http://www.direct.gov.uk/en/MoneyTaxAndBenefits/Taxes/TaxOnSavingsAndInvestments/DG_4016453
A guide from two different countries on how dividends are taxed and treated by the revenue authorities.

http://www.itpaysdividends.co.uk/
A site that mails subscribers details of the dividend payments and policies of companies listed on the London Stock Exchange.

http://www.investorschronicle.co.uk/
Has a company dividend announcement service.

http://www.cfoeurope.com/displayStory.cfm/2477928
The tensions between various stakeholders regarding dividends versus retention.

KEY TERMS

agency cost/contracting model of dividends
announcement date
capitalization issue
constant nominal payment policy
constant payout ratio dividend policy

date of record
dividend payout ratio
ex-dividend
extra dividend/special dividend
low-regular-and-extra policy
residual theory of dividends
reverse stock split

share repurchase programme
signalling model of dividends
stock dividend
target dividend payout ratio
wealth tax

SELF-TEST PROBLEMS

ST13-1 What do record date, ex-dividend date and payment date mean, related to dividends? Why would you expect the price of a share to drop by the amount of the dividend on the ex-dividend date? What rationale has been offered for why this does not actually occur?

ST13-2 What has happened to the total volume of share repurchases announced by US public companies since 1982? Why did that year mark such an important milestone in the history of share repurchase programmes in the United States?

ST13-3 What has happened to the average cash dividend payout ratio of corporations worldwide over time? What explains this trend? How would your answer change if share repurchases were included in calculating dividend payout ratios?

ST13-4 What does it mean to say that corporate managers 'smooth' cash dividend payments? Why do managers do this?

ST13-5 What are the key assumptions and predictions of the signalling model of dividends? Are these predictions supported by empirical research findings?

ST13-6 What is the expected relationship between dividend payout levels and the growth rate and availability of positive-NPV projects, under the agency cost model of dividends? What about the expected relationship between dividend payout and the diffuseness of firm shareholders? Free cash flow? Consider a firm, such as Microsoft, awash in free cash flow, available positive-NPV projects, and a relatively diffuse shareholder base in an industry with increasing competition. Does either the agency model or the signalling model adequately predict the dividend policy of Microsoft? Which does the better job?

QUESTIONS

Q13-1 Compare and contrast the constant payout ratio dividend policy and the constant nominal dividend payment policy. Which policy do most public companies actually follow? Why?

Q13-2 What is a low-regular-and-extra dividend policy? Why do firms pursuing this policy explicitly label some cash dividend payments as 'extra'?

Q13-3 What is a stock dividend? How does this differ from a capitalization issue (or stock split)?

Q13-4 What factors have contributed to the growth in share repurchase programmes by US public companies over the past 15 years?

Q13-5 How do the industrial patterns observed for dividend payouts compare with the patterns observed for capital structures? For example, are industries characterized by high dividend payouts also characterized by high leverage?

Q13-6 What is a firm's dividend yield? How does this compare with that firm's dividend payout ratio?

Q13-7 What is the average stock market reaction to: (a) a dividend initiation; (b) a dividend increase; (c) a dividend termination; and (d) a dividend decrease (cut)? Are these reactions logically consistent?

Q13-8 What are the key assumptions and predictions of the agency cost/contracting model of dividend payments? Are these predictions supported by empirical research findings?

Q13-9 Around the world, utilities generally have the highest dividend payouts of any industry, yet they also tend to have massive investment programmes to finance through external funding. How do you reconcile high payouts and large-scale security issuance?

Q13-10 Why do firms with diverse shareholder bases typically pay higher dividends than private firms or public firms with concentrated ownership structures? How are fixed dividends used as a bonding (commitment) mechanism by managers of firms with dispersed ownership structures and large amounts of free cash flow?

PROBLEMS

Dividend fundamentals

P13-1 Beta Limited has the following shareholders' equity accounts:

Ordinary shares at par	€ 5 000 000
Paid-in capital in excess of par	€ 2 000 000
Retained earnings	€25 000 000
Total shareholders' equity	€32 000 000

a What is the maximum amount that Beta Limited can pay in cash dividends without impairing its legal capital, if its capital is defined as the par value of shares?

b What is the maximum amount that Beta Limited can pay in cash dividends without impairing its legal capital, if its capital is defined as the par value of shares plus paid-in capital in excess of par?

P13-2 What are alternative ways in which investors can receive a cash return from their investment in the equity of a company? From a tax standpoint, which of these would be preferred, assuming that investors pay a 35 per cent tax rate on dividends and a 15 per cent tax rate on capital gains? What if investors faced the same 15 per cent tax on income and capital gains? What are the pros and cons of paying out cash dividends?

P13-3 Delta Limited earned €2.50 per share during fiscal year 2005 and paid cash dividends of €1.00 per share. During the fiscal year ended on 31 December 2006 Delta earned €3.00 per share, and the firm's managers expect to earn this amount per share during fiscal years 2007 and 2008, as well.

a What was Delta's payout ratio for fiscal year 2005?

b If Delta's managers want to follow a constant nominal dividend policy, what dividend per share will they declare for fiscal year 2006?

c If Delta's managers want to follow a constant payout ratio dividend policy, what dividend per share will they declare for fiscal year 2007?

d If Delta's managers want to follow a partial-adjustment strategy, with a target payout ratio equal to FY 2005's, how could they change dividend payments during 2006, 2007 and 2008?

P13-4 General Manufacturing Company (GMC) follows a policy of paying out 50 per cent of its net income as cash dividends to its shareholders each year. The company plans to do so again this year, during which GMC earned €100 million in net profits after tax. The company has 40 million shares outstanding and pays dividends annually.

a What is the company's nominal dividend payment per share each year?

b Assuming that GMC's share price is €54 per share immediately before its ex-dividend date, what is the expected price of GMC shares on the ex-dividend date if there are no personal taxes on dividend income received?

P13-5 General Manufacturing Company (GMC) follows a policy of paying out 50 per cent of its net income as cash dividends to its shareholders each year. The company plans to do so again this year, during which GMC earned €100 million in net profits after tax. The company has 40 million shares outstanding and pays dividends annually. Assume that an investor purchased GMC shares a year ago at €45. The investor, who faces a personal tax rate of 15 per cent on both dividend income and on capital gains, plans to sell the shares very soon. Transaction costs are negligible.

a Calculate the after-tax return this investor will earn if she sells GMC shares at the current €54 share price prior to the ex-dividend date.

b Calculate the after-tax return the investor will earn if she sells GMC shares on the ex-dividend date, assuming that the price of GMC shares falls by the dividend amount on the ex-dividend date.

c Calculate the after-tax return the investor will earn if she sells GMC shares on the ex-dividend date, assuming that the price of GMC shares falls by one half the dividend amount on the ex-dividend date.

P13-6 General Manufacturing Company (GMC) pays out 50 per cent of its net income as cash dividends to its shareholders once each quarter. The company plans to do so again this year, during which GMC earned €100 million in net profits after tax. If the company has 40 million shares outstanding and pays dividends quarterly, what is the company's nominal dividend payment per share each quarter?

P13-7 Twilight Company's shares sell for €60.25 each, and the firm's managers have just announced a €1.50 per share dividend payment.

a What should happen to Twilight Company's share price on the ex-dividend date, assuming that investors do not have to pay taxes on dividends or capital gains and do not incur any transaction costs in trading shares?

b What should happen to Twilight Company's share price on the ex-dividend date, assuming that it follows the historical performance of US share prices on ex-dividend days?

c If the historical 'ex-dividend-day-price effect', observed in US stock markets, was indeed a tax effect, what should happen to Twilight Company's share price on the ex-dividend date, given the tax changes embodied in the Jobs and Growth Tax Relief Reconciliation Act of 2003?

P13-8 Global Financial Company (GFC) has 10 million shares outstanding, each currently worth €80 per share. The firm's managers are considering a 2-for-1 capitalization issue (stock split), but they are concerned with the effect this announcement will have on the firm's stock price.

a If GFC's managers announce a 2-for-1 issue, what exactly will the company do, and what will GFC's share price likely be after the split?

b How many GFC shares will be outstanding after the split?

c If GFC's managers believe the 'ideal' share price for the firm's shares is €20 per share, what should they do? How many shares would be outstanding after this action?

d Why do you think GFC's managers are considering a stock split?

P13-9 Maggie Fiduciary is a shareholder in the Superior Service Company (SSC). The current price of SSC's shares is €33 each, and there are 1 million shares outstanding. Maggie owns

10 000 shares, or 1 per cent of the total, which she purchased one year ago for €30 per share. Assume that SSC makes a surprise announcement that it plans to repurchase 100 000 of its own shares at a price of €35 per share. In response to this announcement, SSC's share price increases €1 per share, from €33 to €34, but this price is expected to fall back to €33.50 per share after the repurchase is completed. Assume that Maggie faces marginal personal tax rates of 15 per cent on both dividend income and capital gains.

a Calculate Maggie's (realized) after-tax return from her investment in SSC shares, assuming that she chooses to participate in the repurchase programme and that all of the shares she tenders are purchased at €35 per share.

b How many shares will Maggie be able to sell if all SSC's shareholders tender their shares to the firm as part of this repurchase programme, and the company purchases shares on a pro-rata basis?

c What fraction of SSC's total equity will Maggie own after the repurchase programme is completed if she chooses not to tender her shares?

Patterns observed in payout policies worldwide

P13-10 Go to the home page of Oracle Corporation (www.oracle.com) and link to its financial reports page. Download the most recent annual report and observe the capital investment and dividend policies of Oracle. Now, do the same for ChevronTexaco. Which of the two firms appears to have more high-growth, positive-NPV investment opportunities? Which pays the higher relative dividend? Do these results support the agency cost/contracting model? The signalling model?

P13-11 Go to the home page of ExxonMobil Corporation (http://www.exxonmobil.com) ands link to its financial reports page. Now, do the same for Royal Dutch Petroleum Company (http://www.shell.com), BP plc (http://www.bp.com) and Total Group (http://www.total.com/ho/en). Compare the dividend and the capital investment policies of these four major international oil companies. How do the dividend payment policies of the

three European-based companies differ from the US-based company, regarding payout percentages, absolute amount and payment frequency? Why do you think that BP's accounts are denominated in US dollars, even though the group is headquartered in London?

P13-12 Go to the home page for Dogs of the Dow (http://www.dogsofthedow.com), look at the year-to-date figures, and observe the dividend yields of the 30 shares of the Dow Jones Industrial Average. Which industries contain the higher-dividend-yielding shares, and which contain the lower-yielding shares? Are there differences in the growth prospects between the high- and low-yielding shares? Is this what you expected? Explain.

P13-13 A publicly traded firm announces an increase in its dividend, with no other material information accompanying the announcement. What information is this announcement likely to convey, and what is the expected share price effect as the market assimilates this information?

P13-14 Stately Building Company's shares are selling for €75 each, and its dividend yield is 2.0 per cent. What is the amount of Stately's dividend per share?

P13-15 The stock of Up-and-Away Ltd is selling for €80 per share, and it is currently paying a quarterly dividend of €0.25 per share. What is the dividend yield on Up-and-Away shares?

P13-16 Well-Bred Service Company earned €50 000 000 during 2005 and paid €20 000 000 in dividends to the holders of its 40 million shares. If the current market price of Well-Bred's shares is €31.25, calculate the following: (a) the company's dividend payout ratio; (b) the nominal dividend per share, assuming Well-Bred pays dividends annually; (c) the nominal dividend per share, assuming Well-Bred pays dividends in equal quarterly payments; and (d) the current dividend yield on Well-Bred shares.

Dividend irrelevance in a world with perfect capital markets

P13-17 It is 1 January 2006. Boomer Equipment Company (BEC) currently has assets of €250 million and expects to earn a 10 per cent return on assets during the year. There are 20 million BEC shares outstanding. The firm has an opportunity to invest in a (minimally) positive-NPV project that will cost €25 million over the course of 2006. BEC needs to determine whether it should finance this investment by retaining profits over the course of the year or pay the profits earned as dividends and issue new shares to finance the investments. Show that the decision is irrelevant in a world of frictionless markets.

P13-18 Swelter Manufacturing Company (SMC) currently has assets of €200 million and a required return of 10 per cent on its 10 million shares outstanding. The firm has an opportunity to invest in (minimally) positive-NPV projects that will cost €20 million. SMC needs to determine whether it should withhold this amount from dividends payable to finance the investments or pay out the dividends and issue new shares to finance the investments. Show that the decision is irrelevant in a world of frictionless markets. What happens to the dividend-irrelevance result if a personal income tax of 15 per cent is introduced into the model?

P13-19 On 1 January 2006, you examine two unlevered firms that operate in the same industry, have identical assets worth €80 million that yield a net profit of 12.5 per cent per year, and have 10 million shares outstanding. During 2006, and all subsequent years, each firm has the opportunity to invest an amount equal to its net income in (slightly) positive-NPV investment projects. The Beta Company wants to finance its capital spending through retained earnings. The Gamma Company wants to pay out 100 percent of its annual earnings as cash dividends and to finance its investments with a new share offering each year. There are no taxes or transaction costs to issuing securities.

a Calculate the overall and per-share market value of the Beta Company at the end of 2006 and each of the two following years (2007 and 2008). What return on investment will this firm's shareholders earn?

b Describe the specific steps that the Gamma Company must take today (1 January 2006), and at the end of each of the next three years (year-end 2006, 2007 and 2008), if it pays out all of its net income as dividends and still grows its assets at the same rate as that of the Beta Company.

c Calculate the number and per-share price of shares that the Gamma Company must sell today, and at the end of 2006, 2007 and 2008, if it pays out all of its net income as dividends and still grows its assets at the same rate as that of the Beta Company.

d Assuming that you currently own 100 000 shares (1 per cent) of Gamma Company, compute the fraction of the company's total outstanding equity that you will own three years from now if you do not participate in any of the share offerings the firm will make during this holding period.

P13-20 Investors anticipate that Sweetwater Manufacturing's next dividend, due in one year, will be €4 per share. Investors also expect earnings to grow at 5 per cent in perpetuity, and they require a return of 10 per cent on their shares. Use the Gordon growth model (see Equation 5.4) to calculate Sweetwater's share price today.

P13-21 Super-Thrift Pharmaceuticals Company traditionally pays an annual dividend equal to 50 per cent of its earnings. Earnings this year are €30 000 000. The company has 15 million shares outstanding. Investors expect earnings to grow at a 5 per cent annual rate in perpetuity, and they require a return of 12 per cent on their shares.

a What is Super-Thrift's current dividend per share? What is it expected to be next year?

b Use the Gordon growth model (see Equation 5.4) to calculate Super-Thrift's share price today.

P13-22 Casual Construction Company (CCC) earned €60 000 000 during 2006. The firm expects to earn €63 000 000 during 2007, in line with its long-term earnings growth rate. There are 20 million CCC shares outstanding, and the firm has a policy of paying out 40 per cent of its earnings as cash dividends. Investors require a 10 per cent return on CCC shares.

a What is CCC's current dividend per share? What is it expected to be next year?

b Use the Gordon growth model (see Equation 5.4) to calculate CCC's share price today.

Real world influences on dividend policy

P13-23 Universal Windmill Company (UWC) currently has assets worth €50 million and a required return of 10 per cent on its 2 million shares outstanding. The firm has an opportunity to invest in (minimally) positive-NPV projects that will cost €5 million. UWC needs to determine whether it should withhold this amount from dividends payable to finance the investments or pay out the dividends and issue new shares to finance the investments. Show that the decision is irrelevant in a world of frictionless markets. What happens if a personal income tax of 15 per cent on dividends (but not capital gains) is introduced into the model?

P13-24 Sam Sharp purchased 100 shares of Electric Lighting International (ELI) one year ago for €60 per share. He also received cash dividends totalling €5 per share over the past 12 months. Now that ELI's share price has increased to €64.50 per share, Sam has decided to sell his holding. What is Sam's gross (pre-tax) and net (after-tax) return on this investment, assuming that he faces a 15 per cent tax rate on dividends and capital gains?

THOMSON ONE Business School Edition

For instructions on using Thomson ONE, refer to the introductory text provided with the Thomson ONE problems at the end of Chapters 1–6, or in *A Guide for Using Thomson ONE – Business School Edition*.

P13-25 Compare the dividend policies of Novartis AG (ticker: S:NOVN), AstraZeneca PLC (AZN), Aventis SA (F:RPP) and Merck and Company Inc. (U:MRK) over the past five years. Determine the annual dividend payout ratios and the dividend yield for the four firms in each year. What do the dividend payout ratios tell you about investment opportunities available to each company? Do the payout ratios change significantly over time? Which of these firms, if any, follows a constant payout ratio policy or a constant nominal payment policy? Did any of these firms pay out an extra or special dividend over the past five years? Was it paid in a year with higher than normal earnings?

P13-26 Do any of the four companies in Problem 25 change dividends over the last five years? Do dividends change (in the same direction) every time earnings change? What does this say about a manager's expectations of changes in company earnings?

MINICASE *Dividend policy*

After working for the past four years as a financial analyst for Nevada Power Corporation, you receive a well-deserved promotion. You have been appointed to work on special projects for Mr Watkins, the chief financial officer (CFO). Your first assignment is to gather information on dividend theory and policy, because the CFO wants to reassess the firm's current dividend policy.

Assignment

1 What are the different types of dividend policies? Provide examples of situations in which each of these dividend policies could be used.

2 Describe the difference between cash dividends, stock dividends, capitalization issues (stock splits) and share repurchases. Provide examples when each of these forms of dividends can be used.

3 Discuss the theory of dividend irrelevance. How do taxes affect the dividend-irrelevance theory?

4 How do managers use dividend policy to convey information to the market-place? Why is dividend policy, instead of a press release, used to communicate information?

PART 5

Additional Topics in Corporate Finance

PART 5

Overview

Throughout the last 13 chapters we have concerned ourselves with a number of interlinked questions: how to value basic securities; how to ensure that we choose appropriate investments; and how to ensure that we manage the mixture of financing. We now move to three topics that, to a certain degree, sit outside those concerns. In Chapter 14 we examine the particular issues and concerns of raising capital for early-stage investments. This venture capital issue is one that has gained increased prominence in Europe over recent years, as the European venture capital industry has matured and grown in importance. However, even the smallest company is exposed to fluctuations in the economy, many of these originating outside the home country. Thus Chapters 15 and 16 look at the sources of and solutions to international financial exposure. In Chapter 15 we see how companies are exposed to fluctuations in exchange rates in particular. We note how interest rates, exchange rates and inflation are all interlinked, and revisit the issue of capital budgeting from Part 3 in the light of these relationships. Chapter 16 introduces us to the main techniques that companies, large and small, can use to deal with these fluctuations. We focus on the pricing and usage of options, swaps and futures contracts, and show how these can be used to minimize the exposure of companies to fluctuations in exchange and interest rates. Chapter 17 concludes our journey, examining the nature and effects of mergers and acquisitions. In essence this is a special case of capital budgeting, but the size and economic effect of these transactions warrant a chapter of their own.

SMART FINANCE
Use the learning tools at www.cengage.co.uk/megginson

Chapter 14

Entrepreneurial Finance and Venture Capital

Sources: The information is drawn from the publications of the two associations noted above, available on www.nvca.org and www.bvca.com.

OPENING FOCUS

Flying, webcrawling and dancing through the venture capital maze

The old adage is true – from little acorns mighty oaks do grow. Although we often think of venture capital companies as small and fast-growing, many large companies that are familiar corporate brands were beneficiaries of venture capital. A great source concerning these companies is the National Venture Capital Association Hall of Fame (for the USA) and the *Entrepreneurs' Case Studies* of the British Venture Capital Association.

Take for example FedEx, the distribution company. FedEx was founded by Fred Smith who had a vision to create an overnight delivery service. Fred was lucky enough to have significant funds to invest, some $4 million, but he also sourced $8 million from early-stage investors. He incorporated the business in 1971 and, by1975, FedEx had its first profitable month. Its growth was boosted by deregulation of the US airline industry, and throughout the 1980s and 1990s, FedEx continued to grow with expansion into Europe, Latin America and Asia. FedEx became the first company in US history to reach $1 billion in revenues without benefit of an acquisition or merger. Today, FedEx has grown into a $25 billion network of companies offering transportation, information, document management and supply chain solutions.

Another company that benefited was Cisco Systems, which was founded by engineers from Stanford University in 1984, and benefited from both university start-up and venture capital investment. Going public in 1990 positioned Cisco financially to benefit from the growth of the internet. Today Cisco is a $22 billion business.

Luminar is the UK's largest operator of dance clubs and late-night venues, with brand names such as Jumpin Jaks. It was founded by Stephen Thomas in 1987 with a £200 000 loan and £20 000 of private equity, and benefited from further venture capital support when it expanded beyond its King's Lynn base in 1990, receiving £1.4 million from HgCapital (then Mercury). It floated in a £30 million IPO in 1996 and is now capitalized at over £400 million.

LEARNING OBJECTIVES

After studying this chapter you should be able to:

- Describe how the financing of entrepreneurial growth companies differs from the financing techniques used by more mature, publicly traded corporations.

- Explain why venture capitalists almost always use convertible preference shares as their investment vehicle.

- Discuss how Western European venture capital processes, practices, funding sources and target industries differ from those in the United States, and describe the profitability of venture capital investments in these two major economies.

- Describe why a vibrant market for initial public offerings is a vital prerequisite for a healthy venture capital industry.

entrepreneurial finance
Study of the special challenges and problems involved with investment in and financing of entrepreneurial growth companies.

entrepreneurial growth companies (EGCs)
Rapidly growing private companies that are usually technology-based and that offer both high returns and high risk to equity investors. These are the companies typically funded by venture capitalists.

private equity
Funds raised for companies from individuals, institutions and other intermediaries where the fundraising is not carried out via organized exchanges.

The past three decades have been kind to finance generally, but perhaps no area of the profession has prospered quite as much as the field of **entrepreneurial finance**. From the proliferation of venture capital investors, to the boom and bust in internet-related IPOs, the financial performance of **entrepreneurial growth companies (EGCs)** has offered spectacular theatre over the past 30 years. In this chapter we outline the particular challenges faced by financial managers of EGCs and the ways that venture capitalists (VCs) help meet these challenges. The topic is an important one, even for students who are not aspiring venture capitalists. Formerly the near-exclusive domain of small, highly specialized venture capital limited partnerships, the financing of EGCs now affects professionals working for mutual funds, pension funds and even large companies concerns. Increasingly, large corporations have internal venture capital units that finance, nurture and grow new business opportunities. This is particularly the case in the USA, where companies such as Intel, Microsoft, Cisco Systems, Pfizer and General Electric spend billions each year investing in EGCs. In the UK, whose venture capital market accounts for over half that of the entire EU, large companies, most notably 3i, also engage in venture capital financing. In Europe the UK, then France and Germany are the largest players in venture capital.

Deciding which EGCs to invest in, as well as how to structure and monitor those investments, presents a difficult problem. By studying how VCs approach these issues, we can learn lessons that extend well beyond the venture capital industry. A generic term often used interchangeably with venture capital is **private equity**, to distinguish it from equity raised on the stock or other security exchanges.

14.1 THE CHALLENGES OF FINANCING ENTREPRENEURIAL GROWTH COMPANIES

How does entrepreneurial finance differ from 'ordinary' finance? Entrepreneurial growth companies differ from large, publicly traded firms in at least four important ways. First, EGCs often achieve compound annual growth rates of 50 per cent, or more, in sales and assets. Though it is somewhat counter-intuitive, companies growing that rapidly usually consume more cash than they generate. Growth requires ongoing investments in fixed assets and working capital. Recall from the analyses performed in Chapter 2 that such investments are net users of cash. In fact, there is an old saying that the leading causes of death for young firms are (1) not enough customers and (2) too many customers. Too many customers, or very rapid growth, can lead to bankruptcy if firms do not have adequate financing in place. This is the phenomenon of overtrading. Privately owned EGCs often plan to convert to public ownership, either through an initial public offering (IPO) or by selling out to a larger firm. Once they become publicly traded, EGCs tend to rely on external equity funding much more than do older, larger firms. In other words, EGCs grow rapidly and require a great deal of cash, much of which must be obtained externally.

Secondly, the most valuable assets of many of these firms are often patents, entrepreneurial know-how and other (intangible) intellectual property rights. We know these are inherently difficult to finance externally. This poses a huge challenge to those professionals who must obtain adequate funding on attractive terms. Companies such as Amazon.com reflect this very well, with fixed assets representing a small percentage of the overall company value.

Thirdly, many entrepreneurial growth companies seek to commercialize highly promising, but untested technologies. This inevitably means that both the risk of failure and the potential pay-off from success are dizzyingly high. It is only by investing in a wide variety and large number of EGCs that venture capital funders can 'play the numbers' and gain a significant return on the overall investment.

Fourthly, EGCs must attract, motivate, remunerate and retain highly skilled technical and entrepreneurial talent – but must do so in a way that minimizes cash outflow, since EGCs are often severely cash constrained. Not surprisingly, these companies rely very heavily on share option grants for remuneration.

These distinctive features of entrepreneurial finance imply that EGCs rely heavily on equity financing and that financial contracting between these companies and their financiers will always be plagued with information problems. As we saw in Chapter 12, growth opportunities cannot easily be financed with borrowed money. Instead, they must be funded with equity capital. Whereas almost all technology- and knowledge-based companies struggle to finance growth opportunities with equity, mature firms can obtain the bulk of the equity funding they need each year by reinvesting profits. EGCs, by definition, grow very rapidly. They must rely on *external* equity financing to fund investments, which vastly exceed the amount of internal funding the companies can generate. Finally, because most EGCs are privately held, they lack access to public stock markets and rely instead on private equity financing. Private equity generally means either capital investments by current owners or funding by professional venture capitalists.

We should point out that the vast majority of firms, even those that subsequently emerge as EGCs, begin life on a modest scale, often with little or no external equity financing besides that provided by the founder's friends and family. This is what Professor Amar Bhide calls 'bootstrap finance'.[1] Only after entrepreneurs exhaust these sources of personal equity can they expect to obtain debt financing from banks or other financial institutions. Table 14.1 describes the results of an empirical study that examines the sources of start-up capital for a sample of 132 companies founded during 1987. The table shows that personal equity financing and loans from financial institutions constitute the two most important sources of start-up capital, accounting for almost 80 per cent of funds raised. This study does not explicitly examine whether the institutions are personally guaranteed by the entrepreneurs (rather than being limited liability loans directly to the company). However, this is almost always the only way that entrepreneurs can borrow money for newly formed businesses.

1 What are the most important ways that entrepreneurial finance differs from 'ordinary' finance? What special burdens confront financial managers of EGCs?

2 Why do firms usually finance intangible assets with equity rather than with debt?

CONCEPT
REVIEW
QUESTIONS

1 See Amar Bhide (1992) 'Bootstrap Finance: The Art of Start-ups', *Harvard Business Review* (November/ December), pp. 109–117. A reader interested in a recent survey article on entrepreneurial finance should also see David J. Denis (2004) 'Entrepreneurial Finance: An Overview of the Issues and Evidence', *Journal of Corporate Finance* 10:301–326. Finally, a potential entrepreneur seeking guidance to determine how much money he or she needs to raise before starting a new venture should refer to the classic article by James McNeill Stancill (1986) 'How Much Money Does Your New Venture Need?' *Harvard Business Review* (May/June), pp. 122–139.

TABLE 14.1

Sources of start-up capital for a sample of 132 small companies

Source: Richard B. Carter and Howard E. Van Auken (1990) 'Personal Equity Investment and Small Business Financial Difficulties', *Entrepreneurship: Theory and Practice* 15: 51–60. Reproduced with permission.

CAPITAL SOURCES[a]	MEAN PERCENT	STANDARD DEVIATION
Equity		
Personal equity	35.6	40.8
Partnerships	5.2	17.9
Issuance of shares	3.2	14.5
Miscellaneous	2.7	13.6
	46.7	
Debt		
Institutional loans	43.8	40.5
Loans from individuals	5.3	19.1
Issuance of bonds	1.1	8.6
Miscellaneous	2.7	12.8
	52.9	

[a] Capital sources are stated as percentages of the total start-up capital. Means do not add to 100%, due to rounding.

14.2 VENTURE CAPITAL FINANCING IN THE UNITED STATES

Defined broadly, venture capital has been a fixture of Western civilization for many centuries. In this context, the decision by Spain's Ferdinand and Isabella to finance the voyage of Christopher Columbus can be considered one of history's most profitable venture capital investments (at least for the Spanish). However, modern **venture capital** – defined as a professionally managed pool of money that is raised for the sole purpose of making actively managed direct equity investments in rapidly growing private companies – is a recent financial innovation. Until recently, only the United States had an active venture capital market. This is changing rapidly, as many countries have experienced significant growth in venture capital financing over the past ten years.

venture capital
A professionally managed pool of money raised for the sole purpose of making actively managed direct equity investments in rapidly growing private companies.

The birth of America's venture capital industry can be traced to the American Research and Development Company (ARDC) that began operating in Boston shortly after the end of World War II. As often happens with pioneers, ARDC had to invent the practices of modern venture capital and made many unprofitable investments in its early years. However, ARDC more than made up for its early mistakes with a single, spectacularly successful $70 000 investment in Digital Equipment in 1957, which grew in value to $355 million over the next 15 years. Through the late 1970s, the total pool of venture capital was quite small. Most of the active funds were sponsored either by financial institutions (e.g. Citicorp Venture Capital) or non-financial corporations (e.g. Xerox). Most of the money raised by these funds came from their corporate backers and from wealthy individuals or family trusts. There are two features of early venture capital funds that we still observe today: (1) these funds' investments were mostly intermediate-term, equity-related investments targeted at technology-based private companies; and (2) the venture capitalists (VCs) played a unique role as active investors, contributing both capital and expertise to portfolio companies. Also, from the very start, VCs looked to invest in those rare companies that not only had the potential of going public or being acquired at a premium within a few years, but also offered investment returns of 25–50 per cent per year.

A fundamental change in the US venture capital market occurred during the late 1970s. Two seemingly unrelated public policy innovations contributed to this change. First, Congress lowered the top personal income tax rate on capital gains from

35 per cent to 28 per cent in 1978, thereby increasing the return to entrepreneurship. Second, the Labor Department adopted its 'Prudent Man Rule' in 1979, effectively authorizing pension fund managers to allocate a moderate fraction of fund assets to private equity investments. Neither of these changes appears revolutionary, but their effect on venture capital funding was dramatic. There was an increase in the total venture capital funds raised, from $68.2 million in 1977 to $978.1 million in 1978 (both figures are in 1987 dollars). In 1981, a further capital gains tax reduction contributed to venture capital funding growth, from $961.4 million in 1980 to $5.1 billion in 1983. Fundraising then remained in the $2–$5 billion range for the rest of the 1980s. After falling to $1.3 billion in 1991, venture capital fundraising began a steady climb to $105.4 billion in 2000, before falling all the way back to $10.8 billion during 2003. Because the Jobs and Growth Tax Relief Reconciliation Act of 2003 significantly lowered the effective tax rate on personal investment income, this recent tax law change could well promote venture capital investment over the next few years, just as the 1978 capital gains tax reduction did.

Types of venture capital funds

In discussing venture capital, we must carefully differentiate between institutional venture capital funds and angel capitalists. **Institutional venture capital funds** are formal business entities in which full-time professionals seek out and fund promising ventures, whereas **angel capitalists** (or 'angels') are wealthy individuals who make private equity investments on a more ad hoc basis. A vibrant market for 'angel capital' exists and routinely provides over $50 billion per year in total equity investment to private businesses in the United States. Apart from the boom years of 1998–2000, angel capitalists have generally provided far more total investment to entrepreneurial companies each year than have institutional venture capital firms. Nonetheless, we focus on the latter group

institutional venture capital funds
Formal business entities with full-time professionals dedicated to seeking out and funding promising ventures.

angel capitalists
Wealthy individuals who make private equity investments on an ad hoc basis.

Source: Adapted from 'Halos Burn Brighter in a Group for Business Angels', *Financial Times*, 12 April 2005.

Real World

The collective noun for a group of angels is traditionally given as being a chorus. One that sings loud and clear is the Kaufmann Group. This is a US-based group of angel capitalists, formed after the 2000 bubble, to provide support and advice to both sides in angel finance. Angel financiers are often classified as 'friends, family or fools', but the average round of angel finance in the USA in 2005 was just under $1 million. This, however, contrasts with the average venture capital round of $8 million. One of the innovative features of the Kaufmann Group is that it also allows for economies of scale, as angels can flock together to fund projects that may individually be too large or too risky for any one to take on.

throughout this text because these firms operate nationally and provide the performance benchmark against which all private equity investment is compared.

There are four categories of institutional venture capital funds. First, **small business investment companies (SBICs)** are federally chartered corporations established as a result of the Small Business Administration Act of 1958. Since then, SBICs have invested over $14 billion in approximately 80 000 small firms. Historically, these venture capitalists have relied on their unique ability to borrow money from the US Treasury, at very attractive rates. SBICs were the only types of VCs that structured

small business investment companies (SBICs)
Federally chartered corporations established as a result of the Small Business Administration Act of 1958.

their investments as debt rather than equity. This feature seriously hampered their flexibility. But a revision of the law in 1992 has made it possible for SBICs to obtain equity capital from the Treasury in the form of preferred equity interests and also to organize themselves as limited partnerships. Recent evidence suggests that this change, by itself, has not been enough for SBICs to regain venture capital market share.

Secondly, **financial venture capital funds** are subsidiaries of financial institutions, particularly commercial banks. These are generally set up both to nurture portfolio companies, which will ultimately become profitable customers of the corporate parent, and to earn high investment returns, by leveraging the financial expertise and contacts of existing corporate staff. Though many financial venture capital funds are organized as SBICs, their orientation is sufficiently specialized that they are generally classified separately. Thirdly, **corporate venture capital funds** are subsidiaries or stand-alone firms, established by non-financial corporations, which are eager to gain access to emerging technologies by making early-stage investments in high-tech firms. Finally, **venture capital limited partnerships** are funds established by professional venture capital firms. These firms act as the general partners – organizing, investing, managing and ultimately liquidating the capital raised from the limited partners. Most limited partnerships have a single-industry focus that is determined by the expertise of the general partners.

Limited partnerships dominate the venture capital industry, partly because they make their investment decisions free from outside influences. The SBICs have been hampered by their historical reliance on inappropriate funding sources and by the myriad regulations that apply to government-sponsored companies. The financial and corporate funds tend to suffer because their ultimate loyalty rests with their corporate parents rather than their portfolio companies. Divided loyalties lead to conflicts of interest between financier and entrepreneur, and between the corporate funds and other venture capital investors. Remunerating employees who work in corporate venture capital funds also frequently poses a challenge. The remuneration of venture capitalists is likely to be much higher and more directly related to performance than is the case for most corporate employees. Finally, corporate funds have histories of only intermittent commitment to venture capital investing. Corporate funds tend to scale back dramatically when business conditions sour. For all these reasons, limited partnerships now control over 75 per cent of total industry resources, and their sway over fundraising seems to be increasing.

US investors typically favour convertible preference shares or convertible debt when they invest in companies. There are a number of reasons for this. First, there is the issue of seniority. These types of security are senior to ordinary shares, in that in the event of liquidation or bankruptcy they enjoy distribution of any assets prior to the ordinary shareholders. Secondly, convertible security investors can negotiate covenants and other arrangements with the company without the need for shareholder approval. Finally, the convertibility of the security means that the company

financial venture capital funds
Subsidiaries of financial institutions, particularly commercial banks.

corporate venture capital funds
Subsidiaries or stand-alone firms established by non-financial corporations eager to gain access to emerging technologies by making early-stage investments in high-tech firms.

venture capital limited partnerships
Funds established by professional venture capital firms, and organized as limited partnerships.

Real World

In recent years the A1 racing circuit has made some significant inroads into the audience for Formula 1 GP racing. In 2006 the company behind it raised some $250 million in venture capital funding, as a preliminary to going public. $120 million of this was in the form of convertible stock. Part of the funding was to cover losses that were larger than expected. Analysts stated that the planned IPO had a very wide spread of funding needs and possible returns due to the fundamental uncertainty of the business proposition.

Source: Adapted from 'Nomura Buys Into A1 GP Series', *Financial Times*, 31 May 2006.

can write off the debt payments, which benefits the cash flow and survivability of the venture, while allowing the investor to share in the upside.

Investment patterns of US venture capital firms

Given the media attention lavished on venture capital in the United States, most people are surprised to learn just how small the industry actually was before 1998. Figure 14.1 plots the total amount of capital invested each year, from 1995 through the first quarter of 2006. Annual disbursements naturally differ from total fundraising. The total amount of money available for investment is the sum of realized investment returns (from IPOs and mergers of portfolio companies) as well as new fund inflows from investors. Figure 14.1 reveals that total investments by VCs never exceeded $6 billion until 1996. Total investment spending then surged dramatically in the internet boom years, exceeding $100 billion in 2000. By this time the average investment per company was over four times larger than the levels in 1995. With the internet bubble over, venture capital declined again, but has been gradually increasing since 2003.

The bulk of venture capital funding once came either from corporate sponsors (in the case of financial or corporate funds) or wealthy individuals. However, institutional investors have become the dominant sources of funding today. Pension funds alone typically account for 25–40 per cent of all new money raised by institutional venture capital firms. Even though few pension funds allocate more than 5 per cent of their total assets to private equity funding, their sheer size makes them extremely important investors. Their long-term investment horizons make them ideal partners for venture capital funds. Financial and non-financial corporations usually represent the second-largest contributors of capital to venture funds, accounting for 10–30 per cent of the total. Foundations (endowments) are the third important source of venture capital funding, usually accounting for 10–25 per cent of the total. Foreign investors have recently become more important. In combination with 'other' investors, they now account for about one-fifth of total funding. Individuals and family trusts are the final major group of venture capital investors. These two groups together generally contribute 10–20 per cent of the total venture capital funding.

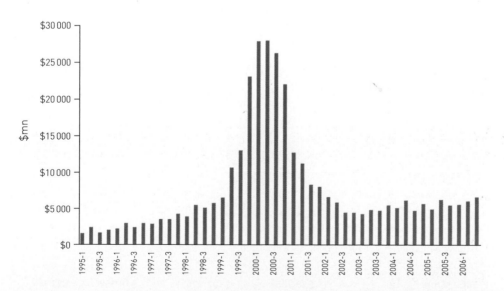

FIGURE 14.1

Annual venture capital investments in the United States, 1995–2006

In $bn current dollars.

Source: National Venture Capital Association http://www.nvca.com.

Industrial and geographic distribution of venture capital investment One reason for the success enjoyed by institutional VCs is that they usually invest only in those industries where they have some competitive advantage and where their involvement in portfolio company management can create real economic value. Table 14.2 lists the industries that received the most venture capital funding in 1998, 2000, 2003 and 2005. Typical of the history of venture capital, the majority of investment flowed into information technology industries (communications and computers) during the first three periods. Internet-specific investments accounted for a whopping 46.4 per cent of the total in year 2000, but for much lower fractions in 1998 and 2003/2005. Reductions in venture capital spending in this sector made room for expanded investments in 2003 in industries such as biotechnology, telecommunications, and medical devices and equipment. In 2005 the bulk of the monies went to the category that includes healthcare and financial services.

Another striking pattern in venture capital investment concerns the geographical distribution of portfolio companies. Firms located in California consistently receive more venture capital backing than firms in any other state, followed by firms in the New England area.

Venture capital investment by stage of company development The popular image of VCs holds that they specialize in making investments in start-up or very early-stage companies. This is only partly true. In fact, as Figure 14.2 documents, early-stage financing accounted for only 11 per cent of total investment in 2006, down from 25 per cent in 2000 and 24 per cent in 1997. Truly early-stage (start-up and seed-stage) financing represented a mere 4 per cent in 2006, and similarly small fractions were allocated in prior years. Being rational investors, venture capitalists are as leery as anyone else of backing extremely risky new companies. They will do so only if the entrepreneur/founder is well known to the venture capitalists or the venture is exceptionally promising, or both. Later-stage investments in more mature private companies, or expansion financing for more established but still venture firms, account for the vast bulk of funds allocated in each year.

Although the distribution between early- and later-stage funding varies from year to year, one principle of venture capital funding never changes – the earlier the development stage of the portfolio company, the higher must be the expected return on the venture capitalist's investment. Professional VCs typically demand compound annual investment returns in excess of 50 per cent on start-up investments. But they

TABLE 14.2

US venture capital investment by industry: 1998, 2000, 2003 and 2005

Source: Data for years 2000/2003/2005 are from the PricewaterhouseCoopers/ Venture Economics/National Venture Capital Association *MoneyTree*™ quarterly description of venture capital investment in the United States (http://www.pwcmoneytree. com). Data for 1998 are drawn from the NVCA website (http://www.nvca.com).

INDUSTRY	1998	2000	2003	2005
Computer software and services	21.6%	14.0%	19.6%	1.6%
Biotechnology	5.2	2.7	18.5	16.7
Other products and services	12.7	5.1	11.2	39.1
Telecommunications	17.6	17.1	10.9	11.1
Networking and equipment	13.4	46.4	9.3	6.5
Medical devices and equipment	12.8	3.5	8.1	9.5
Semiconductor	4.2	5.9	6.5	8.4
Computer hardware	3.1	2.2	<5	2.1
Industrial/energy	2.4	1.4	<5	3.5
Consumer-related	6.9	1.6	<5	1.6
Total ($mn)	$18 705	$102 976	$18 352	$22 652

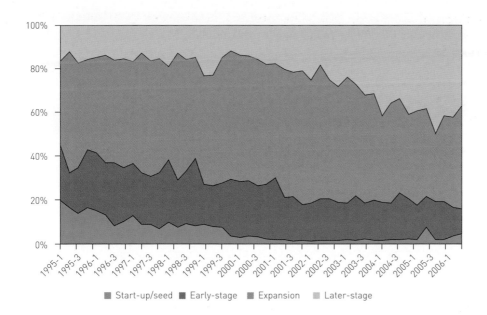

FIGURE 14.2

US venture capital investments by stage of company development, 1995–2006

Source: Adapted from PricewaterhouseCoopers/ Venture Economics/National Venture Capital Association *MoneyTree*™ quarterly description of venture capital investment in the United States (http://www.pwcmoneytree.com).

■ Start-up/seed ■ Early-stage ■ Expansion ☐ Later-stage

will accept returns of 20–30 per cent per year on later-stage deals because the risk is far lower in more established companies. VCs extract a higher expected return on early-stage investments, in part, by requiring entrepreneurs to sell them a higher ownership stake for a given investment amount in these deals.

Usually, there is not a stark choice between early- and later-stage investments. Most VC funds that invest in a company during its early years remain committed to the firm as it develops. VCs typically participate in many financing rounds as the portfolio company matures. On average, the prices venture capitalists pay to acquire additional shares in portfolio companies rise in each subsequent round of financing.

The economic effect of venture capital investment

Before moving on, we should briefly assess whether venture capital investments have really been as large and influential as is generally believed. A study published by the National Venture Capital Association documented the scale and economic effect of 30 years of VC investment in the United States.[2] The key results of that study are presented in Table 14.3. Over the period 1970–2000 American venture capitalists invested $273.3 billion into 16 278 companies in all 50 states. No less than $192 billion of that investment occurred during the six-year period 1995–2000. Venture capital-backed firms employed 7.6 million people and generated $1.3 trillion in sales during 2000, representing 5.9 per cent of the nation's jobs and 13.1 per cent of America's GDP for that year. The study also found that, over the 30-year period, 'venture capital-financed companies had approximately twice the sales, paid almost three times the federal taxes, generated almost twice the exports, and invested almost three times as much in R&D per $1000 in assets as did the average non-venture capital-backed companies.' Finally, the study documented that, on average, every $36 000 in-VC investment created one new job.

---

[2] See Jeanne Metzger and Channa Brooks (2001) 'Three Decades of Venture Capital Investment Yields 7.6 Million Jobs and $1.3 Trillion in Revenue', National Venture Capital Association, downloaded at http://www.nvca.com.

TABLE 14.3

The economic effect of three decades of US venture capital funding, 1970–2000

Cumulative investment (1970–2000); year 2000 sales and employment of venture-backed companies, year 2001 VC investment and growth rate.

STATE	CUMULATIVE VC INVESTED, 1970–2000 ($ MILLIONS)	SALES OF VC-BACKED FIRMS, 2000 ($ MILLIONS)	EMPLOYMENT BY VC-BACKED FIRMS, 2000 (NO OF WORKERS)	VENTURE CAPITAL INVESTED, 2001 ($ MILLIONS) [EST]	5-YR COMPOUND ANNUAL VC GROWTH RATE, 1996–2001
California	$108 810	$ 207 616	1 415 748	$14 431	24.3%
Mass	25 986	48 848	381 433	4 456	35.7
Texas	17 189	158 183	676 158	2 679	29.8
New York	16 070	65 848	369 314	2 080	33.1
Colorado	9 881	14 565	62 971	1 227	32.1
New Jersey	9 138	38 151	260 114	1 207	23.3
Washington	7 383	75 392	263 585	908	20.9
Virginia	7 215	35 689	207 777	972	14.5
Pennsylvania	7 187	58 037	424 652	na	na
Georgia	6 435	62 797	338 188	996	34.5
US total	**$273 300**	**$1 300 000**	**7 600 000**	—	—

Source: Adapted from Jeanne Metzger and Channa Brooks, 'Three Decades of Venture Capital Investment Yields 7.6 Million Jobs and $1.3 Trillion in Revenue', National Venture Capital Association (October 22, 2001) http://www.nvca.com.

Much the same pattern is observed in Western Europe, the other major international market for venture capital. A study by the European Private Equity and Venture Capital Association found that VC-backed European companies generated significantly higher growth rates in sales, research spending, exports and job creation during the 1990–1995 period than did otherwise comparable non-VC-backed companies.[3] Recent updates of this study show that European private equity funds invested €47 billion in 10 915 VC-stage companies during 2005. A very large element of this went to MBOs (management buyouts). Of the remainder, the largest part went to expansion-stage finance.

CONCEPT REVIEW QUESTIONS

3 What is an angel capitalist, and how does this type of investor differ from a professional (institutional) venture capitalist?

4 Why do you think that private limited partnerships have come to dominate the US venture capital industry? Can you think of any weaknesses this organizational form may have as a vehicle for financing entrepreneurial growth companies?

5 Why do venture capitalists almost always use convertible securities to finance entrepreneurial companies?

[3] The study is entitled 'The Economic Impact of Venture Capital in Europe', and is available for downloading at http://www.evca.com. Updates of this study include the *Survey of the Economic and Social Impact of Venture Capital in Europe*, published by EVCA on 20 June 2002, and the *EVCA Final Survey of Pan-European Private Equity and Venture Capital Activity 2002*, published by EVCA on 4 June 2003.

14.3 INTERNATIONAL MARKETS FOR VENTURE CAPITAL AND PRIVATE EQUITY

Although 'classic' venture capital investment by privately financed partnerships has traditionally been a distinctly US phenomenon, private equity financing has long been an established financial specialty in other developed countries, especially in Western Europe. Because Europe is the birthplace of both the industrial revolution and modern capitalism, it is not surprising that a highly sophisticated method of funnelling growth capital to private (often family-owned) businesses evolved there. The largest venture capital company in Europe is 3i (which stands for Investors in Industry), a UK-based public company. In fact, private equity fundraising in Europe compared quite well with that in the United States, until 1997, and showed far less annual variability. The chief differences between European and American venture capital lie in (1) the principal sources of funds for venture capital investing, (2) the organization of the venture funds themselves, (3) the development stage of the portfolio companies able to attract venture financing and (4) the principal method of harvesting venture capital investments. These differences are all related and help explain why the volatility of venture capital investment in the United States is so much higher than in Europe.

There is also a difference in the definition of the term 'venture capital' in Europe, as opposed to the United States. American commentators tend to refer to all professionally managed, equity-based investments in private, entrepreneurial growth companies as venture capital. European commentators typically apply the term only to early- and expansion-stage financing. Later-stage investments and funding for management buyouts are called 'private equity investment' in Europe. Where necessary, we maintain this distinction. In general, we refer to both venture capital and private equity investment as simply 'European venture capital'.

European venture capital and private equity fundraising and investment

As in the United States, venture capital fundraising and investment in Europe have grown rapidly since the mid-1990s. Figure 14.3 describes the growth in total private equity investment over the period 1996–2005. As can be seen there was a decline in the total amount invested after the burst of the dot-com bubble, but the fall was smaller in percentage terms than in the US and indeed the market has more than recovered.

Historically, European venture capital has been funnelled to different industries and different types of companies than is the norm for the United States, though this has been changing lately. As recently as 1996, less than one-quarter of European venture capital went into high-technology investments. In 2001, the fraction allocated to high-tech industries topped 55 per cent, but this dropped back to about one-third in 2003. Table 14.4 describes the industry breakdown of European private equity investments in industrial sectors, for the years 2000, 2003 and 2005. As in the United States, over two-thirds of European high-tech venture capital investment is channelled into computers and communications businesses.

In one important respect, venture capital funding patterns in Europe and in the United States have long been similar. Both are highly concentrated geographically. In Europe, the UK plays the same dominant source role as does California in the USA. In 2005, of the €47 billion invested, some €23 billion were invested in the UK (48 per cent) with €7 billion going to France and €5 billion to Germany. The sourcing of European venture capital funds differs from that of its US counterparts, primarily in Europe's greater reliance on financial institutions. Banks, insurance companies and other corporate investors accounted for more than one-third (35.0 per cent) of all European

FIGURE 14.3

European private
equity investment,
1996–2005

Source: European Private
Equity and Venture Capital
Association website –
http://www.evca.com.

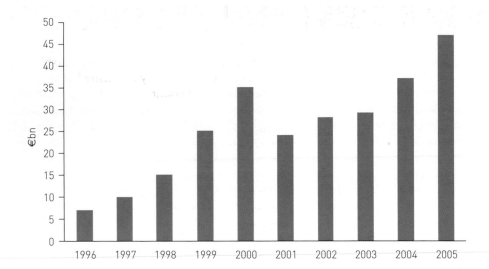

venture funding in 2003, whereas pension fund money represented less than one-fifth (19.4 per cent) of total fundraising. Government agencies accounted for 6.8 per cent of total capital raised.

For a mix of cultural and legal reasons, European venture capital funds are rarely, if ever, organized according to the US model of investment trusts. Instead, funds are generally organized as investment companies under various national laws. Their approach to dealing with portfolio companies is much more akin to the reactive style of US mutual fund managers than to the proactive style of America's venture capitalists. The relative lack of a vibrant entrepreneurial high-technology sector in Europe also hampers continental VCs' efforts to attract technologically savvy fund managers or entrepreneur/founders who want to use their expertise to grow new firms.

Another important element in the financial mix of venture capital in Europe is the role that state and semi-state organizations play. Consider, as an example, Israel. In Israel, unlike in the US, government policy was critical for the emergence of a venture capital industry, rooted however in the high-technology sector that had emerged through military R&D, significant investment by foreign multinationals in R&D laboratories in the country and a consciously orchestrated process to expand R&D and innovation in the business sector, following the establishment of the Office of the Chief Scientist (OCS) at the Ministry of Industry and Trade in 1969. The 1992 Inbal programme represented the first significant Israeli government effort to create a VC industry. It was perceived as being over-bureaucratic and as not having enough downside risk mitigation for companies and was only a modest success. These failures were mitigated in the Yozma Programme that began in 1993. Yozma was a $100 million government-owned fund: $80 million was invested in ten private funds, which had to be matched by a total of $120 million in private funding from 'significant foreign partners'. The second function saw $20 million retained in the government-owned Yozma Venture Fund to be invested directly in early-stage activities. This represented the backbone of an industry that invested in excess of $1 billion in Israel in 2001. This Israeli approach has also recently been adopted by Enterprise Ireland, the Irish government body responsible for encouraging start-ups.

European venture capital investment by stage of company development
Partly for the reasons previously detailed, European venture capital has historically been less focused on early-stage investments than has America's. As in other areas,

SECTOR	2000	2003	2005
Consumer-related	18.50%	19.40%	27.56%
Industrial products and services	10.00	6.80	1.94
Communications	13.80	16.90	15.48
Non-financial services	5.60	9.80	5.64
Medical/health-related	7.90	6.00	7.44
Other manufacturing	9.30	7.70	6.14
Computer-related	13.30	6.00	5.19
Biotechnology	2.90	2.30	1.85
Financial services	1.80	2.40	3.44
Chemicals and materials	2.90	2.30	1.94
Transportation	1.20	5.30	2.15
Other electronics-related	3.90	1.90	1.32
Construction	1.80	3.40	3.08
Total value(€mn)	**€34 926**	**€29 096**	**€47 000**

TABLE 14.4
European private equity investment by industry, 2000, 2003 and 2005

Source: European Venture Capital Association at http://www.evca.com.

however, this is changing fast (see Figure 14.4). Buyouts accounted for more than 40 per cent of European private equity investment during 1997 and 2000, and then surged to 73.6 per cent of 2003's total investment. In 2005 this large percentage had fallen only slightly, to 68 per cent. After spiking upwards during the 1997–2001 period, early-stage companies in 2005 attracted less than 6 per cent of total investment, much less than the fraction of US venture capital investment targeted at early-stage companies.

Venture capital markets outside the United States and Western Europe

The key venture capital markets outside the United States and Europe are Canada, Israel, Japan, China and India.[4] The venture capital industries of Israel and Canada differ dramatically from other advanced countries. Canadian government policies led to its venture capital system being based on funds sponsored by labour unions. Rapid growth in Canada's VC market during the late 1990s, however, weakened the union funds' grip on VC funding. Total investment grew at a compound annual rate of 60 per cent between 1994 and 2000. In 2000, Canada was the world's fifth largest recipient of VC financing and attracted almost as much investment ($4.3 billion versus $4.4 billion) as Germany, a nation five times larger. This pre-eminence was not to last, however. By 2002, Canada had fallen to ninth place overall, having attracted only $1.57 billion in total private equity investment, though it still ranked fourth in high-tech investment. As the Comparative Corporate Finance panel discusses, the fact that Canada has an English common law legal system is a key reason why its venture capital industry has prospered historically.

---

[4] This section draws heavily on material presented by one of the authors in a recently published paper. See William L. Megginson (2004) 'Towards a Global Model for Venture Capital?' *Journal of Applied Corporate Finance* 16:89–107.

COMPARATIVE CORPORATE FINANCE
Does a nation's legal system influence the size of its venture capital industry?

This table details how a country's legal system effects the relative importance of venture capital investment, stock market capitalization, and R&D spending for the 20 countries that received the most VC investment during 2002. Family of legal origin refers to the four main legal families (English common law, French civil law, German law and Scandinavian law) that the nation's commercial code is based on. Expressed as a fraction of GDP, venture capital investment was much higher in countries with legal systems based on English common law (0.47 per cent of GDP) than

in the three types of civil law countries (0.26 per cent). A similar pattern is observed for stock market capitalization as a percentage of GDP, where the average ratio is 110.64 per cent of GDP in common law, versus 68.65 per cent in civil law countries, but not for R&D spending as a percentage of GDP. This ratio is actually higher in civil law countries, which suggests that a nation's legal system does not influence the relative amount of national output invested in research, but it does influence the propensity to channel research investment through venture capitalists.

COUNTRY	FAMILY OF LEGAL ORIGIN	VENTURE CAPITAL AND PRIVATE-EQUITY INVESTMENT		STOCK MARKET CAPITALIZATION AS A % OF GDP	R&D SPENDING AS AS A % OF GDP
		$bn	% OF GDP		
Israel	English common law	$0.98	0.951	39.59	2.72
United Kingdom	English common law	9.58	0.616	115.80	1.90
United States	English common law	62.68	0.600	105.84	2.82
Sweden	Scandinavian law/Civil	1.39	0.584	75.26	4.27
Hong Kong SAR	English common law	0.75	0.460	284.08	0.21
Korea	German law/Civil	1.95	0.416	45.98	2.96
France	French civil law	5.53	0.390	104.02	2.20
Netherlands	French civil law	1.63	0.388	165.87	1.94
South Africa	English common law	0.37	0.356	112.06	0.70
Finland	Scandinavian law/Civil	0.43	0.326	105.17	3.40
Indonesia	French civil law	0.56	0.324	17.38	0.65
Australia	English common law	1.21	0.308	96.71	1.53
India	English common law	1.05	0.228	52.79	0.50
Canada	English common law	1.57	0.215	78.22	1.94
Italy	French civil law	2.48	0.209	40.23	1.07
Spain	French civil law	0.92	0.140	70.57	0.96
Belgium	French civil law	0.34	0.137	74.90	1.96
Germany	German law/Civil	2.37	0.120	34.53	2.49
Japan	German law/Civil	2.38	0.060	52.44	3.09
China	German law/Civil	0.35	0.028	37.44	4.85
Average, English common law countries		—	**0.47%**	**110.64%**	**1.60%**
Average, all civil law countries		—	**0.26%**	**68.65%**	**2.10%**

Sources: 1. GDP data, Institute for International Management World Competitiveness 2003 (http://www01.imd.ch/documents/wcy/content/GDP.pdf). 2. Venture capital investment data, PricewaterhouseCoopers (http://www.pwcmoneytree.com/moneytree/pdfs/gpe_report_2003.pdf). 3. Stock market capitalization data, World Federation of Exchanges (http://www.world-echanges.org), except France, Netherlands, and Belgium, whose data are estimates from Euronext. 4. R&D spending data, OECD statistics (http://www.oecd.org), except India, Israel, Hong Kong, Indonesia, South Africa and China, whose data are from national statistical agencies.

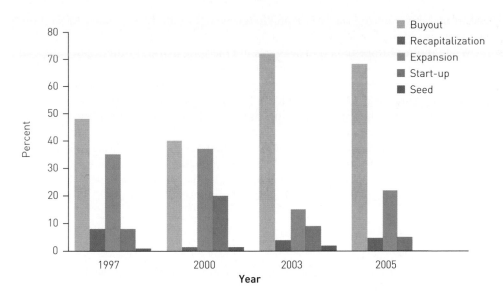

FIGURE 14.4

Distribution of European private equity investment by stage of company development, as a percentage of total investment, 1997–2005

Source: European Private Equity and Venture Capital Association at http://www.evca.com.

In a relative sense, Israel has achieved the greatest success in venture capital and private equity. It was the sixth largest recipient of PE funding in 2000 (receiving $3.2 billion). It was the world's largest recipient, if VC financing is expressed as a percentage of GDP (3.17 per cent). Even during 2002, Israel attracted almost $1 billion and remained the leader, if private equity investment is expressed as a percentage of GDP (0.95 per cent). As discussed, part of Israel's success can be traced to deliberate policy decisions in the early 1990s by the Likud government, which took concrete steps to commercialize defence-related technology developed with public funding. The influx of trained engineers and scientists from the former Soviet Union also helped, as did the pioneering steps taken by Israeli entrepreneurs to go public in the United States, opening a path to public markets that others could and did follow.

Venture capital fundraising and investment in Asia grew significantly between 1995 and 2000, though much less rapidly than in Europe or the United States because of a moribund VC industry in Japan. Elsewhere in Asia, growth was more robust, although from a low base. Japan has a financial specialty referred to as 'venture capital', but most of the firms involved are commercial or investment bank subsidiaries that make few truly entrepreneurial investments. Venture capital shows no real sign of taking root in Japan, and the world's second largest economy attracted only $2.38 billion (0.06 per cent of GDP) in venture funding in 2002. Although China is the fastest-growing major economy in the world, venture capital and private equity play very little role in its development. The country lacks the basic legal infrastructure needed to support a vibrant VC market, and the Chinese stock markets remain inefficient and politicized.

In many ways, India is the most interesting and promising private equity market in the world today. It ranked twelfth overall in total investment during 2002, up from nineteenth in 2000. The total amount invested ($1.05 billion) was more than twice that of 2000. India's history, as a former British colony, gave it a common law legal system, multiple stock exchanges and a heritage of English as the native tongue of its educated classes. Since 1991, India's rapid economic development has been propelled both by the macroeconomic and market opening reforms adopted that year and by relatively large inflows of foreign investment, which were, in turn, attracted by India's vast potential and by the quality of the graduates of its elite universities and technical institutes. Crucially, much of India's growth has been in the IT sector, which is the traditional target of true venture capital investment. For all these reasons, India should become one of the five leading venture capital markets by the end of this decade.

What about venture capital investment in emerging markets other than China and India? A recent study by Josh Lerner and Antoinette Schoar presents an empirical analysis of the transaction structures employed by private equity investors in developing countries.[5] From a sample of 210 transactions, they find that convertible securities are rarely used in developing countries. Investors are much more likely to invest in traditional, low-tech industries in emerging markets than are American venture capitalists. Lerner and Schoar also find that a nation's legal system significantly effects the transaction structure chosen for investments. Investors in countries with French or socialist legal systems show much greater determination to achieve majority voting control than do investors in English common law countries.

CONCEPT REVIEW QUESTIONS

6 Why do you think European governments and stock exchanges want to promote a vibrant entrepreneurial sector? Can you think of any competitive advantages that may accrue to Europe, due to its relatively late start in developing IPO markets?

7 Compare some of the competitive strengths and weaknesses of venture capital, as practised in Europe, Japan and Canada, with those of the United States.

8 How has the European venture capital industry changed over the past five years? Do you think these changes have made it more or less competitive and efficient?

9 What type of growth in venture capital funding and investment have China and India experienced during recent years? What is their future outlook for venture capital growth?

14.4 THE PROFITABILITY AND ULTIMATE DESTINATION OF VENTURE CAPITAL INVESTMENTS

The data on venture capital returns are rather sketchy, but it is clear that investments made by venture capital funds during the mid-1990s earned average compound annual returns of up to 30 per cent. There have been repeated examples of boom-and-bust investment cycles, in which high realized returns prompt excessive new capital inflows into venture capital funds, which in turn cause returns to drop sharply over the next harvest cycle. Although 30 per cent annual returns were also typical for venture capital funds during the late 1970s and early 1980s, data from the European Venture Capital Association indicate that returns fell short of 30 per cent every year from 1984 to 1994. Returns were again at target levels in 1995 and 1996, and then surged to nearly 150 per cent in 1999. However, as Table 14.5 demonstrates, returns for the three years that followed the collapse of the NASDAQ market in March 2000 were very poor in general; they only turned positive again during 2003. The table shows the returns on different types of venture capital investments over various horizons. Think of these horizons as the time span since the venture capital investments were made. Thus, on average, investments made at the earliest stage, seed capital, in European companies, return nearly 40 per cent after one year.

---

[5] See Josh Lerner and Antoinette Schoar (2003) 'Transaction Structures in the Developing World: Evidence from Private Equity', Working Paper, Harvard University and MIT (December).

Fund	1 YEAR		3 YEARS		5 YEARS		10 YEARS	
	USA	EUROPE	USA	EUROPE	USA	EUROPE	USA	EUROPE
Early/seed-stage	9.70	39.70	5.00	4.20	−8.60	−2.00	41.40	10.00
Balanced	31.00	100.80	13.50	9.50	−1.00	5.80	18.00	16.80
Later stage	17.40	36.60	10.70	6.00	−1.80	1.40	10.70	18.80
All venture	19.80	47.90	9.40	6.50	−4.40	1.50	22.70	15.80
Buyouts	25.50	38.10	17.60	14.00	6.30	10.50	8.90	23.30
Mezzanine	11.90	58.80	6.10	10.30	3.10	−4.70	6.60	11.50
All private equity	22.80	41.10	14.70	10.30	3.00	5.30	11.80	18.40

TABLE 14.5

Venture capital and private equity returns by fund type and investment as at mid-2006

Source: National Venture Capital Association http://www.nvca.com and European Venture Capital Association http://www.evca.org.

A strong positive correlation exists between venture returns and returns on small stock mutual funds. It highlights the importance of a healthy public stock market for new ventures, in general, and for initial public offerings in particular. Because VCs prefer to exit via an IPO, and because 'recycled' returns partially flow into new venture investments, any decline in the stock market's appetite for new issues has an immediate negative effect on the venture capital industry.

We also note that while in general returns in Europe are somewhat higher than those of the USA, this arises mostly from the higher returns to European buyouts and later-stage venture capital. The US returns are concentrated in the more risky, but ultimately more rewarding, earlier-stage financing.

Exit strategies of venture capitalists

Venture capital investors are not long-term equity investors. They seek to add value to a private company and then to harvest their investment. They use three principal methods to exit an investment: (1) through an initial public offering of shares to outside investors; (2) through a sale of the portfolio company directly to another company; or (3) through selling the company back to the entrepreneur/founders, known as the **redemption option**. IPOs are by far the most profitable and visible option for US-based venture capitalists. However, we have seen that the IPO market typically moves in waves, and as such so too do venture capital-backed IPOs.

Perhaps surprisingly, the evidence for US-based VCs is that they do not exit immediately at the time of an IPO. Instead, they retain shares for several months, or even years, and then typically distribute shares back to the limited partners, rather than sell the shares on the open market. The distributions usually occur after a period of sharply rising share prices, and the average share price response to distribution announcements is significantly negative.

One of the greatest disappointments of European policymakers, wanting to duplicate the success of the United States in high-technology development, has been the continent's failure, until very recently, to establish a large liquid market for the shares of entrepreneurial growth firms. Many national stock markets exist, and these collectively rival US exchanges in total capitalization of listed companies. This has had a direct effect on the exit strategies that European venture capitalists followed in harvesting their investments in portfolio companies.

Whereas IPOs have long been the preferred method of exit for US venture funds, public offerings accounted for only 21 per cent of European venture capital divestments in 1996, with comparable fractions in earlier years. The number of European IPOs surged after these markets matured, especially the Neuer Markt, which had attracted over 300 listings by early 2000. Unfortunately, the Neuer Markt collapsed

redemption option Option for venture capitalists to sell a company back to its entrepreneur or founders.

SMART IDEAS VIDEO

Steve Kaplan, University of Chicago

Venture capitalists' control, cash flow and liquidation rights.

See the entire interview at **www.cengage.co.uk/ megginson**

almost as fast as it took off. By January 2003, the market's total capitalization had fallen by over 95 per cent from its March 2000 peak, amid a series of accounting scandals and great acrimony between entrepreneurs, exchange officials and investors. The Neuer Markt was officially shut down in June 2003. The European IPO market is now effectively closed to all but the most profitable and established firms. A few European (and many Israeli) technology companies have been able to execute IPOs on US markets. Unfortunately, this is not an option for most entrepreneurial companies.

This is not the case in the UK, where the AIM (Alternative Investment Market) continues to grow and thrive. AIM has proven itself as a resilient market for new, small companies over the years since its inception in 1985. AIM is a branch of the London Stock Exchange, but the listing requirements on AIM are significantly less stringent than on the main exchange. By end-2005 AIM listed more than 1000 companies with an aggregate market capitalization of over €60 billion. AIM has established itself as the premier market for small company IPOs in Europe, with over 60 per cent of all such offerings routed through this market.

14.5 SUMMARY AND CONCLUSIONS

- Entrepreneurial finance requires specialized financial management skills because entrepreneurial growth companies are unlike other private or publicly traded companies. In particular, EGCs must finance much higher asset growth rates than other firms and tap external financial markets much more frequently.

- In addition to providing risk capital to entrepreneurial growth firms, professional venture capitalists (VCs) provide managerial oversight, coupled with technical and business advice, assistance in developing and launching new products, and valuable help recruiting experienced management talent.

- US venture capital investments are highly concentrated, both geographically and industrially.

- US venture capitalists endeavour to make intermediate-term (3–7 years), high-risk investments in entrepreneurial growth firms. Then, they exit these investments, either by selling the portfolio companies to another firm or (preferably) by executing an initial public offering. During recent years, VCs have, on average, achieved their target compound annual returns of over 30 per cent.

- Phenomenal growth in venture capital fundraising and investment has occurred over the past decade in the United States, Western Europe and in certain Asian countries, but not in Japan or in most developing countries. In recent years, the two largest venture capital markets, the United States and Europe, have seen significant convergence in contracting practices, investment patterns and returns.

- The funding of European venture capital is moving rapidly towards greater reliance on pension funds (rather than commercial banks). Today, a higher fraction of European venture capital investment is being targeted towards early-stage investment than in the past. More of Europe's total funding is also being directed towards high technology, rather than management buyouts, again mirroring practices in the United States.

- After a long period of relative underperformance, returns on European private equity investment have increased steadily in recent years. However, the collapse of Germany's Neuer Markt has temporarily closed what once was the most promising exit route for European venture capitalists.

- Although Canada and Israel successfully promoted venture capital funding and investment, growth in venture capital in Asia, Latin America and Africa has lagged behind that of Europe and North America. Venture capital funding and investment in developing countries has been growing from its low base during recent years.

INTERNET RESOURCES

For updates to links in this section and elsewhere in the book, please go to the book's website at **www.cengage.co.uk/megginson.**

http://www.bbaa.org.uk/portal/
British business angels association.

http://www.evca.com
Website of the European Venture Capital & Private Equity Association, which presents detailed information about Europe's venture capital industry and provides numerous reports about the European venture capital scene.

http://www.nvca.com
Website of the National Venture Capital Association, which presents a wide range of data and provides reports about the US venture capital industry, much of it current.

http://www.pwcmoneytree.com
Website of PricewaterhouseCoopers *MoneyTree*™, which presents details about the company's quarterly and annual venture capital surveys, and offers the company's electronic publication, *Global Private Equity Report*, which can be downloaded.

KEY TERMS

angel capitalists	financial venture capital funds	small business investment
corporate venture capital funds	institutional venture capital funds	companies (SBICs)
entrepreneurial finance	private equity	venture capital
entrepreneurial growth	redemption option	venture capital limited partnerships
companies (EGCs)		

ST14-1 You are seeking €1.5 million from a venture capitalist to finance the launch of your online financial search engine. You and the VC agree that your venture is currently worth €3 million. When the company goes public in an IPO in five years, it is expected to have a market capitalization of €20 million. Given the company's stage of development, the VC requires a 50 per cent return on investment. What fraction of the firm will the VC receive in exchange for its €1.5 million investment in your company?

ST14-2 An entrepreneur seeks €12 million from a VC fund. The entrepreneur and fund managers agree that the entrepreneur's venture is currently worth €30 million and that the company is likely to be ready to go public in four years. At that time, the company is expected to have a net income of €9 million. Comparable firms are expected to be selling at a price/earnings ratio of 25. Given the company's stage of development, the venture capital fund managers require a 40 per cent compound annual return on their investment. What fraction of the firm will the fund receive in exchange for its €12 million investment?

ST14-3 Suppose that six out of ten investments made by a VC fund are a total loss, meaning that the return on each of them is −100 per cent. Of the remaining investments, three break even, earning a 0 per cent return. One investment pays off spectacularly and earns a 650 per cent return. What is the realized return on the VC fund's overall portfolio?

QUESTIONS

Q14-1 List and describe the key financial differences between entrepreneurial growth companies and large publicly traded firms.

Q14-2 How does the financing of entrepreneurial growth companies differ from that of most firms in mature industries? How does the concept of 'bootstrap finance' relate to this difference?

Q14-3 What is an angel capitalist? How do the financing techniques used by angels differ from those used by professional venture capitalists?

Q14-4 Distinguish between the four basic types of venture capital funds. Which type has emerged as the dominant organizational form? Why?

Q14-5 What are some of the common characteristics of those entrepreneurial growth companies that are able to attract venture capital investment? In which industries and states is the majority of venture capital invested?

Q14-6 What is meant by early-stage and later-stage venture capital investment? What proportions of venture capital have been allocated between the two in recent years? Which stage requires a higher expected return? Why?

Q14-7 List the major differences between venture capital financing in the United States and in Western Europe. What major changes have been occurring recently in the European venture capital industry?

Q14-8 Why is a vibrant IPO market considered vital to the success of a nation's venture capital industry? What effect will the collapse of Germany's Neuer Markt likely have on the European venture capital industry?

Q14-9 Describe the recent levels of venture capital activity in Canada, Israel, Asia and developing countries. What is the outlook for each of them?

PROBLEMS

P14-1 Access the National Venture Capital Association website at http://www.nvca.com and the European Venture Capital Association website at http://www.evca.com. Update the figures and tables in the chapter using the most recent data available. What general trends do you see regarding sources of venture capital funding and patterns of investing?

P14-2 Access the European Private Equity & Venture Capital Association website at http://www.evca.com. Update Table 14.4 and Figures 14.3 and 14.4, using the most recent data available. What general trends do you see regarding sources of venture capital funding and patterns of investing from this website and its links?

MINICASE *Entrepreneurial finance and venture capital*

Through your financial services firm, Vestin Capital, you have raised a pool of money from clients. You intend to invest it in new business opportunities. To prepare for this endeavour, you decide to answer the following questions.

Assignment

1 What are some of the challenges of financing entrepreneurial growth companies?

2 What are the different types of venture capital funds?

3 What are some choices for organizing a venture capital firm?

4 In what ways should a venture capital firm structure its investments?

5 Should venture capital firms use convertible securities?

6 What are some of the exit strategies that may be available to a venture capital firm?

Chapter 15
International Financial Management

OPENING FOCUS

Dollar's fall creates winners and losers

The German motor manufacturer BMW is associated with stylish, superbly engineered, sporty yet practical luxury motorcars. One of its main markets is the USA. In mid-2005 the company, after a record run of profitability, announced a drop in profits. BMW attributed this to two factors. First, they found that increased labour and raw material costs had finally begun to erode their productivity. Secondly, however, they noted that the weaker US dollar had also impacted on their sales in the USA. BMW sells into the USA and receives dollars, which they then have to convert into euros. Changes in the relative price of dollars and euros therefore affects the euro value of dollar sales. And companies cannot just increase and decrease sticker prices for goods each day. The company also noted that they had hedged over 50 per cent of their exposure against the dollar and were increasing the level of production in the USA to create greater hedges.

Also in 2005, the French defence contractor Thales SA reported that the strengthening euro had resulted in a reduction in profits of some €30 million, as currency hedges had expired.

The lessons here are two-fold. First, though the media reports changes in currency values as though they were somehow a symbol of national vigour or lack thereof, currency movements are neither unambiguously good nor unambiguously bad. Rather, major swings in currency values create winners and losers. Secondly, companies can take actions through the financial markets to reduce the impact of these movements. Understanding the factors that cause currency values to move and the mechanisms by which firms can hedge against those movements is the primary purpose of this chapter.

Sources: 'Costs and Dollar Weakness Squeeze BMW Profits', *Financial Times*, 3 May 2005; 'Thales SA', *Wall Street Journal*, 14 March 2005.

LEARNING OBJECTIVES

After studying this chapter you should be able to:

- Describe the difference between fixed and floating exchange rates, and interpret exchange rate quotes taken from the web or financial newspapers.

- Explain how the four parity relationships in international finance tie together forward and spot exchange rates, interest rates and inflation rates in different countries.

- List the types of risks that multinational corporations face when they conduct business in different countries and currencies.

- Revise the NPV decision rule for capital budgeting analysis to incorporate the added complexity that arises when an investment is undertaken in a foreign currency.

SMART FINANCE

Use the learning tools at www.cengage.co.uk/megginson

Think of routine transactions – using your bank debit card to withdraw cash, taking that cash to purchase a new pair of fashionable boots in a chain store and then going to the cinema with the remaining money. In each of these activities, chances are that you will be dealing with products and services provided by **multinational corporations (MNCs)**, businesses that operate in many countries around the world. In recent decades, international trade in goods and services has expanded dramatically, and so too have the size and scope of MNCs. Although all the financial principles covered in this text thus far apply to MNCs, companies operating across national borders also face unique challenges. Primary among them is coping with exchange rate risk. An **exchange rate** is simply the price of one currency in terms of another, and for the past 30 years the exchange rates of major currencies have fluctuated daily. These movements create uncertainty for firms that earn revenues and pay operating costs in more than one currency. Currency movements also add to the pressures faced by wholly domestic companies that compete with foreign firms.

This chapter focuses on the problems and opportunities firms face as a result of globalization, with special emphasis on currency-related issues. First, we explain the rudimentary features of currency markets, including how and why currencies trade and the rules governments impose on trading in their currencies. Secondly, we describe factors that drive currency values, at least for those countries that allow their currencies to float in response to market forces. Third, we discuss the special risks faced by MNCs and the strategies they employ to manage those risks. We conclude by illustrating how operating across national borders affects capital budgeting analysis.

15.1 EXCHANGE RATE FUNDAMENTALS

We begin our coverage of exchange rate fundamentals by describing the 'rules of the game' as dictated by national governments.

Fixed versus floating exchange rates

Since the mid-1970s, the major currencies of the world have had a **floating exchange rate** relationship with respect to one another, which means that forces of supply and demand continuously move currency values up and down. The opposite of a floating exchange rate regime is a **fixed exchange rate** system. Under a fixed-rate system, governments fix (or peg) their currency's value, usually in terms of another currency or to a weighted average of major trading partners' currencies. Once a government pegs the currency at a particular value, it must stand ready to implement the economic and financial policies necessary to maintain that value. For example, if demand for the currency increases, the government must be ready to sell currency so that the increase in demand does not cause the currency to **appreciate**. If demand for the currency falls, the government must be prepared to buy its own currency to prevent the currency from depreciating. In many countries with fixed exchange rates, governments impose restrictions on the free flow of currencies into and out of the country. Even so, maintaining a currency peg can be quite difficult. For example, in response to mounting economic problems, the government of Argentina allowed the peso, which had been linked to the US dollar, to float freely for the first time in a decade on 11 January 2002. Within one day the peso had lost more than 40 per cent of its value relative to the dollar. Within the European Exchange Rate Mechanism, the system of semi-fixed exchange rates that preceded the euro, there were periodic crises where eventually the bands of allowable fluctuations of currencies were required to be lifted and new bands put in place.

---

multinational corporations (MNCs)
Businesses that operate in many countries around the world.

exchange rate
The price of one currency in terms of another currency.

floating exchange rate
An exchange rate system in which a currency's value is allowed to fluctuate in response to market forces.

fixed exchange rate
An exchange rate system in which the price of one currency is fixed relative to all other currencies by government authorities.

appreciate
A currency appreciates when it buys more of another currency than it did previously.

Some countries have adopted hybrid currency systems in which the currency is neither pegged nor allowed to float freely. A managed floating rate system is a hybrid in which a nation's government loosely 'fixes' the value of the national currency in relation to that of another currency, but does not expend the effort and resources that would be required to maintain a completely fixed exchange rate regime. Other countries simply choose to use another nation's currency as their own, such as Montenegro, which has adopted the euro, while others have adopted a currency board arrangement. In such an arrangement, the national currency continues to circulate, but every unit of the currency is fully backed by government holdings of another currency.

The International Monetary Fund regularly provides detailed analyses of exchange rate arrangements. As of December 2006, 41 countries had no separate currency, including the 12 eurozone members, seven had currency board systems, 40 pegged their currency to an individual currency and 5 to a basket, 53 had managed floating arrangements and 30 free floating arrangements. A number of other countries had composite arrangements.

In terms of trading volume, the major currencies in international finance today include the British pound sterling (£), the Swiss franc (SF), the Japanese yen (¥), the Canadian dollar (C$), the US dollar (US$, or simply $) and the euro (€).

managed floating rate system
A hybrid currency system in which a government loosely fixes the value of the national currency.

currency board arrangement
An exchange rate system in which each unit of the domestic currency is backed by a unit of some foreign currency.

Exchange rate quotes

One of the complications with exchange rates in practice is that they can be quoted in two different but essentially identical ways. Where we express the rate as domestic currency per unit of foreign, this is called a direct quote, and where we express the rate as how much foreign currency is required to purchase one unit of domestic, that is called an indirect quote. The direct quote for euros then would be given as '€ equivalent' and the indirect quote would be 'currency per €'.

Table 15.1 shows exchange rate values quoted on MSNBC on 3 November 2006 for major currencies against the euro. The first column shows 'In euro', which is the

direct quote
An exchange rate quoted in terms of units of domestic currency per unit of foreign currency.

indirect quote
An exchange rate quoted in terms of foreign currency per unit of domestic currency.

CURRENCY	IN EURO	PER EURO
Argentine peso	0.25365	3.94249
Australian dollar	0.60518	1.65240
Brazilian real	0.36677	2.72652
British pound	1.49503	0.66888
Canadian dollar	0.69046	1.44831
Chinese yuan	0.09946	10.05482
Euro	1.00000	1.00000
Hong Kong dollar	0.10062	9.93802
Indian rupee	0.01746	57.28179
Japanese yen	0.00668	149.68689
S Korean won	0.00084	1 197.63568
Mexican peso	0.07215	13.85968
Russian rouble	0.02931	34.12141
Swedish krona	0.10908	9.16767
Swiss franc	0.62816	1.59195

TABLE 15.1

Direct and indirect exchange rate quotes

The table shows direct (euro per unit of foreign currency) and indirect (units of foreign currency per euro) exchange rate quotes.

Source: MSN Money website 3 November 2006.

value of each currency expressed in euro terms, or what we have called earlier the indirect quote. The last column shows the direct quote, or the value of one euro in each of the target currencies. We see that on Friday 3 November, one Argentine peso cost €0.25365. One day earlier, one peso cost $0.2540. Because the value of one peso in terms of euros fell slightly, we say that the peso **depreciated** against the euro.

depreciate
A currency depreciates when it buys less of another currency than it did previously.

Of course, the exchange rate quotes in the two columns reveal exactly the same information. Each of these methods of quoting exchange rates is simply the reciprocal of the other:

$$\frac{Euro}{Sterling} = \frac{1}{Sterling/Euro}$$

Spot and forward rates   There is more than one exchange rate for each currency pair. For each currency, the first exchange rate is the **spot exchange rate**. The spot exchange rate is just another word for the current exchange rate. That is, if you are going to trade currencies right now – 'on the spot' – the relevant exchange rate is the spot exchange rate. In many currencies, it is possible to enter a contract today to trade foreign currency at a fixed price at some future date. The price at which that future trade will take place is called the **forward exchange rate**. For example, a US trader wishing to exchange dollars for British pounds could do so at a spot exchange rate of $1.7733/£ (or equivalently, £0.5639/$). Alternatively, that trader could enter into an agreement to trade dollars for pounds one month later at the forward rate of $1.7686/£ (or equivalently, £0.5654/$). If the trader chooses to transact through a forward contract, no cash changes hands until the date specified by the contract.

spot exchange rate
The exchange rate that applies to immediate currency transactions.

forward exchange rate
The exchange rate quoted for a transaction that will occur on a future date.

We can also examine differences in the spot exchange rate for current transactions and the forward rate for future transactions. For example, consider exchange rate quotes for Japanese yen versus the euro. On the spot market, one yen costs €0.00668/¥, but the exchange rate for trades that will take place six months later is €.00675/¥. One yen buys slightly more euros on the forward market than on the spot market. When one currency buys more of another on the forward market than it does on the spot market, traders say that the first currency trades at a **forward premium**. The forward premium is usually expressed as a percentage relative to the spot rate, so for the yen, we can calculate the six-month forward premium as follows:

forward premium
When one currency buys more of another on the forward market than it buys on the spot market.

$$\frac{F - S}{S} = \frac{0.00675 - 0.00668}{0.00668} = 0.0104 = 1.04\%$$

where F is the symbol for the forward rate and S stands for the spot rate, both quoted in terms of €/¥. Recognizing that the yen's 1.04 per cent forward premium refers to a six-month contract, we could restate the premium in annual terms by multiplying the premium by 2, which would yield an annualized forward premium of 2.08 per cent.

If the yen trades at a forward premium relative to the dollar, then the dollar must trade at a **forward discount** relative to the yen, meaning that one dollar buys fewer yen on the forward market than it does on the spot market. To calculate the forward discount on the dollar, we use the same equation as above, but we express the exchange rate in terms of yen per dollar:

forward discount
When one currency buys less of another on the forward market than it buys on the spot market.

$$\frac{F - S}{S} = \frac{148.148 - 149.706}{149.706} = -0.0104 = -1.04\%$$

The euro trades at a –1.04 per cent forward discount for a six-month contract. In other words, the forward discount on the euro is opposite in sign and similar in magnitude to the forward premium on the yen, though the discount is smaller in absolute value than the premium (this is not apparent here due to rounding). In general, to calculate the annualized forward premium or discount on a currency, based on a forward contract to be executed in N days, use the following equation:

$$\left(\frac{F-S}{S}\right)\left(\frac{360}{N}\right)$$

EQUATION 15.1

The forward discount or premium gives traders information about more than just the price of exchanging currencies at different points in time. The forward premium is tightly linked to differences in interest rates on short-term, low-risk bonds across countries. We explore that relationship in depth in the next section.

Spot rates can also tell us one last piece of information. What if someone wants to know the exchange rate between British pounds and Canadian dollars, but does not have that information in an exchange rate table? In fact, all the information needed to calculate this exchange rate is available from spot rates. We simply need to calculate a **cross exchange rate** by dividing the euro exchange rate for one currency by the exchange rate for the other currency. For example, with spot rates we can determine the £/C$ exchange rate:

cross exchange rate
An exchange rate between two currencies calculated by taking the ratio of the exchange rate of each currency, expressed in terms of a third currency.

$$\frac{€1.49503/£}{€.69046/C\$} = C\$2.1653/£$$

How can we be sure that one pound buys 2.1653 Canadian dollars simply by taking this ratio? The answer is that if the exchange rate between pounds and Canadian dollars was any other number, then currency traders could engage in **triangular arbitrage**, trading currencies simultaneously in different markets to earn a risk-free profit. Because currency markets operate virtually 24 hours per day, and because currency trades take place with lightning speed and with very low transaction costs, arbitrage maintains actual currency values in different markets relatively close to this theoretical ideal.

triangular arbitrage
A trading strategy in which traders buy a currency in a country where the value of that currency is too low and immediately sell the currency in another country where the currency value is too high.

Applying the Model

Suppose that on Friday 3 November 2006, a trader learns that the exchange rate offered by a London bank is C$2.2000/£ rather than C$2.1653/£ as calculated previously. What is her arbitrage opportunity? First, note that the figure C$2.2000/£ is 'too high' relative to the theoretically correct rate. This means that in London, one pound costs too much in terms of Canadian dollars. In other words, the pound is overvalued, and the Canadian dollar is undervalued. Therefore, a trader could make a profit by executing the following steps.

1 Convert euros to British pounds at the prevailing spot rate as given in Table 15.1. Assume that the trader starts with €1 million, which will convert to £668 883 (€1 000 000 ÷ €1.49503/£).

2 Simultaneously, the trader sells £668 883 in London (because pounds are overvalued there) at the exchange rate of C$2.2000/£. The trader will then have C$1 471 542.

3 Convert the Canadian dollars back into euros in New York at the correct rate. Given the spot rate of €0.69046/C$ in Table 15.1, the trader will receive €1 016 041.

> After making these trades, all of which can occur with the touch of a keystroke, the trader (or more probably her employer) winds up €16 041 richer, all without taking risk. As long as the exchange rates do not change, the trader can keep making a profit over and over again.

The preceding example shows that a trader can repeatedly make a profit if the exchange rates do not change. Of course exchange rates do change, and they change in a way that brings the market back into equilibrium.

Source: Adapted from 'Squeeze the Pips for Profit', *Financial Times*, 30 October 2006.

Real World

Foreign exchange arbitrage is a game that everybody can play, via currency spread betting. The UK's largest spread betting company, Capital Spreads, in late 2006 noted that currency trading had become its largest product. Currency spread betting is in essence what we described above except that people spread betting do not have to actually own the currency prior to trading. Spread betting exploits two factors: first the movements can be very small, and secondly each person has a perspective on how a part of a currency pair is likely to move. The consequence is that people perceive arbitrage profits (which may or may not be realized of course depending on how accurate is their forecast) and act accordingly.

With this basic understanding of foreign exchange rates in place, let us now turn to some important institutional features of the foreign exchange market.

The foreign exchange market

The foreign exchange (forex) 'market' is not actually a physical exchange but a global telecommunications market. In fact, it is the world's largest financial market, with total volume of almost $2 trillion per day. The forex market operates continuously during the business week, with trading beginning each calendar day in Tokyo. As the day evolves, trading moves westward as major dealing centres come online in Singapore, Bahrain, continental Europe, London and finally North America (particularly New York and Toronto). Prices for all the floating currencies are set by global supply and demand. Trading in fixed-rate currencies is more constrained and regulated and frequently involves a national government (or a state-owned bank) as counterparty on one side of the trade.

The players in the forex market are numerous, as are their motivations for participating in the market. We can break market participants into six distinct (but not mutually exclusive) groups: (1) exporters and importers, (2) investors, (3) hedgers, (4) speculators, (5) dealers and, at times, (6) governments.

Businesses that export goods to or import goods from a foreign country need to enter the foreign exchange market to pay bills denominated in foreign currency or to convert foreign currency revenues back into the domestic currency. Along with all the other participants in the market, exporters and importers influence currency values. For instance, if Europeans develop a taste for California wines, then European importers will exchange euros (or perhaps pounds, kroner, francs, etc.) for dollars to purchase wine. Other factors held constant, these trades would tend to put upward pressure on the value of the dollar and downward pressure on European currencies.

Investors also trade foreign currency when they seek to buy and sell financial assets in foreign countries. For example, when foreign investors want to buy South African shares or bonds, they must first sell their home currencies and buy rand. Buying pressure from investors causes the rand to appreciate against foreign currencies. In general, the pressures exerted on currencies by investors are much larger than those exerted by exporters and importers because investors account for a larger fraction of currency trading volume. For example, the total value of goods and services traded internationally each year is about $10 trillion, whereas the aggregate value of currency trading is 50 times that, some $500 trillion annually.

Sometimes traders in the foreign exchange market buy and sell currency to offset other risks to which they are exposed during the normal course of business. Hedging refers to the practice of trading an asset for the sole purpose of reducing or eliminating the risk associated with some other asset. For example, suppose that a US firm expects to receive a £1 000 000 payment from a customer in the United Kingdom. The payment is due in 90 days. This receivable is risky from the US firm's perspective because the exchange rate between dollars and pounds may fluctuate over the next 90 days. To hedge the risk of its pound-denominated receivable, the US firm might enter a forward contract to sell pounds for dollars in 90 days. By doing so, the firm essentially locks in a dollar value for the £1 000 000 payment.

Hedgers influence currency values when they take positions to offset the risks of their existing exposures to certain currencies. In contrast, speculators take positions not to reduce risk but to increase it. Speculators sell a currency if they expect it to depreciate, and they buy if they expect it to appreciate. Some speculators, such as George Soros, have become famous for the enormous profits (or losses) they have earned by taking large positions in certain currencies. When external pressures force a country with a pegged currency to devalue its currency, speculators often take the blame. Whether or not they deserve blame for causing, accelerating or exacerbating currency crises, speculators play a useful economic role by taking the opposite side of a transaction from that of hedgers. Speculators help make the foreign currency market more liquid and more efficient.

As in all financial markets, dealers play a crucial role in the foreign exchange business. Most foreign currency trades go through large international banks in the leading financial centres around the globe. These banks provide a means for buyers and sellers to come together, and as their reward they earn a small fee – the bid–ask spread, on each round-trip buy-and-sell transaction they facilitate. The ask price is the price at which a currency dealer is willing to sell foreign currency, and the bid price is the price at which the dealer is willing to buy currency. Because the ask price is slightly higher than the bid (hence the term, bid–ask spread), dealers make a small profit each time they buy and sell currency.

Finally, governments intervene in financial markets to put upward or downward pressure on currencies as circumstances dictate. Governments that attempt to maintain a fixed exchange rate must generally intervene more frequently than those that intervene only in times of crisis. As this chapter's Opening Focus illustrates, currency movements create winners and losers, not only across national boundaries but also within a given country. For example, a rise in the value of the Swiss franc makes Swiss exports more expensive and foreign imports cheaper. Remember, an exchange rate is simply a price, the price of trading one currency for another. Though the financial press dramatizes changes in exchange rates by attaching adjectives such as 'strong' or 'weak' to a given currency, this practice is rather odd when you recognize that they are just talking about a price. For instance, if the price of apples rises and the price of bananas falls, we do not refer to apples as being strong and bananas as being weak! If the price of apples is high, that is good for apple producers and bad for apple consumers. In the same way, a rise in the value of a particular currency benefits some and harms others. Therefore, at least for the major, free-floating currencies, governments are reluctant to intervene because doing so does not unambiguously improve welfare across the board.

Even when governments want to intervene in currency markets, intervention is complicated by the fact that currency values are not set in a vacuum but are linked to other economic variables such as interest rates and inflation. In the next section, we discuss four parity relationships that illustrate the linkages that should hold in equilibrium between exchange rates and other macroeconomic variables.

CONCEPT REVIEW QUESTIONS

1 Explain how a rise in the euro might affect a French company exporting wine to the United States, and compare that with the impact on a German firm importing semiconductors from the United States.

2 Holding all other factors constant, how might an increase in interest rates in Sweden affect the value of the krona?

3 If someone says, 'The exchange rate between yen and pounds increased today', can you know with certainty which currency appreciated and which depreciated? Why or why not?

4 Define spot and forward exchange rates. If a trader expects to buy a foreign currency in one month, can you explain why the trader might prefer to enter into a forward contract today rather than simply wait a month and transact at the spot rate prevailing then?

15.2 THE PARITY CONDITIONS OF INTERNATIONAL FINANCE

In this section we discuss the major forces that influence the values of all the world's free-floating currencies. Theory suggests that when markets are in equilibrium, spot and forward exchange rates, interest rates and inflation rates should be linked across countries. Market imperfections, such as trade barriers and transaction costs, may prevent these parity conditions from holding precisely at all times, but they are still powerful determinants of exchange rate values in the long run.

Forward–spot parity

If the spot rate governs foreign exchange transactions in the present and the forward rate equals the price of trading currencies at some point in the future, intuition suggests that the forward rate might be useful in predicting how the spot rate will change over time. For example, suppose that a British firm intends to import US wheat, for which it must pay $1.5 million in one month. Imagine that the pound currently trades at a forward premium, and the prevailing spot and forward exchange rates are as follows:

$$\text{Spot} = \$1.4/£, \text{ 1-month forward} = \$1.50/£$$

The UK firm faces a choice. Either it can lock in the forward rate today, guaranteeing that it will pay £1 million for its wheat ($1.5 million ÷ $1.50/£), or it can wait a month and transact at the spot rate prevailing then. Let us suppose that the UK firm in this example does not care about exchange rate risk so it will enter the forward contract only if it believes that trading at the forward rate will be less expensive than trading at the spot rate in 30 days.[1]

This results in a simple decision rule for the UK importer. First, it must form a forecast of what the spot exchange rate will be in one month. Let's call that the expected spot rate and denote it with the symbol $E(S)$. We can now determine the UK firm's decision rule:

1 Enter the forward contract today if $E(S) < \$1.50/\pounds$.

2 Wait and buy dollars at the spot rate if $E(S) > \$1.50/\pounds$.

For example, assume that the firm's forecast is that the spot rate will not change from its current level of $\$1.40/\pounds$. Given this forecast, the expected cost of purchasing $1.50 million in 30 days is £1 071 429 ($1.5 million ÷ $1.40/£); and given that the firm will need only £1 million if it locks in the forward rate, it does not pay to wait. Conversely, assume that the UK firm believes that over the next 30 days the pound will appreciate to $1.60/£. In that case, the expected cost of paying for the wheat is just £937 500 ($1.5 million ÷ $1.60/£), and the firm should wait. Only if the firm's forecast of the expected spot rate is $1.50/£, equal to the current forward rate, will it be indifferent to whether it locks in the forward contract now or waits 30 days to transact.

If we look at this problem from the perspective of a US firm that must pay in pounds in 30 days to import some good from the United Kingdom, we get just the opposite decision rule. For the US firm, entering a forward contract to buy pounds makes sense if it expected the spot rate in 30 days to be greater than the current forward rate ($E(S) > \$1.50/\pounds$). Appreciation in the pound increases the cost of importing from Britain, so if a US firm expects the pound to appreciate above the current forward rate, it will lock in a forward contract immediately. On the other hand, if the US firm expects the spot rate to be less than $1.50/£ in 30 days, it will choose to wait rather than lock in at the forward rate.

Now we broaden the example to include all US and UK firms who face a future need to buy foreign currency. Ideally, US firms who need to buy pounds to import British goods could trade with UK firms who must sell pounds and buy dollars to import US goods. However, there is a problem because the circumstances under which firms in each country prefer to trade in the spot market rather than the forward market are mirror images of each other:

1. If $E(S) > F$, the UK firms do not want the forward contract, but US firms do.

2. If $E(S) < F$, the UK firms want the forward contract, but US firms do not.

Equilibrium will occur in this market only when the forecast of the spot rate is equal to the current forward rate. In that case, US and UK firms are indifferent to whether they transact in the spot or the forward market. This yields our first parity condition, known as **forward–spot parity**. It says that the forward rate should be an unbiased predictor of where the spot rate is headed:

forward–spot parity
An equilibrium relationship that predicts that the current forward rate will be an unbiased predictor of the spot rate on a future date.

$$E(S) = F$$

EQUATION 15.2

It would certainly be convenient for currency traders if the forward exchange rate provided a reliable forecast of future spot rates. Unfortunately, most studies suggest

---

[1] This is clearly an abstraction. Firms may decide to enter a forward contract, even if they think that transacting later at the spot rate might be more profitable, because they value the certainty that the forward contract gives them. In this example, we are considering the hypothetical case of a firm that does not care about uncertainty and makes currency trading decisions solely on the basis of expected profitability.

that this is not the case. Changes in spot exchange rates are not closely tied to the forward exchange rate. For that matter, most researchers and practitioners agree that it is nearly impossible to predict how most exchange rates will move most of the time, at least in the short run.

If forward rates do not accurately predict movements in currency values over time, perhaps something else does. Economists have long observed a correlation between currency movements and inflation rate differentials across countries. To illustrate, Table 15.2 reports the cumulative inflation that occurred in the United States, Japan, Germany and France from 1984 to 1996. Beside those figures we show the difference between the US inflation and that which occurred in the other countries, as well as the cumulative change in the values of the yen, the German mark and the French franc against the dollar over the same period.

Notice the remarkable correspondence between the numbers in the third and fourth columns. Japan's was the only currency that appreciated against the dollar from 1984 to 1996, and it was the only country on the list with less inflation than the United States. German and US inflation was about equal, and the dollar–mark exchange rate was about the same in 1996 as it was in 1984. French inflation was roughly 50 percentage points higher than US inflation, about equal to the decline in the franc.

These figures suggest that differences in inflation do a good job of explaining currency movements, at least over a long period of time. The second parity relationship reveals why.

Purchasing power parity

law of one price
A theory that says that the identical good trading in different markets must sell at the same price.

One of the simplest ideas in economics is that identical goods trading in different markets should sell at the same price, absent any barriers to trade. This **law of one price** has a natural application in international finance. Suppose that a DVD of a hit movie retails in the United States for $20, and the identical DVD can be purchased in Italy for €40. Does the law of one price hold? It depends on the exchange rate. If the spot rate of exchange equals €2/$, then the answer is yes. A US consumer can spend $20 to purchase the DVD in the United States, or he can convert $20 to €40 and purchase the item in Milan. We can generalize this example as follows. Suppose that the price of an item in domestic currency is P_{dom} and the price of the identical item in foreign currency is P_{for}. If the spot exchange rate quoted in foreign currency per domestic is $S_{for/dom}$, then the law of one price holds if the following is true:

EQUATION 15.3

$$\frac{P^{foreign}}{P^{domestic}} = Spot^{foreign/domestic}$$

Naturally, the law of one price extends to any pair of countries, not just the United States and Italy. When Equation 15.3 does not hold, traders may engage in arbitrage to exploit price discrepancies across national boundaries.

TABLE 15.2

Inflation and exchange rate movements

Source: Authors' calculations using data from 1984–1996.

	% CUMULATIVE INFLATION	% US INFLATION – FOREIGN INFLATION	% APPRECIATION/DEPRECIATION AGAINST THE $
United States	51	NA	NA
Japan	17	+34	+46
Germany	52	−1	−4.5
France	100	−49	−50

Real World

One of the problems with the law of one price is finding non-financial commodities that are truly global and homogenous. For many years *The Economist* magazine has suggested that the relative price of Big Mac hamburgers from McDonald's should be a good indicator, they being pretty much the same worldwide. *The Economist* regularly publishes an index of currency over and undervaluation on the basis of the dollar-adjusted price of a Big Mac in various countries.

Applying the Model

Suppose that a pair of Maui Jim sunglasses sells for $200 in the United States and for €180 in Italy. The exchange rate between dollars and euros is €0.95/$. Does the law of one price hold? Apparently not, because:

$$180/200 < 0.95$$

How can arbitrageurs exploit this violation of the law of one price? The previous equation reveals that the price of sunglasses in Italy is too low, or the price in the United States is too high, relative to the current exchange rate. Therefore, suppose that a trader buys sunglasses in Italy for €180 and ships them to the United States. After selling them for $200, the trader can convert back to euros, receiving €190 ($200 × €0.95/$). The arbitrage profit is €10. As long as the transaction costs of making these trades is less than €10, and as long as there are no other barriers to trade, then the process will continue until the market reaches equilibrium. Figure 15.1 illustrates how arbritrage trades push the market back towards an equilibrium in which the law of one price holds.

FIGURE 15.1

Arbitrage and the law of one price

If sunglasses sell for $200 in the US and €180 in Italy, then the law of one price holds only if the exchange rate equals €0.90/$. If the exchange rate is €0.95, then traders can make a profit by purchasing the sunglasses in Italy, shipping them to the US and selling them there, and converting the proceeds back into euros.

sell for $200 ← exchange rate (€0.95 = $1) ← buy for €180.000

buy sunglasses in Italy and ship to the United States

$200

exchange $200 for €190

€180

Cost of sunglasses in Italy	− €180
Revenue from selling in US	+ €190
Profit	€ 10

Now we will add a new wrinkle to the law of one price. Suppose that prices in different countries satisfy Equation 15.3 not just at one moment in time, but all the time. We do not necessarily expect this to be the case for every type of good sold in two countries, but if price discrepancies for similar goods become too large, the forces of arbitrage should push them back into line. Of course, the prices of goods and services change every day due to inflation (or deflation), and there is no reason to expect the inflation rate in one country to be the same as in another. If different countries are subject to different inflation pressures, how can the law of one price hold on an ongoing basis? The answer is that the exchange rate adjusts to maintain equilibrium.

Applying the Model

Suppose that the forces of arbitrage have influenced the prices of Maui Jim sunglasses in the United States and in Italy so that the law of one price now holds. Specifically, the US price is $195 and the Italian price is €185.25. If the exchange rate is still €0.95/$, then the law of one price holds because:

$$185.25/195 = 0.95$$

Now suppose that the expected rate of inflation in Italy over the next year is 12 per cent, but no inflation is expected in the United States. One year from today, Maui Jim sunglasses will still sell for $195 in the United States, but with 12 per cent inflation, the price in Italy will rise to €207.48 (185.25×1.12). If these forecasts are correct, then in a year the exchange rate must rise to €1.064/$ for the law of one price to hold and:

$$207.48/195 = 1.064$$

Remember that this exchange rate is expressed in euros per dollar, so an increase from E0.95/$ to E1.064/$ represents appreciation of the dollar and depreciation of the euro.

purchasing power parity
An equilibrium relationship that predicts that currency movements are tied to differences in inflation rates across countries.

EQUATION 15.4

Purchasing power parity is an extension of the law of one price. Purchasing power parity says that if the law of one price holds at all times, then differences in expected inflation between two countries are associated with expected changes in currency values. Mathematically, we can express this idea as follows:

$$\frac{E(S^{foreign/domestic})}{S^{foreign/domestic}} = \frac{1 + E(i_{for})}{1 + E(i_{dom})}$$

where, as before, the expected spot rate is $E(S)$, the current spot rate is S, the expected rate of inflation in the foreign country is $E(i_{for})$ and the expected rate of inflation in the domestic country is $E(i_{dom})$. Notice that the left-hand side of this equation exceeds 1.0 if traders expect the domestic currency to appreciate, and it is less than 1.0 if traders expect the foreign currency to appreciate. Likewise, the right-hand side of the equation exceeds 1.0 when expected inflation is higher abroad than it is at home, and the ratio falls below 1.0 when the opposite is true. Therefore, the equation produces the already familiar prediction that if inflation is higher in one country than another, then the currency of the country with higher inflation will depreciate. The equation advises traders who want to forecast currency movements to invest resources in forecasting inflation rates.

How accurately does purchasing power parity predict exchange rate movements? As we have already seen, over the long term there is a strong relationship between currency values and inflation rates. Countries with high inflation see their currencies depreciate over time, whereas the opposite happens for countries with lower inflation. This is no accident. If we did not observe this pattern in the data it would signal gross violations of the law of one price and indicate that arbitrage was not working to bring prices back into line.

But purchasing power parity does not fare as well in the short run. Violations of the law of one price do occur frequently, and many studies suggest that they persist from three to four years on average. Again, arbitrage, or in this case, limits to arbitrage, explain why. When goods prices in different countries are out of equilibrium, arbitrageurs must trade the goods, moving them across national borders, to earn a profit. This process cannot occur without investments in time and money, and for certain goods, trade may be impossible due to legal restrictions or the physical impediments to transporting goods. Accordingly, there is no reason to expect goods to flow from one market to the other instantaneously at any moment when the law of one price does not hold. Only if price discrepancies across markets are large enough and persistent enough will arbitrageurs find it profitable to trade. Hence, purchasing power parity does a good job of explaining long-run movements in currencies, but not day-to-day, or even year-to-year, fluctuations.

Interest rate parity

Although it is both time-consuming and expensive to move goods across borders, the same cannot generally be said about purely financial transactions. Large institutional investors can buy and sell currencies very rapidly and at low cost, and they can buy and sell financial assets denominated in different currencies just as quickly. Interest rate parity applies the law of one price to financial assets, specifically to risk-free assets denominated in different currencies.

To illustrate, assume that a German insurance company has €10 million that it wants to invest for 180 days in a risk-free government bill. The current annual interest rate on six-month German government stock is 2 per cent per year (1 per cent for six months), so if the institution chooses this investment, it will have €10.1 million six months later:

$$10000000 \left(1 + {}^{r_g}/_2\right) = 10000000 \left(1 + {}^{0.02}/_2\right) = 10100000$$

Alternatively, the institution might choose to convert its €10 million into another currency and invest abroad. However, even if it invests in a risk-free government bill issued by a foreign government, the institution must enter into a forward contract to convert back into dollars when the investment matures. Otherwise, the return on the foreign investment is not risk-free and will depend on changes in currency values over the next six months.

For example, suppose that the annual interest rate on a six-month British government bill is 5.26 per cent per year (2.63 per cent for six months). Suppose also that the spot and six-month forward exchange rates are £0.5639/€ and £0.5730/€, respectively. The German company converts €10 million into £5 639 000 at the spot rate. It invests the pounds for six months at the UK interest rate and enters into a forward contract to convert those pounds back into dollars when the UK bill matures. At the end of six months, the institution has the following:

$$10000000 \; S^{£/€} \left(1 + {}^{r_{uk}}/_2\right) \left(\frac{1}{F^{£/€}}\right)$$

$$= 10000000(0.5639)(1 + 0.0526/2)\left(\frac{1}{0.5730}\right) = 10100010$$

Source: Adapted from 'Carry on Speculating', *The Economist*, 22 February 2007.

interest rate parity
An equilibrium relationship that predicts that differences in risk-free interest rates in two countries must be tied to differences in currency values on the spot and forward markets.

There is a €10 difference between the return that our investor earns in Germany and the return earned in the UK. This is really nothing more than a rounding error because we do not carry exchange rates past the fourth decimal place. Also, note that we first multiply the €10 000 000 times the spot exchange rate to determine the quantity of pounds available for investing. Next, we increase this amount by multiplying times one plus the UK interest rate. Finally, we have to divide the total by the forward rate to convert the currency back into euros. Given the prevailing interest rates and given current spot and forward exchange rates, investors are more or less indifferent to whether they invest in the United States or the United Kingdom. In other words, with respect to short-term, risk-free financial assets, the law of one price holds. This relationship is called **interest rate parity**, which simply means that risk-free investments should offer the same return (after converting currencies) everywhere. As usual, we can express interest rate parity in mathematical terms. Letting R_{for} and R_{dom} represent the risk-free rate on foreign and domestic government debt, we obtain the following equation:[2]

EQUATION 15.5

$$\frac{F^{foreign/domestic}}{S^{foreign/domestic}} = \frac{1 + r_{foreign}}{1 + r_{domestic}}$$

What is the intuitive interpretation of this expression? Observe that if the left-hand side of the equation is greater than 1.0, the domestic currency trades at a forward premium. If domestic investors send money abroad, when they convert back to domestic currency they will realize an exchange loss because the foreign currency buys less domestic currency than it did at the spot rate. Domestic investors know this, so they require an incentive in the form of a higher foreign interest rate before they will send money abroad. To maintain equilibrium, the right-hand side must also be greater than 1.0, which means that the foreign interest rate must exceed the domestic rate. The bottom line is that when a nation's currency trades at a forward premium (discount), risk-free interest rates in that country should be lower (higher) than they are abroad.

As is the case with purchasing power parity, deviations from interest rate parity create arbitrage opportunities. However, these arbitrage opportunities involve buying and selling financial assets rather than physical commodities. Naturally, trade in securities can occur rapidly and much less expensively than trade in goods, so the forces of arbitrage are more powerful in maintaining interest rate parity.

Real World

In late 2006 and early 2007 much concern was expressed about the stability of the world 'carry trade'. That is the term given to the selling of currencies with low interest rates and the purchase of currencies with high rates. Yen weakness is often cited as a consequence of this trade. The carry trade emerges from the interest rate parity we have discussed. Countries with high interest rates should be compensating investors for the risk that their currency will depreciate, but in the real world, uncovered interest parity tends not to apply. Research from the London Business School suggests that this is a consequence of behavioural factors: if investors engage in momentum trading, then if they sell yen and buy dollars, they drive the former down and the latter up. The findings are that the more volatile the markets the weaker the carry trade relationships.

---

[2] Be careful to match the term of the forward rate to the term of the interest rate in this expression. For example, if you are comparing interest rates on 180-day government bills, you must use a 180-day forward rate.

Applying the Model

Suppose that the six-month, risk-free rate in the United States is 2 per cent, and in Canada it is 6 per cent. The spot exchange rate is C$1.5855/$, and the 180-day forward rate is C$1.5937/$. Interest rate parity does not hold, as shown in the following equation:

$$\frac{C\$1.5973/\$}{C\$1.5855} < \frac{1 + 0.06/2}{1 + 0.02/2}$$

Because the right-hand side of this equation is 'too large' relative to parity, the interest rate in Canada is 'too high' or the rate in the United States is 'too low'. The arbitrage opportunity is as follows. An investor borrows money (say $1 million) at 2 per cent in the United States, then converts the proceeds into Canadian dollars, and invests them at 6 per cent. Six months later, the investor converts the Canadian dollars back into US currency to repay the loan. Anything left over is pure arbitrage profit.

Borrow $1 million in the US at 2 per cent for six months → must repay $1 010 000

$1 million → converted at spot rate → C$1 585 500

C$1 585 500 invested for six months at 6 per cent → (C$1 585 500)(1.03) → C$1 633 065

C$1 633 065 converted to US$ at the forward rate → $1 024 700

$1 010 000 needed to repay US loan → leaves $14 700 arbitrage profit

The effect of all these transactions, repeated again and again, is to push exchange rates and interest rates back towards parity. As investors borrow in the United States, the US interest rate will rise from 2 per cent to a higher level. Similarly, as investors purchase Canadian government bonds, the bond prices will rise and the risk-free rate in Canada will fall. When investors sell US dollars to buy Canadian dollars on the spot market, the spot rate (in terms of Canadian dollars per US dollar) will rise, and just the opposite happens on the forward market as investors sell Canadian dollars to buy US dollars. In terms of the interest rate parity equation, we can see how these forces drive markets to equilibrium:

$$increasing \Rightarrow \frac{C\$1.5973/\$\uparrow}{C\$1.5855 \downarrow} < \frac{1 + 0.06/2}{1 + 0.02/2} \Leftarrow decreasing$$
$$\downarrow$$

When this inequality becomes an equality equilibrium is restored.

The process illustrated in the preceding example is known as **covered interest arbitrage** because traders attempt to earn arbitrage profits arising from differences in interest rates across countries, and they 'cover' their currency exposures with forward contracts. Implicit in this example was the assumption that investors could borrow and lend at the risk-free rate in each country. Not all investors can do this, but large, creditworthy institutions can get very close to this ideal. Moreover, they can execute the trades described in the example at very high speed and at low cost. In the real world, deviations from interest rate parity are small and transitory.

SMART CONCEPTS

See the concept explained step-by-step at **www.cengage.co.uk/megginson**

covered interest arbitrage
A trading strategy designed to exploit deviations from interest rate parity to earn an arbitrage profit.

Real interest rate parity (the Fisher effect)

If nominal rates of return on risk-free investments are equalized around the world, after adjusting for currency translation, perhaps real rates of return are also equalized. **Real interest rate parity** means that investors should earn the same real rate of return on risk-free investments no matter the country in which they choose to invest. Recall from Chapter 5 that the real rate of interest is defined as follows:

real interest rate parity
An equilibrium relationship that predicts that the real interest rate will be the same in every country.

$$1 + \text{Real} = \frac{1 + r}{1 + E(i)}$$

If market forces equalize real rates across national borders, then the ratio on the right-hand side should be the same in every country. Continuing to use the notation for foreign and domestic nominal interest rates and expected inflation rates, we can write the following equation:

$$\frac{1 + r_{foreign}}{1 + E(i_{foreign})} = \frac{1 + r_{domestic}}{1 + E(i_{domestic})}$$

Then by cross multiplying we obtain

EQUATION 15.6

$$\frac{1 + r_{foreign}}{1 + r_{domestic}} = \frac{1 + E(i_{foreign})}{1 + E(i_{domestic})}$$

This equation says that if real rates are the same in the domestic and the foreign country, then the ratio of (1 plus) nominal interest rates in the two countries must equal the ratio of (1 plus) expected inflation rates. If expected inflation is higher in one country than in another, then the country with higher inflation must offer higher interest rates to give investors the same real return.

Applying the Model

Suppose that expected inflation in Germany equals zero and expected inflation in Denmark is 12 per cent. Suppose also that the one-year, risk-free rate in the Germany is 3 per cent. What would the one-year, risk-free rate have to be in Denmark to maintain real interest rate parity?

$$\frac{1 + r_{denmark}}{1 + 0.03} = \frac{1 + 0.12}{1 + 0.00}; \ r_{denmark} = 0.1536$$

As with purchasing power parity, real interest rate parity need not hold at all times, because when deviations from parity occur, limits to arbitrage prevent market forces from quickly reaching a new equilibrium. In the long run, we expect that real interest rate parity will hold, at least approximately, but that will not necessarily be the case in the short run.

We conclude this section with a quick review of the four parity relationships, highlighting how they are linked together. If we combine Equations 15.2, 15.4, 15.5 and 15.6, we have the following relationships:[3]

EQUATION 15.7

$$\frac{E(S)}{S} = \frac{F}{S} = \frac{1 + r_{foreign}}{1 + r_{domestic}} = \frac{1 + E(i_{foreign})}{1 + E(i_{domestic})} = \frac{E(S)}{S}$$

Real interest rate parity, forward–spot parity, purchasing power parity and interest rate parity are all interlinked.

---

[3] Notice that to create this equation we divided Equation 15.2 by S, the spot rate. This does no harm to the equality, and it allows us to highlight the connection between the four parity relationships.

The first equality simply restates the forward–spot parity relationship. The second equality is the expression for interest rate parity, and the third and fourth equalities define real interest rate parity and purchasing power parity, respectively. Here we see for the first time that if markets are in equilibrium, spot and forward exchange rates, nominal interest rates and expected inflation rates are all linked internationally. If we want to understand why currency values change, Equation 15.7 gives us a number of clues. The equation also illustrates how difficult it can be for countries to manage their exchange rates. Attempts to push the exchange rate in a particular direction invariably lead to changes in other macroeconomic variables that policy makers may not desire.[4]

---

5 Explain the logic behind each of the four parity relationships.

6 Explain the role of arbitrage in maintaining the parity relationships.

7 In what sense is interest rate parity an application of the law of one price?

8 An investor who notices that interest rates are much lower in Japan than in the United States borrows in Japan and invests the proceeds in the United States. This is called uncovered interest arbitrage, but is it really arbitrage? Why or why not?

CONCEPT
REVIEW
QUESTIONS

15.3 LONG-TERM INVESTMENT DECISIONS

In earlier chapters we emphasized the importance of sound capital budgeting practices for a corporation's long-term survival. The same lessons covered in those chapters apply to multinational corporations. Whether investing at home or abroad, MNCs should evaluate investments based on their incremental cash flows and should discount those cash flows at a rate that is appropriate given the risk of the investment. However, when a company makes investments denominated in many different currencies, this process becomes a bit more complicated. First, in what currency should the firm express a foreign project's cash flows? Secondly, how does one calculate the cost of capital for an MNC, or for a given project?

SMART IDEAS VIDEO

Ike Mathur, University of Southern Illinois at Carbondale
'What I find very interesting is that for a long time in international finance we have talked about the first mover advantage.'

See the entire interview at **www.cengage.co.uk/megginson**

Capital budgeting

Suppose that a US firm is weighing an investment that will generate cash flows in euros. The company's financial analysts have estimated the project's cash flows in euros as follows:

INITIAL COST	YEAR 1	YEAR 2	YEAR 3
−€2 million	€900 000	€850 000	€800 000

---

[4] In October 1997, market pressure was building for a devaluation of the Hong Kong dollar. Hong Kong's currency board reacted by purchasing vast amounts of Hong Kong currency. One consequence of their activity was that overnight interest rates in Hong Kong briefly reached 280 per cent. A year later a similar spike in short-term interest rates occurred in Russia as the government there unsuccessfully tried to prevent a sharp drop in the value of the rouble.

To calculate the project's NPV, the US firm can take either of two approaches. First, it can discount euro-denominated cash flows using a euro-based cost of capital. Having done this, the firm can then convert the resulting NPV back to dollars at the spot rate. For example, assume that the risk-free rate in Europe is 5 per cent, and the firm estimates that the cost of capital (expressed as a euro rate) for this project is 10 per cent (in other words, there is a 5 per cent risk premium associated with the investment). The NPV, rounded to the nearest thousand euros, equals €122 000:

$$NPV = -2000000 + \frac{900000}{1.1^1} + \frac{850000}{1.1^2} + \frac{800000}{1.1^3} = 121713$$

Assume that the current spot rate equals $0.95/€. Multiplying the spot rate times the NPV yields a dollar-based NPV of $116 000 (rounded to the nearest thousand dollars).

In this example, we did not make specific year-by-year forecasts of the future spot rates. Doing so is unnecessary because the firm can choose to hedge its currency exposure through a forward contract. Hedging the currency exposure allows the firm to separate the decision to accept or reject the project from projections of where the dollar-to-euro exchange rate might be headed. Of course, the firm may have a view on the exchange rate question, but even so, it is wise to first consider the investment on its own merits. For instance, suppose that this project has a negative NPV, but managers believe that the euro will appreciate over the life of the project, increasing the project's appeal in dollar terms. Given that belief, there is no need for the firm to undertake the project. Instead, it could purchase euros directly, invest them in safe financial assets in Europe, and convert back to dollars several years later. That is, if the firm wants to speculate on currency movements, it need not invest in physical assets to accomplish that objective.

A second approach for evaluating the investment project is to calculate the NPV in dollar terms, assuming that the firm hedges the project's cash flows using forward contracts. To begin this calculation, we must know the risk-free rate in the United States. Suppose that this rate is 3 per cent. Recognizing that interest rate parity must hold, we can calculate the one-year forward rate:

$$\frac{F^{foreign/domestic}}{S^{foreign/domestic}} = \frac{1 + r_{foreign}}{1 + r_{domestic}}$$

$$\frac{F^{foreign/domestic}}{0.95} = \frac{1.03}{1.05} \Rightarrow F = \$0.9319/€$$

Similarly, we can calculate the two-year and three-year forward rates as follows:

$$\frac{F^{foreign/domestic}}{0.95} = \frac{1.03^2}{1.05^2} \Rightarrow F = \$0.9142/€$$

$$\frac{F^{foreign/domestic}}{0.95} = \frac{1.03^3}{1.05^3} \Rightarrow F = \$0.8967/€$$

Next, multiply each period's cash flow in euros times the matching spot or forward exchange rate to obtain a sequence of cash flows in dollars (rounded to the nearest thousand dollars):

CURRENCY	INITIAL INVESTMENT	YEAR 1	YEAR 2	YEAR 3
€	2 000 000 × 0.95	900 000 × 0.9319	850 000 × 0.9142	800 000 × 0.8967
$	1 900 000	839 000	777 000	717 000

All that remains is to discount this project's cash flows at an appropriate risk-adjusted US interest rate. But how do we determine that rate? Recall that the European discount rate used to calculate the euro-denominated NPV was 10 per cent, 5 per cent above the European risk-free rate. Intuitively, we might expect that the comparable US rate is 8 per cent, representing a 5 per cent risk premium over the current risk-free rate in the United States. That intuition is more or less correct. To be precise, use the following formula to solve for the project's required return in US dollar terms:

$$(1 + r) = (1 + 0.10)\left(\frac{1.03}{1.05}\right); r = 0.079$$

This equation takes the project's required return in euro terms, 10 per cent, and rescales it to dollar terms by multiplying by the ratio of risk-free interest rates in each country. We can verify that discounting the dollar-denominated cash flows using this rate results in the same NPV (again, rounding to the nearest thousand dollars) that we obtained by discounting the cash flows in euros and converting to dollars at the spot rate.

These calculations demonstrate that a company does not have to 'take a view' on currency movements when it invests abroad. Whether the company hedges a project's cash flows using forward contracts, or whether it calculates a project's NPV in local currency before converting to the home currency at the spot exchange rate, future exchange rate movements need not cloud the capital budgeting decision.

Cost of capital

In the preceding example, we assumed that the project's cost of capital in Europe was 10 per cent, which translated into a dollar-based discount rate of 7.9 per cent. But where did the 10 per cent come from? We return to the lessons of Chapter 10, namely that the discount rate should reflect the project's risk. One way to assess that risk is to calculate a beta for the investment. However, calculating the beta for an international project raises some questions for which finance as yet has no definitive answers.

For example, we know that there are major biases in the holdings of portfolios. In particular, there is home bias, where investors hold disproportionately more securities from their home country than would be strictly optimal. Thus shareholders of a UK firm investing in Europe hold mostly UK securities in their portfolios. Perhaps the costs of diversifying internationally are prohibitively expensive for many investors. In that case, when a firm diversifies internationally, it creates value for its shareholders. That stands in sharp contrast to the case when a firm diversifies domestically. Because UK investors can diversify their domestic investments at very low cost, they may not realize any benefit if a firm diversifies on their behalf.

If a firm's shareholders cannot diversify internationally, when the firm invests abroad, it should calculate a project's beta by measuring the movement of similar European investments in relation to the UK market, not the European market. The reason is that from the perspective of UK investors, the project's systematic risk depends on its relationship with the other assets that US investors already own. Therefore a US firm planning to build an electronics manufacturing facility in Germany might compare the returns of existing German electronics firms with returns on a US stock index to estimate a project beta.

In contrast, if the firm's shareholders do hold internationally diversified portfolios, the firm should calculate the project's beta by comparing the relationship between its returns (or returns on similar investments) with returns on a worldwide stock index. This generates the project's 'global beta'. Next, to estimate the project's required return, the firm should apply the CAPM, multiplying the global market risk premium times the project's beta, and adding the risk-free rate. In all likelihood, because a globally diversified portfolio is less volatile than a portfolio containing only domestic securities, the risk premium on the global market will be less than the domestic risk premium.

Source: Adapted from 'Vodafone Chief Dials "I" for India and Hears the Sweet Tones of Victory', *Financial Times*, 13 February 2007.

Real World

Vodafone, the telecoms giant, is also a very acquisitive company. In 2007 it purchased an Indian telecoms company, Hutchinson Essar. Commentators on the purchase noted that one of the key elements that would determine its success was that Vodafone was basing its calculations on the local, Indian cost of capital, or 11–12 per cent. Contrast that with the company's overall costs of capital of around 8 per cent and you see the difference between global and local costs.

Applying the Model

A Japanese car manufacturer decides to build a plant to make cars for the North American market. The firm estimates two project betas. The first calculation takes returns on US car stocks and calculates their betas relative to those on the Nikkei stock index. Based on these calculations, the Japanese firm decides to apply a beta of 1.1 to the investment. The risk-free rate of interest in Japan is 2 per cent, and the market risk premium on the Nikkei index is 8 per cent, so the project's required return is calculated as:

$$R = 2\% + 1.1(8\%) = 10.8\%$$

The second calculation takes the returns on US car manufacturers and determines their betas relative to those on a world stock index. It turns out that US car stocks are more sensitive to movements in the world market than they are to the Nikkei. This leads to a higher estimate of the project beta, say 1.3. However, offsetting this effect is the fact that the risk premium on the world market portfolio is just 5 per cent. Therefore, the second estimate of the project's required return is calculated as:

$$R = 2\% + 1.3(5\%) = 8.5\%$$

CONCEPT
REVIEW
QUESTIONS

9 Why does discounting the cash flows of a foreign investment using the foreign cost of capital, then converting that to the home currency at the spot rate, yield the same NPV as converting the project's cash flows to domestic currency at the forward rate and then discounting them at the domestic cost of capital?

10 Why is it not surprising to find that the risk premium on the world market portfolio is lower than the domestic risk premium?

15.4 SUMMARY AND CONCLUSIONS

- Though the major currencies of the world float freely against each other, many countries have adopted exchange rate policies that fix the value of their currency relative to the currencies of other nations.

- A currency appreciates when it buys more of another currency over time. A currency depreciates when it buys less of another currency over time.

- The spot exchange rate applies to immediate currency transactions, whereas the forward exchange rate applies to trades that take place at some future time.

- The foreign exchange market is the world's largest financial market and attracts many types of participants, including exporters and importers, investors, hedgers, speculators, governments and dealers.

- The four parity relationships in international finance spell out how spot and forward exchange rates are linked to inflation and interest rates in different countries.

- When a firm analyzes a capital investment in a foreign currency, it can either discount the foreign currency cash flows using a foreign cost of capital, or it can calculate the domestic currency equivalent of those cash flows using forward rates and discount them at the domestic cost of capital.

INTERNET RESOURCES

For updates to links in this section and elsewhere in the book, please go to the book's website at www.cengage.co.uk/megginson.

http://www.bis.org
This is the Bank for International Settlements' website. It offers a wide range of information related to the banking industry as well as interest data on international financial markets.

http://www.economist.com
Click on the 'Markets and Data' link and then launch the foreign exchange map. The map provides a wealth of information such as the name of each nation's currency and (using colour codes) how the value of each currency has changed relative to a base currency (which you can choose).

http://www.euribor.org
This site provides data on the Euribor (Euro Interbank Offered Rate), a rate on loans between prime banks within the European Monetary Union.

http://www.euroland.com
This site provides data on eleven different European stock exchanges.

http://www.oanda.com
This site offers an enormous amount of information on the foreign exchange markets.

http://www.securities.com
The site for ISI Emerging Markets specializes in providing data on emerging markets around the world.

http://www.x-rates.com
At this site you can create charts and graphs showing historical data on most of the world's major currencies.

www.economist.com/markets/Bigmac/Index.cfm
This gives the Economist Big Mac PPP index, a fun, widely quoted, if limited measure of relative exchange rate value.

http://www.imf.org/external/pubs/ft/staffp/2002/00–00/pdf/lane.pdf
A paper that examines the extent and nature of international financial integration.

KEY TERMS

appreciate	floating exchange rate	managed floating rate system
covered interest arbitrage	forward discount	multinational corporations (MNCs)
cross exchange rate	forward exchange rate	
currency board arrangement	forward premium	purchasing power parity
depreciate	forward–spot parity	real interest rate parity
direct quote	indirect quote	spot exchange rate
exchange rate	interest rate parity	triangular arbitrage
fixed exchange rate	law of one price	

SELF-TEST PROBLEMS

ST15-1 Use Table 15.1 to determine the cross exchange rate between the British pound and the Japanese yen.

ST15-2 Suppose the spot exchange rate equals ¥100/$, and the six-month forward rate equals ¥101/$. An investor can purchase a US T-bill that matures in six months and earns an annual rate of return of 3 per cent. What would be the annual return on a similar Japanese investment?

QUESTIONS

Q15-1 Define a multinational corporation (MNC). What additional factors must be considered by the manager of an MNC that a manager of a purely domestic firm is not forced to face?

Q15-2 Who are the major players in foreign currency markets, and what are their motivations for trading?

Q15-3 Suppose that an exchange rate is quoted in terms of euros per pound. In what direction would this rate move if the euro appreciated against the pound?

Q15-4 Explain how triangular arbitrage ensures that currency values are essentially the same in different markets around the world at any given moment.

Q15-5 In what sense is it a misnomer to refer to a currency as weak or strong? Who benefits and who loses if the yen appreciates against the pound?

Q15-6 What does a spot exchange rate have in common with a forward rate, and how are they different?

Q15-7 What does it mean to say that a currency trades at a forward premium?

Q15-8 Explain how the law of one price establishes a relationship between changes in currency values and inflation rates.

Q15-9 Why does purchasing power parity appear to hold in the long run but not in the short run?

Q15-10 In terms of risk, is a US investor indifferent about whether to buy a US government bond or a UK government bond? Why or why not?

Q15-11 If the euro trades at a forward premium against the yen, explain why interest rates in Japan would have to be higher than they are in Europe.

Q15-12 Suppose that the US Federal Reserve suddenly decides to raise interest rates. Trace out the potential impact that this action might have on (1) interest rates abroad, (2) the spot value of the dollar and (3) the forward value of the dollar.

Q15-13 Interest rates on risk-free bonds in the United States are about 2 per cent, whereas interest rates on Swiss government bonds are 6 per cent. Can we conclude that investors around the world will flock to buy Swiss bonds? Why or why not?

Q15-14 A Japanese investor decides to purchase shares in a company that trades on the London Stock Exchange. The investor's plan is to hold these shares for one year, sell them and convert the proceeds to yen at the year-end. During the year, the pound appreciates against the yen. Does this enhance or diminish the investor's return on the shares?

Q15-15 Suppose that the dollar trades at a forward discount relative to the yen. A US firm must pay a Japanese supplier ¥10 million in three months. A manager in the US firm reasons that because the dollar buys fewer yen on the forward market than it does on the spot market, the firm should not enter a forward hedge to eliminate its exchange rate exposure. Comment on this opinion.

PROBLEMS

Exchange rate fundamentals

P15-1 One month ago, the Mexican peso (Ps)–US dollar exchange rate was Ps 9.0395/$ ($0.1107/Ps). This month, the exchange rate is Ps 9.4805/$ ($0.1055/Ps). State which currency appreciated and which depreciated over the last month, and then calculate both the percentage appreciation of the currency that rose in value and the percentage depreciation of the currency that declined in value.

P15-2 Using the data presented in Table 15.1, calculate the spot exchange rate between Canadian dollars and British pounds (in pounds per Canadian dollar).

P15-3 Using the data presented in Table 15.1, specify whether the following currencies sell at a discount or a premium (against the euro): the Japanese yen, the Swiss franc and the Brazilian real.

P15-4 Go to http://www.economist.com. Under the 'Markets & Data' section, activate the foreign exchange map. On the menu at the far left, choose the US dollar as the base currency.

a Click on the '1-month' selection to show the appreciation or depreciation of the world's currencies relative to the dollar. Does the dollar appear to be appreciating or depreciating against most of the world's currencies, or is the answer mixed?

b Next, choose the '1-year' option, and identify two or three countries whose currencies have depreciated the most against the US dollar and two or three whose currencies have appreciated the most. Search the web to try to find out those countries' most recent inflation figures. What lesson does this reveal?

P15-5 Recently, a financial newspaper reported the following spot and forward rates for the Japanese yen (¥).

SMART EXCEL

See this problem explained in *Excel* at www.cengage.co.uk/megginson

Spot:
$0.007556/¥ (¥132.34/$)

| 1-month: | $0.007568/¥ (¥132.14/$) |
| 3-month: | $0.007593/¥ (¥131.71/$) |

Supply the forward yen premium or discount (specify which it is) for both the one- and three-month quotes as an annual percentage rate.

P15-6 You are quoted the following series of exchange rates for the US dollar ($), the Canadian dollar (C$) and the British pound (£):

SMART SOLUTIONS

See the problem and solution explained step-by-step at www.cengage.co.uk/megginson

$0.6000/C$	C$1.6667/$
$1.2500/£	£0.8000/$
C$2.5000/£	£0.4000/C$

Assuming that you have $1 million in cash, how can you take advantage of this series of exchange rates? Show the series of trades that would yield an arbitrage profit, and calculate how much profit you would make.

The parity conditions in international finance

SMART EXCEL

See this problem explained in *Excel* at www.cengage.co.uk/ megginson

P15-7 Use the data presented in Table 15.1 to answer this problem. A particular commodity sells for $5000 in the United States and ¥600 000 in Japan.

a Does the law of one price hold? If not, explain how to profit through arbitrage.

b If it costs ¥60 000 to transport the commodity from the United States to Japan, is there still an arbitrage opportunity? At what exchange rate (in yen per dollar) would buying the commodity in the United States and shipping it to sell in Japan become profitable?

c Given shipping costs of ¥60 000, at what exchange rate would it be profitable to buy the commodity in Japan and ship it to the United States to sell? Comment on the general lesson from parts (a)–(c).

d Taking the commodity prices in the United States and Japan as given, at what exchange rate (in terms of yen per dollar) would the law of one price hold ignoring shipping costs?

P15-8 If the expected rate of inflation in the United States is 1 per cent, the one-year risk-free interest rate is 2 per cent, and the one-year risk-free rate in the UK is 4 per cent, what is the expected inflation rate in the UK?

P15-9 Go to http://www.economist.com. Under the 'Markets & Data' section, find the link for the 'Big Mac Index'. After exploring this part of the site, explain why the Big Mac Index might foreshadow changes in exchange rates. What features of the Big Mac would suggest that Big Macs may not satisfy the law of one price?

P15-10 Shortly after it was introduced, the euro traded just below parity with the dollar, meaning that one dollar purchased more than one euro. This implies

a that US inflation was lower than European inflation

b that US interest rates were lower than European rates

c that the law of one price does not hold

d none of the above.

P15-11 Assume that the following information is known about the current spot exchange rate between the US dollar and the British pound (£), inflation rates in the UK and the USA, and the real rate of interest – which is assumed to be the same in both countries:

Current spot rate, $S = \$1.4500/£$ (£0.6897/$)

US inflation rate, $i_{US} = 1.5$ per cent per year (0.015)

British inflation rate, $i_{UK} = 2.0$ per cent per year (0.020)

Real rate of interest, $real = 2.5$ per cent per year (0.025)

Based on this data, use the parity conditions of international finance to compute the following:

a expected spot rate next year

b US risk-free rate (on a one-year bond)

c British risk-free rate (on a one-year bond)

d one-year forward rate.

Finally, show how you can make an arbitrage profit if you are offered the chance to sell or buy pounds forward (for delivery one year from now) at the current spot rate of $1.4500/£ (£0.6897/$). Assuming that you can borrow $1 million or £689 700 at the risk-free interest rate, what would your profit be on this arbitrage transaction?

Long-term investment decisions

P15-12 A German company manufactures a specialized piece of manufacturing equipment and leases it to a UK enterprise. The lease calls for five end-of-year payments of £1 million. The German firm spent €3.5 million to produce the equipment, which is expected to have no salvage value after five years. The current spot rate is €1.5/£. The risk-free interest rate in Germany is 3 per cent, and in the United Kingdom it is 5 per cent. The German firm reasons that the appropriate (German) discount rate for this investment is 7 per cent. Calculate the NPV of this investment in two ways.

a First, convert all cash flows to pounds, and discount at an appropriate (UK) cost of capital. Convert the resulting NPV to euros at the spot rate.

b Second, calculate forward rates for each year, convert the pound-denominated cash flows into euros using those rates, and discount at the German cost of capital. Verify that the NPV obtained from this approach matches (except perhaps for small rounding errors) that obtained in part (a).

THOMSON ONE Business School Edition

For instructions on using Thomson ONE, refer to the introductory text provided with the Thomson ONE problems at the end of Chapters 1–6, or in *A Guide for Using Thomson ONE – Business School Edition*.

P15-13 How do changes in exchange rates affect the consolidation of financial statements of a multinational corporation? BP plc (ticker: BP) has operations all over the world. Look at BP's sales and operating income from US operations for the past five years.[5] The default currency for all figures is BP's home currency, British pounds. Convert these numbers to US dollars. The bottom of the page gives you the exchange rate at which the numbers have been converted from British pounds to US dollars in each year. Has the US dollar strengthened or weakened over the past five years? Convert US sales and operating income for each of the past five years to British pounds using both the minimum and maximum of the five exchange rates. Which of the two exchange rates gives BP the larger sales and operating income in British pounds in each year? As a multinational corporation, does BP prefer a stronger or a weaker US dollar relative to the British pound?

P15-14 How do changes in exchange rates affect an international investor's returns? Calculate Deutsche Telekom's (ticker: D:DTE) annual share returns using the closing share price in euros at the end of each of the past five fiscal years. Convert the closing stock price to US dollars. You can change currency by clicking on the dollar sign ($) on the right side of the menu at the top and then selecting 'US dollars'. Calculate the annual share returns using US dollar prices. Which years have a higher return in US dollars and which years in euros? As a US investor, do you prefer a strong or a weak US dollar relative to the euro?

MINICASE *International financial management*

Five years after completing your college degree you accept an exciting new job with the multinational firm Rangsit Trading International. This new position will involve a great deal of travel, along with some other challenging responsibilities. Part of your job function is to set company policy to manage exchange rate risk. As such, you decide that you need to become fluent in the following topics.

Assignment

1 First, you decide to review basic exchange rate terminology.

a Describe fixed and floating exchange rate systems. What are some problems with these systems?

b Describe a managed floating rate system.

c Describe a currency board arrangement system.

2 Next, you review the following parity relationships.

a Describe forward–spot parity.

b Describe purchasing power parity.

c Describe interest rate parity.

d Describe real interest rate parity.

e Describe how these four parity relationships link together.

---

[5] Geographic segment data can be found under the Financial tab. Click on 'More', go to Worldscope Reports & Charts, and select 'Geographic Segment Review'.

Chapter 16
Risk Management

Source: 'Ryanair Pays for Delay in Hedging its Fuel Needs', *Financial Times*, 27 September 2006; David A.Carter, Betty Simkins and Daniel A. Rogers (2006) 'Does Hedging Affect Firm Value? Evidence From the US Airline Industry', *Financial Management* 35(2):53–86.

OPENING FOCUS

Flying into the black?

One of the main problems that an airline faces is the unpredictability of fuel prices. This point has been illustrated dramatically in recent years, where the timing of some hedging strategies has been to dramatically reduce the price of fuel while others have been badly mistimed. Take the example of US low-cost carrier Southwest, which hedged its fuel costs at the equivalent of $25 a barrel in 2005. Most other US carriers waited, hoping that oil prices would decline and eventually had to lock in prices at close to or double that which Southwest enjoyed.

Consider the contrast with Ryanair, which has modelled itself on Southwest. After having had strong hedges in place throughout 2005 Ryanair allowed its hedges to run out in 2006. The company had given conflicting views to the market. While the chief financial officer suggested that they would hedge only when oil fell below $60 per barrel, the charismatic chief executive, Michael O'Leary, dismissed this strategy with a suggestion that they expected high fuel prices to continue. This timing issue cost Ryanair dearly, as they were eventually forced to hedge until the end of October at $70 a barrel and were 90 per cent hedged for November and December at $74 a barrel. This timing issue therefore resulted in Ryanair hedging at what became the peak of the oil market in 2006.

Hedging properly is thus important for airlines. Cash spent on fuel cannot be spent on other things such as increased investment. Given that jet fuel costs are hedgeable, airlines with a desire for expansion should find value in hedging future purchases of jet fuel. The results of a recent paper show that airline fuel hedging is indeed positively related to airline firm value. For a variety of airlines, engaging in hedging can result in an increase in firm value of between 12 and 16 per cent.

LEARNING OBJECTIVES

After studying this chapter you should be able to:

- Describe the types of risks that can adversely affect a firm's cash flows and explain why firms might choose to hedge those risks.
- Calculate the price of a forward contract and illustrate how to use such a contract to hedge a risk exposure.
- Explain the differences between forward and futures contracts.
- Describe the basic features of options and swaps and explain how they can be used to hedge risk exposure.

SMART FINANCE

Use the learning tools at www.cengage.co.uk/megginson

Trading in virtually all types of financial instruments has increased over the past two decades, but no markets have experienced growth rates as explosive as those for the financial instruments used for hedging and risk management. Since the collapse of the Bretton Woods fixed exchange rate regime in 1973, corporations have been exposed to extreme fluctuations in interest rates, in exchange rates and in the prices of important raw materials. This increased risk has led to a mushrooming demand for financial instruments and strategies that corporations can use to hedge, or offset, their underlying operating and financial exposures.

This chapter discusses risk management and financial engineering in the modern corporation. Traditionally, **risk management** has meant the process of identifying firm-specific risk exposures and managing those risk exposures. In recent years, however, the risk management function has expanded to include identifying, measuring and managing all types of risk exposures, including interest rate, commodity and currency risk exposures. There are three ways to minimize a firm's risk exposures – diversifying, insuring and hedging; this chapter focuses on hedging. Derivative securities, including forwards, futures, options and swaps, are the financial instruments commonly used for hedging and risk management. Figure 16.1 illustrates the growth in the market for these types of products. Currency and interest rate swaps have experienced especially rapid growth.

Though the financial press often portrays derivatives in a negative light, these securities can be an effective means of hedging risk exposures. We will discuss each of these instruments, but we begin with an overview of risk management. We also describe each of the major types of derivative securities and discuss how each can be used to manage a firm's risk exposures.

risk management
The process of identifying firm-specific risk exposures and managing those exposures by means of insurance products. Also includes identifying, measuring and managing all types of risk exposures.

16.1 OVERVIEW OF RISK MANAGEMENT AND RISK FACTORS

Risk management involves identifying potential events that represent a threat to a firm's cash flows and either minimizing the likelihood of those events or minimizing

FIGURE 16.1

Selected over-the-counter derivatives contracts outstanding (notional amounts), 1998–2006

Source: Bank for International Settlements, *BIS Quarterly Review*, various issues.

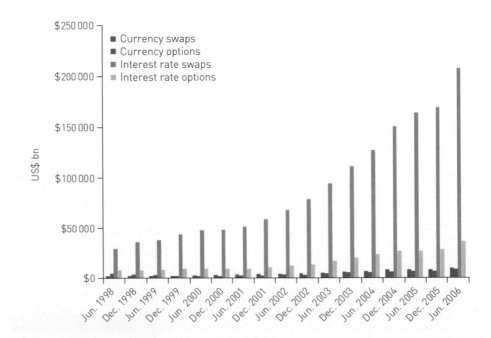

their impact on the firm's cash flows. In the past, this process has focused on firm-specific events such as workers' compensation claims, product recalls, product liability claims, and loss from fire or flood. In recent years, risk management has come to include the process of identifying, measuring and managing market wide sources of exposure. In this section, we provide an overview of this type of risk management.

Transactions risk

Any firm that might experience an adverse change in the value of any of its cash flows as a result of exchange rate movements faces exposure to exchange rate risk. Almost every firm is exposed to exchange rate risk to some degree, even if it operates strictly in one country and has cash flows in only one currency. Such a firm will face exchange rate risk if (1) it produces a good or service that competes with imports in the home market, or (2) it uses as a production input an imported product or service.

Nonetheless, some types of companies face greater exchange rate risk than do others. MNCs obviously face this risk in all aspects of their business, but they also have many opportunities to minimize that risk by, for example, moving production facilities to the countries where their products are sold so that costs and revenues can be in the same currency. The greatest exchange rate exposure occurs when a firm's costs and revenues are largely denominated in different currencies.

As usual, it is easiest to describe the importance of exchange rate risk to an exporter with an example. Assume that Airbus Industries has just sold an airplane to a Japanese airline, with the following details. First, when Airbus sells to Japanese customers it prices its planes in yen. Airbus wants to set the yen price high enough so that the payment it receives converts back into at least €1 million. This allows Airbus to cover costs and earn an acceptable profit. Secondly, assume that the current exchange rate is ¥100.00/€. Airbus therefore negotiates a price of ¥100 million for the airplane. However, the company is primarily concerned with how many euros it will collect when payment is made in yen and then converted into euros on the foreign exchange market.

If Airbus negotiates the terms of this sale at the same time that it receives payment, it does not face any foreign exchange risk. The company will simply exchange ¥100 million for €1 million on the spot market. In reality, Airbus will probably negotiate payment terms months before it expects payment from the Japanese customer. This simple fact creates exchange rate risk, because between the dates when Airbus sets the price in yen for the plane and when it receives payment, the exchange rate can move. Because the contract is denominated in yen, Airbus bears this exchange rate risk, but the risk would not be eliminated by denominating the sales contract in euro – the risk would simply be shifted to the Japanese buyer.

Suppose that after Airbus agrees to a price, it must wait six months for payment. In that time, the exchange rate changes to ¥110.00/€, meaning that the euro has appreciated and the yen has depreciated. Airbus will still receive the same ¥100 million, but now that converts to just €909 091. Appreciation in the euro results in Airbus realizing an exchange rate loss of €90 909. If the yen appreciates, say to ¥90.00/€, Airbus will receive €1 111 111 and will realize an exchange rate gain of €111 111.

This exchange rate risk cannot be eliminated, but it can be hedged (transferred to a third party) using financial contracts. Assume that immediately after Airbus agrees to sell the plane it enters a six-month forward contract to sell yen in exchange for euros. Airbus's forward contract is not with its Japanese customer, but rather with a money-centre bank, such as Citigroup, that serves as a dealer in the foreign exchange market. If the forward rate that Airbus agrees to equals ¥99/€, Airbus promises to deliver ¥100 million in exchange for €1 010 101 exactly six months from now. Once this forward contract is executed, Airbus is no longer exposed to exchange rate risk. The risk has not disappeared; it has simply been transferred from Airbus to Citigroup. But why would Citigroup be willing to assume this risk?

International banks – and, increasingly, other types of financial institutions – are uniquely positioned to bear exchange rate risk because they can create what amounts to a natural hedge, or offsetting risk exposure, as a normal course of their business. Offsetting risk means they are able to easily arrange mirror-image positions with other customers. To see this, consider what type of foreign exchange contract Nintendo might demand from Citigroup. The exchange rate risk problem for Nintendo (one of Japan's biggest exporters) is the opposite of Airbus: Nintendo exports from Japan and sells in the USA, the UK and Europe. The company receives foreign currency as payment, but its costs are in yen, so it would need to *sell currency forward* (locking in a yen price) in order to cover its costs and make an acceptable profit. Citigroup can thus buy euros forward (sell yen) from Nintendo and simultaneously sell euros forward (buy yen) to Airbus, and thus net out the exchange rate exposure on its own books. This is a simplified example because Citigroup may not have a perfectly offsetting exposure, but in that case it would simply execute its own forward contract with another bank – perhaps with Nintendo's main bank.

transactions exposure
The risk that movements in exchange rates will adversely affect the value of a particular transaction.

We have discussed how to measure exchange rate risk as it applies to specific transactions and have briefly discussed one method of dealing with it using a forward market hedge. However, this **transactions exposure** is but one of many types of exchange rate risk.

Source: C&C Annual Report 2005.

Real World

The Irish-based drinks and snacks food company, C&C, reported a profit for the 2005 financial year of €114 million. However, more careful reading indicates that there was also a loss due to unhedged transaction exposure to the Canadian and US dollars of some €6.9 million, equivalent to just over 6 per cent of profits.

Translation and economic risk

MNCs must deal with additional complexities if they have affiliates or subsidiaries on the ground in a foreign country. One such complication arises when MNCs translate costs and revenues denominated in foreign currencies in their financial statements, which, of course, are denominated in the home currency. This type of risk is called **translation exposure or accounting exposure**. In other words, foreign exchange rate fluctuations affect individual accounts in the financial statements. A more important risk element concerns **economic exposure**, which is the overall impact of foreign exchange rate fluctuations on the firm's value. A firm faces economic exposure when exchange rate changes affect its cash flows, even those cash flows not specifically tied to transactions in other currencies. For example, a rise in the value of the dollar against the euro makes European wines less expensive to US consumers, and it makes US wine more expensive for European consumers. A winery operating in the United States, even one that does not sell directly to foreign customers, may realize a decline in cash flows due to competition from suddenly less expensive European vintners.

translation exposure or accounting exposure
The risk that exchange rate movements will adversely impact reported financial results on a firm's financial statements.

economic exposure
The risk that a firm's value will fluctuate due to exchange rate movements.

What can managers do about these risks? Hedging economic exposure is more difficult than hedging transactions exposure, in part because measuring the exposure is more difficult. For instance, a US winery concerned about the declining prices of foreign wines could engage in currency trades that would result in a profit if the dollar appreciates against the euro. In theory, these profits could offset the decline in earnings that occurs when European wines become less expensive, but exactly how large will these losses be for a given change in the exchange rate? Increasingly, MNCs manage their economic exposures both by using sophisticated currency derivatives and by matching costs and revenues in a given currency. For instance, a foreign company exporting to Japan might issue yen-denominated bonds, so-called **Samurai bonds**, to create a yen-based liability that would partially or fully offset the exposure resulting from yen-based receivables. However, it is important to emphasize that unless the cash inflows and outflows match exactly, some residual yen exposure will remain.

Samurai bonds
Yen-denominated bonds issued by non-Japanese corporations.

Political risk

Another important risk facing MNCs is **political risk**, which refers to actions taken by a government that have a negative impact on the value of foreign companies operating in that country, such as raising taxes on a firm's activities or erecting barriers that prevent a firm from repatriating profits back to the home country. In its most extreme form, political risk can mean confiscation of a corporation's assets by a foreign government.

political risk
The risk that a government will take an action that negatively affects the values of firms operating in that country.

Political risk has two basic dimensions: macro and micro. Macro political risk means that *all* foreign firms in the country will be subject to political risk because of political change, revolution or the adoption of new policies by a host government. In other words, no individual country or firm is treated differently. An example of macro political risk occurred when communist regimes came to power in China in 1949 and in Cuba in 1959–1960, or when right-wing governments took over in Chile in 1973. More recently, the near collapse of Indonesia's currency in late 1997 and early 1998, plus the attendant political and economic turmoil elsewhere in Asia, highlights the real and present danger that macro political risk can pose to MNCs and international investors alike. Micro political risk, on the other hand, refers to a foreign government targeting punitive action against an individual firm, a specific industry or companies from a particular foreign country. Examples include the nationalization by a majority of the oil-exporting countries of the assets of the international oil companies in their territories during the 1970s.

Although political risk can take place in any country, the political instability of many developing countries generally makes the positions of multinational companies most vulnerable there. At the same time, some of the countries in this group have the most promising markets for the goods and services being offered by MNCs. The main question, therefore, is how to engage in operations and foreign investment in such countries and yet avoid or minimize the potential political risk.

MNCs may adopt both positive and negative approaches to cope with political risk. Negative approaches include taking a trade dispute with a host country to the World Trade Organization (described later) or threatening to withhold additional investments from a country unless an MNC's demands are met. Firms may also negotiate agreements with host governments that build in costs that the host government must bear if it breaches the terms of the original agreement. Positive approaches for MNCs include working proactively to develop environmental and labour standards in a country, and generally attempting to become perceived as a domestic company by the host country's citizenry.

European monetary union and the rise of regional trading blocks

As a result of the Maastricht Treaty of 1991, 11 of the 15 European Union (EU) nations adopted a single currency, the **euro**, as a continent-wide medium of exchange

euro
The currency used throughout the countries that make up the European Union.

monetary union
An agreement between many European countries to integrate their monetary systems including using a single currency.

beginning 2 January 1999. In early 2002, the national currencies of the 12 (now including Greece) countries participating in **monetary union** were replaced by the euro. Slovenia became the 13th member in 2007. At the same time that the European Union is learning to implement monetary union (which also involved creating a new European Central Bank), it must also deal with a wave of new applicants from Eastern Europe and the Mediterranean region. Whatever its final shape, the new community of Europe will offer both challenges and opportunities to a variety of players, including multinational firms. MNCs, especially those based in the United States, will face heightened levels of competition when operating inside the EU.

COMPARATIVE CORPORATE FINANCE
How risky are different countries?

How much risk do companies face when they decide to do business in a particular country? Twice each year, the magazine *Euromoney* tries to answer this question when it publishes its semi-annual country risk rankings. The rankings, which range from 0 to 100 with higher numbers indicating less risk, evaluate several elements of the risk of investing in each country. The factors that *Euromoney* considers in its rankings include the expected economic growth rate, political risk, various measures related to the country's indebtedness, and measures indicating the access to capital from banks and capital markets in the country. The following table lists some of the results from the September 2006 rankings.

The rankings contain few surprises. The top 10 (safest) countries are primarily European and North American nations. At the bottom of the list are hot spots such as Iraq and Afghanistan, lingering communist regimes in Cuba and North Korea, and troubled African nations like Congo, Liberia, Sudan and Guinea-Bissau.

COUNTRY	SCORE	COUNTRY	SCORE	COUNTRY	SCORE	COUNTRY	SCORE
Luxembourg	99.651	Bermuda	84.127	Slovak Republic	65.407	Antigua & Barbuda	51.100
Norway	98.160	Portugal	82.886	Lithuania	63.658	Egypt	50.777
Switzerland	98.060	Slovenia	80.907	Barbados	63.027	Turkey	50.438
Denmark	95.192	Hong Kong	80.557	Oman	62.990	Costa Rica	50.345
United States	94.441	Greece	80.551	Mexico	62.649	Panama	49.845
Sweden	93.937	Taiwan	79.362	Malaysia	62.624	Macau	49.346
Finland	93.408	Malta	77.969	Latvia	62.395	El Salvador	48.402
Ireland	92.720	UAE	76.763	Botswana	62.338	Colombia	47.595
Netherlands	92.645	Qatar	75.321	Trinidad & Tobago	61.361	Peru	46.248
Austria	92.511	Cyprus	74.747	Croatia	60.049	Jordan	45.697
United Kingdom	92.236	Kuwait	74.118	South Africa	59.892	Algeria	45.518
Canada	91.685	Bahamas	72.607	China	59.890	Ukraine	44.912
Belgium	90.876	Hungary	69.320	Thailand	56.840	Fiji	44.842
Germany	90.718	Bahrain	69.239	Bulgaria	56.809	Vietnam	44.836
France	90.376	Czech Republic	68.923	Russia	56.497	Philippines	44.239
Australia	90.114	South Korea	68.783	India	55.992	Macedonia	43.822
Iceland	89.454	Estonia	68.315	Kazakhstan	55.723	Guatemala	43.407
Japan	89.056	Israel	68.167	Tunisia	55.421	Uruguay	43.307
Singapore	88.105	Saudi Arabia	68.012	Mauritius	54.611	Indonesia	43.212
Spain	88.087	Brunei	67.176	Romania	54.521	St Lucia	42.578
New Zealand	87.116	Chile	66.257	Morocco	52.454	Seychelles	42.530
Italy	85.153	Poland	65.984	Brazil	51.583	Azerbaijan	41.662

COUNTRY	SCORE	COUNTRY	SCORE	COUNTRY	SCORE	COUNTRY	SCORE
Iran	41.135	Honduras	36.970	Georgia	32.577	Sudan	27.031
Ghana	40.965	Lesotho	36.942	Niger	32.369	Gambia	27.015
St Vincent &		Nigeria	36.614	Moldova	32.367	Tajikistan	26.980
Grenadines	40.612	Tanzania	36.560	Uzbekistan	32.367	Malawi	26.799
Sri Lanka	40.326	Dominican Republic	36.444	Burkina Faso	31.930	Eritrea	26.538
Serbia	40.129	Uganda	36.411	Cambodia	31.891	Guinea	26.109
Jamaica	40.053	Armenia	36.284	Nepal	31.576	Haiti	25.419
Cape Verde	39.952	Albania	36.096	Belarus	31.568	Principe	25.313
Grenada	39.920	Yemen	35.850	Ethiopia	31.176	Libya	24.873
Pakistan	39.464	Dominica	35.680	Namibia	31.047	Burundi	22.655
Venezuela	39.387	Bolivia	35.511	Laos	30.389	Solomon Islands	22.077
Senegal	39.361	Bangladesh	35.463	Zambia	30.379	Guinea-Bissau	21.241
Argentina	39.237	Benin	35.403	Nicaragua	29.986	Zimbabwe	19.900
Maldives	39.207	Mongolia	35.251	Mauritania	29.093	Micronesia	19.279
Swaziland	38.790	Eq. Guinea	34.948	Angola	28.841	Congo	17.828
Samoa	38.765	Bhutan	34.617	Sierra Leone	28.611	Liberia	17.581
Tonga	38.599	Ecuador	34.485	Gabon	28.579	DR Congo	16.409
Bosnia-Herzegovina	38.451	Syria	34.395	Chad	28.577	Marshall Islands	12.097
Lebanon	38.065	Cameroon	34.343	Suriname	28.544	Cuba	11.749
N. Caledonia	37.859	Mail	34.268	Myanmar	28.441	Somalia	11.108
Turkmenistan	37.843	Madagascar	34.259	Rwanda	28.440	Iraq	5.172
Mozambique	37.525	Kenya	34.148	Togo	28.364	Afghanistan	4.235
Vanuatu	37.406	Belize	34.071	Kyrgyzstan	27.305	N. Korea	3.655
Papua New Guinea	37.288	Guyana	32.975	Ivory Coast	27.299		
Paraguay	37.268	Djibouti	32.872	C.A.R	27.259		

Source: Euromoney Magazine

Another major trading block that arose during the 1990s is the Mercosur group of countries in South America. Beginning in 1991, the nations of Brazil, Argentina, Paraguay and Uruguay began removing tariffs and other barriers to intraregional trade. The second stage of Mercosur's development began at the end of 1994 and involved the development of a customs union to impose a common tariff on external trade while enforcing uniform and lower tariffs on intragroup trade. To date, Mercosur has been even more successful than its founders had imagined, though the economic collapse of Argentina in early 2002 has obviously placed Mercosur's near-term viability at risk. The long-term importance of Mercosur will likely depend on whether the US Congress overcomes its reluctance to extend the North American Free Trade Agreement (NAFTA) throughout Latin America. In any case, the Mercosur countries represent well over half of total Latin American GDP, and thus will loom large in the plans of any MNC wishing to access the growth markets of this region.

Although it may seem that the world is splitting into a handful of trading blocs, this is less dangerous than it may appear because many international treaties are in force that guarantee relatively open access to at least the largest economies. The most important such treaty is the **General Agreement on Tariffs and Trade (GATT)**, which celebrates its 60th anniversary in May 2008. The current agreement extends free trading rules to broad areas of economic activity – such as agriculture, financial services and intellectual property rights – that had not previously been covered by international treaty and that were thus effectively off-limits to foreign competition. The 1994 revised GATT treaty also established a new international body, the **World Trade Organization (WTO)**, to police world trading practices and to mediate disputes between member countries. The WTO began operating in January 1995, and one extremely important nation, the People's Republic of China, became a member in 2002.

General Agreement on Tariffs and Trade (GATT)
A trade treaty that extends free trade principles to broad areas of economic activity in many countries.

World Trade Organization (WTO)
An organization established by GATT to police world trading practices and to settle disputes between GATT member countries.

CONCEPT REVIEW QUESTIONS

1　Distinguish between transactions, translation and economic exposure.

2　Describe how a domestic firm might use a forward contract to hedge an economic exposure. Why does uncertainty about the magnitude of the exposure make this difficult?

3　Consider a US firm that has for many years exported to European countries. How does the creation of the euro simplify or complicate the management of transactions exposure for this firm?

interest rate risk
The risk that changes in market interest rates will cause fluctuations in a bond's price. Also, the risk of suffering losses as a result of unanticipated changes in market interest rates.

Types of risk exposure

If a change in the level of interest rates will adversely affect the cash flows of a company (perhaps by raising its cost of borrowing), that firm is exposed to **interest rate risk**. This is the single most common concern among managers engaged in risk management. Interest rate risk is the risk of suffering losses as a result of unanticipated changes in market rates of interest. The most often cited example of losses caused by interest rate risk is the experience of the US savings and loan (S&L) industry in the 1980s. S&Ls suffered from a mismatch in terms of the maturity of their assets and liabilities because they funded long-term assets (e.g. 30-year, fixed-rate mortgages) with short-term liabilities (e.g. passbook savings deposits and short-term certificates of deposit). When interest rates spiked in the late 1970s and early 1980s, firms in the industry suffered tremendous losses because they were paying high rates on their short-term deposits while continuing to earn low rates on the long-term mortgages in their portfolio.

Interest rate risk is of particular concern to financial firms. However, more and more non-financial firms are recognizing that they also are exposed to this type of risk. For example, a retailing firm that funds its seasonal build-up of inventories with floating-rate debt will face higher interest expenses if market rates of interest increase. This is an example of transactions exposure (introduced earlier in this chapter) – the risk that a change in prices will negatively affect the value of a specific transaction or series of transactions.

Although most corporations focus on the possibility that changes in market rates of interest will increase interest expenses, changes in interest rates can also affect cash inflows. Some firms have revenue streams that are sensitive to changes in interest rates. For example, a building products manufacturer may experience lower demand when interest rates increase. This is an example of economic exposure (also introduced earlier) – the risk that a change in prices will negatively impact the value of all cash flows of a firm. As we will see later in this chapter, corporations can minimize both their transaction and economic exposures to interest rate risk in several ways.

At the same time that currency exchange rates were becoming more volatile, world economies were becoming more integrated. In recent years, currency exchange rates have remained volatile, and the pace of global integration has continued to accelerate. This means ever increasing exposure to foreign exchange risk, as discussed in Chapter 15. Consider another example of transactions exposure. A US-based company with manufacturing operations in Canada denominates the products it sells in international markets in the buyer's home currency. Suppose that it books a sale, denominated in euros, to a buyer in Germany, requiring delivery and payment in three months. If the euro depreciates in value relative to the Canadian dollar (C$) over the next three months, this company will receive fewer C$ than expected when it converts the euros received in payment into C$ to cover its own production costs.

As another example of economic exposure, if this US manufacturing firm faces stiff competition from a Japanese manufacturer and the value of the yen declines, the Japanese firm may be able to reduce the prices it charges in European markets, thereby hurting demand for the products manufactured by the US firm. Again, most firms concentrate on minimizing transactions exposure, but economic exposures are usually much more important. Unfortunately, these exposures are also much harder to hedge, or otherwise manage, because they are systemic.

Although most discussions of risk management focus on interest rate risk and foreign exchange risk, commodity price risk is also very important for many firms. Any firm that uses a commodity as a production input is potentially exposed to losses if the price of the commodity increases. Likewise, commodity producers are also exposed to the risk that the price of the commodity could decline.

Source: Adapted from 'Hedging Gains Give FL Group War Chest', *Financial Times*, 15 August 2006.

Real World

Small can sometimes be beautiful. There is not a very active market in trading the Icelandic currency, and as is common with such currencies there can be significant swings in very short periods. But when you get it right, even small currencies can provide big opportunities if one hedges correctly. The Icelandic investment group FL Group announced that it had made 'significant gains' from bets on rising foreign currencies as well as short positions in Iceland's krona, which fell 30 per cent in February 2006. The company announced that having made the correct hedging decisions they had withstood the turbulence of the currency fall and were well placed to make international investments.

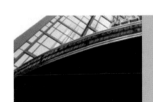

COMPARATIVE CORPORATE FINANCE
International differences in foreign exchange risk management emphasis

The two charts summarize the concerns of managers in multinational corporations in the United Kingdom, the United States and in Asia/Pacific countries. Generally, US companies seem to be more concerned with transaction exposures than companies in the UK or Asia. Asia/Pacific companies, on the other hand, are more concerned about economic exposure than managers in the United States or the United Kingdom.

The differences in emphasis can be attributed, in part, to differences in product markets and the location of production facilities. For example, US multinationals often have product markets that are primarily domestic, but their production facilities are commonly in other countries. Consequently, US multinationals tend to focus more on how changes in exchange rates affect their cost structure and less on how changes in exchange rates affect their revenue stream. Asia/Pacific multinationals, on the other hand, often have domestic production facilities and foreign product markets. Therefore, they tend to worry less about the impact of exchange rates on their cost structures and more about the impact of exchange rates on their revenue stream.

▶

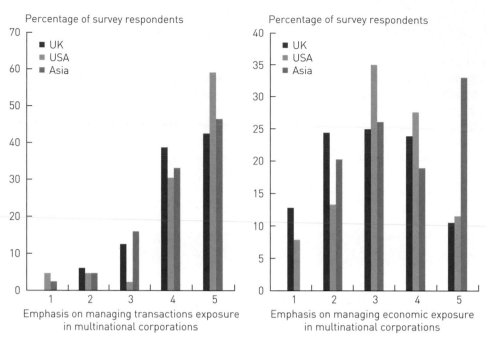

Least important = 1 to Most important = 5

Source: Andrew P. Marshall (2000) 'Foreign Exchange Risk Management in UK, USA, and Asia Pacific Multinational Companies', *Journal of Multinational Financial Management* 10:185–211. Reproduced with permission.

The hedging decision

Although it is clear that the corporate demand for hedging and risk management products has grown dramatically in recent years, it is less clear why a public company would choose to hedge at all. In Chapters 12 and 13 we learned that, in perfect markets, investors can effectively unwind managers' decisions regarding capital structure and dividends. Modigliani and Miller (1958) showed that managers could not increase firm value by choosing an optimal capital structure or dividend policy. The same conclusion applies to risk management when markets are perfect. If managers use derivative securities to hedge a particular risk, investors can trade on their own to undo what managers have done. The explanation for firms' hedging activities could be either that markets are imperfect or that managers hedge for their own benefit rather than for the benefit of shareholders. This section discusses the various potential motivations for hedging and possible hedging strategies.

Motivations for hedging The motivations for buying insurance are similar to those for hedging. However, there are some crucial differences. By purchasing insurance, a corporation benefits from the insurance company's expertise in terms of its ability to evaluate and price certain types of risks. Therefore, insurance companies have a comparative advantage in bearing these sources of risk. Similarly, insurance companies have the ability to process claims more efficiently and effectively than other corporations.

For example, insurance companies have expertise in negotiating, settling and providing legal representation in liability suits.

Hedging marketwide sources of risk, on the other hand, does not seem to provide any real service other than reduced volatility. In addition, this risk reduction is costly in terms of the resources required to implement an effective risk management programme. There are direct costs associated with hedging – transaction costs of buying and selling forwards, futures, options and swaps – and indirect costs in the form of managers' time and expertise.

According to modern hedging theory, value-maximizing firms hedge because hedging can increase firm value in several ways. The principal reason most firms hedge, however, is to reduce the likelihood of financial distress. Figure 16.2 illustrates the impact of hedging on the likelihood of financial distress, showing the range of possible cash flows for the firm in a given period and the associated probability distribution. If the firm's cash flows are below point *A* on the *x*-axis, the firm experiences financial distress. By hedging, the firm is able to reduce the probability of the firm's cash flows being below point *A*.

Reducing the likelihood of financial distress benefits the firm by also reducing the likelihood it will experience the costs associated with this distress. Direct costs of distress include out-of-pocket cash expenses that must be paid to third parties (lawyers, auditors, consultants, court personnel, etc.) in the event of bankruptcy or severe financial distress. Many of the indirect costs are contracting costs involving relationships with creditors, suppliers and employees. For example, a credible promise to hedge can sometimes entice creditors to lend the firm money on more favourable terms than they would be willing to lend to an unhedged borrower. Similarly, suppliers are more likely to extend trade credit when the likelihood of financial distress is low. In addition to potential cost savings, hedging may increase revenue for firms that sell products with warranties or service contracts. Warranties or service contracts are more likely to be honored, and customers will place a higher value on them, if the firm has a lower likelihood of financial distress. Similarly, if the products will require replacement parts or if there is the possibility of future upgrades, minimizing the likelihood of financial distress can promote sales.

Hedging can also reduce a firm's expected tax liability. If a firm's tax rate increases as income increases, hedging can reduce the expected tax liability and increase expected after-tax earnings. For example, suppose that a firm thinks its taxable earnings over the coming year will be one of three equally likely levels, depending on the actual realized price of a key input. If the input price is very high, the firm will generate no earnings at all. If the input price is very low, then earnings will be €20 000. In the intermediate case with a medium price for the key input, the firm's

SMART
IDEAS
VIDEO

John Eck, President of Broadcast and Network Operations NBC

How NBC used options to structure a deal that allowed the company to spread out the gains over time.

See the entire interview at
www.cengage.co.uk/ megginson

SMART
PRACTICES VIDEO

Howard Millar, Ryanair

Ryanair's dilemma: if and when to hedge fuel oil.

See the entire interview at
www.cengage.co.uk/ megginson

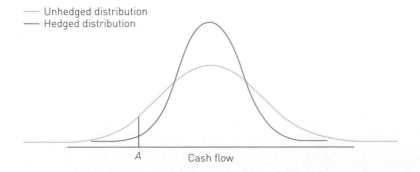

A   Cash flow

— Unhedged distribution
— Hedged distribution

FIGURE 16.2

Probability distribution of possible cash flows for a company

Source: This Figure was published in the Journal of Multinational Financial Management, Volume 10, Andrew P. Marshall, 'Foreign exchange risk management', pp. 185–211, copyright Elsevier 2000

earnings are €10 000. Managers believe that each of these outcomes is equally likely (i.e. probability = 1/3). To highlight the tax incentive to hedge, we will make two assumptions. First, assume that by hedging the firm can lock in the price of its key input at the medium level and thereby ensure that its pre-tax earnings will be €10 000. Secondly, assume that the firm pays a 10 per cent tax rate on the first $10 000 in earnings and a 20 per cent tax rate on all earnings above €10 000. Table 16.1 illustrates how the firm's hedging decision can affect its value.

If the firm hedges to lock in the key input price, then its after-tax earnings equal €9000. The tax schedule drives the difference in the two scenarios. When the firm does not hedge, it pays a higher tax rate when the input price is low and earnings are high than at other times. As a result, the expected tax bill is higher and earnings are lower than when the firm hedges and earns €10 000 before taxes. Hedging can also reduce expected tax liabilities by smoothing the profit stream and reducing the likelihood that the firm will pay high taxes in one period while having to forego (or delay) the benefits of tax shields in another period. Current tax laws limit the extent to which corporations can use losses in one period to offset gains in another period. For this reason, it is in the interest of some corporations to hedge their risk exposures, otherwise they could lose some of the tax benefits associated with losses experienced in periods of poor performance.

Closely held firms are more likely to hedge risk exposures because owners have a greater proportion of their wealth invested in the firm. Because the owners of these firms are less diversified, they generally seek to minimize the risk exposures faced by the firm. Similarly, if the managers of the firm are risk averse, the firm is more likely to pursue strategies that minimize risk exposures. Research studies confirm these expectations. The hedging activities of firms increase as share ownership by managers increases.

Another benefit of hedging is that it makes it easier for the board of directors and outsiders to evaluate the performance of managers. Absent an effective risk management programme, it is difficult to disentangle firm performance due to the manager's performance from firm performance due to external factors. A manager can make his or her performance more observable by minimizing the firm's exposure to external risk factors. For this reason, superior managers may be more inclined to hedge, whereas inferior managers may prefer to disguise their performance behind the firm's unhedged performance.

TABLE 16.1

The tax incentive to hedge

Table 16.1 illustrates that when firms face higher tax rates as their earnings increase, the tax schedule creates an incentive to hedge. If the firm does not hedge, its expected after-tax earnings equal €8667, but if it does hedge, it can lock in after-tax earnings of €9000.

NO HEDGING SCENARIO			
Input price	High	Medium	Low
Taxable earnings	€0	€10 000	€20 000
Taxes due	0	1 000	3 000
After-tax earnings	0	9 000	17 000
Expected after-tax earnings	1/3(€0) + 1/3(€9 000) + 1/3(€17 000) = €8 667		

HEDGING SCENARIO (INPUT PRICE LOCKED IN AT MEDIUM)	
Taxable earnings	€10 000
Taxes due	1 000
After-tax earnings	9 000
Tax schedule	
Tax rate on first €10 000	10%
Tax rate on earnings > €10 000	20%

Finally, even though shareholders can hedge the exposures they face as a result of owning shares in a risky firm, there are some circumstances under which it may be less costly for the firm to minimize risk than for the shareholders to hold a diversified portfolio. For some firms, however, the costs of hedging outweigh the benefits. There are substantial fixed costs associated with hedging, including the costs of acquiring the necessary expertise to implement a successful risk management programme, and small firms are therefore less likely to hedge than large firms.

Hedging strategies In some circumstances, a firm may not hedge a risk exposure if it is confident that the risk factor will be changing in a positive direction or that it has a comparative advantage in bearing the risk. For example, if a silver-mining company is convinced that the price of silver will increase in the coming months, it may choose not to hedge its exposure to changes in the price of silver. When the price of silver increases, the mining company will benefit from the higher price it will receive for silver. In other circumstances, a firm may overhedge if it is certain that a risk factor will be changing in a negative direction. For example, if the mining company is convinced that the price of silver will decrease in the coming months, it may overhedge by taking a position in a derivative security that will more than offset the reduced price it receives for silver, thereby generating a profit on the price decrease. These examples illustrate that derivatives are an effective means for managers to take a position in a risk factor based on their expectations. It is important to note that if a firm chooses *not* to hedge a risk exposure, or chooses to overhedge, it is speculating on changes in the risk factor.

How a firm chooses to hedge a given risk exposure will depend on the costs of the alternative hedging strategies. The firm needs to consider transaction costs, the effectiveness and accuracy of alternative strategies in offsetting underlying risk exposures, and the liquidity and default risks associated with those strategies. Customized hedging strategies, especially those that are financially engineered, are effective and accurate but suffer from greater transaction costs and low liquidity. Off-the-shelf solutions, such as exchange-traded derivative securities, while attractive because of their low transaction costs, high liquidity and low default risk, may not effectively and accurately offset the risk exposure.

---

4 Some legislators have described the markets for derivative securities as an electronic pyramid scheme. How do you respond?

5 Contrast hedging and speculation.

CONCEPT REVIEW QUESTIONS

16.2 FORWARD CONTRACTS

A forward contract involves two parties agreeing today on a price, called the **forward price**, at which the purchaser will buy a specified amount of an asset from the seller at a fixed date sometime in the future. This is in contrast to a cash market transaction in which the buyer and seller conduct their transaction today at the **spot price**. The buyer of a forward contract has a long position and has an obligation to pay the forward price for the asset. The seller of a forward contract has a short position and has an obligation to sell the asset to the buyer in exchange for the forward price. The future date on which the buyer pays the seller (and the seller delivers the asset to the

forward price
The price to which parties in a forward contract agree. The price dictates what the buyer will pay to the seller on a future date.

spot price
The price that the buyer pays the seller in a current, cash market transaction.

settlement date
The future date on which the buyer pays the seller and the seller delivers the asset to the buyer.

buyer) is referred to as the **settlement date**. It is important to note that, unlike options, forward contracts are obligations, and failure to make or take delivery of the underlying asset represents default. In addition, no cash changes hands in a forward contract until the contract settlement date. For these two reasons, default risk is a concern in forward contracts, and market participants enter into such contracts only with parties that they know and trust.

Most forward contracts are individually negotiated between corporations and financial intermediaries, but there are active markets for standard denomination and maturity forward contracts on several currencies and raw materials that institutions (including the bank market-makers themselves) can use to hedge their own exposures.

Forward prices

The forward price is the price that makes the forward contract have zero net present value. The key to determining a security's fair forward price is being able to form an alternative to the forward contract that has identical cash flows. For example, consider an asset that pays no income (e.g. a discount bond) and does not cost anything to store (e.g. financial assets). Rather than buy the asset six months forward, we could borrow the current price of the asset and buy it today. Six months from now, we would repay the loan plus interest. Whether we buy the asset six months forward or borrow and buy it today, we end up in the same position – owning the asset in six months. Because both strategies have identical cash flows in all circumstances, we can make the argument that the value of both strategies must be the same. This argument is based on **arbitrage**, which involves generating a riskless profit by simultaneously buying the strategy with the low value and selling the strategy with the high value. In a well-functioning market, these opportunities are quickly eliminated. Therefore, the forward price, F, for an asset that pays no income and does not cost anything to store should be the following:

arbitrage
The process of buying something in one market at a low price and simultaneously selling it in another market at a higher price to generate an immediate, risk-free profit.

EQUATION 16.1

$$F = S_0(1+R_f)^n$$

where S_0 is the current spot price of the asset, R_f is the current risk-free rate, and n is the number of years until the forward contract is to be settled. If this equation does not hold and $F > S_0(1+R_f)^n$ we can make a riskless profit by simultaneously borrowing an amount equal to S_0, using the borrowed funds to buy the asset, and selling the asset forward. On the settlement date, assuming we are able to borrow at the risk-free rate, we would sell the asset for F by delivering on the forward contract and pay our debt (including interest) of $S_0(1 + R_f)^n$. This arbitrage strategy would generate $F - S_0(1 + R_f)^n > 0$ in riskless profits on the settlement date without requiring any up-front investment.

Alternatively, if F is less than $S_0(1 + R_f)^n$, we would simultaneously short-sell the asset for S_0, lend the proceeds from the short sale at the risk-free rate, and buy the asset forward. On the settlement date, we would collect $S_0(1 + R_f)^n$ from the loan, pay F for the asset and close out our short-sale position. This arbitrage strategy would generate $S_0(1 + R_f)^n - F > 0$ in riskless profits on the settlement date without requiring any up-front investment.

Applying the Model

Helen Komazu is a portfolio manager in Cape Town who plans to buy one-month government debt in two months with a total face amount of R5 million.

The current price for three-month Treasury bills is R985 149 per R1 million face amount. The current risk-free rate is 6.17 per cent. The fair forward price is calculated as follows:

$$F = \text{R985 149} \times (1+0.0617)^{2/12} = \text{R995 029}$$

Therefore, the total forward price Helen should pay is R4 975 145 (R995 029 × 5). If this is not the forward rate quoted to her, Helen or another arbitrageur has an opportunity to earn a riskless profit.

A similar approach can be used to determine the forward price for an asset that pays income (e.g. a coupon bond) or is costly to store (e.g. commodities). In this case, we must account for the receipt of income and/or the payment of storage cost before the contract matures. If an investor purchases an asset through a forward contract rather than through a spot market transaction, the investor incurs certain costs and benefits. If the asset generates any income, then an investor who owns the asset receives the income whereas the investor who owns the futures contract does not. Similarly, if the asset is costly to store, then the owner of the asset must bear those costs and the futures contract holder avoids them. Therefore, a fair future contract price strikes a balance between the marginal benefits and costs of owning the asset. We determine the appropriate forward price for these assets as follows:

$$F = (S_0 - I + W)(1 + R_f)^n$$

EQUATION 16.2

where I is the present value of income to be paid by the asset during the life of the forward contract, and W equals the present value of the cost of storing the asset for the life of the contract.

Applying the Model

Consider a forward contract to purchase a ten-year bond in one year. Currently, an 11-year bond has a coupon rate of 8 per cent and a price of €1100, and will thus make two €40 coupon interest payments over the coming year. The current effective annual risk-free rate of interest over the next year is 5 per cent. The fair forward price is calculated as follows:

$$F = \left[1100 + \frac{40}{(1.05)^{0.5}} - \frac{40}{(1.05)} \right](1.05) = 1074.01$$

Of course, we have made a number of assumptions to arrive at Equations 16.1 and 16.2. First, we have assumed that market participants are able to borrow and lend at the risk-free rate, though most individual and institutional investors are unable to do so. However, a sufficiently large number of institutional investors can borrow at or near the risk-free rate, such that Equations 16.1 and 16.2 should hold. Secondly, we have assumed that there are no transaction costs associated with establishing these positions, which will tend to widen the bounds on futures prices. Thirdly, we have assumed that we can use the proceeds from short-selling and that short-selling does not involve any costs. In reality, only institutional investors can use all the proceeds

SMART CONCEPTS
See the concept explained step-by-step at **www.cengage. co.uk/megginson**

from short-selling, and there are transaction costs associated with short-selling. These costs can be incorporated into the model by discounting the right-hand side of Equations 16.1 and 16.2.

Currency forward contracts

currency forward contract
Exchange of one currency for another at a fixed date in the future.

forward rate
In a currency forward contract, the forward price.

Currency forward contracts, which involve exchanging one currency for another at a fixed date in the future, express the forward price as a **forward rate**. Table 16.2 presents hypothetical spot and forward exchange rates between the US dollar, the British pound and the euro. For example, the spot rate between pounds and dollars is $1.6450/£ (or equivalently £0.6079/$), and the spot rate between euros and dollars is $1.1100/€ (or €0.9009/$).

Figures 16.3 and 16.4 show pay-off diagrams for the buyer and seller of a one-month forward contract on the British pound where the forward rate, which is agreed upon at contract origination, is $1.6845/£. The x-axis of these diagrams represents possible spot rates for the British pound on the settlement date (one month in the future). The y-axis represents the profit or loss to the parties involved in the transaction. The buyer's profit is the spot rate for the British pound on the settlement date minus the forward rate. The seller's profit is the forward rate minus the spot rate on the settlement date. For example, if the spot rate is $1.7500/£ in one month, the buyer's profit is $0.0655/£ ($1.7500/£ − $1.6845/£). The seller would have a loss of $0.0655/£.

Currency forward rates   Determining the fair forward rate in a currency contract is slightly more complicated than for a financial asset that pays no income. Unlike the financial asset discussed previously, currencies generate income in the form of interest earned from investing the currency. However, the principle of how we determine the fair forward price still applies. For example, rather than buy British pounds three months forward, we could borrow dollars, convert the dollars to British pounds at the spot rate, and invest the pounds in the UK at the risk-free rate. These transactions guarantee a fixed amount of British pounds in three months, just as a forward contract does.

In fact, we have already studied a pricing relationship for forward exchange rates. In Chapter 15, we saw that interest rate parity established conditions under which an investor was indifferent between investing in a risk-free asset at home or abroad. These conditions are expressed mathematically as follows:

$$\frac{F}{S} = \frac{1 + r_{for}}{1 + r_{home}}$$

TABLE 16.2

Spot and forward exchange rates

CURRENCY	US$ EQUIVALENT	CURRENCY PER US$
Pound	1.6450	0.6079
1-month fwd	1.6516	0.6055
3-month fwd	1.6647	0.6007
6-month fwd	1.6845	0.5936
Euro	1.1100	0.9009
1-month fwd	1.1144	0.8973
3-month fwd	1.1233	0.8902
6-month fwd	1.1366	0.8798

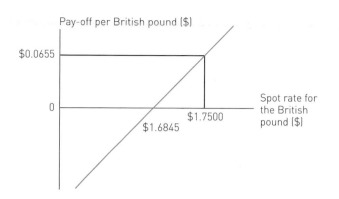

FIGURE 16.3

Pay-off diagram for the buyer of a one-month forward contract on the British pound

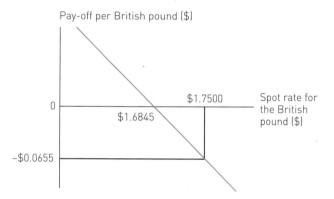

FIGURE 16.4

Pay-off diagram for the seller of a one-month forward contract on the British pound

This equation says that the ratio of the forward rate to the spot rate (expressed in foreign currency per unit of domestic currency) must equal the ratio of one plus the foreign risk-free rate divided by one plus the domestic risk-free rate. If this equation does not hold, then an arbitrage opportunity exists, and traders can borrow in one country and simultaneously invest in another country to make a quick profit. Rearranging this equation slightly, we can derive the formula for the fair price of a forward exchange contract:

$$F = S\frac{1 + r_{for}}{1 + r_{home}}$$

EQUATION 16.3

Applying the Model

Suppose that the current spot exchange rate on the Swiss franc (SF) is $0.5800/SF, or SF1.7241/$. The one-year risk-free rate for borrowing in dollars is 6 per cent, and the rate for borrowing in Swiss francs is 5 per cent. According to Equation 16.3, the following is the one-year forward exchange rate on the Swiss franc:

$$F = 1.7241\frac{1.05}{1.06} = SF1.7078/\$$$

Hedging with currency forward contracts To see how forward contracts can be used to hedge foreign exchange risk, consider a UK multinational company's treasurer who expects to receive a 10 million Swiss franc (SF) payment in 90 days. Suppose the spot rate is currently £0.6050/SF. In 90 days, however, the spot rate may be lower. For example, if the spot rate declines to £0.5800/SF, then the SF10 million payment will be worth only £5 800 000 (£0.5800/SF × SF10 000 000) rather than the £6 050 000 (£0.6050/SF × SF10 000 000) it would be worth today.

This type of foreign exchange risk can be hedged by selling the payment forward. Suppose the three-month forward rate for exchanging Swiss francs into pounds is £0.6051/SF. In three months, after receiving the SF10 million payment, the company will deliver SF10 million to the counterparty in the forward contract and receive in exchange £6 051 000 (£0.6051/SF × SF10 000 000), regardless of what the spot rate happens to be at that time. The treasurer has hedged the company's foreign exchange risk associated with this payment by locking in the pound price the company will receive for its foreign currency cash flow.

Interest rate forward contracts

The underlying asset in an interest rate forward contract is either an interest rate or a debt security. Contracts involving an interest rate as the underlying security are cash settled, which simply means that the underlying security is not transferred from the seller to the buyer. Instead, the buyer and seller exchange the cash value of the contract. Either way, interest rate forward contracts are used to hedge an interest rate risk exposure in much the same way that currency forward contracts are used to hedge a currency risk exposure.

forward rate agreement (FRA)
A forward contract in which the underlying asset is not an asset at all but an interest rate.

Forward rate agreements A **forward rate agreement (FRA)** is an example of a forward contract where the underlying asset is not an asset at all but an interest rate. An FRA is an agreement between two parties to exchange cash flows based on a reference interest rate and principal amount at a single point in time in the future. In an FRA, the first party will pay the second party if the market rate of interest at a specified future time is greater than the forward rate specified in the contract. If, however, the market rate of interest is less than the forward rate, the second party will pay the first party. The size of the payment will depend on the hypothetical principal amount, called the notional principal, and the difference between the market rate of interest and the forward rate. Equation 16.4 shows how to determine the cash flow in an FRA (CF_{FRA}). Note that, by convention, this computation uses a 360-day year.

EQUATION 16.4

$$CF_{FRA} = \frac{np(r_s - r_f)\left(D/360\right)}{1 + \left[r_s\left(D/360\right)\right]}$$

In this equation, np stands for the contract's notional principal, r_s is the reference rate on the contract settlement date (e.g. the three-month Treasury bill rate), r_f is the forward rate established at the beginning of the contract and D is the number of days in the contract period.

Hedging with interest rate forward contracts To see how FRAs can be used to hedge interest rate risk, consider CFE Manufacturing (CFE). The company is planning to borrow €10 million in six months at LIBOR plus 100 basis points and is concerned that LIBOR will increase before the company borrows. To hedge this exposure, CFE and SloveniaFinance enter into a six-month FRA with a notional principal of €10 million. The terms of the contract are such that CFE will pay SloveniaFinance if three-month LIBOR six months from now is less than the forward rate of 6 per cent. If three-month LIBOR exceeds 6 per cent, SloveniaFinance must pay CFE. The size of the cash flow is determined by Equation 16.4. For example, if three-month LIBOR six months from now is 7 per cent, SloveniaFinance must pay CFE the following:

$$CF_{FRA} = \frac{\$10m(0.07 - 0.06)\left(^{92}/_{360}\right)}{1 + \left[0.07\left(^{92}/_{360}\right)\right]} = €25\ 106.43$$

However, if three-month LIBOR six months from now is 5 per cent rather than 7 per cent, CFE must pay SloveniaFinance €25 233.14.

---

6 If Equation 16.2 does not hold, how might an arbitrageur earn a riskless profit?

7 What is the difference in the timing of cash flows in a forward contract and a spot market transaction?

CONCEPT REVIEW QUESTIONS

16.3 FUTURES CONTRACTS

For firms trying to hedge risk exposures, forward contracts suffer from two important problems: default risk and liquidity. Futures contracts solve these problems. Like a forward contract, a **futures contract** involves two parties agreeing today on a price at which the purchaser will buy a given amount of a commodity or financial instrument from the seller at a fixed date sometime in the future. In fact, the contracts are so similar that, for most purposes, we can use the same pricing formulas to price futures contracts that we used for forward contracts. Similarly, we can use the same pay-off diagram for futures that we used for forwards.

Although futures and forwards serve the same economic function, there are differences in the characteristics of the two contracts. In contrast to a forward contract, a futures contract is an exchange-traded contract that promises the delivery of a specified volume of a commodity or financial instrument on a standardized date of the month in which the contract expires. The futures exchange acts as a guarantor for all transactions, eliminating the forward contract's problem of counterparty risk. Because futures exchanges offer a limited set of contracts for trading, futures contracts are relatively liquid compared with forward contracts.

For example, gold futures contracts are traded on the New York Mercantile Exchange. The standard gold futures contract size is 100 troy ounces. Contracts are available for delivery in the current month; the next two months; any February, April, August and October falling within the next two years; and any June and December falling within the next five years.

Table 16.3 provides an example. Let's say that these are the prices of gold futures contracts on a particular day in November 2006. The first trade of the day, called the **opening futures price**, was $678.10 per troy ounce for delivery in January 2007. The highest price for the day was $683.70/oz, and the low for the day was $676.80/oz.

futures contract
Involves two parties agreeing today on a price at which the purchaser will buy a given amount of a commodity or financial instrument from the seller at a fixed date sometime in the future.

opening futures price
Price on the first trade of the day.

TABLE 16.3

Gold futures prices, November 2006: Gold (Comex) 100 troy oz; $ per troy oz

	OPEN	HIGH	LOW	SETTLE	CHANGE	OPEN INTEREST
Jan 07	678.10	683.70	676.80	679.60	2.50	147 694
Feb 07	678.50	684.70	678.40	680.60	2.50	27 992
Apr 07	681.50	685.00	681.50	681.70	2.50	6 565
Jun 07	681.40	686.80	680.50	682.90	2.50	30 148
Aug 07	687.50	688.50	683.50	684.30	2.50	3 072
Oct 07	691.20	692.00	687.50	687.50	2.50	13 637

closing futures price
The price used to settle all contracts at the end of each day's trading.

settlement price
The average price at which a contract sells at the end of a trading day.

open interest
The number of contracts that are currently outstanding.

The last January 2007 futures price for the day was $679.60/oz. This **closing futures price** is the result of a $2.50/oz increase in the settle price from the previous day, as indicated by the change column. The closing price is also known as the **settlement price** and is used to settle all contracts at the end of each day's trading, in a process called 'marking-to-market' (described below). The **open interest** represents the number of contracts that are currently outstanding. This number changes every day as contracts are bought and sold.

Table 16.4 provides some examples of the types of available futures contracts and the exchanges on which they are traded. All the contracts traded on these exchanges are standardized with respect to size and delivery date. The economic rationale for designing futures contracts in this way is that it provides a standardized, high-trading-volume (hence low transaction cost) financial instrument that can be used by both individuals and businesses to hedge underlying commercial risks, as well as by speculators wishing to place a highly leveraged bet on the direction of commodity prices. Contract sizes are small enough for individuals to be able to participate in futures markets, and the volume is high enough for businesses to take significant positions by buying or selling multiple contracts.

marking-to-market
Daily cash settlement of all futures contracts.

Although both futures and forwards impose obligations on their holders, the default risk of a futures contract is much lower, for two reasons. First, every major futures exchange operates a clearing house that acts as the counterparty to all buyers and sellers. This means that traders need not worry about the creditworthiness of the party they trade with (as forward market traders must), but only about the credit-worthiness of the exchange itself. Secondly, futures contracts feature daily cash settlement of all contracts, called **marking-to-market**. By its very nature, a futures contract is a zero-sum game because whenever the market price of a commodity changes, the underlying value of a long (purchase) or short (sale) position also changes – and one party's gain is the other party's loss. By requiring each contract's loser to pay the winner the net amount of this change each day, futures exchanges eliminate the possibility that large, unrealized losses will build up over time. In a forward contract, on the other hand, there are no cash flows until termination of the contract.

Applying the Model

As an example of marking-to-market, consider the gold futures discussed previously. Recall that the settle price for the January 2007 contract was $679.60 per troy ounce. If the settle price on the next business day is $680.20/oz, the person with the long position will receive $0.60/oz (the new futures price minus the original futures price), or a total of $60.00 per contract ($0.60/oz × 100 troy ounces). The person with the short position must pay $0.60/oz. In effect, the new contract with a futures price of $680.20/oz replaces the original contract. The party with

CONTRACT	EXCHANGE	FACE AMOUNT
Grains and oilseeds		
Corn	Chicago Board of Trade	5000 bushels
Corn	Euronext LIFFE	50 tons
Oats	Chicago Board of Trade	5000 bushels
Wheat	Chicago Board of Trade	5000 bushels
Canola	Winnipeg Commodity Exchange	20 metric tons
Rapeseed	Euronext LIFFE	50 metric tons
Livestock and meat		
Cattle – feeder	Chicago Mercantile Exchange	50 000 lbs
Cattle – live	Chicago Mercantile Exchange	40 000 lbs
Pork bellies	Chicago Mercantile Exchange	40 000 lbs
Food and fibre		
Cocoa	Coffee, Sugar & Cocoa Exchange, New York	10 metric tons
Cocoa	Euronext LIFFE	10 metric tons
Coffee	Coffee, Sugar & Cocoa Exchange, New York	37 500 lbs
Coffee, robusta	Euronext LIFFE	10 tons
Sugar – world	Coffee, Sugar & Cocoa Exchange, New York	112 000 lbs
Sugar – domestic	Coffee, Sugar & Cocoa Exchange, New York	112 000 lbs
Cotton	New York Cotton Exchange	50 000 lbs
Orange juice	New York Cotton Exchange	15 000 lbs
Metals and petroleum		
Copper	Comex, New York Mercantile Exchange	25 000 lbs
Gold	Comex, New York Mercantile Exchange	100 troy oz
Platinum	New York Mercantile Exchange	50 troy oz
Silver	Comex, New York Mercantile Exchange	5000 troy oz
Crude oil	New York Mercantile Exchange	1000 bbls
Natural gas	New York Mercantile Exchange	10 000 MMBtu
Copper	London Metal Exchange	1000 kg
Aluminium	London Metal Exchange	1000 kg
Interest rate		
Treasury bonds	Chicago Board of Trade	$100 000
5-year Treasury notes	Chicago Board of Trade	$100 000
30-day federal funds	Chicago Board of Trade	$5 million
LIBOR	Chicago Mercantile Exchange	$3 million
UK government long gilt	Euronext LIFFE	£100 000
Eurodollars	Chicago Mercantile Exchange	$1 million
Index		
Dow Jones Industrial Average	Chicago Board of Trade	$10 × average
S&P 500	Chicago Mercantile Exchange	$250 × average
Nikkei 225	Chicago Mercantile Exchange	$5 × average
FTSE 100	Euronext LIFFE	£10 × average
MSCI Euro Index	Euronext LIFFE	€20 × average
Currency		
Japanese yen (¥)	Chicago Mercantile Exchange	¥12.5 million
British pound (BP)	Chicago Mercantile Exchange	£62 500
Swiss franc (SF)	Chicago Mercantile Exchange	SF125 000
Euro (€)	Euronext LIFFE	€20 000

TABLE 16.4

Examples of exchange-traded futures contracts

the long position is compensated (and the person with the short position must pay) for the increase in the futures price. This type of daily settlement takes place on every trading day until delivery takes place. It is important to note that the party with the long position ultimately ends up paying a total of $679.60/oz, and the party with the short position receives a total of $679.60/oz upon delivery if each party holds his or her contract until maturity.

initial margin
The minimum monetary amount required of an investor when taking a position in a futures contract.

margin account
The account into which the investor must deposit the initial margin.

maintenance margin
Margin level required to maintain an open position.

When taking a position in a futures contract, the investor must deposit a minimum monetary amount called the **initial margin**, which varies by contract, in a **margin account**. The investor deposits gains in or withdraws losses from this account. Each exchange has margin requirements, and brokerage firms may require additional margin above the minimum specified. If losses deplete the margin below the level needed to maintain an open position, the **maintenance margin**, the investor must deposit additional funds in the account to bring the account back to the initial margin. Failure to deposit additional funds before the next day's trading results in the position being closed out by the exchange.

In addition to these distinctions, futures differ from forward contracts in two other important respects. First, futures contracts are designed to have a value that will appeal to a 'retail' market of individuals and smaller companies, whereas most actively traded forward contracts have significantly larger minimum denominations. This small contract size is rarely a problem for futures traders, however, as those wishing to hedge large exposures can simply purchase multiple contracts. Secondly, most forward contracts are settled by actual delivery, but this rarely occurs with futures contracts. Instead, futures market hedgers will execute an offsetting trade to close out their position in the futures market whenever they have closed out their underlying commercial risk through delivery in the normal course of business.

fungibility
The ability to close out a position by taking an offsetting position.

The ability to close out a position by taking an offsetting position is referred to as **fungibility**. Fungibility is made possible because the counterparty in a futures contract is the clearing house and because futures contracts are settled daily. If an investor were to take a long position in a futures contract and subsequently take a short position in the same contract, the contracts would cancel each other out for two reasons: (1) after marking-to-market, the futures prices of the two contracts would be the same, and (2) the clearing house is the counterparty to both contracts. It is important to note that unless buyers or sellers close out their positions, they are required to make or take delivery of the underlying asset.

Hedging with futures contracts

Futures contracts are a very effective mechanism for hedging. In addition to futures markets for metals, there are futures markets for foreign currencies, interest rates, stock indexes and commodities. 'Long hedges' involve buying a futures contract to offset an underlying short (sold) position. 'Short hedges' involve selling a futures contract to offset an underlying long (purchased) position.

Hedging with foreign currency futures The multinational company with the SF10 million exposure discussed earlier could have chosen to hedge that exposure in the futures market rather than with a forward contract by selling 80 Swiss franc futures contracts (each mandating delivery of SF125 000). Recall that the multinational company will be receiving a payment of SF10 million in ninety days. By selling 80 SF futures contracts that expire after the date on which it will receive the SF payments (because futures contracts have fixed delivery periods, they will only rarely exactly match a trader's desired payment date), the company can hedge this exposure using futures rather than forwards. Suppose that the current settle price for Swiss franc futures is £0.6057/SF. When the SF payment is received, the company will exchange it for pounds at whatever the spot £/SF exchange rate happens to be at the time and will simultaneously buy 80 SF futures contracts with the same delivery date as the contracts purchased earlier – thereby offsetting, or closing out, its futures position. If the pound value of the Swiss franc declines from £0.6050/SF to, say, £0.5000/SF during the 60 days in question, then the company will lose £0.1050/SF, or a total of £1 050 000, on its spot market sale of the SF payment. But this loss will be offset by the profit the company will achieve on its futures position. If the futures price declines from £0.6057/SF to £0.5007/SF, the profit in the futures position will be £0.1050/SF, or a total of £1 050 000, exactly offsetting the loss in the cash market position. If the Swiss franc appreciates rather than depreciates against the pound, then the company will gain on its cash market transaction and lose on its futures contracts. Either way, hedgers can use a futures contract to hedge an underlying commercial risk without actually having to take physical delivery on the futures contract.

Hedging with interest rate futures We can use futures contracts to hedge interest rate risk in much the same way that we hedged foreign exchange risk. Consider a corporate treasurer who anticipates borrowing $1 million in five months. The loan will be at 100 basis points over the three-month LIBOR at the time of borrowing. LIBOR is currently at 5 per cent. Eurodollar futures contracts for delivery in six months are trading at a yield of 5.2 per cent. By selling one Eurodollar futures contract, the treasurer can effectively lock in a borrowing rate of 6.2 per cent (5.2 per cent plus 100 basis points) for the three months beginning in six months. As in the currency contract, the treasurer would close out the position in Eurodollar futures and borrow at the same time.

Concerns when using futures contracts

In the previous examples we ignored several potential problems associated with using futures markets to hedge. We discuss some of these problems in the following sections.

Basis risk The basis in a futures contract is the difference between the futures price and the spot price. **Basis risk** arises from the possibility of unanticipated changes in the basis. As the maturity date approaches, the basis goes to zero. This simply means that when a futures contract is about to expire, the futures price must equal the spot price. If this were not the case, a trader could easily make an instant profit. For example, if the futures price is greater than the spot price, then a trader could buy the underlying asset on the spot market and sell it at the higher futures price.

> **basis risk**
> The possibility of unanticipated changes in the difference between the futures price and the spot price.

If a futures contract is closed out prior to maturity, as in the previous examples, basis risk can cause gains (losses) in the underlying position to differ from the offsetting losses (gains) in the futures position. In the currency hedging example, if the futures price had not changed by exactly the same amount as the spot price, the loss in the cash position would have differed from the gain in the futures position.

Cross-hedging The underlying securities in the futures contracts were identical to the assets being hedged in the two previous examples. However, the underlying securities in the futures contract and the assets being hedged often have different characteristics. This practice is called **cross-hedging**. For example, a farmer who uses orange juice futures to hedge his crop of grapefruits is cross-hedging. Some traders use cross-hedging strategies because there is no futures contract available that precisely matches the asset exposure that the trader wants to hedge, or because one futures

> **cross-hedging**
> The underlying securities in a futures contract and the assets being hedged have different characteristics.

contract is more liquid than another one that matches the underlying asset being hedged. To minimize basis risk in a cross-hedge, we need to determine the relation between changes in the value of the asset being hedged and changes in the value of the asset in the futures contract. It is possible to estimate this relation using historical data. Once we measure the sensitivity of the asset being hedged to changes in the price of the underlying asset in the futures contract, we can use that information to adjust the number of futures contracts to buy or sell in order to achieve an effective hedge.

Tailing the hedge Because of the marking-to-market feature of futures contracts, interest is earned on gains to the futures position as they are paid in and interest is lost on losses as they are paid out. This causes gains on a long position in futures to be slightly greater than the losses on a short position in the underlying asset because of the interest earned on the gains. To avoid overhedging, we can **tail the hedge**, or purchase enough futures contracts to hedge the risk exposure, but not so many that we overhedge. To achieve a perfect hedge in the currency hedging example, we would need to sell slightly fewer than 80 Swiss franc futures contracts.

tailing the hedge
Purchasing enough futures contracts to hedge risk exposure, but not so many as to cause overhedging.

Delivery options The deliverable instrument in some futures contracts can take a variety of forms. For example, the underlying security in a Treasury bond futures contract is a 20-year Treasury bond. However, a variety of US government bonds can actually be delivered. When delivery occurs, a conversion factor is used to account for differences in the characteristics of the deliverable instruments.

Another delivery option is the timing option. Many futures contracts allow delivery to take place at any time during the delivery month.

Because delivery rarely takes place in a futures contract, delivery options are not generally a major concern for the manager who is using futures to hedge risk. However, these delivery options do affect futures prices and are important for those market participants who are planning to make or take delivery of the underlying asset in the futures market.

CONCEPT REVIEW QUESTIONS

8 What is the difference in the cash flows for a forward contract and a futures contract?

9 What features of a futures contract tend to reduce default risk?

16.4 OPTIONS AND SWAPS

This section discusses options and swaps, and describes how they can be used to hedge risk exposures.

Options

A bit of folk wisdom says, 'Always keep your options open'. This implies that choices have value. Having the right to do something is better than being obligated to do it. In their most basic forms, options give investors the right to buy or to sell an asset at a fixed price, for a given period of time.

An option is one of the three main types of **derivative securities**, a class of financial instruments that derive their value from other assets. An option, like a forward rate contract or a future, is a derivative instrument. This is because its value depends on

derivative securities
Securities such as options, futures, forwards and swaps that derive their value from some underlying asset.

the price of the underlying asset that the option holder can buy or sell. The asset from which a derivative security obtains its value is called the **underlying asset**. A **call option** on equity grants the right to purchase a share at a fixed price, on or before a certain date. The price at which a call option allows an investor to purchase the underlying share is called the **strike price** or the **exercise price**. It is not too hard to see how a call option's value derives from the value of the underlying share. For example, if a particular call option has an exercise price of €25, then the holder of the option can purchase one underlying share for €25. If the market price of the share rises above €25, the call option's value will increase because it allows the option holder to purchase the share at a bargain price. On the other hand, if the underlying share price stays below €25, then the call option holder will not exercise the right to buy the share for €25. Because it is cheaper to buy the share at the market price than at the exercise price, the call option's value is low (perhaps even zero).

Call options grant investors the right to purchase a share for a fairly short time period, usually just a few months. The point at which this right expires is called the option's **expiration date**. An **American call option** gives holders the right to purchase a share at a fixed price, on or before its expiration date, whereas a **European call option** grants that right only on the expiration date. If we compare the prices of two options that are identical in every respect, except that one is American and one is European, the price of the American option should be at least as high as the European option because of the American option's greater flexibility.

A **put option** grants the right to sell a share at a fixed price, for a specific period of time. The right to sell a share at a fixed price becomes more and more valuable as the price of the underlying share decreases. Thus, we have the most basic distinction between put and call options – put options rise in value as the underlying share price goes down, whereas call options increase in value as the underlying share price goes up. Just like call options, put options specify both an exercise price at which investors can sell the underlying share and an expiration date at which the right to sell vanishes. Also, put options come in American and in European varieties, just as call options do.

The most distinctive feature of options, both puts and calls, can be deduced from the term 'option'. Investors who own calls and puts have the right to buy or sell shares, but they are not obligated to do so. We have already said that having the option to do something is better than being obligated to do it, and that intuition is important in understanding options. Because option holders can choose whether to exercise their option, an asymmetry exists in option pay-offs. This means that an option behaves very differently, depending on whether the underlying share price is above or below the option's strike price. This trait is central to understanding how to use options effectively and how to price them.

An important feature distinguishing calls and puts from other securities we've studied, such as shares and bonds, is that options are not necessarily issued by firms. Rather, an option is a contract between two parties, neither one having any connection to the company whose securities serve as the underlying asset for the contract. For example, suppose Tony and Oscar, neither one working for Aviva, decide to enter into an option contract. Tony agrees to pay Oscar £5 for the right to purchase one Aviva share for £50 at any time during the next month. As the option buyer, Tony has a **long position** in a call option. He can decide at any point whether he wants to **exercise the option**. If he chooses to exercise his option, he will pay Oscar £50, and Oscar will deliver one Aviva share to Tony. Naturally, Tony will choose to exercise the option only if Aviva shares are worth more than £50. If Aviva shares are worth less than £50, Tony will let the option expire worthless and will lose his £5 investment.

Now let's look at Oscar's side of this transaction. As the seller of the option, Oscar has a **short position** in a call option. If Tony decides to exercise his option, Oscar's

underlying asset
The asset from which an option or other derivative security derives its value.

call option
An option that grants the right to buy an underlying asset at a fixed price.

strike price
The price at which an option holder can buy or sell the underlying asset.

exercise price
The price at which an option holder can buy or sell the underlying asset.

expiration date
The date on which the right to buy or to sell the underlying asset expires.

American call option
An option that grants the right to buy an underlying asset, on or before the expiration date.

European call option
An option that grants the right to buy the underlying asset only on the expiration date.

put option
An option that grants the right to sell an underlying asset at a fixed price.

long position
To own an option or another security.

exercise the option
Pay (receive) the strike price and buy (sell) the underlying asset.

short position
To sell an option or another security.

obligation is to follow through on his promise to deliver one Aviva share for £50. If Oscar does not already own an Aviva share, he can buy one in the market. Oscar agrees to this arrangement because he receives the **option premium**, the £5 payment that Tony made at the beginning of their agreement. If Aviva shares rise above £50, Oscar will lose part or all of the option premium because he must sell Tony an asset for less than what it is worth. On the other hand, if Aviva shares do not rise above £50, then Tony will not attempt to buy the asset, and Oscar can keep the £5 option premium.

For our purposes, the key feature of an option as a hedging tool is that it provides protection against adverse price risk (an investor has the right to exercise the option if price changes make it optimal to do so) without having to forfeit the right to profit if the price on the underlying commodity moves in the investor's favour (in which case, the investor allows the option to expire unexercised). Of course, this one-sided protection against risk comes at a price. To acquire an option, unlike a forward contract, a trader must first pay the premium to the option seller.

Options trades do not usually occur in face-to-face transactions between two parties. Instead, options trade either on an exchange or on the over-the-counter market. Most investors who trade options never exercise them. An investor who holds an option and wants to convert that holding into cash can do so in several ways. First, one investor can simply sell the option to another investor, as long as there is some time remaining before expiration. Secondly, an investor can receive a **cash settlement** for the option. When a call option's strike price is less than the current share price, options traders say that the option is **in the money**. For puts, an option is in the money if the strike price exceeds the share price. Using these definitions, we can say that the call options in the upper three rows of Table 16.5 are in the money, whereas the put options in the lower six rows are in the money. Similarly, options traders say that a call option is **out of the money** when the strike price exceeds the current share price. Puts are out of the money when the strike price falls short of the share price. Finally, an option is **at the money** when the share price and the strike price are equal.

So far, our discussion of options has been mostly descriptive. Now we turn to the problem of determining an option's market price. Valuing an option is an extraordinarily difficult problem, so difficult in fact that the economists who solved the problem won a Nobel Prize for their efforts.

Call option pay-offs   We define an option's **pay-off** as the price an investor would be willing to pay for the option the instant before it expires. An option's pay-off is

TABLE 16.5

Option price quotes for Opti-Tech Corp.

The table list prices for call and put options that expire in April, May and July, with strike prices of $27.50, $30.00, $32.50 and $35.00.

COMPANY	EXPIRATION	STRIKE	CALLS	PUTS	
OPTI	April	27.50	3.26	0.67	when X = $27.50, calls are in
30.00	May	27.50	3.91	1.23	the money and puts are out of
30.00	July	27.50	4.91	2.04	the money (X = strike price).
30.00	April	30.00	1.77	1.67	
30.00	May	30.00	2.53	2.33	When X = $30, calls and puts
30.00	July	30.00	3.62	3.23	are both at the money.
30.00	April	32.50	0.85	3.24	
30.00	May	32.50	1.55	3.83	When X = $32.50 or $35, calls are
30.00	July	32.50	2.62	4.69	out of the money and puts are in
30.00	April	35.00	0.36	5.24	the money.
30.00	May	35.00	0.90	5.67	
30.00	July	35.00	1.86	6.40	

distinct from its price, or premium, because the pay-off refers only to the price of the option at a particular instant in time, the expiration date. Graphs that illustrate an option's pay-off as a function of the underlying share price are called **pay-off diagrams**. Pay-off diagrams are extremely useful tools for understanding how options behave and how they can be combined to form portfolios with fascinating properties.

Suppose an investor purchases a call option with a strike price of $75 and an expiration date in three months. To acquire this option, the investor pays a premium of $8. When the option expires, what will it be worth? If the underlying share price is less than $75 on the expiration date, the option will be worthless. No one would pay anything for the right to buy this share for $75 when they can easily buy it for less in the market. What if the share price equals $76 on the expiration date? In that case, owning the right to buy the share at $75 is worth $1, the difference between the share's market price and the option's exercise price. Ignoring transaction costs, an investor who owns the option can buy the share for $75 and immediately sell it in the market for $76, earning a $1 pay-off. In general, the pay-off of this option will equal the greater of:

- $0, if the share price is less than $75 at expiration or
- the difference between the share price and $75, if the share price is more than $75 at expiration.

The top line in Figure 16.5 shows a pay-off diagram for the option buyer, or the long position. This picture is a classic in finance, known as the 'hockey-stick diagram'. It shows that the option, at worst, will be worth $0, and at best, the option's value is unlimited. The lower graph in the figure represents the investor's **net pay-off**. The net pay-off line appears $8 lower than the solid line, reflecting the $8 premium the investor paid to acquire the option. On a net basis, the holder of the call option makes a profit when the price of the share exceeds $83.

Figure 16.5 also shows the call's pay-off from the seller's perspective, or the short position. Options are a zero-sum game, meaning that profits on the long position represent losses on the short side, and vice versa. In this part of the figure, the lower line illustrates that the seller's pay-off equals $0 when the share price is below $75. It decreases as the share price rises above $75. The incentive for the seller to engage in this transaction is the $8 premium, as shown in the figure's upper line. If the option expires out of the money, the seller earns an $8 profit. If the option expires in the money, the seller may realize a net profit or a net loss, depending on how high the share price is at that time. Whereas the call option buyer enjoys the potential for unlimited gains, the option seller faces exposure to the risk of unlimited losses. Rationally, if $8 is sufficient to induce someone to sell this option and thereby face the potential of huge losses, it must be the case that the seller perceives the probability of a large loss to be relatively low.

Put option pay-offs Figure 16.6 shows pay-offs for put option buyers (long) and sellers (short). We maintain the assumption that the strike price equals $75, but, in this figure, the option premium is $7. For an investor holding a put option, the pay-off rises as the share price falls below the option's strike price. However, unlike a call option, a put option's potential gains are limited by a share price that cannot fall below zero (because the law provides limited liability for a firm's shareholders). The maximum gain on this particular put equals $75 (or $68 on a net basis after subtracting the premium), whereas the maximum loss is the $7 option premium.

Again, the seller's perspective is just the opposite of the buyer's. The seller earns a maximum net gain of $7, if the option expires worthless, because the share price

pay-off diagram
A diagram that shows how the expiration date pay-off from an option or a portfolio varies, as the underlying asset price changes.

net pay-off
The difference between the payoff received when the option expires and the premium paid to acquire the option.

FIGURE 16.5

Pay-off of a call option with $X = \$75$

The top graph illustrates, from the option buyer's point of view, how a call option's pay-off varies as the underlying share price changes. The lower graph shows the seller's perspective. The pay-off line shows that a call option, with a strike price of $75, will be worthless on the expiration date, if the share price is $75, or less. For the buyer, the call's value rises dollar for dollar with the share price, as long as the share is worth more than $75. For the seller, the pay-off falls as the share price rises above $75. The net pay-off line reflects the $8 option premium that the call buyer must pay (or that the seller receives). The buyer and seller break even when the share price is $83. At higher share prices, the buyer earns a net gain at the seller's expense. At share prices below $83, the seller realizes a net gain, at the buyer's expense.

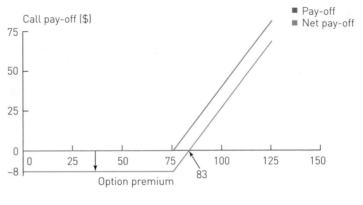

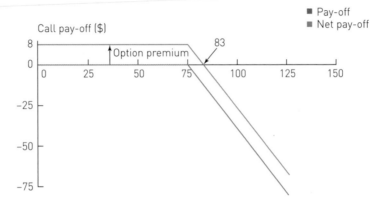

exceeds $75 on the expiration date, and the seller faces a maximum net loss of $68 if the firm goes bankrupt and its shares become worthless.

Pay-offs for portfolios of options and other securities

Experienced option traders know that by combining different types of options they can construct a wide range of portfolios with unusual pay-off structures. Think about what happens if an investor simultaneously buys a call option and a put option on the same underlying share and with the same exercise price. We've seen before that the call option pays off handsomely if the share price rises, whereas the put option is most profitable if the share price falls. By combining both into one portfolio, an investor has a position that can make money whether the share price rises or falls.

Cybil can't predict whether Internet Phones Corporation (IPC) shares will rise or fall from their current value of $30. Suppose Cybil decides to purchase a call option and a put option on IPC shares, both having a strike price of $30 and an expiration date of 20 April. Cybil pays premiums of $4.50 for the call and $3.50 for the put, for a total cost of $8. Figure 16.7 illustrates Cybil's position. The pay-off of her portfolio equals $0 if the IPC share price is $30 on 20 April. Should that occur, Cybil will experience a net loss of $8. But if the share price is higher or lower than $30 on 20 April, at least one of Cybil's options will be in the money. On a net basis, Cybil makes a profit if the IPC share price either falls below $22 or rises above $38, but she doesn't have to take a view on which outcome is more likely.

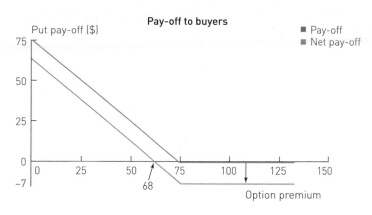

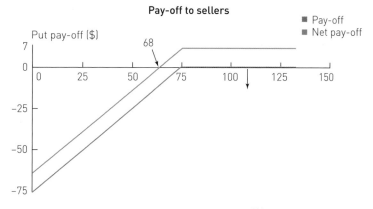

FIGURE 16.6

Pay-off of a put option with X = $75

The top graph illustrates, from the option buyer's point of view, how a put option's pay-off varies as the underlying share price changes. The lower graph shows the seller's perspective. The pay-off line shows that a put option, with a strike price of $75, will be worthless on the expiration date, if the share price is $75 or more. For the buyer, the put's value rises as the share price falls, as long as the share is worth less than $75. For the seller, the pay-off falls as the share price falls below $75. The net pay-off line reflects the $7 option premium that the put buyer must pay (or that the seller receives). The buyer and seller break even when the share price is $68. At higher share prices, the seller earns a net gain at the buyer's expense. At share prices below $68, the buyer realizes a net gain at the seller's expense.

In this example, Cybil is speculating, but not on the direction of the IPC share price. Rather, Cybil's gamble is on the volatility of IPC shares. If the shares move a great deal, either up or down, she makes a net profit. If the shares do not move much by 20 April, she experiences a net loss. Option traders refer to this type of position as a 'long straddle', a portfolio consisting of long positions in calls and puts on the same share with the same strike price and expiration date. Naturally, creating a 'short straddle' is possible, too. If Cybil believed that IPC shares would not move far from their current value, she could simultaneously sell a put and a call option on IPC shares, with a strike price of $30. She would receive $8 in option premiums from this trade. If IPC shares were priced at $30 on 20 April, both of the options she sold would expire worthless. On the other hand, if IPC shares moved up or down from $30, one of the options would be exercised, reducing Cybil's profits from the sale of the options.

Now let's look at what happens when investors form portfolios by combining options with other securities such as shares and bonds. To begin, examine Figure 16.8, which displays pay-off diagrams for a long position in ordinary shares and bonds. Remember, a pay-off diagram shows the total value of a security (in this case, one share or one bond) on a specific future date on the y-axis, and the value of a share on that same date on the x-axis. In Figure 16.8, the pay-off diagram from holding a share is a 45-degree line emanating from the origin because both axes of the graph are plotting the same thing – the value of the share on a future date.

The pay-off diagram for the bond requires a little more explanation. The type of bond in this example is very special. It is a risk-free, zero-coupon bond with a face

FIGURE 16.7

Pay-off to a portfolio containing one call and one put (X = $30)

By purchasing a call and a put option, each with a strike price of $30, an investor creates a position that can be profitable whether the share price rises or falls. Because the total cost of the call and put options is $8, the share price must either fall below $22 or rise above $38 before the trader makes a net profit.

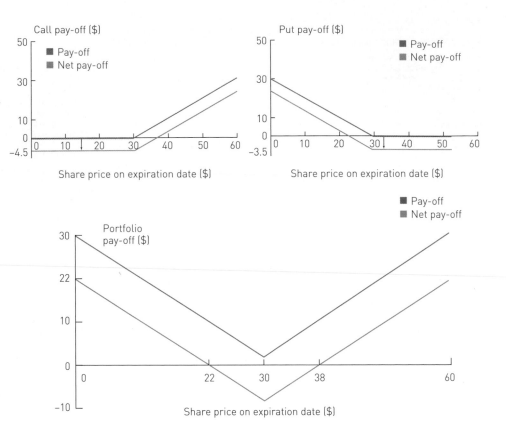

value of $75. The pay-off for an investor who purchases this bond is simply $75, no matter what the price of the share underlying the put and call options turns out to be. That's why the diagram shows a horizontal line at $75 for the long bond's pay-off.

Next, consider a portfolio consisting of one share and one put option on that share, with a strike price of $40. If, on the expiration date of the option, the share price is $40, or more, the put option will be worthless. Therefore, the portfolio's total value will equal the value of the share. What happens if the share price is less than $40 on the option's expiration date? In that case, the put option has a positive pay-off, which ensures that the portfolio's value cannot drop below $40, even if the share price does. Imagine that the share price falls to $30. At that point, the put option's pay-off is $10, leaving the combined portfolio value at $40 ($30 from the share + $10 from the put). Simply stated, the put option provides a kind of portfolio insurance, because it guarantees that the share can be sold for at least $40. However, if the price of the share rises, the portfolio value will rise along with it. Though the put option will be worthless, any increase in the share price beyond $40 increases the portfolio's value as well, as shown in Figure 16.9. This strategy is known as a **protective put**.

protective put
A portfolio containing a share and a put option on that share.

Investors can construct portfolios containing options, shares and bonds in ways that generate a wide range of interesting pay-offs. We have illustrated how investors could construct a portfolio not only to profit from a share's volatility, but to protect themselves from that volatility, using put options. No matter what kind of pay-off structure an investor wants to create, there is always more than one way to form a portfolio that generates the desired pay-offs.

Valuation of an option is an exceptionally difficult task, one indeed that resulted in a Nobel Prize being awarded for a partial solution. Over the years significant research has determined how options respond to various influences. We now know that option prices usually increase as time to expiration increases. Option values also rise as the volatility of the underlying asset increases. Call option prices increase as the

FIGURE 16.8

Pay-off diagrams for bonds and shares

The graphs show the pay-off for long and short positions in ordinary shares and in risk-free, zero-coupon bonds. The pay-off diagram for shares is a 45-degree line (upward sloping for the buyer and downward sloping for the seller) because the pay-off of the shares simply equals the price of the shares. Similarly, the bond pay-off lines are horizontal because the bond pays $75 to the buyer (or requires the seller to pay $75) with certainty. The bond's pay-off is not affected by changes in the share price.

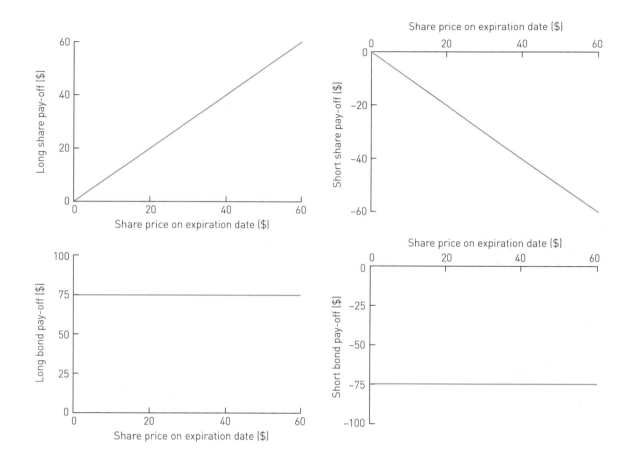

difference between the share price and the strike price grows larger, whereas put prices increase as this difference decreases.

Hedging with currency options Recall the multinational corporation that is expecting to receive a payment of SF10 million. Earlier, we demonstrated how this foreign exchange risk could be hedged using forwards or futures. We can also hedge this risk using options. The multinational company could have purchased 160 Swiss franc put options (each granting the right to deliver SF62 500) that expire after the date on which it will receive the SF payment (like futures contracts, exchange-traded options have fixed expiration dates and will only rarely exactly match a trader's desired payment date). When the SF payment is received, the company will exchange it for pounds at the current spot £/SF exchange rate and will simultaneously sell 160 SF put options with the same delivery date as the contracts purchased earlier – thereby offsetting, or cancelling out, its options position. If the pound value of the Swiss franc has declined from £0.6050/SF to, say, £0.50/SF during the 60 days in question, then the company will lose on its cash market transaction and gain on its options contract. If the Swiss franc appreciates against the pound, the company will gain on its cash

FIGURE 16.9

Pay-off from one long share and one long put (X = $40)

The graphs show the pay-off on a protective put, a portfolio that combines a long position in the underlying share and a long position in a put option on that share, with a strike price of $40. If the share price increases above $40, the investor's portfolio goes up. However, if the share falls below $40, the put option gives the investor the right to sell the share at $40, essentially placing a floor on the portfolio's value.

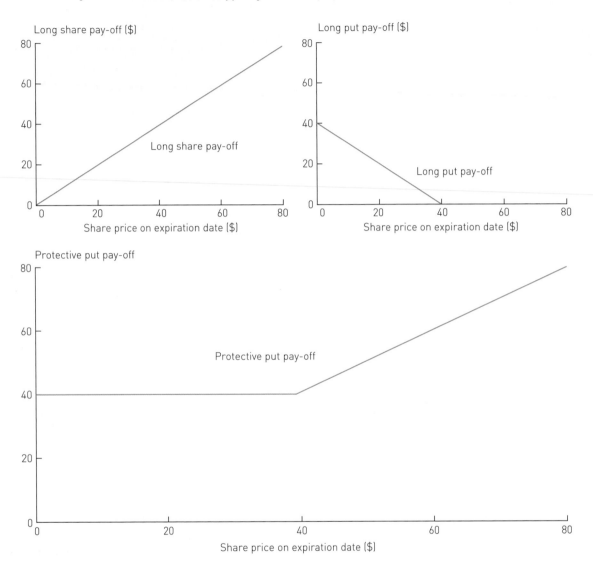

market transaction, and its losses on the options contract will be limited to the premium paid for the option. By using an option to hedge this foreign exchange risk, the multinational corporation minimizes its downside risk without giving up its upside potential. The cost of this hedge is the premium paid for the option.

Hedging with interest rate options In addition to hedging foreign exchange risk, options are commonly used to hedge interest rate risk. For example, a retailer that has borrowed using a variable-rate loan is probably concerned about interest rates rising. If the loan rate is tied to ECB rates, the firm could hedge this interest rate risk by purchasing a call option on a short-dated euro-denominated French government bond. Call options on interest rates are called **interest rate caps**.

Just as an interest rate cap is a call option on interest rates, an **interest rate floor** is a put option on interest rates. Recall that a put option represents the right to sell

interest rate cap
A call option on interest rates.

interest rate floor
A put option on interest rates.

an asset for a specified price within a specified period of time. In the case of interest rate options, which involve cash settlement, a put option will generate a positive pay-off for the buyer when the underlying value declines below the strike price.

One common strategy, called an **interest rate collar**, is to buy an interest rate cap and simultaneously sell an interest rate floor. The purpose of this strategy is to use the proceeds from selling the floor to purchase the cap. Of course, by selling the floor, an investor forgoes some upside potential.

interest rate collar
A strategy involving the purchase of an interest rate cap and the simultaneous sale of an interest rate floor, using the proceeds from selling the floor to purchase the cap.

Swaps

In a **swap contract**, two parties agree to exchange payment obligations on two underlying financial liabilities that are equal in principal amount but differ in payment patterns. Investors use swaps to change the characteristics of cash flows, most often to change the characteristics of cash outflows. We will concentrate on the most common types, interest rate swaps and currency swaps. According to a survey by the Bank for International Settlements, the total notional volume of over-the-counter derivative contracts outstanding totalled more than $284 trillion at the end of 2005, with interest rate swaps accounting for 60 per cent ($172 trillion) of this total. Like forward contracts, swap contracts are over-the-counter instruments and subject to default risk. For this reason, swap market participants enter into contracts only with parties that they know and trust. By far the largest amount of swaps are quoted in terms of US dollar principal amounts, with Japanese yen and euro-denominated principals together accounting for less than half that of US dollar-denominated total.

swap contract
Agreement between two parties to exchange payment obligations on two underlying financial liabilities that are equal in principal amount but differ in payment patterns.

Interest rate swaps As we see above, an **interest rate swap** is the most common type of swap transaction. In a typical interest rate swap, one party will make fixed-rate payments to another party in exchange for floating-rate payments. This is often called a **fixed-for-floating interest rate swap**. As in the FRAs discussed earlier, the interest payments on a fixed-for-floating swap will be based on a hypothetical principal amount called the notional principal.

Figure 16.10 illustrates the structure of a fixed-for-floating swap. The party making fixed-rate payments, Company A, promises to make fixed-rate payments based on some notional principal amount to a financial intermediary in exchange for floating-rate payments. In this example, as in many swap transactions, an intermediary has arranged the swap and is acting as the counterparty to both contracts. The contract calls for Company A to pay the intermediary 8 per cent per year based on a notional principal of $10 million. In return, the intermediary will pay Company A six-month LIBOR applied to the same $10 million notional principal amount. In practice, only the **interest differential** is exchanged between the intermediary and Company A.

At the same time that the intermediary and company agree to swap interest payments, the intermediary enters into an agreement to pay a fixed rate of interest to the floating-rate payer, Company B, in exchange for a floating rate. In this example, the intermediary agrees to pay Company B 7.85 per cent in exchange for six-month LIBOR. The intermediary's compensation is the spread between the fixed rate received from Company A and the fixed rate paid to Company B.

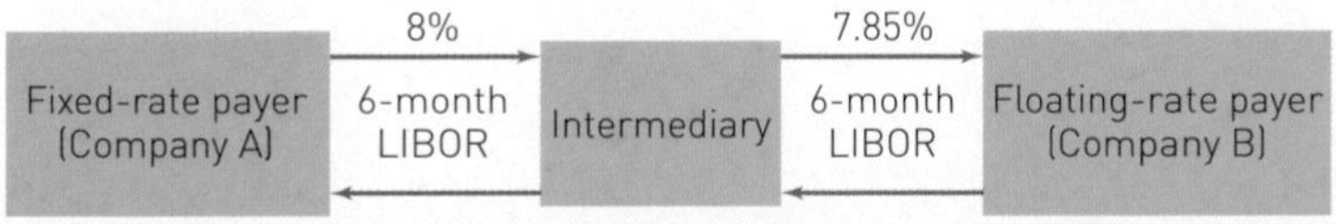

interest rate swap
A swap contract in which two parties exchange payment obligations involving different interest payment schedules.

fixed-for-floating interest rate swap
Typically one party will make fixed-rate payments to another party in exchange for floating-rate payments.

interest differential
In an interest rate swap, only the differential is exchanged.

FIGURE 16.10

Typical structure of a fixed-for-floating swap

Figures 16.11 and 16.12 show pay-off diagrams for Company A and Company B in the interest rate swap. The x-axis of these diagrams represents possible spot rates for six-month LIBOR at the end of each six-month period. The y-axis represents the cash flow to the parties involved in the transaction. If the contract calls for semi-annual payments, the cash flow for Company A is [$10 000 000 × (LIBOR − 0.08) ÷ 2]. The cash flow for Company B is [$10 000 000 × (0.0785 − LIBOR) ÷ 2]. If six-month LIBOR is 7 per cent at the end of the first six-month period, Company A will pay the intermediary $50 000 [$10 000 000 × (0.07 − 0.08) ÷ 2]. The intermediary will pay Company B $42 500 [$10 000 000 × (0.0785 − 0.07) ÷ 2]. Six months later, if six-month LIBOR is 8.5 per cent, the intermediary will pay Company A $25 000 [$10 000 000 × (0.085 − 0.08) ÷ 2]. Company B will pay the intermediary $32 500 [$10 000 000 × (0.0785 − 0.085) ÷ 2]. These exchanges will take place every six months until the termination date.

Typically, these interest rate swaps arise because one party wanted to issue fixed-rate debt but chose instead to issue floating-rate debt, either because the fixed-rate market was closed to this issuer or was more costly. By entering a swap agreement, the floating-rate issuer can effectively obtain a fixed-rate payment obligation. By paying a fixed rate and receiving a floating rate, this firm can use the cash inflows in the form of floating-rate payments to make the floating-rate payments on the debt that is outstanding. The net effect of the swap agreement is to offset the floating-rate payments being paid on the floating-rate debt with the floating-rate payments received on the swap. The fixed-rate payments being made on the swap are all that remain. The counterparty in the swap contract (who has better access to fixed-rate debt markets) achieves a preference floating-rate pattern of payments. As mentioned previously, rather than exchange gross amounts, the two parties will exchange only the net difference between the two payment obligations, the interest differential; therefore, the party that has swapped a fixed-rate payment obligation for one with a floating rate will lose (have to increase payment amounts) if market rates rise and will benefit if market rates fall.

FIGURE 16.11

Semi-annual net cash flow for the fixed-rate payer in a fixed-for-floating swap with a notional principal of $10 000 000

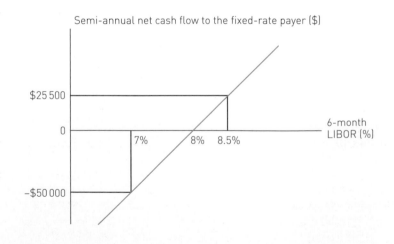

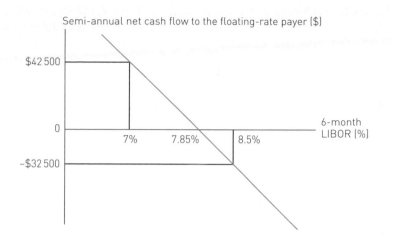

Fait as Dirikers spurn breezers,
Financial Times, 16 June 2004.

FIGURE 16.12

Semi-annual net cash flow for the floating-rate payer in a fixed-for-floating swap with a notional principal of $10 000 000

Real World

Bacardi, the international drinks company, provides a good example of how an interest rate swap can assist a company's bottom line. Consider the 2003 results, when they reported a 21 per cent drop in profits. The chief executive blamed this on a number of one-off issues, including the unwinding (ending) of an interest rate swap.

Currency swaps The second most common type of swap contract is the **currency swap**, in which two parties exchange payment obligations denominated in different currencies. For example, a US company wishing to invest in Germany would prefer to borrow in euros rather than in dollars. If, however, the company could borrow on more attractive terms in dollars (as is often the case) than in euros, a logical strategy would be to borrow the money needed for investment in dollars, say, by issuing bonds, and then swap payment obligations with a German company seeking dollars for investment in the United States. The German company would issue bonds that are denominated in euros.

The US company would make periodic euro payments to the German company. The German company would make periodic dollar payments to the US company. The dollar payments made by the German company would cover the interest and principal payments on the dollar borrowing by the US company, and the euro payments made by the US company would cover the interest and principal payments on the euro borrowing by the German company. By engaging in the swap, the US company has transformed its dollar liabilities into euro liabilities, and the German company has transformed its euro liabilities into dollar liabilities.

Suppose that the US company issues $7 million in ten-year bonds that have a coupon rate of 8 per cent. The German company issues €10 million in ten-year bonds that also have a coupon rate of 8 per cent. In this example, we will assume that the companies have agreed on a fixed exchange rate in the swap contract of $0.70/€. The two parties will exchange the principal amounts at contract origination. At the end of the first six-month period, the US company will pay €400 000 (€10 000 000 × 0.08 ÷ 2) to the German company in exchange for $280 000 ($7 000 000 × 0.08 ÷ 2).

currency swap
A swap contract in which two parties exchange payment obligations denominated in different currencies.

These payments will occur every six months until the termination date. On the termination date, the two parties will exchange principal amounts again to terminate the contract. The principal amounts will then be used to retire the bonds each company originally issued.

Note that unlike interest rate swaps, the notional principal in a currency swap is often exchanged at the origination and termination dates of the contract. If the notional principal were not exchanged at the termination date, the US company would still be faced with a dollar liability when the dollar-denominated bonds mature, and the German company would be faced with a euro liability.

fixed-for-floating currency swap
A combination of a currency swap and an interest rate swap.

Another variant of the currency swap is the **fixed-for-floating currency swap**. This is simply a combination of a currency swap and an interest rate swap. In this transaction, the first party pays a fixed rate of interest denominated in one currency to the second party in exchange for a floating rate of interest denominated in another currency. For example, if the US company in the previous example preferred to borrow in euros at a floating rate of interest, and the Germany company preferred to borrow in dollars at a fixed rate of interest, the two firms could engage in a fixed-for-floating currency swap.

Suppose that the US company was able to borrow $7 million in ten-year bonds with a coupon rate of 8 per cent. The German company borrows €10 million in ten-year bonds with a coupon rate of LIBOR + 100 basis points. As in the currency swap, the two parties will exchange the principal amounts at contract origination. At the end of the first six-month period, if LIBOR is 6.5 per cent, the cost of the loan will be 7.5 per cent (0.065 + 0.01). The US company will pay €375 000 [€10 000 000 × (0.065 + 0.01) ÷ 2] to the German company in exchange for $280 000 ($7 000 000 × 0.08 ÷ 2). For both parties, the semi-annual cash inflows from the swap contract are used to make the interest payments on the bonds that were issued in the cash market. Upon termination of the swap contract, the principal amounts are exchanged again and the bonds are retired.

Source: Adapted from 'Flood of New Issue Hedging Squashes Dollar Spreads Down', *Euroweek*, 12 May 2006.

Real World

Wells Fargo Bank is one of the older American banks, and has a long-standing practice of engaging in swaps. In May 2006 it entered into a €600 million five-year swap at fixed rates, which was swapped to floating-rate dollars. It was priced at just over 0.1 of a percentage point over mid-swap floating rate. Despite the cost of the swap, this was cheaper funding than it could get in dollars.

CONCEPT REVIEW QUESTIONS

10 Describe how an interest rate swap is just a portfolio of FRAs.

11 Why would any corporation hedge with forwards, futures or swaps if it can keep its upside potential by hedging with options?

16.5 SUMMARY AND CONCLUSIONS

- Increased volatility in interest rates, currency exchange rates and commodity prices has led to mushrooming demand for financial instruments that corporations can use to hedge their exposure to these risk factors.

- It is not always in the corporation's best interest to hedge. However, hedging can reduce the likelihood of financial distress, thereby reducing the expected costs of financial distress.

- A forward contract is an over-the-counter instrument that involves two parties agreeing on a price at which the purchaser will buy a specified amount of an asset from the seller at a fixed date sometime in the future. A futures contract is similar to a forward contract but is traded on an organized exchange.

- The fair forward price (or rate) in a forward contract is the price that eliminates the possibility of an arbitrageur generating riskless profits by trading in the forward contract.

- Unlike forward contracts, which are customized instruments, futures are standardized. Several issues to consider when using futures to hedge include basis risk, cross-hedging, tailing the hedge and delivery options.

- Options offer a company the opportunity to hedge its downside risk without giving up its upside potential. However, this comes at a cost in the form of the premium paid for the option. Swap contracts are longer-term hedging instruments that allow companies to change the characteristics of their periodic cash flows.

- In some cases, a company may not be able to hedge its risk exposure using off-the-shelf forwards, futures, options or swaps. In these cases, the company may turn to financial engineering in an effort to create a specialized financial instrument that will hedge the exposure. Financial engineering, however, is beyond the scope of this text.

INTERNET RESOURCES

For updates to links in this section and elsewhere in the book, please go to the book's website at www.cengage.co.uk/megginson.

http://www.cboe.com
Offers price quotes for many options and provides several tutorials that explain the characteristics of options and how they are traded.

http://www.cbot.com
Website of Chicago Board of Trade (CBOT), the oldest major futures exchange, which lists futures contracts for both commodities (corn, wheat, soybeans, gold) and financial instruments (two-, five-, ten- and 30-year Treasury bonds, Eurodollars).

http://www.cme.com
This is the site of the Chicago Mercantile Exchange, another leading market for derivative securities.

http://www.derivativesone.com
Comprehensive derivatives valuation service aimed at the non-professional user, which has over 50 derivatives models and provides help on every input to each model.

http://www.eurexchange.com
Website of the Eurex futures exchange, which began trading in December 1996 as a joint venture between the Swiss Exchange and Deutsche Börse, and within a short period of time emerged as a leading international futures market.

The website for what was the London International Financial Futures Exchange, now part of the Euronext group.

The International Swaps and Derivatives Association.

KEY TERMS

American call option	forward rate agreement (FRA)	option premium
arbitrage	fungibility	out of the money
at the money	futures contract	pay-off
basis risk	General Agreement on Tariffs and	pay-off diagrams
call option	Trade (GATT)	political risk
cash settlement	in the money	protective put
closing futures price	initial margin	put option
cross-hedging	interest differential	risk management
currency forward contract	interest rate cap	Samurai bonds
currency swap	interest rate collar	settlement date
derivative securities	interest rate floor	settlement price
economic exposure	interest rate risk	short position
euro	interest rate swap	spot price
European call option	long position	strike price
exercise price	maintenance margin	swap contract
exercise the option	margin account	tailing the hedge
expiration date	marking-to-market	transactions exposure
fixed-for-floating interest rate	monetary union	translation exposure or accounting
swap	net pay-off	exposure
forward price	open interest	underlying asset
forward rate	opening futures price	World Trade Organization (WTO)

SELF-TEST PROBLEMS

ST16-1 A certain commodity sells for €150 today. The present value of the cost of storing this commodity for one year is €10. The risk-free rate is 4 per cent. What is a fair price for a one-year forward contract on this asset?

ST16-2 The spot exchange rate is $1.6666/£. The risk-free rate is 4 per cent in the United States and 6 per cent in the United Kingdom. What is the forward exchange rate (assume a one-year contract)?

QUESTIONS

Q16-1 Historically, what types of risk were the focus of most firms' risk management practices?

Q16-2 Distinguish between the motivations for purchasing insurance and the motivations for hedging marketwide sources of risk.

Q16-3 Distinguish between transactions exposure and economic exposure.

Q16-4 In what way can hedging reduce the risk of financial distress? How might reducing the risk of financial distress increase firm value?

Q16-5 Explain how hedging can reduce a firm's tax liability.

Q16-6 Why do closely held firms tend to hedge more than firms with diffuse ownership?

Q16-7 How can hedging make it easier to evaluate a manager's performance?

Q16-8 What are the advantages of using exchange-traded derivatives to hedge a risk exposure? What are the advantages of over-the-counter derivatives?

Q16-9 Conceptually, how do we determine the fair forward price for an asset? What are the necessary assumptions to arrive at a fair forward price?

Q16-10 Conceptually, what are the differences between Equations 16.1, 16.2, and 16.3? Which equation would you use to determine the fair forward price for an asset that does not earn any income but is costly to store, such as gold or silver? How would you modify the equation?

Q16-11 Describe the features of a futures contract that make it more liquid than a forward contract.

Q16-12 Explain the features of a futures contract that make it have less credit risk than a forward contract.

Q16-13 Why is fungibility an important feature of futures contracts?

Q16-14 Describe the delivery process for futures contracts. Why does delivery rarely take place in futures contracts?

Q16-15 Why is a call option on an interest rate called an interest rate cap and a put option called an interest rate floor?

Q16-16 Explain how a fixed-for-floating swap can be considered a portfolio of forward contracts on six-month discount bonds.

Q16-17 Go to the CBOT website (http://www.cbot.com) and determine the contract specifications for soybean meal futures and ten-year US Treasury note futures. Apart from the difference in the type of asset, what is the difference between the two contracts in terms of what qualifies as deliverable grades?

Q16-18 Go to the CBOT website (http://www.cbot.com) and determine the minimum initial margin requirements for speculators in the contracts traded on that exchange. Which contracts have the smallest margin requirements? Which contracts have the largest requirements? Why do you suppose these contracts have such different margin requirements?

PROBLEMS

P16-1 Suppose that an investor has agreed to pay €94 339.62 for a one-year discount bond in one year. Two years from now, the investor will receive the bond's face value of €100 000. The current effective annual risk-free rate of interest is 5.8 per cent, and the current spot price for a two-year discount bond is €88 999.64. Has the investor agreed to pay too much or too little? How might an arbitrageur capitalize on this opportunity?

P16-2 Company A's stock will pay a dividend of €5 in three months and €6 in six months. The current stock price is €200, and the risk-free rate of interest is 7 per cent per year with monthly compounding for all maturities. What is the fair forward price for a seven-month forward contract?

> **SMART SOLUTIONS**
>
> See the problem and solution explained step-by-step at **www.cengage.co.uk/ megginson**

P16-3 The current price of gold is €588 per troy ounce. The cost of storing gold is €0.03/oz per month. Assuming an annual risk-free rate of interest of 12 per cent compounded monthly, what is the approximate futures price of gold for delivery in four months?

P16-4 Following is the current yield to maturity on Treasury bills of various maturities:

TIME TO MATURITY (MONTHS)	YIELD (%)
1	5.0
3	5.2
6	5.4
9	5.8

Assuming monthly compounding, what should the forward interest rate of a three-month T-bill be if it is to be delivered at the end of three months? What if it is to be delivered at the end of six months?

P16-5 Using the information in Table 16.2, determine whether the three-month forward rate on euros is fair if the annualized yield for risk-free borrowing over the next three months is 8 per cent in Europe and 5 per cent in the United States. If the price is not fair, how could you capitalize on the arbitrage opportunity? What is the potential profit? Assume monthly compounding for borrowing and lending.

P16-6 A US automobile importer is expecting a shipment of custom-made cars from Britain in six months. Upon delivery, the importer will pay for the cars in pounds. Using the information in Table 16.2, suggest a hedging strategy for the importer. Explain the consequences for the spot market transaction and the forward market transaction if the €/£ spot exchange rate increases over the next six months.

P16-7 Suppose that KF Exports enters into an FRA with Interfirst Bank with a notional principal of €50 million and the following terms: in six months, if LIBOR is above 6 per cent, KF will pay Interfirst according to the standard FRA formula. On the other hand, if LIBOR is less than 6 per cent, Interfirst will pay KF. If LIBOR is 5.5 per cent in six months, who pays and how much will the company pay? What if LIBOR is 6.5 per cent?

P16-8 Consider the following scenarios, determine how to hedge each scenario using bond futures, and comment on whether it would be appropriate to hedge the exposure.

a A bond portfolio manager will be paid a large bonus if her €10 million portfolio earns 6 per cent in the current fiscal year. She has done very well through the first nine months. However, she is concerned that interest rates might increase over the next few months.

b The manager of a company is selling one of its warehouses. The deal will close in two months. The manager plans to buy six-month Treasury bills when the company receives payment for the warehouse space, but the manager is worried that interest rates might decline in the next two months.

c Sam Blackwell plans to retire in a year. Upon retirement, he will be paid a lump sum based on the value of the securities in his defined-contribution retirement plan. Sam's portfolio consists largely of Treasury bonds, and he is worried that interest rates will be increasing in the coming year.

Options and swaps

P16-9 Chipman Products Company will suffer an increase in borrowing costs if the 13-week T-bill rate increases in the next six months. Chipman Products is willing to accept the risk of small changes in the 13-week T-bill rate but wishes to avoid the potential losses associated with large changes. The company plans to hedge its risk exposure using an interest rate collar. If the company buys a call option on the 13-week T-bill rate with a strike price of €60 and sells a put option with a strike price of €50, describe how this strategy will limit the company's exposure to changes in the T-bill rate. The premium on the call is 0.75, and the premium on the put is 0.85. What is the company's profit (or loss) in the option market if the T-bill rate is 4.5 per cent in five months? If the T-bill rate is 5.5 per cent? If the T-bill rate is 6.5 per cent?

P16-10 Go to the Euronext website (http://www.euronext.com) and determine the contract specifications for FTSE futures. Determine the current futures price for the next available contract month. What would your profit or loss be if you bought one contract today, and the FTSE increased by 100 points before the last settlement date?

P16-11 Company A, based in Switzerland, would like to borrow $10 million at a fixed rate of interest. Because the company is not well known, however, it has been unable to find a willing US lender. Instead, the company can borrow SF17 825 000 at 11 per cent per year for five years. Company B, based in the United States, would like to borrow SF17 825 000 for five years at a fixed rate of interest. It has not been able to find a Swiss lender. However, it has been offered a loan of $10 million at 9 per cent per year. Five-year government bonds are yielding 9.5 per cent and 8.5 per cent in Switzerland and the United States, respectively. Suggest a currency swap that would net the financial intermediary 0.5 per cent per year.

P16-12 Citibank and ABM Company enter into a five-year interest rate swap with a notional principal of €100 million and the following terms: every year for the next five years, ABM agrees to pay Citibank 6 per cent and receive from Citibank LIBOR. Using the following information about LIBOR at the end of each of the next five years, determine the cash flows in the swap.

YEAR	LIBOR (%)
1	5.0
2	5.5
3	6.2
4	6.0
5	6.4

P16-13 Based on the type of swap ABM entered into in the previous problem, what type of liabilities do you think ABM has? Long-term or short-term?

THOMSON ONE Business School Edition

For instructions on using Thomson ONE, refer to the introductory text provided with the Thomson ONE problems at the end of Chapters 1–6, or in *A Guide for Using Thomson ONE – Business School Edition*.

P16-14 Review Coca-Cola Company's (ticker: U:KO) most recent 10K filing. What types of risk does Coca-Cola hedge with derivative instruments? What does the filing say about the types of derivative instruments Coca-Cola uses to hedge these risks? If the filing does not say anything about the types of derivative instruments used, what would your choice of derivative instruments be?

MINICASE *Risk mangement*

Basic International Group Ltd has been involved in international trade for the past four years. Recently, the CEO has come to realize that Basic needs better risk management, and he asks you to investigate ways to manage risk through hedging. You remember that derivative securities, including forwards, futures, options and swaps, are the financial instruments commonly used for hedging and risk management. However, to gain more insight into risk management, you decide to answer the following questions.

Assignment

1 What are the types of risk factors that a company faces?

2 If risk aversion cannot explain why firms choose to hedge, then what are their motivations?

3 Explain how a firm's management can limit risk exposure through using a forward contract. What types of forward contracts are available?

4 What are the differences between forward and futures contracts?

5 How do managers use futures contracts to limit risk exposure?

6 How do managers use options to limit risk exposure?

7 How do managers use swaps to limit risk exposure?

Chapter 17
Mergers, Acquisitions and Corporate Control

The world's largest merger?

Mergers are among the largest and most commented upon financial transactions on the stock markets. However, it is not easy to identify the 'world's largest merger'. There are at least two criteria that can be used size of the merged entity, measured by total assets the amount of money in the transaction.

For example, consider the largest mergers by total assets. A pair of mergers announced between late 2003 and early 2004 created the second and third US-based banks with assets of at least $1 trillion, joining America's Citigroup and Japan's Mizuho Holdings as the only companies in the world with assets so vast. In October 2003, Bank of America announced plans to acquire FleetBoston Financial in a friendly, stock-swap merger where Bank of America agreed to pay $47 billion to acquire all of FleetBoston's outstanding stock. The merger would give the combined institution total assets of about $1 trillion, as well as a near-nationwide retail banking presence. The banks' executives predicted that the integration of their operations would yield important operating synergies as well as cost savings in excess of $1.1 billion per year. Although analysts generally praised BofA's strategy, they were appalled by the high 42 per cent premium BofA offered FleetBoston's shareholders, and BofA's shares promptly dropped by 10 per cent the day the merger was announced. Both companies' shareholders approved the merger in April 2004.

Three months later, JP Morgan Chase and Bank One announced their own plans to merge to create a banking behemoth with $1.1 trillion in assets. As with the Bank of America/FleetBoston merger, this was to be a friendly, stock-swap deal with JP Morgan offering $60 billion worth of its shares to acquire Bank One. Executives predicted that the merger would yield major operating synergies as well as

cost savings of $2.2 billion over three years, mostly through the elimination of some 10 000 jobs. Analysts praised this merger as well, though the stock market reaction to the announcement was more balanced than it had been for BofA/FleetBoston. Bank One's stock rose 13 per cent on the news, while JP Morgan's fell by 3 per cent. The merger was approved by both companies' shareholders in May 2004.

Measured on total assets, banking and financial service institutions tend to be inherently large. The sums paid of $47 billion and $60 billion are however dwarfed by a number of other mergers. Two in particular take precedence. Vodafone grew very aggressively via mergers and acquisitions. In 1999 it paid €56 billion for AirTouch, a US wireless telephone company, and in 2000 it announced its intention to purchase Mannesmann, a German company that had diversified from engineering into telecommunications. The merger was bitterly contested by the Mannesmann board right up to the very last minute, when concessions in regard to board membership and management structures allowed the Mannesmann board to accept the deal. The total paid by Vodafone was the equivalent of €183 billion, which analysts even at the time considered high, given the total annual savings were estimated to be of the order of €500 million, with very little coming from staff reductions. By contrast with the trillion dollar asset base of the banking behemoths, the total 2001 asset value of the merged company was only £171 billion, or $230 billion.

Shortly after the Vodafone deal, a merger worth $181 billion was announced between AOL and TimeWarner. At the time this was seen as a move of strategic genius, with both companies' shares jumping by double digit figures. However, the essence of the deal was that the companies could marry internet (clicks) and real economy business (mortar) to form a new business model. The collapse of the tech bubble and problems at AOL made the deal a disaster, with AOL's name eventually disappearing and many elements of the merged business being sold off.

LEARNING OBJECTIVES

After studying this chapter you should be able to:

- Describe the most important forms of corporate control transactions and distinguish between transactions that integrate two businesses and those that split up an existing single business.

- Discuss the differences between horizontal, vertical and conglomerate mergers.

- Explain the different methods of payment acquirers use to execute mergers and acquisitions, and discuss how returns to target and bidder firm shareholders differ between cash and share mergers.

- Contrast the motivations of managers who implement value-maximizing mergers and acquisitions with those who execute non-value-maximizing combinations.

- Describe the most important laws and regulations that govern corporate control activities, and the increasing internationalization of these regulatory regimes.

SMART FINANCE

Use the learning tools at www.cengage.co.uk/megginson

17.1 HISTORY OF MERGERS AND ACQUISITIONS

Merger activity has been defined more by waves of concentrated intensity rather than by continuous activity over time. These waves tend to be positively related to high growth rates in the overall economy and are also related to 'industry shocks', or industry-wide events such as deregulation that affect the corporate control activities of whole industries and lead to these merger waves. In this section, we identify the key merger waves in US and European history and discuss the factors that led to their occurrence, as well as the corporate control regulation that has evolved over time.

Historically there have been a number of 'merger waves' in the UK and the USA. For a variety of reasons, mostly relating to regulatory structures and fiscal conservatism, other European nations have not seen the aggressive cycles of mergers and acquisitions witnessed by these two countries. Merger and takeover waves are generally accepted to have taken place in the early 1900s, the 1920s, the 1960s, the 1980s and the mid to late 1990s.

economies of scale
Relative operating costs are reduced for merged companies because of an increase in size that allows for the reduction or elimination of overlapping resources.

industry shock theory of takeovers
Explains much of the activity in a wave of mergers as a reaction to some external shock to the industry, such as a change in regulation or the introduction of a fundamentally new technology.

Merger waves typically begin with a robust stock market, and the types of mergers occurring in each wave reflect the then current regulatory environment. Activity is generally concentrated in industries undergoing changes (shocks), and the merger waves tend to end with significant declines in the stock market. An excellent overview of the historical forces behind these merger waves is contained in the publications of the European Corporate Governance Institute. In essence, the first wave was characterized by the creation of combines and cartels to achieve market power; the second by horizontal mergers to achieve economies of scale; the third wave was characterized by the creation of conglomerates in the USA and by horizontal mergers in the UK, reflecting the differential approaches of anti-trust legislation. The fourth wave of the 1980s was remarkable for the vastly increased use of debt, the emergence of a more complex market for corporate control, the unwinding (in the USA) of the conglomerate structure in a search for increased focus, and the greatly increased number of hostile and reverse takeovers. The fifth takeover wave was unprecedented in its scale and scope; for the first time it was a truly global phenomenon, with very significant activity in the USA, the UK and continental Europe, along with emerging trends in China and India. Friendly stock-swap mergers became the transaction method of choice in the fifth wave of mergers, which began in 1993 and ended with the sharp drop in takeovers during 2001. Following the trend of specialization and focus from the fourth wave, the vast majority of mergers in this wave occurred between companies in the same industry. The industry shock theory of takeovers seems to explain much of the activity in this wave. The industries with heavy merger activity were healthcare, banking and telecommunications, each having gone through a recent technological shock. Merger activity in this wave surpassed that in all the others, reaching $3.4 trillion in aggregate transaction value in the peak year of 2000. Of this aggregate value, slightly less than $1.8 trillion was generated from deals completed in the United States and about $1.6 trillion from deals outside the United States. Deals involving European companies were approximately as large as those involving US companies, and cross-border activy for the first time equalled domestic activity. The total value of mergers worldwide fell by half to $1.7 trillion in 2001, then to $1.21 trillion in 2002, before recovering slightly to $1.33 trillion in 2003. During the first quarter of 2004, however, global M&A volume picked up significantly. Table 17.1 details the ten largest corporate mergers of all time.

Regulation of corporate control activities

The legal environment affecting mergers evolved from a state of virtually no regulation during the first merger wave to what is currently a relatively complex nexus of

ACQUIRER	TARGET	VALUE ($bn)	YEAR
Vodafone AirTouch plc (UK)	Mannesmann AG (Germany)	183.0	2000
America Online Inc. (US)	Time Warner Inc. (US)	181.0	2001
Pfizer Inc. (US)	Warner-Lambert Co. (US)	89.2	2000
Exxon Corp. (US)	Mobil Corp. (US)	78.9	1999
Glaxo Wellcome plc (UK)	SmithKline Beecham (UK)	76.0	2000
Travelers Group Inc. (US)	Citicorp (US)	72.6	1998
SBC Communications Inc. (US)	Ameritech Corp. (US)	62.6	1999
NationsBank Corp. (US)	BankAmerica Corp. (US)	61.6	1998
Vodafone Group plc (UK)	AirTouch Communications (US)	60.3	1999
Pfizer (US)	Pharmacia (US/Europe)	58.0	2003

TABLE 17.1
The ten largest corporate takeovers, ranked by transaction value

Sources: *Mergers & Acquisitions* (SDC Publishing) and *Mergers and Acquisitions Report* (Thomson Financial).

interrelated legal issues, including anti-trust enforcement, tender offer regulation, and laws regarding the actions of managers and directors and actions of state and international regulators. US merger legislation is extremely complex and also tends to be enforced more or less laxly depending on the political climate. An important element that runs throughout the US mergers and anti-trust legislation and processes is the concept of concentration. Mergers, takeovers and combinations that are likely to generate very concentrated sectors are much more likely to be challenged than those that do not have this effect.

Real World

The failed 1997 merger attempt of Staples and Office Depot exemplifies the role of US regulatory agencies in preventing what are deemed to be anti-competitive combinations. On 4 September 1996, Staples and Office Depot announced their intent to merge in a $3.4 billion deal. At the time, Office Depot and Staples were the largest and second-largest office supply superstores, respectively. Of the $14.0 billion in sales in this market, Office Depot had a market share of $6.6 billion, followed by Staples with $4.1 billion, and the only other major competitor, Office-Max, had sales of $3.3 billion.

The Federal Trade Commission (FTC) reviewed the proposed merger and concluded that it should be rejected because it would have an anti-competitive impact if allowed. One of the key points cited by the FTC in its rejection was the market power that the merged firm would be able to wield in those markets where no stores other than Staples or Office Depot existed (the 5 per cent rule). The companies and the FTC engaged in a series of legal battles, the grounds moving to technical details of concentration and whether the firms should be compared to other office stores or if discount retailers such as Wal-Mart and Kmart should be included. Although the judges ultimately sided with the companies, the outcome was that the merger was abandoned.

Individual US states have become more active participants in the oversight of anti-competitive business practices since the 1990s. State attorneys general from 14 states joined the anti-trust lawsuit first lodged against Microsoft by the Justice Department in 1994. Even after the federal government abandoned its case against Microsoft in 2001 in an effort to settle the case out of court, many of the states refused to abandon their status as plaintiffs against Microsoft. Although only California has

Source: *Fortune* magazine, various issues.

expressed an open willingness to file suit in opposition to a merger on the grounds of anti-competitiveness, the vigilance of the plaintiff states in the anti-trust case against Microsoft indicates that state regulators could become an impediment to future mergers.

Federal securities laws also regulate the actions of managers in corporate control events. The high-profile insider trading scandals of the 1980s generated a keen interest in these laws.

COMPARATIVE CORPORATE FINANCE
Searching for effective corporate governance and value-enhancing mergers

Enron, WorldCom, Adelphia, Global Crossing, Qwest Communications, Tyco. These are but a few of the high-profile corporate bankruptcies or near failures that have destroyed shareholder wealth and shaken investor confidence in the years after the great 1990s bull market. Underlying the much-publicized accounting scandals and extraordinary executive remuneration paid out in these American corporate failures is the ultimate factor that led to their demise – ineffective corporate governance. Shareholders, bondholders, employees, journalists and politicians (of course) are all demanding to know, 'Where were the boards of directors who were supposed to be monitoring the managers?' These same groups are demanding reforms to restore confidence in corporate America, and both domestic and international groups are also seeking corporate reforms.

One domestic reform had already taken place before the spate of corporate failures began. Beginning in 2001, the Financial Accounting Standards Board (FASB) enacted Standards 141 and 142 to update and codify merger and acquisition accounting and the goodwill account created in these transactions. However, these two new standards were promulgated too late to prevent the old tricks being used in merger and acquisition accounting in the 1990s. Before the new standards were enacted, firms could manipulate merger and acquisition accounting rules to overstate their true financial performance. When the merger wave waned and the firms could no longer use their overvalued shares to fund acquisitions, the firms' true financial performance was revealed. Even with the new rules in place, Sam DiPiazza, CEO of accounting firm PricewaterhouseCoopers, has called for even more stringent accounting rules and implementation of international best accounting practices for US corporations.

International proposals for corporate governance reform are also being considered. Governance structures in the United Kingdom and continental Europe are being discussed as possible alternatives to the typical governance structure in place in publicly traded US corporations. In particular, two major British committees issued guidelines for more effective corporate governance during the 1990s. The three basic recommendations of the Cadbury Committee on the Financial Aspects of Corporate Governance (1992) and the Hempel Committee (1998) were that a corporation's chairman of the board and chief executive officer (CEO) always be separate persons, that the board of directors should have a majority of independent directors and that no corporate insiders should serve on the board's audit committee. The similarity of capital markets in the UK and the USA appears to make these guidelines implementable as listing policies for either the New York Stock Exchange or NASDAQ.

In many continental European corporations (especially in Germany), management responsibilities are split between two mutually exclusive groups – a management board and a supervisory board consisting of representatives from the government, financial institutions, labour unions and other interested parties. Corporate managers do not serve on the supervisory board, which is charged with overseeing the management team. However, the continental European governance system is much less consistent with the US model than is the British system. First, hostile takeovers are virtually unheard of in continental Europe, whereas these are commonly used as a disciplining device in the United Kingdom and the United States. Secondly, unlike US corporations, financial institutions (and oftentimes the government) have substantial ownership stakes in European corporations. On the other hand, the complete separation of a supervisory board and managers offers an appealing alternative for those seeking to reform US corporate governance.

As the search continues for effective corporate governance structures in the United States and abroad, it has become clear that no country or system has perfected a corporate governance structure. Concurrent with the spectacular US corporate failures that occurred during the spring and summer of 2002 were the precipitous declines in shareholder value and CEO oustings witnessed at French conglomerate Vivendi and German telecom giant Deutsche Telekom. These were followed by major scandals at Accord and Parmalat in 2003 and at Royal Dutch Shell in early 2004. Especially disconcerting to the European business community was the saga of Sir Christopher Gent, CEO of British telecom firm Vodafone. Gent had led Vodafone through the takeover of Mannesmann AG, the largest takeover in history. Unfortunately, the merger was ill-advised and led to a significant loss in shareholder wealth, but an increase in Gent's compensation and share options. While US reformers were looking to the United Kingdom for ideas on more effective corporate governance, British shareholders and institutional investors were complaining of the ineffective corporate governance that had allowed Gent to enhance his own wealth while shareholders continued to lose money. And the search for effective corporate governance goes on.

The internationalization of M&A regulation

Within the UK and other countries that are members of the European Union, the EU commission has a potentially major role to play in mergers and takeovers. The European Commission (EC) first signalled its more stringent anti-trust regulatory authority in 1999, when it vetoed the proposed merger of US communications giants WorldCom and Sprint. The EC expressed concerns about the pricing power that the combined firm could have if the second- and third-largest US communications firms (behind industry leader AT&T) merged to become the first- or second-largest communications firm in many European markets. The managers of both WorldCom and Sprint abandoned their effort to merge after the EC's decision. EC Competition Commissioner Mario Monti created an international stir in 2001 when he denied the petition to merge filed by General Electric and Honeywell, although the merger had already been approved by US anti-trust authorities. Monti's stern defence of his position and denial of the petition on appeal sends a clear message that firms with international operations that are considering a merger must account for anti-trust authorities outside the United States, even if the merger is between US firms. Monti caused an even bigger stir when in early 2004 his Commission sued Microsoft in an attempt to force the company to uncouple application packages from its operating system (Windows). The Commission maintained that this tie gave Microsoft monopoly power, and fined Microsoft €500 million, with a subsequent fine of €280 million in 2006 for non-compliance.

In the UK the main domestic merger regulatory bodies are the Competition Commission, the Secretary of State (Minister) for Trade and Industry and the Director of Fair Trading. As is typically the case in the UK, the powers of these overlap and are interrelated. In essence, the role of the Secretary of State is to decide whether to refer a proposed merger to the Competition Commission. The Commission can also initiate its own investigations, and can receive submissions from the Director of Fair Trading. The guiding principle for the UK authorities is that mergers should not lessen competition. The Takeover Panel, the self-regulatory body of the UK financial services companies, also has very substantive powers of sanction and persuasion, although these do not have the force of statute law. Mergers that have significant European

SMART PRACTICES VIDEO

David Baum, Co-head of M&A for Goldman Sachs in the Americas

"When the poison pill was introduced, it changed the landscape related to hostile takeovers."

See the entire interview at **www.cengage.co.uk/ megginson**

dimensions are examined directly by the Competition Commission or, if large, by the EU Commission. However, the EU Commission can be overruled by EU legal entities.

Sources: *Financial Times*; EU Commission website.

Real World

In 2006 there were significant political and business manoeuvnrings in France regarding a €72 billion merger proposed between two giant utilities, Gaz de France and Suez, who together would have a dominant position in the gas markets of France and Belgium. Despite the merger being friendly, there was significant negotiating between the companies regarding management structures. Conditional on the company undertaking to dispose of gas and gas supply companies, and on the companies selling off methane production facilities, the European Commission approved the merger.

CONCEPT REVIEW QUESTIONS

1 Which industries do you anticipate will experience industry shocks that will spur merger activity in the near future?

2 How does the dynamic interpretation of anti-trust laws affect managers' acquisition strategies? What impact does the involvement of individual states have on the acquisition decision?

3 Do you believe that increasing global competition will further heighten merger activity?

17.2 THE MARKET FOR CORPORATE CONTROL

Corporate control transactions

corporate control
The monitoring, supervision and direction of a corporation or other business organization.

As its name implies, **corporate control** refers to the monitoring, supervision and direction of a corporation or other business organization. The most common change in corporate control results from the combination of two or more business entities into a single organization, as happens in a merger or acquisition. A change in corporate control also occurs with the consolidation of voting power within a small group of investors, as found in going-private transactions such as leveraged buyouts (LBOs) and management buyouts (MBOs). It can also be found when companies go public for the first time, or when they change from a partnership form of organization to a limited liability form. Transfer of ownership of a business unit with a divestiture and the creation of a new corporation through a spin-off are other ways to bring about such a change.

The forces effecting changes in corporate control and the resulting impact on the business community present some of the most interesting and hotly contested debates in the field of finance. For example, the corporate control contest for RJR Nabisco captivated corporate America in the autumn of 1988, spawned a book and a movie about the takeover, and remains a source of debate for academics and politicians over the social benefit of corporate control activities. Changes in corporate control are frequent sources of political involvement in the financial markets. A good example of this was the intervention by senior French politicians regarding the merger between Indian-based Mittal and Arcelor, the French steelmaker. We address the causes and consequences of changes in corporate control in this chapter, as well as provide real-world examples of the merger/acquisition process and the technical aspects a corporate manager must consider before making decisions regarding corporate control changes.

A **takeover** simply refers to any transaction in which the control of one entity is taken over by another. Thus, a friendly merger negotiated between the boards of directors and shareholders of two independent corporations is a takeover, as is a successful entrepreneur selling out her enterprise to a corporation. The terminology of corporate control can be easily misconstrued and must be clearly defined to prevent such ambiguities. In the following discussion, we will define the many terms and concepts encountered in the corporate control arena.

Changes in corporate control occur through several mechanisms, most notably via acquisitions. An **acquisition** is simply the purchase of additional resources by a business enterprise. These resources may come from the purchase of new assets, the purchase of some of the assets of another company, or the purchase of another whole business entity, which is known as a merger. **Merger** is a general term applied to a transaction in which two or more business organizations combine into a single entity. Oftentimes, however, the term 'merger' is reserved for a transaction in which one corporation takes over another upon the approval of both companies' boards of directors and shareholders after a friendly and mutually agreeable set of terms and conditions and a price are negotiated. Payment is in the form of an exchange of ordinary shares. In actuality, there are many different types of mergers, and they (as well as other corporate control activities) can be differentiated according to several criteria. We define mergers by the mode of target integration used by the acquiring firm, by the level of business concentration created by the merger and by other transaction characteristics for which mergers are commonly known.

There are a variety of ways to integrate the assets and resources of an acquired firm into the acquiring company (the acquirer).

Subsidiary merger An acquirer may wish to maintain the identity of the target as either a separate subsidiary or division. A **subsidiary merger** is often the integration vehicle when there is brand value in the name of the target, such as the case of PepsiCo's merger with Pizza Hut in 1977. Sometimes, separate 'tracking' or 'target' shares are issued in the subsidiary's name. Sometimes, these shares are issued as new shares in exchange for the target's shares, as occurred when General Motors issued new Class E and Class H shares to acquire, respectively, Electronic Data Systems and Hughes Electronics during the 1980s. Alternatively, a new class of preference shares may be issued by the bidding firm to replace the ordinary shares of the target as well.

Real World

Liberty is a media and telecoms conglomerate that has a very active mergers and acquisitions history. Its complicated business structure was simplified, for investors at least, in May 2006 when it created two tracking shares. Liberty Capital is basically the Starz and Encore television networks while Liberty Interactive is a share that tracks the QVC home shopping channel and the Expedia travel company. In late 2006 IDT Entertainment was sold to Liberty and its activities were added to the Liberty Interactive portfolio. In all cases of Liberty's subsidiaries they trade on their own identity and it is not at all obvious that the company is in fact a subsidiary of a much larger corporation. See, for example, www.starz.com or www.expedia.co.uk.

Consolidation **Consolidation** is another integrative form used to effect a merger of two publicly traded companies. Under this form, both the acquirer and target disappear as separate corporations and combine to form an entirely new corporation with new ordinary shares. This form of integration is common in mergers of equals where

takeover
Any transaction in which the control of one entity is taken over by another.

acquisition
The purchase of additional resources by a business enterprise.

merger
A transaction in which two or more business organizations combine into a single entity.

subsidiary merger
A merger in which the acquirer maintains the identity of the target as a separate subsidiary or division.

consolidation
A merger in which both the acquirer and target disappear as separate corporations, combining to form an entirely new corporation with new ordinary shares.

reverse merger
A merger in which the acquirer has a lesser market value than the target.

going-private transactions
The transformation of a public corporation into a private company through issuance of large amounts of debt used to buy all (or at least a voting majority) of the outstanding shares of the corporation.

the market values of the acquirer and target are similar. Many of these new corporations adopt a name that is merely a hybrid of the former names, such as the 1985 consolidation of Allied Corporation and Signal Companies to become AlliedSignal. But some managers of newly created companies want a 'fresh start' with a company name, as in the case of Sandoz and Ciba-Geigy when they merged in 1997 to form Novartis.

Another type of merger that warrants mention, even though it is not a separate integrative form, is the **reverse merger**. In this transaction, the acquirer has a lesser market value than the target. Differences in size can be substantial in a reverse merger but are often the result of a merger of equals where the 'control premium' paid by the acquirer causes the market value of the target to exceed that of the acquirer. At other times, however, a reverse merger is an audacious coup by a smaller company to take itself to a new level by acquiring on a large scale.

Real World

In late 2006 a David and Goliath merger was announced when Riverdeep, the Irish educational software company announced it was taking over Houghton Mifflin, the US education publisher of textbooks under the Pearson and McGraw Hill imprints. The total deal was structured around a debt assumption by Riverdeep of around $1.6 billion and some $1.75 billion in other consideration. An indication of the relative size of the companies is that in 2003 Riverdeep delisted from NADSAQ in a deal that valued it at €400 million.

management buyout (MBO)
The transformation of a public corporation into a private company by the current managers of the corporation.

employee stock ownership plan (ESOP)
The transformation of a public corporation into a private company by the employees of the corporation itself.

reverse LBO
A formerly public company that has previously gone private through a leveraged buyout and then goes public again. Also called a second IPO.

tender offer
The structured purchase of a target's shares in which the acquirer announces a public offer to buy a minimum number of shares at a specific price.

Leveraged and management buyouts

Changes in corporate control also occur when voting power is concentrated in the hands of one individual or a small group. Going-private transactions are one way to achieve this concentration of control. Just as they sound, **going-private transactions** transform public corporations into private companies through issuance of large amounts of debt used to buy all (or at least a voting majority) of the outstanding shares of the corporation. The acquiring party may be a leveraged buyout (LBO) firm, such as Kohlberg, Kravis, and Roberts (KKR), which specializes in such deals; the current managers of the corporation (known as a **management buyout** or **MBO**); or even the employees of the corporation itself through an **employee stock ownership plan (ESOP)**. A prime example of both an LBO and an MBO attempt is the 1988 corporate control contest for RJR Nabisco. H. Ross Johnson, the CEO of RJR Nabisco, led a management team that attempted to take the company private but was outbid by KKR in a $29 billion LBO. An LBO that sells shares to the public again is known as a **reverse LBO**.

Tender offers, acquisitions and proxy fights

An acquirer can also attain control of a public corporation through a non-negotiated purchase of the corporation's shares in the open market or through the voting control of other shareholders' shares via proxy. Theoretically, an acquirer can gain control simply through open-market purchases of a target firm's shares, though regulation severely restricts this form of 'creeping acquisition' in most developed countries. Generally, an acquirer must explicitly bid for control through a tender offer for shares. A **tender offer** is a structured purchase of the target's shares in which the acquirer announces a public offer to buy a minimum number of shares at a specific price. Interested shareholders may then 'tender' their shares at the offer price. If at least the minimum number of shares is tendered, then the acquirer buys those shares at the offer price. The acquirer has the option of buying the shares tendered at the offer price or cancelling the offer altogether if the minimum number of shares is not tendered. A two-tiered offer results when the acquirer offers to buy a certain number of shares at one price and then more shares at another price. These offers are especially popular in situations where the acquirer wishes to purchase 100 per cent of the shares outstanding as quickly as possible and offers to buy 51 per cent at a higher price and the remaining 49 per cent at a lower price in an attempt to provide an incentive for shareholders to tender their shares early in order to receive the higher price. A **tender-merger** is a merger that occurs after an acquirer secures enough voting control of the target's shares through a tender offer to effect a merger.

Tender offers are often associated with hostile takeovers, but these are the highly publicized minority cases. Yet, open-market purchases, tender offers and proxy fights may all be used in combination to launch a 'surprise attack' on an unwitting (and often unwilling) target. Most stock exchanges allow for stakes of small, but significant amounts – such as 5 per cent or 7 per cent – to be built up before the identity of the purchaser is made known to the company in which the stake is being built. Thus, an interested potential acquirer could accumulate a substantial number of shares (known as a 'foothold') without the knowledge of the target's management and then follow a number of acquisition strategies. First, the interested acquirer could simply initiate a tender offer to purchase the remaining shares of the target required for voting control and then effect a merger (a tender-merger as mentioned previously). Secondly, the potential acquirer could approach the target with both a merger offer and the threat of a proxy fight and/or hostile tender offer to gain the remaining shares needed to obtain voting control of the target if the merger offer is refused. This tactic is known as a **bear hug**. Thirdly, the acquirer could also threaten the target with a hostile tender offer and/or proxy fight in order to gain initial or greater access to the board of directors or to sell its shares to the target firm at a premium price (a type of targeted share repurchase known as 'greenmail'). Target firms employ defensive measures such as **anti-takeover amendments** to their corporate charters (also known as **shark repellents**), **poison pills**, the pursuit of **white knights** ('friendly' acquirers who will top the price of an unwelcome bidder), MBOs, stock buybacks, payment of greenmail and other defensive tactics. See Table 17.2 for greater detail on anti-takeover mechanisms. Obviously, there are many different acquisition strategies and methods for integrating the resources of the acquiring and acquired firms.

tender-merger
A merger that occurs after an acquirer secures enough voting control of the target's shares through a tender offer to effect a merger.

bear hug
The potential acquirer approaches the target with both a merger offer and the threat of a proxy fight and/or hostile tender offer to gain the remaining shares needed to obtain voting control of the target if the merger offer is refused.

anti-takeover amendments
Adding defensive measures to corporate charters to avoid a hostile takeover.

shark repellents
Anti-takeover measures added to corporate charters.

poison pills
Defensive measures taken to avoid a hostile takeover.

white knights
'Friendly' acquirers who will top the price of an unwelcome bidder to avoid a hostile takeover.

Real World

Examples of the takeover defences noted are legion:

- News Corporation, the international media conglomerate behind Fox and Sky television, has a poison pill defence that allows existing shareholders to purchase shares at half the prevailing share price if a new shareholder takes a stake of more than 15 per cent of the company, which would of course massively dilute the shareholding.

- When EMI launched a takeover bid in 2006 for its larger rival Warner Music, Warner countered with a takeover attempt of its own and the mutual bids stalled each other.

Source: Authors' own research at FT.com.

- Elan, the Irish drugs company, issued convertible loan notes outstanding that were seen by investors as a poison put in 2003.
- The French marketing services companies Publicis and Aegis signed a standstill agreement in late 2005.
- Capitalia, the Italian bank, let it be known that it had a white squire in the wings in the shape of a French business magnate, Vincente Bellore, when it was under takeover speculation in early 2006.
- Nissin, the Japanese company that invented the instant noodle, launched a white knight bid for its smaller rival noodle manufacturer Myojo in late 2006, defending the company from a US takeover.

divestiture
Assets and/or resources of a subsidiary or division are sold to another organization.

Divestitures and spin-offs

Sometimes, managers prefer to transfer control of certain assets and resources through divestitures, spin-offs, split-offs, equity carve-outs, split-ups or bust-ups. A **divestiture**

TABLE 17.2

Commonly used anti-takeover measures

DEFENCE	DETAILS
Fair price amendments	Corporate charter amendments mandating that a 'fair price', usually defined as the highest price paid to any shareholder, be paid to all of the target firm's shareholders in the event of a takeover
Golden parachutes	Valuable termination arrangements made for executives that are activated after a takeover
Greenmail	The payment of a premium price for the shares held by a potential hostile acquirer but not paid to all shareholders
Just-say-no defence	Refusal to entertain a takeover offer on the grounds that no consideration offered is sufficient to relinquish control
Pac-man defence	The initiation of a takeover attempt for the hostile acquirer itself
Poison pills	Dilution of the value of shares acquired by a hostile bidder through the offer of additional shares to all other existing shareholders at a discounted price
Poison puts	Deterrent to hostile takeovers through put options attached to bonds that allow the holders to sell their bonds back to the company at a prespecified price in the event of a takeover
Recapitalization	A change in capital structure designed to make the target less attractive by increasing firm leverage
Staggered director elections	Corporate charter amendments designed to make it more difficult for a hostile acquirer to replace members of the board of directors with persons sympathetic to a takeover
Standstill agreements	Negotiated contracts that prevent a substantial shareholder from acquiring more shares for a defined period of time
Supermajority approvals	Corporate charter amendments that require the approval of large majorities (67% or 80%) for a takeover to occur
White knight defence	The pursuit of a friendly acquirer to take over the company instead of a hostile acquirer
White squire defence	The sale of a substantial number of shares to an entity that is sympathetic to current management but has no intention of acquiring the firm

SMART IDEAS VIDEO

Francesca Cornelli, London Business School

'There is an example that shows how crucial risk arbitrage can be to the success at a takeover.'

See the entire interview at
www.cengage.co.uk/ megginson

occurs when the assets and/or resources of a subsidiary or division are sold to another organization. Divestitures are extremely common.

In a **spin-off**, a parent company creates a new company with its own shares by spinning off a division or subsidiary. Existing shareholders receive a pro rata distribution of shares in the new company. The aim is to allow management to focus on the areas they are best suited to. This happened when PepsiCo spun off its restaurant operations (Pizza Hut, Taco Bell and KFC) in 1997 as a new company named Tricon Global Restaurants (with the catchy ticker symbol YUM). A **split-off** is similar to a spin-off in that a parent company creates a newly independent company from a subsidiary, but ownership of the company is transferred to only certain existing shareholders in exchange for their shares in the parent. Equity carve-outs (described more fully in Chapter 11) bring a cash infusion to the parent through the sale of a partial interest in a subsidiary through a public offering to new shareholders. Split-ups and bust-ups are the ultimate transfers of corporate control. As it sounds, the **split-up** of a corporation is the split-up and sale of all its subsidiaries so that it ceases to exist (except possibly as a holding company with no assets). A **bust-up** is the takeover of a company that is subsequently split up.

spin-off
A parent company creates a new company with its own shares to form a division or subsidiary, and existing shareholders receive a pro rata distribution of shares in the new company.

split-off
A parent company creates a new, independent company with its own shares, and ownership of the company is transferred to certain existing shareholders only, in exchange for their shares in the parent.

split-up
The division and sale of all of a company's subsidiaries, so that it ceases to exist (except possibly as a holding company with no assets).

Real World

In 2002 Barnes and Noble, the bookseller and retailer, refocused its activities. One of the effects was that it span off its video games division as a new company, GameStop. The IPO raised over $300 million in November 2004 and the result of the refocus was greatly increased returns for shareholders. Barnes and Noble shares rose by 16 per cent in the year and those of GameStop by over 90 per cent.

Source: Adapted from 'Just a Mention of Spin-Off Can Unlock Value for Shareholders', *Financial Times*, 1 March 2006.

4 Why are acquired resources integrated into a company in so many different forms? What transaction-specific circumstances might lead to a preference of one integrative form over another?

5 How does a tender offer differ from a proxy fight? Why might these two corporate control actions be considered different ways to achieve the same objective?

CONCEPT
REVIEW
QUESTIONS

17.3 A TYPOLOGY OF MERGERS

We can classify mergers and acquisitions by a number of methods. Two main approaches are to classify via the relatedness of business activities and by how the transactions are financed.

bust-up
The takeover of a company that is subsequently split up.

Horizontal mergers

horizontal merger
A combination of competitors within the same geographic market.

We can define a **horizontal merger** as a merger between companies that produces identical or closely related products in any geographic market. For example, a merger between two telescope retailer companies, one in France and the other in Italy, would be classified as horizontal. Similarly in the UK, the merger between Carlton and Granada television companies to form ITV plc was a horizontal merger, as was the Daimler and Chrysler link-up.

market power
A benefit that might arise from a horizontal merger when competition is too weak (or non-existent) to prevent the merged company from raising prices in a market at will.

Horizontal mergers both have the greatest potential for wealth creation and usually attract most media and regulator attention. Firms with similar businesses and assets have the ability to benefit from economies of scale and scope from combining their resources. These mergers also have the greatest possibility of realizing cost savings through the reduction or elimination of overlapping resources. **Market power** is another obvious benefit that might arise from a horizontal merger. Increased market power results when competition is too weak (or non-existent) to prevent the merged company from raising prices in a market at will. Of course, this is exactly the kind of anti-competitiveness that regulators will wish to examine closely.

Real World

A good example of horizontal mergers would be the recent suite of European airline mergers. Airlines in Europe increasingly operate in essentially the same market-place. The Lufthansa–Swiss International link-up, the Air France–KLM merger and the takeover of Buzz by Ryanair all represent horizontal mergers in the airline industry.

Source: Authors' research.

Vertical mergers

vertical merger
Companies with current or potential buyer–seller relationships combine to create a more integrated company.

A **vertical merger** occurs when companies with current or potential buyer–seller relationships combine to create a more integrated company. These mergers are easiest to think of in terms of steps in the production process. Consider the process of producing and selling finished petroleum products. Petroleum exploration and production is followed by transportation, refining and end-use sales. If a company in the drilling business acquires a company that refines crude oil, then the driller is moving forward in the production process by purchasing the potential buyer of its crude oil. This type of vertical merger is a **forward integration**. Had a refiner and distributor acquired a driller, then the merger would be a **backward integration**, as exemplified by the 1984 merger between Texaco and Getty Oil. Texaco needed Getty's drilling operations and reserves to complement its own refineries and distribution and marketing outlets in order to be a fully integrated oil company. The Ford Motor Company takeover of Kwik-Fit car centres would also be a vertical merger.

forward integration
A merger in which the acquired company provides a later step in the production process.

backward integration
A merger in which the acquired company provides an earlier step in the production process.

There are several obvious potential benefits to vertical integration via merger. One advantage to a vertical merger is that product quality and procurement can be ensured from earlier stages of the production process with backward integration. For instance, a manufacturer of precision surgical devices might wish to ensure the high-quality standards required of an input such as a laser beam by acquiring the company that manufactures the laser beam. Or, a manufacturer with great sensitivity to inventory conversion cycles could more efficiently monitor an orderly inventory flow by acquiring a supplier of raw materials. Another advantage to backward integration is the reduction of input prices. The 'middleman' and associated price mark-up are eliminated.

Forward integration may also offer benefits. Whereas backward integration emphasizes inputs, forward integration focuses on output quality and distribution. Provision of an outlet for a product is an advantage to forward integration. One reason for Disney's merger with Capital Cities/ABC was to gain access to a television network as an outlet for Disney's television entertainment production. Vertical integration can also be used as a marketing tool. Many retail stores and car manufacturers have acquired financing subsidiaries to make it easier for a customer to obtain credit to purchase their products (e.g. Ford Motor Credit).

However, there are also disadvantages to vertical mergers. The major disadvantage is the entry into a new line of business. Acquiring managers are likely to have some knowledge of the target firm's business because it is part of the same production process, but similarities do not always imply compatibility. A manager of a car manufacturer might find that what works well for manufacturing cars does not work well for renting them, even though both businesses revolve around cars (as Chrysler found out with its Thrifty Rent-a-Car unit). Managers might also find that the cost savings from 'eliminating the middleman' are not as great as expected. Eliminating the mark-up might reduce costs for the acquirer, but it also means that the acquired subsidiary is no longer producing profits for the parent company. The acquirer might overlook or underestimate this factor when attempting to value a target. Finally, vertical mergers may also be subject to anti-trust regulation, albeit with a smaller probability than with horizontal mergers.

Real World

In 2006 the two main derivatives exchanges in the USA, Chicago Board of Trade (CBOT) and Chicago Mercantile Exchange (CME), agreed to merge. In addition to being a clear horizontal merger, there is also a vertical element. CME operates its own clearing house, the mechanism whereby trades are settled. In merging and with the new company also using the CME system, there is a vertical element to the merger.

Chicago'. *Financial Times*, 19 October 2006.

Conglomerate mergers

Other mergers are conglomerate, which in the USA is divided into two types. **Product extension mergers**, or related diversification mergers, are combinations of companies with similar but not exact lines of business. **Pure conglomerate mergers**, or unrelated diversification mergers, occur between companies in completely different lines of business. The latter are what are often considered the classic conglomerate merger.

Pure conglomerate mergers marry two companies that operate in totally unrelated businesses. Although popular in the 1960s, these mergers have significantly declined in frequency since the 1980s. Based on the principles of portfolio diversification, the purpose of these mergers is to put together two companies that operate in businesses so different that if some systematic or idiosyncratic event has an adverse effect on one business, then the other business will be minimally (or even positively) impacted. Merging these two firms is expected to make earnings and cash flows less volatile. The 1984 merger of carmaker General Motors and computer/business service consulting firm Electronic Data Systems is a prime example of a pure conglomerate merger.

product extension mergers
Diversification mergers that combine companies with similar but not identical lines of business.

pure conglomerate mergers
Unrelated diversification mergers that occur between companies in completely different lines of business.

CONCEPT
REVIEW
QUESTIONS

6 What is the purpose of classifying mergers by degree of business concentration? Why do you think these classifications have changed over time?

7 As conglomerate mergers and corporate diversification have proved to be failures in general, why would any manager pursue these objectives? Can you think of any cases where corporate diversification has worked successfully? What distinguishes these cases from the norm?

Further classifications

Corporate control events can also be categorized according to certain defining characteristics of the transactions, including the method of payment used to finance a transaction and the attitude or response of target management to a takeover attempt.

Method of payment Just like any other type of investment, a merger must be financed with capital components – including debt, retained earnings and newly issued ordinary shares. These components comprise the consideration offered in a transaction and add up to the transaction value – the monetary value of all forms of payment offered to the target for control of the company. Cash on hand from retained earnings and/or generated from an issue of debt is used in financing a cash-only deal, where the target's shareholders receive only cash for their shares in a public company or the target's owner(s) receives cash for the private enterprise. More rarely, the target receives a new issue of debt in exchange for control in a debt-only transaction.

pure share exchange merger
A merger in which shares are the only mode of payment.

Conversely, shares are the only mode of payment in a share-swap or **pure share exchange merger**. The general share-swap merger involves the issuance of new shares in exchange for the target's ordinary shares, but payment may come in the form of either preference shares or subsidiary tracking shares. The number of shares of the surviving firm's ordinary shares that target shareholders receive is determined by the exchange ratio. The surviving firm is either the acquiring firm or the new firm created in a consolidation. For instance, an acquirer with a current share price of €20 that sets an exchange ratio of 0.75 for a target with a current share price of €12 and 100 million shares outstanding will issue 75 million new shares in exchange for the target's shares. The transaction value of this merger would be €1.5 billion (€20 × 75 million). An individual who owns 100 shares (€1200) of the target company would receive acquirer shares worth €1500 (€20 × 75 shares), a 25 per cent control premium.

mixed offerings
Offerings in which some of the shares come from existing shareholders and some are new. Also, a merger financed with a combination of cash and securities.

Mergers may also be financed with a combination of cash and securities, in transactions known as **mixed offerings**. Research by Tim Loughran and Anand Vijh reveals that 24.1 per cent of US acquisitions are mixed, compared with 33.2 per cent cash-only deals and 42.8 per cent share-swap mergers.[1] Martynova and Renneboog found much the same proportions in the European context.[2] The 1995 Disney–Capital Cities/ABC merger is an example of a mixed offering. Capital Cities/ABC shareholders were offered $65 and one Disney share for each of their shares.

Sometimes, target shareholders are also offered a choice for the medium of exchange. For example, target shareholders could be offered the choice of either £30 cash or 1.25 of the surviving company's shares for each share that they hold. This

[1] Tim Loughran and Anand Vijh (1997) 'Do Long-Term Shareholders Benefit From Corporate Acquisitions?' *Journal of Finance* 52:1765–1790.
[2] Marina Martynova and Luc Renneboog (2006) 'Mergers and Acquisitions in Europe', *European Corporate Governance Institute – Finance Working Paper No. 114/2006.*

way, the shareholders can decide whether the exchange ratio is sufficient for them to remain shareholders in the surviving company or whether they should 'take the money and run' with the cash offer. In many cases the issue resolves to the tax liabilities of the most important shareholders and whether one method or another exposes them to more or less tax liabilities. In many jurisdictions, share-based payments are useful as they allow the tax liability, if any, to be deferred until the new shares are sold on.

Attitude of target management Takeover attempts (successful and unsuccessful) are often classified by the degree of resistance offered by the management of the target firm. Uncontested offers are generally referred to as 'friendly' deals, whereas resisted offers are termed 'hostile' transactions. As it seems that everyone likes a good fight, hostile deals receive a disproportionate share of attention. Considering the more recent corporate trend of adopting anti-takeover measures to thwart hostile bidders and the fact that takeovers of private or closely held firms are friendly by nature, hostile deals represent an ever-decreasing (but highly publicized) percentage of corporate control activities.

17.4 SHAREHOLDER WEALTH EFFECTS AND TRANSACTION CHARACTERISTICS

How do the shareholders of companies involved in mergers and acquisitions generally fare? The consensus result obtained in merger studies is that the ordinary shareholders of target firms in successful takeovers experience large and significant wealth gains. Acquirer returns are much smaller and not as generalized, and we discuss the theories offered to explain the cross-sectional differences in acquirers' returns. We also explore the wealth effects of various transaction characteristics.

Effects on target and bidding firm shareholders' wealth

Target returns Target firm shareholders almost always experience substantial wealth gains due to the premium offered for giving up control of their company. Typically the analysis of these returns, and returns to other elements, are measured over a two-month window ending on the day of the announcement. An early survey article by Michael Jensen and Richard Ruback finds that, on average, target firm ordinary shareholders receive takeover premiums of 29.1 per cent in successful tender offers and 15.9 per cent in successful mergers, while more recent studies find that the average takeover premium is 31.8 per cent in tender offers, and that the average premium has risen over time.[3] Target returns are also higher when there are multiple bidders and when managerial resistance leads to a higher offer, but takeover premiums are lost when resistance is too great and prevents a takeover. Work on European mergers and acquisitions by Martynova and Renneboog[4] examines the situation in the 1990s.

---

[3] See Michael Jensen and Richard Ruback (1983) 'The Market for Corporate Control: The Scientific Evidence', *Journal of Financial Economics* 11:5–50; Michael Bradley, Anand Desai and Han Kim (1988) 'Synergistic Gains from Corporate Acquisitions and Their Division between the Stockholders of Target and Acquiring Firms', *Journal of Financial Economics* 21:3–40, and Yen-Sheng Huang and Ralph Walking (1987) 'Target Abnormal Returns Associated with Acquisition Announcements: Payment, Acquisition Form, and Managerial Resistance,' *Journal of Financial Economics* 19:329–349.

[4] Marina Martynova and Luc Renneboog (2006) 'Mergers and Acquisitions in Europe', *European Corporate Governance Institute – Finance Working Paper No. 114/2006.*

They find that target firm returns are lower at around 9 per cent on the day of announcement and 21 per cent over the analysis period.

Acquirer returns Results concerning the ordinary share returns of acquiring firms are not as conclusive as those for target shareholders. Studies show that, on average, the ordinary shareholders of acquiring firms experience positive returns in successful tender offers and virtually zero returns in successful mergers. However, in contrast to the rising trend of target returns, a negative trend in acquirer returns occurs over time. Thus Martynova and Renneboog find a return of only 0.5 per cent in the window, a finding replicated worldwide.[5] However, as the target returns are unanimously positive and the bidder returns essentially zero, the overall effect of bidding and the takeover process is to create wealth.

Hostile and friendly bids Martynova and Renneboog also examine this, finding that hostile bids generate the highest returns to the target – on the day of announcement some 15 per cent and some 30 per cent over the two months prior.[6] Friendly bids and announced mergers by contrast generate much lower returns. This dichotomy is also seen in the returns to bidding firms, where there is a positive return of some 2–3 per cent to the bidder shares when the bid is hostile or there is a tender announcement. Friendly or agreed mergers show a negative return to the bidder shares. These findings are also replicated outside the European context.

Mode of payment The mode of payment used to finance an acquisition is believed to explain much of the cross-sectional variance in acquirers' returns. Multiple studies find higher returns in cash transactions than in share transactions. These studies also show that the higher returns observed by both acquirers and targets in tender offers relative to negotiated mergers are attributable to the fact that most tender offers are financed by cash, whereas most negotiated mergers are equity financed. Announcement-period target returns in the USA are typically some 13 per cent greater for cash deals, acquirer returns in cash-financed deals are near zero, and those in share-financed deals are significantly negative. In Europe the data indicate that cash deals are slightly less valuable to the target, returning 10–12 per cent depending on the extent of cash versus loans, while all-equity returns are only some 7 per cent. Long-term results are even more startling: shareholders in cash tender offers outperform those in share-swap mergers by over 100 per cent through the fifth post-acquisition year – a finding that is worldwide.

Researchers have proposed several theories to explain the differential returns between cash and share offers. The most prominent of these theories revolves around a signalling model. In the context of this model, the mode of payment offered by acquiring firms signals inside information to the capital markets. Managers will finance acquisitions with the cheapest source of capital available. Financing an acquisition with equity signals to the market that bidder managers believe equity is a (relatively) cheap source of capital because they think the target share price is overvalued. Receiving this signal, the capital markets will make a downward revision of the value of the bidder equity. Cash payments by comparison indicate that the bidder's management perceive that the target company has significant potential, and thus they wish to subsume to their shareholders those increases in wealth that will come from the merger and not share these with the existing target company shareholders.

---

[5] Ibid.
[6] Ibid.

Price volatility We have seen earlier in this book that the volatility of a share or asset is also important for the effect that it has on any derivatives, particularly options. Yet there is surprisingly little research on the effects of mergers, tender announcements, etc. on the volatility of target or bidder shares. Early studies[7] indicated that target company returns show significant increases in volatility in the days immediately prior to the announcement. There is also some Australian evidence that these volatility levels subsequently reduce and indeed decline below the level they were at before the announcement and that the volatility of the bidder's stock is unaffected.[8]

---

8 What are the two most important methods of paying for corporate acquisitions?

9 Who wins and who loses in corporate takeovers? Why do acquiring firm shareholders generally lose in share-swap mergers but either benefit or at least break even in acquisitions paid for with cash?

CONCEPT
REVIEW
QUESTIONS

17.5 RATIONALE AND MOTIVES FOR MERGERS AND ACQUISITIONS

As we have seen, the primary objective of any corporation's management team should be the maximization of shareholder wealth. Management should undertake a potential merger or acquisition, like any other investment, as long as its net present value is positive and enhances shareholder value. Mergers may be value enhancing in several ways. However, we know that corporate managers do not always act as proper agents for their shareholders, and agency problems arise when managers engage in non-value-maximizing behaviour. In this section, we examine both the value-maximizing and non-value-maximizing motives that lead managers to pursue mergers and acquisitions.

Value-maximizing motives

Mergers create value when managers seek goals such as increasing operating profit, realizing gains from restructuring poorly managed firms, or creating greater barriers to entry in their industry. These and other value-enhancing objectives can be achieved through mergers and acquisitions that garner access to new geographic markets, increase market power, capitalize on economies of scale or create value through the sale of underperforming target resources.

---

[7] B.F. Smith, R. White, M. Robinson and R. Nason (1997) 'Intraday Volatility and Trading Volume After Takeover Announcements', *Journal of Banking and Finance* 21(3):337–368.

[8] E. Hutson and C. Kearney (2001) 'Volume and Volatility in Stocks Subject to Takeover Bids: Australian Evidence Using Daily Data', *Journal of Empirical Finance* 8(3):273–296; and E. Hutson and C. Kearney (2005) 'Merger Arbitrage and the Interaction Between Target and Bidder Stocks During Takeover Bids', *Research in International Business and Finance* 19(1):1–26.

Expansion Geographic expansion (both domestic and international) may enhance shareholder wealth if the market entered is subject to little or no competition. Managers considering expansion must first evaluate two mutually exclusive alternatives: internal versus external expansion. Internal expansion into a new market, also known as **greenfield entry**, involves acquiring and organizing all resources required for each stage of the investment. These stages encompass contracting with an engineering firm to build a new plant, hiring new employees to staff the plant, implementing training programmes for the new staff, establishing distribution outlets, and so on.

External expansion is the acquisition of a firm with resources already in place. Acquirers pay a control premium to the owners of the acquired firm for relinquishing control, but the payment of this premium ensures that many of the potential problems of greenfield entry are avoided. For instance, external expansion avoids construction delays in the building of a new plant or the inability to adequately staff a new facility. Usually, external expansion is the better option in situations where rapid expansion is desired or when great uncertainty exists about the success of any stage of greenfield entry. International expansion is another good reason to choose external expansion over internal expansion. The business operations, political climate and social mores differ so greatly between some countries that an acquisition is often the only viable alternative for international expansion.

Synergy, market power and strategic mergers A **strategic merger** is one that seeks to create a more efficient merged company than the two premerger companies operating independently. This efficiency-enhancing effect is known as **synergy**. Michael Eisner, CEO of Disney, provided the best definition of synergy with his perception of the value created by his company's merger with Capital Cities/ABC: '1 + 1 = 4'. There are three types of merger-related synergies – operational, managerial, and financial.

Synergies The main sources of **operational synergy** are economies of scale, economies of scope and resource complementarities. Economies of scale result when relative operating costs are reduced because of an increase in size that allows for the reduction or elimination of overlapping resources. For example, the reason given for the elimination of 12 000 positions in the 1995 merger of Chemical Bank and Chase Manhattan Bank was the cost savings generated from the elimination of overlapping jobs. **Economies of scope** are other value-creating benefits of increased size. The ability for a merged firm to launch a national advertising campaign that would not have been feasible for either of the premerger firms is such a benefit. **Resource complementarities** exist when a firm with a particular operating expertise merges with a firm with another operating strength to create a company that has expertise in multiple areas. A good example of such a complementarity is the merger of two pharmaceutical companies, the first a specialist in researching and developing new drugs and the second a master marketer of drug products. Operating synergies are most likely to be achieved in horizontal mergers and least likely to be realized in conglomerate mergers. However, resource complementarities are just as likely to be realized in vertical mergers as horizontal mergers, because vertical combinations pair companies that specialize in different areas.

Managerial synergies, like operating synergies, cause two firms to have greater value when combined than when they are independent. Managerial synergies, however, result in efficiency gains from the combination of management teams. Similar to resource complementarities, managerial synergies arise when management teams with different strengths are paired together. Consider a merger between two retailing firms with differing managerial expertise. The first retailer has a management team that emphasizes revenue growth and excels in recognizing customer trends. The second

greenfield entry
Internal expansion into a new market.

strategic merger
Seeks to create a more efficient merged company than the two premerger companies operating independently.

synergy
An efficiency-enhancing effect resulting from a strategic merger.

operational synergy
Economies of scale, economies of scope and resource complementarities.

economies of scope
Value-creating benefits of increased size for merged companies.

resource complementarities
A firm with a particular operating expertise merges with a firm with another operating strength to create a company that has expertise in multiple areas.

managerial synergies
Efficiency gains from combining the management teams of merged companies.

retailer has a technically oriented management team that excels in cost containment and has perfected inventory control with its superior information systems. A merger between these two firms should benefit from managerial synergies with a joint emphasis on and expertise in revenue growth and cost containment, assuming the two management teams can mesh together smoothly.

Financial synergies occur when a merger results in less volatile cash flows, lower default risk and a lower cost of capital. As financial synergies are largely the anticipated result of conglomerate mergers, we defer this discussion to the section on the diversification motive for mergers. There may also be some tax advantages to merging, if the financial structure of the merged entity would have a lower tax burden than the combined burden of the two separate companies.

financial synergies
A merger results in less-volatile cash flows, lower default risk and a lower cost of capital.

Big Deals Dominate Industry',
Financial Times, 29 November 2006.

Real World

Synergies can be (or can be forecast to be) very large. Take the merger of AT&T with Bell South – the forecast synergies for these two companies, mainly through economies of scale, were forecast to be $2 billion per annum.

Market power Other, more controversial, motives support increasing firm size through mergers and acquisitions. As we have seen, horizontal mergers have the potential to create more efficient companies through size-related operational synergies. Horizontal mergers may also profit from size in another fashion: increased market power. As horizontal mergers are those that take place between competitors, the number of competitors in an industry will necessarily decline. Presumably, price competition will also decline if the merger creates a dominant firm that has the power to control prices in a market.

In 2006 Ryanair launched a takeover bid for the irish flag-carrier, Aer Lingus. While there was significant union opposition, which ultimately derailed the plan, there was also significant concern expressed that the merged entity would have over 75 per cent of flights out of Ireland. Regulatory authorities must balance the corporate benefit of increased efficiency against the consumer cost of increased market power when making decisions on allowing a merger to take place – especially a horizontal merger.

Other strategic rationales Other strategic reasons also motivate managers to pursue mergers. As we mentioned earlier, in vertical mergers, product quality can sometimes be more closely monitored. Another strategic motive is defensive consolidation in a mature or declining industry. As consumer demand declines in an industry, competitors may seek each other out for a merger in order to survive the permanent industry downturn. Not only does the merged firm stand to benefit from economies of scale and scope, but it will also benefit from the reduction of competition. Of course, this does introduce the market power issue for regulators. But recent history has seen regulators adopt a more permissive attitude towards defensive consolidation – for example, the consolidation in the US defence industry in the post-Cold War period.

Cash flow generation Financial mergers are motivated by the prospect of uncovering hidden value in a target through a major restructuring or the generation of free cash flow from merger-related tax advantages. Many of the hostile deals of the 1980s were junk bond-financed financial mergers aimed at either 'busting up' undervalued firms by selling off the assets of the acquired firm for a value greater than the acquisition price or restructuring the acquired firm to increase its corporate focus. A typical financial merger involves a focused acquirer that acquires a diversified firm with some

managerialism theory of mergers
Poorly monitored managers will pursue mergers to maximize their corporation's asset size because managerial remuneration is usually based on firm size, regardless of whether or not these mergers create value for shareholders.

free cash flow theory of mergers
Michael Jensen hypothesizes that managers will use free cash flow to invest in mergers that have negative net present values in order to build corporate empires from which the managers will derive personal benefits, including greater remuneration.

managerial entrenchment theory of mergers
Shleifer and Vishny propose that unmonitored managers will try to build corporate empires through the pursuit of negative-NPV mergers, with the motive of making the management team indispensable to the firm because of its greater size and the team's supposed expertise in managing a large company.

hubris hypothesis of corporate takeovers
Richard Roll contends that some managers overestimate their own managerial capabilities and pursue takeovers with the belief that they can better manage their takeover target than the target's current management team can.

business operations in the acquirer's line of business. The acquirer then sells the non-core businesses and uses the cash flow to pay down the cost of the acquisition.

Non-value-maximizing motives

Unfortunately, not all mergers are motivated for the purpose of maximizing shareholder wealth. Although the motives of managers may not be intentionally value reducing, most revolve around agency problems between managers and shareholders. We discuss these improper motives next.

Agency issues Managers will sometimes disguise their attempts to derive personal benefits from creating and managing larger corporations as the need to expand through mergers and acquisitions. Academic research confirms the importance of this motive, with findings that merger activity is positively related to growth in sales and assets but not related to increased profits or share prices. Considering these findings, Dennis Mueller offered the **managerialism theory of mergers**.[9] According to this theory, poorly monitored managers will pursue mergers to maximize their corporation's asset size because managerial remuneration is usually based on firm size, regardless of whether or not these mergers create value for shareholders.

Michael Jensen further advanced the managerialism theory with his **free cash flow theory of mergers**.[10] Jensen hypothesizes that managers will use free cash flow to invest in mergers that have negative net present values in order to build corporate empires from which the managers will derive personal benefits, including greater remuneration. Obviously, investing in negative-NPV projects is not value enhancing for shareholders. Another variation on this theme is the **managerial entrenchment theory of mergers** proposed by Andrei Shleifer and Robert Vishny.[11] Like the free cash flow theory, this theory holds that unmonitored managers will try to build corporate empires through the pursuit of negative-NPV mergers. However, the entrenchment theory holds that the motive is to make the management team indispensable to the firm because of its greater size and the team's supposed expertise in managing a large company. All three theories have a common theme: agency problems motivate managers to seek mergers that benefit themselves but not shareholders.

Richard Roll offers a similar rationale with his **hubris hypothesis of corporate takeovers**.[12] Roll contends that some managers overestimate their own managerial capabilities and pursue takeovers with the belief that they can better manage their takeover target than the target's current management team can. Acquiring managers then overbid for the target and fail to realize the gains expected from the merger in the post-merger period, thereby diminishing shareholder wealth. Thus, the intent of the managers is not incongruent with the best interests of shareholders (the managers think they will create value), but the result is nonetheless value decreasing.

Diversification As recently as the late 1960s, diversification was actually considered a value-maximizing motive for merger. Over time, however, the capital markets have learned of the failure of corporate diversification strategies, especially those emphasizing unrelated diversification. Given these empirical discoveries, we must now consider that diversification is a non-value-enhancing motive for merger.

---

[9] Dennis Mueller (1969) 'A Theory of Conglomerate Mergers', *Quarterly Journal of Economics* 83:643–659.

[10] Michael Jensen (1986) 'Agency Costs of Free Cash Flow, Corporate Finance and Takeovers', *American Economic Review* 76:323–329.

[11] Andrei Shleifer and Robert Vishny (1989) 'Management Entrenchment', *Journal of Financial Economics* 25:123–139.

[12] Richard Roll (1986) 'The Hubris Hypothesis of Corporate Takeovers', *Journal of Business* 59:197–217.

As previously discussed, corporate diversification and conglomerate mergers were an experiment in portfolio theory applied to corporations. The basic premise of corporate diversification is that the combination of two businesses with less than perfectly correlated cash flows will create a merged firm with less volatile cash flows and inherently lower business risk, where bad outcomes in one business can be offset by good outcomes in another business. Diversification supporters contend that these less volatile cash flows make debt service less risky, lowering default risk and the required return on debt. As described by Wilbur Lewellen, financial synergy is created by this **co-insurance of debt**, as the debt of each combining firm is now insured with cash flows from two businesses.[13] Other proponents of unrelated diversification cite the existence of internal capital markets as another reason to pursue conglomerate mergers. **Internal capital markets** are created when the high cash flows ('cash cow') businesses of a conglomerate generate enough cash flow to fund the 'rising star' businesses. Since this financing is accomplished internally, underwriting costs are avoided and riskier business ventures can be financed with 'cheaper' capital generated from more mature and less risky businesses.

Additional research on corporate diversification generated theories describing the flaws in the diversification motive for merger. Realizing that conglomerate mergers are not likely to benefit from any synergies other than financial, researchers showed that the net effect of conglomerate mergers is zero wealth creation and that any wealth gains experienced by bondholders due to financial synergies are merely redistributed from shareholders. Further, internal capital markets fell into disrepute when it became obvious that managerial control over free cash flow created its own, often severe, agency problems. In particular, capital attained and invested without having to pass a market test is often wasted.

In the early 1980s, researchers theorized that managers pursue conglomerate mergers for risk reduction motives that are personal instead of corporate. Managers recognize that less volatile cash flows result in a lower probability of a substantially poor performance in any single year and the concomitant threat of management dismissal. Therefore, managers are motivated to pursue conglomerate mergers in order to reduce their employment risk. Given the failing results of diversified firms, the **managerial risk reduction theory** seems to be quite insightful and implies that the diversification motive, once thought to be beneficial to shareholders, must now be viewed as a value-destroying rationale caused by agency problems.

co-insurance of debt
The debt of each combining firm in a merger is insured with cash flows from two businesses.

internal capital markets
Created when the high-cash-flow businesses of a conglomerate generate enough cash to fund the riskier business ventures internally.

managerial risk reduction theory
Implies that acquiring firm managers acquire other firms primarily to reduce the volatility of the combined firm's earnings, thus reducing the risk that they will be dismissed due to an unexpected decline in earnings.

CONCEPT REVIEW QUESTIONS

10 What characteristics surrounding a merger would lead you to conclude that it is motivated by value-maximizing managers rather than non-value-maximizing managers? What actions could directors or shareholders take to prevent non-value-maximizing mergers?

11 If you wanted to expand your operations into a foreign country with nebulous laws and an unstable political climate, would you favour internal or external expansion? Why?

12 What is the free cash flow theory of mergers? Why do you think that managers might be tempted to pursue size-increasing mergers even when these do not maximize value?

---

[13] Wilbur Lewellen (1971) 'A Pure Financial Rationale for the Conglomerate Merger', *Journal of Finance* 26:531–537.

17.6 SUMMARY AND CONCLUSIONS

- Mergers and acquisitions are major corporate finance events that, when executed efficiently and with the proper motives, can help managers realize their ultimate goal of maximizing shareholder wealth. Merging firms may be integrated in a number of ways, and the circumstances surrounding the merger determine the means of integration. Transactions may be hostile or friendly; may be financed by cash, shares, debt or some combination of the three; and may increase, preserve or decrease the acquirer's level of business concentration.

- Research on corporate control is bountiful. Major empirical findings include the following: target shareholders almost always win but acquirers' returns are mixed. The combined value of merging firms also increases, especially in non-conglomerate combinations. The highest announcement-period returns are found in mergers between well-managed acquirers and poorly managed targets. Long-term performance is highest for focus-increasing deals financed with cash and lowest for diversifying mergers financed with shares.

- Managers have either value-maximizing or non-value-maximizing motives for pursuing mergers. Value-maximizing motives include expansion into new markets, capturing size economies and other synergies, establishing market power, or generating free cash flow to make better investments. Agency problems result in such non-value-maximizing motives as empire building, entrenchment, hubris and diversification.

- Merger activity occurs in waves spurred by industry-wide events such as deregulation. Historically, we have witnessed five major merger waves: a turn-of-the-20th-century wave of horizontal mergers, a 1920s wave of vertical mergers, the 1960s wave of conglomerate mergers, the 1980s wave that deconstructed many of the 1960s conglomerates, and a recent wave of deregulation-based mergers and consolidations made in preparation for an increasingly global economy. Anti-trust enforcement at the time affects activity in each of these waves.

- Corporate control activities are regulated by layers of different authorities. Increasingly the European Commission plays a significant role.

INTERNET RESOURCES

For updates to links in this section and elsewhere in the book, please go to the book's website at www.cengage.co.uk/megginson.

http://www.sec.gov/about/laws.shtml
'The Laws That Govern the Securities Industry' section of the US Securities and Exchange Commission's website; provides a brief overview of the six key laws that the SEC enforces, including those relating to tender offers and M&A regulations.

http://ec.europa.eu/comm/competition/mergers/overview_en.html
The 'Competition' section of the European Union's official website; provides an overview of the Commission's enforcement philosophy, and describes key ongoing cases.

http://www.mergerstat.com/newsite/
Provides a summary overview of worldwide merger activity.

http://www.uni-kiel.de/ifw/forschung/dome/dome_e.htm
A database of mergers in Europe.

http://www.pwc.com/extweb/home.nsf/docid/C544AD9BF220A37D80257114004A6084
A survey and analysis of central and eastern European mergers and acquisitions.

KEY TERMS

acquisition	hubris hypothesis of corporate takeovers	pure conglomerate mergers
anti-takeover amendments		pure share exchange merger
backward integration	industry shock theory of takeovers	resource complementarities
bear hug		reverse LBO
bust-up	internal capital markets	reverse merger
co-insurance of debt	management buyout (MBO)	shark repellents
consolidation	managerial entrenchment theory of mergers	spin-off
corporate control		split-off
economies of scale	managerial risk reduction theory	split-up
economies of scope	managerial synergies	strategic merger
employee stock ownership plan (ESOP)	managerialism theory of mergers	subsidiary merger
	market power	synergy
financial synergies	merger	takeover
forward integration	mixed offerings	tender offer
free cash flow theory of mergers	operational synergy	tender-merger
going-private transactions	poison pills	vertical merger
horizontal merger	product extension mergers	white knights

SELF-TEST PROBLEMS

ST17-1 Mega Service Company (MSC) is offering to exchange 2.5 of its own shares for each share of target firm Norman Corporation as consideration for a proposed merger. There are 10 million Norman Corporation outstanding, and its share price was €60 before the merger offer. MSC's pre-offer share price was €30. What is the control premium percentage offered? Now suppose that when the merger is consummated eight months later, MSC's share price drops to €25. At that point, what is the control premium percentage and total transaction value?

ST17-2 You are the director of capital acquisitions for Morningside Hotel Company. One of the projects you are deliberating is the acquisition of Monroe Hospitality, a company that owns and operates a chain of bed-and-breakfast inns. Susan Sharp, Monroe's owner, is willing to sell her company to Morningside only if she is offered an all-cash purchase price of €5 million. Your project analysis team estimates that the purchase of Monroe Hospitality will generate the following after-tax marginal cash flow:

YEAR	CASH FLOW
1	€1 000 000
2	1 500 000
3	2 000 000
4	2 500 000
5	3 000 000

If you decide to go ahead with this acquisition, it will be funded with Morningside's standard mix of debt and equity, at the firm's weighted average (after-tax) cost of capital of 9 per cent. Morningside's tax rate is 30 per cent. Should you recommend acquiring Monroe Hospitality to your CEO?

Q17-1 What is meant by a change in corporate control? List and describe the various ways in which a change of corporate control may occur.

Q17-2 What is a tender offer, and how can it be used as a mechanism to orchestrate a merger?

Q17-3 Differentiate between the different levels of business concentration created by mergers.

Q17-4 Elaborate on the significance of the mode of payment for the shareholders of the target firm and their continued interest in the surviving firm. Specifically, which form of payment retains the shareholders of the target firm as shareholders in the surviving firm? Which payment form receives preferential tax treatment?

Q17-5 What is the signalling theory of mergers? What is the relationship between signalling and the mode of payment used in acquisitions? Is there a relationship between the mode of payment used in acquisitions and the level of insider shareholdings of acquiring firms?

Q17-6 Empirically, what are the wealth effects of corporate control activities? Who wins and who loses in corporate control contests? What explanations or theories are offered for the differences in returns of acquiring firms' ordinary shares? Why are higher takeover premiums paid in cash transactions than in share transactions? How do other security-holders fare in takeovers?

Q17-7 Relate the industry shock theory of mergers to the history of merger waves. What were the motivating factors for increased merger activity during each of the five major merger waves?

Q17-8 Under what conditions would external expansion be preferable to internal expansion? What is the ultimate decision criterion for determining the acceptability of any expansion strategy?

Q17-9 Delineate the value-maximizing motives for mergers. How are these motives interrelated?

Q17-10 Define the three types of synergy that may result from mergers. What are the sources of these synergies?

Q17-11 Explain how agency problems may lead to non-value-maximizing motives for mergers. Discuss the various academic theories offered as the rationale for these agency problem-induced motives.

Q17-12 Describe the relationship between conglomerate mergers and portfolio theory. What is the desired result of merging two unrelated businesses? Has the empirical evidence proved corporate diversification to be successful?

Q17-13 What is the role of the European Commission in mergers?

Overview of corporate control activities

P17-1 Bulldog Industries is offering, as consideration for a merger, target Blazerco 1.5 of its shares for each share of Blazerco. There are 1 million shares of Blazerco outstanding, priced at was €50 before the merger offer. Bulldog's pre-offer share price was €40. What is the control premium percentage offered? Now suppose that when the merger is consummated six months later, Bulldog's share price drops to €30. At that point, what is the control premium percentage and total transaction value?

P17-2 You are the director of capital acquisitions for Crimson Software Company. One of the projects you are considering is the acquisition of Geekware, a private software company that produces software for finance professors. Dave Vanzandt, the owner of Geekware, is amenable to the idea of selling his enterprise to Crimson, but he has certain conditions that must be met before selling. The primary condition set forth is a non-negotiable, all-cash purchase price of €20 million. Your project analysis team estimates that the purchase of Geekware will generate the following marginal cash flow:

YEAR	CASH FLOW
1	€1 000 000
2	3 000 000
3	5 000 000
4	7 500 000
5	7 500 000

Of the €20 million in cash needed for the purchase, €5 million is available from retained earnings, with a required return of 12 per cent, and the remaining €15 million will come from a new debt issue yielding 8 per cent. Crimson's tax rate is 40 per cent. Should you recommend acquiring Geekware to your CEO?

P17-3 Firm A plans to acquire Firm B. The acquisition would result in incremental cash flows for Firm A of €10 million in each of the first five years. Firm A expects to divest Firm B at the end of the fifth year for €100 million. The ß for Firm A is 1.1, which is expected to remain unchanged after the acquisition. The risk-free rate, R_f, is 7 per cent, and the expected market rate of return, R_m, is 15 per cent. Firm A is financed by 80 per cent equity and 20 per cent debt, and this leverage will also remain unchanged after the acquisition. Firm A pays interest of 10 per cent on its debt, which will also remain unchanged after the acquisition.

a Disregarding taxes, what is the maximum price that Firm A should pay for firm B?

b Firm A has a share price of €30 and 10 million shares outstanding. If Firm B shareholders are to be paid the maximum price determined in part (a) via a new share issue, how many new shares will be issued, and what will be the post-merger stock price?

THOMSON ONE **Business School Edition**

For instructions on using Thomson ONE, refer to the introductory text provided with the Thomson ONE problems at the end of Chapters 1–6, or in *A Guide for Using Thomson ONE – Business School Edition.*

P17-4 There were many large write-downs of goodwill on the balance sheet after FASB 142 went into effect at the beginning of 2002. Specifically, this chapter refers to JDS Uniphase Corp. (ticker: @JDSU), AOL Time Warner (U:TWX), and Nortel Networks (C:NT) having to take multi-billion-dollar write-downs in 2002 for acquisitions completed in previous years. Look at the financial statements for the three companies for the fiscal year ending in 2002. How much do intangible assets on the balance sheet change for the companies between 2001 and 2002 (between 2000 and 2001 for Nortel)? How much of a corresponding change do you observe under extraordinary charge – pre-tax on the income statement? Did the companies perform as badly as suggested by their net incomes in the year they took the extraordinary charge [look at Inc.(Dec.) in Cash & Short Term Investments in the cash flow statement]? Does this tell you if the goodwill write-down is a cash or a non-cash expense?

MINICASE *Mergers, acquisitions and corporate control*

Corporate control activities through merger and acquisition have recently changed the landscape of casino ownership with the acquisition of Mirage Resorts, Incorporated and then Mandalay Resort Group by MGM Grand, Incorporated and the acquisition of Caesars Entertainment Incorporated by Harrah's Entertainment Incorporated. As chief financial officer (CFO) of a competing casino, you feel that you should know all the particulars about corporate control activities, both to protect your company from takeover and to evaluate potential takeover targets. As such, you decide to find the answers to the following questions.

Assignment

1 What are the different types of corporate control activities?

2 What are horizontal, vertical and conglomerate mergers?

3 What returns do target and bidding firm shareholders realize around the announcement of acquisitions?

4 What are some of the motives for value-maximizing mergers and acquisitions?

5 What are some of the motives for mergers and acquisitions that are not value maximizing?

6 What are the reasons for the various merger waves that have occurred throughout history?

7 Discuss the regulation of corporate control activities.

Appendix A:
Financial Tables

TABLE A1

Future value factors for one euro compounded at r per cent for n periods

$$FVF_{r\%,n} = (1+r)^n$$

PERIOD	1%	2%	3%	4%	5%	6%	7%	8%	9%	10%	11%	12%	13%	14%	15%
1	1.010	1.020	1.030	1.040	1.050	1.060	1.070	1.080	1.090	1.100	1.110	1.120	1.130	1.140	1.150
2	1.020	1.040	1.061	1.082	1.103	1.124	1.145	1.166	1.188	1.210	1.232	1.254	1.277	1.300	1.323
3	1.030	1.061	1.093	1.125	1.158	1.191	1.225	1.260	1.295	1.331	1.368	1.405	1.443	1.482	1.521
4	1.041	1.082	1.126	1.170	1.216	1.262	1.311	1.360	1.412	1.464	1.518	1.574	1.630	1.689	1.749
5	1.051	1.104	1.159	1.217	1.276	1.338	1.403	1.469	1.539	1.611	1.685	1.762	1.842	1.925	2.011
6	1.062	1.126	1.194	1.265	1.340	1.419	1.501	1.587	1.677	1.772	1.870	1.974	2.082	2.195	2.313
7	1.072	1.149	1.230	1.316	1.407	1.504	1.606	1.714	1.828	1.949	2.076	2.211	2.353	2.502	2.660
8	1.083	1.172	1.267	1.369	1.477	1.594	1.718	1.851	1.993	2.144	2.305	2.476	2.658	2.853	3.059
9	1.094	1.195	1.305	1.423	1.551	1.689	1.838	1.999	2.172	2.358	2.558	2.773	3.004	3.252	3.518
10	1.105	1.219	1.344	1.480	1.629	1.791	1.967	2.159	2.367	2.594	2.839	3.106	3.395	3.707	4.046
11	1.116	1.243	1.384	1.539	1.710	1.898	2.105	2.332	2.580	2.853	3.152	3.479	3.836	4.226	4.652
12	1.127	1.268	1.426	1.601	1.796	2.012	2.252	2.518	2.813	3.138	3.498	3.896	4.335	4.818	5.350
13	1.138	1.294	1.469	1.665	1.886	2.133	2.410	2.720	3.066	3.452	3.883	4.363	4.898	5.492	6.153
14	1.149	1.319	1.513	1.732	1.980	2.261	2.579	2.937	3.342	3.797	4.310	4.887	5.535	6.261	7.076
15	1.161	1.346	1.558	1.801	2.079	2.397	2.759	3.172	3.642	4.177	4.785	5.474	6.254	7.138	8.137
16	1.173	1.373	1.605	1.873	2.183	2.540	2.952	3.426	3.970	4.595	5.311	6.130	7.067	8.137	9.358
17	1.184	1.400	1.653	1.948	2.292	2.693	3.159	3.700	4.328	5.054	5.895	6.866	7.986	9.276	10.761
18	1.196	1.428	1.702	2.026	2.407	2.854	3.380	3.996	4.717	5.560	6.544	7.690	9.024	10.575	12.375
19	1.208	1.457	1.754	2.107	2.527	3.026	3.617	4.316	5.142	6.116	7.263	8.613	10.197	12.056	14.232
20	1.220	1.486	1.806	2.191	2.653	3.207	3.870	4.661	5.604	6.727	8.062	9.646	11.523	13.743	16.367
21	1.232	1.516	1.860	2.279	2.786	3.400	4.141	5.034	6.109	7.400	8.949	10.804	13.021	15.668	18.822
22	1.245	1.546	1.916	2.370	2.925	3.604	4.430	5.437	6.659	8.140	9.934	12.100	14.714	17.861	21.645
23	1.257	1.577	1.974	2.465	3.072	3.820	4.741	5.871	7.258	8.954	11.026	13.552	16.627	20.362	24.891
24	1.270	1.608	2.033	2.563	3.225	4.049	5.072	6.341	7.911	9.850	12.239	15.179	18.788	23.212	28.625
25	1.282	1.641	2.094	2.666	3.386	4.292	5.427	6.848	8.623	10.835	13.585	17.000	21.231	26.462	32.919
30	1.348	1.811	2.427	3.243	4.322	5.743	7.612	10.063	13.268	17.449	22.892	29.960	39.116	50.950	66.212
35	1.417	2.000	2.814	3.946	5.516	7.686	10.677	14.785	20.414	28.102	38.575	52.800	72.069	98.100	133.176
40	1.489	2.208	3.262	4.801	7.040	10.286	14.974	21.725	31.409	45.259	65.001	93.051	132.782	188.884	267.864
45	1.565	2.438	3.782	5.841	8.985	13.765	21.002	31.920	48.327	72.890	109.530	163.988	244.641	363.679	538.769
50	1.645	2.692	4.384	7.107	11.467	18.420	29.457	46.902	74.358	117.391	184.565	289.002	450.736	700.233	1083.657

TABLE A1 (cont.)

PERIOD	16%	17%	18%	19%	20%	25%	30%	35%	40%	45%	50%
1	1.160	1.170	1.180	1.190	1.200	1.250	1.300	1.350	1.400	1.450	1.500
2	1.346	1.369	1.392	1.416	1.440	1.563	1.690	1.823	1.960	2.103	2.250
3	1.561	1.602	1.643	1.685	1.728	1.953	2.197	2.460	2.744	3.049	3.375
4	1.811	1.874	1.939	2.005	2.074	2.441	2.856	3.322	3.842	4.421	5.063
5	2.100	2.192	2.288	2.386	2.488	3.052	3.713	4.484	5.378	6.410	7.594
6	2.436	2.565	2.700	2.840	2.986	3.815	4.827	6.053	7.530	9.294	11.391
7	2.826	3.001	3.185	3.379	3.583	4.768	6.275	8.172	10.541	13.476	17.086
8	3.278	3.511	3.759	4.021	4.300	5.960	8.157	11.032	14.758	19.541	25.629
9	3.803	4.108	4.435	4.785	5.160	7.451	10.604	14.894	20.661	28.334	38.443
10	4.411	4.807	5.234	5.695	6.192	9.313	13.786	20.107	28.925	41.085	57.665
11	5.117	5.624	6.176	6.777	7.430	11.642	17.922	27.144	40.496	59.573	86.498
12	5.936	6.580	7.288	8.064	8.916	14.552	23.298	36.644	56.694	86.381	129.746
13	6.886	7.699	8.599	9.596	10.699	18.190	30.288	49.470	79.371	125.252	194.620
14	7.988	9.007	10.147	11.420	12.839	22.737	39.374	66.784	111.120	181.615	291.929
15	9.266	10.539	11.974	13.590	15.407	28.422	51.186	90.158	155.568	263.342	437.894
16	10.748	12.330	14.129	16.172	18.488	35.527	66.542	121.714	217.795	381.846	656.841
17	12.468	14.426	16.672	19.244	22.186	44.409	86.504	164.314	304.913	553.676	985.261
18	14.463	16.879	19.673	22.901	26.623	55.511	112.455	221.824	426.879	802.831	1477.892
19	16.777	19.748	23.214	27.252	31.948	69.389	146.192	299.462	597.630	1164.105	2216.838
20	19.461	23.106	27.393	32.429	38.338	86.736	190.050	404.274	836.683	1687.952	3325.257
21	22.574	27.034	32.324	38.591	46.005	108.420	247.065	545.769	1171.356	2447.530	4987.885
22	26.186	31.629	38.142	45.923	55.206	135.525	321.184	736.789	1639.898	3548.919	7481.828
23	30.376	37.006	45.008	54.649	66.247	169.407	417.539	994.665	2295.857	5145.932	11222.741
24	35.236	43.297	53.109	65.032	79.497	211.758	542.801	1342.797	3214.200	7461.602	16834.112
25	40.874	50.658	62.669	77.388	95.396	264.698	705.641	1812.776	4499.880	10819.322	25251.168
30	85.850	111.065	143.371	184.675	237.376	807.794	2619.996	8128.550	24201.432	69348.978	191751.059
35	180.314	243.503	327.997	440.701	590.668	2465.190	9727.860	36448.688	130161.112	444508.508	*
40	378.721	533.869	750.378	1051.668	1469.772	7523.164	36118.865	163437.135	700037.697	*	*
45	795.444	1170.479	1716.684	2509.651	3657.262	22958.874	134106.817	732857.577	*	*	*
50	1670.704	2566.215	3927.357	5988.914	9100.438	70064.923	497929.223	*	*	*	*

* Not shown because of space limitations.

TABLE A2

Present value factors for one euro discounted at r per cent for n periods

$$PVF_{r\%,n} = 1/(1+r)^n$$

PERIOD	1%	2%	3%	4%	5%	6%	7%	8%	9%	10%	11%	12%	13%	14%	15%
1	0.990	0.980	0.971	0.962	0.952	0.943	0.935	0.926	0.917	0.909	0.901	0.893	0.885	0.877	0.870
2	0.980	0.961	0.943	0.925	0.907	0.890	0.873	0.857	0.842	0.826	0.812	0.797	0.783	0.769	0.756
3	0.971	0.942	0.915	0.889	0.864	0.840	0.816	0.794	0.772	0.751	0.731	0.712	0.693	0.675	0.658
4	0.961	0.924	0.888	0.855	0.823	0.792	0.763	0.735	0.708	0.683	0.659	0.636	0.613	0.592	0.572
5	0.951	0.906	0.863	0.822	0.784	0.747	0.713	0.681	0.650	0.621	0.593	0.567	0.543	0.519	0.497
6	0.942	0.888	0.837	0.790	0.746	0.705	0.666	0.630	0.596	0.564	0.535	0.507	0.480	0.456	0.432
7	0.933	0.871	0.813	0.760	0.711	0.665	0.623	0.583	0.547	0.513	0.482	0.452	0.425	0.400	0.376
8	0.923	0.853	0.789	0.731	0.677	0.627	0.582	0.540	0.502	0.467	0.434	0.404	0.376	0.351	0.327
9	0.914	0.837	0.766	0.703	0.645	0.592	0.544	0.500	0.460	0.424	0.391	0.361	0.333	0.308	0.284
10	0.905	0.820	0.744	0.676	0.614	0.558	0.508	0.463	0.422	0.386	0.352	0.322	0.295	0.270	0.247
11	0.896	0.804	0.722	0.650	0.585	0.527	0.475	0.429	0.388	0.350	0.317	0.287	0.261	0.237	0.215
12	0.887	0.788	0.701	0.625	0.557	0.497	0.444	0.397	0.356	0.319	0.286	0.257	0.231	0.208	0.187
13	0.879	0.773	0.681	0.601	0.530	0.469	0.415	0.368	0.326	0.290	0.258	0.229	0.204	0.182	0.163
14	0.870	0.758	0.661	0.577	0.505	0.442	0.388	0.340	0.299	0.263	0.232	0.205	0.181	0.160	0.141
15	0.861	0.743	0.642	0.555	0.481	0.417	0.362	0.315	0.275	0.239	0.209	0.183	0.160	0.140	0.123
16	0.853	0.728	0.623	0.534	0.458	0.394	0.339	0.292	0.252	0.218	0.188	0.163	0.141	0.123	0.107
17	0.844	0.714	0.605	0.513	0.436	0.371	0.317	0.270	0.231	0.198	0.170	0.146	0.125	0.108	0.093
18	0.836	0.700	0.587	0.494	0.416	0.350	0.296	0.250	0.212	0.180	0.153	0.130	0.111	0.095	0.081
19	0.828	0.686	0.570	0.475	0.396	0.331	0.277	0.232	0.194	0.164	0.138	0.116	0.098	0.083	0.070
20	0.820	0.673	0.554	0.456	0.377	0.312	0.258	0.215	0.178	0.149	0.124	0.104	0.087	0.073	0.061
21	0.811	0.660	0.538	0.439	0.359	0.294	0.242	0.199	0.164	0.135	0.112	0.093	0.077	0.064	0.053
22	0.803	0.647	0.522	0.422	0.342	0.278	0.226	0.184	0.150	0.123	0.101	0.083	0.068	0.056	0.046
23	0.795	0.634	0.507	0.406	0.326	0.262	0.211	0.170	0.138	0.112	0.091	0.074	0.060	0.049	0.040
24	0.788	0.622	0.492	0.390	0.310	0.247	0.197	0.158	0.126	0.102	0.082	0.066	0.053	0.043	0.035
25	0.780	0.610	0.478	0.375	0.295	0.233	0.184	0.146	0.116	0.092	0.074	0.059	0.047	0.038	0.030
30	0.742	0.552	0.412	0.308	0.231	0.174	0.131	0.099	0.075	0.057	0.044	0.033	0.026	0.020	0.015
35	0.706	0.500	0.355	0.253	0.181	0.130	0.094	0.068	0.049	0.036	0.026	0.019	0.014	0.010	0.008
40	0.672	0.453	0.307	0.208	0.142	0.097	0.067	0.046	0.032	0.022	0.015	0.011	0.008	0.005	0.004
45	0.639	0.410	0.264	0.171	0.111	0.073	0.048	0.031	0.021	0.014	0.009	0.006	0.004	0.003	0.002
50	0.608	0.372	0.228	0.141	0.087	0.054	0.034	0.021	0.013	0.009	0.005	0.003	0.002	0.001	0.001

TABLE A2 (cont.)

PERIOD	16%	17%	18%	19%	20%	25%	30%	35%	40%	45%	50%
1	0.862	0.855	0.847	0.840	0.833	0.800	0.769	0.741	0.714	0.690	0.667
2	0.743	0.731	0.718	0.706	0.694	0.640	0.592	0.549	0.510	0.476	0.444
3	0.641	0.624	0.609	0.593	0.579	0.512	0.455	0.406	0.364	0.328	0.296
4	0.552	0.534	0.516	0.499	0.482	0.410	0.350	0.301	0.260	0.226	0.198
5	0.476	0.456	0.437	0.419	0.402	0.328	0.269	0.223	0.186	0.156	0.132
6	0.410	0.390	0.370	0.352	0.335	0.262	0.207	0.165	0.133	0.108	0.088
7	0.354	0.333	0.314	0.296	0.279	0.210	0.159	0.122	0.095	0.074	0.059
8	0.305	0.285	0.266	0.249	0.233	0.168	0.123	0.091	0.068	0.051	0.039
9	0.263	0.243	0.225	0.209	0.194	0.134	0.094	0.067	0.048	0.035	0.026
10	0.227	0.208	0.191	0.176	0.162	0.107	0.073	0.050	0.035	0.024	0.017
11	0.195	0.178	0.162	0.148	0.135	0.086	0.056	0.037	0.025	0.017	0.012
12	0.168	0.152	0.137	0.124	0.112	0.069	0.043	0.027	0.018	0.012	0.008
13	0.145	0.130	0.116	0.104	0.093	0.055	0.033	0.020	0.013	0.008	0.005
14	0.125	0.111	0.099	0.088	0.078	0.044	0.025	0.015	0.009	0.006	0.003
15	0.108	0.095	0.084	0.074	0.065	0.035	0.020	0.011	0.006	0.004	0.002
16	0.093	0.081	0.071	0.062	0.054	0.028	0.015	0.008	0.005	0.003	0.002
17	0.080	0.069	0.060	0.052	0.045	0.023	0.012	0.006	0.003	0.002	0.001
18	0.069	0.059	0.051	0.044	0.038	0.018	0.009	0.005	0.002	0.001	0.001
19	0.060	0.051	0.043	0.037	0.031	0.014	0.007	0.003	0.002	0.001	*
20	0.051	0.043	0.037	0.031	0.026	0.012	0.005	0.002	0.001	0.001	*
21	0.044	0.037	0.031	0.026	0.022	0.009	0.004	0.002	0.001	*	*
22	0.038	0.032	0.026	0.022	0.018	0.007	0.003	0.001	0.001	*	*
23	0.033	0.027	0.022	0.018	0.015	0.006	0.002	0.001	*	*	*
24	0.028	0.023	0.019	0.015	0.013	0.005	0.002	0.001	*	*	*
25	0.024	0.020	0.016	0.013	0.010	0.004	0.001	0.001	*	*	*
30	0.012	0.009	0.007	0.005	0.004	0.001	*	*	*	*	*
35	0.006	0.004	0.003	0.002	0.002	*	*	*	*	*	*
40	0.003	0.002	0.001	0.001	0.001	*	*	*	*	*	*
45	0.001	0.001	0.001	0.001	*	*	*	*	*	*	*
50	0.001	*	*	*	*	*	*	*	*	*	*

* PVF is zero to three decimal places.

TABLE A3

Future value factors for a one-euro ordinary annuity compounded at *r* per cent for *n* periods

$$FVFA_{r\%,n} = PMT \times \frac{(1+r)^n - 1}{r}$$

PERIOD	1%	2%	3%	4%	5%	6%	7%	8%	9%	10%	11%	12%	13%	14%	15%
1	1.000	1.000	1.000	1.000	1.000	1.000	1.000	1.000	1.000	1.000	1.000	1.000	1.000	1.000	1.000
2	2.010	2.020	2.030	2.040	2.050	2.060	2.070	2.080	2.090	2.100	2.110	2.120	2.130	2.140	2.150
3	3.030	3.060	3.091	3.122	3.153	3.184	3.215	3.246	3.278	3.310	3.342	3.374	3.407	3.440	3.473
4	4.060	4.122	4.184	4.246	4.310	4.375	4.440	4.506	4.573	4.641	4.710	4.779	4.850	4.921	4.993
5	5.101	5.204	5.309	5.416	5.526	5.637	5.751	5.867	5.985	6.105	6.228	6.353	6.480	6.610	6.742
6	6.152	6.308	6.468	6.633	6.802	6.975	7.153	7.336	7.523	7.716	7.913	8.115	8.323	8.536	8.754
7	7.214	7.434	7.662	7.898	8.142	8.394	8.654	8.923	9.200	9.487	9.783	10.089	10.405	10.730	11.067
8	8.286	8.583	8.892	9.214	9.549	9.897	10.260	10.637	11.028	11.436	11.859	12.300	12.757	13.233	13.727
9	9.369	9.755	10.159	10.583	11.027	11.491	11.978	12.488	13.021	13.579	14.164	14.776	15.416	16.085	16.786
10	10.462	10.950	11.464	12.006	12.578	13.181	13.816	14.487	15.193	15.937	16.722	17.549	18.420	19.337	20.304
11	11.567	12.169	12.808	13.486	14.207	14.972	15.784	16.645	17.560	18.531	19.561	20.655	21.814	23.045	24.349
12	12.683	13.412	14.192	15.026	15.917	16.870	17.888	18.977	20.141	21.384	22.713	24.133	25.650	27.271	29.002
13	13.809	14.680	15.618	16.627	17.713	18.882	20.141	21.495	22.953	24.523	26.212	28.029	29.985	32.089	34.352
14	14.947	15.974	17.086	18.292	19.599	21.015	22.550	24.215	26.019	27.975	30.095	32.393	34.883	37.581	40.505
15	16.097	17.293	18.599	20.024	21.579	23.276	25.129	27.152	29.361	31.772	34.405	37.280	40.417	43.842	47.580
16	17.258	18.639	20.157	21.825	23.657	25.673	27.888	30.324	33.003	35.950	39.190	42.753	46.672	50.980	55.717
17	18.430	20.012	21.762	23.698	25.840	28.213	30.840	33.750	36.974	40.545	44.501	48.884	53.739	59.118	65.075
18	19.615	21.412	23.414	25.645	28.132	30.906	33.999	37.450	41.301	45.599	50.396	55.750	61.725	68.394	75.836
19	20.811	22.841	25.117	27.671	30.539	33.760	37.379	41.446	46.018	51.159	56.939	63.440	70.749	78.969	88.212
20	22.019	24.297	26.870	29.778	33.066	36.786	40.995	45.762	51.160	57.275	64.203	72.052	80.947	91.025	102.444
21	23.239	25.783	28.676	31.969	35.719	39.993	44.865	50.423	56.765	64.002	72.265	81.699	92.470	104.768	118.810
22	24.472	27.299	30.537	34.248	38.505	43.392	49.006	55.457	62.873	71.403	81.214	92.503	105.491	120.436	137.632
23	25.716	28.845	32.453	36.618	41.430	46.996	53.436	60.893	69.532	79.543	91.148	104.603	120.205	138.297	159.276
24	26.973	30.422	34.426	39.083	44.502	50.816	58.177	66.765	76.790	88.497	102.174	118.155	136.831	158.659	184.168
25	28.243	32.030	36.459	41.646	47.727	54.865	63.249	73.106	84.701	98.347	114.413	133.334	155.620	181.871	212.793
30	34.785	40.568	47.575	56.085	66.439	79.058	94.461	113.283	136.308	164.494	199.021	241.333	293.199	356.787	434.745
35	41.660	49.994	60.462	73.652	90.320	111.435	138.237	172.317	215.711	271.024	341.590	431.663	546.681	693.573	881.170
40	48.886	60.402	75.401	95.026	120.800	154.762	199.635	259.057	337.882	442.593	581.826	767.091	1013.704	1342.025	1779.090
45	56.481	71.893	92.720	121.029	159.700	212.744	285.749	386.506	525.859	718.905	986.639	1358.230	1874.165	2590.565	3585.128
50	64.463	84.579	112.797	152.667	209.348	290.336	406.529	573.770	815.084	1163.909	1668.771	2400.018	3459.507	4994.521	7217.716

TABLE A3 (cont.)

PERIOD	16%	17%	18%	19%	20%	25%	30%	35%	40%	45%	50%
1	1.000	1.000	1.000	1.000	1.000	1.000	1.000	1.000	1.000	1.000	1.000
2	2.160	2.170	2.180	2.190	2.200	2.250	2.300	2.350	2.400	2.450	2.500
3	3.506	3.539	3.572	3.606	3.640	3.813	3.990	4.173	4.360	4.553	4.750
4	5.066	5.141	5.215	5.291	5.368	5.766	6.187	6.633	7.104	7.601	8.125
5	6.877	7.014	7.154	7.297	7.442	8.207	9.043	9.954	10.946	12.022	13.188
6	8.977	9.207	9.442	9.683	9.930	11.259	12.756	14.438	16.324	18.431	20.781
7	11.414	11.772	12.142	12.523	12.916	15.073	17.583	20.492	23.853	27.725	32.172
8	14.240	14.773	15.327	15.902	16.499	19.842	23.858	28.664	34.395	41.202	49.258
9	17.519	18.285	19.086	19.923	20.799	25.802	32.015	39.696	49.153	60.743	74.887
10	21.321	22.393	23.521	24.709	25.959	33.253	42.619	54.590	69.814	89.077	113.330
11	25.733	27.200	28.755	30.404	32.150	42.566	56.405	74.697	98.739	130.162	170.995
12	30.850	32.824	34.931	37.180	39.581	54.208	74.327	101.841	139.235	189.735	257.493
13	36.786	39.404	42.219	45.244	48.497	68.760	97.625	138.485	195.929	276.115	387.239
14	43.672	47.103	50.818	54.841	59.196	86.949	127.913	187.954	275.300	401.367	581.859
15	51.660	56.110	60.965	66.261	72.035	109.687	167.286	254.738	386.420	582.982	873.788
16	60.925	66.649	72.939	79.850	87.442	138.109	218.472	344.897	541.988	846.324	1311.682
17	71.673	78.979	87.068	96.022	105.931	173.636	285.014	466.611	759.784	1228.170	1968.523
18	84.141	93.406	103.740	115.266	128.117	218.045	371.518	630.925	1064.697	1781.846	2953.784
19	98.603	110.285	123.414	138.166	154.740	273.556	483.973	852.748	1491.576	2584.677	4431.676
20	115.380	130.033	146.628	165.418	186.688	342.945	630.165	1152.210	2089.206	3748.782	6648.513
21	134.841	153.139	174.021	197.847	225.026	429.681	820.215	1556.484	2925.889	5436.734	9973.770
22	157.415	180.172	206.345	236.438	271.031	538.101	1067.280	2102.253	4097.245	7884.264	14961.655
23	183.601	211.801	244.487	282.362	326.237	673.626	1388.464	2839.042	5737.142	11433.182	22443.483
24	213.978	248.808	289.494	337.010	392.484	843.033	1806.003	3833.706	8032.999	16579.115	33666.224
25	249.214	292.105	342.603	402.042	471.981	1054.791	2348.803	5176.504	11247.199	24040.716	50500.337
30	530.312	647.439	790.948	966.712	1181.882	3227.174	8729.985	23221.570	60501.081	154106.618	383500.118
35	1120.713	1426.491	1816.652	2314.214	2948.341	9856.761	32422.868	104136.251	325400.279	987794.463	*
40	2360.757	3134.522	4163.213	5529.829	7343.858	30088.655	120392.883	466960.385	*	*	*
45	4965.274	6879.291	9531.577	13203.424	18281.310	91831.496	447019.389	*	*	*	*
50	10435.649	15089.502	21813.094	31515.336	45497.191	280255.693	*	*	*	*	*

* Not shown because of space limitations.

TABLE A4

Present value factors for a one-euro ordinary annuity discounted at r per cent for n periods

$$PVFA_{r\%,n} = \frac{PMT}{r} \times \left[1 - \frac{1}{(1+r)^n} \right]$$

PERIOD	1%	2%	3%	4%	5%	6%	7%	8%	9%	10%	11%	12%	13%	14%	15%
1	0.990	0.980	0.971	0.962	0.952	0.943	0.935	0.926	0.917	0.909	0.901	0.893	0.885	0.877	0.870
2	1.970	1.942	1.913	1.886	1.859	1.833	1.808	1.783	1.759	1.736	1.713	1.690	1.668	1.647	1.626
3	2.941	2.884	2.829	2.775	2.723	2.673	2.624	2.577	2.531	2.487	2.444	2.402	2.361	2.322	2.283
4	3.902	3.808	3.717	3.630	3.546	3.465	3.387	3.312	3.240	3.170	3.102	3.037	2.974	2.914	2.855
5	4.853	4.713	4.580	4.452	4.329	4.212	4.100	3.993	3.890	3.791	3.696	3.605	3.517	3.433	3.352
6	5.795	5.601	5.417	5.242	5.076	4.917	4.767	4.623	4.486	4.355	4.231	4.111	3.998	3.889	3.784
7	6.728	6.472	6.230	6.002	5.786	5.582	5.389	5.206	5.033	4.868	4.712	4.564	4.423	4.288	4.160
8	7.652	7.325	7.020	6.733	6.463	6.210	5.971	5.747	5.535	5.335	5.146	4.968	4.799	4.639	4.487
9	8.566	8.162	7.786	7.435	7.108	6.802	6.515	6.247	5.995	5.759	5.537	5.328	5.132	4.946	4.772
10	9.471	8.983	8.530	8.111	7.722	7.360	7.024	6.710	6.418	6.145	5.889	5.650	5.426	5.216	5.019
11	10.368	9.787	9.253	8.760	8.306	7.887	7.499	7.139	6.805	6.495	6.207	5.938	5.687	5.453	5.234
12	11.255	10.575	9.954	9.385	8.863	8.384	7.943	7.536	7.161	6.814	6.492	6.194	5.918	5.660	5.421
13	12.134	11.348	10.635	9.986	9.394	8.853	8.358	7.904	7.487	7.103	6.750	6.424	6.122	5.842	5.583
14	13.004	12.106	11.296	10.563	9.899	9.295	8.745	8.244	7.786	7.367	6.982	6.628	6.302	6.002	5.724
15	13.865	12.849	11.938	11.118	10.380	9.712	9.108	8.559	8.061	7.606	7.191	6.811	6.462	6.142	5.847
16	14.718	13.578	12.561	11.652	10.838	10.106	9.447	8.851	8.313	7.824	7.379	6.974	6.604	6.265	5.954
17	15.562	14.292	13.166	12.166	11.274	10.477	9.763	9.122	8.544	8.022	7.549	7.120	6.729	6.373	6.047
18	16.398	14.992	13.754	12.659	11.690	10.828	10.059	9.372	8.756	8.201	7.702	7.250	6.840	6.467	6.128
19	17.226	15.678	14.324	13.134	12.085	11.158	10.336	9.604	8.950	8.365	7.839	7.366	6.938	6.550	6.198
20	18.046	16.351	14.877	13.590	12.462	11.470	10.594	9.818	9.129	8.514	7.963	7.469	7.025	6.623	6.259
21	18.857	17.011	15.415	14.029	12.821	11.764	10.836	10.017	9.292	8.649	8.075	7.562	7.102	6.687	6.312
22	19.660	17.658	15.937	14.451	13.163	12.042	11.061	10.201	9.442	8.772	8.176	7.645	7.170	6.743	6.359
23	20.456	18.292	16.444	14.857	13.489	12.303	11.272	10.371	9.580	8.883	8.266	7.718	7.230	6.792	6.399
24	21.243	18.914	16.936	15.247	13.799	12.550	11.469	10.529	9.707	8.985	8.348	7.784	7.283	6.835	6.434
25	22.023	19.523	17.413	15.622	14.094	12.783	11.654	10.675	9.823	9.077	8.422	7.843	7.330	6.873	6.464
30	25.808	22.396	19.600	17.292	15.372	13.765	12.409	11.258	10.274	9.427	8.694	8.055	7.496	7.003	6.566
35	29.409	24.999	21.487	18.665	16.374	14.498	12.948	11.655	10.567	9.644	8.855	8.176	7.586	7.070	6.617
40	32.835	27.355	23.115	19.793	17.159	15.046	13.332	11.925	10.757	9.779	8.951	8.244	7.634	7.105	6.642
45	36.095	29.490	24.519	20.720	17.774	15.456	13.606	12.108	10.881	9.863	9.008	8.283	7.661	7.123	6.654
50	39.196	31.424	25.730	21.482	18.256	15.762	13.801	12.233	10.962	9.915	9.042	8.304	7.675	7.133	6.661

TABLE A4 (cont.)

PERIOD	16%	17%	18%	19%	20%	25%	30%	35%	40%	45%	50%
1	0.862	0.855	0.847	0.840	0.833	0.800	0.769	0.741	0.714	0.690	0.667
2	1.605	1.585	1.566	1.547	1.528	1.440	1.361	1.289	1.224	1.165	1.111
3	2.246	2.210	2.174	2.140	2.106	1.952	1.816	1.696	1.589	1.493	1.407
4	2.798	2.743	2.690	2.639	2.589	2.362	2.166	1.997	1.849	1.720	1.605
5	3.274	3.199	3.127	3.058	2.991	2.689	2.436	2.220	2.035	1.876	1.737
6	3.685	3.589	3.498	3.410	3.326	2.951	2.643	2.385	2.168	1.983	1.824
7	4.039	3.922	3.812	3.706	3.605	3.161	2.802	2.508	2.263	2.057	1.883
8	4.344	4.207	4.078	3.954	3.837	3.329	2.925	2.598	2.331	2.109	1.922
9	4.607	4.451	4.303	4.163	4.031	3.463	3.019	2.665	2.379	2.144	1.948
10	4.833	4.659	4.494	4.339	4.192	3.571	3.092	2.715	2.414	2.168	1.965
11	5.029	4.836	4.656	4.486	4.327	3.656	3.147	2.752	2.438	2.185	1.977
12	5.197	4.988	4.793	4.611	4.439	3.725	3.190	2.779	2.456	2.196	1.985
13	5.342	5.118	4.910	4.715	4.533	3.780	3.223	2.799	2.469	2.204	1.990
14	5.468	5.229	5.008	4.802	4.611	3.824	3.249	2.814	2.478	2.210	1.993
15	5.575	5.324	5.092	4.876	4.675	3.859	3.268	2.825	2.484	2.214	1.995
16	5.668	5.405	5.162	4.938	4.730	3.887	3.283	2.834	2.489	2.216	1.997
17	5.749	5.475	5.222	4.990	4.775	3.910	3.295	2.840	2.492	2.218	1.998
18	5.818	5.534	5.273	5.033	4.812	3.928	3.304	2.844	2.494	2.219	1.999
19	5.877	5.584	5.316	5.070	4.843	3.942	3.311	2.848	2.496	2.220	1.999
20	5.929	5.628	5.353	5.101	4.870	3.954	3.316	2.850	2.497	2.221	1.999
21	5.973	5.665	5.384	5.127	4.891	3.963	3.320	2.852	2.498	2.221	2.000
22	6.011	5.696	5.410	5.149	4.909	3.970	3.323	2.853	2.498	2.222	2.000
23	6.044	5.723	5.432	5.167	4.925	3.976	3.325	2.854	2.499	2.222	2.000
24	6.073	5.746	5.451	5.182	4.937	3.981	3.327	2.855	2.499	2.222	2.000
25	6.097	5.766	5.467	5.195	4.948	3.985	3.329	2.856	2.499	2.222	2.000
30	6.177	5.829	5.517	5.235	4.979	3.995	3.332	2.857	2.500	2.222	2.000
35	6.215	5.858	5.539	5.251	4.992	3.998	3.333	2.857	2.500	2.222	2.000
40	6.233	5.871	5.548	5.258	4.997	3.999	3.333	2.857	2.500	2.222	2.000
45	6.242	5.877	5.552	5.261	4.999	4.000	3.333	2.857	2.500	2.222	2.000
50	6.246	5.880	5.554	5.262	4.999	4.000	3.333	2.857	2.500	2.222	2.000

Appendix B: Cumulative Probabilities From the Standard Normal Distribution

TABLE B1

Cumulative probability, $N(d)$, of drawing a value less than or equal to d from the standard normal distribution

d	0	0.01	0.02	0.03	0.04	0.05	0.06	0.07	0.08	0.09
0	0.5000	0.5040	0.5080	0.5120	0.5160	0.5199	0.5239	0.5279	0.5319	0.5359
0.1	0.5398	0.5438	0.5478	0.5517	0.5557	0.5596	0.5636	0.5675	0.5714	0.5753
0.2	0.5793	0.5832	0.5871	0.5910	0.5948	0.5987	0.6026	0.6064	0.6103	0.6141
0.3	0.6179	0.6217	0.6255	0.6293	0.6331	0.6368	0.6406	0.6443	0.6480	0.6517
0.4	0.6554	0.6591	0.6628	0.6664	0.6700	0.6736	0.6772	0.6808	0.6844	0.6879
0.5	0.6915	0.6950	0.6985	0.7019	0.7054	0.7088	0.7123	0.7157	0.7190	0.7224
0.6	0.7257	0.7291	0.7324	0.7357	0.7389	0.7422	0.7454	0.7486	0.7517	0.7549
0.7	0.7580	0.7611	0.7642	0.7673	0.7704	0.7734	0.7764	0.7794	0.7823	0.7852
0.8	0.7881	0.7910	0.7939	0.7967	0.7995	0.8023	0.8051	0.8078	0.8106	0.8133
0.9	0.8159	0.8186	0.8212	0.8238	0.8264	0.8289	0.8315	0.8340	0.8365	0.8389
1	0.8413	0.8438	0.8461	0.8485	0.8508	0.8531	0.8554	0.8577	0.8599	0.8621
1.1	0.8643	0.8665	0.8686	0.8708	0.8729	0.8749	0.8770	0.8790	0.8810	0.8830
1.2	0.8849	0.8869	0.8888	0.8907	0.8925	0.8944	0.8962	0.8980	0.8997	0.9015
1.3	0.9032	0.9049	0.9066	0.9082	0.9099	0.9115	0.9131	0.9147	0.9162	0.9177
1.4	0.9192	0.9207	0.9222	0.9236	0.9251	0.9265	0.9279	0.9292	0.9306	0.9319
1.5	0.9332	0.9345	0.9357	0.9370	0.9382	0.9394	0.9406	0.9418	0.9429	0.9441
1.6	0.9452	0.9463	0.9474	0.9484	0.9495	0.9505	0.9515	0.9525	0.9535	0.9545
1.7	0.9554	0.9564	0.9573	0.9582	0.9591	0.9599	0.9608	0.9616	0.9625	0.9633
1.8	0.9641	0.9649	0.9656	0.9664	0.9671	0.9678	0.9686	0.9693	0.9699	0.9706
1.9	0.9713	0.9719	0.9726	0.9732	0.9738	0.9744	0.9750	0.9756	0.9761	0.9767
2	0.9772	0.9778	0.9783	0.9788	0.9793	0.9798	0.9803	0.9808	0.9812	0.9817
2.1	0.9821	0.9826	0.9830	0.9834	0.9838	0.9842	0.9846	0.9850	0.9854	0.9857
2.2	0.9861	0.9864	0.9868	0.9871	0.9875	0.9878	0.9881	0.9884	0.9887	0.9890
2.3	0.9893	0.9896	0.9898	0.9901	0.9904	0.9906	0.9909	0.9911	0.9913	0.9916
2.4	0.9918	0.9920	0.9922	0.9925	0.9927	0.9929	0.9931	0.9932	0.9934	0.9936
2.5	0.9938	0.9940	0.9941	0.9943	0.9945	0.9946	0.9948	0.9949	0.9951	0.9952

Example: Let $d = 1.15$. There is an 87.49 per cent chance of drawing a value less than or equal to d from the standard normal distribution.

Appendix C: Key Formulas

Free cash flow

A firm's free cash flow (FCF) is derived from operating cash flow (OCF) and changes in asset and liability accounts as:

$$FCF = OCF - \Delta FA - (\Delta CA - \Delta A/P - \Delta accruals)$$

Present value of an ordinary annuity

The present value of an n-year ordinary annuity of €1 per year is:

$$PV = \frac{PMT}{r} \times \left[1 - \frac{1}{(1-r)^n}\right]$$

Present value of a perpetuity

The present value of a perpetual stream of €1 annual payments is:

$$PV = PMT \times \frac{1}{r} = \frac{PMT}{r}$$

Present value of a growing perpetuity

The present value of a perpetual stream of payments, which grows at an annual rate g, is:

$$PV = \frac{CF_1}{r-g}, \quad r > g$$

Effective annual interest rate

The effective annual interest rate (EAR) can be derived from the stated rate r (given m compounding periods) as:

$$EAR = \left(1 + \frac{r}{m}\right)^m - 1$$

Expected return on a portfolio

If the expected returns for individual assets in a portfolio are known, the expected return of an n-asset portfolio (with individual asset weights w_i) can be found as:

$$E(R_p) = w_1 E(R_1) + w_2 E(R_2) + \cdots + w_N E(R_N)$$

The capital asset pricing model

The CAPM yields a unique expected return for an asset or portfolio as a linear function of that asset's beta (β_i) and the risk-free rate R_f:

$$E(R_i) = R_f + \beta_i(E(R_m) - R_f)$$

Net present value

Finance's basic valuation model computes the NPV of a project or an asset, usually by subtracting the sum of a series of discounted cash inflows $\dfrac{CF_i}{(1+r)^i}$ from a single cash outflow (CF_0):

$$NPV = CF_0 + \frac{CF_1}{(1+r)^1} + \frac{CF_2}{(1+r)^2} + \frac{CF_3}{(1+r)^3} + \ldots + \frac{CF_N}{(1+r)^N}$$

Weighted average cost of capital (without taxes)

The WACC is a weighted average of the cost of debt and equity financing for a firm, in which the weights are the fractions of debt and equity in the firm's capital structure:

$$WACC = \left(\frac{D}{D+E}\right)r_d + \left(\frac{E}{D+E}\right)r_e$$

The weighted average cost of capital (with taxes)

Incorporating corporate taxes allows calculation of a firm's WACC when it must pay taxes at rate T_c on its income:

$$WACC = \left(\frac{D}{D+E}\right)(1 - T_c)r_d + \left(\frac{E}{D+E}\right)r_e$$

M&M Proposition I

Modigliani and Miller's famous Proposition I says that a firm's value (V) is given by capitalizing its expected net operating income (EBIT) at the rate r, and is independent of capital structure:

$$V = (E + D) = \frac{EBIT}{r}$$

M & M Proposition II

Proposition II determines the rate at which the expected return on a levered firm's equity (r_l) must increase as debt is substituted for equity in its capital structure:

$$r_l = r + (r - r_d)\frac{D}{E}$$

Value of a levered firm (including only corporate taxes)

In the presence of corporate income taxes, the value of a levered firm is equal to the value of an otherwise equivalent unlevered firm plus the value of the interest tax shields on its debt:

$$V_L = V_U + PV \text{ tax shield} = V_U + T_c D$$

Gain from leverage

In the presence of both corporate and personal taxes, the gain from leverage for a firm is a function of the effective tax rates on corporate profits (T_c), equity income received by investors (T_{ps}) and interest income received by investors (T_{pd}):

$$G_L = \left[1 + \frac{(1 - T_c)(1 - T_{ps})}{(1 - T_{pd})}\right] \times D$$

The forward premium or discount (exchange rates)

The annualized forward discount or premium of a currency is:

$$\frac{F-S}{S} \times \frac{360}{N}$$

The parity conditions of international finance

Forward-spot parity

In equilibrium, the forward rate (F) observed for a currency should be equal to the expected future spot exchange rate, $E(S)$, for that currency:

$$E(S) = F$$

Purchasing power parity

PPP expresses a currency's expected future spot exchange rate $[E/(S^{\text{for/dom}})]$, relative to today's spot rate ($S^{\text{for/dom}}$), as a function of the relative expected inflation rates in the foreign, ($E(i_{\text{for}})$ and domestic, $E(i_{\text{dom}})$, markets:

$$\frac{E(S^{\text{for/dom}})}{S^{\text{for/dom}}} = \frac{1 + E(i_{\text{for}})}{1 + E(i_{\text{dom}})}$$

Interest rate parity

IRP expresses a currency's forward exchange rate ($F^{\text{for/dom}}$), relative to today's spot rate ($S^{\text{for/dom}}$), as a function of the relative interest rates in the foreign (R_{for}) and domestic (R_{dom}) markets:

$$\frac{F^{\text{for/dom}}}{S^{\text{for/dom}}} = \frac{1 + R_{\text{for}}}{1 + R_{\text{dom}}}$$

Real interest parity

The real interest parity relationship expresses interest rate parity in real rather than nominal terms:

$$\frac{1 + F_{\text{for}}}{1 + R_{\text{dom}}} = \frac{1 + E(i_{\text{for}})}{1 + E(i_{\text{dom}})}$$

Forward price of an asset

Given a risk-free rate of interest R_f, the forward price (F) of an asset or commodity to be delivered n periods in the future can be derived from the current spot price (S_0) as:

$$F = S_0(1+R_f)^n$$

Appendix D: Answers to Self-Test Problems

Chapter 2 Financial Statement and Cash Flow Analysis

ST2-1 Use the financial statements below to answer the questions about S&M Manufacturing's financial position at the end of the calendar year 2006.

S&M Manufacturing
Balance sheet at 31 December 2006 (€000)

Assets		Liabilities and equity	
Current assets		Current liabilities	
Cash	€ 140 000	Accounts payable	€ 480 000
Marketable securities	260 000	Notes payable	500 000
Accounts receivable	650 000	Accruals	80 000
Inventories	800 000	Total current	€1 060 000
Total current assets	€1 850 000	liabilities	
Fixed assets		Long-term debt	
Gross fixed assets	€3 780 000	Bonds outstanding	€1 300 000
Less: Accumulated	1 220 000	Bank debt (long-term)	260 000
depreciation		Total long-term debt	€1 560 000
Net fixed assets	€2 560 000	Shareholders' equity	
Total assets	**€4 410 000**	Preference shares	€180 000
		Par value of shares	200 000
		Paid-in capital	810 000
		in excess of par	
		Retained earnings	600 000
		Total shareholders'	€1 790 000
		equity	
		Total liabilities	**€4 410 000**
		and equity	

S&M Manufacturing
Income statement for year ended 31 December 2006 (€000)

Sales revenue		€6 900 000
Less: Cost of goods sold		4 200 000
Gross profits		€2 700 000
Less: Operating expenses		
Sales expense	€ 750 000	
General and administrative expense	1 150 000	
Leasing expense	210 000	
Depreciation expense	235 000	
Total operation expenses		2 345 000
Earnings before interest and taxes		€ 355 000
Less: Interest expense		85 000
Net profit before taxes		€ 270 000
Less: Taxes		81 000
Net profits after taxes		**€ 189 000**
Less: Preference shares dividends		10 800
Earnings available for		**€ 178 200**
ordinary shareholders		
Less: Dividends		75 000
To retained earnings		**€ 103 200**
Per share data		
Earnings per share (EPS)	€	1.43
Dividends per share (DPS)	€	0.60
Price per share	€	15.85

a How much cash and near cash does S&M have at year-end 2006?

b What was the original cost of all of the firm's real property that is currently owned?

c How much in total liabilities did the firms have at year-end 2006?

d How much did S&M owe for credit purchases at year-end 2006?

e How much did the firm sell during 2006?

f How much equity did the common stockholders have in the firm at year-end 2006?

g What was the cumulative total of earnings reinvested in the firm from its inception through to the end of 2006?

h How much operating profit did the firm earn during 2006?

i What was the total amount of dividends paid out by the firm during the year 2006?

j How many shares did S&M have outstanding at year-end 2006?

Answer ST2-1

a €400 000 (only cash and marketable securities should be included €140 000 + €260 000)

b €3 780 000 (net asset position + depreciation)

c €2 620 000 (current liabilities + long-term debt)

d €480 000 (accounts payable)

e €6 900 000 (sales)

f €1 010 000 (ordinary shares at par + paid-in capital)

g €600 000 (retained earnings)

h €355 000 (EBIT)

i €85 800 (preference + ordinary share dividends)

j 124 615 shares outstanding (178 200/1.43)

ST2-2 The partially complete 2006 balance sheet and income statement for Challenge Industries are set out below, followed by selected ratio values for the firm based on its completed 2006 financial statements. Use the ratios along with the partial statements to complete the financial statements. *Hint*: Use the ratios in the order listed to calculate the missing statement values that need to be installed in the partial statements.

Challenge Industries
Balance sheet at 31 December 2006 (in €000)

Assets		Liabilities and equity	
Current assets		Current liabilities	
Cash	€ 52 000	Accounts payable	€150 000
Marketable securities	60 000	Notes payable	?
Accounts receivable	200 000	Accruals	80 000
Inventories	?	Total current liabilities	?
Total current assets	?	Long-term debt	€425 000
Fixed assets (gross)	?	Total liabilities	?
Less: Accumulated	240 000	Shareholders' equity	
depreciation		Preference shares	?
Net fixed assets	?	Par value of shares	150 000
Total assets	**?**	Paid-in capital in excess of par	?
		Retained earnings	390 000
		Total shareholders' equity	?
		Total liabilities and	**?**
		shareholders' equity	

Challenge Industries
Income statement for the year ended 31 December 2006 (in €000)

Sales revenue		€4 800 000
Less: Cost of goods sold		?
Gross profits		?
Less: Operating expenses		
Sales expense	€690 000	
General and administrative expense	750 000	
Depreciation expense	120 000	
Total operating expenses		1 560 000
Earnings before interest and taxes		?
Less: Interest expense		35 000
Earnings before taxes		?
Less: Taxes		?
Net income (Net profits after taxes)		**?**
Less: Preference dividends		15 000
Earnings available for ordinary shareholders		**?**
Less: Dividends		60 000
To retained earnings		**?**

Challenge Industries
Ratios for the year ended 31 December 2006

Ratio	Value
Total asset turnover	2.00
Gross profit margin	40%
Inventory turnover	10
Current ratio	1.60
Net profit margin	3.75%
Return on equity	12.5%

Answer ST2-2

Challenge Industries
Balance sheet at 31 December 2006 (in €000)

Assets		Liabilities and equity	
Current assets		Current liabilities	
Cash	52 000	Accounts payable	150 000
Marketable securities	60 000	Notes payable	145 000
Accounts receivable	200 000	Accruals	80 000
Inventory	288 000	Total current liabilities	375 000
Total current assets	600 000	Long-term debt	425 000
Fixed assets (gross)	2 040 000	Total liabilities	800 000
Less: Accumulated	240 000	Shareholders' equity	
depreciation		Preference shares	160 000
Net fixed assets	1 800 000	Ordinary shares (at par)	150 000
Total assets	**2 400 000**	Paid-in capital in excess of par	900 000
		Retained earnings	390 000
		Total shareholders' equity	1 600 000
		Total liabilities and	**2 400 000**
		shareholders' equity	

Challenge Industries
Income statement for the year ended 31 December 2006 (in €000)

Sales revenue		4 800 000
Less: Cost of goods sold		2 880 000
Gross profits		1 920 000
Less Operating expenses		
Selling expense	690 000	
General and administrative expense	150 000	
Depreciation	120 000	
Total operation expenses		1 560 000
Earnings before interest and taxes		360 000
Less: Interest expense		35 000
Earnings before taxes		325 000
Less: Taxes		130 000
Net income (Net profits after taxes)		**195 000**
Less: Preference dividends		15 000
Earnings available for ordinary shareholders		**180 000**
Less: Dividends		60 000
To retained earnings		**120 000**

Chapter 3 Present Value

ST3-1 Starratt Alexander is considering investing specified amounts in each of four investment opportunities described below. For each opportunity, determine the amount of money Starratt will have at the end of the given investment horizon.

Investment A: Invest a lump sum of €2750 today in an account that pays 6 per cent annual interest and leave the funds on deposit for exactly 15 years.

Investment B: Invest the following amounts at the beginning of each of the next five years in a venture that will earn 9 per cent annually and measure the accumulated value at the end of exactly five years:

BEGINNING OF YEAR	AMOUNT
1	€ 900
2	1000
3	1200
4	1500
5	1800

Investment C: Invest €1200 at the end of each year for the next ten years in an account that pays 10 per cent annual interest and determine the account balance at the end of year 10.

Investment D: Make the same investment as in investment C but place the €1200 in the account at the beginning of each year.

Answer ST3-1

Investment A: Future value is €6590 = (€2750 × FV(15, 6%) = 2.3966)
Investment B: Future value = €900 × $(1.09)^5$ + €1000 × $(1.09)^4$ + €1200 × $(1.09)^3$ + €1500 × $(1.09)^2$ + €1800 × (1.09) = €8094.53
Investment C: Future value is €19116 (€1200 × FVAF(10, 10%) = 15.93)
Investment D: €19116 × 1.09 = €20836

ST3-2 Gregg Snead has been offered four investment opportunities, all equally priced at €45 000. Because the opportunities differ in risk, Gregg's required returns (i.e. applicable discount rates) are not the same for each opportunity. The cash flows and required returns for each opportunity are summarized below.

OPPORTUNITY	CASH FLOWS	REQUIRED RETURN
A	€7500 at the end of 5 years	12%
B	Year Amount	15%
	1 €10 000	
	2 12 000	
	3 18 000	
	4 10 000	
	5 13 000	
	6 9 000	
C	€5000 at the end of each year for the next 30 years.	10%
D	€7000 at the beginning of each year for the next 20 years.	18%

   a Find the present value of each of the four investment opportunities.

   b Which, if any, opportunities are acceptable?

   c Which opportunity should Gregg take?

Answer ST3-2

   a PV of A: €7500 × PV(5, 12%) = 0.5674 = €4255.50
      PV of B: €10 000/(1.15) + €12 000/(1.15)^2 + €18 000/(1.15)^3 +
      €10 000/(1.15)^4 + €13 000/(1.15)^5 + €9 000/(1.15)^6 = €45 676.44
      PV of C: €5000 × PVAF(30, 10%) = 9.4269 = €47 134
      PV of D: €7000 × PVAF(20, 18%) = 5.3527 = €37 468 × 1.18 = €44 213

   b Opportunities B and C are acceptable because the present value of their cash flows is in excess of their current cost of €45 000. Opportunities A and D are not acceptable because their present values are below their €45 000 cost.

   c None.

ST3-3 Assume you wish to establish a university scholarship of €2000 paid at the end of each year for a deserving student at the school you attended. You would like to make a lump-sum gift to the school to fund the scholarship into perpetuity. The school's treasurer assures you that they will earn 7.5 per cent annually forever.

   a How much must you give the school today to fund the proposed scholarship programme?

   b If you wanted to allow the amount of the scholarship to increase annually after the first award (end of year 1) by 3 per cent per year, how much must you give the school today to fund the scholarship programme?

   c Compare, contrast and discuss the difference in your response to parts (a) and (b).

Answer ST3-3

   a The present value of the proposed perpetuity is €2000/0.075 = €26 667

   b The present value of the growing perpetuity is
      €2060/(0.075 − 0.03) = €2060/0.045 = €45 778

   c The amount you need to give the high school if you want the scholarship to grow at 3 per cent per year indefinitely, assuming they will be able to earn the proposed interest rate, is almost double the amount needed if the scholarship does not grow. This effect is due to the fact that we discount the annual cash flow by a smaller number in order to account for the annual growth in the scholarship.

ST3-4 Assume that you deposit €10 000 today into an account paying 6 per cent annual interest and leave it on deposit for exactly eight years.

   a How much will be in the account at the end of eight years if interest is compounded

      1 annually?

      2 semi-annually?

      3 monthly?

      4 continuously?

   b Calculate the effective annual rate (EAR) for (1) to (4) above.

   c Based on your findings in parts (a) and (b), what is the general relationship between the frequency of compounding and EAR?

Answer ST3-4

  a **1** FV = €10 000 × FV (8, 6%) = 1.5938 = €15 938

      2 FV = €10 000 × FV (16, 3%) = 1.6047 = €16 047

      3 FV = €10 000 × FV (96, 0.5%) = 1.6141 = €16 141

      4 FV = €10 000 × $e^{(8 \times 0.06)}$ = €10 000 × $2.7182^{0.48}$ = €10 000 × 1.6161 = €16 160

  b **1** EAR = $(1+0.06/1)^1 - 1$ = 6%

      2 EAR = $(1+0.06/2)^2 - 1$ = 6.09%

      3 EAR = $(1+0.06/12)^{12} - 1$ = 6.17%

      4 EAR = $e^{0.06} - 1$ = 6.18%

  c The observable pattern shows that the more frequent the compounding, the higher the effective annual rate. Consequently, the higher annual rate is obtained when the compounding is continuous.

ST3-5   Imagine that you are a professional personal financial planner. One of your clients asks you the following two questions. Use time value of money techniques to develop appropriate responses to each question.

  a I borrowed €75 000, am required to repay it in six equal (annual) end-of-year instalments of €3344 and want to know what interest rate I am paying.

  b I need to save €37 000 over the next 15 years to fund my three-year-old daughter's university education. If I make equal annual end-of-year deposits into an account that earns 7 per cent annual interest, how large must this deposit be?

Answer ST3-5

  a 9% (calculated with a financial calculator)

  b The amount of the annual, end-of-year deposits should be:
€37 000/FVAF (15, 7%) = 25.129 = €1472

Chapter 4 Valuing Bonds

ST4-1   A five-year bond pays interest annually. The par value is €1000 and the coupon rate equals 7 per cent. If the market's required return on the bond is 8 per cent, what is the bond's market price?

Answer ST4-1

$$P = \frac{€70}{1.08^1} + \frac{€70}{1.08^2} + \frac{€70}{1.08^3} + \frac{€70}{1.08^4} + \frac{€1070}{1.08^5} = €960.07$$

You could also obtain this answer by valuing the annuity of coupon payments and the lump sum principal amount separately as follows.

$$P_0 = €70 \left[\frac{1 - \frac{1}{(1 + 0.08)^5}}{0.08} \right] + \frac{€1000}{(1 + 0.08)^5}$$

$$= €279.49 + €680.58 = €960.07$$

ST4-2 A bond that matures in two years makes semi-annual interest payments. The par value is €1000, the coupon rate equals 4 per cent and the bond's market price is €1019.27. What is the bond's yield to maturity?

Answer ST4-2

The YTM is the value of r that solves this equation.

$$€1019.27 = \frac{€20}{\left(1 + \frac{r}{2}\right)^1} + \frac{€20}{\left(1 + \frac{r}{2}\right)^2} + \frac{€20}{\left(1 + \frac{r}{2}\right)^3} + \frac{€1020}{\left(1 + \frac{r}{2}\right)^4}$$

Because the bond sells at a premium, the YTM must be less than the coupon rate. We can try to find the YTM by trial and error. Inserting $r = 0.035$ into the equation produces a price of €1009.58. This price is too low, so we have chosen a YTM that is too high. Next try $r = 0.03$. At that interest rate, the market price is €1019.27, so the YTM = 3 per cent.

An alternative approach to this problem uses the *Excel* function, =IRR. This function requires that you input the price of the bond as a negative value, followed by the positive cash flows that the bond promises.

	A
1	−1019.27
2	20
3	20
4	20
5	20

Now in an empty cell type the function, =IRR(A1:A5), and *Excel* will return the value 1.5 per cent. This is the YTM stated on a semi-annual basis (equivalent to r/2 in the equation above), so multiply it times 2 to get the annual YTM of 3 per cent. Note, you need to be sure that the cell in which you type the IRR formula is formatted in a way that allows you to see several decimal places. Otherwise, *Excel* may round off the YTM and you will not know it.

ST4-3 Two bonds offer a 5 per cent coupon rate, paid annually, and sell at par (€1000). One bond matures in two years and the other matures in ten years.

a What are the YTMs on each bond?

b If the YTM changes to 4 per cent, what happens to the price of each bond?

c What happens if the YTM changes to 6 per cent?

Answer ST4-3

Because the bonds currently sell at par, the coupon rate and the YTM must be equal at 5 per cent. If the YTM drops to 4 per cent, both bonds will sell at a premium, but the price of the ten-year bond will increase more than the price of the two-year bond.

$$P_{2-yr} = €50 \left[\frac{1 - \frac{1}{(1 + 0.04)^2}}{0.04} \right] + \frac{€1000}{(1 + 0.04)^2}$$

$$= €94.30 + €924.56 = €1018.86$$

$$P_{10-yr} = €50 \left[\frac{1 - \frac{1}{(1 + 0.04)^{10}}}{0.04} \right] + \frac{€1000}{(1 + 0.04)^{10}}$$

$$= €405.55 + €675.56 = €1081.11$$

Repeating the calculations above at $r = 0.06$ we find that the two-year bond's price falls to €981.67 and the ten-year bond's price falls to €926.40. This illustrates that long-term bond prices are more sensitive to changes in interest rates than are short-term bond prices.

Chapter 5 Valuing Shares

ST5-1 Omega Healthcare Investors (ticker symbol, OHI) pays a dividend on its Series B preference shares of $0.539 per quarter. If the price of Series B preference shares is $25 per share, what quarterly rate of return does the market require on this share, and what is the effective annual required return?

Answer ST5-1

The preference share valuation formula says that the price equals the dividend divided by the required rate of return. Therefore, using the quarterly dividend and the quarterly required rate, we have

$$\$25 = \$0.539/r$$
$$r = 0.02156$$

This means that the effective annual required rate on the stock equals

$$(1.02156)^4 - 1 = 0.089 \text{ or } 8.9\%$$

ST5-2 The restaurant chain Applebee's International, Inc. (ticker symbol, APPB) announced an increase of their quarterly dividend from $0.06 to $0.07 per share in December 2003. This continued a long string of dividend increases. Applebee's was one of few companies that had managed to increase its dividend at a double-digit clip for more than a decade. Suppose you want to use the dividend growth model to value Applebee's shares. You believe that dividends will keep growing at 10 per cent per year indefinitely, and you think the market's required return on this share is 11 per cent. Let's assume that Applebee's pays dividends annually and that the next dividend is expected to be $0.31 per share. The dividend will arrive in exactly one year. What would you pay for Applebee's shares right now? Suppose you buy the shares today, hold them just long enough to receive the next dividend, and then sell them. What rate of return will you earn on that investment?

Answer ST5-2

To calculate the price of the shares now, we simply divide next year's expected dividend, $0.31, by the difference between the required rate of return and the dividend growth rate. This yields a price of $0.31 ÷ (0.11 − 0.10) = $31.00. Next, we have to calculate the expected price a year from now after the $0.31 dividend has been paid. To do that, we need an estimate of the dividend two years in the future. If next year's dividend is $0.31, then the following year's dividend should be 10 per cent more or $0.341 per share. This means that the price of Applebee's shares, just after the $0.31 dividend is paid should be $0.341 ÷ (0.11 − 0.10) = $34.10. Now calculate your rate of return. You purchase the shares for €31. One year later you receive a dividend of $0.31 and you immediately sell the shares for $34.10, generating a capital gain of $3.10. Your total return is therefore ($34.10 + $0.31 − €31.00) ÷ $31.00 = 0.11 or 11 per cent. That shouldn't be a surprise because this is exactly the market's required return on the shares.

Chapter 6 The Trade-Off Between Risk and Return

ST6-1   Download from Thomson ONE the data for the five shares analysed over the 1986–2006 period. Calculate the standard deviation of these share returns over the four five-year periods. Have these shares become more or less volatile over time?

Answer ST6-1

The table below illustrates the calculations needed to solve this problem. First, calculate the average return. Next, subtract that average from each year's actual return, then square that difference. Add up the squared differences and divide by four to get the variance, and take the square root of the variance to get the standard deviation. Returns were more volatile over the past five years compared to the past ten years.

YEAR	RETURN (%)	RETURN − AVERAGE	SQUARED DIFFERENCE
1999	23.6	21.1	445.2
2000	−10.9	−13.4	179.6
2001	−11.0	−13.5	182.2
2002	−20.9	−23.4	547.6
2003	31.6	29.1	847.8
Sum	12.4		2201.4
Average return (%)	2.5		
Variance			550.3
Standard dev. (%)			23.4

ST6-2   Suppose that short-term government debt returns follow a normal distribution with a mean of 4.1 per cent and a standard deviation of 2.8 per cent. This implies that, 68 per cent of the time, short-term government debt returns should fall within what range?

Answer ST6-2

For any normal distribution, 68 per cent of the observations should fall within plus or minus one standard deviation of the mean. This means 68 per cent of annual short-term government debt returns should fall within 1.3 per cent and 6.9 per cent.

Chapter 7 Risk, Return and the Capital Asset Pricing Model

ST7-1 Calculate the arithmetic mean, variance and standard deviations for a share with the probability distribution outlined in the accompanying table:

OUTCOME	PROBABILITY	SHARE RETURN
Recession	10%	−40%
Expansion	60%	20%
Boom	30%	50%

Answer ST7-1

The expected return is $0.10(-0.40) + 0.60(0.20) + 0.30(0.50) = 0.23$. The variance equals $0.10(-0.4 - 0.23)^2 + 0.60(0.2 - 0.23)^2 + 0.30(0.50 - 0.23)^2 = 0.0621$. The standard deviation is the square root of the variance, or 0.2492.

ST7-2 You invest €25 000 in T-bills and €50 000 in the market portfolio. If the risk-free rate equals 2 per cent and the expected market risk premium is 6 per cent, what is the expected return on your portfolio?

Answer ST7-2

The portfolio is invested one-third in T-bills (€25K/€75K) and two-thirds in shares (€50K/€75K). The risk-free rate is 2 per cent. If the market risk premium is 6 per cent, then the market's expected return is 8 per cent. Therefore, the portfolio's expected return is: $0.33(2\%) + 0.67(8\%) = 6\%$

ST7-3 The risk-free rate equals 4 per cent, and the expected return on the market is 10 per cent. If a share's expected return is 13 per cent, what is the share's beta?

Answer ST7-3

Plug the known values into Equation 7.2:

$$13\% = 4\% + B(10\% - 4\%)$$

which implies that the beta equals 1.5.

Chapter 8 Capital Budgeting Process and Techniques

ST8-1 Nader International is considering investing in two assets – A and B. The initial outlay, annual cash flows and annual depreciation for each asset is shown in the table below for the assets' assumed five-year lives. As can be seen, Nader will use straight-line depreciation over each asset's five-year life. The firm requires a 12 per cent return on each of those equally risky assets. Nader's maximum payback period is 2.5 years, its maximum discounted payback period is 3.25 years and its minimum accounting rate of return is 30 per cent.

	ASSET A			ASSET B	
INITIAL OUTLAY (CF_0)	€200 000			€180 000	
YEAR (t)	CASH FLOW (CF_t)	DEPRECIATION		CASH FLOW (CF_t)	DEPRECIATION
1	€ 70 000	€40 000		€80 000	€36 000
2	80 000	40 000		90 000	36 000
3	90 000	40 000		30 000	36 000
4	90 000	40 000		40 000	36 000
5	100 000	40 000		40 000	36 000

a   Calculate the accounting rate of return from each asset, assess its acceptability and indicate which asset is best, using the accounting rate of return.

b   Calculate the payback period for each asset, assess its acceptability, and indicate which asset is best, using the payback period.

c   Calculate the discounted payback for each asset, assess its acceptability, and indicate which asset is best, using the discounted payback.

d   Compute and contrast your findings in parts (a), (b) and (c). Which asset would you recommend to Nader, assuming that they are mutually exclusive? Why?

Answer ST8-1

		ASSET A				ASSET B	
INVEST		€200 000				€180 000	
YEAR	CF	12% PV	DEPR.		CF	12% PV	DEPR.
1	€ 70 000	62 500	€40 000		€80 000	71 429	€36 000
2	80 000	63 776	40 000		90 000	71 747	36 000
3	90 000	64 060	40 000		30 000	21 353	36 000
4	90 000	57 196	40 000		40 000	25 420	36 000
5	100 000		40 000		40 000		36 000

a   Accounting rate of return

	ASSET A	ASSET B
YEAR	NPAT	NPAT
1	€70 000 − €40 000 = €30 000	€80 000 − €36 000 = €44 000
2	€80 000 − €40 000 = €40 000	€90 000 − €36 000 = €54 000
3	€90 000 − €40 000 = €50 000	€30 000 − €36 000 = −€6 000
4	€90 000 − €40 000 = €50 000	€40 000 − €36 000 = €4 000
5	€100 000 − €40 000 = €60 000	€40 000 − €36 000 = €4 000
	Average = €46 000	Average = €20 000

$\dfrac{€46000}{100000}$ = 46% Acceptable $\dfrac{€20000}{90000}$ = 22.22% Not accpetable

MAX

2.50   **b** Payback   2.56 years /   2.33 years / Acceptable

Not acceptable

3.25   **c** Discounted   3.17 years/Acceptable   3.62 years / Not acceptable

payback at 12%

d They should take asset A because its accounting rate of return is acceptable as is its discounted payback.

ST8-2 JK Products is considering investing in either of two competing projects that will allow the firm to eliminate a production bottleneck and meet the growing demand for its products. The firm's engineering department narrowed the alternatives down to two – Status Quo (SQ) and High Tech (HT). Working with the accounting and finance personnel, the firm's CFO developed the following estimates of the cash flows for SQ and HT over the relevant six-year time horizon. The firm has an 11 per cent required return and views these projects as equally risky.

	PROJECT SQ	PROJECT HT
INITIAL OUTFLOW (CF_o)	€670 000	€940 000
YEAR (t)	CASH INFLOWS (CF_t)	
1	€250 000	€170 000
2	200 000	180 000
3	170 000	200 000
4	150 000	250 000
5	130 000	300 000
6	130 000	550 000

a Calculate the net present value (NPV) of each project, assess its acceptability, and indicate which project is best, using NPV.
b Calculate the internal rate of return (IRR) of each project, assess its acceptability and indicate which project is best, using IRR.
c Calculate the profitability index (PI) of each project, assess its acceptability and indicate which project is best, using PI.
d Draw the NPV profile for project SQ and HT on the same set of axes and use this diagram to explain why the NPV and the IRR show different preferences for these two mutually exclusive projects. Discuss this difference in terms of both the 'scale problem' and the 'timing problem'.
e Which of the two mutually exclusive projects would you recommend that JK Products undertake? Why?

Answer ST8-2

	PROJECT SQ	PROJECT HT
a NPV	€87 313.87	€142 254.07*
b IRR	16.07%*	15.17%
c PI	1.13	1.15*

All measures indicate project acceptability:
NPV > 0
IRR > 11%
PI > 1.00
*Indicates the preferred project using each measure.

d

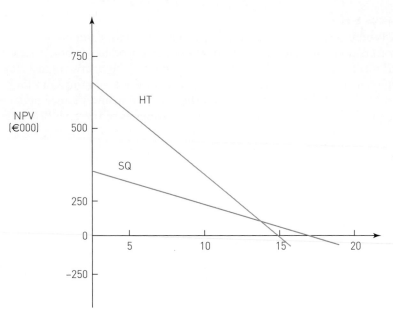

	PROJECT	
RATE	**SQ**	**HT**
0%	€ 360 000	€ 710 000
11%	€ 87 313.87	€ 142 254.07
15.17%	—	0
16.07%	0	—

At 11 per cent HT is preferred over SQ, but because the profiles cross somewhere beyond 11 per cent and before the functions cross the required return axis, the IRR of SQ exceeds the IRR of HT. This behaviour can be explained by the fact that HT's larger scale causes its NPV to exceed that of SQ. The smaller project and the timing of SQ's cash flows – more in the early years – causes its IRR to exceed that of HT, which has more of its cash flows in later years.

e   Project HT is recommended because it has the higher NPV, the better technique. In addition, its PI is higher than that of Project SQ.

Chapter 9 Cash Flow and Capital Budgeting

ST9-1 Claross Ltd wants to determine the relevant operating cash flows associated with the proposed purchase of a new piece of equipment that has an installed cost of €10 million and is depreciated over five years. The firm's financial analyst estimated that the relevant time horizon for analysis is six years. She expects the revenues attributable to the equipment to be €15.8 million in the first year and to increase at 5 per cent per year through year 6. Similarly, she estimates all expenses, other than depreciation attributable to the equipment, to total €12.2 million in the first year and to increase by 4 per cent per year through year 6. She plans to ignore any cash flows after year 6. The firm has a marginal tax rate of 40 per cent and its required return on the equipment investment is 13 per cent. (Note: round all cash flow calculations to the nearest €0.01 million.)

a Find the relevant incremental cash flows for years 0 through 6.

b Using the cash flows found in part (a), determine the NPV and IRR for the proposed equipment purchase.

c Based on your findings in part (b), would you recommend that Claross Ltd purchase the equipment? Why?

Answer ST9-1

a

				YEAR			
	0	**1**	**2**	**3**	**4**	**5**	**6**
Initial investment	−10						
Revenue (+5%/yr)		15.80	16.59	17.42	18.29	19.21	20.17
Expenses (+4%/yr)		12.20	12.69	13.20	13.72	14.27	14.84
EBDT		3.60	3.90	4.22	4.57	4.94	5.33
−Depreciation		2.00	3.20	1.92	1.15	1.15	0.58
EBT		1.60	0.70	2.30	3.42	3.79	4.75
−Taxes (40%)		0.64	0.28	0.92	1.37	1.52	1.90
EAT		0.96	0.42	1.38	2.05	2.27	2.85
+Depreciation		2.00	3.20	1.92	1.15	1.15	0.58
Total cash flow	−10	2.96	3.62	3.30	3.20	3.42	3.43

b NPV at 13% = 3.21
   IRR = 24%

c Accept the project because the NPV is greater than zero and the IRR is greater than 13%.

ST9-2 Atech Industries wants to determine whether it would be advisable for it to replace an existing, fully depreciated machine with a new one. The new machine will have an after-tax installed cost of €300 000 and will be depreciated under a three-year schedule. The old machine can be sold today for €80 000, after taxes. The firm is in the 40 per cent marginal tax bracket and requires a minimum return on the replacement decision of 15 per cent. The firm's estimates of its revenues and expenses (excluding depreciation) for both the new and the old machine (in € thousands) over the next four years are given below.

	NEW MACHINE		OLD MACHINE	
YEAR	**REVENUE**	**EXPENSES (EXCLUDING DEPRECIATION)**	**REVENUE**	**EXPENSES (EXCLUDING DEPRECIATION)**
1	€925	€740	€625	€580
2	990	780	645	595
3	1 000	825	670	610
4	1 100	875	695	630

Atech also estimates the values of various current accounts that could be impacted by the proposed replacement. They are shown below for both the new and the old machine over the next four years. Currently (at time 0), the firm's net investment in these current accounts is assumed to be €110 000 with the new machine and €75 000 with the old machine.

NEW MACHINE

	YEAR			
	1	**2**	**3**	**4**
Cash	€20 000	€25 000	€ 30 000	€ 36 000
Accounts receivable	90 000	95 000	110 000	120 000
Inventory	80 000	90 000	100 000	105 000
Accounts payable	60 000	65 000	70 000	72 000

OLD MACHINE

	YEAR			
	1	**2**	**3**	**4**
Cash	€15 000	€15 000	€15 000	€15 000
Accounts receivable	60 000	64 000	68 000	70 000
Inventory	45 000	48 000	52 000	55 000
Accounts payable	33 000	35 000	38 000	40 000

Atech estimates that after four years of detailed cash flow development, it will assume, in analysing this replacement decision, that the year 4 incremental cash flows of the new machine over the old machine will grow at a compound annual rate of 2 per cent from the end of year 4 to infinity.

a Find the incremental operating cash flows (including any working capital investment) for years 1 to 4, for Atech's proposed machine replacement decision.

b Calculate the terminal value of Atech's proposed machine replacement at the end of year 4.

c Show the relevant cash flows (initial outlay, operating cash flows and terminal cash flow) for years 1 to 4, for Atech's proposed machine replacement.

d Using the relevant cash flows from part (c), find the NPV and IRR for Atech's proposed machine replacement.

e Based on your findings in part (d), what recommendation would you make to Atech regarding its proposed machine replacement?

Answer ST9-2

a

	YEAR				
	0	**1**	**2**	**3**	**4**
NEW MACHINE					
Investment	−300 000				
Revenue		925 000	990 000	1 000 000	1 100 000
−Expenses (excl. depr.)		740 000	780 000	825 000	875 000
−Depreciation*		99 990	133 350	44 430	22 230
EBT		85 010	76 650	130 570	202 770
EAT [(1−0.40) × EBT]		51 006	45 990	78 342	121 662
−W/C investment**		20 000	15 000	25 000	19 000
(1) Operating CF		31 006	30 990	53 342	102 662

OLD MACHINE

A/T sale proceeds	+ 80,000				
Revenue		625 000	645 000	670 000	695 000
−Expenses(excl. depr.)		580 000	595 000	610 000	630 000
−Depreciation		0	0	0	0
EBT		45 000	50 000	60 000	65 000
EAT [(1−0.40) × EBT]		27 000	30 000	36 000	39 000
−W/C investment***		12 000	5 000	5 000	3 000
(2) Operating CF		15 000	25 000	31 000	36 000
INCR. CF[(1)−(2)]	−220 000	16 006	5 990	22 342	66 662

* New asset depreciation:

YEAR	RATE	COST	DEPRECIATION
1	0.3333	€300 000	€ 99 990
2	0.4445	300 000	133 350
3	0.1481	300 000	44 430
4	0.0741	300 000	22 230

** New machine working capital investment:

NWC = Cash + Accounts Receivable + Inventory − Accounts Payable
ΔNWC = NWC – [Prior year's NWC]
Year 1 Δ NWC = €20 000 + €90 000 + € 80 000 −€60 000 – [€110 000] = €20 000
Year 2 Δ NWC = €25 000 + €95 000 + € 90 000 −€65 000 – [€130 000] = €15 000
Year 3 Δ NWC = €30 000 + €110 000 + €100 000 – €70 000 – [€145 000] = €25 000
Year 4 Δ NWC = €36 000 + €120 000 + €105 000 – €72 000 – [€170 000] = €19 000

*** Old machine working capital investment:

NWC = Cash + Accounts Receivable + Inventory − Accounts Payable
ΔNWC = NWC – [Prior year's NWC]
Year 1 Δ NWC = €15 000 + €60 000 + €45 000 – €33 000 – [€75 000] = €12 000
Year 2 Δ NWC = €15 000 + €64 000 + €48 000 – €35 000 – [€87 000] = €5 000
Year 3 Δ NWC = €15 000 + €68 000 + €52 000 – €38 000 – [€92 000] = €5 000
Year 4 Δ NWC = €15 000 + €70 000 + €55 000 – €40 000 – [€97 000] = €3 000

b Year 5 operating CF = €66 662 × $(1+.02)^1$ = €67 995

Terminal value at end of Year 4 = $\dfrac{€67\ 995}{0.15 - 0.02}$ = €523 038

c Relevant cash flows:
Total year 4 CF = €66 662 + €523 038 = €589 700

YEAR	CASH FLOW
0	−€220 000
1	16 006
2	5 990
3	22 342
4	589 700

d NPV @ 15% = €150 301
IRR = 31.92%

e Atech should undertake the proposed machine replacement because the NPV of €150 301 is greater than €0 and the IRR of 31.92 per cent is above the firm's 15 per cent required return.

ST9-3 Performance Ltd is faced with choosing between two mutually exclusive projects with differing lives. It requires a return of 12 per cent on these projects. Project A requires an initial outlay at time 0 of €5 000 000 and is expected to require annual maintenance cash outflows of €3 100 000 per year over its two-year life. Project B requires an initial outlay at time 0 of €6 000 000 and is expected to require annual maintenance cash outflows of €2 600 000 per year over its three-year life. Both projects are acceptable investments and provide equal quality service. The firm assumes that the replacement and maintenance costs for both projects will remain unchanged over time.

a Find the NPV of each project over its life.
b Which project would you recommend, based on your finding in part (a)? What is wrong with choosing the best project based on its NPV?
c Use the equivalent annual cost (EAC) method to compare the two projects.
d Which project would you recommend, based on your finding in part (c)? Compare and contrast this recommendation with the one you gave in part (b).

Answer ST9-3

a Project A NPV = −€10 239 158
   Project B NPV = −€12 244 761
b Project A would be recommended because it has the lower cost NPV. The problem with this comparison is that Project A provides service for only two years versus Project B's three-year service life.
c EAC for Project A = €6 058 490
   EAC for Project B = €5 098 094
d Project B is preferred based on its lower EAC, which means that when costs are viewed on an annual basis it is less expensive than Project A. This recommendation is superior to the one made in part (b) because by looking at annual cost it resolves the issue of differing service lives when the replacement and maintenance costs are assumed unchanged over time.

Chapter 10 Capital Cost and Capital Budgeting

ST10-1 A financial analyst for Quality Investments, a diversified investment fund, has gathered the following information for the years 2005 and 2006 on two firms – A and B – that it is considering adding to its portfolio. Of particular concern are the operating and financial risks of each firm.

	2005		2006	
	FIRM A	**FIRM B**	**FIRM A**	**FIRM B**
Sales (€mn)	10.7	13.9	11.6	14.6
EBIT (€mn)	5.7	7.4	6.2	8.1
Assets (€mn)			10.7	15.6
Debt (€mn)			5.8	9.3
Interest (€mn)			0.6	1.0
Equity (€mn)			4.9	6.3

a Use the data provided to assess the operating leverage of each firm (using 2005 as the point of reference). Which firm has more operating leverage?

b Use the data provided to assess each firm's ROE (cash to equity/equity), assuming the firm's return on assets is 10 per cent and 20 per cent in each case. Which firm has more financial leverage?

c Use your findings in parts (a) and (b) to compare and contrast the operating and financial risks of Firms A and B. Which firm is more risky? Explain.

Answer ST10-1

a
$$\text{Operating leverage} = \frac{\overline{\Delta \text{EBIT}}}{\text{EBIT}} \div \frac{\overline{\Delta \text{Sales}}}{\text{Sales}}$$

Firm A: $[(6.2 - 5.7) \div 5.7] \div [(11.6 - 10.7) = 10.7] = 0.0877 = 0.0841 = 1.0428$
Firm B: $[(8.1 - 7.4) \div 7.4] \div [(14.6 - 13.9) = 13.9] \div 0.0946 = 0.0504 = 1.8770$

Firm B has more operating leverage than Firm A given its considerably higher ratio noted above. Based on 2005 sales, Firm B would experience a 1.8770 per cent change in its EBIT for every 1 per cent change in sales, whereas Firm A would only experience a 1.0428 per cent change in EBIT for a 1 per cent change in sales.

b

	FIRM A	FIRM B
When return on assets equals 10%		
EBIT ($)	0.10 × 10.7 = 1.07	0.10 × 15.6 = 1.56
Less: Interest ($)	0.60	1.00
Cash to equity ($)	0.47	0.56
ROE	0.47 ÷ 4.9 = 9.59%	0.56 ÷ 6.3 = 8.89%
When return on assets equals 20%		
EBIT ($)	0.20 × 10.7 = 2.14	0.20 × 15.6 = 3.12
Less: Interest ($)	0.60	1.00
Cash to equity ($)	1.54	2.12
ROE	1.54 ÷ 4.9 = 31.43%	2.12 ÷ 6.3 = 33.65%

Firm B has more financial leverage as demonstrated by the broader range of ROEs it experiences when the return on assets moves from 10 per cent to 20 per cent. Note that Firm B's ROE is lower than Firm A's at the 10 per cent return on assets and it is higher than Firm B's ROE at the 20 per cent return on assets. Firm B's ROE has greater variability – is more responsive to changes in return on assets – than Firm A's ROE. Simply stated, Firm B has more financial risk than Firm A.

c Based on the findings in parts (a) and (b), it is clear that Firm B is riskier than Firm A given that both its operating leverage (risk) and financial leverage (risk) are greater than that of Firm A.

ST10-2 Sierra Vista Industries (SVI) wishes to estimate its cost of capital for use in analysing projects that are similar to those that already exist. The firm's current capital structure, in terms of market value, includes 40 per cent debt, 10 per cent preference shares and 50 per cent ordinary shares. The firm's debt has an average yield to maturity of 8.3 per cent. Its preference shares have a €70 par value, an 8 per cent dividend, and are currently selling for €76 per share. SVI's beta is 1.05, the risk-free rate is 4 per cent and the return on the S&P 500 (the market proxy) is 11.4 per cent. SVI is in the 40 per cent marginal tax bracket.

a What are SVI's pre-tax costs of debt, preference shares and ordinary shares?

     b Calculate SVI's weighted average cost of capital (WACC) on both a pre-tax and an after-tax basis. Which WACC should SVI use when making investment decisions?

     c SVI is contemplating a major investment that is expected to increase both its operating and financial leverage. Its new capital structure will contain 50 per cent debt, 10 per cent preference shares and 40 per cent ordinary shares. As a result of the proposed investment, the firm's average yield to maturity on debt is expected to increase to 9 per cent, the market value of preference shares is expected to fall to their €70 par value and its beta is expected to rise to 1.15. What effect will this investment have on SVI's WACC? Explain your finding.

Answer ST10-2

     a Cost of debt = 8.30%

Cost of preference shares = $(0.08 \times €70) \div €76 = €5.60 \div €76 = 7.37\%$

Cost of ordinary shares (using CAPM) $= 4.00\% + [1.05 \times (11.40\% - 4.00\%)]$
$$= 4.00\% + 7.77\%$$
$$= 11.77\%$$

     b WACC (pre-tax) $= (0.40 \times 8.30\%) + (0.10 \times 7.37\%) + (0.50 \times 11.77\%)$
$$= 3.32\% + 0.74\% + 5.89\%$$
$$= 9.95\%$$

WACC (after-tax) $= [(1.00 - 0.40) \times (0.40 \times 8.30\%)] + (0.10 \times 7.37\%)$
$$+ (0.50 \times 11.77\%)$$
$$= 1.99\% + 0.74\% + 5.89\%$$
$$= 8.62\%$$

     c Cost of debt = 9.00%

Cost of preference shares = $(0.08 \times €70) \div €70 = €5.60 \div €70 = 8.00\%$

Cost of ordinary shares (using CAPM) $= 4.00\% + [1.15 \times (11.40\% - 4.00\%)]$
$$= 4.00\% + 8.51\%$$
$$= 12.51\%$$

WACC (after-tax) $= [(1.00 - 0.40) \times (0.50 \times 9.00\%)] + (0.10 \times 8.00\%)$
$$+ (0.40 \times 12.51\%)$$
$$= 2.70\% + 0.80\,\% + 5.00\%$$
$$= 8.50\%$$

As a result of the proposed risk-increasing investment, SVI's after-tax WACC drops slightly from 8.62 per cent to 8.50 per cent. This result may seem a bit inconsistent with expectations, but can be explained by the fact that the increased financial leverage resulted in a higher proportion of debt in the firm's capital structure. In spite of the increased pre-tax costs of each source of financing, the tax-deductibility of the increased proportion of debt more than compensated for them, thereby lowering SVI's WACC.

Chapter 11 Raising Long-Term Equity Financing

ST11-1 Last year Guaraldi Instruments conducted an IPO, issuing 2 million ordinary shares with a par value of €0.25 to investors, at a price of €15 per share. During its first year of operation, Guaraldi earned net income of €0.07 per share and paid a dividend of €0.005 per share. At the end of the year, the company's shares were selling for €20 each. Construct the equity account for Guaraldi at the end of its first year in business and calculate the firm's market capitalization.

Answer ST11-1

Immediately after the IPO, during which Guaraldi Instruments sold 2 million shares with a par value of €0.25 each at a price of €15 each, the company's equity account would have the following entries:

Ordinary shares, at par value (€0.25 × 2 million)	€ 500 000
Paid-in capital surplus ((€15.00 – €0.25) × 2 million)	29 500 000
Retained earnings	0
Total shareholders' equity	30 000 000

After the first year's net income (after dividend payments) are credited to Guaraldi's balance sheet, the equity accounts will have the following entries:

Ordinary shares, at par value (€0.25 × 2 million)	€ 500 000
Paid-in capital surplus ((€15.00 – $0.25) × 2 million)	29 500 000
Retained earnings ((€0.07 – $0.005) × 2 million)	130 000
Total shareholders' equity	30 130 000

Guaraldi's market capitalization at the end of the first year would be €40 million (€20/share × 2 million shares).

ST11-2 The Bloomington Company needs to raise €20 million of new equity capital. Its share price is currently €42. The investment bankers require an underwriting spread of 7 per cent of the offering price. The company's legal, accounting and printing expenses associated with the seasoned offering are estimated to be €450 000. How many new shares must the company sell to net €20 million?

Answer ST11-2

The Bloomington Company needs to raise €20 000 000 + €450 000 = €20 450 000

$7\% \times 42 = €2.94$

The shares will net €39.06 a share (€42.00 – €2.94)

€20 450 000/€39.06 = 523 554 shares

ST11-3 Assume that Zurich Semiconductor Company (ZSC) wants to create a sponsored ADR programme, worth $75 million, to trade its shares on the NASDAQ stock market. Assume that ZSC is currently selling on the SWX Swiss Exchange for SF25.00 per share, and the current dollar/Swiss franc exchange rate is $0.8000/SF. American Bank and Trust (ABT) is handling the ADR issue for ZSC and has advised the company that the ideal trading price for high-technology shares on the NASDAQ is about $60 per share (or per ADR).

a Describe the precise steps ABT must take to create an ADR issue that meets ZSC's preferences.

b Assume that ZSC's share price declines from SF25.00 to SF22.50. If the exchange rate does not also change, what will happen to ZSC's ADR price?

c If the Swiss franc depreciates from $0.8000/SF to $0.7500/SF, but the price of ZSC's shares remains unchanged in Swiss francs, how will ZSC's ADR price change?

Answer ST11-3

a ZSC wants to start an ADR programme equivalent to about $75 million.
Current ZSC stock price = SF25.00
Exchange rate: $0.8000/SF
Current ZSC stock price in dollars = SF25.00 × $0.8000 = $20.00/share
Since the preferred ADR price is about $60/share, bundle three ZSC shares into each ADR
ADR price in dollars = 3 × $20/share = $60
To raise roughly $75 million, ZSC must sell about 1 250 000 ADRs at $60 each.
To begin ADR creation process, ABT would purchase 3 750 000 shares of ZSC (1.25 ADR × shs/ADR).

Step 1: Purchase 3 750 000 ZSC shares = 3 750 000 × SF25.00/share = SF93 750 000

Step 2: Package shares into 1 250 000 ADRS and sell to US buyers for $60/ADR, raising 1 250 000 ADRs × $60/ADR = $75 000 000.

Step 3: Convert dollar proceeds from selling ADRs into Swiss francs to cover cost of purchasing stock $75 000 000 ÷ $0.8000/SF = SF93 750 000; this covers ABT's costs.

b New ADR price in dollars: SF22.50/share × 3 shares/ADR × $0.8000/SF = $54/ADR

c New ADR price in dollars: SF25.00/share × 3 shares/ADR × $0.7500/SF = $56.25/ADR

Chapter 12 Capital Structure

ST12-1 As financial director of the United Service Corporation (USC), you are considering a recapitalization plan that would convert USC from its current all-equity capital structure to one including substantial financial leverage. USC now has 150 000 shares outstanding, which are selling for €80.00 each. The recapitalization proposal is to issue €6 000 000 worth of long-term debt, at an interest rate of 7.0 per cent, and use the proceeds to repurchase 75 000 shares worth €6 000 000. USC's earnings in the next year will depend on the state of the economy. If there is normal growth, EBIT will be €1 200 000. EBIT will be €600 000 if there is a recession, and EBIT will be €1 800 000 if there is an economic boom. You believe that each economic outcome is equally likely. Assume there are no market frictions such as corporate or personal income taxes.

a If the proposed recapitalization is adopted, calculate the number of shares outstanding, the per-share price and the debt-to-equity ratio for USC.

b Calculate the earnings per share (EPS) and the return on equity for USC shareholders, under all three economic outcomes (recession, normal growth and boom), for both the current all-equity capitalization and the proposed mixed debt/equity capital structure.

c Calculate the breakeven level of EBIT, where earnings per share for USC shareholders are the same, under the current and proposed capital structures.

d At what level of EBIT will USC shareholders earn zero *EPS*, under the current and the proposed capital structures?

Answer ST12-1

a If USC issues €6 000 000 worth of debt and repurchases 75 000 shares worth €6 000 000, this implies that the shares will be repurchased at a price of €80 each (€6 000 000 ÷ 75 000 shares). After this transaction, 75 000 shares will remain outstanding, each worth €80, for a total equity value of €6 000 000. The debt-to-equity ratio will therefore be 1.0 (€6 000 000 debt ÷ €6 000 000 equity).

b Expected operating profits, cash flows to shareholders and bondholders under current and proposed capital structure for USC for three equally likely economic outcomes:

	RECESSION		NORMAL GROWTH		BOOM	
EBIT	€600 000		€1 200 000		€1 800 000	
	ALL-EQUITY FINANCING	**50% DEBT: 50% EQUITY**	**ALL-EQUITY FINANCING**	**50% DEBT: 50% EQUITY**	**ALL-EQUITY FINANCING**	**50% DEBT: 50% EQUITY**
Interest (7.0%)	€ 0	€ 420 000	€ 0	€420 000	€ 0	€420 000
Net income	€600 000	€180 000	€1 200 000	€780 000	€1 800 000	€1 380 000
Shares outstanding	150 000	75 000	150 000	75 000	150 000	75 000
Earnings per share	€4.00	€2.40	€8.00	€10.40	€12.00	€18.40
% Return on shares (P_0 = €80.00/share)	**5.0%**	**3.0%**	**10.0%**	**13.00%**	**15.0%**	**23.0%**

c The breakeven point is EBIT equal to twice the interest payment, or €840 000 (2 × €420 000 interest). At that level of EBIT, earnings per share will be €5.60 per share under both the current all-equity capitalization (€840 000 EBIT ÷ 150 000 shares O/S) and under the 50% debt, 50% equity capital structure [(€840 000 EBIT − €420 000 interest) ÷ 75 000 shares O/S].

d Under the current all-equity capitalization, shareholders will earn positive EPS for any EBIT above zero, so EBIT = €0 is where EPS = €0. Under the proposed capital structure, EPS = €0 where EBIT = interest payments = €420 000.

ST12-2 An unlevered company operates in perfect markets and has net operating income (EBIT) of €2 000 000. Assume that the required return on assets for firms in this industry is 8 per cent. The firm issues €10 million worth of debt, with a required return of 6.5 per cent, and uses the proceeds to repurchase outstanding shares. There are no corporate or personal taxes.

a What is the market value and required return of this firm's shares before the repurchase transaction, according to M&M Proposition I?

b What is the market value and required return of this firm's remaining shares after the repurchase transaction, according to M&M Proposition II?

Answer ST12-2

a Before the share repurchase, the value of the firm is
EBIT/r = €2 000 000/0.08 = €25 000 000. The required return on the shares
(all-equity financing) is 8.0%.

b After the repurchase, the firm has €10 000 000 debt and €15 000 000
equity, so the debt-to-equity ratio is 0.6667 and the new required return on
equity is
$r_l = r + (r - r_d)D/E = 0.08 + (0.08 - 0.065) \times 0.6667 = 0.08 + 0.01 = 0.09$ or 9%

ST12-3 Westside Manufacturing has EBIT of €10 million. There is €60 million of
debt outstanding, with a required rate of return of 6.5 per cent. The required
rate of return on the industry is 10 per cent. The corporate tax rate is 30
per cent. Assume there are corporate taxes but no personal taxes.

a Determine the present value of the interest tax shield of Westside Manufacturing,
as well as the total value of the firm.

b Determine the gain from leverage, if personal taxes of 10 per cent on share
income and 35 per cent on debt income exist.

Answer ST12-3

	LEVERED	UNLEVERED
EBIT	€10 000 000	€10 000 000
− Interest paid (0.065 × €60,000,000)	(3 900 000)	0
= Taxable income	€ 6 100 000	€10 000 000
− Taxes ($T_c = 0.30$)	(1 830 000)	(3 000 000)
= Net income	€ 4 270 000	€ 7 000 000
+Interest paid	3 900 000	0
= Total income available to investors	€ 8 170 000	€ 7 000 000

a Present value of tax shield = Debt × T_C = €60 000 000 × 0.30 = €18 000 000
Value unlevered firm = Net income ÷ Capitalization rate
$\qquad$ = €7 000 000 ÷ 0.10
$\qquad$ = €70 000 000
Value of levered firm = Value unlevered firm + PV tax shields
$\qquad$ = €70 000 000 + €18 000 000
$\qquad$ = €78 000 000.

b
$$G_L = \left[1 - \frac{(1 - T_c)(1 - T_{ps})}{(1 - T_{pd})}\right] \times = \left\{1 - [(1 - 0.3)(1 - 0.1)] \div (1 - 0.35)\right\}$$

$$\times \$60\ 000\ 000$$

$$= \{1 - [(0.7)(0.0)] \div 0.65\} \times €60\ 000\ 000$$

$$= 0.0308 \times €60\ 000\ 000$$

$$= €1\ 846\ 153.85$$

ST12-4 You are the manager of a financially distressed company with €10 million
in debt outstanding, which will mature in one month. Your firm currently

has €7 million cash on hand. Assume that you are offered the opportunity to invest in either of the two projects described below.

- **Project 1:** the opportunity to invest €7 million in risk-free government stock, with a 4 per cent annual interest rate (or a 0.333 per cent per month interest rate).
- **Project 2:** a high-risk gamble, which will pay off €12 million in one month, if it is successful (probability = 0.25), but will only pay €4 million if it is unsuccessful (probability = 0.75).

a Compute the expected pay-off for each project and state which one you would adopt if you were operating the firm in the shareholders' best interests? Why?

b Which project would you accept if the firm was unlevered? Why?

c Which project would you accept if the firm was organized as a partnership rather than a company? Why?

Answer ST12-4

a Pay-off for Project 1: €7 000 000 × 1.00333 = €7 023 333

Pay-off for Project 2: 0.25 × €12 000 000 + 0.75 × €4 000 000 = €6 000 000

If you were operating in the shareholders' interests, Project 2 would be accepted. It gives a higher potential pay-off to shareholders if the project does well. Project 1 has a sure, but lower return, but its pay-off will accrue to bondholders, rather than shareholders. This is in spite of the fact that Project 2 clearly has a negative NPV – it pays off only €6 million and requires a €7 million investment. Note that these are future pay-offs – they need to be discounted at the appropriate cost of capital to determine NPV.

b If the firm were unlevered, the firm would prefer Project 1. The pay-off for Project 1 is higher than the pay-off for Project 2. If the firm is unlevered, all of the return will accrue to shareholders, since there are no bondholders. An unlevered firm would reject Project 2.

c If the firm were organized as a partnership rather than a company, then it would accept Project 1. In partnerships, the owners do not have the option to default on the firm's debt (i.e. they don't have limited liability), leaving the firm's assets in the hands of creditors. Therefore, without the option to default, partners have no incentive to underinvest. They will accept Project 1 because doing so reduces their expected losses when the firm goes bankrupt.

ST12-5 Run-and-Hide Detective Company currently has no debt and expects to earn €5 million in EBIT each year, for the foreseeable future. The required return on assets for detective companies of this type is 10.0 per cent, and the corporate tax rate is 35 per cent. There are no taxes on dividends or interest at the personal level. Run-and-Hide calculates that there is a 5 per cent chance that the firm will fall into bankruptcy in any given year. If bankruptcy does occur, it will impose direct and indirect costs, totalling €8 million. If necessary, they will use the industry required return for discounting bankruptcy costs.

a Compute the present value of bankruptcy costs for Run-and-Hide.

b Compute the overall value of the firm.

c Recalculate the value of the company assuming that the firm's shareholders face a 15 per cent personal tax rate on equity income.

Answer ST12-5

a For any given year, the expected value of bankruptcy costs will be equal to the probability of bankruptcy ($p = 0.05$) times the cost to the firm if bankruptcy occurs (€8 000 000), or €400 000 per year. Since direct bankruptcy (B/R) costs are usually only incurred by unprofitable firms – that are not currently paying corporate income taxes – and since indirect B/R costs are things such as opportunity costs like lost sales, loss of reputational capital and loss of key personnel, we will assume that all B/R costs are after-tax costs. The present value of bankruptcy costs, PV_{BR}, will then be equal to the sum of the stream of discounted expected annual bankruptcy costs, where the discount rate will be the industry required return ($r = 0.10$). Since this stream is a perpetuity, PV_{BR} will simply be the expected annual B/R costs divided by the discount rate:

$$PV_{BR} = \left[\frac{€400000}{0.10}\right] = €4\ 000\ 000$$

b The overall value of the firm is computed using Equation 12.7, where V_U is the value of an unlevered firm (computed using Equation 12.3), V_L is the value of a levered firm, and PVTS equals the present value of debt tax shields. Since there are, at present, no debt tax shields, we will simply compute firm value, V:

$$V_L = V = V_U + PV_{TS} - PV_{BR} \qquad \text{(Equation 12.7)}$$

$$V_U = \left[\frac{EBIT(1 - T_c)}{r}\right] = \frac{€5000000(0.65)}{0.10} = \frac{€3250000}{0.10} = €32\ 500\ 000$$

$$V = V_U - PV_{BR} = €32\ 500\ 000 - €4\ 000\ 000 = €28\ 500\ 000$$

c Incorporating a personal tax rate on equity income into the valuation model of an unlevered firm presented in Equation 12.3 yields:

$$V_U = \left[\frac{EBIT(1 - T_c)(1 - T_{PS})}{r}\right]$$

$$= \frac{€5000000(0.65)(0.85)}{0.10} = \frac{€2762500}{0.10} = €27\ 625\ 000$$

And the new value of the firm, V, taking account of bankruptcy costs as well, becomes:

$$V = V_U - PV_{BR} = €27625000 - €4000000 = €26\ 400\ 000$$

Chapter 13 Dividend Policy

ST13-1 What do record date, ex-dividend date and payment date mean, related to dividends? Why would you expect the price of a share to drop by the amount of the dividend on the ex-dividend date? What rationale has been offered for why this does not actually occur?

Answer ST13-1

When companies announce dividend payments, they state that the dividend will be paid to shareholders of record on a certain date, with payment to be made several days later. This means the cheque will be made out to shareholders on the company's registry as at, say 5 July, with payment actually being made on 15 July. About three days before the record date, the company's shares will trade ex-dividend, meaning that someone who purchases shares before this ex-dividend date will be recorded on the company's books before the record date and will receive the dividend payment. Someone who purchases shares on or after the ex-dividend date will not receive the dividend payment (it will go to the previous owner), as there will be insufficient time to record the new owner on the shareholders' registry before payment is made. The share price should therefore drop by about the amount of the dividend payment on the ex-dividend date, because the new purchaser must be compensated for the fact that the upcoming cash payment will be made to the previous owner. Historically, the average price drop on the ex-dividend day for US companies has been 50–65 per cent of the amount of the dividend paid, and this has been interpreted as a personal income tax effect. Since personal tax rates on dividend income have traditionally been taxed at a higher rate than on realized capital gains, most individual investors eager to sell shares would prefer to sell before the ex-dividend date – receiving their return as capital gains – rather than wait to receive the highly taxed cash dividend. For some expected ex-dividend day price drop investors will be indifferent between receiving €1 worth of capital gains rather than €0.50−€0.65 worth of cash dividends.

ST13-2 What has happened to the total volume of share repurchases announced by US public companies since 1982? Why did that year mark such an important milestone in the history of share repurchase programmes in the United States?

Answer ST13-2

The total value of share repurchases in the United States increased dramatically after 1992. During that year, the US Securities and Exchange Commission (SEC) spelled out the legal rules covering share repurchases, and this 'safe harbour' ruling clarified when corporate managers could execute repurchases without fear of being charged with insider trading by the SEC.

ST13-3 What has happened to the average cash dividend payout ratio of corporations worldwide over time? What explains this trend? How would your answer change if share repurchases were included in calculating dividend payout ratios?

ANSWER ST13-3

Not only has the fraction of corporations worldwide that pay dividends been declining steadily for the past 50 years, those companies that do pay regular cash dividends tend to pay out lower fractions of their earnings today than in the past. Focusing on the US market, a relative handful of 200 or so NYSE listed firms account for over half of the value of dividend payments in the United States, though these companies are truly enormous and also account for the bulk of corporate profits each year. Several factors seem to account of this decline in the 'propensity to pay' among dividend-paying firms, including the rise of institutional investors worldwide (who presumably have less need for a regular cash payment than individual investors) and the increasing importance of technology and entrepreneurship in global business. These factors suggest both that corporate managers would have greater need to retain earnings for investment and that investors would have less desire to receive dividends. On the other hand, if share repurchases are included with regular cash dividends, than the picture of declining dividend payments reverses itself. By this measure, the aggregate 'payout ratio' of corporations worldwide has been steadily (if slightly) increasing over time, though it is still the same relative handful of companies that pay dividend and execute share repurchase programmes.

ST13-4 What does it mean to say that corporate managers 'smooth' cash dividend payments? Why do managers do this?

Answer ST13-4

Most firms will maintain a constant nominal dividend payment until the company's managers are convinced that corporate earnings have permanently changed. If the firm's 'permanent earnings' increase, then managers will increase the nominal dividend payment a little each quarter or year until a new equilibrium level of dividend payments close to the target payout ratio is reached. The company will then maintain the quarterly or annual dividend at this nominal level until the firm's permanent earnings change again. This pattern of stable nominal dividend payments, followed by slow and steady increases as the firm's managers adjust to new levels of permanent earnings, gives the observed dividend series a smooth pattern, so managers are said to smooth dividends if they follow a constant nominal dividend payment policy with a partial adjustment strategy – as most do.

ST13-5 What are the key assumptions and predictions of the signalling model of dividends? Are these predictions supported by empirical research findings?

Answer ST13-5

The signalling model of dividends predicts that managers will begin paying dividends in order to differentiate their 'strong' firms from weaker firms (with lower cash flows) in a market characterized by information asymmetries between managers and shareholders. In such an environment, investors cannot distinguish strong from weak companies, so managers of strong firms will incur all the costs (taxes, foregone investment, transaction costs of issuing new securities) of paying high dividends because their firms can afford to bear these costs while weaker firms cannot. Signalling with dividends is comparable to burning €100 bills in public; only the wealthiest individuals can afford to commit such a wasteful act, so the signal is credible to all who witness it. The signalling model predicts that the most profitable and most promising firms will pay the highest dividends. The prediction that more profitable firms will pay the highest dividends is partially supported by empirical research, but the most promising firms (high-tech and entrepreneurial companies) have low payouts, which contradicts the signalling model's predictions.

ST13-6 What is the expected relationship between dividend payout levels and the growth rate and availability of positive-NPV projects, under the agency cost model of dividends? What about the expected relationship between dividend payout and the diffuseness of firm shareholders? Free cash flow? Consider a firm, such as Microsoft, awash in free cash flow, available positive-NPV projects, and a relatively diffuse shareholder base in an industry with increasing competition. Does either the agency model or the signalling model adequately predict the dividend policy of Microsoft? Which does the better job?

Answer ST13-6

The agency cost model predicts that firms with many positive-NPV investment projects will have less need to pay out cash as dividends in order to overcome agency costs than will firms with few positive-NPV projects. Thus high-growth firms will have low dividend payouts. Firms with a tight ownership structure have few agency problems between managers and shareholders, so have less need to make large dividend payments. Most economists agree that Microsoft should pay out more of its cash holdings as dividends, and the firm recently has raised its payout level – though the current payments will not seriously reduce Microsoft's cash mountain in the foreseeable future.

Chapter 14 Entrepreneurial Finance and Venture Capital

ST14-1 You are seeking €1.5 million from a venture capitalist to finance the launch of your online financial search engine. You and the VC agree that your venture is currently worth €3 million. When the company goes public in an IPO in five years, it is expected to have a market capitalization of €20 million. Given the company's stage of development, the VC requires a 50 per cent return on investment. What fraction of the firm will the VC receive in exchange for its €1.5 million investment in your company?

Answer ST14-1

Expected market value in 5 years = €20 million

Required return on investment = 50%

Value of VC investment in 5 years = €1500000 $\times$ 1.50^5 = €1500000 $\times$ 7.594 = €11 390 625

Fraction equity received = €11390625 $\div$ €20000000 = 56.95%

ST14-2 An entrepreneur seeks €12 million from a VC fund. The entrepreneur and fund managers agree that the entrepreneur's venture is currently worth €30 million and that the company is likely to be ready to go public in four years. At that time, the company is expected to have a net income of €9 million. Comparable firms are expected to be selling at a price/earnings ratio of 25. Given the company's stage of development, the venture capital fund managers require a 40 per cent compound annual return on their investment. What fraction of the firm will the fund receive in exchange for its €12 million investment?

Answer ST14-2

Value of firm = Net income $\times$ P/E multiple = €6 million $\times$ 25 = €150 million

40% return is required on the investment
12000000 × (1.40)^4 = €12000000 × 3.842 = €46 099 200
€46099200 ÷ €150000000 = 30.73% of the firm.

ST14-3 Suppose that six out of ten investments made by a VC fund
are a total loss, meaning that the return on each of them is –
100 per cent. Of the remaining investments, three break even,
earning a 0 per cent return. One investment pays off spectacularly and
earns a 650 per cent return. What is the realized return on the VC fund's
overall portfolio?

Answer ST14-3

This solution assumes that each of the ten investments are for equal euro; amounts.
Therefore, each investment gets a portfolio weight of 10 per cent.
6 of 10 earn − 100%, so expressed as a fraction of total portfolio (p/f) return:
   (0.6 × –1.00) = –0.60

3 of 10 earn 0% return, so expressed as a fraction of total p/f return:
   (0.2 × 0) = 0
One investment earns 650% (0.1 × 6.50)

Portfolio return (R) is thus calculated as:
R = (0.6 × −1.00) + (0.3 × 0) + (0.1 × 6.50)
  = −0.60 + 0 + 0.65 = 0.05
The portfolio's realized return will be 5.0%

Chapter 15 International Financial Management

ST15-1 Use Table 15.1 to determine the cross exchange rate between the British
pound and the Japanese yen.

Answer ST15-1

(£/€0.6)/(¥/€149.6) = £0.004/¥

ST15-2 Suppose the spot exchange rate equals ¥100/$, and the six-month forward
rate equals ¥101/$. An investor can purchase a US T-bill that matures in
six months and earns an annual rate of return of 3 per cent. What would
be the annual return on a similar Japanese investment?

Answer ST15-2

In order for interest rate parity to hold, we get:

$$101/100 = (1 + x)/1.015$$

$$x = 0.0252$$

Therefore, the annualized return on Japanese investment will be 2 × 0.0252 = 5.03%.

Chapter 16 Risk Management

ST16-1 A certain commodity sells for €150 today. The present value of the
cost of storing this commodity for one year is €10. The risk-free

rate is 4 per cent. What is a fair price for a one-year forward contract on this asset?

Answer ST16-1

Use Equation 16.2 to solve this problem:

$$F = (150 + 10)(1.04) = 166.40$$

ST16-2 The spot exchange rate is $1.6666/£. The risk-free rate is 4 per cent in the United States and 6 per cent in the United Kingdom. What is the forward exchange rate (assume a one-year contract)?

Answer ST16-2

Use Equation 16.3 here, but remember that we need to express the exchange rates in terms of foreign currency per unit of domestic currency. If we treat the $ as the domestic currency, then the spot rate is 1/($1.6666/£) or £0.6000/$. So we have:

$$F = 0.6000(1.06)/1.04 = 0.6115$$

Chapter 17 Mergers, Acquisitions and Corporate Control

ST17-1 Mega Service Company (MSC) is offering to exchange 2.5 of its own shares for each shares of target firm Norman Corporation as consideration for a proposed merger. There are 10 million Norman Corporation shares outstanding, and its share price was €60 before the merger offer. MSC's pre-offer share price was €30. What is the control premium percentage offered? Now suppose that when the merger is consummated eight months later, MSC's share price drops to €25. At that point, what is the control premium per centage and total transaction value?

Answer ST17-1

The pre-offer value of Norman Corporation is €600 million (10 million shares × €60/share) and Mega Service Company offered 2.5 of its own shares (worth €30/share) as payment, or €75 per share of Norman Corporation. The initial control premium offered is thus €15/share (€75 offer price – €60 market price) of Norman Corporation, which is a control premium percentage of 25 per cent (€15 premium ÷ €60 initial market price).

When the merger is completed, and MSC's share price has fallen to €25/share, the value actually received by Norman Corporation shareholders is only €62.50/share (€25/share MSC shares × 2.5 shares MSC for each Norman Corporation share). Norman shareholders will thus actually receive a control premium of €2.50/share or 4.17 per cent (€2.50 premium ÷ €60 initial market price). At that point the total transaction value is €625 million (10 million shares × €62.50/share).

ST17-2 You are the director of capital acquisitions for Morningside Hotel Company. One of the projects you are deliberating is the acquisition of Monroe Hospitality, a company that owns and operates a chain of bed-and-breakfast inns. Susan Sharp, Monroe's owner, is willing to sell her company to Morningside only if she is offered an all-cash purchase price of €5 million. Your project analysis team estimates that the purchase of Monroe Hospitality will generate the following after-tax marginal cash flow:

YEAR	CASH FLOW
1	$1 000 000
2	1 500 000
3	2 000 000
4	2 500 000
5	3 000 000

If you decide to go ahead with this acquisition, it will be funded with Morningside's standard mix of debt and equity, at the firm's weighted average (after-tax) cost of capital of 9 per cent. Morningside's tax rate is 30 per cent. Should you recommend acquiring Monroe Hospitality to your CEO?

Answer ST17-2

We use the 9 per cent WACC to find the present value of the forecast marginal cash flow.

$$\text{Present value} = \frac{€1000000}{(1.09)^1} + \frac{€1500000}{(1.09)^2} + \frac{€2000000}{(1.09)^3} + \frac{€2500000}{(1.09)^4} + \frac{€3000000}{(1.09)^5}$$

$$= €917431 + €1262520 + €1544367 + €1771063 + €1949794$$

$$= €7445175$$

Because the present value of the marginal cash flow from the purchase of Monroe Hospitality of €7 445 175 is more than its €5 000 000 all-cash purchase price, the CEO should purchase Monroe.

Glossary

Accounting rate of return Calculation of a hurdle rate by dividing net income by the book value of assets, either on a year-by-year basis or by taking an average over the project's life.

Accrual-based approach Revenues are recorded at the point of sale and costs when they are incurred, not necessarily when a firm receives or pays out cash.

Acquisition The purchase of additional resources by a business enterprise.

Actively managed An approach to running a mutual fund in which the fund manager does research to identify undervalued and overvalued shares.

Activity ratios A measure of the speed with which a firm converts various accounts into sales or cash.

Additional paid-in capital The difference between the price the company received when it sold shares in the primary market and the par value of the shares, multiplied by the number of shares sold. This represents the amount of money the firm received from selling shares, above and beyond the share's par value.

Agency bonds Bonds that are issued by an agency of government, such as a housing, investment or other quasi-commercial entity.

Agency cost/contracting model of dividends A theoretical model that explains empirical regularities in dividend payment and share repurchase patterns, based on agency problems between managers and shareholders.

Agency cost/tax shield trade-off model of corporate leverage This model expresses the value of a levered firm as the value of an unlevered firm, plus the present values of tax shields and the agency costs of outside equity, minus the present value of bankruptcy costs and the agency costs of debt.

Agency costs Costs that arise due to conflicts of interest between shareholders and managers.

Agency costs of debt Costs that must be weighed against the benefits of leverage in reducing the agency costs of outside equity.

Agency costs of (outside) equity In an efficient market, informed investors only pay a price per share that fully reflects the perks an entrepreneur is expected to consume after the equity sale, so the entrepreneur bears the full costs of her or his actions.

Agency problems The conflict between the goals of a firm's owners and its managers.

American call option An option that grants the right to buy an underlying asset, on or before the expiration date.

American depositary receipts (ADRs) Dollar-denominated claims, issued by US banks, that represent ownership of shares of a foreign company held on deposit by the US bank in the issuing firm's home country.

Angel capitalists Wealthy individuals who make private equity investments on an ad hoc basis.

Announcement date The day a firm releases the details of the dividend amount and the record and payment dates to the public.

Annual percentage rate (APR) The stated annual rate calculated by multiplying the periodic rate by the number of periods in one year.

Annual percentage yield (APY) The annual rate of interest actually earned reflecting the impact of compounding frequency. The same as the effective annual rate.

Annuity A stream of equal periodic cash flows.

Annuity due An annuity for which the payments occur at the beginning of each period.

Anti-takeover amendments Adding defensive measures to corporate charters to avoid a hostile takeover.

Appreciate A currency appreciates when it buys more of another currency than it did previously.

Arbitrage The process of buying something in one market at a low price and simultaneously selling it in another market at a higher price to generate an immediate, risk-free profit.

Asset substitution An investment that will increase firm value but does not earn a return high enough to fully redeem the maturing bonds.

Assets-to-equity (A/E) ratio A measure of the proportion of total assets financed by a firm's equity. Also called the equity multiplier.

At the money An option is at the money when the share price equals the strike price.

Average age of inventory A measure of inventory turnover, calculated by dividing the turnover figure into 360.

Average collection period The average amount of time that elapses from a sale on credit until the payment becomes usable funds for a firm. Calculated by dividing accounts receivable by average sales per day. Also called the average age of accounts receivable.

Average payment period A measure of the average length of time it takes a firm to pay its suppliers.

Backward integration A merger in which the acquired company provides an earlier step in the production process.

Bankruptcy costs The direct and indirect costs of the bankruptcy process.

Basis risk The possibility of unanticipated changes in the difference between the futures price and the spot price.

Bear hug The potential acquirer approaches the target with both a merger offer and the threat of a proxy fight and/or hostile tender offer to gain the remaining shares needed to obtain voting control of the target if the merger offer is refused.

Best efforts The investment bank promises to give its best effort to sell the firm's securities at the agreed-upon price; but if there is insufficient demand for the issue, then the firm withdraws it from the market.

Beta A standardized measure of the risk of an individual asset, one that captures only the systematic component of its volatility.

Boards of directors Elected by shareholders to be responsible for hiring and firing managers and setting overall corporate policies.

Bond ratings Grades assigned to bonds by specialized agencies that evaluate the capacity of bond issuers to repay their debts. Lower grades signify higher default risk.

Book-building A process in which underwriters ask prospective investors to reveal information about their demand for the offering. Through conversations with investors, the underwriter tries to measure the demand curve for a given issue, and the investment bank sets the offer price after gathering all the information it can from investors.

Book value The value of a firm's equity as recorded on the firm's balance sheet.

Breakeven analysis The study of what is required for a project's profits and losses to balance out.

Breakeven point (BEP) The level of sales or production that a firm must achieve in order to avoid losses by fully covering all costs. Calculated by dividing total fixed costs (FC) by the contribution margin.

Brokers Agents who facilitate secondary market trading by bringing buyers and sellers together.

Bulge bracket Consists of firms that generally occupy the lead or co-lead manager's position in large, new security offerings, meaning that they take primary responsibility for the new offering (even though other banks participate as part of a syndicate), and as a result they earn higher fees.

Business risk Refers to the variability of a firm's cash flows, as measured by the variability of EBIT.

Bust-up The takeover of a company that is subsequently split up.

Call option An option that grants the right to buy an underlying asset at a fixed price.

Call price The price at which a bond issuer may call or repurchase an outstanding bond from investors.

Callable Bonds that the issuer can repurchase from investors at a predetermined price known as the call price.

Cannibalization Loss of sales of an existing product when a new product is introduced.

Capital asset pricing model (CAPM) States that the expected return on a specific asset equals the risk-free rate plus a premium that depends on the asset's beta and the expected risk premium on the market portfolio.

Capital budgeting The process of identifying which long-lived investment projects a firm should undertake.

Capital budgeting function Selecting the best projects in which to invest the resources of the firm, based on each project's perceived risk and expected return.

Capital gain The increase in the price of an asset that occurs over a period of time.

Capital investment Investments in long-lived assets such as plant, equipment and advertising.

Capital loss The decrease in the price of an asset that occurs over a period of time.

Capital rationing The situation where a firm has more positive NPV projects than its available budget can fund. It must choose a combination of those projects that maximizes shareholder wealth.

Capital spending Investments in long-lived assets such as plant, equipment and advertising.

Capital surplus The number of ordinary shares outstanding times the original selling price of the shares, net of the par value.

Capitalization issue Termed a 'stock split' in the USA. Involves a company splitting the par value of its shares and issuing new shares to existing investors. For example, in a 2-for-1 issue, the firm doubles the number of shares outstanding.

Cash flow approach Used by financial professionals to focus attention on current and prospective inflows and outflows of cash.

Cash flow from operations Cash inflows and outflows directly related to the production and sale of a firm's products or services. Calculated as net income plus depreciation and other non-cash charges.

Cash settlement An agreement between two parties in which one party pays the other party the cash value of its option position, rather than forcing it to exercise the option by buying or selling the underlying asset.

Chief executive officer (CEO) The top company manager with overall responsibility and authority for managing daily company affairs and carrying out policies established by the board.

Closing futures price The price used to settle all contracts at the end of each day's trading.

Co-insurance of debt The debt of each combining firm in a merger is insured with cash flows from two businesses.

Collateral The specific assets pledged to secure a loan.

Collateral trust bonds A bond secured by financial assets held by a trustee.

Collective action problem When individual shareholders expend time and resources monitoring managers, bearing the costs of monitoring management while the benefit of their activities accrues to all shareholders.

Competitively bid offer The firm announces the terms of its intended equity sale, and investment banks bid for the business.

Compound interest Interest earned both on the principal amount and on the interest earned in previous periods.

Consolidation A merger in which both the acquirer and target disappear as separate corporations, combining to form an entirely new corporation with new ordinary shares.

Constant nominal payment policy Based on the payment of a fixed euro dividend in each period.

Constant payout ratio dividend policy Used by a firm to establish that a certain percentage of earnings is paid to owners in each dividend period.

Continuous compounding Interest compounds at literally every moment as time passes.

Contribution margin The sale price per unit (SP) minus variable cost per unit (VC).

Convertible bond A bond that gives investors the option to redeem their bonds for the issuer's shares rather than cash.

Corporate bonds Bonds issued by corporations.

Corporate charter The legal document created at the corporation's inception to govern its operations.

Corporate control The monitoring, supervision and direction of a corporation or other business organization.

Corporate finance The activities involved in managing money in a business environment.

Corporate governance function Developing ownership and corporate governance structures for companies that ensure that managers behave ethically and make decisions that benefit shareholders.

Corporate venture capital funds Subsidiaries or stand-alone firms established by non-financial corporations eager to gain access to emerging technologies by making early-stage investments in high-tech firms.

Corporation A separate legal entity with many of the same economic rights and responsibilities as those enjoyed by individuals.

Coupon A fixed amount of interest that a bond promises to pay investors.

Coupon rate The rate derived by dividing the bond's annual coupon payment by its par value.

Coupon yield The amount obtained by dividing the bond's coupon by its current market price (which does not always equal its par value).

Coverage ratio A debt ratio that focuses more on income statement measures of a firm's ability to generate sufficient cash flow to make scheduled interest and principal payments.

Covered interest arbitrage A trading strategy designed to exploit deviations from interest rate parity to earn an arbitrage profit.

Cross exchange rate An exchange rate between two currencies calculated by taking the ratio of the exchange rate of each currency, expressed in terms of a third currency.

Cross-hedging The underlying securities in a futures contract and the assets being hedged have different characteristics.

Currency board arrangement An exchange rate system in which each unit of the domestic currency is backed by a unit of some foreign currency.

Currency forward contract Exchange of one currency for another at a fixed date in the future.

Currency swap A swap contract in which two parties exchange payment obligations denominated in different currencies.

Current ratio A measure of a firm's ability to meet its short-term obligations, defined as current assets divided by current liabilities.

Date of record The date on which the names of all persons who own shares in a company are recorded as shareholders and thus eligible to receive a dividend.

Dealers Also called market-makers, dealers facilitate secondary market trading by standing ready to buy and sell securities with other investors.

Debentures Unsecured bonds backed only by the general faith and credit of the borrowing company.

Debt capital Borrowed money.

Debt ratio A measure of the proportion of total assets financed by a firm's creditors.

Debt-to-equity ratio A measure of the firm's financial leverage, calculated by dividing long-term debt by shareholders' equity.

Decision tree A visual representation of the sequential choices that managers face over time with regard to a particular investment.

Default risk The risk that the corporation issuing a bond may not make all scheduled payments.

Deferred taxes Reflect the discrepancy between the taxes that firms actually pay and the tax liabilities they report on their public financial statements.

Depreciate A currency depreciates when it buys less of another currency than it did previously.

Derivative securities Securities such as options, futures, forwards and swaps that derive their value from some underlying asset.

Direct costs of bankruptcy Out-of-pocket cash expenses directly related to bankruptcy filing and administration.

Direct quote An exchange rate quoted in terms of units of domestic currency per unit of foreign currency.

Discount A bond sells at a discount when its market price is less than its par value.

Discounted payback The amount of time it takes for a project's discounted cash flows to recover the initial investment.

Discounting Describes the process of calculating present values.

Diversification The act of investing in many different assets rather than just a few.

Dividend A periodic cash payment that firms make to investors who hold the firms' preference or ordinary shares.

Dividend payout ratio The percentage of current earnings available for ordinary shareholders paid out as dividends. Calculated by dividing the firm's cash dividend per share by its earnings per share.

Double taxation problem A situation where company profits (out of which dividends are paid) are subject to taxation, and the dividends themselves are also subject to taxation.

DuPont system An analysis that uses both income and balance sheet information to break down the ROA and ROE ratios into their component parts.

Economic exposure The risk that a firm's value will fluctuate due to exchange rate movements.

Economies of scale Relative operating costs are reduced for merged companies because of an increase in size that allows for the reduction or elimination of overlapping resources.

Economies of scope Value-creating benefits of increased size for merged companies.

Effective annual rate (EAR) The annual rate of interest actually paid or earned, reflecting the impact of compounding frequency. Also called the true annual return.

Efficient markets hypothesis (EMH) Asserts that financial asset prices fully reflect all available information (as formally presented by Eugene Fama in 1970).

Employee stock ownership plan (ESOP) The transformation of a public corporation into a private company by the employees of the corporation itself.

Entrepreneurial finance Study of the special challenges and problems involved with investment in and financing of entrepreneurial growth companies.

Entrepreneurial growth companies (EGCs) Rapidly growing private companies that are usually technology-based and that offer both high returns and high risk to equity investors. These are the companies typically funded by venture capitalists.

Equipment trust certificates A secured bond often used to finance transportation equipment.

Equity capital An ownership interest usually in the form of ordinary or preference shares.

Equity carve-out Occurs when a parent company sells shares of a subsidiary corporation to the public through an initial public offering. The parent company may sell some of the subsidiary shares that it already owns, or the subsidiary may issue new shares.

Equity claimants Owners of a company's equity securities.

Equity multiplier A measure of the proportion of total assets financed by a firm's equity. Also called the assets-to-equity (A/E) ratio.

Equivalent annual cost (EAC) method Represents the annual expenditure over the life of each asset that has a present value equal to the present value of the asset's annual cash flows over its lifetime.

Euro The currency used throughout the countries that make up the European Union.

Eurobond A bond issued by an international borrower and sold to investors in countries with currencies other than that in which the bond is denominated.

European call option An option that grants the right to buy the underlying asset only on the expiration date.

Exchange rate The price of one currency in terms of another currency.

Exchangeable bonds Bonds issued by corporations that may be converted into shares of a company other than the company that issued the bonds.

Ex-dividend A purchaser of a share does not receive the current dividend.

Exercise price The price at which an option holder can buy or sell the underlying asset.

Exercise the option Pay (receive) the strike price and buy (sell) the underlying asset.

Expectations theory In equilibrium, investors should expect to earn the same return whether they invest in long-term government bonds or a series of short-term government bonds.

Expected return A forecast of the return that an asset will earn over some period of time.

Expiration date The date on which the right to buy or to sell the underlying asset expires.

External financing function Raising capital to support companies' operations and investment programmes.

Extra dividend/special dividend The additional dividend that a firm pays if earnings are higher than normal in a given period.

Federal funds rate The interest rate that US banks charge each other for overnight loans.

Fiduciary Someone who invests and manages money on someone else's behalf.

Financial deficit More financial capital for investment and investor payments than is retained in profits by a corporation.

Financial intermediary (FI) An institution that raises capital by issuing liabilities against itself. Also, a commercial bank or other entity that lends to corporations.

Financial leverage Using debt to magnify both the risk and expected return on a firm's investments. Also, the result of the presence of debt when firms finance their operations with debt and equity, leading to a higher stock beta.

Financial management function Managing firms' internal cash flows and its mix of debt and equity financing, both to maximize the value of the debt and equity claims on firms and to ensure that companies can pay off their obligations when they come due.

Financial risk Refers to how a firm chooses to distribute the business risk affecting a firm's cash flows between shareholders and bondholders.

Financial synergies A merger results in less-volatile cash flows, lower default risk and a lower cost of capital.

Financial venture capital funds Subsidiaries of financial institutions, particularly commercial banks.

Financing flows Result from debt and equity financing transactions.

Firm-commitment An offering in which the investment bank underwrites the company's securities and thereby guarantees that the company will successfully complete its sale of securities.

Fixed asset turnover A measure of the efficiency with which a firm uses its fixed assets, calculated by dividing sales by the number of euros of net fixed asset investment.

Fixed exchange rate An exchange rate system in which the price of one currency is fixed relative to all other currencies by government authorities.

Fixed-for-floating interest rate swap Typically one party will make fixed-rate payments to another party in exchange for floating-rate payments.

Fixed-price offer An offer in which the underwriters set the final offer price for a new issue weeks in advance.

Flip To buy shares at the offer price and sell them on the first trading day. Also called stagging.

Floating exchange rate An exchange rate system in which a currency's value is allowed to fluctuate in response to market forces.

Floating-rate bonds Bonds that make coupon payments that vary over time. The coupon payments are usually tied to a benchmark market interest rate. Also called variable-rate bonds.

Foreign bond A bond issued in a host country's financial market, in the host country's currency, by a non-resident corporation.

Forward discount When one currency buys less of another on the forward market than it buys on the spot market.

Forward exchange rate The exchange rate quoted for a transaction that will occur on a future date.

Forward integration A merger in which the acquired company provides a later step in the production process.

Forward premium When one currency buys more of another on the forward market than it buys on the spot market.

Forward price The price to which parties in a forward contract agree. The price dictates what the buyer will pay to the seller on a future date.

Forward rate agreement (FRA) A forward contract in which the underlying asset is not an asset at all but an interest rate.

Forward rate In a currency forward contract, the forward price.

Forward–spot parity An equilibrium relationship that predicts that the current forward rate will be an unbiased predictor of the spot rate on a future date.

Free cash flow (FCF) The net amount of cash flow remaining after the firm has met all operating needs and paid for investments, both long term (fixed) and short term (current). Represents the cash amount that a firm could distribute to investors after meeting all its other obligations.

Free cash flow theory of mergers Michael Jensen hypothesizes that managers will use free cash flow to invest in mergers that have negative net present values in order to build corporate empires from which the managers will derive personal benefits, including greater remuneration.

Fundamental principle of financial leverage States that substituting long-term debt for equity in a company's capital structure increases both the level of expected returns to shareholders – measured by earnings per share or ROE – and the risk (dispersion) of those expected returns.

Fungibility The ability to close out a position by taking an offsetting position.

Future value The value of an investment made today measured at a specific future date using compound interest.

Futures contract Involves two parties agreeing today on a price at which the purchaser will buy a given amount of a commodity or financial instrument from the seller at a fixed date sometime in the future.

General Agreement on Tariffs and Trade (GATT) A trade treaty that extends free trade principles to broad areas of economic activity in many countries.

General cash offerings Shares are offered for sale to any and all investors. Most equity sales fall under this category.

Glass-Steagall Act Congressional Act of 1933 mandating the separation of investment and commercial banking.

Global depositary receipts (GDRs) Local currency-denominated claims, issued by local banks, that represent ownership of shares of a foreign company held on deposit by that bank in the issuing firm's home country.

Going-private transactions The transformation of a public corporation into a private company through issuance of large amounts of debt used to buy all (or at least a voting majority) of the outstanding shares of the corporation.

Gordon growth model The valuation model, named after Myron Gordon, that views cash flows as a 'growing perpetuity'.

Gramm-Leach-Bailey Act Act that allowed commercial banks, securities firms and insurance companies to join together.

Green Shoe option An option to sell more shares than originally planned.

Gross profit margin A measure of profitability that represents the percentage of each sales euro remaining after a firm has paid for its goods.

Growing perpetuity An annuity promising to pay a growing amount at the end of each year forever.

Hedging Procedures used by firms to offset many of the more threatening market risks.

Horizontal merger A combination of competitors within the same geographic market.

Hostile takeover The acquisition of one firm by another through an open-market bid for a majority of the target's shares where the target firm's senior managers do not support (or, more likely, actively resist) the acquisition.

Hubris hypothesis of corporate takeovers Richard Roll (1986) contends that some managers overestimate their own managerial capabilities and pursue takeovers with the belief that they can better manage their takeover target than the target's current management team can.

In the money A call (put) option is in the money when the share price is greater (less) than the strike price.

Incremental cash flows Cash flows that directly result from a proposed investment. They effectively represent the marginal costs (MC) and marginal benefits (MB) expected to result from undertaking a proposed investment.

Indenture A legal document stating the conditions under which a bond has been issued.

Index fund A passively managed fund that tries to mimic the performance of a market index such as the FTSE-100.

Indirect bankruptcy costs Expenses or economic losses that result from bankruptcy but are not cash outflows spent on the process itself.

Indirect quote An exchange rate quoted in terms of foreign currency per unit of domestic currency.

Industry shock theory of takeovers Explains much of the activity in a wave of mergers as a reaction to some external shock to the industry, such as a change in regulation or the introduction of a fundamentally new technology.

Initial margin The minimum monetary amount required of an investor when taking a position in a futures contract.

Initial public offering (IPO) A corporation offers its shares for sale to the public for the first time; the first public sale of company shares to outside investors.

Initial return The gain when an allocation of shares from an investment banker is sold at the first opportunity because the offer price is consistently lower than what the market is willing to bear.

Institutional venture capital funds Formal business entities with full-time professionals dedicated to seeking out and funding promising ventures.

Interest differential In an interest rate swap, only the differential is exchanged.

Interest rate cap A call option on interest rates.

Interest rate collar A strategy involving the purchase of an interest rate cap and the simultaneous sale of an interest rate floor, using the proceeds from selling the floor to purchase the cap.

Interest rate floor A put option on interest rates.

Interest rate parity An equilibrium relationship that predicts that differences in risk-free interest rates in two countries must be tied to differences in currency values on the spot and forward markets.

Interest rate swap A swap contract in which two parties exchange payment obligations involving different interest payment schedules.

Internal capital markets Created when the high-cash-flow businesses of a conglomerate generate enough cash to fund the riskier business ventures internally.

Internal rate of return (IRR) The compound annual rate of return on a project, given its up-front costs and subsequent cash flows.

International shares Equity issues sold in more than one country by non-resident corporations.

Inventory turnover A measure of how quickly a firm sells its goods.

Investment bank A bank that helps firms acquire external capital.

Investment banks Financial institutions that assist firms in the process of issuing securities to investors. Investment banks also advise firms engaged in mergers and acquisitions, and they are active in the business of selling and trading securities in secondary markets.

Investment flows Cash flows associated with the purchase or sale of both fixed assets and business equity.

IPO underpricing Occurs when the offer price in the prospectus is consistently lower than what the market is willing to bear.

Joint and several liability A legal concept that makes each partner in a partnership legally liable for all the debts of the partnership.

Junk bonds Bonds rated below investment grade (also known as high yield bonds).

Law of one price A theory that says that the identical good trading in different markets must sell at the same price.

Lead underwriter The investment bank that takes the primary role in assisting a firm in a public offering of securities.

League table Ranks investment banks, based on the total value of securities they underwrote globally during a given year.

Limited partners One or more totally passive participants in a limited partnership, who do not take any active role in the operation of the business and who do not face personal liability for the debts of the business.

Liquidity preference theory States that the slope of the yield curve is influenced not only by expected interest rate changes, but also by the liquidity premium that investors require on long-term bonds.

Liquidity ratios Measure a firm's ability to satisfy its short-term obligations as they come due.

Listed securities Securities that trade on major stock exchanges.

Loan amortization A borrower makes equal periodic payments over time to fully repay a loan.

Loan amortization schedule Used to determine loan amortization payments and the allocation of each payment to interest and principal.

London Interbank Offered Rate (LIBOR) The interest rate that banks in London charge each other for overnight loans. Widely used as a benchmark interest rate for short-term floating-rate debt.

Long position To own an option or another security.

Long-term debt Debt that matures more than one year in the future.

Low-regular-and-extra policy Policy of a firm paying a low regular dividend supplemented by an additional cash dividend when earnings warrant it.

Maintenance margin Margin level required to maintain an open position.

Majority voting system System that allows each shareholder to cast one vote per share for each open position on the board of directors.

Managed floating rate system A hybrid currency system in which a government loosely fixes the value of the national currency.

Management buyout (MBO) The transformation of a public corporation into a private company by the current managers of the corporation.

Managerial entrenchment theory of mergers Shleifer and Vishny propose that unmonitored managers will try to build corporate empires through the pursuit of negative-NPV mergers, with the motive of making the management team indispensable to the firm because of its greater size and the team's supposed expertise in managing a large company.

Managerial risk reduction theory Implies that acquiring firm managers acquire other firms primarily to reduce the volatility of the combined firm's earnings, thus reducing the risk that they will be dismissed due to an unexpected decline in earnings.

Managerial synergies Efficiency gains from combining the management teams of merged companies.

Managerialism theory of mergers Poorly monitored managers will pursue mergers to maximize their corporation's asset size because managerial remuneration is usually based on firm size, regardless of whether or not these mergers create value for shareholders.

Margin account The account into which the investor must deposit the initial margin.

Marginal tax rate The percentage of taxes owed on the next euro of income.

Market capitalization The value of a company's shares that are owned by the shareholders: the total number of shares issued multiplied by the current price per share.

Market portfolio A portfolio that contains some of every asset in the economy.

Market power A benefit that might arise from a horizontal merger when competition is too weak (or non-existent) to prevent the merged company from raising prices in a market at will.

Market risk premium The additional return earned (or expected) on the market portfolio over and above the risk-free rate.

Market/book (M/B) ratio A measure used to assess a firm's future performance by relating its market value per share to its book value per share.

Marking-to-market Daily cash settlement of all futures contracts.

Maturity date The date when a bond's life ends and the borrower must make the final interest payment and repay the principal.

McFadden Act Congressional Act of 1927 that prohibited interstate banking.

Merchant bank A bank capable of providing a full range of financial services.

Merger A transaction in which two or more business organizations combine into a single entity.

Minority interest The value of shares that a company holds in subsidiaries of the company.

Mixed offerings Offerings in which some of the shares come from existing shareholders and some are new. Also, a merger financed with a combination of cash and securities.

Mixed stream A series of unequal cash flows reflecting no particular pattern.

Monetary union An agreement between many European countries to integrate their monetary systems including using a single currency.

Monte Carlo simulation A sophisticated risk assessment technique that provides for calculating the decision variable, such as net present value, using a range or probability distribution of potential outcomes for each of a model's assumptions.

Mortgage bonds A bond secured by real estate or buildings.

Multinational corporations (MNCs) Businesses that operate in many countries around the world.

Municipal bonds Issued by US state and local governments. Interest received on these bonds is exempt from federal income tax.

Mutually exclusive projects The situation that occurs when the IRRs of several projects exceed the hurdle rate (or the NPVs exceed €0), but only a subset of those projects can be undertaken at the given time.

National Association of Securities Dealers Automated Quotation (NASDAQ) System An electronic system that facilitates trading in OTC shares.

Negotiated offer The issuing firm negotiates the terms of the offer directly with one investment bank.

Net pay-off The difference between the pay-off received when the option expires and the premium paid to acquire the option.

Net present value (NPV) The sum of the present value of all of a given project's cash flows, both inflows and outflows, discounted at a rate consistent with the project's risk. Also, a method for valuing capital investments.

Net present value (NPV) profile A plot of a project's NPV (on the y-axis) against various discount rates (on the x-axis). It is used to illustrate the relationship between the NPV and the IRR for the typical project.

Net profit margin A measure of profitability that represents the percentage of each sales euro remaining after all costs and expenses, including interest, taxes and preference share dividends, have been deducted.

Net working capital The difference between a firm's current assets and its current liabilities. Often used as a measure of liquidity.

Nominal return The stated return offered by an investment unadjusted for the effects of inflation.

Non-cash charges Expenses, such as depreciation, amortization and depletion allowances, that appear on the income statement but do not involve an actual outlay of cash.

Non-cash expenses Tax-deductible expenses for which there is no corresponding cash outflow. They include depreciation, amortization and depletion.

Open interest The number of contracts that are currently outstanding.

Opening futures price Price on the first trade of the day.

Operating cash flow (OCF) The amount of cash flow generated by a firm from its operations. Mathematically, earnings before interest and taxes (EBIT) minus taxes plus depreciation.

Operating flows Cash inflows and outflows directly related to the production and sale of a firm's products or services.

Operating leverage Measures the tendency of the volatility of operating cash flows to increase with fixed operating costs.

Operating profit margin A measure of profitability that represents the percentage of each sales euro remaining after deducting all costs and expenses other than interest and taxes.

Operational synergy Economies of scale, economies of scope and resource complementarities.

Opportunity costs Lost cash flows on an alternative investment that the firm or individual decides not to make.

Option premium The market price of the option.

Ordinary annuity An annuity for which the payments occur at the end of each period.

Ordinary shares The most basic form of corporate ownership. Called common stock in the USA.

Out of the money A call (put) option is out of the money when the share price is less (greater) than the strike price.

Oversubscribe When the investment banker builds a book of orders for shares that is greater than the amount of shares the firm intends to sell.

Par value (bonds) The face value of a bond, which the borrower repays at maturity.

Par value (of ordinary shares) An arbitrary value assigned to shares on a firm's balance sheet.

Passively managed An approach to running a mutual fund in which the fund manager makes no attempt to identify overvalued or undervalued shares, but instead holds a diversified portfolio and attempts to minimize the costs of operating the fund.

Payback period The amount of time it takes for a given project's cumulative net cash inflows to recoup the initial investment.

Payment date The actual date on which a firm posts the dividend payment to the holders of record.

Pay-off The value received from exercising an option on the expiration date (or zero), ignoring the initial premium required to purchase the option.

Pay-off diagram A diagram that shows how the expiration date pay-off from an option or a portfolio varies, as the underlying asset price changes.

Perpetuity A level or growing cash flow stream that continues forever.

Poison pills Defensive measures taken to avoid a hostile takeover.

Political risk The risk that a government will take an action that negatively affects the values of firms operating in that country.

Portfolio weights The percentage invested in each of several securities in a portfolio. Portfolio weights must sum to 1.0 (or 100 per cent).

Pre-emptive rights These hold that shareholders have first claim on anything of value distributed by a corporation.

Preference shares A form of ownership that has preference over ordinary shares with regard to income and assets.

Preferred habitat theory A theory that recognizes that the shape of the yield curve may be influenced by investors who prefer to purchase bonds having a particular maturity regardless of the returns those bonds offer compared to returns available at other maturities.

Premium A bond that sells for more than its par value.

Present value The value today of a cash flow to be received at a specific date in the future, assuming an opportunity to earn interest at a specified rate.

Price stabilization Purchase of shares by an investment bank when a new issue begins to falter in the market, keeping the market price at, or slightly above, the offer price.

Price/earnings (P/E) ratio A measure of a firm's long-term growth prospects that represents the amount investors are willing to pay for each euro of a firm's earnings.

Primary market transactions Sales of securities to investors by a corporation to raise capital for the firm.

Primary security issues Security offerings that raise capital for firms.

Prime rate The rate of interest charged by banks on loans to business borrowers with excellent credit records.

Principal The amount of money on which interest is paid.

Private equity Funds raised for companies from individuals, institutions and other intermediaries where the fundraising is not carried out via organized exchanges.

Product extension mergers Diversification mergers that combine companies with similar but not identical lines of business.

Profitability index (PI) A capital budgeting tool, defined as the present value of a project's cash inflows divided by its initial cash outflow.

Proposition I The famous 'irrelevance proposition', which imagines that a company is operating in a world of frictionless capital markets, and in a world where there is uncertainty about corporate revenues and earnings.

Proposition II Asserts that the expected return on a levered firm's equity is a linear function of that firm's debt-to-equity ratio.

Prospectus A document that describes the securities being offered for sale and the company offering them.

Protective covenants Provisions of the bond indenture that stipulate actions that the borrower must do (positive covenants) or actions that the borrower must not do (negative covenants).

Protective put A portfolio containing a share and a put option on that share.

Proxy fight A ploy used by outsiders to attempt to gain control of a firm by soliciting a sufficient number of votes to unseat existing directors.

Proxy statements A document mailed to shareholders that describes the matters to be decided by a shareholder vote in a forthcoming annual meeting. Shareholders can sign their proxy statements and grant their voting rights to other parties.

Public company A corporation, the shares of which can be freely traded among investors without obtaining the permission of other investors and whose shares are listed for trading in a public securities market.

Purchasing power parity An equilibrium relationship that predicts that currency movements are tied to differences in inflation rates across countries.

Pure conglomerate mergers Unrelated diversification mergers that occur between companies in completely different lines of business.

Pure discount bonds Bonds that pay no interest and sell below par value. Also called zero-coupon bonds.

Pure share exchange merger A merger in which shares are the only mode of payment.

Put option An option that grants the right to sell an underlying asset at a fixed price.

Putable bonds Bonds that investors can sell back to the issuer at a predetermined price under certain conditions.

Quarterly compounding Interest compounds four times per year.

Quick (acid-test) ratio A measure of a firm's liquidity that is similar to the current ratio except that it excludes inventory, which is usually the least liquid current asset.

Ratio analysis Calculating and interpreting financial ratios to assess a firm's performance and status.

Real interest rate parity An equilibrium relationship that predicts that the real interest rate will be the same in every country.

Real return Approximately, the difference between an investment's stated or nominal return and the inflation rate.

Recapitalization Alteration of a company's capital structure to change the relative mix of debt and equity financing, leaving total capitalization unchanged.

Redemption option Option for venture capitalists to sell a company back to its entrepreneur or founders.

Relevant cash flows All of the incremental, after-tax cash flows (initial outlay, operating cash flow and terminal value) associated with a proposed investment.

Reserves (retained earnings) The cumulative total of the earnings that a firm has reinvested since its inception.

Residual claimants Investors who have the right to receive cash flows only after all other claimants have been satisfied. Shareholders are typically the residual claimants of corporations.

Residual theory of dividends States that observed dividend payments will simply be a residual; the cash left over after corporations have funded all their positive-NPV investments.

Resource complementarities A firm with a particular operating expertise merges with a firm with another operating strength to create a company that has expertise in multiple areas.

Return on equity (ROE) A measure that captures the return earned on the common shareholders' (owners') investment in a firm.

Return on total assets (ROA) A measure of the overall effectiveness of management in generating returns to shareholders with its available assets.

Reverse LBO (or second IPO) A formerly public company that has previously gone private through a leveraged buyout and then goes public again. Also called a second IPO.

Reverse LBO A formerly public company that has previously gone private through a leveraged buyout and then goes public again. Also called a second IPO.

Reverse merger A merger in which the acquirer has a lesser market value than the target.

Reverse stock split Occurs when a firm replaces a certain number of outstanding shares with just one new share. This is done to increase the share price.

Rights offering/rights issue A special type of seasoned equity offering that allows the firm's existing owners to buy new shares at a bargain price or to sell that right to other investors.

Risk management The process of identifying firm-specific risk exposures and managing those exposures by means of insurance products. Also includes identifying, measuring and managing all types of risk exposures.

Risk management function Managing firms' exposures to all types of risk, both insurable and uninsurable, in order to maintain optimum risk–return trade-offs and thereby maximize shareholder value.

Risk premium The additional return that an investment must offer, relative to some alternative, because it is more risky than the alternative.

Road show A tour of major cities taken by a firm and its bankers several weeks before a scheduled offering.

Required rate of return The rate of return that investors require from an investment given the risk of the investment.

Rule 144A offering A special type of offer, first approved in April 1990, that allows issuing companies to waive some disclosure requirements by selling shares only to sophisticated institutional investors, who may then trade the shares among themselves.

Samurai bonds Yen-denominated bonds issued by non-Japanese corporations.

Sarbanes-Oxley Act 2002 (SOX) Act of Congress that established new corporate governance standards for US public companies, and that established the Public Company Accounting Oversight Board (PCAOB).

Scenario analysis A more complex form of sensitivity analysis that provides for calculating the decision variable, such as net present value, when a whole set of assumptions changes in a particular way.

Seasoned equity offering (SEO) An equity issue by a firm that already has shares outstanding.

Secondary market transactions Trades between investors that generate no new cash flow for the firm.

Secondary offering An offering whose purpose is to allow an existing shareholder to sell a large block of shares to new investors. This kind of offering raises no new capital for the firm.

Securitization The repackaging of loans and other traditional bank-based credit products into securities that can be sold to public investors.

Selling group Consists of investment banks that may assist in selling shares but are not formal members of the underwriting syndicate.

Selling short Borrowing a security and selling it for cash at the current market price. An investor who sells short must eventually return the security to the lender by purchasing it at the then-current market price. Therefore, a short seller hopes that either (1) the price of the security sold short will fall, or (2) the return on the security sold short will be lower than the return on the asset in which the proceeds from the short sale were invested.

Semi-annual compounding Interest compounds twice a year.

Sensitivity analysis A tool that allows exploration of the impact of individual assumptions on a decision variable, such as a project's net present value, by determining the effect of changing one variable while holding all others fixed.

Settlement date The future date on which the buyer pays the seller and the seller delivers the asset to the buyer.

Settlement price The average price at which a contract sells at the end of a trading day.

Shareholders Owners of ordinary and preference shares of a company.

Share issue privatization (SIP) A government executing one of these will sell all or part of its ownership in a state-owned enterprise to private investors via a public share offering.

Share premium account The number of ordinary shares outstanding times the original selling price of the shares, net of the par value.

Share repurchase programme A company announcing this kind of programme states that it will buy some of its own shares over a period of time.

Shares authorized The amount of a company's shares that shareholders and the board authorize the firm to sell to the public.

Shares issued Shares that have been issued or sold to the public.

Shark repellents Anti-takeover measures added to corporate charters.

Short position To sell an option or another security.

Signalling model of dividends Assumes that managers use dividends to convey positive information to poorly informed shareholders.

Simple interest Interest paid only on the initial principal of an investment, not on the interest that accrues in earlier periods.

Sinking fund A provision in a bond indenture that requires the borrower to make regular payments to a third-party trustee for use in retiring the bond.

Small business investment companies (SBICs) Federally chartered corporations established as a result of the US Small Business Administration Act of 1958.

Spin-off A parent company creates a new company with its own shares to form a division or subsidiary, and existing shareholders receive a pro rata distribution of shares in the new company.

Split-off A parent company creates a new, independent company with its own shares, and ownership of the company is transferred to certain existing shareholders only, in exchange for their shares in the parent.

Split-up The division and sale of all of a company's subsidiaries, so that it ceases to exist (except possibly as a holding company with no assets).

Sponsored ADR (or GDR) A depository receipt for which the issuing (foreign) company absorbs the legal and financial costs of creating and trading the security.

Spot exchange rate The exchange rate that applies to immediate currency transactions.

Spot price The price that the buyer pays the seller in a current, cash market transaction.

Spread The difference between the rate that a lender charges for a loan and the underlying benchmark interest rate. Lenders charge higher spreads to less creditworthy borrowers.

Standard deviation A measure of volatility equal to the square root of variance.

Stated annual rate The contractual annual rate of interest charged by a lender or promised by a borrower.

Stock dividend The payment to existing owners of a dividend in the form of stock.

Strategic merger Seeks to create a more efficient merged company than the two premerger companies operating independently.

Strike price The price at which an option holder can buy or sell the underlying asset.

Subordinated debentures An unsecured bond that has a legal claim inferior to other outstanding bonds.

Subsidiary merger A merger in which the acquirer maintains the identity of the target as a separate subsidiary or division.

Sunk costs Costs that have already been paid and are therefore not recoverable.

Swap contract Agreement between two parties to exchange payment obligations on two underlying financial liabilities that are equal in principal amount but differ in payment patterns.

Synergy An efficiency-enhancing effect resulting from a strategic merger.

Systematic risk Risk that cannot be eliminated through diversification. (Also termed market or undiversifiable risk.)

Tailing the hedge Purchasing enough futures contracts to hedge risk exposure, but not so many as to cause overhedging.

Takeover Any transaction in which the control of one entity is taken over by another.

Target dividend payout ratio Under this policy, the firm attempts to pay out a certain percentage of earnings, but rather than let dividends fluctuate, it pays a stated euro dividend and adjusts it towards the target payout slowly as proven earnings increases occur.

Tender offer The structured purchase of a target's shares in which the acquirer announces a public offer to buy a minimum number of shares at a specific price.

Tender-merger A merger that occurs after an acquirer secures enough voting control of the target's shares through a tender offer to effect a merger.

Term structure of interest rates The relationship between yield to maturity and time to maturity among bonds having similar risk.

Terminal value The value of a project at a given future date.

Time line A graphical presentation of cash flows over a given period of time.

Time value of money The financial concept that recognizes the fact that a euro received today is more valuable than a euro received in the future.

Times interest earned ratio A measure of the firm's ability to make contractual interest payments, calculated by dividing earnings before interest and taxes by interest expense.

Total asset turnover A measure of the efficiency with which a firm uses all its assets to generate sales; calculated by dividing the euros of sales a firm generates by the euros of asset investment.

Total return A measure of the performance of an investment that captures both the income it pays and its capital gain or loss over a stated period of time.

Tracking stocks Equity claims based on (and designed to mirror, or track) the earnings of wholly owned subsidiaries of diversified firms.

Transactions exposure The risk that movements in exchange rates will adversely affect the value of a particular transaction.

Translation exposure or accounting exposure The risk that exchange rate movements will adversely impact reported financial results on a firm's financial statements.

Treasury bills Debt instruments issued by the US federal government that mature in less than one year.

Treasury bonds Debt instruments issued by the US federal government with maturities longer than ten years.

Treasury notes Debt instruments issued by the US federal government with maturities ranging from one to ten years.

Treasury shares Shares that were issued and later reacquired by the firm through share repurchase programmes and are therefore being held in reserve by the firm.

Treasury STRIP A zero-coupon bond representing one coupon payment or the final principal payment made by an existing Treasury note or bond.

Triangular arbitrage A trading strategy in which traders buy a currency in a country where the value of that currency is too low and immediately sell the currency in another country where the currency value is too high.

Underinvestment A situation of financial distress in which default is likely, yet a very profitable but short-lived investment opportunity exists.

Underlying asset The asset from which an option or other derivative security derives its value.

Underwrite The investment banker purchases shares from a firm and resells them to investors.

Underwriting spread The difference between the net price and the offer price.

Underwriting syndicate Consists of many investment banks that collectively purchase the firm's shares and market them, thereby spreading the risk exposure across the syndicate.

Unseasoned equity offering An initial offering of shares by a company that does not currently have a public listing for trading its shares.

Unsponsored ADR (or GDR) A now rare type of depositary receipt in which the issuing firm is not involved with the issue at all, and may even oppose it.

Unsystematic risk Risk that can be eliminated through diversification.

Variable growth model Assumes that the dividend growth rate will vary during different periods of time, when calculating the value of a firm's shares.

Venture capital A professionally managed pool of money raised for the sole purpose of making actively managed direct equity investments in rapidly growing private companies.

Venture capital limited partnerships Funds established by professional venture capital firms, and organized as limited partnerships.

Venture capitalists Professional investors who specialize in high-risk/high-return investments in rapidly growing entrepreneurial businesses.

Vertical merger Companies with current or potential buyer–seller relationships combine to create a more integrated company.

Wealth tax A tax levied on share appreciation every period, regardless of whether the shares are sold or not.

Weighted average cost of capital (WACC) The after-tax, weighted average required return on all types of securities issued by a firm, in which the weights equal the percentage of each type of financing in a firm's overall capital structure.

White knights 'Friendly' acquirers who will top the price of an unwelcome bidder to avoid a hostile takeover.

Working capital Refers to what is more correctly known as net working capital.

World Trade Organization (WTO) An organization established by GATT to police world trading practices and to settle disputes between GATT member countries.

Yield curve A graph that plots the relationship between yield to maturity and maturity for a group of similar bonds.

Yield spread The difference in yield to maturity between two bonds or two classes of bonds with similar maturities.

Yield to maturity The discount rate that equates the present value of the bond's cash flows to its market price.

Zero growth model The simplest approach to share valuation that assumes a constant dividend stream.

Name index

Subject index